whatever happened to america?

Also by
Jon Christian Ryter:
The Baffled Christian's Handbook
Prince Albert, Prophet of Utopia

whatever happened to america?

By
Jon Christian Ryter

HALLBERG PUBLISHING CORPORATION

Nonfiction Book Publishers—ISBN 0-83719
Tampa, Florida 33623

ISBN NUMBER 0-87319-049-1
Library of Congress
Catalog Card Number 99-097279

Cover design by EKGraphics,
Frederick, Maryland

Printed in the
United States of America
10 9 8 7 6 5 4 3 2 1

For information concerning Rights and
Permissions, or other questions contact:

HALLBERG PUBLISHING CORPORATION
P.O. Box 23985 • Tampa, Florida 33623
Phone: 1-800-633-7627 • Fax 1-800-253-READ

This book is dedicated to concerned Americans everywhere who see their nation and their liberty threatened by forces they cannot comprehend which seek to create a system of global governance for"the betterment of mankind" at the expense of America.

In particular, this book is dedicated to a selfless group of Americans who have aided me with advise or have allowed me to take advantage of their investigative labors as they examined the hidden agenda of the United States government as our legislators, at both State and federal levels, penned the questionable and sometimes unconstitutional legislation that is now being used to abrogate our rights under the Constitution of the United States.

To this group, who on their own time and of their own expense, have tirelessly pored through the files of the National Archives, various State archives and other portals of information to secure many of the documents cited in this text I dedicate this book.

These Americans include:
M.J. "Red" Beckman
Sam Bitz
Congresswoman Helen Chenoweth-Hage
A. Ralph Epperson
Linda Liotta
Congressman Ron Paul
Larry Pratt
Dr. Eugene Schroder
Joan Veon

with a special thanks to the Plymouth Rock Foundation and Gun Owners of America

❖ Author's Note ❖

An Explanation

Since I have written under the pen name of Jon Christian Ryter for several years, and because I am known by that pen name to the many thousands of Americans who have followed my writing over the past few years, I have elected to use that name entirely because of its recognition to those people who would likely pick up this book because of the author's name rather than the book's title (catchy as it is).

In the opinion of the publisher, because the information contained within the pages of this book is so explosive, and because the information is so well supported by history, by documents, and by such incontrovertible circumstantial "evidence" that no other logical conclusion can be drawn from the premises advanced, the people and organizations whose actions and agendas are detailed in this book will not be able to successfully attack the message and will, therefore, attack the messenger. As the history of the Clinton Administration has verified, the publisher is, of course, very likely correct. This is a book that the globalists within the halls of Congress will feel hard pressed to ignore.

In the publisher's view, presenting this book under a pseudonym would raise the question why, if the author stands behind the accuracy what he has written, is it necessary for him to hide behind a pseudonym? The solution, then, was finding a means by which the fans of the writing of Jon Christian Ryter could immediately identify a book whose author is, in reality, Jon Spokes, a former newspaper reporter turned Advertising Executive with *The Washington Times*. This appeared to be the best solution.

Jon L. Spokes
writing under the name
Jon Christian Ryter
August 11, 2000

❖ Table of Content ❖

ed the States from the equation of power in the nation's capitol, and destroyed the balance of power between the States and the federal government. This chapter clearly demonstrates how the federal government, which was created inferior to the States, was able to assume supra-authority over the States, and over the people of the United States that it does not Constitutionally possess.

tating effect it had in the realignment of power in Europe, bringing to power Benito Mussolini in Italy and Adolph Hitler in Germany.

its published agenda and its timeline to create a the well-publicized agenda of the most powerful transnational bankers, industrialists, and the former nobility of Europe to usurp the sovereignty of the nation-states and create a global government ruled by them.

❖ INTRODUCTION ❖

The Basis

This effort, *Whatever Happened To America?* was not written for the sufficiently alarmed, rapidly growing conservative militia groups in America. Probably more than anyone else, the faction of our society — the backbone and grit of America, the common, ordinary patriotic folks — have been more aware of the plight of this great nation and its planned destruction, than the rest of us. Although most Americans who proudly call themselves the *citizen militia* are not aware that the globalists of the New World Order actually have an established, agendized timeline that mandates the destruction of the national sovereignty of the United States no later than 2012, and optimistically believe world government can be peacefully achieved between 2008-10, those within the *citizen militia* ranks know with unfailing certainty that the central government of the United States is attempting to destroy the rule of law in America, and for that reason alone, it can no longer be trusted.

Whatever Happened To America? was written to inform a complacent, apathetic public about what has, over the past eighty years, happened to America, and where the road upon which this nation is traveling will ultimately lead the United States as we cross the utopian's toll bridge to the totalitarian reality on the other side.

If this book does what it is supposed to do, and the American people become sufficiently alarmed and provoked, they have one course to follow — they must act — and act quickly. Through the elective process, Americans must disenfranchise elected officals who would, by deceit, disenfranchise America. To accomplish this, we must look beyond political affiliations. Being a liberal is not necessarily evil, nor is being a conservative inherently good. We must also ignore the trite polite political party pandering of "Democrat" or "Republican." We need to explore new words to describe those who are willing to defend America's right to exist as a separate and independent nation, and those who would surrender that right for the sake of global unity in a merged socialist, one-world economic global state headed not by those we constitutionally elected, but rather, by the United Nations whose laws are diametrically opposed to ours.

We need to re-examine the credentials of those to whom we have entrusted our lives, our families and our futures—not based on their positions on abortion, civil rights, homosexual rights, or how much pork they are able to bring home to their State; but rather on whether or not they are ideologically a "nationalist" or a "globalist." The defining issues that shape what remains of the future of America will be determined by this factor alone. Everything else is merely a divisive smoke screen.

Second, the American public needs to take a strong, hard look at those who interpret the Constitution of the United States, as well as the federal magistrates who, with lifetime appointments to the bench, casually reinterpret the Constitution to fit the politically-correct whims of a politically-correct society based on a politically-correct agenda that was clearly initiated in the international arena to ultimately serve the needs of a socialist global society based on the utopian principles of a communist world government that restricts rather than imputes liberty.

When America finds a federal judge or Supreme Court justice who is determined to either rewrite the Constitution based on political whim, or who legislates from the bench, that judge or justice must, for the security of the Constitution, be impeached by the House of Representatives and tried by the Senate. If the House and Senate refuse to do so, then the electorate needs to empower a new Senator or a new Representative in order to get the job done. That, as U.S. Senate Majority Leader Trent Lott so aptly said shortly after the 1996 national elections, is part of the checks and balance system of the Constitution. It is, regretfully, an important part of that system that has been sorely neglected by the Congress of the United States since 1935. The blame, however, rests not with the Senate or the House of Representatives, but with us. We elected them.

Third, America needs to permanently disenfranchise the unconstitutional bureaucracy Congress allowed to be created, and return the power to govern to the States and to the people themselves who were granted that authority by the Constitution. The fourth branch of the United States government, the administrative branch, was instituted by short-sighted Congressmen who blindly allowed a myriad of Congressionally-unsupervised, unelected bureaucrats to write the regulations that, when codified, became as much a part of the law as the legislation Congress enacted. Since the American people cannot fire the bureaucrats, they must consider the alternatives: either to allow the continuous growth of a burdensome and exorbitantly expensive government, or fire those responsible for its unsupervised growth.

While the members of Congress have not been doing their jobs as defined by their Constitutional job descriptions, "we the people" have not been doing our jobs, either. We, like many of the politicians we continue to elect, have our hands outstretched towards the Mecca of entitlements, and our faces are buried so deep in the public trough that we have no idea at all what happened to America.

On our lips are the words: "What's in it for me?" or "What's in it for my special interest group?" It's no wonder that we, as a people, can no longer recognize the lack of ethics and moral character in our national leaders. We have none with which to compare. Our leaders are, after all, only a mirror image of the constituency that elected them.

When I began this work the subject of the text, according to my outline, was to discuss the ramifications of "political correctness" on the societal, political, and religious issues that affect the lives and families of Americans. It was to be a study of liberalism in America, as well as the effects of globalism on the economy of the United States as we prepare to enter the next century. Nothing more.

However, as I began my research, I discovered far more questions than answers. Each answered question led to a new series of pertinent inquiries: why did a particular event in history which— superficially at least—appears to contradict either common sense or logic, occur? And, since these events did occur who, logically, would profit most from the event—and where would the evidence linking that individual or group of individuals to the event be found, if such evidence even existed?

My investigation led me down a thousand paths, many of them fruitless detours that cost valuable research time and produced no tangible evidence—only more unsupported theories that could not be factually corroborated. However, my preliminary studies yielded one very important and immensely valuable piece of information that ultimately determined the direction of the text.

There appears to be a common thread woven throughout most "conspiracy-oriented" books and papers that, in most cases, render them worthless. Why? Because most of these otherwise well-intentioned writers based far too many of their conclusions not on facts that had been uncovered either by themselves or someone else, but on theories advanced by other writers who have previously written on the subject. Unfortunately, the unsupported references of one writer by another neither legitimizes the second reference, nor do they become more credible because footnotes or endnotes exists.

The credibility of a text that is 90% verifiable can easily be destroyed by the 10% that cannot since it is that portion of the text which will be attacked by its detractors. Cries of rightwing extremism by the liberal elitists who smugly ridicule the allegations of militia-type patriotic nationalists who insist that military "black helicopters" are holding "civil unrest" maneuvers over American cities in preparation of an anticipated citizens' revolt when the Constitution of the United States is scrapped in favor of the UN Declaration on Human Rights, are viewed as being far more credible than the warnings of the radical right for three reasons despite the fact that such "maneuvers" have actually been reported in the mainstream media in Florida, Texas and Maryland.

First, the patriotic nationalists who have shouted their allegations from the rooftops and over the Internet are not content with reporting only that which they can support as fact—and can prove with documented evidence. They also report that which they surmise will ultimately become true as fact as well. Thus, it has been rather easy for the globalist to shoot down the patriots in just about any utopian debate since the nationalists so thoughtfully provides most of the ammunition the globalist requires to get the job done.

Second, the globalists, who appear to be much better equipped in public relations than most of the militia-type nationalists, get much better press since they are attempting only to destroy the Constitution (in the name of fairness and equality to the downtrodden).

Third, the media—or at least the mainstream media—is clearly on the socialist side of every political debate. The "news" that is spoon-fed to America on a daily basis is a carefully laundered litany of elitist prose that artistically paints the liberal, and the all too clearly socialist agenda as a polyunsaturated blend of Santa Claus and Jesus Christ. The crimes and sins of the elitist are either overlooked or mitigated with self-serving rhetoric. The misgivings of the extremist are magnified and intensified until even minor infractions are made to look like heinous crimes against humanity.

Many of the writers who have penned some of the more recent "conspiracy" titles that have been ridiculed by the left as being long on theory and short on substance went to school during a time when the curriculum was still at least in part focused on the 3-R's: reading, 'riting and 'rithmetic. Most of those writers could add 2 + 2 and come up with 4. Since the "radical extremists" can put 2 and 2 together, they can logically see where globalism + black helicopters + the abrogation of our constitutional rights will lead. However, black helicopters by themselves, without an overt act from the military or the government of the United States, are only one element of a textbook logic equation—half of a premise without a verifiable conclusion. The "extremists" cannot prove their allegations that those who currently lead this nation, on both sides of the aisle, are determined to make America a puppet State among the puppet states of the United Nations. However, not being able to prove their allegations has not hindered their zeal to level charges, believing that everyone can see the issues as clearly as they do, and that they, too, can add 2 + 2.

The globalists among us are a very intelligent, very articulate group. And, why not? They represent the *intelligentsia*. Many are ranking members of some of the most prestigious think tanks in the world. Many are well-credentialed academicians. Others are leaders in business and industry. Many are bankers. Still others are wealthy financiers, or the owners and managers of some of the largest media companies in the United States and the world. And some of them are your neighbors just down the street who, after listening to the socialist peace and prosperity rhetoric, choose to believe the promise of utopian bliss without either questioning the cost of this global prosperity or asking who will be required to pay for it.

The material you will find in this book is, I believe, well-researched and documented. Theories, when proposed, are presented as theories and not as fact. Each theory is corroborated with relevant evidence or events that clearly support the conclusions which are drawn. If you are a *globalphite*, you will not like what you read, and will in all likelihood attempt to dismiss *Whatever Happened To America?* as just one more book about "black helicopters." Clearly however, it is not. It is a factual history of a global shadow government that began before the birth of the United States. It is not a fantasy about organizations called the Illuminati, the Bilderbergers, the Trilateral Commission or the Council on Foreign Relations. It is the history of the political movement of the United States from beginning—to end.

If you are a *globalphobe* this book will both shock and frighten you. And, rightly it should. The globalists succeeded in their century-old effort to steal America. All that remains is to transfer the sovereignty of the United States to the New World Order.

❖ ONE ❖

Creating the Republic

I am absolutely convinced that if the politicians who gave us the New Deal and the Great Society had been among the Founding Fathers of this great nation, the United States of America would not exist in any form today.

First, the colonies would have quickly repudiated the socialist agenda advocated by both, and the nation would have died before it was even born. Second, had a nation somehow been formed, America would likely have been embroiled in Civil War within one or two decades of its birth. However, rather than fighting a war to prevent eleven states from seceding from the Union, it would have been a war in which a socialist federal bureaucracy would have sought military assistance from the power brokers of Europe to prevent its thirteen colonies from seceding from the federal government.

To some, my remarks might appear to be the statements of a malcontent who is obviously feels disenfranchised from the form of government created by our Founding Fathers some 220-odd years ago. However, those who understand precisely what type of government was created with the enactment of the Constitution of the United States in 1789, compared to the form of government which now exists in America, are equally concerned not only with the losses of personal liberties we are now experiencing, but also about the continued state of the Union.

Before examining the events which precipitated the decision of colonial America to seek its independence from England it is important to understand the options for self-governance which were available to the colonies once the decision to secede from Great Britain was reached, and why our Founding Fathers elected to form a Constitutional Republic of granted limited rights and powers rather than a democracy. Contrary to common belief, they are not the same forms of government.

In a "political science" sense, there are four traditional forms

1

of government. First, there is a theocracy. In a theocracy, God is the regent. In a pure Biblical sense that has never happened. For God to be regent, He would have to create the laws as He did when He ordered Moses to the summit of Mount Sinai to receive the Ten Commandments. God would then have to be able to physically enforce the laws He created. The world will not see a true theocracy until Jesus Christ returns to Jerusalem and establishes His Millennial Kingdom on Earth.

In our contemporary world theocracies do exist, but none of them are theological from a Biblical perspective. Those who hold power may incorporate a religious texture to their laws but their edicts, although seemingly theologically-based, are still the laws of man created by men to promote a human rather than divine political agenda. Every Islamic society claims to be a theocracy, but in every instance they are governed by the laws of those who control the reins of power. None, in other words, are true theocracies.

The second form is the monarchy, or dictatorship. One individual rules. Most modern monarchies evolved from singular rule into the third method of governance: the oligarchy. Oligarchies are societies in which a handful of people control the government. Most true socialist countries are oligarchies. Fourth, is the democracy. Democracies are societies which are theoretically ruled by the "will" of the majority through the process of "election."

Most Americans, if asked what form of government is found in the United States, would respond that it is a democracy. While that is not the form of government that was created by our Founding Fathers, they would nevertheless be partially correct in their answer. Our Founding Fathers created a Constitutional Republic. In a Constitutional Republic, government is granted limited power over its citizens. On April 8, 1913 the Republic of the United States of America became a democracy when the power of the States and the power reserved for the people of these United States passed into the hands of the federal government.

Today, absolute power is vested in a handful of strongly tenured politicians backed by powerful and very wealthy financial interests determined to pursue their own agendas. The electorate is now powerless to stop them.

R evolutions are fought for a complex variety of reasons. Ask anyone who has ever been involved in one what they hoped to gain from it. The answer you receive will depend entirely upon which layer of society the respondent belongs. Most commonly, I suppose, those who did most of the fighting and dying during the Revolutionary War would probably have replied with a one word answer: "Freedom."

Yet, those who instigated the Revolution, like Samuel Adams, John Hancock, Patrick Henry and Thomas Jefferson, would more likely have answered the question with the word: "Liberty."

Freedom. Liberty. Are they one and the same thing? Of course not. Freedom is merely an exemption from arbitrary control. Freedom, as most blacks in America know and all too clearly understand, is simply the act of unshackling the human mind and spirit, and the setting free of the human body from those external controls that would otherwise restrict the free movement of their human body.

Even with the newly found freedom ostensibly brought about by the ratification of the 13th Amendment of the Constitution of the United States in 1865, the freed slaves of the South did not possess liberty. Granted, they were free to go wherever they pleased — provided, of course, that access or opportunity was not restricted by the free exercising of personal liberty by others within the same society. Freedom without liberty is a shallow gift.

Freedom is simply one of benefits of liberty. Liberty is, on the other hand, an inherent right. Rather, it is a inherent right with certain responsibilities that must necessarily be attached to it. Because without those responsibilities, *liberty* becomes *license,* and license leads to dictatorship.

The followers of John Locke in colonial America recognized that for them to enjoy freedom government had to be restricted. This was accomplished by laying down a series of guidelines that established precisely what the rights of each man were, and to what extent those rights could be exercised before they infringed on the rights of others.

In a simpler form, God did this in the deserts of Sinai when he gave Moses the Ten Commandments. These commandments, or laws, did not outline the rights the Jews were to enjoy in their newly established freedom. Rather, they detailed an abridgement of those rights because it is only through the control of personal freedom that liberty is actually achieved.

3

All of the ten commandments are restrictive and begin with, or contain, variations of the phrase *thou shall not.* These commandments all deal with what might otherwise be construed as the free exercise of man's prerogatives, or the infringement of those rights upon others within that society.

Liberty offers rights together with responsibilities. License, or anarchy, is the free exercising of implied rights without restriction or responsibility. Liberty was guaranteed by our Constitutional Republic; license is imputed by a democracy.

Historians traditionally ignore the greed that many times compels men into action, and centers instead on the patriotic rhetoric that more often than not shrouds the real motives behind the events that shaped our history.

Traditional historians would have us believe that the United States was the result of historical happenstance; that a series of events simply occurred, by accident, and that nations and rulers were powerless to alter the course of those events through intervention. The reality is, most of the events of history have been the result of design, for reasons usually not generally known, and many times deliberately concealed by those who created the circumstances that influenced change.

Historians delight in patriotic rhetoric concerning the birth of this nation. The reality is our Founding Fathers, if they lived today, would be branded as right wing extremists, tax dodgers and criminals. In today's politically-correct society, John Adams and Thomas Jefferson would more likely have spent four to eight years in prison than four or eight years in the White House. And John Hancock, who signed his name with such flourish on the Declaration of Independence, would likely have been viewed as the Continental Congress' Webster Hubbell, or perhaps even as Massachusetts' Jim Guy Tucker.

Hancock, who was guilty of both smuggling and tax evasion, served first as the presiding officer of the Continental Congress, and then from 1780 to 1785 as the first elected governor of the State of Massachusetts. Hancock and Samuel Adams, who were recognized by the British as the primary conspirators of sedition in America, were the only two colonists exempted from the offer of amnesty made by the British after the Battles of Lexington and Concord in April, 1775 at the start of the war.

To more fully understand the forces that invisibly govern our lives and economic welfare today, it is important to peel back the shroud of patriotic rhetoric from the past and examine the real reasons the Revolutionary War was fought. Once we are able to appreciate the motives behind the events that shaped our nation, we will have a more clear picture of how those same forces are working in the world today, and how they are bringing about the dissolution of our society and the traditional American way of life.

There are two basic philosophies concerning history. The first view is that every event recorded in history happened accidently. The second view is that every major event in the history of the world was the result of one or more conspiracies — people, with well-devised agendas, working together to affect contrived goals or objectives for personal gain. The two schools are evenly divided.

Economist James P. Warburg, in *The West In Crisis* (Doubleday & Company; pg. 20) declared that "...History is written more by accident than design, often by the wholly irrational acts of madmen." Franklin D. Roosevelt, who was himself part of at least two conspiracies that have been uncovered in recent years, has been quoted in the press as saying, "In politics, nothing happens by accident. If it happens, it was planned to happen."

It is difficult for the casual observer to comprehend that catastrophic events might actually be planned, and that actions which will adversely affect thousands, if not millions, of people could be deliberately staged and allowed to happen; or that such power actually exists within our society today. Poll 100 people today, and 99 of them will confidently tell you such power does not exist. They are wrong. It does.

The historically stated reason for the Revolutionary War was taxation without representation. Or, more simply put, taxes. In reviewing the history books, one might even suggest it was fought over the abrogation of personal liberty by the British with the passing of the *Intolerable Acts in 1774*, since the Revolutionary War started the following year. These may well have been the reasons the common Continental soldier thought about as he shouldered his musket and marched off to battle. They were most likely the reasons provided him by his commanders.

They were not, however, the reasons the war was fought. Nor can we take the high moral ground by insisting it was fought to create a new nation in which all men were endowed by their Creator with certain inalienable rights that would grant them the free pursuit of life, liberty and happiness. It wasn't. The *Declaration of Independence* was a purely political document created a year after the Revolutionary War began. It was designed not to express the patriotic reasons that colonists were shedding their blood in places like Lexington, Concord, Bunker Hill and Stony Point; but rather, it was designed to influence public opinion in Europe, particularly in France, where the Americans looked for both the military and financial support they needed to wage their war for independence.

The patriotic verbage we read in this document was carefully crafted by Thomas Jefferson not to tug at the heartstrings of Americans, but to appeal to the European community's court of public opinion. The John Locke rhetoric that permeates the Declaration of Independence represented the political philosophy of such men as Jefferson and Thomas Paine.

While the radical elements in all militant societies argue that civil unrest is justified whenever governments encroach on human rights, Jefferson's document presented the argument that resistance is justified only when government attempts to establish tyranny. Jefferson attempted to show those to whom he wrote that it was the intent of the Americans to create an orderly, functional society based on natural law rather than natural rights.

This was a key phrase in the document, and was carefully crafted from the writings of Emerich deVattel, the Swiss legal philosopher. Jefferson emphasized natural law rather than natural rights to make it clear that an orderly, republican form of government was being created.

What made the language of the *Declaration of Independence* so important is that it was to be used by Benjamin Franklin, the unofficial diplomat of the unofficial nation, to approach the banking families of Europe in search of financial support for the American war effort. Without funds and military assistance, the fledgling republic would be lost before it was created. For the European bankers to invest in America, they had to be certain, at least in their own minds, that the money they invested in this new nation would not be lost.

6

Franklin had spent a total of eleven years in Europe as the chief representative of the American colonies. Known throughout England as a loyalist, he became friends with many of the most influential people in Britain, and was able to successfully lobby the Tories in Parliament to follow a path of conciliation with the colonists when most would have preferred to take a more iron-fisted approach to solving their problems in America.

While Franklin was still arguing with the British that America was not planning an armed rebellion against the Crown, the colonists, on September 5, 1774, assembled the first Continental Congress in Philadelphia. Each of the thirteen colonies and Canada, which was also a colony of England, were invited to send delegates. Canada and Georgia, whose loyalties to the Crown were above reproach, refused to send delegates to debate what options, legal or extralegal, were open to them. While each of them might have agreed that the measures leveled against them by the British parliament were oppressively harsh, neither was willing to engage in what each viewed as sedition to debate them.

Convention radicals, headed by Samuel Adams and armed with a copy of the *Suffolk Resolves* which had been adopted a month earlier by the Massachusetts Assembly when it called the constitutional convention, favored armed conflict if necessary to protect their rights. On May 27, 1774 the Virginia House of Burgesses adopted a formal resolution calling for the creation of a Congress of the Colonies. Two days later Patrick Henry introduced a series of resolutions in the House of Burgesses similar to the *Suffolk Resolves* that denounced four British mandates: the *Sugar Act* which taxed importation of sugar. Interestingly, the *Sugar Act* actually cut the tax on molasses, but called for strict enforcement of the law. The *Colonial Currency Act* depreciated the value of the colonial script making it virtually worthless outside the colonies. The Act further forbade the colonies from issuing what it called "unsound money." The *Stamp Act* required stamps on all commercial and legal documents, and on the publication of all almanacs, phamphlets, and newspapers, as well as a stamp on playing cards and dice. The stamp which appears on every new deck of playing cards today is a carryover from the *Stamp Act*. And finally, Henry offered a resolution decrying *The Quartering Act* which would allow the British Army to billet its troops in civilian hostelries if there was not sufficient military billeting available. The resolutions, send to each of the co-   7 lonial governments, led to the creation of the Continental Congress on September 5 of that year.

Contrary to popular myth, it was not taxation without representation in the British Parliament that angered the colonies most, but rather it was the heavy-handed manner in which the Crown, or its agents, chose to enforce the oppressive tax laws it had enacted. When George Grenville assumed power in England in 1763 the Seven Year War had just ended. England's national debt — owed to the Rothschilds and others who had financed both sides of the conflict, stood at £133 million, more than double the £60 million it previously owed. It was the costliest war England had ever fought. The tax load amounted to £18 for every man, woman and child living in England. Grenville viewed the disparity between the taxes paid by Crown subjects in England and those in America as an unfathomable anomaly since the American citizens' tax burden amounted to less than 18 shillings per person and yet, in his view, the Americans had benefited more from the Seven Year War than the British citizens who lived in England.

It was common knowledge in England that the Americans avoided most of the taxes which were imposed on them by smuggling — particularly molasses and rum. Grenville's actuaries estimated that smuggling in the colonies cost the Crown over £700,000 each year. Grenville was determined to end the practice that had made men like John Hancock wealthy. Additional troops were sent to the colonies and a new Vice-Admiralty Court was set up in Halifax to try the offenders. American courts were made inferior to the military tribunals and the Crown tax collectors — who were previously paid by the colonies — were now paid by the Crown from the tax receipts they collected.

The Suffolk Convention met in August, 1774 to protest the *Intolerable Acts*. The convention resolved that the four laws which constituted the *Intolerable Acts* — particularly the *Currency Act* — should be "rejected as the attempts of a wicked administration to enslave America." (It should come as no surprise to anyone that the Suffolk Convention was called by Adams.) Both Adams and John Hancock knew the *Massachusetts Government Act*, which abrogated the rights of the colonists to trials in America for acts of sedition against the Crown, was specifically

8

directed against them. In fact, after the Battles of Lexington and Concord, the British government offered a blanket grant of amnesty to all of the colonists engaged in acts of sedition against the Crown except Adams and Hancock, who alone were viewed by the British as the ringleaders of the revolution.

Surprisingly, although Adams advocated armed conflict to protect the civil rights of the colonists during the convention, not a single delegate, Adams included, ever mentioned the word *independence*. The debate was entirely centered on the *Suffolk Resolves*, the issues of civil rights, and how best to safeguard them.

Joseph Galloway, the delegate from Pennsylvania, unsuccessfully argued that a conciliatory gesture be made to the British government through which the difficulties between the Crown and the colonies might be successfully and peacefully adjudicated. Adams, his radical advocates solidly behind him, debated his point of view so successfully that Galloway's conservatives were soundly defeated when the matter came up for a vote.

Instead, the convention formally renounced the *Intolerable Acts*, and drafted both a list of grievances and a declaration of rights which would be presented to the Crown. In addition, the petition asked George III to prevent Parliament from violating the rights of the colonists, who were free Englishmen, and detailed a total of thirteen instances in which Parliament had previously done so.

To put teeth in their demands the delegates formally agreed that none of the colonies would import any English goods whatsoever after December 1, 1774. Furthermore they stipulated that in the event the British government did not accede to their demands by September 11, 1775, the colonies would no longer allow any American goods, which included tobacco and pelts, to be exported to England. This threat proved to be a serious miscalculation on the part of the colonists. War was now inevitable, and the doomsday clock was ticking.

Rhetoric aside, wars are more often fought over money than patriotic principles. War, or the need to suffer war, is more often decided by the power brokers behind the seats of government than by those who theoretically control them. The American Revolution was no exception. That the colonies were going to war was an inescapable fact from as early as 1764. It is only because neither side wanted war that the events which triggered the American Revolution fermented for eleven years before finally erupting into pitched battles at Lexington and Concord, Massachusetts on April 19, 1775 and ultimately, after the declaration of independence from England a year later, the launching of full-scale war.

From the moment England passed the *Currency Act of 1764* and replaced the legal currency of the colonies with English pounds, war with England was inevitable. No measures taken by either side from that point could effect a peaceful solution.

For war to be avoided by the colonists, their right to print and control their own money supply, taken from them when the *Currency Act* was passed, would necessarily had to have been restored by the Crown—a right which, from 1694 until March 1, 1946[1], it did not itself possess. The money barons of Europe had clearly impressed on the Crown that the control of the colonial monetary system was to be their exclusive domain. Clearly, they would have suffered an extreme and unacceptable financial loss by surrendering that right, and those profits, back to the colonies— something they did not intend to do. For war to be avoided by the Crown, the right to control the money supply of the colonies, and the ability to tax the colonies, had to remain vested in the Bank of England. Due to the vast sum owed it by the Crown, the privately owned bank had more than enough economic clout to determine the course of the political actions that would be taken by the Crown. Since neither side was willing to surrender the right to control the monetary system of the colonies, war was inevitable.

---

[1]At the end of WW II the British discovered that the Bank of England had participated in secret ventures with several other European central banks to loan money to the Third Reich. Angered at the thought that the British taxpayers—the victims of Hitler's aerial reign of terror—might have been paying for the bombs that were dropped on London during the war, the House of Commons voted overwhelmingly to reject the Bank of England's charter which had existed since July 27, 1694, and the British government assumed "ownership" of the bank. It was a largely "ceremonial" "takeover" because all of the key figures in the Bank of England remained "in charge." But, even in their indignation, the members of Parliament knew not to cross the line too far. Taken from thebankers briefly was their profits. On March 1, 1946 the British government seized the capital stock of the Bank of England and surrendered it to the British Treasury, effectively nationalizing the Bank. As the European economy stagnated in the late 1940s, the stock was quietly returned with the government function-

A lthough the colonists did not view themselves as seeking independence from the British Empire, their petition reeked of independence. In the eyes of the Crown the stipulations put forth pretty much amounted to the same thing. By demanding that the *Intolerable Acts* be repealed, the colonists were, in essence, demanding both political and economic freedom from England.

In addition, by refusing to buy British goods, the colonists refused to pay British taxes. This meant that for the Crown to meet its obligations to the bankers from whom it had heavily borrowed, additional taxes would have to be levied against the English citizen—something the Crown was not prepared to do since it would likely cause civil unrest at home. Furthermore, by refusing to buy English goods, whether subject to taxation or not, the colonists were disrupting the economy of Britain. British merchants would be clamoring for action from their elected officials in both the House of Commons and the House of Lords—something Parliament was not prepared to deal with. And, finally, since the colonists were also demanding all of the rights of a sovereign nation, the money overlords in the Bank of England demanded that the sedition in America be put down once and for all time.

Major General Thomas Gage had been quietly collecting intelligence on the colonists for quite some time, and had recently learned from loyalists to the Crown that the First Provincial Congress of Massachusetts had formed an organization called the Committee of Safety in October, 1774 whose stated purpose was to collect arms and munitions to supply a Continental army should the need arise. The Committee of Safety, headed by none other than Gage's old nemesis Samuel Adams, would reportedly func-

---

ing from that point on as the silent "overseer" rather than as an owner of the bank.

The Bank of England today, however, is about as "nationally" owned as the American Federal Reserve System. Clearly, the House of Commons was "showboating" for the British press. The Bank of England's Board of Governors operates precisely as the American Fed governors. The Bank of England is administered by a governor, a deputy governor and 16 directors who are appointed by the Crown. Today, the Bank of England functions as it did prior to 1946—the profits belong to the European banking cartel.

tion as the governing body of Massachusetts should war with England erupt.

Learning that John Hancock had vast stores of muskets and ammunition stored in his warehouse in Concord, Gage dispatched a detachment of 800 troops under the command of Lt. Col. Francis Smith from Boston to destroy them. Because Gage also knew the colonists had formed a citizen's militia known as the Minutemen, Smith was ordered to confiscate any arms and munitions from any person that might fight in any of the patriot militias — which, as far as Smith was concerned, meant anyone and everyone. (It was specifically the confiscatory action on the part of Smith on April 18, 1775 that resulted in the inclusion of the 2nd Amendment into the United States Constitution.)

As Smith's troops moved through the countryside confiscating arms, word of their advance was spread quickly by Minutemen like Paul Revere. When Smith's troops reached the outskirts of Concord on the morning of April 19, 1775 the colonists were waiting. As Smith's troops crossed the bridge that spanned the Concord River the colonists opened fire, killing two soldiers outright and wounding several others. The handful of farmers were no match for Smith's regular army troops. Eight Americans died in the brief skirmish.

However, the Minutemen had bought Hancock all of the time he needed. By the time Smith's troops fought their way to Hancock's warehouse, most of the munitions and supplies had been evacuated. Smith sent a runner back to Boston for reinforcements and, with his remaining troops, attempted to cordon off the town of Concord and hold it until help arrived. At that time, Smith reasoned, he would conduct a house-to-house search for the military stores, arrest the seditionists, and the rebellion would be over.

Instead, Smith discovered his problems were just beginning. Hundreds of colonial militiamen suddenly appeared from all over the Massachusetts countryside and launched a surprise counterattack against Smith's regulars.

However, unlike the British troops who were trained in the European school of warfare to fight encounters with other regular troops who fought in mechanical formations utilizing the lethal practice of volley-firing, the colonial Minutemen were untrained and accustomed only to using firearms for hunting game. The colonists did not stand and fight like trained regulars. They fired and disappeared, only to reappear in a different spot minutes later to fire again.

The British troops were unnerved. That any force of irregular troops, of any size, could seriously threaten a troop of British regulars unsettled not only the troops under his command, but Smith as well, who stood helplessly as his well-trained soldiers fell under the deadly fire of the colonists. Defeated, Smith ordered a retreat. As the retreat sounded, Smith's troops broke into disorganized flight with the Minutemen in hot pursuit.

Smith's troops did not stop running until they met up with the reinforcements from Boston under the command of Sir Hugh Percy at Lexington. Percy's troops, totalling 1,200 men, were able to momentarily check the advance of the Minutemen, but Percy was likewise no match for the unorthodox fighting style of the colonists. Percy's troops engaged the colonists several times in rear guard actions covering the British retreat, an event which now under the command of Percy was much more orderly. It would not look good for British soldiers to be seen scurrying for safety like hounds being chased by the rabbit.

The American offensive did not end when the British troops reached Boston. Militia forces continued to arrive. On April 20, 1775 the colonists laid siege to the city and held it until the British evacuated Boston eleven months later, on March 17, 1776, under a flag of truce.

When the casualties from the Battles of Concord and Lexington were tallied, America was credited with its first military victory — and, it was a decisive victory at that. The British suffered 73 killed, 174 wounded, and 26 missing in action. Colonial forces suffered 49 killed, 39 wounded and 5 missing in action. Militiamen from 23 towns and villages in Massachusetts participated in the call-to-arms. But more important was the effect the uprising had on Gage, the commander of the British troops. Gage was paralyzed by the impact the colonists made on Smith's seasoned troops. Untrained farmers had devastated some of England's finest forces with a new form of warfare that even the field commander, Smith, could not describe. The attacks were so lightning fast and lethal, Smith's troops could not defend themselves against it. In fact, Smith was at least partially responsible for Gage's decision not to attempt to break the siege lines that strangled Boston.

Shortly after the siege began, General Artemas Ward of the Massachusetts militia assumed temporary command of the be- 13 sieging colonial forces. Eventually the colonial army would swell to include units from New Hampshire under the command of Colonel John Stark, from Rhode Island under the command of General Nathanael Greene, and from Connecticut under the command of General Israel Putnam.

Unlike Ward, who was not an experienced soldier, Greene was a self-taught military expert who earned his stripes during the French and Indian War, as did both Stark and Putnam and most of the New England militiamen under their commands.

When news of the outbreak of war reached England, Franklin made one final appeal to Parliament to hold their forces in check. It was this effort which resulted in the blanket offer of amnesty to all of the colonists except Samuel Adams and Hancock. His power of conciliation with the Crown exhausted, Franklin sorrowfully returned to Philadelphia on May 5, 1775, carrying with him the knowledge that his homeland was doomed. America lacked both the finances and experience to win a protracted war with England.

Five days later on May 10 the second Continental Congress met in Philadelphia to discuss the events which were rapidly unfolding in America. During this convention, which lasted some 40 days, a Congress was established as the central government of the United Colonies of America. Since the new government would be required to finance the cost of war, it immediately granted itself authority to issue paper currency. This fiat money, backed by nothing except patriotic zeal, immediately replaced the English script as legal tender. In a show of solidarity, most of the colonial legislatures passed laws requiring their citizens to accept the Colonial script. While the power brokers behind the Bank of England would not lose any sleep over the shooting of 247 British soldiers or the entrapment of over 3200 more soldiers within Boston, they would become insomniacs when they learned that the rebel Congress had replaced the British currency with their own — and repudiated the bond issue that financed the British script. War was now inevitable.

The troops which laid siege to Boston were officially commissioned as the Continental Army, and by a unanimous voice vote, George Washington was appointed the commander of it.

Benjamin Franklin was immediately dispatched to Canada to seek both financial and military aid from the Canadian colonists. His efforts proved to be fruitless. While Canada shared

America's aspirations, they believed the British army could not be defeated and would not put themselves in jeopardy. Britain was at that time the most powerful nation in the world. It possessed a well organized government, a vast, competent army, a sizeable treasury, and the largest, most powerful navy in the world. In addition, its subjects enjoyed a prosperous lifestyle and would support the decisions of the Parliament. In contrast, the Canadians pointed out to Franklin that the colonists were a loose-knit, ragtail confederation with no chief executive, no organized government, no organized army — and most of all, no money with which to fight a war, sustained or otherwise.

In addition, the newly formed Continental Congress had political rivals in the thirteen colonial assemblies that would likely not cooperate with their own delegates in Philadelphia. The Canadians even suggested it might be in Franklin's best interests to return to England and wait out the conflict — which they assured him would not take long.

When he returned to Philadelphia, Franklin was appointed, along with John Adams, Thomas Jefferson, Roger Sherman, and Robert Livingstone to draft what was to become the Declaration of Independence. Jefferson, who was an advocate of the principles of John Locke and who was known as a literary craftsman in his own right, was assigned the task of actually writing the document that was to be created.

The idea itself originated with Richard Henry Lee of the Virginia delegation to the Continental Congress who made a motion on the floor of Congress on June 7, 1776 that "...these united colonies are, and of right ought to be, free and independent states, and that they are absolved from all allegiance to the British Crown, and that all political connection between them and the State of Great Britain is, and ought to be, totally dissolved."

In patriotic zeal, John Adams quickly seconded the motion, but action on the resolution was deferred until July 1. A committee of the above named delegates was established on June 11 to prepare the resolution suggested by Lee — who would, eleven years later, argue that the Constitution as it was written by James Madison infringed too much on states' rights.

Lee would not be alone in his thinking. Samuel Adams and Patrick Henry would also oppose the creation of a strong central government, and refused to attend the Constitutional Convention. In defense of his principles Lee proposed, much in the

15

same words that it would eventually be adopted, the 10th Amendment to the Constitution which states: "The power not delegated to the United States by the Constitution, nor prohibited by it to the States, are reserved to the States respectively, or to the people." Unfortunately, during the 20th century Lee's worst fears would be realized as the Congress of the United States assumed for itself authority not only not granted it, but expressly denied to it, by the amendment Lee wrote.

The attorney John Adams and the statesman Franklin made several minor changes in Jefferson's draft of the Declaration of Independence before it was formally submitted. On July 1, 1776 the delegates adopted the document after making several other revisions and alterations, deleting several sections — including one inserted by Adams that condemned Negro slavery. Lee's resolution was incorporated and the revised text was issued as the Declaration of Independence. If John Adams had held more political sway with the Continental Congress, the United States might well have been born as a nation in which slavery did not exist, a land where all men, regardless of the color of their skin, would be born free and equal before the law. Instead, eight-five years later the slavery issue would be cited by the Jacobins as the catalyst that divided the nation and pitted brother against brother in a Civil War whose scars would take a hundred years to heal. In point of fact the Civil War was not fought over slavery. The Civil War erupted over the issue of States' rights[2].

The rewritten document was completed and resubmitted to Congress on July 4, 1776 where it was formally approved by the voice vote of twelve of the thirteen colonies. The New York delegate abstained from voting because they had not been granted authority by their legislature to do so. On July 9 the New York

---

[2]It is important for the reader to understand that from the expiration of the Second National Bank's charter in 1836, with two notable exceptions, it was largely the Southern Senators who opposed rechartering a privately-owned central bank in the United States. In 1832 Henry Clay and Daniel Webster urged Nicholas Biddle, President of the Second National Bank to apply for a charter—four years early—to embarrass Andrew Jackson and damage his chances of being re-elected since the industrial north wanted to keep the central bank—regardless who owned it. Beginning in 1833 Jackson transferred all of America's funds from the Second Bank to

legislature voted to endorse the Declaration. By August 2, it had been signed by 53 of the 56 Congressional delegates. The remaining three delegates, who were not present on August 2, subsequently signed the document. Several copies of the Declaration were transcribed. A copy was sent to each colony and to each of the military commanders of the Continental army.

And copies were entrusted to Franklin who, along with Arthur Lee and Silas Deane, was dispatched to France to solicit economic aid for the new nation.

Arthur Lee, a brother of Richard Henry Lee and a second cousin of Robert E. Lee, traveled as part of Franklin's entourage to France. Lee was actually recruited by Congress as a secret agent to enlist support not only from the various governments of Europe, but also from sympathetic Englishmen who had previously

---

a group of State banks.

As the Jacobins grew in power over the next twenty years issues over States rights verses federal might took the forefront of political debate as the Jacobin Congress attempted, through legislation, to reinterpret its franchise under the Constitution and assume a superior role over the States. While the history books our children study in the classrooms of America's schools today offer a fairly accurate view of the "public" events—the succession of the 11 Confederate States and the firing on and subsequent capture of the federal aresenal at Fort Sumter in Charleston harbor by Confederate General Pierre Beauregard on April 10, 1861—which led to the Civil War, few students realize that South Carolina had a constitutional right to secede from the Union on December 20, 1860 not over the issue of slavery, but over the issue of the superiority of the States. The Northern industrial States wanted, and needed, a central bank in order to build the roads and fund the industrial development they needed to expand commerce. The South, which was largely agrarian, saw no need for a central bank and even less for the increased taxes a central bank would demand to repay them for the loans they would grant the Jacobin Congress which was, in 1861, attempting to "federalize" the States.

On February 4, 1861 Senator John J. Crittenden (D-KY) proposed what became known as the *Crittenden Compromise.* The Compromise, pointed to by historians as the catalyst that would drive the South to secede when it was voted down [to prove that the Civil War was fought over slavery], would have extended the *Missouri Compromise* line to the Pacific Ocean. However, the originator of proposal was not Crittenden, it was Senator Stephen Douglas (D-IL), Lincoln's nemesis, who was seeking the patronage of the railroad barons who wanted to employ slave labor to build the transcontinental railroad.

made substantial financial investments in the colonies that they might wish protected until the conflict ended. Very subtly, Lee wrangled financial support from business interests all over Europe — even from members of the British Parliament.

Franklin, who was now seventy, still had access to most of the French political and social circles, but he was slowing down and no longer possessed the stamina he had only two years earlier when he visited France and convinced a group of French businessmen to buy guns for the colonies. However, he had the zeal of a used car salesman, the wit of a comedian and gracious manner of a statesman. Through his ingenuity, Franklin secured both financial aid and economic concessions from France despite vigorous opposition from Jacques Necker, the French minister of finance — and despite jealous antagonism from Silas Deane, who viewed Franklin as an inept, senile colonial boor who lacked the genteel *bon ton* upbringing expected of those who visited the courts of Europe.

Yet, Deane returned home empty-handed. Franklin returned home with a treaty, negotiated on February 6, 1778 that provided, in addition to three million livre, additional grants and loans, a defense alliance and a willing trading partner for American goods.

Conspiracy advocates insist Franklin's success in France was due entirely to the fact that both he and those with whom he met were Masons, including the French foreign minister Charles Gravier de Vergennes, and that the Masons, together with the Illuminati (a secret society of wealthy intellectuals formed on May 1, 1776), were part of a well-organized, clandestine conspiracy to overthrow all of the nations of the world.

There was a genuine concern in colonial America over the growing influence of the Masons in the United States — almost from the birth of the nation. Franklin was a Mason. So was George Washington, John Adams, and Thomas Jefferson. All totaled, 53 of the 56 signers of the Declaration of Independence were Masons[3].

---

[3]It is by no means strange that so many of the Founding Fathers were Masons since many of those who migrated to America were Masons who did not believe in the hereditary rule of the monarchy, and wanted to escape the totalitarian rule imposed upon them by the kings of Europe. The same is true of many of the aristocrats who belonged to the "gentry" sects, like the Jacobins. But unlike the working class, the arisotcrats enjoyed the privileges of royalty but could not share the power.

So were most of the members of the Constitutional Convention.

Interestingly, Patrick Henry, Samuel Adams and John Hancock were not. Each of these men were consumed with states rights issues. Adams and Henry, although delegates, refused to attend the Constitutional Convention because they did not see the need for forming a national government. On the other hand, Richard Henry Lee was a Mason. And he, like Henry and Adams, resisted the formation of a strong national government.

The first organized third party in the United States was formed in 1827 as the Anti-Mason Party. They threw their support behind John Quincy Adams, who unlike his famous father, was not a Mason. His opponent, Andrew Jackson, was. Jackson lost.

The Anti-Masons offered their own presidential candidate, William Wirt, in 1832 against the extremely popular Jackson. Most of those who belonged to the Anti-Mason Party were extremely influential within their communities, but as a voting block they proved to be insignificant. The power they wielded over those who worked in their shops and factories did not extend into the voting booth. They took 8% of the popular vote and carried only one state, Vermont. Their contribution to the electoral process in America, however, had a far-reaching impact on the American political process.

Because the Anti-Masons could not attract any of the famous patriots who bravely fought during the war of 1812, or those whose names were associated with the American Revolution—perhaps because most of them were Masons—they chose a different venue for selecting their candidate. They held a national convention and selected their candidate by ballot. Prior to 1832, presidential candidates were selected by congressional party members. Both of the major parties quickly adopted the convention process. While the Anti-Mason Party died in 1838 when it merged with the Whigs, the national political convention lived on.

The Anti-Masons were formed to counter what they alleged was an attempt to subvert all public institutions in the United States by the Freemasons. Their movement gained life through the disappearance of a writer, William Morgan, who wrote a book that purportedly exposed the secret agenda of the Masons. While history amply supports the theory that a conspiracy, 19 or collective groups of conspiracies, does and has existed for two hundred years, and that the sole purpose of the conspiracy was the overthrow all of the governments of all of the nations in the world, those attempts have not been the handiwork of the Masons, or any other "structured" organization.

Conspiracy buffs do their theories an injustice by attempting to convince others that a conspiracy exists by labeling those involved as Masons, members of the Illuminati, Bilderbergers, or what nots. Conspiracies, when they exist, are contrived by men for personal reasons and personal gain. The names of the organizations to which they belong are not important. It is the objective of the conspiracy and whether or not those conspiring possess the ability to achieve their objectives that is important. Prior to this moment in history, no organization or groups of organizations has possessed either the ability or the means to overthrow all of the nations of the earth. Today, that is no longer true.

As stated previously, there are two views of history. First, there is the view that every major event in history occurred by happenstance. Catastrophes simply happen. Nobody plans them; nobody controls them. As major events of history unfold, people and societies get caught up in them, and these events simply evolve to their natural conclusions.

Second, there is the view which suggests that absolutely nothing happens by chance. Historical events such as famines, wars, and economic calamities take place because someone wants them to take place; someone has planned for them to take place; and finally, someone is directing the movement to achieve a pre-planned objective.

History treats the Boston Tea Party as one of those unplanned acts of history that was carried out by overzealous patriots caught in the fervor of the moment. It was not. It was a conspiracy, devised for profit, by two men: Samuel Adams and John Hancock. Conspiracies do not have to be national in scope to be conspiracies. A conspiracy occurs anytime one or more people work in secret to devise a scheme which will affect the lives of other people. A conspiracy also occurs when an unplanned or undesired catastrophe, which could have been averted, is allowed to happen. The Boston Tea Party is an example of the first definition. Pearl Harbor is an example of the second.

Hancock was one of Massachusetts' wealthiest importers. He profited from goods carried to the colonies on his ships, as well as on the British trade vessels, since the goods he purchased from the British were stored in his warehouse to be sold to merchants throughout Massachusetts for resale to their customers.

Historians would have us believe that colonials, dressed as Indians, pitched 342 chests of prime East Indies tea worth some £9,000 into Boston harbor because it carried an oppressive tax. Other than the token taxes levied against most trade goods under the *Townshend Act,* there was no tax on tea. *The Tea Act,* which triggered the Boston Tea Party, was not about taxes. Rather, it allowed the British East India Company, which was in dire financial straits due to the mismanagement of its principles, to bypass American wholesalers like Hancock and sell direct to the shop owners in the colonies.

Did Hancock and Adams tell those who dumped the tea into the harbor that the reason for the Boston Tea Party was because Hancock would suffer financially if the goods were allowed to be unloaded? Of course not. They used *taxation without representation* to inflame the people.

Adams' motivation was much deeper than Hancock's. Adams was a true anarchist who believed the natural rights of man superseded the authority of all governments. While Hancock's motive was profit, Adams wanted to provoke a war. Adams had, for several years, fanned the flames of discontent in the colonies, and led the vanguard that championed rebellion. He instigated and led the demonstration that resulted in the Boston Massacre. Upon the formation of the Continental Congress, he led the radical faction that demanded a military solution to the problems with Britain.

It was largely the writings of Samuel Adams, written over many years under several different pseudonyms, arguing against any type of reconciliation with England, and demanding that the citizens of the colonies rise up and strike down their oppressors, that colored the mood of rebellion in America.

And finally, was it a coincidence that the first battles of the Revolutionary War occurred on April 19, 1775 — exactly one day after Gage signed an arrest warrant for Adams and Hancock, charging them with smuggling and sedition? Or that the first two battles of that war took place in Concord and Lexington? Hancock lived in Concord. Adams lived in Lexington.   21

Coincidence...or conspiracy?

"The history of liberty is a history of limitations of governmental power, not the increase of it. When we resist, therefore, the concentration of power, we are resisting the powers of death, because concentration of power is what always precedes the destruction of human liberty."
Thomas Woodrow Wilson
The Rebirth of America
By Robert Flood;
The Arthur S. Demoss Foundation, pg. 13

❖ TWO ❖

Churchill, Wilson and Roosevelt

While few Americans realize it, two of the players who helped engineer the United States' involvement in the first world war would also become the key architect's of America's involvement in World War II.

On October 25, 1911 Winston Churchill, who gained early fame for his exploits during the Battle of Omdurman in the Sudan, was appointed First Lord of the Admiralty by British Prime Minister Herbert Asquith. When war broke out in Europe, Churchill became one of its first casualties, being blamed for the British defeat in the Dardanelles in December, 1915 with the staggering loss of 100,000 British and Turkish soldiers. He was demoted to the subservient post as Chancellor of the Duchy of Lancaster.

Churchill resigned, joined the British army and served briefly in France as an infantry major. When Sir David Lloyd George was elected Prime Minister he returned to government service as the Minister of Munitions in 1917. Still festering from his 1915 political battle scars, Churchill viewed the expanding world war as an opportunity for him to gain both power and position in the British government, and he was determined the make the most of the opportunity. He owed no allegiance to party or person. During his early career he changed party affiliation at least three times, always erring to the party in power since the party in power controlled all ministerial appointments.

Interestingly Churchill, as an insider involved in international politics, was convinced that a global conspiracy of sorts was being played out on the world stage and argued that point in a February 8, 1920 interview with the *Illustrated Sunday Herald* where he was quoted as saying: " From the days of Spartacus...to Karl Marx, to Trotsky [there is] a worldwide conspiracy for the overthrow of civilization [and it] has been steadily growing [for years]."

23

On the other side of the ocean, a young man just entering political life, Franklin Delano Roosevelt, caught the attention of Colonel Edward Mandell House, the wealthy author of a book entitled *Phillip Dru, Administrator* that detailed the exploits of a idealistic socialist civil servant, Phillip Dru, who successfully overthrows the government of the United States.

House was the son of Thomas W. House who amassed a fortune during the Civil War as an American agent of the Rothschilds by serving the financial needs of both the North and the South. Like many of the kingmakers of the late 19th and early 20th century, Edward House was a private person who remained so unobtrusively hidden behind the scenes that he was largely ignored by the historians who recorded the events of his day. However, House was a major shaper of policy in both the administrations of Woodrow Wilson and Franklin D. Roosevelt—the young man who was to become his protegé in 1916.

As First Lord of the Admiralty, Winston Churchill was assigned the job of negotiating the temporary transfer of the Cunard Lines passenger ship, the *U.S.S. Lusitania,* to the British government to be used as war supplies carrier. This was not an unusual assignment. Since there was a shortage of cargo vessels, many American passenger ships were being used to transport war supplies and materials to Europe.

The ship was routed to New York where it picked up a cargo, reported to be 6,000,000 rounds of ammunition, owned by J.P. Morgan & Co. Before the *Lusitania* was scheduled to sail, the German government ran an advertisement in all of the New York City newspapers warning the American people that anyone planning to sail on the ship would be well advised not to, since the German navy now viewed the *Lusitania* as a British cargo vessel that was sailing into a war zone. If spotted by a German U-boat, it would be sunk.

When the advertisement appeared, Secretary of State William Jennings Bryan requested that the White House issue a warning to all Americans to avoid the *Lusitania,* but no such warning was ever issued by Woodrow Wilson or anyone else in the executive branch.

On December 14, 1914 British intelligence broke the German war code. Within a month, they were able to track the departures of every German ship of war, including their U-boats. This was one of the best kept secrets in the Admiralty, and helped minimize Allied losses during the war. While the British navy did not know the specific locations of the U-boats at any given time, they always knew which areas most likely contained them.

Another incident which, if true, bears directly on the motives of the sinking of the *Lusitania* was discussed in the book *The Lusitania* by Colin Simpson (*Ballantine Books,* 1972; p.134). The author referred to a conversation between Edward Mandell House and Sir Edward Grey, the Foreign Secretary of England concerning the likelihood of America's entrance into the war:

"Grey: 'What will America do if the Germans sink an ocean liner with American passengers on board?'

House: 'I believe that a flame of indignation would sweep the United States and that by itself would be sufficient to carry us into the war.'"

Woodrow Wilson, the former governor of New Jersey and Princeton University president, like his protegé Franklin Roosevelt would thirty years later, spent half of his time assuring the American public he would keep the United States out of the war in Europe and the rest of his time covertly trying to deal them in. And, like Roosevelt, he privately stressed to his allies the need for an *event* to transpire which would serve as a catalyst to propel a reluctant nation into the conflict. After all, he had the 1916 election to worry about—as his protegé Roosevelt would have 1944.

On the morning of May 7, 1915 the *Lusitania* was sunk by a German U-boat off the coast of Ireland in the English Channel with the loss of 1,198 lives, including 128 American citizens. The Lusitania, which had maintained the traditional zig-zag sailing pattern to avoid U-boats throughout the trip across the Atlantic suddenly stopped zig-zagging and even cut its speed in half. An inquiry by the British government conducted in June, 1915 revealed that the *Lusitania* had slowed to await an escort vessel, the *H.M.S. Juno,* which was to lead it to port. However, for reasons which have never been satisfactorily explained, the First Lord of the Admiralty, Winston Churchill, ordered the *Juno* to return to port while the *Lusitania* sat alone and unprotected in the English Channel waiting for its arrival.

Around noon on May 7, Captain Walther Schwieger, who commanded the German U-20 spotted the *HMS Juno.* According to his log, she was zigzagging at top speed. Schwieger knew he would not be able to catch the *Juno,* and gave up the chase. A short time later he spotted the *Lusitana* standing dead in the

25

water. He fired one torpedo. Eighteen minutes later 1,198 of the *Lusitana's* 2,000 passengers were dead. Two separate inquiries were held at the end of the war. Both inquiries were inclusive.

American newspapers, citing the advertisements run by the German government, accused the Germans of deliberately seeking out the *Lusitania*. While the German government vehemently denied the allegation it is probably true. The munitions cargo the Lusitania purportedly carried was not only not kept a secret, neither was the departure date of the *Lusitania*, its course, or its arrival date in England — making it a not only a prime but logical target for the German navy. It was almost as though someone wanted the ship to be sunk. And, of course, the Germans willingly obliged.

The court of inquiry which investigated the disaster in 1915, as well as an American inquiry at the end of the war which included an interview with the U-boat commander who sank the Lusitania, reached the same conclusion from hundreds of pages of otherwise conflicting testimony that contained substantially different versions about what actually transpired that morning. The *Lusitania* was sunk by torpedoes from a German U-boat and not from exploding munitions. What makes that conclusion so striking is the fact that when a torpedo strikes a munitions ship, the munitions explode; and, it is usually the munitions and not the torpedoes that actually sinks the vessel. In the case of the *Lusitania,* it was the conclusion of the experts that there were no munitions in its cargo hold since the explosion that should have resulted did not occur.

The public outcry that was to catapult America into the war did not happen and the *Lusitania* did not become the catalyst that dragged America into the war. One thousand one hundred ninety-eight people died in vain.

On the merry-go-round of world politics, Wilson was to get one shot at the gold ring. While visiting Sir Edward Grey in London during January, 1916, Colonel House, Wilson's "unofficial" advisor, proposed a unique idea that fell on very receptive ears. A world governing body needed to be established at the end of the war. The plenary ruling council would consist of those nations who helped Britain defeat the Germans. They would establish the rules, and they would set the agenda for all of the nations of the world from that point on.

From that group, House proposed, one man, an intellectual visionary with a plan to end war for all time, a man with the wisdom of Solomon who could shape this league of nations into a global society of equal trading partners would logically preside as the head of this elite world forum.

That man, House had previously assured Wilson, would be him—providing he was prepared to commit the full force and might of the United States to end the conflict in Europe. While House was championing his protegé Wilson to Grey, the British foreign secretary envisioned something completely different from that which House described. Grey saw a way through which the power of the British Empire could be forever guaranteed and perpetuated.

On May 17, 1916 President Wilson proposed, in a speech to the League to Enforce Peace, the formation of a world government. The President of this world government, in the President's mind, would be Wilson. Fed by House's vivd imagination, Wilson was hooked by his own ego. Wilson saw himself as the "man of peace" who would end this horrible war. But, to end it, he had to get in it. Any justifiable provocation, Wilson promised Grey, would send American troops to war.

Although he had been trying to find an excuse to enter the war for almost a year, Wilson was re-elected on November 7, 1916 on a platform of peace. However the race was too close and Wilson obviously knew he did not possess a clear mandate from the people. He garnered 49.4% of the popular vote. His opponent, Republican Charles Evans Hughes took 46.2% of the vote and spoilers, who sometimes alter the outcome of elections, took 4.4%. Wilson carried 32 states; Hughes carried 16.

With nothing to lose now except the possible presidency of the League of Nations, Wilson assured the British that if the Germans did not sit down at the peace table, America would enter the war.

On December 12, 1916 the German government notified Wilson that it was prepared to sit down at the peace table with the Allies. Wilson conveyed this message to London. Sir David Lloyd George, the British Prime Minister immediately rejected the advance, claiming the German offer to negotiate did not contain any specific terms and therefore was merely a ploy to elicit support from political doves in America.

It is likely that the real reason the British rejected the overture was that Austro-German and Turkish forces had been winning the war and would likely insist that they be allowed to keep all of the lands they had taken—which included Belgium, Serbia, and Montenegro, as well as portions of France, Italy, Rumania, Macedonia, Czechoslovakia and Bulgaria. This, of course, was totally unacceptable to the British who wanted nothing less than the total capitulation of Germany.

Wilson, on December 18, with his eye forever fixed on the gold ring, transmitted his own proposal to the warring nations. He suggested that Germany, Austria, and Turkey outline their terms for peace and their guarantees against renewed conflict. On December 26 the Austro-German and Turkish governments responded by suggesting that the detailing of terms was premature, and that such negotiations should commence with an exchange of views between all parties. Lloyd George, on the other hand, had no difficulty in dictating terms. He demanded the restoration of lands taken, and the evacuation of all Austro-German and Turkish forces from France, Italy, Russian, Rumanian and Czech soil. In addition, the prime minister demanded reparations to cover the Allied costs of war.

The negotiations broke down before they ever began.

Wilson was incensed. The Allies, who were losing the war, were in no position to make such arrogant demands. The Germans, on the other hand, knew that the Allies would not be able to continue their war effort much longer without American participation. And, they were equally convinced it would not come since the American people were adamantly opposed to sending troops to Europe. If that remained the case, the Allies would be forced to sue for peace. However, the Germans didn't know about Wilson's vision of a world governing body that he would lead. Nor did they know, or care, about the hawkish Assistant Secretary of the Navy, Roosevelt, who impatiently and perpetually pursued the President to declare war on Germany.

Roosevelt was extremely frustrated because his career was moving so slowly. He blamed his boss, Navy Secretary Joseph Daniels. Roosevelt knew Wilson wanted to be a player, and was convinced the American public would support the decision once it was made. He couldn't understand why Wilson was dragging his feet.

28   Daniels resisted every hawkish effort to put American cargo

ships into harm's way. He opposed convoying American ships with those from England because they might accidently be torpedoed by U-boats. And, most of all, he resisted every Wilson Administration effort to arm merchant ships that were sailing into harm's way because he knew such an action would be viewed by the Germans as an overt act of hostility.

Roosevelt favored both. However, the Senate wasn't buying. Roosevelt lobbied the president for Daniel's job, and he lobbied Congress for a declaration of war against Germany—and the hawks outside the government, knowing he was House's protegé with direct access to Wilson lobbied him. Roosevelt was frequently seen dining at the Metropolitan Club in Washington with likes of J.P. Morgan, House, and Elihu Root—supporters he would ultimately use in his own quest for power.

Wilson knew the majority of Americans wanted peace at any price, but he was determined to find a way to enter the war. The Germans, on January 20, 1917 sent him a secret communique detailing what they considered to be acceptable conditions to end the war. The terms, he knew once he read them, would be unacceptable to the British. The Germans wanted restitution for German enterprises damaged by the war, expanded national borders, and the creation of a strategic zone between Germany and Poland on one side and between Germany and Russia on the other; and the granting of colonial territory to Germany based on her population and economic needs.

But, at the same time the Germans were preparing their list of demands for Wilson, a meeting between the highest military and civilian officials in Germany was taking place at Pless. The Germans knew Lloyd George would flatly reject their terms. The conditions were submitted merely to buy time.

Those attending the Pless conference concluded that the only way to bring England to her knees would be through the unrestricted use of the U-boat. The German navy estimated that they could easily sink some 600,000 tons each month, and that within six months at the most England would be forced to sue for peace.

It was soberly understood by everyone present that such action would ultimately bring the United States into the conflict. The military leaders who presided over the meeting were convinced that the war would be over before the full weight of America could be brought to bear.

Chancellor Theobald von Bethmann-Hollweg and Karl Helf-   **29** ferich, the German statesman, weren't convinced. Both felt such blatant action would be viewed by Wilson as provocation enough to join the fray. However, neither had anything better to put on the table. Only Arthur von Zimmermann, the foreign minister did. And it was his solution that finally pulled the United States into the war. He suggested sending instructions to the German ministers in Mexico and Japan to negotiate alliances with both nations directed against the United States. If that objective could be achieved, any threat from America would be effectively counterbalanced.

On January 31, 1917 the United States was officially notified by Germany that unrestricted submarine warfare would commence on February 1, and that America was being advised to stay out of the Atlantic shipping channels. Wilson responded on February 3 by severing diplomatic relations with Germany. Roosevelt demanded that Wilson either arm American merchant ships or declare war on Germany. Roosevelt's frustration clearly showed in a diary notation that voiced the question: how do you make Wilson "...steer a clear course to uphold right?" (*Roosevelt & Churchill* by Joseph Lash; pg. 429.)

Wilson who, at the urging of House, was privately although reluctantly contemplating an unprecedented third try for the White House, did not want to upset the voters by breaking his campaign promise, believing if he was out of office when the war ended, his plan to lead the League of Nations would end as well.

Privately, Wilson was waiting for the right provocation to commit American troops to the war that the voters would be willing to accept. Publicly, he insisted he would not declare war on Germany unless provoked. Yet, several American merchant ships were sunk during both February and March and still Wilson did nothing. Roosevelt wondered what the President was waiting for. So did Lloyd George. In March, British intelligence intercepted and decoded a communique from von Zimmermann to his minister in Japan that detailed his efforts to encourage military action against the United States.

Finally, on April 2, 1917 at the urging of House, Wilson addressed a joint session of Congress and asked for a declaration of war against Germany. It was granted on April 6. The United States finally entered the first world war. On June 13, 1917 the first American troops sailed for France.

Prior to that, on May 18, 1917 Congress passed the *Selective Service Act* that provided for the drafting of American males between the ages of 21 and 31 years of age. On September 12, 1918 the age span was increased to include men from 18 to 48.

Over the next four months a variety of restrictive measures were enacted and the American citizen began to feel the hardships of Mr. Wilson's war. On October 3, 1917 Congress passed the *War Revenue Act* which greatly increased the federal income tax rate — and imposed an excess profits tax on businesses, ending any opportunity a Democrat might have to win the White House in 1920.

B ecause of the war conditions that were now taking their toll on Mainstreet America, Congress enacted the *Lever Act* on August 10 and placed a Republican, Herbert Clark Hoover, in charge of the program as the United States Food Administrator. Hoover was chosen because of his credentials as the director of the Belgium Relief Commission. And, selecting a Republican suggested there was bipartisan support for Wilson's belt-tightening war effort. What makes this piece of legislation noteworthy is that it would serve as the catalyst for the 18th Amendment, and 21 months later, the *National Prohibition Act,* more commonly known as the *Volstead Act,* that was enacted by Congress on October 28, 1920 over Wilson's veto.

---

[4]Because of severe grain shortages in the United States due to greatly increased demand by our allies in Europe, Congress passed the *Lever Act* on August 10, 1917 to conserve grain. To further control prices, Congress created the Grain Corporation which financed the American farmers' grain crops from 1917 to 1919, and fixed the wholesale prices of grain to keep them from skyrocketing. Hoover, who realized that vast amounts of grain were consumed by America's breweries and whiskey distillers, embarked on a campaign to discourage the consumption of alcoholic beverages in 1917, believing if the demand for grain from the breweries fell, the war effort would be served. Hoover's plan was heartily welcomed by Wilson who actively, although not publicly, supported the idea of Prohibition. Fueled by America's disdain for anything German during hte war years, the Prohibitionist movement gained strength during the midterm election of 1918. Prohibition was suddenly a front-burner issue not because Americans were suddenly awakened to the evils of Jim Barleycorn or the dangers of alcoholism, but simply because most of the brewers in America were of German extraction, and their beer had German-sounding names.

There had been a strong prohibition movement growing in the America for well over a decade, championed to a large degree by suffragettes. The Prohibitionists fielded Presidential candidates against both Taft in 1912 and Wilson in 1916, but due largely to the fact that women did not yet possess the right to vote, none received any appreciable support in the voting booths, and the prohibitionist candidates never gained enough momentum to attract any national support until the 19th Amendment was ratified on August 18, 1920.

In 1917 the concept of Prohibition began to gain national support for a much different reason. Hoover, in his attempt to find new ways to conserve food supplies — particularly grain — realized that enormous amounts of grain was being used daily in breweries and distilleries all across the United States to make beer and whiskey. As he explored ways to curb what he viewed as a flagrant waste of grain[1], his efforts became the focus of a great deal of media coverage — largely because he traveled with an entourage of government public relations people — who suddenly focused on the fact that large numbers of the breweries and distilleries were owned by people of German extraction with very German sounding names.

The prohibitionists jumped on this discovery, fanning the flames of resentment for anything German at a time when most Americans were feeling the brunt of the war in Europe with food shortages, fuel shortages, higher taxes, and the loss of loved ones who would never be coming home from strange sounding places in France and Belgium. As a result of the public relations campaign initiated by Hoover, the 18th Amendment to the Constitution was ratified on January 16, 1919. One year later it, with the passage of the *National Prohibition* (or Volstead) *Act*, it became the law of the land. For the first time in the history of the Republic, the federal government used its power to dictate a lifestyle behavior on the American people. It would not be the last. Contrary to the rhetoric that accompanies the passage of "behavioral" legislation [i.e., "Big Brother" laws] that such laws are designed to "protect us" (apparently from ourselves), in reality they are designed to accustom us to having every facet of our lives controlled by an increasingly intrusive central government — the same way control is exercised by any totalitarian government

When a cease-fire ended hostilities on the western front at 11 a.m., November 11, 1918 the known dead totalled some 10,000,000 men. The wounded were at least double that amount. Distributed among the chief combatants, the death tolls by nation were: Germany, 1,808,000; Austria-Hungary, 1,200,000; Turkey, 325,000; Russia, 1,700,000; France, 1,385,000; Great Britain, 947,000; Italy, 460,00; and the United States, 115,000. The total direct cost of the war was estimated at $180,500,000,000.00. Indirect costs added another $151,612,500,000.00. All totaled, some 30 nations were at war during that conflict. Truly, the world had been at war. It was the war to end all wars. Almost.

Establishing a lasting peace would prove to be more difficult. To date, no heads of state have ever been able to achieve it.

The peace conference was formally opened in Paris on January 18, 1919. Twenty-seven of the victor nations were in attendance. Germany was excluded from the conference until the terms of surrender were ready to be signed. The front had been silent for fourteen months, but the cry for German blood that echoed through this plenary gathering was as explosive as those shouted before the last shots of war were fired.

While most of those attending the conference were present to divide the spoils of war and demand their pound of German flesh, Wilson and his personal advisor Edward Mandell House arrived in Paris full of utopian ideas about a new global society, the framework of which was contained within the document Wilson carried with him.

The idealism and objectivity contained within the *Fourteen Points* document, while delivered by Wilson to Congress on January 8, 1918 was actually the vision of Colonel House. The first thirteen points concerned themselves with the establishment of a lasting peace following the ultimate victory by the Allied forces in Europe, together with the terms Wilson felt would be necessary to achieve that goal. The fourteenth point was pure utopianism, and could easily have been taken directly from the pages of House's book, *Phillip Dru, Administrator*.

There is no doubt that Colonel House was an imaginative visionary, nor is there any doubt that there was a master plan behind the proposed League of Nations which he carefully planted in the fertile minds of both Wilson and Grey. One needed only read his book to learn it. It was not a well kept secret.

The *Phillip Dru* storyline evolved around a wealthy financier and a powerfully ambitious United States Senator who was
the likely successor to the incumbent president. However, the
Senator was not content with simply being President. With the
help of a financier, the Senator devised a scheme to take over
both Congress and the Supreme Court after the election and assume the role of dictator — after learning from the financier that
the government is actually run by a small circle of powerful,
wealthy insiders.

The plot was accidently discovered when the financier's secretary played a dictograph recording of a conversation between
the two men that detailed the conspiracy. Being patriotic herself, she turned the recording over to the media. The conspiracy
was exposed in the press, but it was too late. Ignoring Constitutional ascendancy, the Senator was appointed President after the
duly-elected President was forced to flee the country when the
Senator's coup was hurriedly unleashed.

The hero of the book, Phillip Dru, then organized a citizen's

---

[2]Col. Edward Mandell House, the J.P. Morgan hireling and agent of the
Rothschild Bank who served as Wilson's confidant and advisor until Wilson suffered a massive stroke on October 2, 1919, was the "public" visionary behind the League of Nations (whose blueprint was created by
the world's wealthiest transnational industrialists and bankers). Because
of the dire need of England to involve the United States in the war, which
Germany was winning, House convinced Wilson that if the United States
entered the fray and won the war for the Allies, a grateful Europe would
elect him president of the world government that was to be formed with
the signing of the League of Nations charter. Wilson believed him.

So convinced was Wilson of that fact that on January 8, 1918, in an
address to Congress, Wilson outlined his—or rather House's—famous
Fourteen Points that would become the cornerstone of the Treaty of Versailles. The 14th Point, of course, was the planned League of Nations. At
the end of the war, Wilson declared, a "league of nations" would be created in which economic trade barriers between nations would be nonexistent, and nations would be sufficiently disarmed so that while the nation-states would be able to defend themselves from attack, none would
be sufficiently armed to be an aggressor.

But Wilson was equally convinced of two other things. First, that to
achieve that lofty goal, he would have to the President of the United States
when the League of Nations assumed its role as the superior govern-

militia of 500,000 men to restore democracy. Dru's forces headed for Washington where they engaged federal troops and defeated them. The Senator was then forced to surrender to him. Dru allowed the Senator to remain President, but assumed all of the authority of the office for himself, effectively becoming the dictator of the United States.

What makes an otherwise insignificant and otherwise unknown fictional work important is that it reveals both the character and political philosophy of its author—the man who virtually controlled the administration of Woodrow Wilson and greatly influenced that of Franklin Delano Roosevelt.

Wilson would never realize his dream of becoming the first President of the world[2]. Colonel House's League of Nations, artfully concealed within the framework of the *Treaty of Versailles*, was rejected by the United States Senate which saw within it an attempt on the part of Wilson and Sir David Lloyd George, the British prime minister, to form a global government that would ultimately usurp the authority of the Constitution and subjugate the people of the United States to the League of Nations.

On January 25, 1919, the conference participants unanimously adopted a resolution for the creation of the League. A committee of six, headed by Wilson, was appointed to shape a proposed Constitution. Serving with Wilson on the committee was Edward House; Jan Christian Smuts, the prime minister of South Africa; Edgar Algernon Robert, the 1st Viscount Cecil of Chelwood; Leon Victor Auguste Bourgeois, a French statesman; and Eleutherios Venizelos, the Greek prime minister.

---

ment of the world; and second, that he would have to personally forge the union of nations with his own hands to guarantee his role as the leader of the new world government. Wilson arrived in Paris on December 13, 1918, and with only brief sojourns back to the United States over the next six months, largely remaining in Paris until the League of Nations charter was signed on June 28, 1919.

But the Republican dominated Senate, headed by Sen. Henry Cabot Lodge, was not prepared to surrender America's sovereignty—one of the provisions of the League of nations—for the sake of European peace. The League of Nations Treaty languished in legislative limbo as Wilson tried to find the votes to ratify it. After two months of fruitless negotiations with Lodge, Wilson embarked on a whistlestop tour of America, taking his case to the American people. Wilson believed if he convinced the people, they would force the Senate to ratify the Treaty. But America wanted

Colonel House was placed in charge of the committee as Wilson's agent when, in mid-February, the President returned to Washington. On April 28 the League covenant was completed and submitted to the Council of Ten, whose members consisted of representatives from five of the six major powers involved in the war (England, the United States, France, Italy, and Japan) for final approval. (Although Russia suffered more losses than any of her Allies, she was excluded because the revolutionary government of Russia was still in a state of flux. Russia was admitted as a member in 1934, but expelled five years later when it invaded Finland.)

On June 28, 1919 the *Treaty of Versailles* containing the League of Nations, which would come into being on January 10, 1920, was formally submitted to the League's charter member. It was ratified first by Germany, on July 7, 1919 (who, as the loser of the war, was obligated to sign first. Germany would not be granted admission in 1926). France ratified the Treaty on October 13, with Great Britain and Italy following suit two days later. Japan ratified it on October 30. The United States, because of Article Ten of the League's Constitution, which established a world government, never did ratify the Treaty.

The Republican dominated Senate attempted to introduce key amendments to the Treaty that would make it acceptable to the

---

nothing to do with Europe. On September 25, Wilson collapsed, suffering a minor stroke that was reported in the media as "exhaustion." Wilson returned to Washington where he suffered a major stroke on October 2. On November 19, 1919 the Senate rejected the League of Nations for the first time.

Still partially paralyzed and unable to speak coherently (although his mind worked was well as ever), Wilson was determined to seek re-election in 1920 to force the League of Nations through Congress, believing if the Senate did not ratify the Treaty of Versailles it "...would place an ineffable stain upon the gallantry and honor of the United States." The race of 1920 would be, he declared, a "great and solemn referendum" on the League of Nations. Unable to walk, and able to speak only with great effort, Edith Wilson and the President's closest friends quietly scotched his efforts to seek a third term, believing his desire to do so was merely the fantasy of an enfeebled old man. It is unclear at that time whether Wilson, confined to a wheel chair, believed he would still be elected the world's first president; or if at that point, he was merely fueled by a desire to see his dream of world government fulfilled.

American people, but their efforts were successfully thwarted by Wilson. As a result, the League of Nations proved to be an ineffective world governing force throughout its twenty-six year history, and Wilson's place in history as the first president of the world governing body was filled by Sir James Eric Drummond who would serve, not as president, but as Secretary-General of the League of Nations—a title that would carry on into the United Nations. Edward Mandell House, the founder of the vision, would not live to see the one-world government he tried so hard to create.

H ouse, an avowed Marxist, was an employee of John Pierpont Morgan up until Woodrow Wilson's announced candidacy for the White House in the spring of 1912, was reportedly—like his father—also an agent of the House of Rothschild. Thomas House was a representative of the Rothschild banking interests and created substantial personal wealth running Union blockades to bring European trade goods and military supplies to the Confederacy during the Civil War. Whether or not his son remained a paid agent of J.P. Morgan when he acted in an advisory capacity to Wilson has never been firmly established, but few doubted the persistent rumors.

In his book, House's alter ego Phillip Dru initiated a graduated income tax, created Marxist social programs, and rewrote the Constitution of the United States. During Wilson's Administration, the Constitution was largely rewritten with the ratification of the 17th Amendment when power passed from the States, and the people of those States, into the eager hands of the federal government through the direct election of Senators by the people rather than by the State legislatures. The power to coin money was taken from the House of Representatives and surreptitiously given to a group of ravenous, powerful international bankers who had devised scheme after scheme over 100 years to create and control a privately-owned central bank in the United States. And, finally a graduated income tax was levied against untold generations of American citizens with the ratification of the 16th Amendment in order to pay for the socialist programs which would be enacted by House's other protegé, Franklin Delano Roosevelt, some twenty years later.

Biographer Charles Seymour interviewed Edward Mandell House as he collected collateral material for a book on the Wilson Administration. In that interview, House boasted that "...during the last fifteen years I have been close to the center of all things, although few people suspect it. No important foreigner came to America without talking to me. I was close to the movement that nominated Roosevelt..." He was, in fact, an integral part of the mechanism that financed FDR's run for the presidency — the global money machine.

The fact that Roosevelt and House communicated quite often as FDR searched for the most expedient path to political power is readily acknowledged by Arthur Schlesinger, Jr. in his 1958 book, *The Coming New Deal.* And, the fact that House's philosophy influenced Roosevelt is evidenced by a statement FDR made in a letter to House shortly after he declared the bank holiday on March 4, 1933 which effectively closed every banking institution in the United States. In that communique Roosevelt wrote: "The real truth of the matter is, as you and I know, that a financial element in the larger centers has owned the government ever since the days of Andrew Jackson, and I am not excepting the administration of W.W. The country is going through a repetition of Jackson's fight with the Bank of the United States, only on a far bigger and broader basis." Only this time, America would lose.

The American people largely blamed both the bankers and the Wall Street financiers for both the stock market crash of 1929 and the depression which followed. And, Roosevelt, the "big business" candidate, capitalized on that sentiment very well.

One of Roosevelt's early supporters during the 1932 campaign season was Henry Harriman, the President of the United States Chamber of Commerce. Harriman, a Democrat, initially approached Herbert Hoover and offered the endorsement of the Chamber of Commerce in exchange for Hoover's support of several key economic stimulus programs that the Chamber was promoting to the Republican Congress. Hoover refused, insisting Harriman's ideas would foster a socialist state in which the federal government would be granted the right to control the industrial strength of America.

He further argued that it was impossible to have an economic dictatorship within a democracy and expect real economic growth, since it is free enterprise, not government largesse, that deter-

38

mines both the scope and nature of economic progress. Further, he felt that government could not stimulate industry, since they are counterpoised to one another. Government solves problems by levying taxes and imposing regulations. Industry grows only when left unrestrained and allowed to reinvest its profits into job creation. He predicted that if Harriman's plans were ever enacted, chronic unemployment followed by frantic government spending to provide for those unemployed would result, creating even greater havoc and chaos[3].

Hoover was right. Harriman, determined to see his agenda enacted, threw his support and the financial resources of the Chamber of Commerce behind Roosevelt.

Hoover, who was adamantly opposed to any form of government intervention, found his popularity eroding in a direct relation to the jobless statistics, which continued to grow. By December, 1932 unemployment exceeded 12% nationwide. In the heavily industrialized areas, it exceeded 20%. By summer, 90 days after Roosevelt's inauguration, unemployment would exceed 25% nationwide, meaning that in some pockets of the country, local or regional unemployment would had reached a staggering 50% or greater. The blame, of course, was laid at Hoover's doorstep, and he would carry that blame into history.

From 1930 until Roosevelt assumed office, the gross national product (GNP) which had for years grown at an average annual rate of some 3.5%, plummeted over 10% per year. Agricultural

---

[3]Hoover's predictions, which were finally made public in the 1940's, were uncannily accurate. Historians, however hard they have tried try to affix all of the blame of the global devastation of the Great Depression on Hoover, should now be willing to admit that much of the vast unemployment which ultimately resulted must be attributed as much to Roosevelt's bureaucratic "tinkering" with the free enterprise system as the Fed's tight money policies in 1933-34 since money is the fuel that powers the engine of any free market economy.

To date, however, most still attribute the Depression to what they believe was general weakness in the economy throughout the 1920's due to the agricultural segment of the economy, as well as coal mining, railroads and the textile industry. Furthermore, they believe that since the spectacular growth in the stock market was artificially created, it did not accurately reflect the economic conditions which existed in the United States at the time. And, although a great many stock market speculators lost virtual fortunes during the crash in October, 1929, few

prices dropped 53%; and industrial stocks lost some 80% of their pre-crash value.

Hoover, in a belated attempt to rescue industry, urged Congress to pass the *Reconstruction Finance Corporation Act* to provide some $500 million in aid to ailing businesses. However, it was too little, too late. Had Hoover initiated this program in 1930, it is very likely that the full impact of the Depression might not have ever occurred.

Roosevelt, like William Jefferson Clinton sixty years later, would use a clever ploy to win the White House. Roosevelt, the liberal, disguised himself as a moderate whose only concern was the welfare of the citizens of the United States. Clinton, the liberal, would do the same to defeat George Herbert Walker Bush in 1992.

Hoover, in fact, campaigned much like Bush — but for different reasons. Both avoided the character of their opponent. Their opponents didn't. Clinton attacked Bush as a friend of big business who saddled the working man with a tax increase after his infamous 1988 convention promise to "...read my lips...no new taxes." Roosevelt did basically the same thing to Hoover. Clinton campaigned against the most popular incumbent president in the second half of the twentieth century. Roosevelt campaigned against the least popular incumbent in the first half.

Roosevelt attacked an administrative record that could not be defended. And Hoover, who had no record to stand on, had no issues upon which to campaign. Nor did Bush. Both were effectively disarmed and became easy prey for their political opponents.

Even though Hoover refused to support the efforts of the big business interests, the Wall Street fat cats and the international bankers who were already profiting handsomely from the misfortunes of Americans, Roosevelt successfully projected Hoover

---

businesses went under at that time; and rampant unemployment did not begin until 1933 when Roosevelt declared a bank holiday and collapsed the economy. There was no doubt that America was suffering from the worst economic slump in its history, but few economists expected it to last more than a year or two at the most. Without the interference of either government or the major financial interests both in the United States and Europe, it is also very likely that the crash which triggered many of the events that would bring the world to the brink of despair over the next decade, may not have occurred—including Hitler's Third Reich!

as the candidate of big business — although their money was actually supporting him. Roosevelt, the candidate of big business, was portrayed by the media as anti-business, standing solidly behind the working man. Hoover, who was probably one of the most anti-big business Presidents in American history, was painted by the media as the consummate Washington politician who was sleeping with every special interest big business group in the nation — and the American worker was paying the rent for the bed in which the rape of the economy was taking place.

Roosevelt's landslide victory over Hoover can be best compared to Lyndon Johnson's resounding defeat of Barry Goldwater in 1964, and George Bush's searing victory over Michael Dukakis in 1988. In each of these contests, it was negativism that assured victory for the winner.

While Roosevelt took only 57.4% of the popular vote in 1932, he captured 42 of the 48 states, and America took a radical step to the left in a march towards socialism that continues unabated to this day.

W hile Roosevelt prepared for an unprecedented third try for the White House, that part of the world not already entrenched in war was preparing for it. Like the America of 1916, the America of 1940 was decidedly isolationist and Congress intended, this time, to keep it that way.

On January 30, 1933 German President Paul von Hindenburg appointed the very charismatic National Socialist leader, Adolph Hitler, as Chancellor. Although Hitler's faction was rapidly losing ground in the *Reichstag,* Hitler managed to mesmerize the legislative leaders of the Third Reich and was granted extraordinary power to initiate sweeping changes. Hitler ardently campaigned against the *Treaty of Versailles* which he claimed dehumanized the German citizen and made them paupers of the Zionist money overlords who first controlled, and then destroyed, the German economy. One of his first acts as Chancellor was to withdraw from the League of Nations.

Nothing happened.

Prior to the appointment of Hitler, in June, 1932, the German government requested that the war debt of $332,112,500,000.00 be cancelled. The League of Nations agreed to set the debt aside on the condition that Germany post bonds totalling three billion

41

Reichsmarks with the Bank for International Settlement. The United States Congress vetoed the proposition by issuing a resolution that stated "...it is against the policy of Congress that any of the indebtedness of foreign powers to the United States should in any manner be cancelled or reduced."

A year later, Germany simply repudiated the entire debt.

Nothing happened.

On March 16, 1933, Germany formally rejected the clauses of the *Treaty of Versailles* that dealt with its disarmament, and began military conscription. This was followed almost immediately by a massive build-up of war machines and armaments, which supplied thousands of jobs to the impoverished German population.

Again, nothing happened.

Except, that is, Adolph Hitler's popularity with the German people was on a meteoric rise.

On March 7, 1936 German troops overran the Rhineland, claiming the annexation of its former satellite was necessary to protect German nationals living there. A strong protest was launched by France, Belgium and Great Britain—but England, who realized that another world war was looming on the horizon, refused to invoke sanctions against Germany.

And, once again, nothing happened.

Hitler enjoyed a brief moment of popularity in Germany. But soon the German people would learn to fear him as much as their French, Belgium, Czech and English neighbors.

Like Britain, America saw another European conflict brewing.

In May, 1937, Congress passed the *United States Neutrality Act.* It prevented America from supplying arms or munitions to belligerent nations, maintaining strict neutrality in conflicts that did not directly involve the United States. Roosevelt, who had already decided to seek a third term as President, wanted to veto the measure, but to do so would have been political suicide.

In June, 1939 King George VI, the first reigning European monarch of any country of the world to do so, visited to the United States at the suggestion of Roosevelt to lobby Congress for modifications in the *Neutrality Act* which would allow Roosevelt to supply arms and munitions to England. Despite his efforts, Congress refused. In retaliation, Roosevelt took Congress to task in the press, arguing that the *Neutrality Act* provided enough encouragement to aggressor nations against

America's allies, that war could possibly result.

Roosevelt, however, was smart enough make his remarks appear as though he was trying to keep America out of another European war when in fact he intended to involve America in the conflict as a means of jumpstarting an economy which had remained stagnant for an entire decade.

During that period there reportedly existed a well conceived plot that was purportedly aimed at the overthrow of the government and the establishment of a dictatorship in America. This scheme was detailed in a 1973 book, *The Plot to Seize the White House,* by Jules Archer (Hawthorn Books), and again in the 1991 book: *J. Edgar Hoover, The Man and the Secrets* by Curt Gentry (W.W. Norton & Company).

The plot to seize not only the White House, but the nation, began when Major General Smedley Darlington Butler, the former commandant of the U.S. Marines and recipient of two Congressional Medals of Honor (who was forced into premature retirement by FDR because he called Italian dictator Benito Mussolini a "mad dog" while speaking before a civic group in Philadelphia) was approached by two prominent American Legion officials: William Doyle and Gerald MacGuire, who asked him if he would be interested in running for the post of national commander of the American Legion.

Doyle and MacGuire convinced him he was just the man they needed to lead the rank and file members to unseat the entrenched leadership which they felt was taking the Legion in the wrong direction. They planned to hold a national convention in Chicago, they told him. As intrigued and flattered as Butler was, he was also a something of a pessimist and questioned how successfully their effort would be since he knew the average rank and file member of the Legion could not afford to attend such a conference.

MacGuire assured him they had sufficient funds to bring thousands of veterans to the convention, and to prove it he produced a bank deposit book which contained two deposits totaling over $100,000.00. They assured Butler that more money, if needed, would be available.

During their second meeting, MacGuire informed Butler that his campaign was being backed by nine very wealthy businessmen. When Butler pressed the matter, MacGuire identified one of the men as Grayson Mallet-Provost Murphy, the president of a small but prestigious brokerage firm. Although not mentioned at the time, Murphy also sat on the boards of Anaconda Copper Mining, Goodyear and J.P. Morgan Company.

It was during this meeting that Butler became suspicious of the pair. MacGuire handed him the transcript of the speech he was expected to make at the convention. In it was a demand for the nation to be returned to the recently abandoned gold standard. The national scope of the purely political rhetoric contained in the speech waved a red flag to Butler. Butler informed MacGuire that before he could make a decisions about the position, he would have to meet some of the other behind-the-scenes principles. Shortly thereafter, Butler was visited by Robert Sterling Clark. Clark, who controlled the Singer Sewing Machine fortune, was a Wall Street broker. He also served as the chief litigator for J.P. Morgan.

Clark confided that his personal assets consisted of approximately $30,000,000.00. He was willing, he said, to invest half of it in order to protect the other half—which he declared would quickly vanish if Roosevelt remained in the White House. The more he spoke, the more convinced Butler became that there was something very sinister behind the group that wanted to back him as the national head of the American Legion.

Sensing his hesitation, Clark informed Butler that he was not the only candidate being considered for this slot.

"...'Although our group is for you,' Clark told him, 'the Morgan interests say that you cannot be trusted, that you are too radical...They are for Douglas MacArthur.' Deciding there was '...something funny' about the speech, Butler told Clark they'd better pick MacArthur, he wanted no part of it." (*J. Edgar Hoover*; Curt Gentry; W.W. Norton Company © 1991; pg. 202).

That October the convention, headed up by Doyle (who was a veteran) because no high profile American military personality could be found to spearhead their effort, endorsed a return to the gold standard. Had the group left Butler alone, the *American Liberty League* would have passed, unnoticed, into history. However, obscurity was not what the *American Liberty League* wanted.

The following spring, MacGuire again contacted Butler.

"He'd just returned from Europe [MacGuire] said, where he'd studied the role of veterans groups in the formation of the Nazi party in Germany, Fascisti in Italy, and the Croix de Feu movement in France. He and his sponsors had concluded that the

44

American veterans could play a similarly important role. What was needed to save the United States from the 'communist menace', MacGuire said was a complete change of government. To affect this, MacGuire and the men he represented wanted Butler to lead a march of a half million veterans on Washington where they would stage a *coup d' état*. If Roosevelt yielded to their demands, they might allow him to remain as president, MacGuire said, but without any real power. The Secretary of State, who would be their own man, would actually run the government." (*ibid*; pg. 202).

Such a plan, of course, would have entailed the assassinations or removal of at least three men: the vice president, the Speaker of the House of Representatives, and the President Pro-Tem of the Senate. John Nance Garner, the vice president would automatically become President if Roosevelt died in office or became incapacitated. In the unlikely event that Garner and John Bankhead both died or stepped aside, the Senate leader was next in line[4]. Only in the event of his death or resignation would Cordell Hull, the Secretary of State ascend to the Presidency. Hull had been Roosevelt's compatriot for many years, and Wilson's before that. Was he MacGuire's man? Butler found that hard to believe.

Additionally, Butler felt it strange that a man who had spoken out so vehemently against both Fascism and Communism would be asked to head a Fascist movement to overthrow the government of the United States. It was a strange plot indeed.

The cast of players, all of whom signed on as sponsors of the newly formed American Liberty League, was a virtual litany of Roosevelt supporters that included Sewell Avery, S.B. Colgate, Lammont duPont, E. F. Hutton, J. H. Pew, John J. Raskob, and E. C. Sams and Elihu Root—a close and very personal friend of Roosevelt—whose combined wealth was well in excess of $37 billion. All in all, the League had 156 sponsors who were either

---

[4]While ascendancy to the presidency in the event of the death or disablement of both the President and Vice President was not clarified in Article II, Section I of the Constitution prior to the ratification of the 25th Amendment on February 20, 1967, the Constitution provided Congress with the authority to determine too whom the office would devolve in the event of the death or removal of an ascended vice president. In doing so, Congress determined that in the event of the death or removal of both the President and the Vice President, that the Speaker of the House would ascend to the Presidency. In the event of the death of the Speaker, the

45

the heads or directors of many of America's best known corporations including E.I. duPont deNemours, General Motors, Goodyear Tire, J.C. Penney, and Standard Oil.

Butler was, of course, being asked to play the Phillip Dru role
in Colonel House's fictional fantasy to overthrow the government of the United States.

The scenario Butler detailed in his secret November 20, 1934
testimony before the congressional committee that would later
become known as the *House Un-American Activities Committee,*
followed the story line of Phillip Dru to the letter, and could not
have been scripted from anything else. Since Roosevelt was the
handpicked candidate of both the international banking and international business consortiums who were at least publicly well
pleased with his performance, it is not logical that they would
enlist an outsider to attempt an all-out coup, or even attempt to
overthrow Roosevelt's Administration.

Surprisingly, none of the figures named by Butler were called
to testify before this, or any, congressional committee concerning
the Butler matter. In fact, when the committee issued its final report all testimonial references to any of them had been deleted,
and a sanitized report was entered in the Congressional Record.

The conspirators simply denied Butler's allegations — as he
knew they would. However, prior to approaching J. Edgar Hoover
with his fantastic story, Butler enlisted the support of Paul Comly
French, a reporter for the *Philadelphia Record* who launched his
own investigation. Posing as a sympathizer, French worked his
way into the confidence of MacGuire and substantially corroborated Butler's story.

On November 20, the day Butler testified before the House
committee, the *Philadelphia Record* broke the story. But, it was a
story heading nowhere. Hoover announced that since no federal laws had been broken, he had no authority to investigate. If
the Federal Bureau of Investigation did not think there was anything to investigate, why should the press? The story died before most Americans even learned that a story existed.

---

job would then fall, first, on the President Pro-Tem of the Senate and then
the Secretary of State, followed by the Secretary of Defense and Treasury. With the ratification of the 25th Amendment, a new Vice President
iwould be appointed to fill the vacancy, thereby eliminating Congressional
consideration from Article II, Section I.

Were the principles of the American Liberty League disgruntled former Roosevelt supports who wanted him out of office?

Not likely.

Why invest millions of dollars in a surreptitious plan to overthrow the government when an assassin could be hired for a few thousand dollars? Logic suggests the episode was concocted for an entirely different reason. What could that reason be?

Perhaps to provide a media-orchestrated backlash sufficient to create enough mass hysteria that Roosevelt could legally exercise the *War Powers Act,* declare martial law and assume permanent wartime dictatorial control over the United States government. Logic necessarily supports this conclusion since hard proof to confirm or refute that the events described actually occurred does not exist except in the diary entries of those involved — and in J. Edgar Hoover's personal gestapo files on some of America's most important people.

First, if any group of wealthy businessmen decided to overthrow the government of the United States they would not select a highly decorated American military leader who was loyal to the government and also an outspoken foe of the political philosophy of the group attempting to recruit him. Therefore, it is more likely that Butler was selected for the very course of action he followed after being advised that the group wanted to overthrow the government.

Second, it is extremely interesting that the U.S. House of Representatives, when faced with sworn testimony from the highly decorated ex-commandant of the U.S. Marine Corps that not only did a plot to overthrow the government of the United States exist, but that the conspiracy involved some of the most prominent and influential names in America, chose not only to ignore the significance of that testimony, but also decided to expunge the records of that hearing to protect the instigators. Why was that action taken? Unfortunately, the answer to that question rests with those who perpetuated the conspiracy and those who concealed it from the American people.

Third, the Phillip Dru story line which permeated Butler's testimony clearly linked the plot to the Roosevelt Administration, or at least to someone in that administration with close philosophical ties to Colonel House. Only Roosevelt had that much imagination — and only Roosevelt had the link.

Finally, since Roosevelt was recorded discussing his involvement in yet another conspiracy, we know he was capable of such deeds if they served his political purpose.

That conspiracy, outlined in startling detail in the book *Gestapo Chief*, by Gregory Douglas (R. James Bender Publishing; 1996) was culled by the author from U.S. Army Intelligence files as he researched and recorded the top secret 1948 interrogation of Heinrich Muller, the head of the German Gestapo, who was being recruited by the United States government.

In *Gestapo Chief*, Douglas explains that one of AT&T's first telephonic scramblers, called the A-3, was hooked up between #10 Downing Street and the White House. The Germans learned of the device through a *New York Times* article which appeared on October 8, 1939, informing the world that a system that would foil spies abroad, existed within the White House. Apparently each A-3 unit contained uniquely different security systems making eavesdropping virtually impossible.

Because Dr. Wilhelm Ohnesorge, the German Minister of Post had likewise purchased the A-3 system from AT&T before the war, he believed it was possible to break the security system on Roosevelt's A-3 system. Ohnesorge assigned his best technician, Kurt Vetterlain, to the project. Using the Reichpost's A-3 as a guide, Vetterlain successfully broke the security code and began listening to Roosevelt's conversation not only with Churchill, but other diplomats and world leaders as well.

One conversation, bearing Gestapo file number 321/41, detailed in its entirety by Douglas in *Gestapo Chief*, tied Churchill and Roosevelt together in a conspiracy involving the Japanese bombing of Pearl Harbor in which 3,219 Americans either lost their lives or were reported missing in action, and another 1,272 were wounded. The recorded conversation occurred on the night of November 26, 1941.

After a few moments of small talk in which Churchill apologized to Roosevelt for the lateness of his call, he said: "...A powerful Japanese task force [composed of] six of their carriers, two battleships and a number of other units to include tankers and cruisers, has sailed yesterday from a secret base in the northern Japanese islands."

Roosevelt, according to Douglas, replied: "We both knew this was coming. There are also reports in my hands about a force of some size making up in China...obviously intended to go South."

"Yes, we have all of that," Churchill said. There is an inter-ruption in which some of the words are garbled. "...are far more advanced than you in our reading of the Jap naval operations codes. But even without that, their moves are evident. And they will indeed move South but the force I spoke of is not headed South, Franklin, it is headed East..."

"Surely you must be...will you repeat that, please?"

"I said East," Churchill replied. "This force is sailing to the East...towards you."

"Perhaps," Roosevelt countered, "they set an easterly course to fool any observers and then plan to swing South to support the landings in the southern areas. I have..."

"Not at this moment," Churchill replied, interrupting the president, "their forces are moving across the northern Pacific and I can assure you that their goal is the...[conversation broken]...fleet in Hawaii. At Pearl Harbor."

The conversation continues for a few minutes with each dis-cussing other possible targets. Finally Roosevelt asked, "...What do your people give you as the actual date of the attack?"

Churchill answered, "the actual date of the attack is the eighth of December. That's a Monday."

Roosevelt, according to the *Gestapo Chief*, thought that was an odd date. Apparently neither leader realized that the International Date Line separated Pearl Harbor from Tokyo, and while it would be Monday in Japan, it would be Sunday at Pearl Harbor.

The conspiracy thickened when Roosevelt said, "...I will have to consider the entire problem. A Japanese attack on us, which would result in war between us...would certainly fulfill two of the most important requirements of our policy. Harry has told me repeatedly..." [referring to Harry Hopkins, a long time close and personal advisor of Roosevelt who currently served as the Administration's Secretary of Commerce] "...and I have more faith in him than I do in the Soviet ambassador...that Stalin is desperate at this point. The Nazis are at the gates of Moscow, his armies are melting away...the government has evacuated and although Harry and Marshall..." [referring to Gen. George Marshall] "...feel that Stalin can hang on and eventually defeat Hitler, there is no saying what could transpire if the Japs sud-denly fell on Stalin's rear...I think we have to decide what is more important...keeping Russia in the war to bleed the Nazis dry to their eventual destruction...[conversation broken]...supply Stalin with weapons but do not forget, in fact he is your ally, not mine. There are strong isolationist feelings here and there are quite a number of anti-communists..."

"Fascists..." Churchill replied.

"Certainly," Roosevelt agreed, "but they would do all they could to block any attempt on my part to more than give some monetary assistance to Stalin."

The opinion expressed here by Roosevelt concerning the ideology of the conservatives in our Congress is both interesting and revealing of the geopolitical character of the man. To FDR, communism was an acceptable form of government, fascism was not.

That fact was not lost on Churchill. When Roosevelt was questioning the Prime Minister on the reliability of his information, Churchill lied and told him the source was a highly placed German naval officer whom the British had compromised. In something of an apology for refusing more specific information, Churchill said, "We cannot compromise our codebreaking. You understand this. Only myself and a few...[conversation broken]...not even Hopkins. It will go straight to Moscow and I am not sure we want that." (Douglas, in *Gestapo Chief*, footnoted the dialogue with this reference: "Harry Hopkins was Roosevelt's confidant whom the British strongly suspected was selling highly secret material to the Soviets on his visits to Stalin.")

At the end of the war, it was discovered that the German army had captured secret Soviet documents which named highly placed Americans in the Roosevelt Administration as agents of the Soviet government. Hopkins name, as well as that of Harold Ickes and other key Roosevelt officials, including Secretary of Labor Frances Perkins, were on the list. (See *Gestapo Chief II*; Gregory Douglas; R. James Bender Publishing © 1997; pg. 62) Churchill was correct in his assumption that to convey sensitive information to Roosevelt was tantamount to telling the Soviets.

Churchill appealed to Roosevelt: "But we too have our major desperations, Franklin. Our shipping upon which our nation depends, is being sunk by the Huns faster than we could ever replace...[conversation broken]...the Japs attack both of us in the Pacific? We could lose Malaya which is our primary source of rubber and tin. And if the Japs get Java and the oil, they could press south to Australia and I have told you repeatedly, we cannot hold...[conversation broken]...them much but in truth I cannot deliver. We need every man and every ship to fight Hitler in

Europe...India too. If the Japs get into Malaya, they can press on virtually unopposed into Burma and then India. Need I tell you of the resultant destruction of our Empire? We cannot survive on this small island, Franklin...[conversation broken]...allow the Nips to attack, you can get your war declaration through your Congress after all."

A portion of Churchill's remarks and the opening of Roosevelt's reply was lost. The German wiretap picks up at the point when clear transmission returns: "...not as capable as you at translating their messages and the army and navy are very jealous of each other. There is so much coming in that everyone is confused. We have no agents in place in Japan and every day dozens of messages are...[conversation broken]...that contradict each other or are not well translated. I have seen three transmissions... [conversation broken]...address your concern about British holdings in the Pacific...if the Japanese do attack both of us, eventually we will be able to crush them and regain all of the lost territories. As for myself, I will be...glad to be rid of the Philippines."

"I see this as a gamble...[conversation broken]...what would your decision be?" Churchill asked. "We cannot procrastinate over this for too long. Eleven or twelve days are all we have. Can we not agree in principle now? Should I mention that several advisors have counselled against informing you of this and allowing it to happen. You see by my notifying you where my loyalty lies. Certainly to one who is heart and soul with us against Hitler."

It is obvious from the following statement that in a portion of the garbled or missing dialogue between the two leaders that Churchill was asking Roosevelt to do absolutely nothing with the information that was being proffered, and simply allow the event to take place. Roosevelt was torn. But, his quandary was not over the prospect of allowing American naval personnel and civilians to be killed in order to provoke Congress into declaring war on Japan and Germany. Rather, he was in a quandary over the likelihood of being caught in his intrigue.

"I do appreciate your loyalty, Winston. What, on the other hand, will happen here if one of our intelligence people is able to intercept, decipher and deliver to me the same information you just gave me? I cannot ignore it...all of my intelligence people will know about it then. I could not ignore this."

"But if it were just a vague message then?"

51

"No," Roosevelt answered, "a specific message. I could not just sweep it under the rug like that..." [conversation broken].

"Of course not," Churchill agreed. "I think we should let matters develop as they will."

"I think that perhaps I can find a reason to absent myself from Washington while this crisis develops," Roosevelt concluded. "What I don't know can't hurt me and I too can misunderstand messages, especially at a distance..." [conversation broken].

"Completely. My best to you all there."

"Thank you for your call."

The conversation was concluded.

Researcher-author Douglas learned that on Friday, November 28, 1941, carrying the knowledge that an imminent attack on Pearl Harbor would, in nine days, change the course of history, Roosevelt climbed aboard his special armored train for what the press said would be a belated Thanksgiving holiday in Warm Springs, Georgia.

Unfortunately for the Churchill/Roosevelt conspiracy, the Japanese plot was revealed to Secretary of War Henry Stimson by the Soviet ambassador two days later. Roosevelt received a frantic telephone call from Stimson and Cordell Hull advising him that a convoy of Japanese war ships was steaming towards Pearl Harbor. Roosevelt, feigning surprise, returned to Washington on December 1 to deal with the growing crisis.

Actually, everyone who was anyone in the Roosevelt Administration had heard rumors to the same effect on January 27, 1941 — almost one whole year prior to the attack — when Joseph C. Crew, the American ambassador to Japan, revealed to FDR in a diplomatic correspondence that the Peruvian minister informed a member of his staff that he'd heard that in the event that hostilities broke out between the United States and Japan, the Japanese would initiate a pre-dawn, sneak attack against Pearl Harbor.

Roosevelt ignored the warning because diplomatically he was doing everything humanly possible to provoke exactly that type of crisis.

On July 26, 1940 Roosevelt froze all Japanese assets in the United States by presidential decree. Churchill took the same action in Great Britain. As Roosevelt secretly prepared for war, all American and British troops in the Philippine Islands were placed under the control of the United States. General Douglas MacArthur was appointed commander-in-chief of the Far East. It is interesting that an American general would assume command of British troops in a theatre of war in which only Great Britain was actually engaged in conflict.

On September 26, Roosevelt issued a decree that placed an embargo on the export of iron and scrap metal after October 15, 1940 to any nation outside the western hemisphere. Great Britain was exempted. On October 8 the Japanese envoy in Washington officially protested the embargo, calling it an *unfriendly act* towards Japan.

Meanwhile, on September 27, 1940, Japan joined Germany and Italy in a tripartite pact, and the Axis was officially born. The world was now on an irreversible course towards global war.

The question of what Roosevelt knew as commander-in-chief of the military forces of the United States and when he knew it has been hotly disputed for decades. Several books on the subject have been written over the years which suggest that the American government had broken the secret Japanese Purple Code as early as August, 1941 and knew an attack on an American installation in the Pacific was imminent from around the middle of November. They just didn't know where the attack was going to take place.

The likely target was believed to be either Hawaii or a military base in the Aleutians that guarded the largely unpopulated northern access to the North American continent. Convinced that one of these two naval bases was the logical destination of the Japanese attack fleet, a message concerning a fabricated problem with the water treatment plant at Pearl Harbor was broadcast uncoded from CINCPAC to Washington. The following day, reference to the breakdown in water treatment plant was included in a radio dispatch from Tokyo to the Japanese fleet. From this communique, military intelligence concluded that Pearl Harbor was to be the destination of the fleet.

However, a point well argued by Douglas in *Gestapo Chief* is that it is extremely unlikely that the warning of an impending Japanese attack on Pearl Harbor came from within the ranks of the American military since it is unimaginable that if the Joint Chiefs had uncovered the fact that an attacking force was enroute they would have been able to keep it a secret for fifty years given the number of enlisted men and junior grade officers who would ultimately come into contact with the information.

Furthermore, the argument put forth by Douglas concludes that "...In the absence of any concrete evidence to support the receipt of Japanese messages dealing with an attack on any specific American installation, it is not within the realm of belief that these senior officers would passively allow American military units to be attacked."

Logic further suggests that if the military participated in the conspiracy for whatever reason there would have been only one or two *expendable* ships anchored in Pearl Harbor on that fateful Sunday morning — not the entire Pacific fleet.

American losses that day included five battleships and three heavy cruisers sunk or severely crippled, three battleships damaged but still functional, 177 aircraft destroyed, and many smaller vessels either sunk or damaged. Had Japan persisted in its attack against Hawaii, the island group would have almost certainly fallen since it lacked the naval strength to ward off an invasion, nor did it possess a garrison strong enough to repel one had it occurred.

If the American military had been involved in the conspiracy, the only ships lost would have been those they needed to sacrifice in order to provoke Congressional action to declare war on Japan. It is also apparent from Roosevelt's conversation with Churchill that the president did not trust anyone — particularly the military — to understand his logic in allowing the sneak attack to place since he was prepared to move immediately in the event word of the impending invasion leaked out.

Revisionist historians, whose writings are subsequent to the events, created the myth that American military intelligence broke the Japanese code and uncovered the plot to bomb Pearl Harbor by deciphering communiques from Tokyo to their fleet mere hours before the attack was launched. Perhaps they did. Most of those in the nation's capitol who knew precisely what happened during that fateful first week of December, 1941 are now deceased and took their first-hand knowledge to the grave. Whatever records still exist that reveal precisely *who knew what,* and *when they knew it,* remain sealed. Several writers, Douglas among them, have petitioned these files under the *Freedom of Information Act,* but to date the CIA, which has become the custodian of these *top secret* documents has refused anyone access to them.

However, even without the actual government transcripts

which document the roles of each of the key players in the Pearl Harbor disaster in those fateful days prior to December 7, a steady stream of information clearly indicates that Roosevelt was the key, if not sole, conspirator has been trickling out of Washington for the past twenty years or so.

R oosevelt's public position throughout 1940 and 1941 was one in which he maintained strict neutrality because he did not want to jeopardize his standing as a dove. In November, 1940 in one of his famous fireside chats, Roosevelt assured the American public he would not drag them into a war when he said: "...I say to you fathers and mothers — and I will say it again and again and again, your boys will not be sent into foreign wars..."

Yet, a month earlier, in October, 1940 Roosevelt sent Secretary of the Navy Frank Knox on a secret mission to Admiral J.O. Richardson, the CINCPAC commander in Pearl Harbor. Knox advised Richardson that the President wanted him to "...establish a patrol of the Pacific...in such a way as to make it impossible for Japan to reach any of her sources of supply..." (*The Roosevelt Myth*; John T. Flynn; Devon Adair Company © 1948; pg. 296) Richardson knew such an action would provoke war. He also knew that since the instructions were given to him verbally, Roosevelt was trying to circumvent Congress. He refused. His disobedience had a price. He was removed as commander of the Pacific fleet in January, 1941.

In March, Roosevelt was still trying to provoke war. When he was interviewed by Eleanor Roosevelt's protegé, Joseph Lash[5] for his book *Roosevelt and Churchill*, Harold Ickes, Roosevelt's Secretary of the Interior admitted: "At dinner on March 24, [Roosevelt] remarked that 'things are coming to a head; Germany will be making a blunder soon'. There could be no doubt of the President's scarcely concealed desire that there might be an incident which would justify our declaring a state of war against Germany." (*ibid*; pg. 298.)

Churchill was of the same opinion. In the same book, Lash,

---

[5]Joseph Lash met Eleanor Roosevelt in November, 1939 when he was called to testify before the Dies Committee which was investigating subversive organizations in the United States. Lash was the national secretary of the American Student Union, which was affiliated with a known

on page 402, wrote: "The President had said that he would wage war but not declare it, and that he would become more and more provocative. If the Germans did not like it, they could attack [the] American forces.

"The United States Navy was taking over the convoy routes to Iceland...in and of itself, an invitation for U-boat attacks...The President's orders to these escorts were to attack any U-boat which showed itself, even if it were two or three hundred miles away from the convoy...Everything would be done to force an incident."

Hitler, on the other hand, did everything humanly possible to avoid any form of conflict with the United States knowing that even the accidental sinking of an American warship could bring America, with its huge industrial infrastructure and financial strength, into the war.

Churchill and Roosevelt, knowing Hitler would not allow himself to be provoked into making a stupid mistake, turned their attention back to the Pacific.

Churchill, like the rest of the world if they thought about it, knew that the small rocky island called Japan had no oil reserves to speak of: a substance needed to fuel not only their industrial plants but the machines of war whether on land, air or sea. Without oil, the machinery that fueled the Japanese economy would grind to a halt. At the urging of Churchill, Roosevelt placed an embargo on all oil shipments to Japan. Publicly, this was done to promote peace. Privately, it was done to provoke war with Japan.

While the American public failed to see through this ruse, Herbert Hoover did. In one of the few public statements the former president made after his humiliating defeat by Roosevelt

---

communist group, the American Youth Congress. Roosevelt insisted she became involved with the organization only because its goal was obtain federal aid for education and support for those who wished a career in government service.

Lash, at that time, became a personal protegé of Eleanor and visited her on many occasions both at the White House and at Hyde Park. Although he denied it for several years, Lash later admitted that he had "almost" become a member of the Communist Party, but became disillusioned when the Soviets signed a non-aggression pact with the Nazis. From then on he insisted he devoted his effort to lessening their impact in both the American Youth Congress and the American Student Union.

in 1932, Hoover, in August, 1941 said: "The American people should insistently demand that Congress put a stop to this step-by-step projection of the United States into undeclared war with Japan..." (*The Dan Smoot Report;* November 15, 1965; pg. 1). Hoover could very clearly see what America chose to ignore: by attempting to shut down the Japanese economy—which like the American economy—was fueled by oil, Roosevelt was progressively leading American closer to war as he feigned neutrality to the American people.

But, of course, the American people were not paying attention. The economy, due to another war that was festering like an infected boil in Europe, was beginning to improve. Jobs were becoming plentiful once again, and America was going back to work. As far as most American workers were concerned, whatever FDR did was pretty much okay with them. Roosevelt got them through the Depression with a few needed handouts, and now he was providing them with better jobs than those they'd lost in 1933. Life in America was suddenly good again. What did it matter to them what happened in Poland, France or Austria? If war came again, it would be Europe's war.

War, and the causes of war, are much more complex than the analogy "Billy threw a rock at Tommy and Tommy threw two back." Ask anyone who has ever fought in a war who started it and, regardless which side of the conflict they were on, they will tell you it was started by those on the other side of the issue. Few people below the pinnacle of absolute economic power understand how, or why, wars happen; or who profits when nations fight and men die. War is a political device used by transnational industrialists and bankers to achieve an economic objective from which they, and not the nations who fight the wars, will profit. Those who fight the wars are seldom, if ever, told the economic reasons why the wars they fight are fought. Instead, the hyperbole that precedes any conflict usually deals with sociological issues and the rhetoric permeates with words like "human rights" or "freedom" or "civil liberty." Those words are carefully crafted into the spin because, as Americans, we traditionally believe that all men have an inherent right to liberty, and that all men should be free to pursue their dreams.

The "official" reason for our entrance into World War II was the unprovoked attack on Pearl Harbor by the Japanese Navy on December 7, 1941.

57

When the Japanese Emperor Yoshihito died on December 25, 1926 the Taisho dynasty ended. Yoshihito, enthroned in 1912, was a weak ruler and willingly surrendered much of his control over political matters to his premier, Count Okuma in 1914. Okuma strengthened Japan's parliament, the Diet, and began the slow, tedious task of converting a militaristic nation into a capitalist economy. When Yoshihito died and Hirohito was declared Emperor, Wakatsuki, the leader of the Kenseikai Party, became premier. But Watatsuki's government was in trouble before it was even formed. A bank crisis developed shortly after Wakatsuki assumed the mantle of governance due to massive loans secured by Count Okuma from the European central banks which were used both to provide relief for losses suffered during World War I and for the construction of industrial facilities in post-war Japan. On April 17, 1927 the Wakatsuki government fell and General Baron Tanaka, the leader of the Seiyukai Party assumed the dual role as Japan's premier and foreign minister.

Although Tanaka initiated what was viewed as a "positive policy" towards China, Japan slowly repudiated the liberal internationalism of the Taisho period. Repudiated also was the intellectual and cultural diplomacy that had cemented diplomatic ties not only with its Asian neighbors but with the economic powers of the West in order to obtain the oil, gas and coal Japan needed to compete in an industrialized world — not to mention the harvestable grains and other food stuffs Japan required to feed its population.

Japan was a nation in turmoil. Only the West could save it. But the West was not interested in Japan. It had nothing to offer the industrialists and bankers of Europe and America who measured wealth in terms of natural resources. In addition the island nation was bulging at the seams. Unlike China, which had ample land, Japan had too many people. Its population, which was about 50 million in 1927, was doubling every 63 years. By 1930, Japan's population was growing by 1 million each year.

During the Taisho period, the Japanese government encouraged its citizens to emigrate to the United States, Europe, Korea and China as a means of relieving the economic and societal problems caused by the sheer density of its population — not to mention the strain on Japan's natural resources, most of which had to be imported. While limited emigration was allowed by the West, it was not enough to provide Japan with any measurable relief to its population dilemma. By 1930 Japan realized that to provide for the economic and societal needs of its people it needed, first, to increase its industrial base through increased foreign trade; and second, it needed to increase its land mass. The lands which Japan coveted were, of course, those from which the natural resources it needed — rubber, tin, oil and coal — were imported. The problem was that those natural resources, which were worth incalculable billions, were owned not by the governments or the people of those nations, but by the Rothschilds, the Nobels, the Rockefellers, and the banking dynasties of the United States and western Europe. Collectively, they would take their nations to war to protect their assets.

On Tuesday, November 25, 1941 the Japanese attack fleet embarked for Pearl Harbor. That same afternoon, President Franklin D. Roosevelt convened a war room meeting with his key advisors that included Cordell Hull, Henry Stimson, Frank Knox, General George Marshall, head of the Joint Chiefs, and Admiral Harold B. Stark, the Chief of Naval Operations, to discuss the events which were rapidly coming to a boil in the Pacific theatre.

Stimson had been advised earlier that same day by the a contact in the Soviet embassy that it was highly probable that the United States would be attacked by Japan, perhaps within a week or so at the outside, but most likely by Monday, December 1.

The purpose of the meeting was not to discuss the defense of Hawaii and, in particular, Pearl Harbor and Hickam Field, but rather to devise a political strategy that would assure the administration of America's support to declare war without any electoral backlash.

This thought is confirmed by the testimony of Stimson, recorded in *The Final Secret of Pearl Harbor* (Robert A. Theobald; Devon-Adair Company © 1954; pg. 76). "In spite of the risks involved in letting the Japanese fire the first shot,," Stimson said, "we realized that in order to have the full support of the American people, it was desirable to make sure that the Japanese be the ones to do this so that there should remain no doubt in anyone's mind as to who were the aggressors."

The Japanese, who thought the United States was being duped by Churchill, actually believed that Roosevelt would be forced to accept a treaty that would assure mutual harmony between

59

the United States and Japan even though Japan was at war with Great Britain. However, on the morning of Wednesday, November 26, Hull flatly rejected the Japanese overture of peace. It was later that very night that Churchill called Roosevelt to inform him that the Japanese were going to attack Pearl Harbor on Monday, December 8, Tokyo time.

❖ THREE ❖

Conspiratorial Politics

Thomas Woodrow Wilson wanted to go to war with Germany. America went to war. Franklin Delano Roosevelt wanted to go to war with Japan. America went to war. Both men campaigned for the presidency on a pledge to keep America out of war. Both men deliberately deceived America. In both wars, Winston Leonard Spencer Churchill, acting as an agent of the British government in collusion with members of the government of the United States did, through nefarious deceit, conspire to deliberately bring about the deaths of American citizens in order to provoke America into war. Churchill's conspiracy worked. In both instances, America went to war.

Wilson's motive is easy to understand. He wanted to be president of the world. Churchill's motivation is also easy to understand. It was based on the survival of Great Britain. Roosevelt, the etherial president, was motivated by the desire to create a truly classless society administrated by an Orwellean Big Brother — the federal government, of which he was the head.

Conspiratorial politics, whether practiced on the international scene or on a national or regional platform is, quite simply, the art of deliberate, duplicitous chicanery. Unfortunately, it has become all too common for a candidate to campaign on an established standard of values or on a pledge to support a particular political course of action if elected, and simply abandon those promises once elected. Wilson did it. Roosevelt did it. And, George Bush, who was for a brief period, the most popular President of the twentieth century, did it as well.

Roosevelt, the master strategist, concealed his broken promise to keep America out of the war behind the broken bodies of the 4,491 American servicemen who were either killed or wounded at Pearl Harbor in order to create the right "mood" in America — one that would allow him to embark on a course of war without creating a backlash that would drive him from office.

61

Bush, on the other hand, broke a 1988 campaign promise not to raise taxes—and voter backlash, worked to fever pitch by a liberal media that was determined to teach the President a lesson (because of Bush's attempt to control the media during the Persian Gulf War), swept him out of office. Elected instead was a man with very questionable moral ethics—Bill Clinton, a very charismatic liberal elitist—who completely lacked the moral integrity that America has always demanded of its Presidents.

Clinton, who campaigned on a promise of tax relief for the middle class, engineered the largest tax increase in the history of the United States within six months of taking office—a tax increase that was made retroactive to the time when Bush was President. In doing so, Clinton became the first Chief Executive in the history of the United States to tax a former President's administration, the legality of which is still debated. Strangely enough, when Clinton ran for re-election in 1996, the press chose to ignore the fact that he also broke a tax-related campaign pledge. Clinton was rewarded with a second term. Bush, who was blackmailed by the Federal Reserve which threaten increased interest rates if a modest tax increase was not implemented in 1991, caved in when promised by the Democratic leadership in Congress that the tax increase was so critical that they would not use his broken pledge in the 1992 elections. They broke their promise, too.

It is only when we delve into the political personae of men like FDR and Bill Clinton that we are able to understand the logic behind their actions. It is important to understand the principles that guide conspiratorial politics because much of what is wrong with America today happened because of this type of manipulation—whether applied by politicians, military leaders, business leaders, newspapers—or, yes, even the school teachers to whom our children's education is entrusted.

Those who have participated in the non-violent revolution in the United States to overthrow the Republic that was created by our forefathers and replace it with a utopian state controlled not by the people, but by an elite, socialist oligarchy have, regretfully, succeeded.

America is no longer a democracy since democracies are ruled by majorities. America was not paying attention when Lyndon B. Johnson initiated his Great Society. In our rush to provide equality to all minorities we surrendered the Constitutional safe-guards that are protected by the rule of law. In our search for social justice the rule of law was sacrificed along the way, be-cause in a socialist world the rule of law and social justice can-not exist side-by-side.

Throughout the balance of this book, the author will endeavor to peel back the layers of social change which have altered the face and nature of America over the past 100 years, and closely examine the historically preserved reasons for those changes as well as the logic behind the actions taken by those who fostered those changes. Among the motives for change, this book will show that conspiracies have existed — and continue to exist — in which the politicians advocating change do so not for the betterment of the society-at-large, but rather, for personal and political ad-vantage in the struggle to create a single global community. At stake is power. Raw power. Enough power to make any nation subservient to the will of those holding that power; enough power to corrupt the very tenets of the Constitution of the United States and make it worthless except as a relic of our historic past.

We, the former nation of the People, by the People, for the People, cannot restore the Republic if we do not understand how the Republic was lost.

First, we must understand exactly what our Founding Fathers intended to create when the Constitution of the United States was written, and why that particular form of government, as opposed to any other, was important to them.

The colonists, who had personally experienced the abuse of big government, were determined to create a system of govern-ment which prevented any faction — including the people them-selves — from gaining too much power and authority over any other segment of that society. For that reason, their Constitution was the most unique political document ever drafted. It accom-plished precisely that — no more, no less. The power to govern rested jointly with the people (through the House of Represen-tatives), the States (through the Senate) and the federal govern-ment (through the Executive branch). The power to legislate was granted, bicamerally, to the people and the States, but not to the federal government. The role of the federal government was to act as the administrator of the wishes of the people and the various

63

States. The power of the federal government was deliberately limited by the 10th Amendment, since big government was viewed as the worst evil man could endure. Should issues of Constitutional legality arise which could not be satisfied between the federal government and the States, a Supreme Court was created to adjudicate such disputes.

In addition, because the United States government was both a national and international body, the Constitution provided the federal government the right to create superior courts as needed to handle whatever international, national, or interstate disputes might arise that exceeded the jurisdiction or venue of the various State courts.

In creating this body, the framers of the Constitution additionally restrained the federal government with three completely independent chambers: executive, legislative and judicial.

Members of the House of Representatives were most easily influenced by their constituency inasmuch as their term in office was set at two years. This allowed a dissatisfied electorate to quickly replace those who violated their trust or did not perform in the manner expected by those who placed them in office. Since the House directly represented the people, one Congressman was designated for each 30,000 people within the state.

To make certain that the rights of the States were preserved in these United States, and to assure that their representatives in Congress safeguarded those rights, U.S. Senators served at the whim of their state governments, being elected as they were by the State legislatures. Their term in office was set at six years since that length of time usually surpassed the terms of office of the state officials, most of which were either two or four years. This was done to grant the Senators a degree of immunity to pursue legislation which would be beneficial to all of the people of all of the States as well as to those holding the reins of power within their home States.

While the President of the United States is ostensibly elected by the people of the United States, most Americans today realize that is not true. The President of the United States is elected by an Electoral College consisting of delegates appointed by the State's political parties, or by ballot in State elections. The process is simple. Each political party nominates a slate of *electors*. When you cast your ballot for President, you are actually electing one or the other of these slates of *electors* who will, in turn, actually elect the President on the first Monday after the second Wednesday in the December of a Presidential election year.

Most Americans feel this is a moot point; and that, in reality, they are still the ones who place the winner into the White House. That is true only if the candidate for which you cast your vote receives a sufficient amount of electoral votes as well. Candidates may win the lion's share of the popular vote but still lose the election because not enough electoral votes—the votes that actually place the winner in the White House—are received.

This happened in 1876 in the race between Samuel J. Tilden and Rutherford B. Hayes, and again in 1888 between Grover Cleveland and Benjamin Harrison. It came close to happening twice during the 20th century, once in 1948 when Harry S. Truman narrowly defeated New York Governor Thomas E. Dewey, and again in 1960 when John Fitzgerald Kennedy defeated Richard Milhous Nixon. The popular vote during each election was so close that if the election was settled on the popular vote alone, both elections would have experienced recounts. In fact, questions concerning the Cook County, Illinois vote still linger today, with many Illinoians wondering how many votes from Cook County's cemeteries were needed to hand Illinois' 26 electoral votes over to Kennedy in that election.

Tilden, in 1876 gained 4,284,020 popular votes, or 51% of the total ballots cast to Hayes' 4,036,572 votes, or 48% of the total. Although Hayes trailed Tilden by some 250,000 popular votes, he won the election by a majority of one electoral vote[1]. When the vote was tallied, Tilden had 184 electoral votes, one short of a majority. Hayes had only 163. The 22 electoral votes of four states: Florida, Louisiana, Oregon and South Carolina were contested.

The Republican Party charged that the Democrats had achieved popular majorities in Florida, South Carolina and Louisiana only by intimidating Negro voters. Although this was common knowledge throughout the South, hearsay is not valid legal evidence, and the Republicans were not able to prove their

---

[1] Congress determines the total number of Presidential electors from each state. Today, the total number of electoral votes are 538. To win a simple majority, 270 are needed to win the White House. Obviously, in 1876, with a much smaller national population, there were fewer electors and, therefore, fewer electoral votes were needed to win the election.

allegations. Oregon Democrats, to gain Tilden the additional electoral vote he needed to take the White House, used a little known legal technicality to oust a Hayes elector and replace him with a Tilden man. The Republicans disputed this claim as well.

Because neither candidate had a sufficient number of electoral votes to win without the disputed ballots, the election was thrown into the House of Representatives. Although it would seem a simple vote along party lines would have easily placed Tilden in the White House (since the House of Representatives was controlled by the Democrats), gridlock ensued. This resulted because of a serious lobbying effort on the part of House and Senate Republicans, and because the Senate was controlled by the Republicans who made it very clear if the House Democrats voted against Hayes, no Democratic sponsored legislation would be enacted throughout Tilden's administration. Conversely, although most House Democrats were well aware that Hayes' complaints concerning the intimidation of blacks by the Democratic state party organizations in the contested southern states had merit, they were equally determined not to hand the White House over to the Republicans by default when it was within their power to place a Democrat in it. By January 28, 1877, they were still deadlocked.

On January 29, both sides agreed to a bipartisan commission of fifteen men to settle the matter. Five came from the Senate, five from the House and four came from the Supreme Court. These fourteen, evenly divided between Democrats and Republicans, would cast a ballot for a fifth Supreme Court Justice to complete the total. Although normally impartial on political issues, the justice they selected, David Davis, was a Lincoln appointee.

Hayes was unanimously awarded the disputed electoral votes from Oregon and South Carolina; and, in a vote along party lines, he also received the disputed Florida and Louisiana votes, and became the 19th President of the United States.

Grover Cleveland, who defeated Republican James Gillespie Blaine for the White House in 1884 was not a 20th century big government Democrat. The Republicans were the "party of big government" at that time. Cleveland resisted efforts to expand the role of government and likewise fought labor by opposing tariff barriers to free competition. In doing so Cleveland alienated most of the industrial support he needed to get reelected. Campaigning on the ideological fringe of his party in 1888, Cleveland was in trouble in key industrial states, and he knew it. However, because he strongly believed in lowering tariffs and allowing free competition to foster economic growth, he refused to change his campaign tactics and ever so slowly began to lose favor in the key industrial urban centers where the only election issue was jobs.

His opponent, Republican Benjamin Harrison, campaigned for higher tariffs and protectionism, a position which garnered the support of the key industrial states where close elections are usually decided. When the votes were tallied, Cleveland had garnered 48.9% of the popular vote, and Harrison 47.9%. Third party candidates took 3.5%. Although Harrison received 90,628 fewer votes than the incumbent president, he carried the election with a sufficient number of electoral votes to place him in the White House.

Although the majority of the American electorate wanted Tilden in 1876 and Cleveland in 1888, they were denied the candidates of their choice because it is the States, not the people, who elect the president. It is only when the States and the people agree that the total will of the people is actually heard.

On only one occasion in our history was a President elected who had neither a popular nor electoral mandate. It happened in 1824. Four candidates were seeking the office of President of the United States.

John Quincy Adams, the first born son of John and Abigail, was making his second try for the White House. Four years earlier Adams lost in the most lopsided Presidential race in the history of the United States when James Monroe was reelected with the most powerful mandate ever given a United States President. Monroe took every state, and all but one electoral vote. (Prior to the election of 1824, statistics on the popular vote were not kept, since the candidates themselves understood that it was the electoral college, not the people, who elected the President.)

One of the major issues bantered by the candidates in 1824 was the growing influence of Freemasonry in America. Added to that was the growing political strength — and demands — of both the South and the western frontier. Every faction had a candidate. Adams, the establishment's candidate, represented the industrial north on the National Republican ticket. Henry Clay, a very influential senator from Kentucky, represented the party of the Anti-Masons. William Harris Crawford, an attorney from Georgia, represented the political interests of the south on the Democratic-Republican ticket. (The Democratic-Republican party would later merge with *the party of Jackson* and become the Democratic Party of today.) General Andrew Jackson, the popular hero of New Orleans was the frontiersmen's candidate, and headed what was then called the Democratic ticket.

Of all of the candidates offered in 1824, Jackson was not only the most popular, he was the only candidate with any national name recognition. As a result, his campaign was the target of much mudslinging from all of the other candidates — as it would be four years later when he was finally elected the 22nd President of the United States.

Even with the verbal abuse and character assassination, Jackson pulled 43.1% of the popular vote and 99 electoral votes — more than any other candidate. Adams was second with 30.5% of the popular vote, Crawford was third with 13.2%, and Clay mustered 13.1%, mutely testifying to the fact that Americans weren't really concerned about Freemasonry. Obviously, the majority of the Americans who voted in 1824 wanted Andy Jackson, a Freemason, as their president. They did not get their wish.

The election was thrown into the House of Representatives which, due largely to partisan bickering, was unable to select the future President. They turned to James Madison for an answer. Madison, a lame duck President at the end of his second term, used what he viewed was implied authority granted the Presidency under Article II, Section 3 of the Constitution. He advised Congress that only the top three voter-getters should be considered in their deliberation, eliminating Clay from the equation. Clay, who suddenly saw his own dream to be president dashed, threw his support behind Adams to prevent Jackson, whom he despised, from gaining the White House. Adams, the son of a Freemason, became the sixth president of the United States. And Clay became Secretary of State.

Due to the Tilden/Hayes electoral vote dispute, Congress enacted legislation which gave the States the right to settle all controversies concerning the selection of Presidential electors, except those in which the electors voted "irregularly" — that is, voted against their party's candidate; assuring that the ploy used by the State of Oregon to cast the winning electoral vote for Tilden could not happen again. Technically, Presidential electors are free to cast their vote for any Presidential candidate they wish when they cast their ballots in December, although they are committed to the candidate who won the popular vote of that State. Congress, in every case where vote-switching occurred, validated the vote when the ballots were counted before a joint session of Congress on January 6 without contest. No instance of vote-switching by a Presidential elector has, to date, changed the outcome of an election.

O ver the course of the past two or three decades there have been several movements launched to eliminate the Electoral College completely and allow the American people to elect the President by popular vote. The suggestion sounds good on the surface. When it was suggested to the American people in 1912 that they should have the right to directly elect their United States Senators, the same sentiment was echoed.

The 17th Amendment was proposed, debated, passed by both Houses of Congress, and hurriedly sent to the various States for ratification amidst a fanfare of media hype extolling the virtues of direct election unequalled in modern time. Everyone seemed to be in favor of direct election—especially the politicians. Which should have made someone question whether altering the Constitution without fully understanding the consequences of such an action was such a good idea.

It would seem that Americans would have learned by now that when a politician suggests anything that appears on the surface to benefit the electorate, to question the motives. Congress has done nothing, deliberately that is, to benefit the taxpayers of America since the Bill of Rights was ratified in 1787—and even those liberties have ever so slowly been usurped by Congress and the Supreme Court over the past 60 years.

The Founding Fathers, largely because they themselves had suffered under a tyrannical form of government and were familiar with the history of abuse promulgated on the people of Europe by the totalitarian regimes which ruled them, instituted a system of governance which they believed would contain the power of the federal government to limit or destroy the rights and liberty of its citizens. Each of the signers of the Constitution recognized that while the document they had created was not perfect and might even need to be amended in the future, it accomplished exactly what they intended: to severely limit the

69

authority of the federal government.

George Washington, upon leaving the office of the Presidency in 1797 warned the American people not to abuse their right to amend the Constitution, likening the power of the federal government to that of fire; both were useful, but both possessed the ability to totally consume and destroy everything it touched.

"If in the opinion of the people," Washington said, "the distribution or modification of the Constitutional power be in any particular wrong, it be corrected by an amendment in the way the Constitution designates...for though this...may be the instrument of good, it is the customary weapon by which free governments are destroyed."

Somewhere in the course of building a nation, we have lost sight of the fact that the power granted to the federal government of the United States are *enumerated powers,* not *implied powers.* Enumerated powers are those which have been specifically detailed in the Constitution. Those powers not specifically granted are prohibited. Implied powers, on the other hand, grant unlimited authority, and preclude only those powers specifically excluded.

Abuse of power by the federal government was the concern of many of the signers of the Constitution, particularly Thomas Jefferson, James Madison, Patrick Henry and Richard Henry Lee. It was only after Lee drafted the 10th Amendment that Patrick Henry would sign the Constitution since he was adamantly opposed to the document on the grounds that it would threaten both States' rights and individual liberty. It was Henry who proposed the addition of a Bill of Rights, specifically detailing the liberties which could not be taken from the citizens of this new country.

Alexander Hamilton, like Washington and John Adams, advocated a strong central government with power vested in the American aristocracy. According to Hamilton, representation in Congress should be based on wealth and property, much like the House of Lords in the British Parliament. His plan was immediately rejected although the structure he created was adopted and became the framework for the first three Articles. Hamilton understood the principle of implied power and used his influence to make certain the powers ascribed and denied to the federal government remained vague enough that they might be more broadly interpreted by the government once the Constitution was ratified.

70

It was largely because of what Hamilton termed "the deliberate vagueness" of the "legal text" of the preamble of the Constitution and Article I that the federal government has been able to wrest authority from the States and the people. In 1787, the preamble was nothing more than a declaratory statement. It did not provide any enumerated rights. Hamilton was convinced that future generations would very likely link the "implied rights" of the preamble to the specific enumerated rights found in Article I, Section 8 in order to broaden the power of the federal government. He was correct.

And therein lies the problem. The last paragraph in Article I, Section 8 provided the government with the broad stroke brush it sought to legislate superior power for itself not specifically denied it, even though the 10th Amendment categorically denies it any power not specifically granted to it.

If you've ever been embroiled in a contract dispute with anyone, you know that vague or contradictory clauses are always construed against the party who wrote the contract. In this case, it was written by the American people.

George Washington was correct in warning America about what has become, over the last six or seven decades, a common practice of both the Congress and the United States Supreme Court to literally amend the Constitution with self-serving, if not outright unconstitutional laws and judicial decisions that are designed only to expedite their utopian agendas.

Occasionally, issues are offered in the form of Constitutional amendments that are national in scope, universal in nature, and where the benefit or detriment resulting from passage would apply equally to all citizens. That is a right granted the citizens by the Founding Fathers. However, attempts to legislate social or economic justice through Constitutional amendments designed to elevate or protect one group, sect or class of people at the exclusion or detriment of all other classes or groups of people violates the general principles of the Constitution. Issues that beg preferential treatment for one class or segment of the general population, or that seeks to abridge rights guaranteed elsewhere in the Constitution, are not constitutionally valid.

The Equal Rights Amendment, proposed by the National Organization of Women (NOW) in 1970 and approved by the Congress on March 22, 1972 was one such amendment. Dressed up in all of the fancy, politically correct equality rhetoric, there was

71

nothing equal about the *Equal Rights Amendment*. Like most terrible pieces of legislation that will ultimately be used to punish some segment of society rather than to protect all segments, the language was left deliberately vague to grant both Congress and the courts broad interpretative rights. Perhaps America learned its lesson from the illegal adoption of the equally "harmless" 16th Amendment.

When it was offered to the States in 1972, the *Equal Rights Amendment* contained all of the right patriotic, harmless sounding verbage. Unfortunately for both Congress and the feminist movement that had been demanding more equitable representation in the work place since Alice Paul of the National Women's Party drafted the original *Equal Rights Amendment* in 1923, America has had enough affirmative action. The deadline for ratification of the *Equal Rights Amendment* was March, 1979. In 1978, Congress, under pressure from feminists, extended the deadline by three years. On June 30, 1982, the resolution expired three states short of the 38 states required to pass it. On July 14, 1982 it was re-introduced in Congress, but the measure was defeated in the Democratically controlled House of Representatives on November 15, 1983.

What is most intriguing about the affirmative action legislation is that it was ostensibly designed to correct an injustice by setting a specific minority aside for special consideration. If that is so, why was a constitutional amendment needed to assure women, who constitute a majority in America, equality in the work place when only Congressional legislation, and not an amendment to the Constitution, was needed in 1964 to end discrimination in America against blacks and other minorities?[3]

The ERA was promoted as an "equal wages" rather than an equality of rights issue. Why?

Everyone: male or female, black or white, Christian or atheist, is in favor of equal wages for equal productivity. Income disparity for equal labor is an enigma on any modern society. And clearly,

---

[3]The *Civil Rights Act of 1964* banned discrimination in the work place and created the Equal Employment Opportunity Commission to mandate compliance from business and industry. This legislation also prohibited discrimination in public places. Four years later, a second piece of legislation, the The *Civil Rights Act of 1968* extended those guarantees to real estate.

both women and minority males have come up on the short end of the stick in this area far too often. By promoting ERA simply as an equal wages issue, support was fairly easy to muster. However, equal wages was the least of NOW's worries or concerns. The issue of equal wages was simply a smoke screen by which support for the amendment was gained. NOW had a much grander agenda in mind when it offered the *Equal Rights Amendment.*

The language of the proposed 26th Amendment was as simple as it was dangerous: "Equality of rights under the law shall not be denied or abridged by the United States or by any State on account of sex."

Fair enough. But where were the references to wages or career opportunity, etc., which abound in the *Civil Rights Act of 1964?* They don't exist.

But wasn't that the issue?

Not really.

There was no "protection" proposed in the 26th Amendment that could not be construed from either the *Civil Rights Act of 1964* or the 14th Amendment, which clearly stipulates that no State may deny any person within its jurisdiction equal protection under its laws. However, there is much that can be construed from the deliberately vague verbage of the proposed *Equal Rights Amendment.* Unlike the *Civil Rights Act of 1964* which spoke of equal rights, the proposed Constitutional amendment spoke of the *equality of rights.* And while both words, *equal* and *equality* are linguistically parallel, they are distinctly different by definition.

Equal, by definition, means: "To come up; to match. To produce or achieve something on level; to cope on equal terms." (*The Oxford Universal Dictionary;* pg. 625.) The definition of *equality* is: "The condition of being made equal in dignity, privileges, power with others." (ibid; pg. 625.)

One is earned; the other is granted.

The purpose of the 26th Amendment was not to create a track upon which women could compete on a level playing field for opportunities against male co-workers—i.e., equal; but rather, it would have mandated that women simply be *accorded* equality not earned through competition.

Highly publicized flak from feminist groups over the manner in which the Virginia Military Institute at Lexington complied with the June 26, 1996 U.S. Supreme Court ruling that ordered the all-   73 male military college to admit female cadets supports the conclusion that what was really sought by the federal government was not equal rights, or even the "equality" of rights, but rather, federal control over "rights" in general. If the government and not the Constitution is legally construed as the "grantor" of all rights, then the government also possesses the authority to withdraw those rights at its own discretion in order to more effectively control the population at large.

The feminist battle with VMI began quietly on January 31, 1990 when the Bush Justice Department received a complaint from a female high school student who was refused admittance to the college. The Justice Department filed suit in U.S. District Court and argued, on April 4, 1991, that VMI's all-male policy was not only unconstitutional, it was outdated since women were serving more frequently in the miliary and had proven themselves on the battlefield.

U.S. District Court Judge Jackson Kiser ruled, on June 17, that VMI could deny admission to women because co-education could thwart its unique training methods. Not content with this decision, the Justice Department appealed to the 4th U.S. District Court of Appeals. On October 5, 1992 the Court of Appeals ruled that VMI must either admit women, decline State financial support, or offer comparable training for women elsewhere. The matter ended temporarily with VMI clearly the winner. VMI decided to offer a military-type leadership program elsewhere, and selected the all-female Mary Baldwin College in nearby Staunton as the site of the new program.

The newly installed Clinton Justice Department picked up the standard in 1993 and refiled the lawsuit, resulting in a second trial. On April 30, 1994 Judge Kiser accepted the VMI/Mary Baldwin plan with classes scheduled to begin on August 23, 1995.

Not content with this solution, Attorney General Janet Reno petitioned the U.S. Supreme Court to hear the matter, which it did on May 26, 1995. The argument put forth by Justice Department attorney Theodore Olsen was that alternative programs today were just as unequal and unconstitutional as were the segregated schools prior to 1964. After debating the evidence for 13 months, the Court ruled on June 26, 1996 that VMI must either admit female students or give up its State funding.

Triumphantly, Marcia Greenberger of the National Women's Law Center declared that the "...resounding repudiation of Virginia's position is noteworthy..." because the court was not closely divided in its decision.[3] "It is fitting," Greenberger concluded, "to see this opinion written by Justice [Ruth Bader] Ginsberg, because she has dedicated so much of her career to assuring that women would have adequate protection from sex discrimination under the Constitution." (*The Washington Post;* June 27, 1996.)

Janet Gallagher, Director of the Women's Rights Project of the American Civil Liberties Union rejoiced as well, calling the ruling "...a tremendous victory for all women..." that substitutes equal protection for paternalism (ibid).

However, by September 23, 1996 the feminist groups would be up in arms again. VMI, in a series of marathon meetings held to determine the college's course of action, decided on Saturday, September 21 to admit female cadets. However VMI administrators, in a 9 to 8 decision voted that the treatment of cadets, male or female, should be equal.

Eric Lipton of the *Washington Post* reported in its September 24, 1996 issue: "From boxing and wrestling classes to crew cuts, women enrolling at a co-educational Virginia Military Institute are scheduled to face the same requirements that male students have, a plan that administrators say will ensure equality, but that critics say will discourage women from applying to the school ...Civil rights lawyers said that after years of litigation, [VMI Superintendent Josiah] Bunting's pronouncements are merely the latest efforts by VMI to try to prevent the integration of women into the school..."

NOW, in a terse, brief statement, blasted the decision. "VMI is obviously lamenting the downfall of phallocracy — the rule of phallus," commented Karen Johnson, a NOW vice president and a retired Air Force lieutenant colonel. "They don't want women there! We know that women have less muscle mass than men. That has nothing to do with ability." (*The Washington Times;* Sept. 24, 1996.) However, in the opinion of VMI, that had everything to do with it, particularly in light of Ginsberg's written decision. Ginsberg pointed out that some women can perform as well as men, declaring most emphatically that *these women* should have equal access to VMI. (Emphasis, author.)

Kathy Rodgers of the NOW Legal Defense Fund admitted

---

[3]The Court voted 7-1 against VMI. Justice Clarence Thomas abstained from voting because his son attends VMI.

she was disappointed that the court did not provide the same affirmative action legal protection applied in race-bias cases.

Those cases, which deal primarily with employment issues, however well-intended, preferentially impute not equality but superiority to minority candidates. Under affirmative action, if two candidates applying for a position have similar educational backgrounds, the minority candidate is presumed superior and must be hired in preference to the non-minority candidate — unless the employer has met the prescribed federally mandated quotas.

In some cases, employers who have not fully complied with federally mandated affirmative action requirements, or for whatever reason find themselves the targets of affirmative action activists, are pressured to award the positions they offer to a less qualified minority candidates even though more qualified non-minority applicants may have applied. These demands are made on the grounds of *equality of rights*, not equal rights — which is precisely what the feminists sought at VMI. All of the glory, none of the pain. And, therein lies the heart of the dispute — the difference between equal rights and equality of rights.

The conspiratorial politics of the feminist movement is not now, nor has it ever been, one in which equal rights to a level playing field were sought by the feminist. What has been demanded is an affirmative action program for the weaker sex, with less stringent rules, if any rules at all, to allow the feminist, without competition, to usurp a man's role in what they abhorrently view as a male-dominated world.

A perfect example of that occurred in late December, 1992 shortly after William Jefferson Clinton was elected the 42nd President of the United States with a 42% "mandate" to govern.

Although the majority of the American voters were oblivious of the Clintons' ultra-liberal leanings, the feminists and gay rights groups were not. Even before the co-presidency of Bill and Hillary Clinton ascended on Washington, the gay rights activists and feminist groups ascended on the Clintons in Little Rock, demanding an active role in managing the affairs of the United States. The gay rights groups wanted their people entrenched in the new bureaucracy. So did the feminists. But, they were apparently willing to compromise. If appointments to high ranking cabinet positions were filled by women who were also practicing lesbians, so much the better.

76   As the Clintons began selecting their cabinet officials and

other high-ranking inner circle power types, the first four named, on December 11, 1992, were men. Lloyd Bentsen, who had been Michael Dukakis' running mate in 1988, was named as Secretary of the Treasury. Congressman Leon Panetta (D-CA) was named as the new Director of Management & Budget. Roger C. Altman, a New York investment banker, was named as Bentson's assistant; and Robert Rubin, the savy co-chairman of Goldman, Sachs & Company, who outwitted Congressional Republicans during the budget standoff in December, 1995 was named as Chairman of the newly created National Economic Council. The fifth appointment went to a woman when Alice Rivlin, with a well-earned reputation as a deficit hawk, was named as the Director of the Congressional Budget Office. The feminist groups watched anxiously. After all, the Clintons had promised a *well-balanced* cabinet.

With male appointees already outnumbering women in the new cabinet four-to-one, Clinton immediately drew fire from every liberal and feminist group in the country.

One of his most fervent critics in what would be the shaping phase of the Clinton administration was *Newsday's* Robert Reno whose sister, Janet, would be tapped by Clinton to head up the Justice Department after the Zoe Baird embarrassment, wrote this about those being named to Clinton's cabinet: "...they're all male, white and have not been convicted of pig stealing. Still, on paper, it's a curious first step in administration building for a candidate who drew his most lopsided majorities among liberals, blacks, the distressed inner cities, the poor, [and] the feminists..."

The feminists agreed. Patricia Ireland, then President of NOW, dispatched a letter to Clinton when his first appointments were announced, demanding that Clinton appoint no fewer than six women to cabinet posts to break what she called the "glass ceiling" of the Reagan and Bush Administrations which limited female cabinet members to three each.

Clinton, who hates to be criticized by anyone for any reason, issued an icy response to Ireland and others who were attempting to establish either gender or ideological quotas on him, stating most emphatically that his cabinet would be the most diverse cabinet of any president — and, that he would give real clout to both female and minority cabinet members.

Although angered by Ireland's demand that six cabinet level positions be given to women instead of the token two or three,   77

Clinton obliged by naming eight: Alice Rivlin; Donna Shalala (the former chair of the Children's Defense Fund was named Secretary of Health and Human Services); Laura D'Andrea Tyson (an economics professor at Berkeley) as chairperson of the Council of Economic Advisors; Carol Browner as head of the Environmental Protection Agency; the well-traveled Hazel O'Leary as the Secretary of Energy; and, of course, M. Joycelyn Elders, who will long be remembered as the Surgeon General who advocated the legalizing of drugs (at the time her son was being convicted of drug trafficking), and masturbation as a solution to teenage pregnancy. Madeleine Albright, a campaign *groupie* from both George McGovern's and Michael Dukakis' abortive presidential bids, and now the first female Secretary of State, was then tapped as United Nations Ambassador. Finally, Janet Reno was named Attorney General.

The feminists, like most who lobby for special interests inside the beltway, have a conspiratorial agenda. It is conspiratorial in the sense that like most conspiracies its true agenda was promulgated in secret. The true agenda of the feminist is not about equal opportunity, equal wages, or even sexual harassment in the work place. Quite simply, like most who lobby within the vaunted chambers of Congress, its about power, and it's about taking control and reshaping America to fit the perception held by those who hold that power, for whatever purpose.

The problem with the feminist agenda is not that it exists, because quite frankly, on one scale or another, everyone has an agenda. You do. I do. So does your neighbor next door. So does the guy down the street who cuts his grass three times a week so your yard will look shabbier than his. The problem exists when the agenda is camouflaged to look and sound like something else — a conspiracy — in order to secure the support needed to either establish or maintain it.

D uring World War II, an American soldier named Kilroy was sent to Europe. Nobody remembers his first name, although I am certain over a thousand former G.I.'s now claim to be him. Frankly, who he was is not important. Nobody except a trivia buff would even care. He left some graffiti on a wall somewhere in Italy. It was a simple message. "Kilroy was here!" Soon, the phrase was found everywhere: on walls, on overpasses, and even on disabled Panzer tanks on the side of the road—in Italy, in France, in Belgium, and in Germany. Kilroy became a myth. Everyone contributed their own graffiti to the myth. Kilroy was everywhere! But does that mean the original Kilroy did not exist?

The same is true of the organization referred to as the Illuminati. It was, and perhaps still is, striving secretly to carry out its socialist, global one-world agenda. However, if the organization exists today, it exists not as the Illuminati, but rather as several well-known and much respected American institutions: the Carnegie Foundation, the Rockefeller Foundation, the Ford Foundation, the Robert Wood Johnson Foundation, the Council on Foreign Relations, the Fabian Society, the Trilateral Commission, the Institute on Pacific Relations, the Cecil Rhodes Foundation, and many other lesser known entities and foundations that are dedicated to the creation of world government.

The Illuminati, like Kilroy, did exist. As already stated, it still exists, in secret, today. Under the mantra of several diverse global organizations which appear on the surface to have completely dissimilar economical, political, religious or social New World Order objectives and strategies, the Illuminati is today subversively attempting to peacefully overthrow all of the governments of the world. Tomorrow, or next year, or sometime during the next decade, it will succeed.

Many still claim the Illuminati is an ultra-secret society within the secret society of the Masonic Order, known only to 33° degree Masons. Others claim the organization, consisting of Jacobins, works through a dozen or so of the wealthiest families of the world such as the Rothschilds, the Carnegies, the DuPonts, the Vanderbilts, the Mellons, and the Rockefellers who now tutorially control almost every government in the world by manipulating those in power to do their will. It is no secret that money controls power, or that raw power creates money. The argument is valid, and is probably true to a great extent although the word *Illuminati* is no longer part of the venacular spoken by the ultra-rich—except perhaps to ridicule those who still use it.

"There is no art which one government sooner learns of another than that of draining money from the pockets of the people.

Adam Smith
Wealth of Nations, 1776

"Nothing is easier than spending the public money. It does not appear to belong to anyone. The temptation is overwhelming to bestow on somebody."

Calvin Coolidge
Calvin Coolidge: Wit and Wisdom, 1933
John H. McKee

❖ FOUR ❖

The Conspiracy Against America

T he only reason the banking houses of Europe financially supported the American Revolution was the pot of gold at the end of the rainbow. Granted, backing what most of them believed would likely become another power whose untapped wealth could rival the combined wealth of Europe also provided an additional incentive.

But, foremost in their minds was the issue of banking. Who was going to control the currency of this new Republic? Did this new government plan to print and manage their own currency, or were they prepared to allow those with the knowledge and expertise to do it for them?

Colonists like John Adams, Benjamin Franklin, George Washington, Alexander Hamilton, John Jay, and John Marshall were in favor of allowing the banking houses in Europe to create a central bank for two reasons. First, they were realists. They knew that any attempt on the part of America to break from England would require vast financial resources backed by something other than the promises of a nation that did not at the moment exist. Second, they realistically acknowledged that the colonial script they had already issued was worthless. While the script was legal tender in the United Colonies of America, it was not accepted by the foreign companies supplying the Colonial army with supplies and munitions. Wisely, they all demanded payment in gold or silver. In the event America lost the conflict, they would lose nothing.

States' rights advocates like Thomas Jefferson, James Madison, Richard Henry Lee, Samuel Adams, John Hancock and others viewed a central bank as a threat that would grant too much domestic and international power to the foreign banking interests who would be called upon to finance the economic and societal programs of the new nation. Each believed the States, as sovereign entities within the confederation, should possess the right to control their own economies. In their view the sole func-

81

tion of a central government should be confined to the protection of the States and the lives and property of its citizens.

Hamilton's forces won the debate. Recognizing that the colonies had only a few natural advantages, such as a vast reservoir of manpower from which to draw reinforcements, a willingness to fight for freedom, and a local terrain to defend, the Continental Congress was still forced to acknowledge that to succeed, they would need a vast amount of capital—real capital, not script—with which to buy not only arms and supplies, but assistance. Their adversary, the British, possessed a well-established and stable government, a sizeable treasury with sufficient credit to draw from if additional financing was needed, and more than anything else, a competent, experienced army—and the most powerful navy in the world. Without the support of the European banking houses, America didn't have a snowball's chance of winning. Like it or not, the Continental Congress had to deal with the issue. And like it or not, they would have to grant the bankers of Europe their wish.

The first national bank in the United States was formed by an act of the Continental Congress in 1781. Unlike most of the European banks that, while functioning as the central banks of their governments, were privately owned institutions, the newly chartered Bank of North America was owned and controlled by the Continental Congress.

The sole purpose of this bank was to supply a sound national currency and to act as the fiscal agent of the new government. It was through this bank that the Revolutionary War was funded. The funds it borrowed from the central banks of Europe were backed by bonds issued by the States and paid for by taxes and duties levied by the various States on their own populations.

State banks were chartered in New York and Boston in 1784. The Pennsylvania Bank, which was founded by Thomas Paine to fund the purchase of the supplies needed to equip the Continental Army at the start of the war was liquidated in 1781. The bond debt, which promised to pay 6% interest, was transferred to the Bank of North America which continued to function until it was assumed by the Bank of the United States, or as it is more commonly known today, the First Bank of America, in 1791. When it was first proposed, the Bank of the United States, like the Bank of England at that time, would be 100% owned by the private interests that funded it. However, Alexander Hamilton was unable to sell such a package to Congress. The bankers finally relented and offered the United States government a 20% stake in the $10,000,000.00 deal. Urged to do so by Hamilton and John Adams, Congress took the bait.

In return for their $10,000,000.00 investment, this privately owned central bank would become the sole fiscal agent of the United States government. Although the federal government had no legal standing to regulate State chartered banks, the *Assumption Act of 1791* allowed the central bank to redeem the notes of any state bank and demand redemption in species. This oversight authority was ostensibly granted to prevent fiscal abuses by the state banks. In reality this fiscal oversight was a condition demanded by the European bankers because under the U.S. Constitution there was no other way the central bank could legally exercise control over a State bank. The international bankers who owned the stock in the Bank of the United States were able to keep the State banks in check by using this new form of fiscal intimidation.

Thomas Jefferson, who fought the idea of a central bank tooth and nail, saw himself losing this battle in Congress in 1791, and took his argument to the people, hoping to pressure both the Congress and President Washington to forego the notion of creating a central bank. Jefferson clearly recognized the pitfalls of a private banking system that thrived by creating public debt that had to be repaid by the people, and was allowed to charge those taxpayers interest on the money it created. "If the people of the United States," he declared, "ever allow private banks to control the issue of currency, first by inflation, then by deflation, the banks and corporations that will grow up around them will deprive the people of their property until their children will wake up homeless on the continent their fathers conquered." (*The Federal Reserve*; H.S. Keenan; The Noontide Press © 1966; pg. 247.)

Andrew Jackson, a Mason like Jefferson, also fought the central bank, viewing it as a globalist banking plot to indenture future generations of Americans: "The principle of spending money to be paid by posterity, under the name of funding," he declared, "is but swindling futurity on a large scale. It is incumbent upon every generation to pay its own debts as it goes; a principle which, if acted on, would save one half of the wars of the world." (*Andrew Jackson, Hero;* Donald Barr Chidsey; Thomas Nelson Publishers © 1976; pg. 148.)

America, exhausted from war, flushed with victory and focused on growing the nation, wasn't listening to Jefferson. Nor did history pay attention when Andrew Jackson so succinctly identified the cause of war, and laid the blame at the doorstep of the international bankers, the only group in the world with enough power to create and topple governments — and to topple nations.

The task of negotiating the terms of the surrender of America's financial institutions fell on Alexander Hamilton, George Washington's hand-picked Secretary of the Treasury. Jefferson protested, arguing that Congress had no authority under Article I, Section 8 of the Constitution to delegate the money powers of the House of Representatives to private bankers. His argument fell on deaf ears. Had Jefferson taken his argument to the United States Supreme Court, it is likely that the result would have been the same since Washington had stacked the court with like-minded Federalists.

Jefferson was in the minority. Most Americans were simply indifferent since they did not understand the significance of what was taking place in "Washington City." They left it up to their elected officials to look out for their interests. After all, that's why they elected them. The only affect Jefferson had on the Congress was to limit the bank's charter to twenty years. The Congress in 1811 would have to decide if the Bank of the United States would continue to exist.

As a portent of the future, the legislation to create the Bank of the United States was concealed in the *Assumption Bill of 1791*[1].

---

[1]Since 1791, it has been the practice of Congress to hide mandates that will expand the power of the federal government in "gratuity" bills. Such was the case with the *Assumption Act of 1791*. Such was also the case with most of the New Deal legislation of the 1930s when the federal government unconstitutionally assumed for itself the right to regulate the businesses and industries of the United States, and through those regulations, control the lives and conduct of the people—a right specifically denied it under the Constitution of the United States.

To those watching, the *Assumption Bill* was a necessary piece of legislation because it provided for the federal assumption of the debts the States. Although Jefferson argued against its passage, being reimbursed for the cost of their participation in the Revolutionary War was just too hot an issue at State level.

Unobtrusively concealed within that legislation was a little noticed excise tax on all imports, as well as what amounted to a federal sales tax on all domestically produced goods. These taxes were to generate the funds needed to assure the new central bank that obligations to the bank by the citizens of the United States would be met on a timely basis.

The following year Jefferson broke ranks with the Federalists and formed the Republican Party (which would later become the Democratic-Republican Party, and still later, the Democratic Party). Jefferson, from that point on until his election as the third president of the United States, argued that the interests of the Federalists, namely Hamilton and John Adams, were deliberately designed to favor those commercial and financial interests that had rapidly become such an inimical part of the American economy.

H istory recalls the War of 1812 as the Second War for Independence. The reasons for it are vaguely shrouded in the senility of an all too distant past, forgotten perhaps because it lacked the patriotic rhetoric that abounded during the Revolutionary War. It was a conflict few Americans or its leaders completely understood. Ask a dozen historians for the reasons, and you will receive a half dozen different answers.

Few would provide the correct one. Many of those with whom I disagree would likewise disagree with me. Many historians would rightly claim that the War of 1812 started because the British navy, during the Napoleonic Wars, began seizing American merchants ships, confiscating both the ships and the cargoes, and forcibly impressing the American sailors into the British navy. Others might claim that the war started because of a series of skirmishes between the United States and England over the Northwest Territory[2], with each claimstaking the lands

---

[2]The Northwest Territory described here is not to be confused with the the Canadian Northwest Territory. The land area in dispute with England consisted of that lands above the western frontier, and included all of 　　85

between the Ohio and Mississippi Rivers for their respective countries. Both historians would be right. Add to that the firing on the U.S.S. *Chesapeake* by the *H.M.S. Leopard* and you have still another incident. Wars throughout the centuries have been started with even less public provocation.

What makes this question so intriguing, and what begs for an answer, is not the fact that England appeared willing to risk provoking the United States into a war, but rather that she chose to do so at that particular time.

England, like the rest of Europe, was engaged in a very costly war with Napoleon Bonaparte, the Corsican upstart who staged a *coup d'etat* in France on November 9, 1799 and overthrew the people's government that was created during the French Revolution. Napoleon was at the zenith of his power when England began harassing the Administrations of John Adams, Thomas Jefferson and James Madison on the high seas, and could ill-afford to be engaged in another war — particularly one with a nation that was supplying it with much of the vital munitions and goods it required to succeed in its protracted conflict with Napoleon.

The British might logically argue that since America was also supplying the French it was necessary to attack the American merchant ships carrying cargoes headed for France. But, on the high seas, who would know to which port any particular ship was destined? Perhaps the argument might be that England, with its treasury sorely depleted from fifteen years of war with France, remembered not only the wealth of raw materials to be found in America, but a much needed tax base as well?

All arguments of this type aside, there is a much more plausible reason, frightening as it might be, that has been ignored by historians for far too long simply because it is too conspiratorial

---

what is currently the States of Ohio, Michigan, Wisconsin, Indiana and Illinois. Virginia claimed approximately half of the lower peninsula of Michigan, to the 45th parallel. Massachusetts claimed the lower portion of Wisconsin to about the same parallel. Virginia claimed all of what has become Ohio, Indiana and Illinois in 1784. In 1786 Connecticut claimed a portion of that land as its own. In fact, Connecticut even claimed about half of Pennsylvania in 1782. Of all of the colonies, only New Hampshire, Pennsylvania, Rhode Island and Maryland made no territorial demands in the Northwest Territory.

and suggests that much of the history of the modern world occurred not by happenstance, but rather, because the events which transpired were planned. History records, but fails to acknowledge, most of these conspiratorial events.

A s the franchise on the Bank of the United States neared expiration, it was obvious to the bankers that their charter would not be renewed. A massive lobbying effort was launched in the Congress, and even with southern war hawks like Henry Clay[2] and John Caldwell Calhoun clamoring for the charter's extension as a necessary evil to finance the impending conflict with England, Congress could not be persuaded. The central bank had made too many enemies at the State level, and the Senate would not agree to recharter the bank, or even extend its current charter. Here was a stinging lesson in statesmanship the central bankers learned very well in 1811. They were determined not to revisit the problem one hundred years later when the Federal Reserve System was created.

Calhoun, a federalist of the old school, favored a stronger, much more intrusive federal government. He felt it was the government's role to grow industry and commerce legislatively, and he advocated the construction of federally financed east/west roadways, canals and harbors—all of which were to be paid for with funds borrowed from the central bank of the United States and paid for with higher taxes on the American public—even though both Calhoun and Clay, the co-sponsor of the legislation, argued that the economic development program would be paid for entirely by the higher tariffs demanded in the *American System Bill*. Adroitly concealed in the bill was the framework of a new, permanent national bank.

---

[3]Henry Clay (KY-W) was appointed to fill an unexpired term in the U.S. Senate in 1809 when the debate started on renewing the charter of the Bank of the United States. He was adamantly opposed to extending the charter even one day on the grounds that the measure was corrupt, immoral, and unconstitutional. Two years later, as a member of the House of Representatives, Clay and Calhoun (SC-D) championed the re-chartering of the central bank. Clay's reversal subjected him to a considerable amount of criticism from his peers in the Senate. Rumors circulated that Clay had been "bought" by the bankers, but no evidence of any wrongdoing was ever brought forth.

The *American System Bill* went down in defeat.

Although it cannot be verified by documentary evidence, it is obvious to any serious student of history that the War of 1812 was instigated not by the nations who participated in it, but was forced upon those nations by powers none of those nations could control.

Individuals, when they need money, visit a local community bank and secure a loan. To support their application, they are obligated pledge some form of collateral that the bank can seize in the event the loan is defaulted. This is simple banking. Everyone understands the principles and the pitfalls.

International banking, on the other hand, is much more complicated. What does an international banker do when a nation defaults on a debt? He does exactly what the local banker does—he seizes the collateral. Only, more times than not, the collateral offered by that nation is the nation itself.

While the United States did not default on the terms of the loans supplied by the Bank of the United States in 1811, it did default, in the eyes of the bankers who financed the Revolutionary War, on the terms of the agreement. When Benjamin Franklin and Arthur Lee discussed the financial needs of the Continental government with the wealthy elite of Europe, it is doubtful that any of those present spoke of a "test drive" for the American central bank that was demanded as a condition of the loan by the European banking houses. America defaulted on its promise, and the banking houses of Europe that put up the money attempted to repossess the collateral—the United States of America!

To accomplish their task, they enlisted the unwilling support of their biggest debtor, Great Britain, whose central bank was owned by them. Forcing England to respond to them was relatively simple since Britain was engaged in the Napoleonic Wars and could not afford to ignore the wishes of the Bank of England.

The bank had several available options. Because they controlled England's currency, they could arbitrarily inflate its value and cripple Britain's economy through a recession. They could greatly deflate the currency and, by removing the excess from circulation, bring about a depression. Or they could simply collapse the pound and bring down the British Empire overnight. Even more subtly, they could call in their outstanding notes or refuse to extend Parliament additional credit at a time when England's need for liquidity was critical to its survival.

Which ever tactic they applied worked. Great Britain, which could ill afford at that moment to antagonize a critical supplier of war materials and supplies or, for that matter, fight a second war, did just that. England's behavior constituted nothing less than the conduct of a desperate nation with a gun to its head.

James Madison, who was elected President in 1808 on an anti-war pledge was supported by the bankers even though as the hand-picked successor of Jefferson, he was viewed as an advocate of a more limited government. It may well be that the bankers realized that while Madison's opponent, Thomas Pickeney, would support an extension of the central bank's charter, he could not get elected and, for that reason alone, threw their support behind the man they couldn't keep out of the White House in an attempt to incur Madison's favor on the bank issue.

Madison campaigned on an anti-war platform, and he was determined to keep his promise. Immediately after his inauguration on March 15, 1809 he repealed the *Embargo Act* that was enacted under Jefferson believing, he declared, that it would ease tensions between the United States and Great Britain and prevent war. The *Embargo Act* was a major campaign issue for Pickeney — but for a much different reason.

While both England and France encouraged privateers to prey on neutral ships delivering cargoes to the other nation that resulted in the loss of some 1600 merchant ships and $60 million in foreign trade, exports increased in America from some $48 million in 1792 to just under $250 million in 1807. Jefferson's embargo, passed on December 22, 1807, had more of an impact on American businessmen in New York and Boston than it did on France or England. In one year, export trade dropped almost 90%, to $28 million. Agriculture prices dropped sharply, bankrupting several large farmers who had bought additional land on credit and suddenly found themselves without the funds to meet their mortgages. Although a stand against the *Embargo Act* did not do much for Pickeney's candidacy, the issue did carry several Federalist candidates into Congress in 1808. Another change occurred two years later.

The mid-term election of 1810 was a decisive one and Madison got the message. America's mood was changing. Many of the older, pacifistic members of Congress were booted out, and a younger, more aggressive Congress was elected. With it came the War Hawks like Clay and Calhoun. Clay was elected to the

House of Representatives that year. Although he had already served twice in the Senate, this was his first elected position in Congress. Previously he had been appointed to fill unexpired terms, and each time chose not seek re-election.

The War Hawks were concerned with England's aggression in the west, and with Indian uprisings instigated by Britain to stymie the western advance of the Americans beyond the Ohio River. Because British aid to the Algonquins, Iroquois, Chippewas, Muskhogeans and others was coming from Canada, the War Hawks wanted to annex Canada and drive the British completely off the North American continent.

The Election of 1810 sent an unambiguous message to the White House. America was tired of being a pawn in the European war games. But even more than that, America was tired of being kicked around. Madison took a firmer stand against England, not realizing that those who actually wrote the message that was sent from the polling booths were the same money lenders whose franchise was due to expire the following year.

In April, 1812 Congress passed a new temporary embargo that forced all American sea-going vessels to return to an American port within 90 days because they were convinced as they were that within that period of time the United States would be at war.

On June 18, 1812 the United States Congress declared war on Great Britain. As in the Revolutionary War, there was no clear-cut winner in the War of 1812. It was as though each side simply tired of fighting and decided to go home. The War of 1812 ended with the signing of the *Treaty of Ghent* on December 24, 1814. The document was mute on the causes of the war, or even which party was the instigator of the hostilities. It simply restored the *status quo*.

Granted, while the War of 1812 created its history book heroes: General Andrew Jackson, Lieutenant Oliver Hazard Perry and General William Henry Harrison, it did not create a decisive victory for either side. The only victors were the spoilers — the bankers whose conspiratorial manipulation of two governments created the conflict. While Perry became a Commodore, and both Jackson and Harrison became Presidents, the biggest prize went to the money lenders. The Bank of the United States was rechartered.

Many Americans at the time correctly pointed the finger of blame at the European bankers. A few of them even spoke out.

Unfortunately, most of them, including Harvard President Joseph Willard, saw the involvement of the money lenders only as an Illuminati orchestrated conspiracy—and directed their charges against that ghost society to no avail. The Illuminati had succeeded in doing what it set out to do fifty years earlier—it had become invisible.

The Second Bank of the United States was officially chartered in 1816 with capital of $35 million. Like the Bank of the United States before it, its charter was good for only twenty years. And, as with its predecessor, the United States government owned 20% of the stock. However, this time, 20% of the directors were appointed by the President of the United States. It goes without saying that without a majority voice on the central bank's board, the government could no more influence the decisions of the bank now than before. But, somehow it seemed to make President Madison, who signed the legislation into law, feel better.

He shouldn't have, however, because this time Congress surrendered all of its rights. The new bank was given the authority to actually create the money supply of the United States, up to $60 million—from nothing. The bank simply authorized a bond issue to cover the currency being created, and lo, the money existed.

It should have been obvious, even then, that if the bank's charter was not renewed in 1836, America could expect to be involved in another war shortly thereafter[4].

---

[4]In 1836, because of oppressive measures levied against Texicans by Mexico, Texas declared its independence from Mexico.

Hostilities erupted on March 1, 1836 between Mexican troops and Texicans at Washington-on-the-Brazos. Americans, including famous frontiersman Davy Crockett and western legend Jim Bowie, fortified themselves in the mission at the Alamo. In total, 187 Americans, commanded by Colonel William B. Travis, held Santa Ana's army at bay for four days before the mission fell. The defenders of the mission died to the last man, creating a heroic epic unparalleled in American history.

On March 1, 1845, President John Tyler brought about the formal annexation of Texas by a joint resolution of Congress—three days before James K. Polk became the eleventh president of the United States. Polk inherited Tyler's war. Texas voted, on December 29, 1845 to join the union. Mexico responded by declaring war on the United States. The war ended with the signing of the *Treaty of Guadalupe-Hidalgo* in 1848.

The War of 1812 was even more costly than the American Revolution which lasted five times longer. When the charter of the Bank of the United States expired, America's national debt was $45 million. In 1816, it was a staggering $127 million, largely in the form of I.O.U.s to other nations.

Almost immediately, the Second Bank of the United States began making demands on the federal government to retire its outstanding non-financed debt — by borrowing from them. President James Monroe resisted the pressure applied on him by the both the bankers and the Senate — despite warnings that his failure to do so could have catastrophic effects on the economy.

When Monroe rejected the ultimatum, the Second Bank took the nation on its first major economic roller-coaster ride. The bank simply opened the money spigot, and a never-ending stream of currency flooded the land like too much rain in a delta where two rivers converge.

The economy overheated, creating an inflationary spiral that quickly reached dizzying heights. Demand for products far exceeded the young nation's ability to produce them, and prices skyrocketed. Suddenly and without warning the bank slammed on the brakes, throwing the nation into a tailspin. When the brakes were applied, the bank reversed its policy by calling in the loans it had so freely granted, and deliberately contracted the economy. Everything came to screeching halt. America suddenly found itself in its a depression. And the central bank discovered a new weapon that could be used to bring belligerent governments to their knees.

Historically, blame for the Depression of 1819 was placed on the Monroe Administration and on what was termed the "instability of the State chartered banks." In reality, it was instigated by the Second Bank of the United States[5]. It was a weapon they would successfully use again and again in the future.

Thomas Jefferson, well advanced in age, spoke out against the central bank one last time in 1816, this time in a letter to John

---

[5]The Second Bank of the United States was chartered by Congress largely through the efforts of Nicholas Biddle, an agent of Rothschilds of Paris. Biddle was an important figure in European banking, and played an integral role in the creation of several of Europe's central banks, each of which was linked to the House of Rothschild. Biddle was named president of the Second Bank.

Taylor: "...I believe that banking institutions are more dangerous to our liberty than standing armies. Already they have raised up a money aristocracy that has set the Government at defiance. The issuing power should be taken from the banks and restored to the Government, to whom it properly belongs..." (*The Unseen Hand, ibid;* pg. 133.)

Jefferson was not alone in his thinking.

M any other Americans were of the same mind. Among them was Andrew Jackson, who revoked the Second Bank's charter in 1836. Another was Abraham Lincoln who blamed the Civil War on a conspiracy that involved most of the banks of Europe.

Jackson, a States' rights activist, was an outspoken critic of the central bank throughout his first term. That he was not the "candidate of choice" of the Second Bank in 1832 would be a gross understatement. Nicholas Biddle, the president of the Second Bank, was determined to block his re-election at all costs because the election of 1832 was critical to the survival of the Second Bank. Its charter would be coming up for renewal in 1836. Jackson vowed to veto any effort on the part of Congress to extend the life of the central bank.

Biddle selected his own candidate, Henry Clay, to run against Jackson. Clay, who had been influential in the re-chartering of the central bank in 1816, retired from politics in 1829. However, at the request of Biddle, he re-entered the political arena in 1831 and won a Senate seat from Kentucky in order, one might imagine, to have a national platform from which to campaign for the highest office of the land the following year.

What is most interesting about the line-up of candidates in 1832 is that Jackson's running mate both elections was John C. Calhoun[6] who, with Clay, rammed the legislation that created the Second Bank through Congress in 1816.

---

[6]Calhoun became a Jackson convert largely because of the "Tariff of Abominations" which, surprisingly, was framed in 1828 by Jackson supporters in order to embarrass John Quincy Adams who, politically, could afford neither to sign the bill into law nor veto it. To their surprise, not only did the Tariff bill pass both Houses of Congress, Adams signed it into law over the protest of Calhoun who denounced the legislation in the South Carolina Exposition of 1828.

Although the Second Bank acted in a much more restrained manner financially after the Depression of 1819, its members continued to commit what Jackson felt were serious political indiscretions aimed at undermining his Administration throughout most of his first term. These incidents merely exacerbated Jackson's prejudice against the central bank, which he felt wielded far too much power over not only the lives and welfare of the citizens of the United States, but its government as well. And, Jackson was determined to end that monopoly—once and for all!

In a political ploy designed to embarrass Jackson during the 1832 campaign, Clay and Daniel Webster urged the central bank to apply for a renewal of its charter four years early in order to make it a campaign issue they could use against Jackson[7].

They did. It was.

Unlike those along the frontier who possessed little money and even less need for a bank, those who lived in the urban centers were dependent on an economy that required a strong banking system. It didn't seem to matter to them that bankers like Nicholas Biddle exercised too much control over their government as long as they kept the economy moving forward and provided the funds needed to create the jobs demanded by the working class. Not only did the working class not realize precisely how much power bankers like Biddle actually had, they also did not know that most of the economic strife they had suffered in 1819 was due to them. They only knew that the wheels of progress turned when oiled with money, and that those wheels had to turn before they could earn a living. Everything else was secondary.

Inflamed by Clay and Webster, Jackson attacked the Second Bank both privately and publicly Since Clay was now a Presidential candidate, Webster lobbied the bill through both the House and the Senate. The House voted for passage 107 to 85,

---

[7]While many conspiracy theorists insist Biddle devised the scheme to force Jackson to campaign on the central bank issue, it was clearly a strategy created by Clay and Webster. They reasoned if Jackson was forced to campaign against the Second Bank of the United States, the issue would likely siphon off much of his support from industrial and commercial groups who needed to stay in the good graces of Biddle. Jackson's only recourse would be to allow the bank to be rechartered four years early in order to avoid the pitfalls such an issue would present on the campaign trail.

and the Senate passed it 28 to 20. On July 10, 1832, Jackson vetoed the proposition declaring: "Some of the powers and privileges possessed by the Second Bank of the United States are unauthorized by the Constitution, subversive to the rights of the States, and dangerous to the liberties of the people...The bold efforts the present bank has made to control the government, the distress it has wantonly caused are but a premonition of the fate which awaits the American people should they be deluded into the perpetuation of this institution or the establishment of another like it."

Responding to criticism of his veto, he added: "If the American people only knew the rank injustice of our money and banking system, there would be a revolution by morning! It is regrettable that the rich and powerful too often bend the acts of government to their selfish purposes...In the full enjoyment of the gifts of heaven and the fruits of superior industry, economy and virtue, every man is equally entitled to protection by law, but when the law undertakes to...grant...gratuities and exclusive privileges, to make the rich richer and the potent more powerful, the humble members of society — the farmers, mechanics, and laborers — who have neither the time nor the means of securing like favor to themselves, have a right to complain of their injustice to their government."

Jackson, like Jefferson before him, believed there were no provisions within the Constitution that granted Congress the power to create a central bank even though the Second Bank had been adjudged constitutional by the United States Supreme Court in 1819 in the case of *McCulloch v. Maryland*.

E ven though the Supreme Court has assumed for itself special interpretative powers to imply that hidden meaning somehow exists within the phraseology of Constitution, the document itself seems fairly clear and unambiguous in its delegation of authority — particularly in monetary matters.

Contained within Article I, Section 8 is such a provision: "*The Congress shall have power...to coin money [and] regulate the value thereof...*" Congress does not possess the authority to delegate, abrogate, or surrender its power over the creation of currency to private parties. There is no ambiguity in the Section 8 for Constitutional lawyers to trip over. Unlike the legalism of today, the language in the Constitution is quite simple and to the point. And, for good reason. The framers of the Constitution did not want it to be misunderstood — particularly on this point.

In part, the American Revolution was fought over the issue of coinage. As mentioned previously, Britain enacted the *Colonial Currency Act* in 1764 which forbade the colonies from printing or circulating their own currency. That law gave England's privately-owned central bank immense power over the American economy, which it manipulated at will.

It is for precisely that reason that one of the first things any conquering nation does to a defeated foe is to replace its monetary system — which the European Union is now doing in order to control the governments of its member States. The conqueror's script is redeemable only through the largesse of the conqueror — who can inflate it, deflate it, or completely devalue it.

That was a major concern of the Founding Fathers. They clearly understood that whomever controlled their currency controlled them. To safeguard the right to coin money, it was granted not to one person or a small group of people, but rather to all of the people collectively through their elected representatives with oversight by the States through the Senate.

Meyer Amschel Rothschild, who for many years controlled the vast Rothschild financial empire — including the Second Bank of the United States — once said: "Give me the power to coin the money and I care not who controls the reins of government." It would be difficult not to understand precisely what Rothschild meant.

Real power exists behind the seats of government — not in them. Rothschild clearly understood that principle. So do most of the politicians of the world who dance to the pied piper tune of the Rothschilds and others like them.

Politicians in the national or international arenas stand on the precipice of real power in the sense that they have reached a station in life which allows them to witness, first hand, the delegation of global authority by those who control the purse strings of the world. Although difficult if not impossible for most Americans to imagine, little happens on the world level that is not sanctioned by "behind the scenes" global manipulators. As Americans, we believe we are sheltered by the Constitution. We are not, and have not been since April 8, 1913.

❖ FIVE ❖

The Abrogation of Rights

History had clearly illustrated to the banking community that changes in the Constitution needed to be imple mented before the newly created Federal Reserve System could operate with impunity. Even before Wilson was elected the 28th President of the United States, Congress launched the safeguards needed to protect the new, more powerful elitist bureaucracy it was creating in the form of two constitutional amendments that were proposed, promoted and passed through both Houses of Congress due largely by the efforts of one man: Senator Nelson Wilmarth Aldrich.

Both amendments would prove to be very destructive to future generations of Americans. Both will eventually be counted among those catalysts that ultimately destroy the remnants of the fabric of a free society in America. Both are helping to open the door wide for a system of global governance led by foreign interests. And, almost every social problem suffered in America today can be linked, directly or indirectly, to one or the other of those amendments that appeared, on surface, to be pieces of legislation that would not adversely affect the lives of the average working man or woman in America.

Unfortunately Americans have short memories about our elected officials. We forget the unkept promises and broken trusts, and continually elect to office men and women with less moral character than many of those who are incarcerated in the penal institutions of America. And, we do so using the excuse that *all politicians lie, and all politicians break their campaign promises.* As a result, far too often our votes are cast on the basis of which candidate will do the least amount of damage to America while in office, or which promises the best spot at the public feeding trough.

While we complain about the candidates from which we are forced to choose, we quickly forget that we nominated those candidates ourselves, or allowed them to be selected in state prima-

97

ries or by state caucuses. If the candidates are bad, it's our fault. And, when the politician gains more power than we collectively possess as voters, it is time to get rid of the politicians before they, through the abrogation of our electoral rights, deny us that authority — a problem America now faces over term limits.

The most monumental problem facing the bankers who crafted the Federal Reserve legislation in 1913 was how to generate a revenue stream sufficient to cover the costs of their loans to the federal government to finance the social programs that would soon be emanating from Washington. In Europe it was fairly easy since none of the European nations' constitutions were as complex or as protective of its peoples as that of the United States[1]. Each European nation possessed the sovereign right to impose any form of tax or tariff upon its citizenry, whether direct or indirect.

However, Article I, Section 9 of the Constitution prevented direct taxes from being levied against the American citizen. This provision was written for two reasons. First, the Founding Fathers had a healthy, well-founded mistrust of strong central governments. Second, because they had first hand experience dealing with the international money lenders, they viewed the central bank as the most potentially serious evil facing the fledgling nation. Central banks, like central governments, are cancers that feed on the societies they purport to help much the same way a leech feeds on its host. The leech offers nothing in return to the host for its hospitality; and in fact many times actually destroys the host upon which it depends for sustenance.

By limiting the ability of the federal government to grow itself, or assume authority not granted it by the Constitution, the rights of the States and the people to self-governance were guaranteed in perpetuity. By preventing direct taxation, the Founding Fathers eliminated not only much of the immediate threat of the central bank but also any future attempt on the part of the federal bureaucracy to control the States, or the people, through

---

[1] In Europe, the rights of the people come from the largesse of the government. The United States is the only country in which the "rights" of the government are granted by the people, with the superior rights of the people coming directly from God.

the levying of direct taxes — something Great Britain did several times to bring the colonists into submission.

But, it was an easy matter for the bureaucracy to fix. A Constitutional amendment was drafted by the Aldrich forces, hurried through Congress and sent off the States for ratification. Its text was as simple as it was full of pitfalls for the American taxpayer: "*The Congress shall have power to lay and collect taxes on incomes, from whatever source derived, without apportionment among the several States, and without regard to any census of enumeration.*"

Somehow, the promises made by the politicians about precisely who would be paying this new tax was not found in the text of the proposed amendment. Most Americans, if polled at that time, would likely have said they supported the idea believing as they did, it was to be a "rich man's tax." Of course the idea that a tax system could be created by any nation that would exempt both the wealthiest and poorest members of its society and penalize only its middle class was too radical of a concept to even imagine in 1913 — although today one need only look at the socialist states in Europe to see the model. Of course, in 1913 those models did not exist. The Bolshevik Revolution was still four years away.

Not that the 16th Amendment flew through Congress without argument or debate. It was suggested by several Senators who wanted tax perimeters included in the Amendment, that without such built-in safeguards, tax rates could feasibly climb to as much as 20% of the taxpayer's income. Senator William Edgar Borah (R-UT), a co-sponsor of the 16th Amendment and one of the key proponents of the 17th, argued that such preposterous speculation on the part of members of Congress was outrageous and declared that Congress could never impose such a confiscatory rate on the American people and still remain in office.

Not only were federal legislators concerned about the impact of the 16th Amendment on future generations, so were most of the State legislators as well. When the Amendment was being discussed in the Virginia House of Delegates in the closing days of 1910, Democratic Speaker Richard R. Byrd argued that "...a hand from Washington will be stretched out and placed upon every man's business; the eye of the federal inspector will be in every man's counting house...they will compel men of business to show their books and disclose the secrets of their affairs...they will require statements and affidavits...[and] under it, [men] will be hauled into court distant from their businesses [because]...it will extend the federal power so as to reach the citizen in the ordinary business of life."

Byrd likewise opposed the 17th Amendment, viewing it as an attempt on the part of the federal government to strip the States of their right to representation in the Congress. He was correct again. And again, he lost.

The growth of the federal government, and with it, its self-ordained right to use coercion to force its citizens into submission was a gradual process, happening imperceptibly over some four decades in the twentieth century while the people's attention was focused on the task of creating the great American dream for themselves and their families.

The 17th Amendment was promoted to the people of America as an entitlement — their right — to directly elect Senators as they did their Congressmen. Prior to the ratification of the 17th Amendment members of the U.S. Senate, with few exceptions, were elected by the State legislatures as part of a Constitutional checks and balance system that was deliberately and specifically designed to limit federal power by making the United States Senate beholden to the States for their continued employment in Congress.

Prior to the 17th Amendment, any U.S. Senator would have thought twice before voting on any legislation that would grant the federal government additional authority to intrude on the rights of the States. On April 8, 1913 when the 17th Amendment was ratified, the Republic created by our Founding Fathers died. In its place, on May 31, 1913, the date when the 17th Amendment superseded Article I, Section 3 of the Constitution, the balance of power shifted from the States to the federal bureaucracy when an oligarchy was created in the place of the Constitutional Republic so many of our ancestors died to create.

America was sold a phony bill of goods. And, America, gullible as it has historically proven itself to be, bought the media rhetoric that preceded the Amendment hook, line and sinker. Americans were told they had the right to elect their Senators in exactly the same manner they elected their Congressmen. Nobody raised the question: *why then, are our Senators elected by the States?* Nobody asked what would happen to the balance of power once this change was implemented. The 17th Amendment was promoted as an act of empowerment *for the people*. It wasn't. It was an act of empowerment for the federal government. It removed from the people almost all of the real authority they previously possessed.

From 1913 until today the primary focus of the federal government has been to create methods, both legal and illegal, to remove all remaining vestiges of real power from the States — and from the people — through the enactment of one law after another that clearly violates the specific powers both granted and denied the federal government by the Constitution.

Most of the new laws and regulations enacted by Congress from 1933 to 1994 were increasingly designed to expand the intrusive role of the federal government by assuming powers they do not legally possess. However, since the 17th Amendment removed the States' voice from Congress, who was left to contest the constitutionality of the legislation it enacted? Certainly not the United States Supreme Court, which long ago expanded its own franchise to cover not only Constitutional issues, but disputes which rightly are the sole jurisdiction of state courts.

Like both the legislative and executive branches of government, the sphere of the Supreme Court is clearly defined by the Constitution. Nowhere within the Constitution is the Supreme Court explicitly granted the power of judicial review over a State law. In other words, the States did not grant the high court superior authority to reverse decisions made by State courts concerning States issues. Like the implied powers assumed by the federal government, the Supreme Court similarly assumed authority for itself it likewise did not Constitutionally possess.

The Supreme Court was granted appellate rights over all cases in which either Constitutional issues, or violations of federal law arose. While some might logically argue that because some Constitutional issue has invariably been construed to be at stake in every case in the land, the high court has the right to review any court decision, State or federal, particularly since the 14th Amendment placed "federal" restrictions on the States. However, since the Supreme Court is the final resting place for all judicial decisions, it's a moot argument at best, since there is no court beyond it with which to address the argument.

While Congress may neither expand nor diminish the power

provided the Supreme Court by the Constitution, it does possess the authority to expand its realm of jurisdiction — something it has jealously chosen not to do. However, the Supreme Court itself has not hesitated to expand its own jurisdiction whenever it wanted, and has done so repeatedly throughout its history.

In the mid-sixties, the Supreme Court decided that State levied death penalties violated the 8th Amendment provision against "cruel and unusual punishment" — and outlawed it. Yet, the text and tone of the 5th Amendment clearly suggests the Founding Fathers recognized that those convicted of capital offenses would face such a penalty when they said: "No person shall be... deprived of *life*, liberty or property without due process of law." (Emphasis, author.)

Interestingly, criminal courts today are meting out original, if not bizarre, sentences to convicted felons and not an eyebrow is raised from those who decry the execution of killers and serial rapists as "cruel and unusual punishment." In fact, the courts are many times commended for their originality in sentencing by some of the same advocates who hold candlelight vigils outside of state penitentiaries when a convicted murderer is executed, or who flood the offices of governors with letters requesting clemency for those who, without batting an eye, snuffed out the lives of their victims.

The State of California passed a law that mandates the chemical castration of those convicted of sex offenses — both for rape and pedophilia. While I have long advocated this type of punishment — and worse — for sex offenders, this is a textbook case of cruel and unusual punishment. But, because these are crimes against women and children, the punishment is deemed to be politically correct, and the civil rights advocates are noticeably silent.

Judges at both county and state levels are now branding rapists and pedophiles as a condition of their paroles so the community at large knows when one is among them. This is also viewed as politically correct. An Internet website has been launched that tracks sex offenders nationwide. When the feminist wave subsides, the high court will review this type of sentencing and will likely rule such "punishment" unconstitutional as well.

Each year the Supreme Court receives upwards of 5,000 requests for hearings. From them, the Court selects approximately 300 of the most controversial cases — many of which, because they are State matters, it actually has no legal jurisdiction to address.

It goes without saying that every attorney who files for redress before the Court has found a *constitutional link* since the 6th Amendment guarantees the accused a speedy and public trial by an *impartial* jury of his peers; and further, that the State has abided by the law in securing evidence against the accused as provided by the 4th Amendment. Usually somewhere between the 4th, 5th and 6th Amendments a good lawyer can find a reasonable Constitutional argument upon which to seek redress from the Supreme Court.

For the sake of example, this text will cite two cases addressed by the Supreme Court which should never have appeared on its docket.

In the first case, because no genuine Constitutional issue was at stake, one was created. The legal argument was so weak, the plaintiff's attorneys in *Roe v. Wade* and *Doe v. Bolton* were convinced they would lose before the justices even heard their argument. It was, however, a politically correct case at the onset of a politically correct era. Not only did the justices accept their argument, they greatly expanded on it, creating the entire case for the plaintiff. In the second case, because such an unusual Constitutional issue was at stake, the Supreme Court should have excused itself and even forbade any other federal court from addressing the question as well.

The question dealt with the 1st Amendment — the touchiest of all of the amendments to the Constitution. The 1st Amendment specifies that "Congress shall make no law respecting an establishment of religion, *or prohibiting the free exercise thereof,* or abridging the freedom of speech, or of the press, or the right of the people peaceably to assemble, and to petition the Government for a redress of grievances." (Emphasis, author.)

The 1st Amendment has always been viewed as the most sacrosanct amendment contained within the Bill of Rights. Freedom of speech, a free press, and most of all, the right to worship God in the manner of our choosing, without interference or hindrance from the government, has been the cornerstone of liberty in America. Without the 1st Amendment, the protection afforded Americans under the remaining tenets of the Bill of Rights can easily be abrogated by an overzealous, overly protective "Big Brother-type" federal bureaucracy.

The assault on the 1st Amendment began in 1947 when the Supreme Court issued a landmark ruling in the case of *Everson*   103 *v. Board of Education*[2] (330 U.S. 1, 18), saying: "The First Amendment has created a wall between church and state. That wall must be kept high and impregnable. We could not approve the slightest breech."

Most Americans, if asked, would probably insist that somewhere within the Constitution the phrase "a wall of separation," or at least, "separation of church and state," appears. It does not. The phrase, and the concept that an *impregnable wall of separation* somehow exists, was legislatively adjudicated by the high court in 1878 during the case of *Reynolds v. United States* (98 U.S. 145, 164) when the Justices rewrote the 1st Amendment through legal interpretation. The Supreme Court upheld their 1878 interpretation of the 1st Amendment when it ruled in the case of *Pierce v. Society Sisters* in 1925, establishing the *wall of separation* principle they would cite over and over again throughout the 20th century until it became as much a part of the 1st Amendment as freedom of speech or freedom of the press.

In *Everson v. Board of Education*, the high court went one step farther, and coupled the 1st Amendment (1787) with Section 1 of the 14th Amendment (1868), entwining them in order to apply the restrictions directed exclusively at the federal government to the States—although the 14th Amendment dealt with the readmission of the former Confederate states into the Union, and the civil rights of the former slaves. "Coupling" has now become the standard of interpretation practiced by the high court.

In *Everson v. Board of Education* the propensity of the high court to arrogantly abuse the Constitution was clearly depicted. By coupling the 1st and 14th Amendments to support a theoretical wall of separation that does not exist, the Justices proved they could not only rewrite Congressional law, but they could, by interpretation, successfully amend the Constitution as well.

Interestingly, an attempt was made in 1875 by James Gillespie Blaine (R-ME), the Speaker of the House of Representatives to introduce a Constitutional Amendment that would have effectively rewritten the 1st Amendment and expanded it to cover the States.

---

[2]*Everson v. Board of Education* concerned the issue of taxpayer funds being used to support a Christian school. The following year, the high court would hear *McCollum v. Board of Education*, and rule that voluntary classes in religion—held off of school property, but during regular school hours—were likewise unconstitutional.

In essence, the *Blaine Amendment* declared: "No State shall make any law respecting the establishment of religion, or prohibiting the free exercise thereof, or abridging the freedom of speech, or of the press, or the right of the people peaceably to assemble, and to petition the State for a redress of grievances. No public property and no public revenue [of the State] shall be appropriated [by the State] for support of any school...under the control of any religious or anti-religious sect, organization, or denomination...And, no such particular creed or tenets shall be read or taught in any school or institution supported...by such revenue." (*Original Intent* by David Barton. Wallbuilder Press © 1996; pg. 201.) (Parenthesized reference added.)

"This Amendment would have done to the States exactly what the Court did in the 1940's; yet it was *rejected* by the Congress which passed the 14th Amendment. In fact, the McCollum Court [1948] noted that not only the Blaine Amendment but also five similar ones which would have applied the 1st Amendment against the States were *rejected* by Congress. The intent of the legislators who framed the 14th was clear: it was not to be coupled to the 1st.

"Therefore, even though the Court invokes the 14th Amendment as its supposed constitutional authority to intrude into the issue of State and local religious expressions, history proves that the 14th Amendment actually provides the Court *no* legitimate basis for that interference. History factually demonstrates the extent to which the Court has taken into its own hand the complete converting of the Constitution by rewriting the intent of a number of its clauses." (*Original Intent; ibid.*)

In *McCollum v. Board of Education* (333 US 203, 207-209; 1948), Vashti McCollum, an atheist, argued that an Illinois state law that allowed students to be excused from classes one afternoon each week to attend Bible classes at their own church was unconstitutional. McCollum petitioned the court not only to strike down the voluntary classes, but also to forbid any form of religious teaching of children that suggests there is a God.

The Illinois religious training law was enacted only after intense lobbying on the part of a Champaign, Illinois group called the *Council on Religious Education*. The CRE was made up of Roman Catholics, Jews and Protestant clergy and congregationalists who felt that religious education was as essential as reading, writing and arithmetic in the character molding of the children of Illinois. Recognizing the diversity of its citizens, which included monotheists, atheists as well as traditional theists, the Illinois law allowed the school boards to implement a completely voluntarily program of religious education as a completely elective class.

Students would be allowed to participate only if their parents signed authorization cards requesting that their children be allowed to attend. Furthermore, the program was initiated without any use of public funds. All costs were incurred by the Council members, who provided the instructors from within their own congregations.

Those parents who did not wish their children to participate could simply refuse to sign the school release card. McCollum did not sign. But, that was not enough for the Champaign housewife because while her children were not subject to the voluntary religious training, they were required to remain in school while the other students were excused for *church school*. This apparently proved to be a source of embarrassment for her offspring — who, because of parental ancestry, were possibly viewed by some of their peers as *different* — or, at least, that was the case in McCollum's mind.

The religious instruction in Champaign was funded by community churches and the classes were not held on school property. In reality the only issue before the high court was whether or not the Illinois public school system could dismiss classes early one day each week so that the students, who were allowed to do so by their parents, could attend religious instruction at their own churches. Since the State of Illinois sanctioned the practice, the Supreme Court had no genuine Constitutional right to intrude.

It didn't matter. McCollum won.

McCollum's petition, although filed over the issue of religion, was in reality one dealing with racial differences and ethnic stereotypes. Granted, McCollum was an atheist. And, granted, atheism is a form of religion since the atheist believes in the deity of man over God. However, the Supreme Court should not have heard the McCollum case for two reasons. First, the Supreme Court had no Constitutional authority to tell the State of Illinois they could not dismiss the public schools early one day each week since the State was completely neutral on the religious issue. Doing so suggests the high court's motive was based on a federal attempt to control the State's school system by denying the local school board the right to make decisions affecting classroom hours.

And, second, since the Constitution forbids the federal government from passing any laws that interfere with the free exercise of religion, "laws" judicated by the high court are as binding as those legislated by Congress — particularly when the case on the docket was asking the high court to rule in favor of one theological perspective in preference to another. Any abridgement of the free exercise clause of the 1st Amendment violates the Constitutional right of free men to openly practice the tenets of their faith — the fact that others with differing theological views may disagree with those tenets, notwithstanding. That is one of the primary benefits of a free society — we can disagree.

In his concurring opinion, Supreme Court Justice Robert H. Jackson wrote: "The plaintiff, as she has every right to be, is an avowed atheist. What she has asked of the courts is that they not only end the "released time" plan but also ban every form of teaching which suggests or recognizes that there is a God. She would ban all teaching of the Scriptures..." Unfortunately, the "teaching of the Scriptures" McCollum wanted to ban was that which took place in the churches, not the schools, in Champaign, Illinois. But that did not seem to matter to the high court. "...She especially mentions as an example of invasion of her rights 'having pupils [in the *voluntarily* attended, *elective* classes] learn and recite such statements as "The Lord is my Shepherd, I shall not want.' And she objects to teaching that the King James version of the Bible 'is called the Christian's Guide Book, the Holy Writ and the Word of God,' and many other similar matters. This Court is directing the Illinois courts generally to sustain plaintiff's complaint without exception of any of these grounds of complaint." Although McCollum was seeking a national ban on religion, she received little satisfaction other than to see the release time programs stopped not only in Illinois but in every other State which had adopted the program.

The watershed case abrogating most religious rights in America occurred in *Murray v. Baltimore Board of Education* in 1965. In this case, Madelyn Murray, an atheist, argued against the forcing of her son, William, to recite the Pledge of Allegiance in class since it mentioned allegiance not only to America, but to a deity, God. In this case, the Supreme Court expanded its wall of separation to include not only schools, but all local, state or federal government agencies — opening the floodgates for hundreds of court challenges on religious expression. Among them was one

107

that forbade Alaska schools from using the word "Christmas" to describe Christmas, since the name "Christ" is contained within the word; or, an Aldine, Texas school song that expounded such values as honesty, truth and faith in the form of a "prayer" — although it did not mention any deity or expound any religious tenets. Or a decision that forbade a school from displaying a copy of the Ten Commandments — although no attempt was made by the school to indoctrinate anyone. Since children might read or meditate upon them be inclined — completely on their own — to obey them, the Ten Commandments were deemed to be unconstitutional.

When the high court ruled in the case of *McCollum v. Board of Education*, liberal Justice Felix Frankfurter, who wrote the decision, said: "...as we said in the Everson case, the 1st Amendment has erected a wall of separation between Church and State which must be kept high and impregnable...Separation means separation, not something less."

Years before those words were uttered by Frankfurter, former Chief Justice John Marshall said in ruling on *Barron v. Baltimore* in 1833: "In almost every convention by which the Constitution was adopted, amendments to guard against the abuse of power were recommended. These amendments demanded security against the apprehended encroachment of the general government..."

Even before Marshall, Samuel Adams declared that the Bill of Rights was created because those attending the Constitutional Convention needed to know exactly where the line that defined State and federal power was drawn. "Without such distinction," Adams insisted, "there will be danger of the Congress issuing imperceptibl[e laws that] gradually [lead to] a consolidated government." If that happened, Adams declared, the States would no longer be free. The Bill of Rights was not designed to restrict the States — only the general government.

The reason for coupling the 14th Amendment with those concerning other personal liberty issues should be obvious even to a novice student of the Constitution.

The 17th Amendment to the Constitution was created to remove any semblance of real power from the States under the guise of giving people more "power" in the election of those who would represent them in the Senate. The people were hood-winked. For absolute power to be consolidated in Washington, authority had to be taken from the States. It goes without saying that those in power in the United States Senate were in favor of direct elections since they knew the people would be easier to control than the State legislatures. All Congress had to do was provide them a feeding spot at the public trough.

However, the rapidly growing federal bureaucracy still had a problem. It's called the Bill of Rights. Everywhere they turned, the Bill of Rights got in their way. To date, the federal govern-ment has not been able to invalidate its provisions — and, it has not been for the lack of trying! What has stopped them thus far has been the States themselves. The Bill of Rights was designed to curtail the federal bureaucracy, not the States. The Bill of Rights is the States' last vestige of power. To eliminate it, the Court now couples the Bill of Rights with the 14th Amendment when-ever Constitutional issues concerning those amendments arise.

That it was a deliberate plan was affirmed by Associate Jus-tice William O. Douglas in his written opinion in the matter of *Walz v. Tax Commission* when he said: "The result has been a national revolution...in reversing the historic position that the foundation of those liberties [in the Bill of Rights] rested largely in State law...[T]he *revolution* occasioned by the 14th Amend-ment has progressed as Article after Article in the Bill of Rights has been [selectively] incorporated in it [the 14th] and made ap-plicable to the States."

W hile the Court can be counted on to suppress any American's right to the free expression of religious liberty, it will al-most certainly affirm your right to desecrate the American flag, display the most obscene pornography in the name of art in any public building in the nation — or practice witchcraft in any gov-ernment installation. *What's wrong with this picture?*

The Constitution of the United States expressly forbids any-one — legislatively or judicially — from infringing on anyone else's right to freely express their religious beliefs, whether those convic-tions are displayed in someone's front yard, at the local court-house, at the White House — or on the wall of an outhouse. It is a Constitutional right that cannot be abridged by anyone.

There is no clause anywhere within the Constitution that says if I don't like your God you can't worship him. Likewise, there is no clause in the Constitution that gives anyone the right to either take, or deny, life to another human being in order to safeguard what the Court construes as an abhorrent prohibition of the free exercise of personal liberty. Carrying an unwanted child in the womb to the exclusion of a woman's *right to privacy* must have been considered by the nine old men on the Warren Burger Court[6] to be the most horrendous experience a woman could possibly be made to endure, since their solution to the problem was feticide — the killing of the unborn.

In November, 1969 some three and one half years before *Roe v. Wade* (410 US 113) and *Doe v. Bolton* (410 US 179), the U.S. District Court for the District of Columbia ruled that the District's seventy-some year-old abortion statute was *unconstitutionally vague* and threw it out, opening the door for physicians in the Washington, D.C. area to perform abortions with impunity. On appeal, the Supreme Court decided, in a five-to-two decision in April, 1971, that the law was not vague. The high court reinstated the law and rescinded the legal protection from prosecution the District Court decision had afforded doctors only eighteen months earlier. This ruling occurred only twenty-one months before the Supreme Court opened the floodgates to the mass murder of the unborn on January 22, 1973.

H ow could there be such a radical change in the opinions of the justices on the high court in such a short period of time? Quite simply during that period a new *medical ethic* had taken place not only in America but across the globe. This new ethic was based largely on the opinion of the World Health Organization (WHO) of the United Nations which insisted that within a matter of some twenty to thirty years, the world would no longer be able to sustain itself — there would simply be too many people for the world to feed.

Every statistic and supposition published by WHO concerning overpopulation was actively promoted as fact by abortion activist groups like the Abortion Law Reform Association and Planned Parenthood.

Granville Williams, the godfather of abortion-on-demand attempted, in October, 1963, to incite a national referendum on the issue, advocating that abortion be made a legal, private matter between a woman and her physician during the first trimester. His proposal was shot down by every abortion group in the nation who knew that abortion-on-demand, if left to the people to decide, would never be allowed in America. Little did Williams know that in less than ten years the Supreme Court would write into the Constitution a doctrine far more damning than anything his radical mind would have dared imagine.

In writing the majority opinion for *Roe v. Wade/Doe v. Bolton*, Justice Harry A. Blackmun provided America with some insight into his mind. Blackmun, in "...an excusatory preamble states that he is aware of 'the insensitive emotional nature of the abortion controversy' and concludes with an admonition from [Chief Justice Oliver Wendall] Holmes that judges should not brand a statute unconstitutional merely because it embodies opinions which to them are 'novel and even shocking' [*Wade*, pp. 1-2]." (*The Zero People; Raw Judicial Power;* John T, Noonan, Jr.; Servant Books © 1983 by Jeff Lane Hensley; pg. 19.)

The Supreme Court, somewhere within the text of the 14th Amendment, discovered a heretofore unknown Constitutional privilege: the right of a woman to possess such a degree of privacy over her body that she could legally kill a human life within her for daring to intrude upon that privacy. Since the high court itself could not quite define precisely where that right was located in the 14th Amendment, the text of Section I, which deals with the question of individual rights, is included here for your own contemplation: "*All persons born or naturalized in the United States, and subject to the jurisdiction thereof, are citizens of the United States and the State wherein they reside.*" Nothing there. "*No state shall make or enforce any law which shall abridge the privileges or immunities of citizens of the United States, nor shall any State deprive any person of life, liberty, or property, without due process of law; nor deny to any person within its jurisdiction the equal protection of its laws.*" Nothing there, either.

Although the words "privileges," "immunities," and "liberty" are mentioned in the second sentence, there is nothing there that can legally or morally be construed as a *special* right—particularly when the final portion of the sentence qualifies the meaning: "*...without due process of law.*" In fact, if anything, the 14th Amendment should protect the unborn from wanton slaughter.

Anyone who has ever read the entire 14th Amendment understands the intent of the Congress when it was proffered. With the 13th Amendment, Congress formally abolished slavery[3] on December 18, 1865. The 14th Amendment was designed to serve a dual purpose, both of which were related to the Civil War that had just ended. First, the 14th Amendment provided the former slaves the same privileges, immunities and liberties that were extended to all other American citizens. Second, it sought to make certain that the former Confederate states, once re-admitted into the Union, could not enact any State laws which would treat the former slaves any less equal than any other citizen of the State; nor could they deny those new citizens due process under the law.

With respect to content, there is little difference between the guarantees of the 5th Amendment and those of the 14th with one important distinction. The 14th Amendment was directed specifically at the States. All other "Bill of Rights" amendments are directed specifically and exclusively at the federal government.

The sole purpose of coupling the 14th Amendment with any other Amendment cited in any Constitutional issue before the high court is to intertwine them in such a way as to be able to apply the restrictions of the other Amendment against the States. In the case of *Roe v. Wade/Doe v. Bolton,* the 14th Amendment was, strangely, coupled with 9th: "The enumeration of the Constitution, of certain rights, shall not be construed to deny or disparage others retained by the people."

Somewhere within the text of the 14th Amendment, Black-

---

[3]Many people believe that the Emancipation Proclamation, issued by Abraham Lincoln on September 22, 1862 freed all of the slaves on January 1, 1863. It did not. It applied only to those slaves under bondage in the Confederacy. Exempted from the proclamation were those slaves within any Union state. Likewise, the Proclamation did not apply to any slaves within captured Confederate land. Quite naturally, Lincoln's proclamation had no authority in the Confederacy. All tolled, Lincoln's proclamation freed a handful of slaves at best.

The purpose of the Emancipation Proclamation was not to free the slaves from bondage, but rather, to incite them to rebel against their Southern owners. It was entirely a military ploy. Lincoln's sole objective was to save the Union, but he did not want to disrupt its economy.

"My paramount object in this struggle," he said, "is to save the Union. If I could save the Union without freeing any slaves, I would do it." (*The Irony of Democracy, An Introduction to American Politics;* Thomas R. Dye & L. Harmon Zeigler; Duxburg Press © 1972; pg. 73)

mun saw what he described in his decision as the constitutionally protected right to privacy by a woman that allowed her to
decide whether or not to terminate a pregnancy. Not only did
he insist this right actually existed within that text, but that it was a
fundamental right. He did not, however, elaborate on precisely
what words, or series of words, affirmed that special right. By
entwining this special, invisible right with the 9th Amendment,
the high court ruled that the States needed a compelling interest
before they could restrict abortion. Since the only compelling
interest the States could possibly have was in saving the life of
the baby, Blackmun then declared the fetus to be a non-person.
Justifying their action, the Burger Court[4] declared that if those
trained in medicine, philosophy and religion could not arrive at
a consensus on when life begins, then, "...the judiciary is not in a
position to speculate on the answer."

Ignored was an article which appeared in the *Journal of California Medicine* in September, 1970 in which the following quote
appeared: "The process of eroding the old ethic and substituting
[a new one] has already begun. It may be seen most clearly in
changing attitudes about human abortion. In defiance of the long
held Western ethic of intrinsic and equal value for every human
life regardless of its stage, condition, or status, abortion is becoming accepted by society as moral, right, and even necessary.
It is worth noting that this shift in public attitude has affected
the churches, the laws, and public policy rather than the reverse.
Since the old ethic has not yet been fully displaced it has been
necessary to separate the idea of abortion from the idea of killing, which continues to be socially abhorrent. *The result has been
a curious avoidance of the scientific fact which everyone really knows
that human life begins at conception and is continuous whether intra-
or extra-uterine until death. The very considerable semantic gymnas-
tics which are required to rationalize abortion as anything but the taking of human life would be ludicrous if they were not put forth under*

---

[4]Warren Earl Burger joined the Department of Justice in 1953 as
assistant Attorney General under Attorney General Herbert Brownell.
In 1956, Dwight D. Eisenhower appointed Burger to the U.S. Court of
Appeals for the District of Columbia. In 1969, President Richard M.
Nixon selected Burger to succeed Chief Justice Earl Warren. Because
of his former association with the court system of the District of Columbia,
Burger was one of the two justices who recused himself from voting on

socially impeccable auspices. It is suggested that this schizophrenic sort of subterfuge is necessary because while a new ethic is being accepted the old one is not yet rejected." (113:67-68; September, 1970.) (Emphasis, author.)

However, the text of the *Roe v. Wade* petition cited by Blackmun provides some schizophrenic insight of its own. In his decision Blackmun cites population growth, pollution and poverty as issues that complicate the abortion question, maintaining that the decision to allow abortions was consistent with the "...demands of the profound problems of the present day." In conclusion, Blackmun defended the decision by insisting that since something that meant one thing in 1865 might logically be construed a something completely different in 1973 it is necessary to periodically reinterpret the Constitution in order to make it speak to the times.

Tragically, *Roe v. Wade/Doe v. Bolton* was not a judicial decision by the Supreme Court — it was a political one. The Supreme Court callously exceeded its authority when it judicially legislated an incontestable law that could never have been successfully enacted by Congress.

According to Chief Judge Richard A. Posner of the United States Court of Appeals for the 7th Circuit, one of the leading authorities on Constitutional law in the United States, there is no such thing as a constitutional right to privacy anywhere in the Constitution. "No rights to an abortion, or right of privacy is stated in the Constitution. These are unenumerated constitutional rights. Their scope and legitimacy are at the forefront of modern constitutional controversy...[A]s [Ronald] Dworkin contends, the right to use contraceptives and the right to burn the American flag...a right affirmed by many scholars and judges, such as Justice [Anthony] Scalia, who believe that *Roe v. Wade* was de-

---

the abortion matter that originated from the District in 1971.

Burger was personally a conservative. His Court was usually moderate. Unfortunately, he was an extremely weak, ineffective Chief Justice and his views never dominated those of his colleagues. The Burger Court lacked any semblance of dominant philosophy except that, perhaps, of Harry Blackmun who was appointed to the court a year later. Blackmun was a conservative on matters of criminal law, but was extremely liberal in all affirmative action matters. Blackmun wrote the majority opinion in *Roe v. Wade/Doe v. Bolton.*

cided incorrectly, would be seen to stand on the same plane as far as the distinction between enumerated and unenumerated rights is concerned." (*Overlooking Law;* Richard A. Posner; Harvard University Press; © 1995; pgs. 175-76.)

Dworkin, a legal scholar and author of several texts on the subject of constitutional law, argued that "...[t]he Supreme Court has a duty to find some conception of protected liberties, some statement defining which freedoms must be preserved, that is defensible both as a political principle and as consistent with the general form of government established by the Constitution." (*ibid;* pg. 178.)

In other words, according to Dworkin, the Supreme Court does not have the authority to legislate. Any interpretation of select clauses of the Constitution that "...fails to achieve consistency of principle across the whole Constitution, or at least the whole of the Bill of Rights plus the 14th Amendment—must to that extent be coherent, holistic." (*ibid;* pg. 178.)

It is the responsibility of the high court, when rendering judicial decisions, to clearly outline the scope of the constitutional theory they have advanced, and show precisely and specifically from which clauses, and upon what basis, those rights are construed.

According to Posner, despite "...the efforts that Dworkin makes to ground *Roe v. Wade* in a particular clause of the Constitution, he cannot have great confidence that the rights...can be generated by theories limited to individual clauses, such as the due process clause, *Roe's* original home. The substantive construal of that clause stinks in the nostrils of modern liberals and modern conservatives alike...because of its formlessness." (*ibid;* pg. 180.)

Since 1973 Constitutional scholars have attempted to fit *Roe v. Wade*—which Posner aptly describes as the "wandering Jew of constitutional law"—somewhere into the Constitution, much like an extra piece in a jigsaw puzzle. Everyone who has tried has been forced to conclude that it simply doesn't fit anywhere.

The reason is obvious. It doesn't fit because a constitutional right to privacy, as Posner claims, doesn't exist.

By 1972, largely because of the over-population scare promoted by WHO, the Ford, Rockefeller, and Scaife Foundations became deeply dedicated not only to the legalization of abortion, but also to the free distribution of contraceptives to teenag-   **115** ers without parental consent. In fact, these groups even advocated compulsory sterilization to stem the threatening population explosion.

It is frightening to contemplate the thought that the United States Supreme Court could be motivated to render a *politically correct* decision rather than a judicially correct one—particularly in light of the fact that the current Chief Justice, William Rehnquist, (an Associate Justice at the time) insisted in his dissenting opinion on *Roe v. Wade* that the personal liberty described by Blackmun (that had somehow escaped everyone's attention for over a century) would, if noticed in 1868, have invalidated any abortion-rights laws in effect at the time.

What is most ironic about the use of the 14th Amendment to allow abortion is the fact that it was used to overrule an earlier Supreme Court decision: *Dred Scott v. Sandford* (60 US 393 [1856]). In the *Dred Scott* decision, the Supreme Court ruled that even a freed black man has no personal rights. Today the Constitutional amendment that guaranteed the black man not only equal rights, but equal protection under the law as well, is now being used by the high court to deny those same rights to a fetus.

In closing this section dealing with the Supreme Court, it is imperative to leave the reader with one additional thought to contemplate.

When Hillary Rodham Clinton put together the 1993 Health Care Task Force, she utilized the services of The Diebold Institute for Public Policy Studies, Inc.[5] to prepare the study from which the Clinton Healthcare Plan would be fashioned.

Contained within those documents, under the heading of "De-

---

[5]The Diebold Institute Commission consisted of several extremely influential individuals who would ultimately play key, well-rewarded roles in promoting the Clinton agenda. The American members of the Diebold Commission were: Dr. Craig I. Fields, President and CEO of MCC Corporation; Robert M. Galvin, Chairman, Motorola, Inc.; Maurice R. Greenberg, Chairman, President and CEO of American International Group; John D. Macomber, Chairman, President and CEO of the Export-ImportBank of the United States; H. Ross Perot, Chairman, The Perot Group; and Dr. P. Roy Vagelos, Chairman and CEO, Merck & Co., Inc.

Most interesting of all of the above named is Ross Perot, who ran as the "spoiler" against George Bush in 1992. Perot spent $45 million of his own funds. In 1996, using $30 million of federal matching funds and little of his own capital, Perot appeared again as the spoiler against

ployment of Health Care Infrastructure" was a schematic of those who would be serviced under the plan. Below the schematic is a timeline when certain aspects of the program would be achieved.

Somewhere between 1993 and 1996 the Clintons anticipated testing, in federal court, what would become a community-based information utility that would ultimately gather a medical database on all of the people in the United States.

Sometime between 1997 and 2001, the U.S. Supreme Court would rule that collecting medical services information cannot be construed as practicing medicine without a license. It is somewhat intriguing that the Clinton Healthcare Plan was formulating plans based on a Supreme Court decision that has not yet occurred — on a legal action which has not yet been filed!

Compounding that dilemma, the Supreme Court will again rule — this time somewhere between 2002 and 2006 — that patient information, formerly the proprietary property of the patient, is now co-owned by the government insurer! After that decision is made by the Supreme Court, the United Nations will be assigned the task of regulating that information database. *(National Archives; the Clinton White House, Health Care Interdepartmental Working Group, Reproduction Tab: Box 1748.)*

---

former Senate Majority Leader Bob Dole (R-KS).

It was reported by *The Washington Times* that in October,1996 George Carpozi, author of *Clinton Confidential: The Climb To Power*, uncovered evidence that suggested a deal had been cut in 1991 between Arkansas Governor Bill Clinton and Perot for Perot to enter the 1992 race as a spoiler to cut Bush's lead. Clinton's pollsters estimated that Clinton would, at best, gain 45% of the vote. Clinton needed a spoiler who could siphon off at least 12% of Bush's supporters; or at least, throw the election into the House of Representatives which was controlled by the Democrats in 1992. (*Health Security Act Working Papers, Diebold Report; Box 1748, National Archive.*)

In exchange, according to Carpozi, two of Perot's database companies would be awarded the lion's share of the Clinton Healthcare business—worth billions over the next decade. When Carpozi broke the story, Perot called his home to deny the allegation. Unknown to Perot, Carpozi taped the conversation—and later played it in its entirety on the conservative Los Angeles-based talk radio George Putnam Show.

Perot denied any connection with the Clintons, or with the Diebold Group. When Carpozi told him he was listed in the Diebold Report as

The federal assault on the Bill of Rights started on September 3, 1917 when 35 agents of the newly formed Justice Department's Bureau of Investigation, assisted by 2,500 members of the quasi-official American Protection League (APL), together with 500 police officers and close to 2,500 army personnel conducted simultaneous street raids in Brooklyn, Newark, New York and Jersey City in an attempt to round up draft dodgers.

The crackdown on draft dodgers, together with a planned raid on the twenty-four regional offices of the International Workers of the World labor union on September 5, 1917 were the direct result of a growing nationwide anti- German sentiment, complicated by persistent rumors that anyone with a German-sounding name was likely to be either a spy or a saboteur.

Congress declared war on Germany on April 6, and passed the *Selective Service Act* on May 18. By June 5, local Selective Service Boards had registered some 9,586,508 eligible men between the ages of 21 and 31 years who would be subject to the military draft and might well be called upon to fight in Wilson's War. Within another year, a total of 23,815,527 American males — everyone between the ages of 18 and 48 — would be registered for the draft. On June 13, 1917 the first division of American troops left for Europe. The Hun scare was on.

A patriotic zeal erupted in America. The doughboys would go to France, save the English crown, and be home by Christmas. Only, Christmas came and passed. The only doughboys who came home were those who were crippled or maimed in the first

---

one of its Directors, and that his name showed up prominently in the Clinton White House Healtcare interdepartmental working group papers, Perot feigned surprise, declaring that it was news to him, and insisting that "...nobody mentioned anything about it to him."

In 1996, Perot, whose party was now called the Reform Party, was back. This time, however, he refused to spend his own money, since he lost $45 million when the Clinton Health Security Act went down in flaming defeat.

Guaranteed matching funds if the Reform Party held a primary and selected a Presidential candidate by secret ballot, Perot went through the sham of holding one. With only 10% of his theoretical 800,000 party "faithfuls" returning their ballots, Perot won against former Congressman Richard Lamm. Now, armed with $30 million in taxpayer dollars, or $375 for each vote cast in his "primary," Perot was ready to help Bill Clinton win his second Presidential election.

war of the 20th century. Most of those who died would remain behind, buried in strange sounding places in France and Belgium.

American pacifists were either shunned as cowards or treated as spies. Those who complained about food shortages, or the lack of goods in American stores, or bellyached about poor wages in American factories were treated as seditionists. And, those who complained about Wilson's war policies were accused of treason. Neighbors became suspicious of neighbors — particularly if the neighbor had a German-sounding last name. Every state, county and local police agency was flooded with calls or anonymous letters from concerned citizens who were convinced their neighbor was up to no good. Even the Secret Service was besieged with mail identifying this person or that as an enemy agent.

The fear-mongers loved it. On June 15, 1917 Congress passed the *Espionage Act,* allowing the Justice Department to deal with subversives. It was followed, on October 6 with the *Trading With The Enemy Act,* and on May 6, 1918 with the *Sedition Act,* and later that year with the *Alien Deportation Act.* The United States was now ready to deal with the threat.

Only, at the time, no threat existed.

So, the Department of Justice created one with the help of a vigilante group called the American Protection League.

Because the Federal Bureau of Investigation as we know it today did not exist at the time, the Justice Department was in a quandary. It's unofficial and constitutionally-illegal Bureau of Investigation lacked the budget, the manpower, or the legal authority to investigate American citizens unless some sort of evidence directly linked that citizen, or group of citizens, to a violation of a federal law. Rumors were plentiful. Evidence of wrongdoing was almost nonexistent. It was, however, the conviction of those within the government that where there was smoke, there was sure to be fire.

The Bureau of Investigation was certain the evidence existed. They simply needed the manpower to find it.

The APL provided the solution. Within a few short months of its creation, the APL saw its membership grow to some 10,000 overzealous and completely untrained citizen spies who were determined to infiltrate every business in America in order to ferret out all of the German spies. Only, there weren't any.

The fledgling Bureau of Investigation's sedition investigations were placed under the supervision of special assistant At- 119 torney General John L. O'Brian. O'Brian selected a young, aggressive Department of Justice clerk named John Edgar Hoover to head up a unit called the Enemy Alien Registration Section. Hoover's job was to make certain that all "enemy aliens" were properly registered with the government. Hoover, however, saw his assignment as a mission to rid America of its unwanted.

Hoover convinced O'Brian that the persistent rumors concerning spies were genuine. Hoover also convinced O'Brian that the understaffed Bureau should utilize the "free labor" available to it through the APL.

Impressed by Hoover's argument, O'Brian secretly persuaded Attorney General Thomas W. Gregory to make the APL a quasi-official auxiliary of the Justice Department. Officious looking badges were issued to the APL by the Justice Department — which the APL used to increase its membership. By the middle of 1918, the APL had grown from 10,000 to a quarter million completely untrained, unrestrained hometown government vigilantes — each one eager to violate anyone's Constitutional rights in order to create a little excitement in their own life. Also, each was eager to earn the $50.00 bounty the federal government had placed on the capture of any draft dodger, or a much larger reward that could be received for the apprehension of an enemy spy — if such actually existed[6].

Eager to collect the bounty offered for draft dodgers, APL members in Boston, Chicago, and Pittsburgh under the direction of Bureau of Investigation chief A. Bruce Bielaski began round-

---

[6]It should be pointed out that the German government, during World War I, did not have an organized "third column" movement in the United States since it did not perceive the United States as an enemy. Germany was convinced that Wilson would not enter the fray, since he had campaigned on an isolationist platform, and was coming up for re-election the following year. While there were German spies assigned to the German Embassy in Washington as well as some linked to many of the German National groups scattered throughout the country, their primary role was to keep their finger on the pulse of public opinion in America, and to track the movement of freight and munitions from the factories to the freighters which would transport those war materials to England. There were very few instances of sabotage in the United States during the period from 1917 to 1919 that could be attributed to a third column movement, although attempts were made to link every disaster in America to German sabatours.

ing up limited numbers of *suspected* draft dodgers. The experimental program, which was officially sanctioned by Gregory, worked. The dragnet imposed by the APL brought in several citizens who had failed to register for the draft.

Pleased with the initial results, Bielaski got ambitious. Without authorization or clearance from his superiors in the Justice Department, Bielaski's force simultaneously attacked Brooklyn, Newark, New York, and Jersey City.

Without warrants or legal provocation, Bielaski's vigilantes confronted men of all ages on the streets, in pool halls, hotel lobbies, and even in offices while they worked, and demanded that each produce a draft card. If the "suspect" didn't have one, a birth certificate proving that he was either too young or too old for the draft was demanded. Those with neither on their person were summarily arrested and incarcerated.

The Bill of Rights had been suspended.

Congress immediately denounced the raid and demanded an accounting. In his final report of the roundup of "slackers," as the draft dodgers were called, Bielaski reported that a total of 50,000 men of all ages had been arrested and detained. Of those, 1,505 were immediately inducted into the service and 15,000 were referred to their local draft boards. By his own tabulation, Bielaski admitted to the false arrest of some 33,495 American citizens. However, one of Bielaski's assistants admitted in the Congressional Record that out of every 200 arrests, 199 were clearly mistakes.

While it is likely that Bielaski tried to make a case against some 16,000 of those arrested, it appears as though less than 250 of the 50,000 arrested were actually slackers.

Even more shocking is the fact that the action was stoutly defended by New York Bureau superintendent Charles DeWoody who stated that "...the dragnet would have been justified 'if only two or three slackers' had been found."

The International Workers of the World, known to most in the industrial world as the Wobblies, was targeted for a raid on September 5, 1917 not because it was suspected of being a third columnist organization, or agents of the German government. It wasn't. Hoover knew it. The Wobblies were socialists. Their only crime was that they existed at the wrong time — and in the wrong place.

The IWW president in 1917 was William "Big Bill" Dudley Haywood. Haywood was a Mormon by birth and a socialist by persuasion. He promoted a socialist philosophy known as *syndicalism* which, like most Marxist ideologies, advocated a violent class struggle to achieve equality for the working man.

In 1906 Haywood and several other socialists were accused of being implicated in the murder of Frank Steunenberg, the former governor of Idaho. Defended by Clarence Darrow, he was acquitted in 1907. Too radical even for his own supporters, Haywood was fired from his leadership position in the American Socialist Party in 1913 for advocating violence in labor disputes.

As the head of IWW, Haywood and Eugene V. Debs[8], who headed the American Socialist Party, were the biggest fish netted during the IWW raid. Both were charged with sedition. Both stood trial. Both were convicted. Debs was sentenced to ten years in prison. Haywood was fined $20,000.00 and sentenced to twenty years, but appealed his conviction. While awaiting a new trial, Haywood fled to the Soviet Union where he remained until his death in 1928.

The IWW was singled out for the September 7 raid for two reasons. First, Haywood was viewed as one of the most dangerous, subversive men in America. Second, Haywood, who was much respected by the growing labor movement in the United States, was attempting to organize general strikes all over the country at a time when America needed every industrial plant in the nation outputting goods to their maximum capacities. The IWW had to be stopped. The Justice Department believed that by making an example out of Haywood and Debs, other labor unions would think twice about flexing their growing muscle during times of political or military strife. They were right. Labor unrest in America ceased almost immediately.

The history of the Federal Bureau of Investigation is replete with example after example of gestapo-type Constitutional

---

[8]Eugene Victor Debs led a somewhat undistinguished life until he became involved in the labor movement. In 1880, Debs was elected grand secretary and treasurer of the Brotherhood of Locomotive Firemen, a position he held until he resigned in 1893 to form the American Railroad Union. In 1885, after serving as the city clerk of Terre Haute,

abuses. The Bureau itself was illegally conceived and created without Congressional mandate or approval. There was a fear in Congress that by allowing the creation of an Executive branch police force, Congress would be providing the President of the United States with his own Gestapo. History has proven their fears were justified.

Hoover surreptitiously investigated every Presidential candidate from Coolidge to Nixon and stored derogatory information about them in three separate sets of secret files that could be used against any President who threatened to remove him. Using blackmail to keep his job, Hoover held the directorship of the FBI from 1924 until his death on Tuesday, May 2, 1972.

Since his death a myriad of appointees, beginning with L. Patrick Gray III, have been named to fill the six year term as Director since Hoover's death. In 1993 Louis Freeh replaced William Steele Sessions. Sessions was appointed by Ronald Reagan in November, 1987. He was fired by Bill Clinton the day before the mysterious death of Vincent Foster—with six months still remaining in his appointment. Sessions was the first FBI Director ever fired by a President. Sessions, who himself died mysteriously in the summer of 1997, was fired not for malfeasance, but because Clinton wanted someone in the "top cop" slot whose loyalty would not be in question. With one or two exceptions, Freeh proved not to be a disappointment to Clinton.

Recent examples of FBI excesses can be found in the exami-

Indiana Debs was elected to the state legislature.

Under Debs' leadership, the union struck the Great Northern Railroad in 1894. The strike was broken by federal troops on the orders of Grover Cleveland in July, 1894. Debs was arrested and charged with conspiracy to commit murder, although the government never pursued the charge in open court. Instead, Debs was tried for violating an injunction and sentenced to six months in jail. It was there that Debs was introduced to socialism by a cellmate, Victor Louis Berger, who provided Debs with a copy of Karl Marx's *Das Capital.*

In 1897, Debs organized the Social Democratic Party of America, and in 1900, became its candidate for President of the United States. He received 96,116 votes. He ran again in 1904, 1908, and 1912. A pacifist, he was arrested in the seditionist roundup of 1917. Although he was sentenced to ten years in prison for seditionist activities, his sentence was commuted in 1921. While confined to prison in 1920, he ran for President again—and received almost 1,000,000 votes.

nation of two recent and tragic events: the Waco Massacre and Ruby Ridge. The FBI's fingerprints likewise linger on two White House scandals, Travelgate and Filegate. History may also prove its silent complicity in the cover-up of the death of Clinton friend and deputy White House counsel Vincent Foster. In each of those latter incidents, the top cop in the nation ignored the Constitution he was sworn to uphold in order to serve the needs of his political masters in the Department of Justice and the White House.

The FBI now also has a well-earned reputation as an agency prone to extreme rushes to judgement. Such was the case with Richard Jewell, the security guard at the Olympics in Atlanta, Georgia in the summer of 1996. Jewell, a contract employee with AT&T was on duty in Centennial Park when a terrorist bomb exploded, killing one and wounding several others. Initially, Jewell was lauded as the hero of the tragedy. Within two weeks he became the FBI's only suspect in the bombing—due entirely to a tip the FBI received from one of Jewell's former employers who labeled him as an overzealous, power hungry security guard who wanted to play "cops and robbers" just like a "real cop." In point of fact, as the investigation developed, it was learned that Jewell had been a real cop: a deputy sheriff in Habersham County, Georgia. During that period, it was also revealed that because of his overzealousness, he was taken off of patrol and assigned to a desk. Shortly thereafter Jewell resigned and returned to Atlanta. And that, for some strange reason, made him even more suspect.

Based on that "evidence" and apparently nothing else, the FBI decided Jewell fit the profile of a domestic terrorist who would likely plant a bomb or two, save a few people, become a temporary hero and, during his fifteen minutes of fame be offered a real police job again.

To trap him into a confession, the FBI invited Jewell to their Atlanta field office on the pretext of assisting them in making a training video for new agents hoping, one imagines, that by feeding a malcontent's ego, Jewell would either confess, or provide them with enough information that they would have sufficient cause to arrest him. Wanting to make certain that any information they extracted from him under this ploy could be used against him, they conveniently had him sign a waiver of his rights. Jewell appeared to be the only person in America at the time who did

124

not realize he was the suspect.

While he was assisting the FBI with their training project, the FBI leaked the story that he was the prime suspect to the *Atlanta Journal & Constitution*. The following day, in a widely televised media event, FBI agents served Jewell's mother with a search warrant that was nothing more than a legally-obtained fishing license. As Jewell and his mother watched from the street, FBI agents carted off anything and everything that might possibly be construed as evidence — including eight Walt Disney movies that belonged to Jewell's mother.

Even though the FBI insisted that Jewell was simply one of many suspects in the case, the reality was they had no others. Under extreme pressure to find the terrorist — not, as one might imagine, for the sake of bringing the guilty party to justice, but rather, to protect the millions of dollars the city of Atlanta had invested in the Olympics, the FBI opted to go after the closest thing they had to one: Richard Jewell. And, in a rush to judgement to brand Jewell as a domestic terrorist, the FBI all but ended Jewell's chances of again finding permanent, lasting employment in law enforcement. So, in fact, died any chance he had of continuing his work as a security guard or for that matter, as a night watchman in a deserted widget factory.

Americans are supposed to be able to trust their law enforcement agencies, whether federal, state or local. That is no longer possible. During the past six years the FBI, a branch of the Justice Department, has literally become a gestapo arm of the White House. As the basic liberties guaranteed to every American under the Bill of Rights became obscured by a litany of new anti-terrorist laws enacted to protect us from ourselves, even the Constitution of the United States is in jeopardy.

And, unfortunately, while many Americans will disagree, the Constitution is deliberately being eroded. The text of this book will, in minute detail, outline exactly how, and why, it is being destroyed.

If left unchallenged, the federal government will soon legislate an oligarchy in America that is as oppressive as any of those formerly found in the most despotic communist societies of the world, under the rhetoric of *protecting* personal liberty. Not the personal liberty of the *majority*, mind you — but rather, the *special* liberties and *special rights* of both an elitist minority and a greatly enfranchised welfare class — until such time as the utopian society the globalists envision has been achieved. At that time, the welfare class will be permanently disenfranchised since, in all socialist societies, all "citizens" are expected to be contributing members.

In a utopian society the "have-nots" must initially be supported by the "haves" until such time as the "haves" are equal with the "have-nots" (and not the reverse as one might think.) Today, the "haves" are obligated to strive for equally beneath their current level of existence as the government attempts to elevate the bottom-feeders of society up the rungs of the societal ladder as they force the middle-class down the ladder to meet them. When this takes place on a global level, the bureaucrats believe, Utopia will be achieved in the world. At that point they believe all men will truly be equal, and society will then have no further need of any form of national government. Peace and prosperity will permeate through the core fiber of the utopian global society and mankind will live happily ever after.

Socialist rhetoric aside, the utopian pipedream is as flawed as the democratic daydream that trumpets the theory that since all men are created equal in the eyes of God they are somehow entitled to economic equality without the need to earn it.

The promise of America is not an immunity from the circumstances of birth. Rather, it is the opportunity, through the sweat of a man's own labors to overcome those circumstances and become whatever it is he desires to be. Some will succeed. Others will fail. That is the promise of America. Not the promise of success — only the promise of opportunity.

❖ SIX ❖

The 16th Amendment

The American government's second attempt to impose an income tax happened in 1892[1]. Unrest had been growing for over a decade among farmers throughout the United States resulting from the stagnant agricultural economy in America. The farmers blamed the banks and, in particular, the national bank system that controlled the flow of currency in the United States.

In December, 1889 conventions were held in St. Louis, Missouri and Ocala, Florida to decide how the farmers of America could best be represented in Washington. It was felt that the only way the farmers would ever be properly represented was if their own candidate sat in the White House. A third convention was held in Cincinnati in May, 1891 where a grassroots political organization, the Populist Party, was formed.

At their convention in July, 1892 the Populists nominated James B. Weaver, a socialist economist, as their candidate. The platform they drew up demanded a monetary system that was not managed by the bankers. Control would come from the federal government itself through the creation of postal savings banks. The Populists also sought a graduated income tax to support the growing national debt, the free and unlimited coinage of silver, and the nationalization of the railroad, telephone and telegraph.

---

[1]On August 5, 1861, in order to help finance the conflict between the States, Abraham Lincoln imposed an unconstitutional income tax of 3% on all incomes of $800 or more. Within a year, a graduated income tax was imposed, taxing incomes over $5,000 at an even higher rate. Lincoln's tax was supposed to be a temporary measure, lasting only until the Civil War was over. However, the Jacobins, decrying the cost of Reconstruction, resisted efforts to grant tax relief to the American people until Ulysses S. Grant suspended Lincoln's illegal income tax in 1872 in order to incur favor with the electorate.

While their platform was popular with rural America, it did not bode well with entrepreneurial America that viewed the nationalization of anything as abhorrent. Weaver took 22 electoral votes with 10.9% of the popular vote, and tilted the election to Stephen Grover Cleveland, who defeated Republican Benjamin Harrison by a narrow margin. Cleveland, with 46.1% of the popular vote, took 277 electoral votes and denied Harrison the re-election that Harrison had denied him four years earlier.

The populist movement did more than simply re-elect Cleveland, the first Democrat to hold the White House in 24 years — it elected a Democratic Congress as well. The Democrats reciprocated in 1894 by enacting a new 2% federal income tax levied on both individuals and business. This time, however, the income tax was clearly and succinctly a violation of the Constitution. It was challenged before the Supreme Court in *Pollock v. Farmers Loan and Trust Co.* (157 U.S. 429). On May 20, 1895 the income tax was declared unconstitutional, causing much criticism of the high court by Congress.

In the Pollock case, the high court said: "If, as the Constitution now reads, no unapportioned tax be imposed upon real estate, can Congress, without apportionment nevertheless impose taxes upon said real estate under the guise of an annual tax upon its rents or income? Ordinarily, all taxes paid primarily by persons who can shift the burden upon someone else, or who are under no legal compulsion to pay them, are considered indirect taxes; but a tax upon property holders in respect of their estates, whether real or personal, or the income yielded by such estates, and the payment of which cannot be avoided, are direct taxes."

Further, the court said, "A tax upon one's whole income is a tax upon the annual receipts from his whole property, and as such falls within the same class as a tax upon that property, and is a direct tax, in the meaning of the Constitution."

With the Pollock decision, the court blurred the distinction between a man's income and his real property — which, Constitutionally, was exempt from any form of unapportioned federal tax. While it served its purpose in 1895 to end Congress' efforts to levy a new income tax, *Pollock v Farmers Loan & Trust* would be cited by the Justice Department when the 16th Amendment came under fire during the ensuing years to support their contention that the income tax is not a mandatory direct tax but is, instead, a voluntary excise tax.

The nature of politics changed dramatically with the election of Cleveland. The Republicans had run roughshod over the nation almost unabated for a one year shy of a quarter century. The G.O.P. had been the party of J.P. Morgan, Cornelius Vanderbilt, Andrew Carnegie and John D. Rockefeller — and it had been a grand old party. During their 24-year reign, the Republicans maintained a virtual stranglehold on the economy of the nation. They backed big business against labor. They backed the national banks against the state-chartered banks. And, they backed big money against the little man. And, big money returned them to power during every election.

In 1893 that changed. With the reputation of the Republicans now irrefutably tarnished, "big money" jumped ship and joined the Democrats who championed the "little man." No one seemed to notice or, for that matter, cared.

The hallmark of the Harrison Administration was the Depression of 1890. The catalyst was the collapse of the English banking house Baring & Company due to bad investments in Argentina. British investors in American securities were forced to liquidate their holdings to support their financial portfolios in England. It was a repeat of the Jay Cooke & Company debacle 20 years earlier when the investment banker who financed Lincoln's civil war went bankrupt. Now, however, the American dollar was backed by gold rather than debt bonds. Large amounts of gold bullion were suddenly being withdrawn from the country, creating an even greater strain on the American banks who suddenly found themselves starved for cash.

British capital, which had been used to expand the American economy and in particular, the growth of the rail system in the western United States, vanished overnight. The rail boom collapsed as wealthy railroad tycoons floundered for cash just to meet payroll. By 1893 the shortage of currency reverberated throughout the entire economy as one business after another across the nation closed its doors. America was gripped by another depression.

With a new income tax to support vast, sweeping social programs, the Democratic Congress embarked on a campaign to save the working people of America with a series of Roosevelt style programs that included pensions for war veterans. Cleveland balked, declaring that "...although the people support the government, the government should not support the people!"

129

Cleveland refused to modify his essential conservatism, and resisted the efforts of the new Democratic majority to expand the intrusive role of government in the lives and affairs of the American people. Cleveland vetoed every piece of legislation Congress passed that would have expanded government largesse.

By the fall of 1893 unemployment in the cities had reached epidemic proportions and the economy continued to worsen. Meeting with several leading economists, Cleveland concluded the drain on the Treasury was due to a worldwide fear that America would not be able to maintain its gold standard. For some unknown reason it was suggested to Cleveland that the solution to the gold drain might lie in the repeal of the *Sherman Silver Purchase Act of 1889*, which had absolutely nothing to do with gold—except that it allowed the Treasury to arbitrarily pay off the European banks that were redeeming the treasury certificates with silver instead of gold[2].

Had Cleveland opted to so order the Treasury to pay off the redeemed gold certificates with silver, the gold crisis would have ended immediately. Instead, the crisis continued until 1895 when the America's gold vaults were virtually empty[3].

Cleveland called a special session of Congress to repeal the *Silver Act*. After a bitter Congressional debate in which Cleveland expended most of his political capital, the *Silver Act* was repealed on October 30, 1893. The money barons, who wanted gold and not silver for their redeemed treasury certificates, won again.

---

[2]The *Sherman Silver Purchase Act of 1889* provided for the monthly purchase of 4.5 million ounces of silver to be used for coinage in silver dollars, and also to support the use of treasury certificates which were redeemable in silver. The purpose was to standardize the price of silver, and to bolster the sagging silver market. Also, a provision of the Act allowed the federal government, at its discretion, to substitute silver for gold when lawful treasury certificates were presented to the Treasurer of the United States for payment.

[3]Pressure from both foreign investors and European central banks as well as American investment bankers like J.P. Morgan was applied on both the Congress and the White House to repeal the *Silver Purchase Act of 1889* since the Silver Act which allowed the Treasury Department to substitute silver for gold in order to protect the American gold reserves (and likewise to protect the Western silver mining interests who had lobbied Congress hard to enact legislation that viewed silver, like gold, as species).

Not in the least surprising, the repeal of the *Silver Act* did nothing to reduce the exodus of gold from the United States. In fact, it continued to escalate at an alarming rate. America was on the verge of bankruptcy. In a desperate scheme to replenish the Treasury, Cleveland's Secretary of the Treasury arranged a bond sale with the same European bankers who had drained the gold vaults, to return the bullion to America's treasury—for a handsome profit. In February, 1895 the J.P. Morgan/Belmont Syndicate sold over $60 million in gold bonds to themselves and others and netted some $7 million in commissions at the expense of the American taxpayers.

When the news reached the press, an outcry was heard across the nation. In January, 1896 the gold bonds were offered at public subscription, but the profit-taking was already over. The crisis had ended. Cleveland's gold fiasco cost the Democrats the presidency for sixteen more years. It would be 1912 before another Democrat would reside in the White House. That Democrat would be the Princeton liberal, Woodrow Wilson, who would chart the nation's course towards socialism—a course from which the United States deviated only briefly during the Reagan Administration.

During the Cleveland years the basic political approaches of the Democrats and the Republicans reversed themselves. The Democrats, who for years were the dogmatic defenders of States rights, suddenly discovered the source of continuing power came not from the people who cast the votes but from the money that determined how those votes were cast. It would not be until 1933 that the Republicans, who suddenly noticed the massive erosion of States rights due to the ratification of the 17th Amendment, became the defenders of both States rights and personal liberty. Of course, by that time, it was too late.

B ecause they learned so well from their previous attempts to secure both a Constitutional income tax and a permanent, privately-owned, authoritarian central bank in the United States that would not have to answer to petty elected officials or appointed bureaucrats, the international banking community embarked on a secretive campaign to win the votes they needed to secure two Constitutional amendments before pushing for the passage of the legislative needed to create a strong, permanent, self-governing central bank in America.

To accomplish this, the money barons chose a handful of men   131 they could trust. One of those men was Senator Nelson Wilmarth Aldrich, a thirty year veteran of Congress whose son-in-law just happened to be John D. Rockefeller, Jr. The second key player would be Congressman Edward Butterfield Vreeland, who, along with Aldrich, would sponsor the *Federal Reserve Act of 1913*, creating — finally — an impregnable central bank in the United States. The third was Philander C. Knox, Taft's Secretary of State who formerly served as the attorney of such wealthy Americans as Cornelius Vanderbilt and Andrew Carnegie.

Each of these key players knew that the success of their mission to create a failsafe central bank was contingent not only upon absolute secrecy, but also on two very important first steps: the need to create a Constitutionally approved, permanent income tax and the elimination of the States' prerogative to interfere in federal matters, since it had been the States themselves which had thwarted each of the three previous attempts to create a permanent central bank.

B efore the American people would be willing to buy the package Aldrich would soon be peddling, the money barons knew they needed to experience a little economic adversity in order to prepare them for the "cure" that would then be forthcoming. The adversity came in the form of what would become known in financial circles as the Panic of 1907.

The agent used by the money barons to provoke this panic was J.P. Morgan. Morgan visited Europe in March, 1907 and spent two months there. According to the *New York Times* and other major daily newspapers who kept up on such things, the business tycoon was vacationing. What he was actually doing, it appears at least in hindsight, had nothing to do with a vacation. Obviously, what he and other money barons were doing was outlining the strategy Morgan would use later that fall to trigger a nationwide bank panic in the United States.

When Morgan returned he became the source of some wellplaced media-reported "rumors" that the Knickerbocker Bank in New York was insolvent. The bank's depositors became frightened because they thought Morgan, being the best known banker of the day, might very well be right. Their panic started a run on the bank. The run of course proved Morgan right, and the panic at the Knickerbocker also caused runs on other banks, first in New

132

York and then across the nation. The Panic of 1907 was launched.

Life writer Frederick Allen reported in the magazine's April 25, 1949 issue that historians of that day had concluded that Morgan interests took advantage of the very unsettled conditions that existed during the fall of 1907 to "...precipitate the Panic, guiding it shrewdly as it progressed..." in order, they supposed, to kill off rival banks and consolidate more holdings under the banner of J. P. Morgan and Company.

Although those chroniclers failed to grasp the true motive behind the Panic of 1907, at least they had properly identified the culprit who both initiated and perpetuated it. But, in 1907, nobody cared. All they cared about was getting their money out of the Knickerbocker Bank before it closed its doors forever.

When the dust settled during the Panic of 1907, politicians like Aldrich were demanding an investigation of the state-chartered banks. The press pounded the issue, echoing the angry cry of the bureaucrats and the fear of the population. In response to the public outcry, Congress created the *National Monetary Commission* and installed Aldrich as its head to investigate the monetary problems in the United States and to report his findings to Congress.

Instead of investigating the banks that had failed, the Commission—or at least Aldrich—headed for Europe. Over a two year period, from the fall of 1907 until the summer of 1909, Aldrich visited most of the banking houses of Europe several times. It was assumed Aldrich was studying the European banking system to learn why it functioned so well.

Aldrich actually had a much more sinister purpose. He was there to learn how to successfully circumvent the Constitution of the United States. Using their past errors as a guide, the group of bankers and industrialists Aldrich visited were devising a new step-by-step program that would lead to a new, permanent central bank in the United States. To be successful, the bankers needed to start with a Constitutionally approved income tax.

In the summer of 1909 while the recently elected 300-pound President, William Howard Taft, might well have been contemplating how to install a new king-sized porcelain bathtub in the White House bathroom, Aldrich was completing the first leg of his mission: determining precisely how the banking cartel wanted the new central bank of the United States to be structured, and what changes needed to be made in the Constitution to best accommodate them.

During Aldrich's European visit, the question of the American press itself was raised. To control the media, the bankers knew it would ultimately be necessary to own the press. But, each program in its own time. Two things had to be accomplished first. To fund the new central bank, a constitutionally-approved income tax was mandatory. To guarantee its control over the government, the Constitution first had to be diluted to remove any semblance of real authority from the States. This would vest all real power in the hands of an elite few at the national level. Logically, an oligarchy is easier to control than an entire population.

The cartel knew that its success in Europe was due largely to the fact that in each nation where it had established a central bank, an oligarchy controlled the government. Also, in each of those countries an income tax, compelling the people to pay the debts incurred by their governments, had easily been legislated.

France was the first nation to levy a national income tax, doing so in 1793. Great Britain followed in 1798. Switzerland became the third nation to impose a national income tax in 1840, followed by Austria in 1849 and Italy in 1864. By the turn of the century every industrialized nation in Europe except Russia had a national tax on income — and each also had a central bank, privately owned by a small core of international bankers.

William Howard Taft, who had proven to be an ardent foe of the proponents who were attempting to create a new privately-owned central bank in the United States, said little about the Constitutional Amendments being proposed by Aldrich's allies to the newly installed 61st Congress. If Taft associated them either directly or indirectly to the European banking cartel or to the proposal to create a new central bank advanced by Senator Aldrich, he did not publicly voice his thoughts. Taft believed that Constitutional Amendments were matters for the States themselves to decide. They would either ratify the Amendments, or reject them. He neither encouraged the States to ratify them, nor did he advise them to reject them. His official political position was "no official position."

Taft believed the American people, who generally opposed any additional taxes, would strong arm their own State legislatures to reject the proposed 16th amendment and he would not be forced to expend any political capital on the issue himself.

On July 31, 1909 Taft's Secretary of State, Philander Knox, received a Concurrent Congressional Resolution, dated July 27, which stated: "Resolved by the Senate [the House of Representatives concurring], That the President of the United States be requested to transmit forthwith to the executives of the several States of the United States copies of the article of amendment proposed by Congress to the State legislatures to amend the Constitution of the United States, passed July twelfth, nineteen hundred and nine, respecting the power of Congress to lay and collect taxes on incomes, to the end that the said States may proceed to act upon the said article of Amendment: and that he request the executive of each State that may ratify said amendment to transmit to the Secretary of State a certified copy of each ratification." The concurrent resolution was signed by Secretary of the Senate Charles G. Bennett and A. N. McDowell, the Clerk of the House of Representatives.

This resolution set into motion the process of ratification of the most controversial Congressional amendment since the Constitution itself was fully ratified in 1790. Over the past several years, the 16th Amendment has been the subject of much controversy as charges that it was fraudulently ratified have been alleged and largely substantiated[4].

These charges stemmed from the fact that most of the States that ratified the 16th Amendment also deliberately modified the

---

[4] When the controversy first surfaced over two decades ago, M.J. "Red" Beckman, a former Montana legislator, was challenged to discover whether or not fraud existed in the ratification process. Using the membership of an ad hoc organization called the *Montana Historians* that was formed in April, 1980 by Montana businessman Sam Bitz, Beckman and Bitz began the tedious task of contacting State legislatures in June 1980, and requesting photostats of the resolutions used in the ratification. By the fall of 1980 the group possessed the first clear evidence that fraud had been committed. In addition to violating the Montana State Constitution in passage, Montana violated Federal law by

language of the text, thereby changing the legal meaning of the amendment — something they could not do according to federal law. In some instances the changes were minor, dealing primarily with punctuation. In others, entirely different words were substituted. And, in a few instances, the entire amendment was simply re-written. Any amended resolution should have been ruled invalid and either sent back to the State to be re-ratified, or simply rejected as a repudiated vote. Had the proposed amendment dealt with States' rights issues that granted more, not less, power to the States, it is almost certain that any improperly worded resolution would have been ruled invalid by Joshua Reuben Clark, Jr., the Solicitor General, and counted among those ballots that repudiated the proposed amendment.

The instructions to the States were very specific with respect to the language of the amendment that was being ratified. Under the terms of ratification, the legislatures of the States are "...not authorized to alter in any way the amendment proposed by Congress, the function of the legislature consisting merely of the right to approve or disapprove the proposed amendment." In other words, the State legislatures could not change even so much as a comma, semi-colon or period. This is the only proper mode of

---

not sending the Secretary of State a certified copy, negating the resolution. Texas violated enough State laws to reasonably conclude the 16th Amendment was illegally ratified by that State as well. By the summer of 1981, the *Montana Historians* had contacted most of the States and were alarmed, but not surprised, by what they had found. The 16th Amendment to the Constitution has never been legally ratified.

In March, 1983, Beckman was asked to testify at the income tax evasion trial of Allen Lee Buchta. Armed with over 400 documents from each of the 48-continuous states, Beckman arrived in Fort Worth only to find his "evidence" ruled inadmissible by U.S. District Court Judge James T. Moody because none of the documents were notarized, and no companion affidavits from those involved in the original creation of the documents were attached. Moody, in fact, seized the documents. The documents have never been released. In doing so, Moody declared the problem was a political rather than a judicial dilemma, and that it up to Congress, not the courts, to address the problem.

During that trial, Buchta's attorney, Andrew Spiegel, employed a paralegal named Bill Benson. Benson appeared extremely sympathetic to Buchta's plight and was very critical of Judge Moody's suppression of the documents, suggesting to Spiegel and Beckman that even if the documents did not prove outright fraud, they were at least something

136

ratification since by making any alteration, regardless how slight, the State could essentially change the meaning of the proposed amendment and ultimately ratify something completely different from that which was initially proposed.

Document 97-120 of the first session of the 95th Congress entitled *How Our Laws Are Made,* details specifically how bills must be concurred under federal legislative rules. The Solicitor General's instructions to the States in 1909 were based on these principles although the guideline had not yet been written: "Each amendment must be inserted in precisely the proper place in the bill, with the spelling and punctuation exactly the same as it was adopted by the House. Obviously, it is extremely important that the Senate receive a copy of the bill in the precise form in which it passed the House...each [amendment] must be set out in the enrollment exactly as agreed to, and all punctuation must be in accord with the action taken."

Several states lacked the legal authority from their own State Constitutions to ratify any tax bill that obligated the taxpayers of their State to pay a tax that was not to be used exclusively for their benefit. Legally those States were Constitutionally obligated

---

which needed to be further examined by the court. Benson and Beckman hit it off extremely well. Upon the conclusion of the trial—Buchta was found guilty of income tax evasion and sentenced to prison—Benson offered to help Beckman ferret out even more evidence of fraud in the ratification of the 16th Amendment.

Benson impressed Beckman as a top-notch investigator, so he agreed. Using as much of his own funds as he could afford, and financed in part by Connecticut businessman George Sitka, Beckman sent Benson to each of the 48 continuous States to physically collect all of the pertinent documents from within each State's archives, making copies of each. In total, Beckman and Benson collected more than 17,000 documents on both the 16th and 17th Amendments. Most show fraud of some form in the ratification not only of the 16th Amendment, but the 17th Amendment as well.

When they completed their quest at the State level, they went to Washington, D.C. and visited the National Archive, copying documents there as well. Their conclusions—and the evidence which supports their conclusions—is well-documented in a two-volume work entitled *"The Law That Never Was."* What they discovered has been no secret to those who make the laws and chart the course of the "ship of state" of the United States since both the 16th and 17th Amendments were "ratified" in 1913. Both amendments were illegally ratified.

to reject it — but didn't. It also appears from documents found in the archives of at least two States that, although they appear to have repudiated the measure, they were likewise listed among those that ratified the 16th Amendment.

The ratification process was a legal mess that Philander Knox, an attorney and former of Congressman himself, gladly turned over to Clark for clarification. Knox, an Aldrich ally, could not afford to have his fingerprints found on anything that might be construed as irregular or questionable. The legal shenanigans would be left to Clark since that was, after all, his bailiwick.

It is important to note that the role of the Secretary of State in the ratification process was not to determine the legality of the certifications of ratification, or to become the arbitrator of whether or not a State had the legal authority to ratify a tax bill not granted to it by its own State Constitution. His job was simply to count the ballots and determine if enough States voted "yea" to pass the amendment. Nothing more, nothing less.

In *The Law That Never Was, Vol. II,* author Bill Benson observed: "The Constitution of the United States is silent as to who should decide whether a proposed amendment has or has not been passed according to formal provisions of Article V of the Constitution...The duty of the Secretary of State was ministerial, to wit, to count and determine when three-fourths of the states had ratified the proposed amendment. He could not determine that a state, having once rejected a proposed amendment could thereafter approve it, nor could he determine that a state having once ratified that proposal could thereafter reject it. The court and not the Congress should determine such matters." (*The Law That Never Was, Vol. II*; William Benson; Constitutional Research Center © 1986; pg. 166)

The decision of whether or not a State legislature has the legal authority to ratify a tax amendment expressly forbidden by that State's Constitution rests exclusively with the people of that State by plebiscite. None other has the legal standing to determine it.

The position of the federal government is, and has been since 1913, that matters dealing with the suspected bribery of State legislators, obviously suspect ratifications, and other forms of outright fraud concerning the passage of the 16th Amendment are political in nature and therefore must be resolved at State level. Likewise it is the legal opinion of the federal government that even though fraud may be proven, the 16th Amendment will stand *since the government accepted the ratifications "on good faith" from the States who theoretically ratified it.*

This argument was first advanced by Assistant U.S. Attorney David Brown who prosecuted *United States v. George House & Marion House* in June, 1983. The defendants' attorney, Lowell Becraft, set up a conference with Brown prior to a hearing for reconsideration of the charges against his clients. Brown wanted to review the documents that Red Beckman had uncovered concerning the legality of the 16th Amendment, which had been placed in evidence.

"...[A]fter having examined some of the documents...[Brown] admitted that Secretary of State Philander Knox had committed a crime but then rationalized a continued prosecution of the Houses because over 72 years had passed since the crime had been committed." *(ibid;* pg. 60.) In other words, he maintained, because the government accepted the Amendment on good faith, a 72-year old fraud on the part of a long dead Secretary of State was inconsequential, and the government was not obligated to create a red herring by investigating it. "As a prosecutor, Brown knew there was no statute of limitations on fraud prior to its discovery and yet he chose to participate in the fraud. Brown even admitted in that conference that the 16th Amendment issue is not a political question, and properly belongs in the courts." *(ibid;* pg. 60.)

The Department of Justice has been forced for over a decade to address the legality of the 16th Amendment based on the fraud uncovered by Beckman and Benson. In every instance it has argued, and the judges to whom it presented its argument have agreed, that the 16th Amendment is constitutional *not because fraud cannot be proven,* but simply because the 16th Amendment has existed since 1913, *and they have relied on it to render decisions* to either send those convicted to prison, or to confiscate their property to settle awards granted by the federal court to the federal government. Of course the federal government does not want the 16th Amendment overturned.

The Houses were convicted of income tax evasion and appealed their conviction based on the fraud discovered by Beckman and acknowledged by the federal prosecutor Brown, citing 37Am.Jur.2d8, which states:

"Fraud vitiates every transaction and all contracts. Indeed, the   139 principle is often stated, in broad and sweeping language, that fraud destroys everything into which it enters, and that it vitiates the most solemn contracts, and even judgments. Fraud, as it is sometimes said, vitiates every act, which statement embodies a thoroughly sound doctrine when it is properly applied to the subject matter in controversy and to the parties thereto in a proper forum."

Assistant U.S. Attorney General Glenn L. Archer handled the appeal for the government before the United States Court of Appeals for the 6th Circuit and argued what would become the government's new position on the matter. Archer noted that "...Even without regard to the 16th Amendment, Congress would be empowered to impose a tax on income received as compensation for services, without apportionment, pursuant to the broad grant of taxing power under Article I, Section 8, of the Constitution. This taxing power embraces every conceivable power of taxation, including the power to lay and collect income taxes, *Brushaber v. Union Pacific Railroad Co.*, 240 U.S. 1, 12-13 (1916). The 16th Amendment merely eliminates the requirement that, to the extent [that] an income tax constitutes a direct tax, it be apportioned among the states." (*ibid;* pg 4.)

It is interesting that the government brought out their big guns to handle the House appeal, suggesting they were at least a little worried that Becraft might topple the 16th Amendment. Archer was an Assistant Attorney General rather than a mere lawyer from the Justice Department. The government's argument was based on a verbal slight of hand that was nothing more than double talk. But, the court — which was seeking any out — bought Archer's argument and concluded that the income tax can be construed as a nonapportioned, indirect tax.

The government now defends the position that the income tax never was a direct tax. It was instead, they maintain, a *voluntary* excise tax all along. Try to avoid paying the government what they feel they are due from your sweat and labor however, and you will face criminal charges and imprisonment. The only way you can voluntarily avoid paying income tax is to stop working and have no income. Of course, since we live in a society which requires its citizens to pay as they go, it is difficult to survive for long without an income. Even welfare recipients are taxed.

The distinction between the two forms of taxation are thus: a direct, or income, tax is mandatory and cannot be avoided. This was a bone of contention with the American Colonists, and was one of the causes of the American Revolution. The Founding Fathers were determined, first, to make certain the national government they were creating could not impose such a tax without the consent of the American people.

An indirect, or excise, tax is voluntary only in the sense that it is placed on goods, merchandise or commodities that you can avoid paying simply by not buying the good upon which they are assessed. In the United States, it is commonly called a luxury tax, suggesting by its name that it is assessed on non-essential goods or luxury items bought only by the wealthy.

Of course, nothing could be farther from the truth. Those non-essentials include such things as domestically produced automobiles, wrist watches, belts, shoes, computers, television sets, refrigerators and a whole myriad of other items that we, as Americans use in the course of our daily lives. And, needless to say, largely because American labor unions have screamed about the low prices of foreign-made goods, there has also been an excise tax on almost every item that is imported into the United States. Those excise taxes are called tariffs. They are levied to inflate the price of foreign goods to make them as costly as the "union-made" American products.

An indirect tax, because it is not apportioned, can be selectively used to protect an American industry or to punish a trading partner. Usually it is levied to protect an American industry from "unfair" foreign competition. Many times high tariffs are demanded by American industrialists merely to stifle foreign competition—particularly when the targeted products are viewed by the consumers as superior to those found in this country. Tariffs have also been used to discourage American industries from relocating their industrial and manufacturing facilities in neighboring countries that offered cheaper labor and less restrictive labor or environmental laws. Today, NAFTA is forcing American industry to do what the tariffs of the past decades prevented them from doing.

The first challenge levied against the 16th Amendment was *Brushaber v. Union Pacific Railroad Co.* In it, the Supreme Court held that the 16th Amendment conferred no new taxing powers to Congress since an income tax had previously existed and was not successfully challenged. Interestingly, the 1862 Lincoln income tax came about under the emergency powers granted a President in times of national strife, which clearly the Civil War was. Had it been implemented at any other time, under any other circumstances, it would have been challenged in the courts and suffered the same fate as the 1894 attempt. Yet, the high court concurred that the Lincoln tax was a lawful precedent in the House appeal, confirming Archer's opinion that because it existed, the federal government must have had the authority, under Article I, Section 8 of the Constitution, to implement it.

The government would shortly co-mingle *Brushaber* (1916) with *Pollock* (1895) to arrive at the somewhat bizarre and twisted conclusion that not only was the income tax constitutional, the 16th Amendment notwithstanding, but that the government has the right to tax not only a man's current labor, but his acquired wealth (i.e., his personal property) as well.

For that reason, before going any farther, it is important to examine the ratification of the 16th Amendment state-by-state, step-by-step, to see if it was lawfully and legally ratified. After all, nobody thought to check Uncle Sam at the time to make certain that the powerful, invisible money power that was clandestinely working behind the scenes to usurp the Constitution for the third time wasn't somehow manipulating the ratification not only of the 16th but the 17th Amendment as well, since both were critical to the success of the new central bank that was already planned for 1913.

Of course, at that time, America didn't know about the covert, invisible force controlling our politicians. In early Americana we trusted our national political leaders and turned them out of office at the first sign of scandal. Integrity was the most important qualification in running for, or holding, national office.

Imagine how we would feel about George Washington if we suddenly learned he had exposed himself to Betsy Ross as she was sewing the American flag, and asked her to perform oral sex on him between the stars and stripes? Or, to learn that John and Abigail Adams were in collusion with Thomas Jefferson to force Alexander Hamilton to arrange the loan of several million dollars for them to build a community on land they shuffled back and forth between themselves to artificially inflate its value? On land which was so completely desolate and inaccessible that it was absolutely worthless? Financed, say, with a loan agreement that exempted the principals from repayment without penalty? Or, to learn that James Monroe, who warned the European powers to stay out of the western hemisphere, not only cowardly avoided military service during the Revolutionary War, but had also instigated demonstrations against the colonists in England?

Knowing that about them, would America have elected those men to the highest office in the land? Of course not. Yet, now in the waning days of the 20th century, integrity and honesty are no longer important characteristics in our leaders. Is that because we, as American citizens, no longer have integrity ourselves? Have we had our faces buried for so long in the public trough, feeding on the table scraps of the elite, that we have surrendered our own integrity for a handout from the State? It must be. Leaders almost always mirror the constituency that elects them.

It would be a real tragedy to suddenly discover, after 86 years, that the United States government lied to us about the legality of the 16th Amendment; and that we, the taxpayers of America, had paid countless billions of dollars in income taxes and arbitrary penalties to a central government that had neither the right nor legal authority to demand from the American people.

Perhaps that is what former U.S. Senator George Malone (R-NV) meant in 1957 when, in speaking on the record before the United States Congress, he said: "I believe that if the people of this nation fully understood what Congress has done to them over the past 49 years, they would move on Washington. They would not wait for an election...It adds up to a preconceived plan to destroy the economic and social independence of the United States." The discussion on the floor of the Senate that afternoon was centered on the Federal Reserve System and the income tax that fed it.

R ed Beckman was convinced there was something wrong. So were a lot of other people. But, how does a simple American citizen verify the integrity of the ratification of a Constitutional amendment? Does he call his Congressman? Does he call the Chief Justice of the Supreme Court? Or, does he call the independent, unimpeachable auditor whom, one might imagine, certified not only the integrity of the States' votes, but also the legality of them as well?

A citizen who calls the Library of Congress or the National Archives and requests a copy of United States Senate Document

143

240 that details the statistics on the ratification of the 16th Amendment will likely first be asked why he wants the document. Then, regardless of the answer, he or she will also likely be told such a document does not exist. Only, it does. Or at least, it did. S.D. 240 was prepared by a Mr. Fess for the 71st Congress on January 6, 1931. It was the only complete record of each States' voting activity on each of the amendments that was added to the Constitution from 1795 to 1920. Granted, with the subsequent passage of additional amendments, Senate Document 240 has been obsolete for 79 years. Additional ratification chronologies have been recorded and S.D. 240 has been modified and its chronologies are now filed under different House and Senate document names.

After seeing S.D. 240 in the archives of two States, Beckman requested a copy of it from the government under the *Freedom of Information Act*. When he asked for it, he didn't suspect the government would deny its existence—which it did. Nor did he realize that his request would trigger an interest in his past federal income tax filings by the Internal Revenue Service—which it did. At that point, Beckman was certain his investigation would not be in vain. It wasn't.

S am Bitz had been researching the history of the American Republic for several years and, in particular, the evolution of our political system. One of Bitz's concerns was the 16th Amendment. The evidence he had gathered in Montana suggested that State's ratification of the 16th Amendment was not legal due to at least five violations of either State or federal law that occurred during the process. Bitz's concern was that if Montana did not lawfully ratify the 16th Amendment, did the same problem exist with the ratifications of other States as well? Thirty-eight of the 48 States are listed on S.D. 240 as ratifying the amendment—two more than the total needed to grant the federal government the legal right to tax the incomes and accrued assets of its citizens.

Bitz put together a one-hour television documentary entitled *People Controlled Government* on his findings. Bitz, however, lacked the financial resources to complete the project. Enter Beckman.

Martin J. "Red" Beckman shared Bitz's passion for the unique political system that has made the United States the greatest nation in the history of the world. Not only did Beckman agree to produce the special which was to be telecasted on a local Great

144

Falls, Montana television station, he was also the sole sponsor when the program was aired in April, 1980. Through the friendship that quickly developed between Bitz and Beckman, the group, which became known as the Montana Historians, was formed. By the fall of 1981 they had gathered sufficient evidence to successfully argue their point that many of the States had not properly and constitutionally ratified the 16th Amendment.

However, in March, 1983 when Beckman found himself called as an expert witness in the case of *United States v. Allen Lee Buchta* and again in June when he was called by Lowell Becraft as a witness for the defense in *United States v. George House & Marion House*, his argument fell on deaf ears.

B ecause of several obvious legal flaws in the resolutions from most of those 36 States, Philander Knox deferred to Reuben Clark for a legal opinion as to whether the resolutions from the States could be construed as valid. Obviously Knox, an attorney himself, knew almost every resolution was invalid for one reason or another. But Knox also knew it was his job was to "fix" whatever was wrong with the resolutions and declare the 16th Amendment ratified.

According to the statistics presented in a memorandum from the Solicitor General dated February 13, 1913 in which he certified the 16th Amendment as legally ratified, only six states were actually flawless in their mission. The government's own report suggests they were well aware of the fact that they were somewhat shy of the necessary three-fourths of the States needed to successfully ratify any Constitutional amendment, and decided to use a little "interpretative" legal chicanery in order to ignore the voluminous problems found in the resolutions so they could certify them as valid. However, as Beckman and Bill Benson began their exhaustive, although futile, quest for the truth within each State's archives, they quickly discovered that the legal flaws that worried Philander Knox were universal[4].

First, the investigators quickly learned that several States were expressly forbidden by their own State Constitutions from

---

[4]The data compiled by Red Beckman and Bill Benson is so voluminous that it has already required two volumes, plus a third that may be in the offing. The documentation cited in this book is in the possession of the authors of *"The Law That Never Was"*. Volume I of this work, which contains photostats of the actual documents discussed here is available

ratifying any tax legislation that would not be used exclusively to benefit of the citizens of those States. Needless to say, all of the proceeds collected by the federal government's new income tax would not be exclusively funneled into the treasuries of those particular States. In fact it is relatively safe to say that even forgetting the omnibus quality or national character of the federal income tax, that not even the taxes paid by the citizens of those States was funneled, 100%, back to them (except perhaps the State of West Virginia which, due largely to the pork gathering capacity of former Senate Majority Leader Robert Byrd (D-WV), has probably consumed more federal tax dollars than it has contributed). However, the Constitution of the State of West Virginia did not exclude its legislators from voting on any type of tax legislation, regardless who benefits from it.

Nevertheless, West Virginia had its own problems. First, according to Article VII, Section 14 of the West Virginia State Constitution, the resolution had to be signed by its governor, William E. Glasscock, before it was valid. Not only did Glasscock not sign it, neither did the presiding officers of either house of the legislature. Nor did the State send a certified copy of the ratification to the Secretary of State as prescribed by federal law. In addition, also in violation of law, the Resolution which went through both Houses failed to comply with Senate Resolution 40 regarding the language of the text ratified. In fact, the text voted on did not contain anything which even stated the legislators were

from Beckman for $28.00 plus shipping & handling. The book may be ordered by writing:

Common Sense Press
P.O. Box 1544
Billings, MT 59103

or, by telephone: (503) 824-2050. The authors invested an incalculable amount of their precious time, and expended many thousands of dollars of their own money—not to mention the harassment each has endured from the Internal Revenue because of their work to uncover this information. For that reason, the right to present it to America belongs morally, if not legally, exclusively to them. It is to be duly noted that all specific 16th Amendment quotations and statistical data in *Whatever Happened To America?* were either directly or indirectly sourced through *"The Law That Never Was"*. For that reason, because they would be too numerous, reference credits in this one chapter have been deferred with Beckman's permission. The author acknowledges his work in compiling this data.

voting on the 16th Amendment.

But even more important, the State of West Virginia's ratification acknowledgment was not even mailed to the United States Secretary of State's office until April 13, 1913—some 60 days after Knox certified that West Virginia had ratified the 16th Amendment.

Within three weeks of the ratification of the 16th Amendment, Woodrow Wilson was inaugurated, and William Jennings Bryan was confirmed as Secretary of State. Knox was gone. Bryan inherited the mess. Discovering that the government had almost no certifications from the States to substantiate the ratification of the 16th Amendment, he immediately wrote each of the offending States and demanded documentation.

His reply from West Virginia was most interesting because the identity of the letter writer is unknown. The letter, dated April 13, was written on United States Senate letterhead. A note attached to it was addressed to a "Mr. Davis," who did not exist in the Secretary of State's office. The signature was an illegible scribble that did not appear to match the names of the Senators listed on the letterhead. "I beg to inclose..." [sic] the letter began, "herewith resolutions of the legislature of West Virginia ratifying the income tax amendment. *As this amendment has already been ratified by thirty-six states,* I take it that this paper can now serve no useful purpose, but it was sent to me and I received it just today. I had always supposed that West Virginia had been in time to get in the official count. Her intentions were good I know." (Emphasis, author.) The documents attached were all unsigned.

The Senator, his chief of staff or, quite possibly even a legislative aide, acknowledged that the 16th Amendment was already ratified by the necessary 36 States. What he didn't know was that West Virginia was supposedly one of those 36 States that had theoretically ratified it. It seems unlikely that a United States Senator would be unaware of what his State was doing with a Constitutional amendment—particularly one of such significance. Yet, in the mind of this West Virginia Senator, chief of staff, or legislative aide, it had not been ratified as of April 13, 1913.

The final intrigue centers around not only the mysterious Mr. Davis, but the writer of the attached note as well. It, also, was unsigned. Briefly, it said: "As the Senator's letter herewith, appears to be personal, I am submitting this reply instead of a formal acknowledgment [of ratification]..." Of course. No formal   147 acknowledgment of ratification existed. Nor could any statement, notarized or even blessed by God, from any United States Senator of any State legally serve as certification of any State's ratification of any Constitutional amendment since the ratification of a Constitutional amendment is solely a matter of State prerogative. A U.S. Senator is a federal official.

Arizona and New Mexico, which were admitted into the Union in 1912 during the ratification period, were obligated to ratify the 16th Amendment as a condition of statehood.

Arizona was the 48th State to be admitted into the Union. Its first official act as a State was to illegally ratify the 16th Amendment. S.D. 240 does not signify the votes which occurred with its passage on April 9, 1912. As a condition of statehood, the Journal of the Arizona Senate shows only that the amendment, after a third reading, was passed by unanimous consent.

The problem with the Arizona ratification is found in their own State Constitution, in Article IX, Section 9: "Every law which imposes, continues, or revives a tax shall distinctly state the tax and the object for which it shall be applied; and it shall not be sufficient to refer to any other law to fix such tax or object."

It would have been an interesting historic footnote if the Arizona legislature had stipulated the tax rate based on the rhetoric of Aldrich's Congressional hucksters at the time, since the States that did ask were advised that the tax, like Lincoln's tax during the Civil War would never exceed 1% or 2%; and that the income tax, like Lincoln's, would in all likelihood to be applied only when extreme emergencies, such as war, faced the nation. The politically postured sales pitch was that the income tax, by the nature of its creation, was intended to be a tax on the rich.

There were those in the United States Senate who objected to the open-endedness of the amendment. They felt the rate of taxation should be stipulated for two reasons. First, knowing their own propensity to abuse the privileges granted them by the electorate, a small group of Senators felt placing a ceiling on Congress' ability to plunder the American pocketbook was a necessary safeguard. During the floor debate on the measure it was pointed out that because the initial tax was so low Congress would almost certainly be inclined to raise it gradually every year, until finally, the federal income tax would likely consume as much 20% of a man's annual income.

You will recall that Senator William Borah (R-ID), scoffed at such a contemplation, labeling the remark as outrageous fear-mongering, and declared, in defense of the proposed Amendment, that Congress would never impose such a confiscatory rate on the taxpayers of the United States. Borah, a conservative nationalist was, at the time, newly elected to the Senate in 1907. He was a political neophyte who, like most Americans at the time, still believed the oxymoron: "I'm from the government, and I'm here to help you." Because the Aldrich forces told him that the federal income tax would be: (a) a tax on the rich, and (b) that it would never exceed 1% to 2%, he believed them and vigorously fought for the passage of the Congressional resolution which would be offered to the States.

You will recall also that it was promoted as a tax on the rich in the press. If asked at the time, most factory workers would have favored the ratification of the 16th Amendment believing as they did that it would penalize only the wealthy industrialists and business owners whom most believed had too much money. Who would object if the federal government wanted to take money away from someone named Rockefeller or Vanderbilt?

That this was the commonly held belief is corroborated by Mississippi Governor E.F. Noel's words as he addressed a special session of his legislature on January 4, 1910: "The most equitable of all taxes are those upon the net incomes in excess of the few thousands of dollars, exempted to meet expenses of living or unexpected business reversals. This power of the federal government, after its exercise for many years, was nullified by an almost evenly divided decision of the United States Supreme Court. As a revenue collector, in times of war, its use might avert greater disaster...The adoption of this amendment...empowers the federal government, in its discretion, to call for a share of the net incomes of those *who are most able to contribute* to the expense of the government.[5]" (Emphasis, author.)

---

[5]Noel's argument was seriously flawed in one area. The income tax which was overruled by the Supreme Court had not been in existence for many years. It was enacted in a provision added to the *Wilson-Gorman Tariff Act* on August 27, 1894, and provided for a 2% tax on incomes over $4,000. It was repealed by the Supreme Court on May 20, 1895. Noel apparently co-mingled the *Wilson-Gorman* tax with Lincoln's tax, which was in force for approximately ten years during the state of emergency created by the Civil War and the Reconstruction of the South.

Americans were assured that if their annual incomes were below $5,000 they would be exempt. That, in point of fact, remained a literal truism for many years. When their incomes reached that mystical, astronomical $5,000 level, the tax that would be assessed, they were assured, would be minimal: four-tenths of one percent. On $5,000, that amounted to $20. Anyone making $100 per week (when most factory workers did not make that much in a month) could easily afford an annual tax of $20. Few would disagree with the logic. Incomes of $10,000 would be taxed at seven-tenths of one percent—a tax of $70.

Only the wealthy would be obligated to shoulder a larger share of the tax burden. Incomes of $100,000.00 would be taxed at the rate of 2 1/2%, and income in excess of $1,000,000 would pay an annual tax of 5%. Or so the rhetoric said.

N ew Mexico, which was the 47th State admitted into the Union was the last to ratify the 16th Amendment. Again, ratification was the price of Statehood. Yet, it took the New Mexico legislature a full year to ratify it.

In a direct and deliberate violation of New Mexico law the legislators, instead of introducing the Congressional Joint Resolution upon which by federal law they were required to vote, substituted their own abbreviated version. In doing so they violated Article IV, Sections 15 and 21 of the New Mexico Constitution.

The Amendment, as it was sent to all of the States, read: "Article XVI. The Congress shall have the power to lay and collect taxes on incomes, from whatever source derived, without apportionment, among the several States, and without regard to any census or enumeration." The New Mexico resolution simply read: "Ratifying a proposed amendment to the Constitution of the United States authorizing Congress to lay and collect taxes on income." Two key phrases were omitted: "*without apportionment*" and "*without regard to any census or enumeration.*" Without those two key phrases, the 16th Amendment would have merely cloned Lincoln's income tax.

New Mexico law, in Article IV, Section 15 expressly forbade its legislature from altering the language of the bills it passed. So, for that matter, does federal law. New Mexico substituted, and voted on, an entirely different resolution, one that left out the most critical elements of the 16th Amendment — and then, at the conclusion of the vote, re-substituted the original text as passed. Why did that take a full year?

According to Article IV, Section 21, anyone substituting or materially changing any bill pending in, or passed by, the legislature is guilty of a felony, the penalty of which is punishment by imprisonment in the State penitentiary for up to five years.

Without taking this scenario any farther, the evidence produced by Beckman and Benson clearly support their contention that the 16th Amendment was not legally ratified. Thirty-eight States, according to SD. 240, had ratified the 16th Amendment by February 15, 1913. Thirty-six were needed to meet the three-fourths test. Three of those ratifications have, on the preceding pages, been shown to be fraudulent. That leaves 35 states. If every remaining ratification was flawless, the 16th Amendment failed to meet the majority test, and must be ruled null and void.

But in fact, most of the remaining resolutions from the States are equally flawed. Beckman and Benson together and singularly have already written well over 600 pages on the 16th Amendment. Their work outlines, in minute detail, every fraud and flaw, deliberate or accidental, perpetuated by each State in every resolution. Almost none are exempt from some form of disqualifying error. It was for precisely this reason that Knox was forced to seek help from Solicitor General Reuben Clark to find some legal precedent that would allow the federal government to validate what they knew was either fraud or unbridled incompetence, or both, on the part of almost every State legislature in the United States.

It is sufficient to say, in addition to the three States described thus far, at least two other States: Kentucky and Texas were prohibited by their State Constitutions from considering any tax law in which the proceeds of the imposed taxation was not used exclusively for the benefit of the taxpayers of those States.

S.D. 240 lists Kentucky as officially ratifying the 16th Amendment on either February 8 or 9, 1910 based on excerpts of the official State journals that reported a House vote of 70 to 3 in favor of passage; and a Senate vote of 27-2 also in favor of ratified the 16th Amendment. However the Journals themselves, which are the only official chronology of legislative events of each State, very clearly declared the 16th Amendment rejected in the Senate with a registered vote of 9 yeas and 22 nays. Copies of the journals were sent to Knox along with the abbreviated transcript. No records appear to exist in the archives of either the State of Kentucky or the federal government why this inconsistency was not noticed or challenged. Furthermore, there appear to be no records, journals or diaries to explain why Governor Augustus E. Willson was not aware of the Journal discrepancy, or that his State had rejected the 16th Amendment. Willson did not sign the ratification, suggesting someone in the Legislature simply chose to bypass him.

Texas Governor T.M. Campbell, on the other hand, did sign the ratification — in a clear violation of Texas law. Texas passed the resolution in record time — 15 days. Campbell introduced the legislation on August 2, 1910 and it was ratified on August 17. In doing so, the legislators — and Campbell — violated three state laws. Most important was Article III, Section 38 which states:

"The Legislature shall not have the right to levy taxes or impose burdens upon the people, except to raise revenue sufficient for the economical administration of the government, in which may be included the following purposes: The payment of all interest upon the bonded debt of the State; The erection and repairs of public buildings; The benefit of the sinking fund, which shall not be more than two percentile of the public debt, and for the payment of the present floating debt of the State, including matured bonds for the payment of which the sinking fund is inadequate; The support of public schools, in which shall be included colleges and universities established by the State; and the maintenance and support of the Agricultural and Mechanical College of Texas; The payment of the cost of assessing and collecting the revenue; and the payment of all officers, agents and employees of the State government, and all incidental expenses connected therewith; The support of the Blind Asylum, the Deaf and Dumb Asylum, and the Insane Asylum; the State cemetery and the public grounds of the State; The enforcement of quarantine regulations on the coast of Texas; The protection of the frontier."

In addition, the Constitution of the United States requires that constitutional amendments must pass by a majority vote of at least 2/3 of the States' House and Senate. The Mississippi House passed the 16th Amendment with a majority vote of 62.5%; the Senate concurred by a vote of 62.2%. Legally, certification for the 16th Amendment could not be sent to the Secretary of State, since it was not lawfully ratified.

Georgia's Senate voted passage with a 55% majority — there exists no documented record which verifies that the Georgia House of Delegates ever did vote on, or pass, the 16th Amendment. They did vote — 125 to 44 — to pass something purported to be the 16th Amendment, however a completely different text was apparently substituted, and it was for that language that the vote was cast.

Maryland's Senate passed the resolution with a 59% majority. The House version appears to have passed 83-1. However, the Constitution of Maryland requires that all tax bills be passed by a 2/3 vote of each State house, not the collective total of both houses. In addition, according to Maryland law Article II, Section 17 and Article III, Section 30 the Governor is required to sign the bill before it can be recorded in the office of the Secretary of State as enacted. The Maryland legislature did not send the bill to Maryland Governor Austin L. Crothers who, when he delivered his address on the proposed amendment to the January session of the legislature in 1910 made it clear that he did not believe the federal government had the legal authority to impose an income tax, the 16th Amendment notwithstanding. Clearly, Crothers intended to reject the resolution if it was passed by the legislature since he was convinced the power to impose an income tax was exclusively a State prerogative.

His address to the Joint Session, recorded in the State Journal, voiced that conviction. "I approve and endorse the principle of an income tax," he began. "It is a policy supported by the Democratic party and rests upon sound considerations of political economy and right...[H]owever, I am of the opinion that this policy should be adopted as a State policy and a reasonable tax upon incomes and upon direct inheritances should be laid by the State government. The Federal government, exercising powers which have been challenged by many distinguished American citizens from the days of Thomas Jefferson to present time, has laid prohibitive tariff duties at rates so high as to seriously impair the federal revenues. I cannot but regard the proposal upon the part of the federal government to raise additional revenues by the means of a federal income tax as an expedient upon its part to enable it to maintain its present unjust and extortionate tariff system. In the maintenance of that iniquity, I am unwilling to unite. The great masses of the American people, including the people of Maryland, are demanding relief from the

153

oppression of the present federal tariff, and steps should be taken to enforce a revision of existing tariff rates *downward* rather than to enable them to be maintained and perpetuated." (Emphasis on *downward* appeared in the journal transcript.)

"Moreover," Crothers concluded, "the power of imposing taxes upon the inheritances and incomes is clearly reserved to the States...In my judgment, it should be exercised by the States and not delegated to the General Government...[C]onsiderations of revenue and economy upon the part of this State, especially in view of the works of internal improvement upon which they have embarked, certainly justify the retention by the State itself of this important source of revenue." (*Maryland State Congressional Journal,* January, 1910.)

Joseph M. Brown, the governor of Georgia did not sign the resolution which passed his legislature either. He failed to do so because he was prohibited by law from doing so for two reasons. First, Brown was aware of the substitution made by the House of Delegates—a clear cut violation of the State Constitution. Second, neither congressional body approved the amendment with a 2/3 majority. Although S.D. 240 indicates Georgia ratified the 16th Amendment on August 3, 1910, the State itself apparently was not aware that it had, since the matter resurfaced and was re-introduced in the 1912 session of the legislature.

Mississippi had its own problems in passing the 16th Amendment which it solved in a rather unique, albeit illegal, manner. The leadership, in particular Secretary of State Joseph W. Power, Representative L.L. Donnah and United States Senator Leroy Percy were believed by most of those present as being responsible for the 30 fifths of bourbon that were brought into the House cloakroom on March 8, 1910, the day the 16th Amendment was voted on. A legislator identified in the complaint that was filed by State Representative Joseph McDonald the following day, Rep. Blakelee, initially admitted to bringing the liquor into the building, but later recanted. Blakelee then implicated a porter, who was employed by Power, as the culprit. The reason for the liquor was clearly to get the representatives intoxicated in order to influence their vote. But which vote? On that same day, the legislature was also voting on United States Senatorial candidates.

The fact that Percy was involved suggests the ploy was used to influence his renomination to the United States Senate. However Percy, a Democrat, was one of Aldrich's *across-the-aisle* cronies in Congress that actively campaigned for passage of the Joint Resolution which was now being considered by the State of Mississippi.

A document discovered by Beckman and Benson in the Mississippi State archives dated April 16, 1910 suggests that those investigating the whiskey party in the House believed the flack was being generated because of Percy and not the 16th Amendment. The archival journal record states: "In view of the scandalous rumors which have been circulated touching the recent Senatorial contest , the House of Representatives takes pleasure in saying to the people of Mississippi that we are convinced that the conduct of every candidate in the Senatorial contest was dignified and honorable and upright and that no vote in the caucus nomination was procured by any improper means or corrupt influence, and that the election of Senator Percy is free from fraud and corruption...We have examined 67 witnesses...In the examination...we have spared no time or expense in trying to arrive at the truth...and running down each and every rumor that came to our knowledge...We believe that undue influence by the improper use of liquor was used upon at least one member of the House. This member was changed from his original conviction and, being unfortunately addicted to the use of strong drink was, by this improper influence, overpersuaded to vote against his real convictions...The evidence shows further that in other instances other members of the Legislature were approached and asked if money or political position would persuade them to change their vote, and this, we believe, was very improper. Even the patronage of the Federal government is shown to have been brought into play and used in this caucus...Whiskey was used excessively during this caucus. But there is no proof that any intoxicants were dispensed in the headquarters of any candidate. (*1910 House Journal,* Eightieth Day April 10/1910 Duplicate.)"

The 1910 Senatorial race in Mississippi was a heated affair, and opposition against Percy, whom many in the state Democratic organization believed had climbed into bed with the Republicans, was strong. Most grassroots Democrats wanted to dump Percy and nominate a former Mississippi governor as the candidate of the Democratic Party that year.

For that reason, it is very likely that the whiskey party was not engineered to influence the vote on the 16th Amendment. However, inasmuch as the Amendment Resolution was Percy's in the minds of the Mississippi legislators, it is also likely that it   155 rode Percy's bourbon-soaked coattails to passage. It is likely that Percy's supporters in the Senate believed that if their candidate was defeated, so likewise would be the 16th Amendment. For that reason, both were lobbied with equal fervor.

Six states: Utah, Connecticut, Rhode Island, Virginia, Florida, and Pennsylvania flatly rejected the 16th Amendment. Vermont, Massachusetts and New Hampshire ratified it after the fact, bringing the actual total of those in favor to 42. Originally, New Hampshire was one of seven States to reject it. On March 7, 1911 Governor Robert P. Bass wrote to Knox advising him that "...I regret to inform you that the joint resolution 'ratifying the sixteenth amendment to the Constitution of the United States of America' has failed of passage at the present session of the New Hampshire General Court..."

After declaring the 16th Amendment ratified on February 15, 1913, William Jennings Bryan, appealed to those States who had previously rejected it, asking for their unanimous support for what was now a reality in the United States. Bryan, like Knox before him, knew the 16th Amendment was flawed. Additional ratifications from those who had previously rejected it would serve to further secure it from legal challenges in the future.

On January 8, 1913 New Hampshire, understanding that the 16th Amendment had already been ratified and was in fact now the law of the land, readdressed the ratification as a matter of national unity. On March 7, 1913, they became the 42nd, and last, State to ratify it.

The debate that raged for four years in the State legislatures is important for two reasons. First, it shows that a good many State legislators were aware that the federal government could not be trusted with the power of direct taxation, and accurately predicted the abuse that would follow. Second, through the use of intimidation and threats, fraud and corruption, as well as extravagant promises of both personal reward and political patronage for those who acceded to the demands of the political bosses, we are given a rare glimpse of the naked power behind the seats of government — even at State level.

In the Massachusetts debate, Representative James J. Myers argued against the political bosses of his State who insisted that an income tax would be imposed by the federal government only in times of war or other extreme national emergencies. Myers insisted that "...this amendment does much more than provide for an emergency. It goes far beyond that and provides that Congress may levy such a tax without any such need and at any time...[L]et us not...confer on Congress a power...far broader than the case calls for and one fraught with the very dangers about which the framers of our Constitution took such pains to guard themselves and those to come after them."

Massachusetts rejected the 16th Amendment three times before finally ratifying it on March 4, 1913 — again, only after it had been *officially* declared ratified, and only because they were asked to be a voice for national unity.

Vermont, after several failed attempts, finally passed the amendment only after it learned that 36 states — the exact amount needed to ratify it — had already done so. Their vote was likewise a vote for unity.

O ne question remains as yet unanswered. Of each of the 42 states which ultimately ratified the 16th Amendment, only six did so in an incontestable manner. Why? The flaws that exist universally within these resolutions are much too obvious to be errors. From the vast amount and severity of them one can only conclude they were, for the most part, deliberate since the written instructions from Knox that accompanied the Joint Resolution were too specific for at least 36 of the 42 ratifying States to fill their resolutions with such grievous errors.

What each State appeared to be doing was either creating a safety net which they could fall back on if the need to declare the 16th Amendment invalid arose; or, they expected the Secretary of State to nullify their ratifications due to the blatant errors contained within them. Neither happened. And, at this late date, neither is likely to ever take place. The errors, too numerous to detail here, were carefully mitigated by Clark through the use of a precedent that compared frequently misspelled words in the 14th and 15th Amendment resolutions and declared them to be accidents that did not otherwise detract from the desire of the States to ratify the amendment.

These are probably not the best examples for an unbiased Solicitor General to cite since, in point of fact, the 14th and 15th Amendments was foisted on the States by the radical Jacobin Re-

157

publicans who were determined to punish the South. If every State resolution was deficient it is likely the Jacobin Republicans would have nevertheless declared the 14th Amendment ratified. It may well be that they were the best example available. If so, his analogy was very weak at best and suspect at worst.

It was the extreme amount of disqualifying errors, misfilings, missing affidavits and an almost complete lack of certification on the part of almost every state that caused the Solicitor General to seek a loophole through which the government could declare the 16th Amendment ratified. Clark noted that "...A careful examination of the resolutions of the various states on file in the Department, ratifying the 16th Amendment to the Constitution, shows that there are many errors of punctuation and capitalization and some, although not substantial, errors of wording, in quoting the article proposed by Congress..." Eleven of the states changed at least some of the words within the proposed amendment. And while Clark did not feel minor changes in punctuation were important enough to disqualify any State, it should be noted that a well placed comma can alter the meaning of a sentence completely.

It was the opinion of Clark that "...it should be...observed that it seems clearly to have been the intention of the legislatures in each and every case to accept and ratify the 16th Amendment as proposed by Congress. Again, the incorporation of the terms of the proposed amendment in the ratifying resolution seems in every case merely to have been by way of recitation. In no case has any legislature signified in any way its deliberate intention to change the wording of the proposed amendment." Of course they didn't, because they knew they couldn't. The directions they received concerning the ratification process were too specific to make such an error accidently.

"...Each amendment must be inserted in precisely the proper place in the bill with the spelling and punctuation exactly as it was adopted...When the bill has been agreed to in identical form by both bodies...a copy of the bill is enrolled...The preparation of the enrolled bill is a painstaking and important task since it must reflect precisely the effect...agreed to by both parties...The enrolling clerk...must prepare meticulously the final form of the bill, as it was agreed to by both Houses...exactly as agreed to, and all punctuation must be in accord with the action taken."

158   *(United States Senate Document 97-120.)*

Clark concluded "...Furthermore, under the provisions of the Constitution a legislature is not authorized to alter in any way the amendment proposed by Congress, the function of the legislature consisting merely in the right to approve or disapprove the proposed amendment..."

Which is precisely what the States were counting on. According to the same regulations being quoted by Clark to accept the ratifications, the resolutions of each State that violated the guidelines should have been disqualified and counted among those States which rejected the amendment.

Had Knox done so, both the 16th and 17th Amendments would have been soundly rejected. Instead Clark, acting on behalf of Knox, rationalized that there appeared to be a "...necessary presumption, in the absence of express stipulation to the contrary, that a legislature did not intend to do something that it had not the power to do, but rather that it intended to do something that it had the power to do, namely, where its action has been affirmative, to ratify the amendment proposed by Congress. Moreover, it could not be presumed that by a mere change of wording, probably inadvertent, the legislature had intended to reject the amendment."

The argument of Solicitor General Clark, painstakingly developed over a period of two weeks, was simply that although the 14th and 15th Amendments contained an extreme amount of errors, both had successfully withstood court challenges. In neither case did any plaintiff contest the legality of the Amendment itself, only the legal implications of its content.

While the adage *two wrongs don't make a right* has been one of the golden rules most Americans live by, the government of the United States apparently believes two wrongs, if not discovered in time, create an outstanding legal precedent.

In defending the multiplicity of errors in the 14th and 15th Amendments, Clark was quick to point out that one State, Kansas, substituted entirely different wording in its ratification of the 15th Amendment—and the Secretary of State accepted the document as a valid ratification of an entirely different amendment—one which Kansas had not even voted on.

In speaking about the 14th Amendment, the Solicitor General said: "It will be observed that there were many substantial errors of wording in the resolutions of the state legislatures upon which the Secretary of State acted in issuing his declaration an-

159

nouncing the adoption and ratification by the states of the 14th amendment to the Constitution. By announcing the ratification of the 14th amendment the Executive Branch of the Government ruled that these errors where immaterial to the adoption of the amendment, and further, as this amendment has been repeatedly before the courts, and has been enforced, it is clear that the procedure in ratifying that amendment on this point a precedent which may be properly followed in proclaiming the adoption of the present amendment — that is to say, that the Secretary of State may disregard the errors contained in the certified copies of the resolutions of legislatures acting affirmatively on the proposed amendment."

Two wrongs apparently do make a right.

The governors of each State were sent, by Knox, a certified copy of Senate Joint Resolution 40 that specifically detailed, with equally precise clarity, how the ratification process worked. In addition, the exact language of the proposed amendment to be voted on was included. Specific instructions on both the preparation of the bills, the precise text — word-for-word, comma-by-comma, capitalization-by-capitalization, period-by-period — were outlined. It was imperative that each State voted on exactly the same amendment, containing exactly the same words, commas and periods — all in exactly the same place. Otherwise it could, and eventually would, be construed that the States which theoretically ratified the 16th Amendment had actually voted on 42 different resolutions, with only one State concurring on each. That is precisely what happened. While each State voted, in principle, on the idea of a federal income tax, no two States actually voted on the same legal amendment to bring one about.

Each State was officially notified that when their legislature approved or disapproved the proposed amendment, they were to certify the results, including the particulars of the vote and a true copy of the State's legislative journal. This certification was necessary to affirm ratification. Twenty-three states failed to send the required certification to verify the ratification. And although the laws of most of those States required the chief executive to sign all lawfully passed legislation before it could be deemed legally enacted, 20 governors did not affix their signatures to the resolutions which were theoretically passed by their legislatures.

160

In addressing the June 1, 1912 veto of the resolution by Governor George W. Donaghey of Arkansas, Clark wrote: "It will be observed from the above record that the Governor of the State of Arkansas vetoed the resolution passed by the legislature of that State. It is *submitted*, however, that this does not in any way invalidate the action of the legislature or nullify the effect of the resolution, as *it is believed* that the approval of the Governor is not necessary and that he has not the power of veto in such cases." (Emphasis, author.)

Clearly, Clark was advancing nothing more than a personal opinion, since he served only as the chief attorney for the State Department. He was not a judge, and his opinion lacked any binding authority. *"It is submitted..."* advances only a legal argument. No legal precedent had previously been established. Likewise, when he said *"it is believed,"* he was offering nothing more than a non-binding opinion. It is akin to saying: "I don't know if you can legally do that, but I don't think you can..."

Yet interestingly, the President of the United States has the legal authority to veto a Constitutional amendment passed by the Congress (although it would likely be an effort in futility since it requires the same number of votes to enact a Constitutional Amendment as it does to override a veto). But that isn't the point. As the chief executive of the nation, the President represents all of the people simply because he was elected by all of them. Each member of Congress, whether Senator or Representative, represents only his or her constituency and therefore has less power individually than the President. Collectively however, Congress — which theoretically represents all the people — has more power than the President. The same is true at State level.

In one paragraph, the Solicitor General, of his own initiative and not based on any legal opinions by the Supreme Court, decided that with respect to a Constitutional amendment, the Governor of a State does not, in this one instance, legally possess the one Constitutional tool granted him to protect the citizens of his State from overzealous legislation, the right of veto — which Clark assumed was somehow temporarily suspended without legal precedent. In the same statement Clark decided that chief executives of the States are not necessary in the final enactment of bills which have been enrolled in the legislative processes of those States. Yet like the President, the Governor represents all of the people of his sovereign State simply because he, like the President, is

161

elected by all of them.

Nor did it seem to matter to Clark that several States had ratified a resolution that their own Constitutions expressly forbade them from even voting on.

But, what is most surprising is that the Solicitor General's 1913 personal opinion was not challenged by a single State then, nor has it yet been today. Appearing on CNN's *Inside Politics* on November 23, 1996, Michigan Governor John Engler was asked whether he thought a Balanced Budget Amendment might being forthcoming from the G.O.P. Congress during the 1997-98 session, and also whether or not in his opinion such an amendment would be ratified. To which, based somewhat on the questionable precedent established by Clark's unchallenged 1913 personal opinion, he responded: "I believe it's clearly understood that the opinions of Governors carry no weight in Constitutional amendment matters."

The effort expended by Philander C. Knox and his willing accomplice Joshua Reuben Clark, Jr., circumvented not only the Constitutions of the various States by usurping the legal authority of the chief executives of those States, but the Constitution of the United States itself by assuming for themselves the role of *judicator of last resorts* with respect to the legislative processes within the various States. Clearly, without an opinion from the Supreme Court to validate their argument, the actions of the Secretary of State and the Solicitor General in arbitrarily suspending the legislative rules mandated by the various States' Constitutions was not only an abuse of power by the Executive Branch, it was also a clear and unequivocal fraudulent violation of the Constitution of the United States.

The federal guidelines which had to be observed in the passage of a Constitutional amendment were clearly and carefully spelled out to each of the States. The 16th Amendment contains 30 words. It takes less than 30 seconds to read. The myriad of documents retrieved by Beckman and Benson from the various State and National archives clearly indicate it would have been literally impossible for any State not to understand that they could not deviate in any way from the exact wording of the proposed amendment — right down to the commas, capitalizations and periods! Yet, almost every States did. Why? Even a sixth grader

162

can copy, verbatim, 30 words without error. Why was it that the legislators of at least 38 States, most of whom had spent countless years drafting similar legislation that had to be presented in identical form to their own bicameral legislatures, could not correctly copy 30 words?

From their experience as legislators, each knew their resolutions, if improperly submitted, would be legally invalid and would necessarily have to be rejected by the Secretary of State. Such a contemplation may sound somewhat farfetched since obviously, if the State legislature did not want to ratify the 16th Amendment, they needed only to reject it. However in this case there was a very great need for subterfuge.

For a very brief period in the history of the United States, from 1907 until 1913, the invisible money power that has largely influenced the affairs of this nation since the Revolutionary War chose to become more forcibly visible in America. Unfortunately there exists no public letters, minutes of meetings, memos, correspondences or archival records which support the author's opinion, since this group is so powerful that the spoken word is sufficient to achieve its ends. Logic suggests the frightened and albeit illegal acts of otherwise powerful and influential politicians within the State and federal governments adequately testified to that presence.

In his voluminous best-selling work, *Titan: The Life of John D. Rockefeller, Sr.* author Ron Chernow described a secret deal hatched up between Rockefeller (then a struggling, although already well-to-do oil refiner in Cleveland, Ohio) and robber baron Jay Gould who was, at that moment in 1868, attempting to exercise control over the booming railroad industry. Gould, who had just wrested control of the Erie Railroad from Commodore Cornelius Vanderbilt, hatched a deal with Rockefeller and his partner, Henry Morrison Flagler, to financially cripple the Pennsylvania Railroad which was, at that time, carrying most of the crude oil from the oil fields in western Pennsylvania to Philadelphia or New York for refining. The joint venture was called the Alleghany Transportation Company. Rockefeller and Flagler, the salesman, negotiated deals with the drillers in Oil Creek, Pennsylvania to ship their crude through Alleghany. Flagler wrested major concessions from the Pennsylvania Railroad's other competition in the northeast, the New York Central Railroad and the Lakeshore Line—for a staggering 75% rebate that was

163

paid by all three railroads directly to Alleghany on all oil shipped through their system. By dealing exclusively with Rockefeller and Flagler rather than two or three dozen small oil shippers, the railroads were able to ship far more crude oil with far fewer oil tanker cars. The average shipping time from Oil Creek to New York dropped from 30 days to 10, and the number of oil tank cars needed to carry more crude to market dropped from 1,800 per week to 600. (*Titan: The Life of John D. Rockefeller, Sr.;* Ron Chernow; Random House © 1998; pgs. 111-115.)

What makes this snapshot of Rockefeller and Gould important to this text is the fact that, as Chernow notes in his book, the pattern of "hand shake deals" without any written contracts, was already a fact of life of the world of high finance. Multimillion dollar, and many times billion dollar, deals take place on a daily basis throughout the industrial and financial world today without any "paperwork" trails to evidence that those transactions ever took place. Likewise, the backroom deals and leveraging tactics employed by the money barons to gain the concessions they require to obtain their objectives are never recorded for posterity to see since those records are the stuff that antitrust lawsuits are created from.

Those who were exposed to the financial giants at the pinnacle of power knew that a single word, privately uttered, could bring the career of an otherwise prominent and successful politician to an abrupt end. At stake in America at that time was more than simply an income tax, or even a new central bank. The core issue was the Constitution of the United States which placed the real power of this nation in the hands of the people. Two Constitutional resolutions had been introduced—the 16th and 17th Amendments. Both were critical to the plans of the money barons. Both usurped States' rights. Both should have been quickly voted down by every State in the Union. Yet, both—even with flawed and incomplete transmittals—were surreptitiously validated.

The pressure that was applied on the legislators in every State was extraordinarily prodigious. Threats and bribery were commonplace. Promises of personal financial gain and political patronage from the highest levels of the United States government are amply evidenced in the archival documents found in the various States. The power of the king-makers was suddenly and very forcefully brought to bear on local, county and State officials who had heretofore only imagined that such power really existed.

I t is clear from examining the various archival documents that regardless if the errors in the ratifications were deliberate or acts of sheer stupidity, the Executive Branch was determined to declare the 16th Amendment legally ratified — the volume of the errors discovered notwithstanding — even though it wasn't.

Obviously, without the 16th Amendment, the money J.P. Morgan invested in the 1912 presidential campaigns of Woodrow Wilson and Theodore Roosevelt to unseat William Howard Taft would have been wasted, since the plans of the money barons to successfully create a new and virtually impregnable privately owned central bank in the United States depended heavily on the passage of both the 16th and 17th Amendments.

America possessed an agency to collect income tax receipts since 1862, only it had no income taxes to collect since 1874. Interestingly, when Lincoln's tax was suspended during the closing days of Grant's Administration, the Internal Revenue Service was not. While awaiting the rebirth of the income tax, the IRS was used by the Treasury to collect the various tariffs and excise taxes that were now more frequently and more universally imposed on the products sold in America to offset the revenues lost by the suspension of Lincoln's income tax.

Taft himself was placed under extreme pressure by the invisible forces behind the government. Due largely to the Lincoln precedent, Taft did not view the income tax as a tool of the bankers, but rather like Lincoln, he saw it as a means to hold the money barons at bay. While Taft was deliberately vague in his public posturing on the ratification or rejection of the 16th Amendment, he adamantly resisted every effort by the Aldrich forces to legislate a new central bank. And, for that reason alone, he had to go.

Thomas Woodrow Wilson, the somewhat soft-spoken, unobtrusive and all but obscure New Jersey governor and former president of Princeton University was handpicked by J.P. Morgan to run against Taft in 1912 not because, as some say, of his astute intellect and realistic grasp of the need for strong financial and economic reforms in America, but for a completely unrelated reason. That reason was Colonel House. House had been in the employ of the international money barons as a lobbyist of sorts his entire adult life and was one of J.P. Morgan's key point men in the behind the scenes lobbying of legislators for the passage of both the 16th and 17th Amendments.

While William Jennings Bryan, in his own writings, would claim that the Morgan crowd bet their money on Champ Clark, the Democratic Speaker of the House in 1912, the reality is, Morgan put his money on just about everyone that year—except perhaps on the jailhouse presidential bid of socialist Eugene V. Debs, who campaigned from his prison cell. Debs was probably the only candidate in 1912 that Morgan did not back. And Wilson, who campaigned against "Morgan money" and the Wall Street interests, was the only candidate Morgan did not *publicly* finance since Wilson was the candidate Morgan expected to win. Too many Americans still blamed Morgan for the Bank Panic of 1907. But Morgan's most public support went to Taft, whom he expected to lose.

When Morgan privately complained that Taft was taking his position as President of the United States a little too seriously and was becoming extremely difficult to manage, House would later claim in his memoirs that it was he who suggested to Morgan that he create his own President—one who would march lock-step to the beat of the Morgan drum. Such a man, he advanced, might be Wilson.

While it is not known if House and Wilson were acquainted at the time, House had good reason to suggest Wilson's name. During the Panic of 1907 Wilson, as the president of Princeton with an earned reputation as an economist, granted an interview to the press in which he declared: "All this trouble could be averted if we appointed a committee of six or seven public-spirited men like J.P. Morgan to handle the affairs of our country." (*The Federal Reserve, the Most Fantastic Fraud in History*; H.S. Kennan; pg. 105.)

While it has been advanced by a great many conspiracy theorists, particularly Kennan, that Wilson was a "Morgan man" at the time of his 1907 press release, and that the interview itself was staged to mitigate Morgan's role in the national financial crisis he had created, logic suggests otherwise. Although history will probably never really know for certain, it is more likely that the interview, granted by a well-intentioned but nonetheless ignorant economist, brought Wilson to Morgan's attention. This opinion is supported in part by Wilson's own words in *New Freedom*, which was published shortly before the election of 1912. In *New*

Freedom, Wilson articulated his awe of an invisible power he had recently discovered that possessed the extraordinary ability to humble the giants of both industry and commerce. Wilson wrote from the perspective of an outsider seeing this power for the very first time. Had Wilson been the insider many conspiracy theorists claimed he was, such references would not have existed anywhere within the pages of his book, simply because the book itself would likely never have been written. Those accustomed to real power do not openly discuss it. Only those who have recently discovered its existence do.

Wilson, the political neophyte, utilized precisely the same type of rhetoric used by most politicians before and after him, campaigning on issues that were the opposite of his real convictions. You will recall that in 1907 Wilson argued that the nation would be best served by turning control of the government over to J.P. Morgan and the Money Mafia. Yet, five years later he publicly campaigned against the same Morgan interests that were currently financing his effort to take the White House. And Taft, who had resisted Morgan at every turn, was painted as a politician in the hip pocket of the money barons.

Using *New Freedom* as a campaign tool to argue his position that a handful of wealthy men controlled the government, Wilson lambasted Taft as a Morgan hireling. As a portent of things to come, Wilson also campaigned on the issue of States' rights even as those rights were, at that very moment, being drained from the commonwealths with the ratifications of the 16th and 17th Amendments like water through a sieve. A month after Wilson assumed office, States rights would forever be a mute issue. They no longer existed. The separation of powers between the various factions of the government had just been reduced by one third. The States no longer possessed an advocate to adjudicate their interests. The people themselves would be next.

"Where some people are very wealthy and others have nothing, the result will be eitehr extreme democracy or absolute oligarchy, or despotism will come from either of those excesses."

Aristotle
Politics

"And I tell you that virtue does not come from money, but from virtue comes money and all other good things to man, both the the individual and the state."

Socrates
Plato Apology

❖ SEVEN ❖

The Federal Reserve

When the *Federal Reserve Act* was being debated in the House of Representatives, Rep. Charles A. Lindbergh, Sr. declared to Congress: "This Act establishes the most gigantic trust on earth. When the President signs this Act, the invisible government of the money power, proven to exist by the Money Trust investigation, will be legalized. This new law will create inflation whenever the trust wants inflation. From now on depressions will be scientifically created." (*American Opinion Magazine*, March, 1978; pg. 16.)

Lindbergh's fears were confirmed by Congressman Wright Patman, Chairman of the House Banking and Currency Committee who, on the floor of Congress some four decades later, said: "In the United States today, we have in effect two governments. We have the duly constituted government. Then we have an independent, uncontrolled and uncoordinated government in the Federal Reserve System, operating the money powers which are reserved to Congress by the Constitution." (*The Unseen Hand;* A. Ralph Epperson; Publius Press © 1985; pg. 174.)

Patman was not the first head of this particular committee to express that view. Congressman Louis McFadden, who headed the House Banking Committee in 1933 was of the same opinion. Speaking out in the Congressional Record on May 23, 1933 when he brought impeachment charges against the Federal Reserve Board for masterminding the Stock Market Crash in 1929, McFadden said: "We have in this country one of the most corrupt institutions the world has ever known. I refer to the Federal Reserve Board and the Federal Reserve Banks...They are not government institutions. They are private monopolies which prey upon the people of the United States for the benefit of themselves and their foreign and domestic swindlers: rich and predatory moneylenders... When the *Federal Reserve Act* was passed, the 169 people of these United States did not perceive that a world banking system was being set up here. A super-state controlled by international bankers and international industrialists acting together to enslave the world for their own pleasure. Every effort has been made by the Fed to conceal [its] powers but the truth is — the Fed has usurped the government. It controls everything here, and it controls all our foreign relations! It makes and breaks governments at will!

"I charge them with having...taken over $80,000,000,000.00 from the United States government in the year 1928. I charge them...with having arbitrar[il]y and unlawfully raised and lowered the rates on money...increased and diminished the volume of currency in circulation for the benefit of private interests...I charge them...[with] having conspired to transfer to foreigners and international money lenders title to, and control of, the financial resources of the United States." McFadden passionately argued that the Depression, resulting from the Stock Market Crash, was not an accident. "It was a carefully contrived occurrence," he insisted. "The international bankers sought to bring about a condition of despair here so that they might emerge as the rulers of us all." (*Congressional Record*, May 23, 1933.)

McFadden's investigation of the Fed died an abortive death a few days after it commenced when the Congressman himself died shortly after returning home from a banquet where he complained of feeling ill. Those close to the Congressman insist he was poisoned. His death was ruled to have been from natural causes although no autopsy was ever performed to determine precisely what caused it. The allegation of poison arose largely because McFadden had been the victim of two very recent failed assassination attempts. (*The Federal Reserve and Our Manipulated Dollar*; Dr. Martin Larson; Devon-Adair © 1975; pg. 99.)

As mentioned previously, in 1957, U.S. Senator George W. Malone of Nevada, speaking before Congress on the subject of the Federal Reserve declared that he believed that "...if the people of this nation fully understood what Congress has done to them over the past 40 years, they would move on Washington." Malone affirmed that the Fed was "...a preconceived plan to destroy the economic and social independence of the United States."

Henry Ford, founder of Ford Motor Company concurred when he said, "It is well enough that [the] people of [this] nation do not understand our banking and monetary system, for if they did, I believe there would be a revolution before tomorrow morning."

Congress was assured by U.S. Senator Nelson Wilmarth Aldrich, who sponsored the *Federal Reserve Act,* that the legislation would both contain the growing power of the bankers and that it would also give Congress authority over the new banking system. Of course, if any Congressman had actually taken the time to read the legislation they were voting on, they would have realized they were creating a system so completely outside the scope of authority of the United States government that Congress would not even be allowed to demand an audit of its books once the legislation was signed into law by Wilson.

In 1914, shortly after the new law took effect, Aldrich bragged that "...before the passage of this Act, the New York bankers..." (the Rockefeller and Morgan interests) "...could only dominate the reserves of New York. Now we are able to dominate the bank reserves of the entire country."

In *The Capitalist Conspiracy,* author G. Edward Griffin observed that "...By law, the seven members of the Federal Reserve Board are appointed by the President for terms of 14 years. In spite of the incredible length of these appointments, nevertheless, they are supposed to create the illusion that the people, acting through their elected leaders, have some voice in the nation's monetary policies. In practice, however, every President since the beginning of the Federal Reserve System has appointed only those men who were congenial to the financial interests of the international banking dynasties. There have been no exceptions."

The creation of the Federal Reserve System in 1913 stands as a direct violation to the Constitution of the United States, which mandates that only the U.S. government, specifically the House of Representatives, has the right to "coin" money.

Every president from Thomas Jefferson to William Howard Taft resisted the attempt of the money barons to install a permanent, privately owned central bank in the United States. From Wilson to Clinton, every president has defended it. Andrew Jackson, whose defiance of a central bank almost cost him his life from an assassin's bullet, said: "If Congress has the right under the Constitution to issue paper money, it was given to them to use by themselves, not to be delegated to individuals or corporations."

Like most of the unconstitutional acts the United States government has foisted on the American public during the past century, a considerable amount of Congressional soul searching took   171 place over the creation of the Fed. Soul searching not in a theological sense—soul searching for a legal loophole that would allow Congress to circumvent the Constitution. It was found in the wording of Article I, Section 8 § 5.

The mindset of the federal government in 1913 is explained in the 1973 Church Committee Senate Document 43, *Hearings on the Termination of the National Emergency,* that also deals with the logic Roosevelt used to defend his unconstitutional removal of the United States from the gold standard.

The government needed to establish that there was a compelling national need, under Article I, Section 8 of the Constitution to create a privately-owned, non-government central bank. They argued: "The sound construction of the Constitution must allow the National Legislature that discretion with respect to the means by which the powers it confers are to be carried into execution, which will enable that body to perform the high duties assigned to it in a manner most beneficial to the people. Let the end be legitimate, let it be within the scope of the Constitution, and all means which are appropriate, which are plainly adapted to that end, which are not prohibited, but [are within] the letter and spirit of the Constitution...*Congress has the implied power to issue currency* and to provide for uniformity in description and value of its currency, *as well as the express power to coin money and regulate the value thereof...*" (Emphasis, author's.)

Very subtly, Congress drew a distinction between the *printing* and *coining* of money, making them two separate and completely unrelated powers. Congress would argue in 1913 that the power reserved for Congress according to Article I, Section 8 § 5 was not the *printing* of paper money, but was instead merely the power to *coin* money. Once this distinction was clearly established, it was relatively easy to delegate that which they maintained was not specifically implied in the Constitution—the *printing* of paper money—to private bankers.

"For some 70 years of the Government's existence, Congress acted under only one of these powers—that of coining money and regulating its value. Then it acted upon the other power—that relating to currency. The exercise of these different powers resulted in two kinds of national 'money'...If 'money' is the medium for effecting exchanges and is a measure of value, *when the law made both species and currency legal tender, without actual equal purchasing power, gold became a mere commodity or article of commerce...*since it had

172

inherent value as a metal. While currency had no inherent value, only conceptional value as ideal money...[and w]hile the courts cannot control our citizens' preferences for one kind of money over another kind, or prevent them from giving a premium for the one or the other kind of money when the fiscal affairs of the Government necessitate the adoption of a certain policy, expressed in constitutional legislative enactment, such as the maintenance of a monetary system consisting of *specie* and *currency*, to be acceptable interchangeably as to the value of the dollar, the courts should not give effect to a stipulation impugning the power of the legislature to make such laws[1]..." (Emphasis, author.) (*Senate Document 43;* July 24, 1973.)

Clearly, the argument of the government has been merely a play on words since *species* and *currency* are interchangeable nouns. When the Constitution of the United States was drafted, paper money—called *script*—did exist, and was used frequently as money in times of emergency. Script, however, was clearly not recognized by anyone as "lawful" money. It was more or less an I.O.U. from the government. It was reluctantly accepted as money because the bearer knew that at the conclusion of whatever crisis mandated its use—providing, of course, the issuer prevailed—the script could be redeemed at full face value for the lawful species of the realm. In other words, paper money was temporary money. Coined money was species because its value was inherent. Everyone understands the value of gold and silver. When you own it you possess real, tangible wealth. When you possess paper money, its value is arbitrarily determined by fiat and is subject to change on the whims of the power that issued it. Simply stated, when you own gold, you control wealth; when you possess paper money, wealth controls you.

---

[1]The substance of this statement was originally made by the Roosevelt Administration in its successful effort to rob the wealth of America from its citizens by substituting fiat script for its lawful money. Implied was the notion that fiat money had more value as a stable currency than gold because gold, as a commodity of commerce, fluctuated so much that its value, and thus the value of the dollar, could not be controlled.

Nothing could be farther from the truth. Gold, on the world market, was selling for $32.00 per troy ounce in 1933. The global prices of gold and silver were stable largely because their values were fixed by law in the United States.

That was the argument advanced by Daniel Webster against John C. Calhoun on the floor of the United States Senate during the debate on the recharter of the central bank in 1846 when he said: "A disordered currency is one of the greatest political evils. It undermines the virtues necessary for the support of the social system, and encourages propensities destructive to its happiness. It wars against industry, frugality and economy. Of all the contrivances for cheating the laboring classes of mankind, none has been more effectual than that which deludes them with paper money." (*Congressional Record;* March 4, 1846.)

When the Panic of 1907 was orchestrated by J.P. Morgan, America possessed one of only three monetary systems in the world still on the gold standard. The dollar was recognized as the most stable currency in the world since it was the only currency whose value was determined by gold and not indebtedness. It was almost completely immune from any type of manipulation by outside forces. For that reason, Morgan didn't attempt to either inflate or deflate the value of the dollar, but instead attacked the fears of the people who owned the dollars that were safely deposited in the banks of America.

As a banker, Morgan understood the *reserve principle* that governs modern banking. At any given time, because all banks earn their money by loaning out the funds that are on deposit, no bank anywhere in the world will likely have more than a small fraction of its deposits on hand at any given time. Knowing that, it was relatively easy for Morgan to start a run on America's banks. The trick was to confine the run to the United States and not let it spill over into Europe. To a large degree Morgan was successful in his efforts. Only one European bank failed during that period. Later, revisionist historians would single out that one European bank failure as the catalyst for the Panic of 1907 in the United States *although no bank panic occurred in Europe.* They would use the same ploy in 1929 when the collapse of the Credit-Anstalt Bank in Vienna, Austria was cited as the catalyst for the stock market crash in the United States.

In reality the Bank Panic of 1907 and the Stock Market crash in 1929 were both the direct result of deliberate manipulation by international bankers to achieve precisely what happened during those events.

174

To be successful in their efforts to create a banking system which was immune from the State-level political meddling that jeopardized its previous central bank franchises, the money barons of Europe and America needed to accomplish three objectives. Because they had learned so well from previous experiences with the American people and their Constitution, the banking cartels of both Europe and America determined first to erode the power of the States, and thus the people, by first undermining the tenets of the Constitution. For this end they enlisted the willing support of Aldrich.

N ovember 22, 1910 was a blistery cold day in Hoboken, New Jersey. The first snow storm of the year added to the bone-chilling cold. The snow was a somber, quiet warning to those who traditionally wintered in the South that the migratory season had arrived, and it was time to head for a warmer climate.

The Hoboken train station was almost desolate at 10 p.m. as the last train of the day prepared to embark for the South. Only a few passengers scurried across the platform, their chins tucked deep into their coats to ward off the assault of cold, arctic air. Few, if any, took the time to pause and stare at the elaborately ornate railroad car at the far end of the platform. That it was a rich man's private railway car was apparent from its highly polished brass filigree and heavily shaded windows. In warmer weather, almost any coach passenger preparing to board the Hoboken train would have been curious enough to saunter over for a peek. Tonight, it was just too cold. Tonight, they dismissed its presence with a cursory glance and boarded the train.

Perhaps later the mystery car at the end of the train might be a topic of discussion for the travellers in coach. But none of those travelers could have even remotely imagined that the five men who boarded that railway car moments before the train left the Hoboken station — none of whom any of those travelers would likely have recognized — would be among seven men who would forever change not only the course of the economy of the United States, but the nation's political power structure as well.

The train stopped again briefly at New York's Grand Central Station to pick up more southern-bound passengers. Two more men boarded the special car. For a brief moment, the passengers embarking in New York caught a rare glimpse of the opu- 175 lence that the elite take for granted when they travel: rich mahogany paneled walls, plush red carpet and a well-stocked bar. Two white jacketed attendants stood just inside the door as the pair silently climbed on board.

Inside the private railway car that belonged to Rhode Island's junior Senator Aldrich when it pulled out of Grand Central Station were Abraham Piatt Andrews, assistant Secretary of the Treasury; Henry P. Davidson, senior partner of J.P. Morgan Company; Charles D. Norton, president of J.P. Morgan's First National Bank of New York; Benjamin Strong, president of Bankers Trust Company; Frank A. Vanderlip, president of the Rockefeller's National City Bank of New York which was partially owned by Kuhn, Loeb & Company and was recognized, at that time, as the most powerful banking institution in America; and Paul Moritz Warburg who represented the Rothschild dynasty as a senior partner of Kuhn, Loeb & Company. The seventh passenger was Aldrich himself.

The significance of what these men personified has been all but ignored by history for almost a century. Aside from the fact that they collectively represented slightly over one-fourth of the world's wealth, they also represented a merging—for the first time in history—of the world's five major banking cartels: the Rockefellers, the Morgans, the Rothschilds, the Kuhn-Loebs and the Warburgs.

If these men had been industrialists instead of bankers, and if the cartel that resulted from their meeting had been publicly known at the time, each would have been charged with violating the *Sherman Antitrust Act of 1890* which had been enacted by Congress to break up the Rockefeller's Standard Oil monopoly, and was later used by the federal government in 1895 to break not only a strike organized by socialist Eugene V. Debs against Carnegie Steel but to shatter Deb's union, the Amalgamated Association of Iron and Steel Workers, as well.

For this reason, among others, each was sworn to secrecy.

Years later, when Vanderlip spoke about the trip in an interview to the *Saturday Evening Post* that appeared in its February 9, 1935 issue, he admitted this fact. "We were told," he recalled, "to leave our last names behind us. We were told further that we should avoid dining together on the night of our departure. We were instructed to come one at a time and as unobtrusively as possible to the terminal of the New Jersey littoral of the

176

Hudson, where Senator Aldrich's private car would be in readiness, attached to the rear end of the train for the South.

"Discovery we knew, simply must not happen, or else all of our time and effort would be wasted, since it would be fatal to Senator Aldrich's plan to have it known that he was calling on anybody from Wall Street to help in preparing his bill. If it was publicly exposed that our group had gotten together and had written a banking bill, that bill would have no chance whatsoever of passage by Congress."

The reason was obvious. The five most powerful banking families in the world had met to form a cartel strong enough to subdue the United States of America. While their common history had been one of ruthless competition, each realized that the prize at stake—the monetary system of America—could never be singularly captured by any of them; and that to succeed against such a formidable foe, they would have to consolidate their resources and work together. It was a concept that made sense to each of them. If they were successful, there would be ample profit for all.

A meeting at this time was absolutely necessary. Profits in the cartel's government-chartered national banks were rapidly dwindling, and had been since the mid-1890s when a rash of State-chartered banks were launched throughout the South, and particularly in the western United States, to accommodate the migration of America's disillusioned working class into those developing areas with offers of free land and an unlimited opportunity to create their own American dream.

By the turn of the century, almost 70% of the banks that existed in the United States were State-chartered. They held almost 60% of the total funds on deposit in the country. Each year brought several hundred more new State banks, and each year the market shares of the Rockefeller, Morgan, Rothschild, Kuhn-Loeb and Warburg banks shrank in a direct proportion.

To make matters worse, Congress, under the control of the Democrats, enacted several very restrictive pieces of anti-big business legislation, starting with the *Sherman Act of 1890* that specifically targeted John D. Rockefeller's Standard Oil Company. The *Sherman Act* was followed by the *McKinley Tariff Act* which contained within it a reciprocal trade agreement that actually encouraged foreign trade and reduced tax revenues going into the federal treasury.

177

However, the *coup d' etat* came on March 14, 1900 when Congress passed the *Currency Act of 1900* which created a more level playing field in the banking arena by declaring that forms of money other than those created by the national banks were likewise redeemable in gold on demand, thereby reducing the capital requirements of State-charter banks and creating even more competition for the cartel banks in the major urban centers.

In 1910, shortly before the Jekyll Island meeting, Congress stepped on J.P. Morgan's toes even more by enacting the *Mann-Elkins Act* which greatly strengthened the Interstate Commerce Commission—and placed both AT&T and Western Union under the regulatory control of the I.C.C. At the time, Morgan was the single biggest stockholder in AT&T and was recognized, at least in Congress, as the unofficial head of the Bell telephone system. AT&T was currently attempting to strangle all of the competition in the communications arena that would result from the legal expiration of Alexander Graham Bell's patent rights to the telephone at midnight on March 6, 1893. However, due to some legal chicanery on the part of AT&T, those patent rights were extended until 1908.

It is a safe assumption that Morgan and Rockefeller, if not Rothschild and Warburg equally as much, suffered financially under what each viewed as a heavy-handed, overzealous Congress running amuck. Their financial losses were compounded even more as a tidal wave of Congressional free enterprise legislation created puerile opportunities for pubescent entrepreneurs—many of whom used their own capital to start new business enterprises or financed the expansion of existing ventures from earned profits rather than paying the stiff interest rates demanded by the bankers.

While most conspiracy buffs generally view the banking cartel's efforts to create a new central bank in America as a singular event, it wasn't. The Jekyll Island meeting was arranged to strategize a three-pronged attack against America that would ultimately result not only in the creation of a new central bank owned and controlled exclusively by cartel members, but would also assure them of the ratification of the proposed 16th Amendment. At the time of the Jekyll Island meeting, only nine states had ratified the amendment—and, the ratifications of five States were questionable. More pressure had to be applied on the State legislators. The successful ratification of the income tax amendment was critical to the ultimate success of the Jekyll Island meeting.

The bankers knew that the constitutionally mandated income tax would place the people of the United States in perpetual bondage to the new central bank, thus assuring the bank of adequate revenues to support any programs the government might want to initiate. Equally important, the six bankers on their way to Brunswick, Georgia that night in November, 1910 knew the toughest part of their assignment had nothing to do with banking or money — it had to do with power. Before their meeting on Jekyll Island could conclude they had to devise a scheme that would guarantee the ratification of the 17th Amendment. This was by far their most difficult assignment since that ratification would transfer of the power of the Constitution away from the States and into the hands of those whom the bankers felt could be trusted with its awesome power — themselves. It was a tall order. The States would be voting to curb their own power in Washington.

One additional item was on the Jekyll Island agenda. It would likewise require a Constitutional amendment to be successful: the removal of the United States from the gold standard. To make the currency of the United States more plentiful it would be necessary to disconnect it from the regulated price of gold. Two ends would be served. First, the currency of the United States would then become truly elastic. The amount of currency in circulation at any given time could be manipulated at will to either expand or contract the economy. Second, since gold would no longer be species it, like any other metal, would simply become a commodity with an inherent value well in excess of any other metal that was bought and sold on the open market.

The argument that would be advanced by the Aldrich forces in Congress was based on the concept that there was no difference in the minds of the American people between a debt-backed currency and one backed with gold. Money was money. And, while currency had only a conceptual value as "money" it provided a uniform and trustworthy medium of exchange that would not fluctuate with the price of gold. They would further argue that Congress had the discretion under the terms of Article I, Section 8 to regulate the uniformity of its currency; and that only the States, under Section 10, were obligated to coin their legal tender from gold or silver.

It was an argument that would fall on deaf ears in 1910.

One of those in the Senate who helped defeat the proposed

179

gold repeal measure was an Aldrich ally, Senator Elihu Root, who would also become one of the founding members of the Council on Foreign Relations in 1921. Root, like most members of Congress, viewed the proposed elimination of the gold standard as an unconscionable act that would first destroy the monetary system of the nation, and then its economy.

Root also knew if gold was allowed to become simply a commodity to be traded like wheat, corn, lumber or petroleum, there would be an exodus of gold bullion from the United States that would dwarf the Gold Crisis of 1893-95.

Initially a supporter of the re-establishment of a central bank in the United States, Root saw the awesome power which was about to be unleashed against the people of America. A few days before the scheduled Senate vote, Root joined forces with Democratic Senator Louis McFadden to denounce the legislation. "Long before we wake up from our dreams of prosperity through an inflated economy," he declared on the floor of the Senate, "our gold, which alone could have kept us from catastrophe, will have vanished — and no rate of interest will tempt it to return!" (You will recall that to solve the gold crisis in 1895 Grover Cleveland's Secretary of the Treasury had to arrange a bond sale to buy back the gold the European banks had drawn from the federal gold repositories in the United States, paying those bankers an exorbitant rate of interest to return the bullion to Fort Knox.)

T he train carrying the Jekyll Island Special rolled into Raleigh, North Carolina the following afternoon, stopping in the switching yard several hundred yards from the terminal just long enough to back Aldrich's rail car onto an isolated siding. It was quickly uncoupled. By the time the train's regular passengers had detrained at the station, Aldrich's special car was already coupled to another train heading farther south. Nobody was the wiser.

When the Jekyll Island Special was uncoupled later that night in Brunswick, Georgia it was noticed for the first time. Although Brunswick was a very small Atlantic seaboard town, the Sea Islands, which were just off the coast, had become a popular vacationing spot for the ultra-rich. It was not unusual, particularly in the winter months, to catch a glimpse of people like John D. Rockefeller or J.P. Morgan arriving to escape the blistery cold winters of New York, New Jersey and Massachusetts.

For that reason when Aldrich's car was uncoupled on a rail siding in Brunswick, it attracted every available spectator in town. The women wanted to see what the wealthy women from New York or Boston were wearing that season, and the men wanted to catch a glimpse of real power, hoping against hope that some-one named Rockefeller or Vanderbilt or Carnegie would pass the time of day with them, thereby somehow enhancing their own imagined status in the community.

Of course, there were no fancy, high-stepping big city fash-ion molls on the Aldrich car. Its only passengers were seven stuffy old men in duck hunting attire and carrying shotguns. Before Morgan's launch arrived to ferry the seven from the Brunswick dock to Jekyll Island most of the onlookers had dispersed All that remained was a few reporters looking for worthwhile gos-sip to spice up the evening news.

An insignificant blurb in the local newspaper stated only that Mr. Henry P. Davidson and a few friends had arrived at the banker's Jekyll Island retreat on November 23 to enjoy a few days of duck hunting. None of Davidson's "friends" were identi-fied in the press simply because Davidson, who was known to the newspaper, made no attempt to identify them.

The most interesting fact about the Jekyll Island meeting was not revealed until 1916 when members of Morgan's household staff were approached by a young financial reporter named B.C. Forbes who was preparing an article on the Jekyll Island meet-ing for the October 16, 1916 issue of *Leslie's Weekly* (most likely resulting from a tip by the Fed Chairman, Paul Warburg, who liked Forbes and occasionally passed him tips—as well as infor-mation that Warburg sometimes needed to get into print).

Forbes felt he could piece together a reasonably accurate pic-ture of what transpired during those nine days on Jekyll Island by interviewing each of Morgan's servants. However, he quickly discovered that none of them were even on Jekyll Island during that period. They had been granted special Thanksgiving vaca-tions by their benevolent boss, Morgan. For some reason, which simply increased the intrigue, Morgan wanted to be certain that none of the "locals" knew what was taking place at the Morgan retreat on Jekyll Island. Forbes found it interesting that Morgan would furlough not only his permanent caretaker but the entire household staff for ten days when he had a house full of very important guests—only to replace them with a temporary staff   181 of carefully selected and screened domestics that were sent to Jekyll Island from New York.

The intrigue continued throughout the entire ten days. Each of the guests were assigned an "alias," and each addressed the others only by those pseudonyms. Not once were any of them addressed by their real names—not even in private. Not even the temporary servants, who had been tediously screened by private detectives, could be trusted.

The melodramatic charade which took place on Jekyll Island has been the subject of much speculation over the past eighty years—and the subject of an equal amount of conspiracy theories. America has known since Paul Warburg's book, *The Federal Reserve System, Its Origin and Growth,* was published in 1930 that the group met to formulate the concept that was to become the Federal Reserve System. But, what else about that meeting still remains a mystery?

Several things. First, it is not generally known that the legislation that created the Federal Reserve was not written by Congressmen looking out for the best interests of their constituents. It was written on Jekyll Island by the bankers themselves.

Second, although they have heard it mentioned countless times, most Americans remain oblivious of the fact that the Fed is not a part of the federal government of the United States. It is a private corporation whose stock is exclusively owned and controlled by its principle shareholders that include: Bankers Trust Company of New York; Chase Manhattan Bank of New York; First National Bank of New York; Goldman Sachs Bank of New York; Israel Moses Seiff Banks of Italy; Kuhn-Loeb Bank of New York; Lazard Brothers Banks of Paris; Lehman Brothers Bank of New York; National City Bank of New York; the Rothschild Banks of England and Germany; and finally, the M.M. Warburg Banks of Hamburg and Amsterdam. While it is likely that shares are owned by other banks around the world, those listed above are more prominently known. *None of the stock is owned by the United States government.* Not only that, but under the terms of the establishing legislation, Fed stockholders cannot sell, pledge or transfer any of their shares to any other banks, institutions or individuals. The Fed is a closed cartel.

Under the terms of the 1913 Federal Reserve legislation, all "profits" gleaned by the Fed were to be surrendered to the Treasury of the United States. That changed in 1933. Under Roosevelt's *Banking Act of 1933* which was signed into law on June 10, only 67 days after his inauguration, all profits from the Federal Reserve Banks were to be, from that point on, retained by the Fed. The *Banking Act of 1933* and the *Bank Relief Act of 1933* which was signed into law on March 9, five days after Roosevelt's inauguration, were both written by Fed lawyers and enacted largely without debate or change by Congress.

It is not only likely but equally logical that a good portion of the discussions on Jekyll Island during those nine days centered on how to successfully conclude the ratification of the 16th and 17th Amendments, and how to get the United States off the gold standard.

Without the ability to directly tax the earning power of the citizens of the United States the Federal Reserve, like its two predecessor central banks, would have had to limit the credit of the United States to that which the government could repay through the collection of voluntary excise taxes. History clearly supports the contention that when excise taxes on any particular item or groups of items grows too extreme, people merely stop buying the taxed items and the revenue stream of the government simply trickles to a halt.

In the cases of both prior central banks in the United States, pressure applied by either the State-chartered banks or business interests within the sovereign States on the legislators who elected the U.S. Senators, caused the central bank's franchises not to be extended or rechartered. In both instances, the House of Representatives would likely have rechartered them, and perhaps may have even had the votes to enact the legislation over the Presidential vetoes which would have resulted from both James Madison and Andrew Jackson. However in both cases the Senate, under pressure from their States' assemblies back home, would not even bring the matter to the floor for a vote. In both cases it took a war before the Senate seriously entertained the notion of rechartering the central bank. In 1816, the central bank was rechartered as the Second Bank of the United States. But not even the Civil War could force the Senate to surrender America's rights to the international banking cartel again. Instead of caving in to another central bank, Congress legislated a series of national banks which, although run by the same international bankers, were more rigidly controlled by Congressional regulations. Expanded authority to State banks also proved to be an adequate check against 183 the abuses of the national banks.

All banks, State as well as national, were allowed to issue banknotes secured by government bonds emanating from the national banks. However, the State banks were assessed a tax on the banknotes they created, ostensibly to eliminate the risk of their flooding the market with unstable currency due too over-circulation. In reality, the tax was assessed for no other reason than to make the State banks less competitive by forcing them to charge higher interest rates than the national banks.

It is very likely that the bankers at Jekyll Island knew and seriously discussed that the sweeping social agenda and increased federal regulations planned for the future would probably not be welcomed by any of the State governments who would most likely view such legislation as a violation of the Constitutional separation of powers and an infringement of States' rights. If so, then for that reason as much s the first, it would be imperative to take the control of the Senate away from the States and place it in the hands of seasoned national politicians who could more easily be controlled. That, in doing so, they would violate the basic tenets of our Republican form of government would prove to be merely an added benefit.

The Morgan cartel couldn't have been more pleased. The American people had spoken. Morgan's last barrier to a successful passage of the Federal Reserve Act — Taft — had just been booted out of office. Woodrow Wilson would become the 28th President of the United States on March 4, 1913. Thanks to Philander Knox and Solicitor General Reuben Clark, the 16th and 17th Amendments had been certified as ratified. The cartel could now get down to very the profitable business of governing the government of the United States.

On December 23, 1913 Wilson fulfilled his pledge to J.P. Morgan and signed the *Federal Reserve Bank Act* into law. Wilson gave them the Christmas present they had fervently sought for 137 years — an impregnable central bank they could call their very own.

For no other reason than to deceive the American people, the new central bank would be called the "Federal" Reserve, implying by its name that it was an agency of the government of the United States. Also, in an attempt to disguise its true character, the *Federal Reserve Bank Act* divided the nation into twelve bank zones, with separate central banks located in Atlanta, Boston, Cleveland, Chicago, Dallas, Kansas City, Minneapolis, New York, Philadelphia, Richmond, St. Louis and San Francisco to make it appear as though there is not one central bank, but twelve government-sponsored federal banks that operate exclusively in the public's interest. However, although branches of the Fed were located in twelve different cities across the country, they were all part of the same system and were all controlled by one governing board in Washington pretty much the way the branches of any American corporation are controlled by its Board of Directors.

The deceptive name chosen for the new central bank did not originate in the fertile mind of Congress. It was a creation of the Jekyll Island Seven. The bankers were convinced if the electorate realized Congress was legislating another privately-owned central bank in the United States, several key members of both the House and the Senate whose votes would be critical to the future agenda of the money power might not get reelected in 1914.

Congressman Charles A. Lindbergh (D-MI) fought the Fed bill. He argued that Congress was deceiving America by calling the legislation the *Federal Reserve Bank Act of 1913* since it was not, by any stretch of the imagination, a government-owned bank. "It is a common practice," Lindbergh declared, "for Congressmen to make the titles of acts promise aright, but in the body or text of the act to rob the people of what is promised in the title." (*Lindbergh on the Federal Reserve;* Charles A. Lindbergh, Sr. © Noontide Press; 1923; pg. 70.)

Most Americans have difficulty accepting the fact that the Federal Reserve is a privately-owned central bank for several reasons. As any serious student of American government knows, Article I, Section 8 § 6 of the Constitution exclusively reserves the *unassignable authority* to create the money supply of the United States to its government. To grant that authority to an uncontrolled third party would not only violate the Constitution, it would border on rank stupidity—or perhaps even high crimes against the nation.

Yet, that is precisely what the Congress did.

On December 23, 1913 when Woodrow Wilson signed the legislation which created the Federal Reserve System, the United States surrendered all of its monetary policy rights to the same international banking cartel that had operated all of the central banks of

Europe for the better part of one hundred years. Theoretically, safeguards had been built into the *Federal Reserve Act* that would guarantee Congress adequate Congressional oversight of the Fed. Or, at least that's what the Congressmen were told. However, any mention of those oversight privileges were conspicuously absent from the version of the bill that was signed into law.

The Fed had no intention of sharing its secrets with Congress, and has not since its creation. All of its meetings are held in secret. Congress' oversight ended before it ever began.

When Paul Warburg was appointed the first Chairman of the Federal Reserve he even refused to appear before the Senate Banking Subcommittee. Warburg claimed it might impair his usefulness on the Federal Reserve Board if he was required to answer any of the questions typically posed to Presidential appointees. Nobody asked him how answering questions concerning his qualifications to head the Federal Reserve might impair his ability to function as that body's Chairman. Nor did anyone ask him about the directorships he held in ten American corporations, or whether he was planning to resign them once he was confirmed as the Chairman of the Fed.

Since Warburg refused to appear before Congress, he was confirmed without a hearing. He was not required to resign any of his directorships. And, he retained his half-million dollar per year salary with Kuhn-Loeb even though "officially" he had resigned his position.

In 1973 Congressman Wright Patman, Chairman of the House Banking Committee, sponsored legislation that would force the Fed to open its books to Congress. Much to his amazement, Patman discovered his colleagues weren't as concerned about the Fed as he was—or were more afraid of it. Opposition to his bill was landmark. Patman lobbied his colleagues almost as hard as the Fed lobbied Congress. To drum up support from his constituents and the constituents of other House members, Patman's office wrote countless letters to newspapers all over the country. Very few of those letters ever ended up in print.

In one such correspondence, printed in a weekly newsletter to his constituents, he wrote: "Although I had anticipated that officials of the Federal Reserve System would vigorously oppose my bill, I am frankly amazed by the massive lobbying campaign now underway to prevent enactment of this measure. This itself is further proof, if any is needed, that a thorough and independent audit is an absolute necessity in the public interest."

Calling in every favor owed him for thirty years, Patman's bill, or a diluted version of it, finally passed. Due to amendments, riders and deletions, Patman's audit of the Fed would be limited to administrative expenses only. Members of Congress would get to see how much it cost to run the clerical offices in the Federal Reserve. Nothing more. Patman expended all of his political clout for nothing.

He almost lost his reelection bid the following year as well. Coming back to Washington in January, 1975 with the narrowest margin of victory in his career, Patman was soon to discover he had lost his chairmanship of the banking committee as well. The word was out. Patman was too old and too senile to hold such an important chair. And, while his constituents may have wanted Patman to represent them, Patman's colleagues could no longer afford to have him represent them. Chairman Patman, one of the senior most Congressmen in the House of Representatives became Congressman Patman with less congressional pull than the junior-most freshman in the House of Representatives during his final term in office. Patman spent his last term fighting the shadow government of the Fed.

"In its 60-year history," Patman barked on the floor of the House on May 5, 1975, "the Federal Reserve System has never been subjected to a complete, independent audit, and it is the only important agency that refuses to consent to an audit by the Congress' agency, the General Accounting Office...GAO audits of the Federal Reserve will, moreover, fill the glaring gap that now exists in our information about the Fed's activities and programs. As things now stand, the only information that we get on the programs of the Fed is what the Fed itself wants us to have!" [*The Congressional Record*, May 5, 1975.]

When Patman concluded his speech, no one accepted his sanguine challenge to pick up the gauntlet and continue his fight. It was a lost battle, and although Patman uttered truths that each Congressman knew only too well, none were willing to put their careers on the line to fight a war that could not be won.

Over the years a few, like Congressman Phillip Crane (R-IL) have tried, but to no avail. Crane introduced House Resolution Bill H.R. 1468 in the 102nd Congress on March 19, 1991. H.R.

1468 would have directed the G.A.O. to audit not only the Federal Reserve hierarchy but the Federal Advisory Council, the Federal Open Market Committee and each of the twelve member banks. H.R. 1468 never surfaced to see the light of day.

An article written by Congressman Ronald Paul (R-TX), a member of the House Banking and Currency Committee, appeared in the April, 1983 issue of *National Educator*. In it Paul said, "...As a member of the House Banking Committee, I have long believed that present economic difficulties are caused principally by our centralized banking system headed by the Federal Reserve, and by the use of irredeemable paper money...I am convinced that there is no permanent solution to our severe economic problems that does not involve thorough monetary reform. This is why I have introduced [two] major pieces of legislation. The first bill, H.R. 875, would repeal the *Federal Reserve Act of 1913*, thus ending our 70-year experiment with paper money, an experiment that has obviously failed. To achieve this end, I have also introduced a bill requiring, for the first time in history, a complete audit of the Federal Reserve, H.R. 877. I believe that a thorough audit and investigation of the Federal Reserve would reveal enough damning information about the Fed that virtually all members of Congress would support its abolition..." Neither Congressman Paul nor his House Resolutions saw the light of day. Paul was defeated in his bid for re-election in 1984. Re-elected by his constituents in the 14th Congressional District of Texas in 1996, Ron Paul is once again a member of the House Banking Committee.

Paul, like Helen Chenoweth-Hage of Idaho and other strong Bill of Rights advocates in Congress, are facing a monumental battle. More than ever before the Constitution of the United States is under attack—not only from socialist zealots outside of Congress, but from many of those who, when they were elected to serve in our federal legislative body, swore an oath to uphold and protect the very document they are now attempting to destroy. One of the goals of the utopians—on both sides of the aisle—is the abolition of the 2nd Amendment in order to more peacefully pave the way for the final abrogation of the Constitution, the surrender of national sovereignty, and the creation of the global union of nation-states under the political control of the United Nations.

❖ EIGHT ❖

The 17th Amendment

The fraud that was perpetuated on the citizens of the United States by the banking cartel at Jekyll Island was easily achieved. Politicians throughout the world and throughout the ages have learned that the masses, particularly when they are either ill-informed or uninformed, are easily manipulated. After all, man has been gullibly deceived since the days of Adam.

The fraud against the American people could not have been successful without the help of the existing media of the day. It was precisely for that reason that the Rothschilds bought a controlling interest in Reuters International News Service in London, Havas News Agency in France and Wolfe in Germany, and why Fed Chairman Paul Warburg urged his father-in-law Solomon Loeb to buy an interest in the *New York Times*. Rothschild was well aware that there was much truth to the adage that whomever controls the news controls the hearts and minds of the man on the streets. J.P. Morgan apparently wholeheartedly agreed with Rothschild's assessment of the media according to U.S. Congressman Oscar Calloway.

In March, 1915 Calloway placed the following comment in the Congressional Record: "J.P. Morgan interests...got together with twelve men high up in the newspaper world and employed them to select the most influential newspapers in the United States...to control generally the policy of the daily press of the United States. These men...select[ed] 179 newspapers, and then began by an elimination process to retain only those necessary for the purpose of controlling [the news]. They found it was necessary to purchase control of 25 of the greatest newspapers."

The ploy created by Aldrich's people with respect to the 17th Amendment — and promoted equally as heavy in the press — was to convince the American voters that they had a Constitutional right to directly elect those who theoretically represented them in both

189

the House of Representatives and the United States Senate. Of course, those promoting the American wage-earner's right to elect their Senators forgot to tell them that heretofore those in the Senate represented not the citizens of their respective States, but the States themselves—whose interests are sometimes at odds with both those of the federal government and the citizens within their own boundaries.

Citizens of democratic societies are predominantly concerned with individual rights and personal freedom. That is not surprising since we live in ego-centered world where a book entitled *"Looking Out For Number One"* can top the *New York Times* best seller list. We, as a society, have been brainwashed by civil rights hucksters hawking a wide variety of social programs and political agendas aimed at convincing us that our rights as individuals supersede the rights of the communities in which we live. After all, they keep telling us, we live in a democracy.

Needless to say, unbridled individual rights and personal freedom for all members of any society are impossible to achieve since what may be pleasing and acceptable to me may be abhorrent to you. Do I have a legal license to freely exercise my prerogatives when they infringe on your right not to be subjected to my particularly distasteful habits? After all, I live in a democracy, too.

If we are equal, who decides when you and I disagree?

In a democracy, the oligarchy decides.

We have been bombarded with literally tons of political rhetoric over the past eighty years suggesting that the American people hold all of the power and establish the mandates of the nation in the voting booth.

Some Americans actually believe they do.

Our "power" as citizens of the United States extends no farther than selecting between a slate of candidates handpicked to run for elective office by someone other than ourselves. In many cases, as in the last two United States Presidential elections, none of the candidates achieved a majority. In a true democracy that doesn't matter since democracies, which are all oligarchies, are systems ruled by and for the minority, not the majority.

If you doubt that, take a few days to peruse some of the "landmark" pieces of legislation that have become law in the United States over the past fifty years and see precisely whose rights are protected—and whose are abrogated.

Every structured society in the history of the world except two have been oligarchies. Today, all of them are. It is a generally accepted view that even those nations which are viewed as either monarchies or dictatorships are in reality oligarchies since they are all ruled by a small core of elite members of those societies. This includes monarchies like Great Britain, dictatorships like China or Cuba, or even societies like Iran that claim to be theocracies.

Israel, a nation created by God for His purpose was a true theocracy only for a brief, obedient period of time. Solomon prostituted God's reign, and anarchy resulted. The nation split apart and two monarchies were formed. Neither survived.

The United States of America was created in 1787 as a Republic. International moneylenders attempted to destroy it in 1812 and again in 1861, but it survived for another 52 years before it was dismantled by the ignorance and indifference of its caretakers — the people of the United States[1].

While a good many nations call themselves Republics — like the People's *Republic* of China — only the United States, through a Constitution which limited the authority of its federal government by retaining the bulk of the governing power for the people, actually was. What made our Constitution unique was that it divided the power between the federal Executive branch, the States and the People. In doing so, it limited everyone's power, thereby

---

[1] In 1775, the Founding Fathers, in seeking the money they needed to purchase the arms, ammunition, and supplies they needed to field an army strong enough to earn their independence from England, pledged to the moneylenders of Europe the right o create a central bank in the United States at the conclusion of the war. The Constitution, by its own language, prohibited the government from surrendering the right to "coin" the money of the realm to the private banking industry. And although the moneylenders were granted a "temporary" right to "create and manage" the money supply of the United States, it was not the broad "license" the moneylenders had expected. Each time the central bank charter came up for renewal, the State-chartered banks, which greatly influenced the U.S. Senate, resisted the re-chartering of the central bank's franchise.

As this text has shown, each time the central bank's charter came up for renewal, and resistance to the continuation of the charter mounted in the U.S. Senate, America found itself embroiled in a military conflict that required it, once again, to turn to the international moneylenders.

191

protecting the rights of both the majority and the minority. But most important, it limited the power of the federal government to infringe on those rights.

By eliminating the power of the States at the federal level, the 17th Amendment altered the balance of power in Washington and changed what was a Republic into a democracy that is now ruled by an elite oligarchy that sits comfortably behind the seat of government. Today, the agenda of the government is subtly established by this power and carefully spoon-fed to America in small palatable dozes by the mainstream media which has been editorially controlled by those same powers for most of this century. *We the people* have been properly indoctrinated to accept the politically correct views — and the political agenda — of the elitists.

The technique used by the Jekyll Island group to launch their successful public relations campaign to convince the American people that they had a Constitutional right to directly elect their United States Senators is precisely the same methodology being applied today to convince Americans they have a constitutional right to directly elect the President of the United States by popular vote through the abolishment of the Electoral College.

Although the expounded rhetoric sounds like the liberal elitists both in government and in the media want to provide Americans more and not less rights, it is important to examine the consequences of such an action before America surrenders the last vestiges of its democracy and find their "Republic" has become an dictatorship with all power vested in elected leaders it cannot remove from office.

O ver the past seventy-odd years the powers delegated to both the States and the federal government have flip-flopped. The federal government has arbitrarily assumed for itself powers expressly denied it by the 10th Amendment which specifically declares that "[t]he powers not delegated to the United States by the Constitution, nor prohibited by it to the States, are reserved to the States respectively, or to the people." In other words, the federal government of the United States was not a party to its own creation thus granting it the right to reinterpret its franchise. It was not created as the ultimate governing authority — the States, by and through the People, were. That's how our Republic works.

192   Nor was the federal government endowed with the authority

to grant itself power. The narrowly construed power conferred upon the federal government was very specific and very deliberately limited to make certain the people retained the bulk of the power for themselves.

To safeguard the nation from abuses from either the People, the States or the central government, the Founding Fathers created a unique system of governance through which each shared equally in the responsibility of governing. This triune sharing of responsibility and authority was woven throughout the entire fabric of the Republic.

A bicameral legislature was established that consisted of a House of Representatives whose members were elected for two years, and a Senate whose members were elected for six. This was not an accident, nor was it a whim of the moment. The fledging nation had fought a six year war to break the shackles of an intolerable and oppressive oligarchy. The Founding Fathers wanted to make certain the system of government they created was one in which the People, not a small group of self-interested powerful politicians, made the laws and controlled the power. Congressmen, who directly represented the will of the citizens within their congressional districts, were elected to a minimal term of office so the people could quickly replace them if they abused that responsibility or failed to act in the best interests of their constituency.

Senators, who were responsible to protect the rights of the States in the federal arena, were elected by the State legislatures for terms of six year. Senators, with a term of office two years longer than most of the governors and state legislators who elected them, were theoretically insulated from partisan State politicking since their terms exceeded those who elected them. If the people did not like what their Senators were doing, they had to replace the State legislators who elected the Senators.

To offset the powers granted to Congress, a limited amount of clearly specified powers were delegated to the federal government to be exercised through the President of the United States. These duties, responsibilities and authority are specifically detailed in Article II, Section 2 of the Constitution.

Since the States were perfectly capable of governing themselves, all of the powers delegated to the federal government and specifically, to the Executive Branch through the auspices of the President, dealt exclusively with national or international matters. The President, according to the Constitution, was to be the elected official of the States to deal with foreign powers in the name of the various *united* States. The President does not now have, nor has he ever possessed, the Constitutional authority to propose or mandate sweeping and costly social welfare programs or healthcare legislation. Nor for that matter does the Congress of the United States. According to the Constitution, these are pre-rogatives reserved exclusively for the legislatures of the various States — a fact that has been ignored by Congress and the White House since 1933.

According to Article I, Section 8 of the Constitution, Congress has the authority to levy certain taxes, regulate commerce with foreign governments and among the various States, create and define bankruptcy laws, coin money, protect the currency of the United States, establish a Post Office, create a national system of roads, legislate patent laws, determine the rules by which citizenship is granted, define the laws of the admiralty and prosecute felonies on the high seas; raise, support and maintain an army and a navy to protect the confederation, and whenever necessary, to declare war on enemies of the United States in order to protect its sovereign people from the threat of tyranny. Congress was not granted the authority by the Constitution to grant itself any of the powers reserved for either the States or the People.

J ust like everything else the Founding Fathers did to make certain that power was shared equally between the People and the States, they devised a unique dual voting system by which both the People and the States would have a somewhat equal say in the election of the President.

However, because the President is the duly elected constitutional agent of the States, he is directly elected by *electors* selected by the States rather than by popular vote. The popular vote in November determines which slate of electors will be allowed to cast its ballots for the President on the first Monday after the second Wednesday in December. It is at this time that the President of the United States is actually elected.

The political debate questioning the need for an Electoral College has raged in this country for much of this century. Critics of the system have argued, and rightfully so, that in a winner-take-all scenario the candidate who wins the popular vote by a margin of one vote takes the same number of electoral votes as the candidate who wins by a majority of one million votes. And, likewise, the candidate who loses by one vote loses everything. These critics further argue that by allowing such an inequity to exist, the minority vote within any State is disfranchised. Furthermore they argue that a candidate with fewer popular votes could — and has — been elected simply by carrying the key electoral States. Which is precisely why the system was created. When the People and the States agree, *as they have in every two-party race for the Presidency that has ever occurred,* the winning candidate achieves victory with the popular plurality. When the People disagree with the States, the States elect the President.

Three Presidents have been elected in this manner. John Quincy Adams defeated Andrew Jackson in 1824 with fewer popular votes in an election that was ultimately settled in the House of Representatives. The same was true of Rutherford B. Hayes' victory over Samuel J. Tilden. In 1888, Grover Cleveland lost his re-election bid to Benjamin Harrison with 48.6% of the popular vote to 47.9% for Harrison. Third party spoiler candidates took 3.5% of the popular vote — and the election — away from Cleveland[2].

Interestingly, in each of these contests, more than two candidates vied for the office of President. In each contest except one

---

[2]The American electoral system slowly evolved into a three-candidate system after the election of 1824; and then into a "political party" system dominated by two major parties between 1848 and 1856 after the death of the Whigs and the Anti-Masons. While any natural born American citizen over the age of 35 has the right to seek the highest office in the land as an independent candidate, or has the constitutional right to create a political party with a whole slate of candidates vying for national State, county and municipal office, the hierarchy of the "party system" has made it almost virtually impossible for anyone other than one of the two primary party candidates to win an election—at any level of governance.

In 1888 Grover Cleveland incurred the anomosity of the industrialists when he stood against the promulgation of powerful industrialist monopolies like the Standard Oil Trust, the Sugar Trust, the Distillers and Cattle Feeders Trust (also known as the Whiskey Trust), the Lead Trust and the Cotton Oil Trust. At the same time, talks were going on between the British Imperial Tobacco Company and the American Tobacco Company to form an international tobacco trust; and the DeBeers Combination was,

the third party spoilers took the popular votes from the candidate who ultimately lost the election. In two-party races, no Presidential candidate has achieved victory without gaining a plurality of the popular vote. Spoilers, or third party candidates, are usually introduced into national elections to siphon votes from either an incumbent seeking re-election or an extremely popular front-runner. This was the case in 1912 when Woodrow Wilson defeated incumbent William Howard Taft, in 1992 when Bill Clinton defeated George Bush[3], and again it was the same strategy utilized by incumbent Clinton to assure his victory over Republican challenger Bob Dole in 1996.

---

at the same time, attempting to control not only the international price of diamonds but gold as well.

Cleveland's opponent in 1888, Senator Benjamin Harrison [R-IN], was a "party man" who opposed reigning in the trusts. He was the candidate of the industrialists. The media championed Harrison—the Republican—and promoted him as a "man of the people." Cleveland—the Democrat—who fought both the industrialists and the bankers, was painted as the candidate of big business because he resisted congressional efforts to create a taxpayer-funded welfare system in America, with the *Washington Post* and the *New York Times* leading the fight to defeat Cleveland in what the *Post* described as "...a campaign of argument, not of brag or bluster." [*See How They Ran: The Changing Role of the Political Candidate;* Gil Troy © 1996; Harvard University Press, pg. 94.] Cleveland won the popular vote—5,540,050 (or 48.7%) against 5,444,337 votes for Harrison (or 47.8%), but lost the election in the Electoral College 233 votes to 168. In 1884, Republican reformers called the Mugwumps and headed by former Senator Roscoe Conkling (who actually wanted to perpetuate the spoils system), fractured the GOP and brought about the election of Cleveland.

Cleveland, however, refused to pander to the patronage system that got him elected, and fought to keep tariff's low when the industrial interests that Conkling represented wanted higher tariffs. Harrison, who was a "party man" through-and-through, was better suited for the industrialists. The Mugwumps fractured the Democratic vote in 1888, and by taking 3.5% of the popular vote, shifted the electoral college vote in favor of Harrison.

[3]Evidence found in the *Diebold Report* contained within the working papers of the failed Hillary Clinton *Health Security Act* working papers in the National Archive (which will be discussed in greater detail later in this text) clearly suggests that Ross Perot's "spoiler" candidacy in both 1992

The Electoral College represents the last vestige of power the States possess to impact the political process in the United States. Ultimate power was Constitutionally reserved for the people through the most unique system of government in the world: one in which the trappings of governance would be evenly delegated to independent legislative, judicial and executive branches to assure that the strength of the government would never exceed the strength of the people who elected it.

When the 17th Amendment was ratified, the delicate balance of power that had previously existed between the States, the People and the federal government was dramatically tilted. The powers reserved for the States were surreptitiously absorbed by the federal government, creating a lopsided balance of power which favors the bureaucracy through unconstitutionally regulated mandates that are reinforced by a federal court system that now makes a common practice of overruling State courts dealing with State issues. Today, most of the Constitutional rights formerly possessed by the People have been altogether abridged by an ever-increasingly intrusive federal state.

Yet, in the eyes of liberal bureaucrats, the balance of power must still shift more to the left, away from the republican form of government envisioned by our Founding Fathers, and more towards the parliamentary forms of government found in coun-

---

and 1996 was specifically tailored to dilute the popular vote going to Bush in 1992 and Dole in 1996.

An analysis of the voting patterns in 1996 was done by the author in which the votes won by Ross Perot were credited to Bob Dole in each State where either a Democratic Senate or House incumbent lost his or her seat to a Republican, or where a Republican won an open seat in either a House or Senate race, thus indicating a preference for the GOP agenda over that of the Democrats. In doing so, and eliminating Perot from the equation, Dole would have won the popular vote by a 51% to 49% margin, and would have taken 273 electoral votes and the election of 1996. If all of Perot's votes were given to Dole, Dole would have experienced a Ronald Reagan-style landslide over Clinton. (Since the author did not have the state-by-state vote tally for 1992, no such analysis could be made. However, by taking the total votes Perot earned in 1992 and giving them to Bush, it is clear that in a two-party race, Bush would have easily won re-election in 1992.

tries like Great Britain and France.

In the closing days of the 19th century, Princeton scholar Woodrow Wilson lamented over the weakness of the American presidency compared to the power of the Prime Minister of England. Wilson argued that the coalescence of the Executive and Legislative branches of the United States government was the only solution to what he perceived as an inherent weakness in the system of governance created by our Founding Fathers. He complained in his book *Congressional Government* that the separation of the Executive and Legislative branches fractured power too much and prevented accountability to the electorate. "...[P]ower," he concluded, "and strict accountability for its use are the essential constituents of good Government." [*The Frozen Republic: How The Constitution Is Paralyzing Democracy*; Daniel Lazare © 1996; Harcourt & Brace, pgs. 142-148.]

Wilson ignored the fact that absolute power negates both the need and value of accountability. He also ignored the fact that almost all of the parliamentary systems in the world today lack vigilant bipartite legislatures with the power to either investigate or curb abuses by overzealous chief executives. Wilson also conveniently ignored the fact that the more diverse the separation of power, the more real power is retained by the people. Which was, of course, the real point of his argument.

In 1910, the invisible power behind the throne of government embarked on a nationwide public relations campaign to convince the American people that they had a Constitutional right to directly elect those Senators who represented them in the Congress of the United States. If, in fact, the Senate's role in Congress was to represent the rights of the people individually or collectively rather than having a Constitutional obligation to protect the rights of the States, the argument—and the 17th Amendment—would have been valid.

However, it was the duty of the Congress to protect the rights of their constituents. That's how a Republic works. Each separate power: the federal government, the States, and the People, had an advocate in the nation's capitol to protect them. The People had the House of Representatives, the States had the Senate, and the federal government had the President who, with the aid of the United States Supreme Court to weigh the Constitutionality of the laws legislated in the Congress, held the power of veto over any federal legislation he felt was detrimental to the interests of the sovereign nation. Most Americans do not understand the principles which made our Republican form of government work from 1787 to 1913, and why it no longer functions today.

Quite simply, it no longer works because the balance of power was stripped from the States. On March 6, 1933 the federal government *temporarily* assumed all of the powers granted the various States by the Constitution when the newly elected President, Franklin Delano Roosevelt, declared a state of national emergency and enacted the sweeping powers afforded Presidents in times of war under Woodrow Wilson's *Trading With The Enemy Act*. By March 9 Roosevelt, at the urging of the Governors of the Federal Reserve, had already begun the tedious and illegal task of dismantling the Constitution of the United States, thereby eliminating forever the last traces of real power from the States. With it also came the final abrogation of the power of the People.

Would Roosevelt have been allowed to pursue a socialist legislative agenda that violated every precept of the Constitution if the 17th Amendment had not been ratified? Not likely.

Roosevelt, claiming an extreme national emergency existed, began lobbying the governors of the various States as early as mid-November, 1932—only a week or two after his election, and some four and a half months before his inauguration as President, to support what he knew would be dangerously unconstitutional and impeachable actions. It is likely he would have gotten much of his "emergency package" passed regardless, since the nation was frightened and was reacting to the economic crisis promulgated by the Federal Reserve more out of fear than sober deliberation.

Quite possibly, if the Constitutionally created balance of power in Washington had still existed in 1933, much of the more extreme elements of Roosevelt's socialist New Deal agenda, in particular those which the Supreme Court almost immediately declared to be unconstitutional, as well as the repeal of the gold standard which the high court upheld, might not have been proposed—at least, not on the first day of Roosevelt's administration.

Today, the debate is centered on the Electoral College. The same special interest groups that suggested Americans had the right to directly elect their Senators are now advising the American people that the Electoral system should be abolished, and that the American voter has the right to directly elect the President by popular vote without interference from the States. Be-   **199** fore any more Americans jump on the "Abolish the Electoral College" bandwagon, they need to understand precisely how much more it will cost them to eliminate the last vestige of Constitutional power from the States. Anyone who takes the time to analyze the advantages and pitfalls of such an action will discover the cost to abolish the Electoral College will be remarkably high. The price tag will be the Constitution itself.

In the fall of 1980 an article written by former Clinton White House counsel Lloyd N. Cutler appeared in *Foreign Affairs*, the Council on Foreign Relations magazine, in which Cutler discussed the merits of consolidating the Executive and Legislative branches of the United States government to eliminate what Cutler termed the "legislative gridlock" that had plagued the Carter Administration for most of its four years.

Cutler's argument, which he admitted would require "...modest changes that would make our structure work somewhat more in the manner of a parliamentary system..." was fraught with Constitutional inconsistencies. Since Congress, the federal judicial system, and the White House have ignored the legal precepts of that document since 1933 it was not in the least surprising that Cutler simply noted, when casually suggesting that the President should be allowed "...to select 50% of his cabinet from among the members of his party in the Senate and the House, who would retain their seats while serving in the cabinet..." that "...it would require a change in Article I, Section 6, which provides that 'no person holding any office under the United States shall be a member of either house during his continuance in office'."

Cutler, who became an integral part of an Administration that apparently saw no evil in *conflicts of interest,* apparently saw none in his own suggestion that Congressmen be allowed to serve in White House positions at the same time they were purportedly serving their own constituents, viewing such in his own words as merely a "minor infringement on the constitutional principle of separation of powers." Of course, Cutler, who has been close to the seat of power for almost two decades more clearly understands something most Americans are just now beginning to grasp: all power today is vested in the federal government, and the lines of separation between the Executive and Legislative branches are so skewed that they are almost nonexistent. That,

200

of course, is not what our Founding Fathers envisioned, nor is it what the Constitution intended.

Cutler began his argument by declaring that "...under the U.S. Constitution it is not now feasible to 'form a government.' The separation of powers between the legislative and executive branches, whatever its merits in 1793, has become a structure that almost guarantees stalemate today...This difficulty is of course compounded when the president's party does not...hold the majority of the seats in both houses...In such cases the Constitution does not require or even permit the holding of a new election, in which those who oppose the president can seek office to carry out their own program...As a result the stalemate continues." (*American Government: Readings and Cases;* Peter Woll; Scott, Foreman and Company © 1990; pgs. 54-55.)

Cutler failed to note that during Carter's Administration, the gridlock was created by Carter's own party which controlled both houses of Congress. The same is true of the gridlock that permeated the first two years of Clinton's Administration. Gridlock did not cease until the Republicans took control of both Houses in 1994. Hardly a good defense for attorney Cutler's argument—but, very much the reason for it.

"Compare this system," Cutler continued, "with the structure of parliamentary governments. A parliamentary government *may have no written constitution,* as in the United Kingdom...The majority elects a premier or prime minister from among its numbers, and he or she selects the other members of the majority as members of the cabinet. The majority as a whole is responsible for forming and conducting the government...At all times the voting public knows who is in charge and whom to hold accountable for success or failure." (*ibid;* pg. 55.) (Emphasis, author.)

Cutler declared that "...We now vote for a presidential candidate and a vice-presidential candidate as an inseparable team. We could require that in presidential election years voters in each Congressional district vote for a trio of candidates, as a team, for president, vice-president and member of Congress. This would tie the political fortunes of the party's presidential and congressional candidates to one another and give them some incentives for sticking together after they are elected. Such a proposal could be combined with a four-year term for members of the House of Representatives." (*ibid;* pg. 64.)

Cutler's suggestion, which was actually the brainchild of   201

Representative Jonathan Bingham (D-NY), is as logically flawed as Cutler's opening remarks for several reasons.

First, by linking the election of our Congressmen to the election to the President, he or she merely becomes a member of the President's team — the majority. Second, the percentage of Republicans to Democrat in the House of Representatives would then be found to be in a direct proportion to the percentage of popular vote won by the President. In theory, the White House would always control the House of Representatives — and the purse strings of America. It would be impossible for the electorate to give the White House to one political party and both Houses of Congress to another as they did in every election from 1980 to 1996, with the single exception of 1992. Third, since the Congressmen could not be elected without the President, party-line voting would become mandatory, denying the voter the right to choose from the field of candidates seeking office. The voter could not split his or her ticket, voting for the Presidential candidate of one party and a congressional candidate in another. This would also likely preclude any third party candidates from ever being elected, particularly if that nominee did not field a full slate of Congressional candidates as well. Finally, by granting Congressmen a four year term, constituency accountability would be delayed by two years. And even then, the only way the voter could punish the Congressman for malfeasance would be to not vote for his or her party's candidate for President in the next election.

Interestingly, this plan will work only if the Electoral College is eliminated. As long as the States elect the President through the Electoral College, it remains possible for a presidential nominee to win a majority of the popular votes, but lose the key electoral States and with them, the election.

Cutler, in his *Foreign Affairs* article, suggested that his idea, drastic as it sounds, is the only way to eliminate Congressional gridlock — which he attributed to an innate structural defect in our current two-party electoral system. His argument initially and superficially suggests that the *structural defect* manifests itself when one political party takes the White House and the other holds Congress. However, his motives are clarified when he says: "President Carter's party had a much larger majority percentage in both houses of Congress than Chancellor [Helmut] Schmidt or Prime Minister [Margaret] Thatcher ...But this comfortable majority did not even begin to ensure that he or any other president could rely on that majority to vote for each element of his program. *No member of that majority had the constitutional duty or the practical political need to do so. Neither the president nor the leaders of the legislative majority had the means to punish him if he did not."* (*ibid;* pg. 56.) (Emphasis, author.)

Clearly, the gridlock Cutler referred to was not that which might exist when neither party has a clear majority since, as Cutler admitted, Carter had a larger majority in the American Congress than either Schmidt and Thatcher had in their respective parliaments. In fact, other than in 1946-48, 1954-60 and 1968-76, the Democrats have controlled both Houses of Congress in every election in the 20th century until 1994. And, they controlled the House of Representatives unabated from 1946 to 1994. The gridlock Cutler envisioned was that which exists when the majority party rebels against its own chief executive — as the Democrats did against Carter and, again in 1992-94, against Clinton.

The argument Cutler postulated was not one of gridlock, it was accountability. Neither Carter nor Clinton could enact their costly globalist programs simply because Congress was accountable to the electorate. They wanted to get re-elected.

To whom should Congress be accountable? Under our Constitution, Congress is directly accountable to the People who retain the authority to turn their elected representatives out of office if they are not satisfied with their performance (although, admittedly, the voters have not been doing their jobs very well as of late). That is what Cutler would change.

Cutler, and those of his political affinity, would further erode the Constitution — and the power of the People — by making Congress accountable not to them, but to the President in the final *coup d' état* against the Constitution of the United States.

Cutler's final suggestion — and the whole purpose of his article was "...to provide the president with the power, to be exercised not more than once in his term, to dissolve Congress and call for new congressional elections...For obvious reasons, the president would [be able to] invoke such a power only as a last resort, but his ability to do so could have a powerful influence on congressional responses to his initiatives. This...would significantly enhance the president's power to form a government." (*ibid;* pg. 65.) Of course it would. It would also completely erase whatever remnants of the separation of powers that still remain at this time. But then, that was the purpose of the plan.

Cutler's plan advocated a system in which the legislative branch of government would be merged with the executive branch and made answerable to the President of the United States.

Cutler's plan would also necessarily empower the Congress, with a majority of two-thirds of both houses concurring, to call for a new presidential election. This, of course, would create ultimate gridlock. With both factions possessing equal power to call for the new election of the other faction, neither side would likely utilize such a weapon, since it would ultimately mean their own recall as well. But again, the ability of one or both factions in a unicameral government that is accountable only to itself to recall each other isn't really the point.

What is specifically the point is the issue of accountability and whether Congress should be accountable to their constituency or to the White House. If the voter is removed from the equation of accountability, then all power in all matters will be arbitrarily assumed by the federal government. It will no longer matter which political party is in the majority since the entire electorate will become the minority. Power will have passed completely from the people and into the hands of the oligarchy.

Cutler, like so many others, dismissed the separation of power as a unnecessary structural defect in the Constitution, and completely ignored the constituency accountability that is mandated by our Republican form of government. Americans were Constitutionally empowered not only with the authority but the responsibility to control both the power and scope of their government through an intricate system of checks and balances that included the voting booth. Since the ratification of the 17th Amendment and the abrogation of States' rights, the voting booth now remains the only venue Americans possess to right the wrongs foisted on them by their government.

Under a system such as the one envisioned by Cutler, those seeking Congressional office would most likely and ultimately be selected for candidacy not through a traditional primary as they are now but rather, by special interest caucuses backing the national tickets, based on the candidate's political ideology or his or her pledge to support the party's national platform. The issues promoted as germane during the political season would be those fostered by the special interest groups rather those seeking representation before Congress.

And more than ever before, the promises made to the elec-

torate would be only so much Cinderella rhetoric since all legislation would be national in scope and would begin and end at
the White House. Diversity of individuality within all of the
political parties would vanish since none of the Congressional
candidates would possess the power to act outside the party's
proposed mandate. Nor, for that matter, would State, County or
Local officials. Each, regardless of his or her level of officiousness, would be grafted into the national ticket and into national
politics, giving the person at the top of the ticket such far-reaching authority that he could ultimately impact such things as local
zoning regulations and whether or not a residential subdivision,
shop-ping complex or industrial plant could be built. In other
words, the President of the United States could, if he so desired,
decide whether or not you could expand your local business — or
build a new garage on your residential property, therein more directly tying your personal fortunes to your national voting record.

Cutler, in advancing his proposal that the United States adopt
an electoral system like that of England, France or Russia, overlooked one key element. According to the Constitution, the States
are sovereign, and the power of the federal government is subservient to those of the various States. Cutler's plan requires that
the Constitutional rights of the States be completely obliverated,
their borders erased, and each State invisibly absorbed into the
cauldron of a stateless nation. To accomplish this, the Constitution itself must be abolished.

Cutler further argues that there are only two ways to reform the
government of the United States and avoid or eliminate
gridlock: either by a Constitutional amendment, which he admits would be difficult to accomplish since it would interrupt
the Congressional status quo. (It is highly unlikely that any Congressman or Senator would introduce a Constitutional amendment that would entwine their fortunes with the political fate of
any President.) That leaves a Constitutional Convention. Cutler
acknowledges that since his proposal would devastate the concept
of separation of powers "...any idea of a national constitutional convention on the separation of powers is probably a nonstarter." (*ibid;*
pg. 67.)

There is a third, and more permanent, way.

At some point, through some real or artificially created state of emergency the President of the United States, using the special powers granted his office by Wilson's *War Powers Act*, could simply suspend the Constitution.

As unimaginable as it may sound to a reasonable mind, such a contemplation is not only possible, but may very well prove to be imperative to maintain the timetable of the globalists to implement world government by 2012, since one of the key tenets of the New World Order is the abolition of all individual nation-states. As long as the Constitution of the United States rules the conduct of politicians in America, it cannot happen. The Constitution, therefore, must go—sacrificed as a roadblock on the information superhighway that is speeding mankind towards a world dominated by the New World Order.

The first Constitutional cornerstone to be shattered was that which guaranteed the States an equal voice in Congress. This was accomplished with the "successful" ratification of the 17th Amendment on April 8, 1913.

To those who now want to completely dismantle the Constitution, the passage of the 17th Amendment proved its destruction could be accomplished over a period of time providing the American people were properly conditioned by the media to accept the idea that the Constitution is an outmoded, obsolete document that will impede America's progress into the 21st century.

As a student of history for many years it has always intrigued me that the States, which must ratify any Constitutional amendment before it becomes law, would ratify an Amendment to the Constitution of the United States that would silence forever their voice—and authority—in Congress.

Like its 16th Amendment Siamese twin, for the 17th Amendment to be considered legally ratified, 36 States needed to forward Secretary of State Philander Knox a certified copy of the Resolution passed by each State's legislature in accordance with the laws of the sovereign States governing such actions, together with the House and Senate journals verifying their ratification. In other words, the recorded votes of each State must have accompanied the ratified Resolution which, itself, must be passed precisely as it is submitted to the States by Congress. Since the Constitution was mute on the percentage of the majority vote needed to ratify a Constitutional amendment, whether by a simple majority or a 2/3 vote, the laws governing such votes within the sovereign States would necessarily prevail. Most requires a 2/3 majority to ratify a Constitutional amendment.

In our examination of the 16th Amendment we looked at the substance of the text being ratified, the amount of votes required to ratify the amendment, and the questionable legality of some State legislators voting on a tax bill which their own Constitutions denied them the right to vote on.

Our examination of the ratification of the 17th Amendment will deal with only two elements: the number of votes cast in the various States, and the method of notification of ratification to the Secretary of State. Nothing else is needed to show that the 17th Amendment, like the 16th, was fraudulently certified as ratified. As mentioned in a previous chapter, Senate Document 240 details the ratification of each constitutional amendment up to, and including, the 21st Amendment.

The information cited to negate the legality of the 17th Amendment comes from the government's own records — S.D. 240 (pages 12 and 13) which lists each State's ratification and substantiating documentation.

According to S.D. 240, 36 States — the exact number of States required — ratified the 17th Amendment at the time it was certified. The following year, on June 11, 1914 Louisiana was added to the list of States ratifying the amendment. However, at the time that Knox certified the 17th Amendment as ratified, he knew positively that at least two of the ratifications were invalid since the necessary 2/3 vote required by the Constitutions of at least two States — Vermont and Connecticut — had not been achieved. For all practical purposes, the government was still two States short of the required 36 it needed to declare the 17th Amendment legally ratified when they certified it as such.

Two States (Utah and Delaware) formally rejected it; and 9 States (Alabama, Florida, Georgia, Kentucky, Maryland, Mississippi, Rhode Island, South Carolina and Virginia) declined to vote on it. To invalidate the 17th Amendment it is necessary only to show that two of the States counted among those ratifying it did not legally do so.

The first of these States is Connecticut. According to S.D. 240, Connecticut ratified the 17th Amendment on April 8, 1913, and was the State Knox used to certify the passage of the amendment. In the Connecticut House 228 Representatives cast their

207

votes on the amendment. One hundred fifty-one delegates voted for ratification. However, 152 votes were required by their Constitution for a 2/3 majority in the House. The measure failed by one vote. Additionally, no Journal was submitted to verify the actual Senate vote as required by law. According to S.D. 240, the Connecticut Senate passed the amendment without a recorded vote (Connecticut Senate Journal, pg. 648), which invalidates the ratification since a recorded vote is mandatory. However, the ratification falls on the House vote alone.

Vermont is the second state whose recorded vote was not sufficient. According to SD 240, Vermont ratified the 17th Amendment on February 18, 1913 — and then again, a day later. Apparently the State bosses wanted it ratified so bad they declared it such twice. However, neither the House nor the Senate did. One hundred ninety-eight House members cast their votes on the measure. One hundred thirty-two votes were needed for ratification. Only 123 "yeas" were cast. Likewise 16 of the State's 24 Senators needed to vote "yea." It fell one vote short. Even though neither chamber of the Vermont legislature successfully passed the measure, it was certified as ratified.

According to the Louisiana House Journal, page 271, there was no recorded vote on the matter. The Senate Journal was not sent to Knox, suggesting that on an unrecorded voice vote in the Louisiana House only, the 17th Amendment was passed.

Massachusetts, which supposedly ratified the 17th Amendment on May 17, 1912, did so according to S.D. 240 ...without a division..." by acclamation. Yet, documentation shows only a Senate vote although both the Massachusetts House and Senate Journals were forwarded to Knox.

New Hampshire likewise submitted its journals to the Secretary of State on February 18, 1913. The House vote is recorded on page 378 and the Senate vote on pages 110 and 111. Yet, only the Senate vote, 20 to 2 is entered in S.D. 240.

S.D. 240, in acknowledging the ratification on January 24, 1913 by North Carolina noted only that "...The House passed the resolution ratifying this amendment with division...[the] Senate Journal [is] not available." In other words, there existed no documented verification that the North Carolina Senate had either voted on, or passed the amendment even with a simple majority vote. Yet, it was declared "ratified" by the Secretary of State.

In addition to Vermont and Connecticut which did not legally ratify the 17th Amendment, the ratifications of four additional States are also in jeopardy since the recorded votes of the legislatures were never submitted, nor were they acknowledged by the federal government, suggesting if such documentation did exist, the vote was well below that needed for passage. Only 31 States, according to S.D. 240, verifiably ratified the 17th Amendment — 5 states short of the required 3/4th majority.

The 17th Amendment was illegally and improperly certified as ratified on April 8, 1913.

Even though it has been the most destructive assault levied against the Constitution to date, it is not likely that the validity of the 17th Amendment will ever be challenged before the Supreme Court. Eighty-seven years have passed since the "crime" was committed and no injured parties have yet stepped forward. Other than the States themselves, who can legally claim they have been damaged and, more important, how could they prove it?

Clearly, they can easily prove fraud on the part of Philander Knox with respect to the certification. On May 23, 1985 Assistant U.S. Attorney David Brown openly admitted, on the record, that Knox committed a felony by certifying the ratification of the 16th Amendment. The litmus test applied by Knox to the 17th Amendment resolutions was the same. Six of the resolutions offered to secure passage of the 17th Amendment were clearly illegal, yet no protest has ever been launched. Was it a crime without victims?

Or was it, perhaps, a crime in which the victims — the American people — do not yet realize they have been victimized?

In 1913, Charles A. Beard published his now famous text, *An Economic Interpretation of the Constitution,* in which he suggested that the Constitution was the work of a cohesive, conspiratorial group of economic elitists — wealthy landholders, merchants and lawyers — who merely wanted to safeguard their property by placing limitations on majority rule.

Beard's thesis, published shortly after the ratification of the 17th Amendment, claimed that the Constitution, from its initial adoption to its final ratification, was never supported by the majority of the people in the States. He also claimed that those selected to attend the conventions were not selected by universal

209

suffrage, but rather were "handpicked" at the discretion of the various State legislatures. Beard argued that only the wealthy landowners, wealthy merchants, and wealthy lawyers were allowed to attend, precluding any participation from the "popular majority" who did not support the Constitution's ratification. Beard's allegations were closely examined at the time (since in 1913, men in high political positions in America and elsewhere already viewed the Constitution as an outmoded, structurally deficient document that hindered the performance of government). [*American Government, 10th Edition;* Peter Woll © 1990; Scott, Foreman, Little & Brown; pg. 36.]

The evidence, however, simply didn't support Beard's theory. Most of the key leaders of the Constitutional movement, including James Madison, were not wealthy men. (Beard might have been confused with the signers of the Declaration of Independence since most of them, including Thomas Jefferson, John Hancock, Samuel Adams, Patrick Henry, Benjamin Franklin, Richard Henry Lee and others, were.)

Beard's writings clearly affirm he was not an avid fan of the Constitution, yet in a later work entitled *The Economic Basis of Politics and Related Writings by Charles A. Beard;* compiled by William Beard and Miriam B. Vagts; Vintage Books © 1957) he is quoted as saying: "This very system of checks and balances, which is undeniably the essential element of the Constitution, is built upon the doctrine that the popular branch of the government cannot be allowed full sway...The exclusion of the direct popular vote in the election of the President; the creation, again by indirect election, of the Senate...bear[s] witness to the fact that the underlying purpose of the Constitution was not the establishment of popular government by means of parliamentary majorities. What was created — and what the Founding Fathers intended to create — was a constitutional Republic, not a parliamentary democracy. Granted, the ratification of the 17th Amendment in 1913, and the diluting of the separations of powers changed our mode of governance into one, but that it not what our forefathers intended."

Alexander Hamilton, one of those who helped frame both the Declaration of Independence and the Constitution of the United States, noted in *The Federalist Papers:* "The framers of our Constitution attempted to structure the government in such a way that it would meet the needs and aspirations of the people and at the same time check the arbitrary exercise of political power.

The doctrine of separation of powers was designed to prevent any one group from gaining control of the national government apparatus." (*Federalist 1*; October, 1787.)

In his overview of *Federalist 10* penned by James Madison, Peter Woll wrote: "The separation of powers among the executive, legislative and judicial branches is an outstanding characteristic of our constitutional system. A uniquely American separation of powers incorporated an *independent* executive, pitting the president against Congress and requiring their cooperation to make the government work. The separation of powers was a constitutional filter through which political demands had to flow before they could be translated into public policies.

"James Madison clearly saw the separation-of-powers system...as a process that would help prevent arbitrary and excessive governmental actions." (*American Government; ibid;* pg. 52.)

Today, the Republic is dead. It death rattle began on April 8, 1913. From the ashes of the Republic, a democracy began to take root in the fertile soil of American ideology. Democracy, however, was not destined to survive for long. But, before it could be anchored into America's blood-fought heritage, democracy died twenty years later on March 9, 1933, replaced by a socialist oligarchy that still exists today.

Ironically, the United States is an oligarchy with a uniquely written Constitution that still protects its citizens from the abuses of the democratic oligarchy that Americans, through their ignorance of their own Constitution, allowed to assume power.

How long that stalwart protection remains depends entirely on the American people.

"Conviction of politicians—certainly; conviction of civil servants—no."

Lord Bancroft, head of England's Civil Service
In a lecture given, Dec. 1, 1983

"Ninety percentage of the politicians give the other ten percent a bad name."

Henry Kissinger
Washington Post, January 20, 1977, attributed to him

"I was persuaded that government was a practical thing made for the happiness of mankind, and not to furnish out a spectacle of uniformity to gratify the schemes of visionary politicians."

Edmund Burke,
Letters to the Sheriffs of Bristol, 1777

"Among a people generally corrupt, liberty cannot long exist."

Edmund Burke,
Letters to the Sheriffs of Bristol, 1777

❖ NINE ❖

The Disavowed White House Protocol

E ven with a focus group-originated "political make-over" that turned the extremely liberal Arkansas governor Bill Clinton into the safe, moderate "New Democrat," Clinton couldn't squeak above 45% in the honest, private in-house voting pattern polls.

Clinton needed help if he was going to get elected.

That "help" came from an unlikely source.

Texas billionaire H. Ross Perot officially threw his tight-fitting ten gallon hat into the ring after announcing in April, 1992 that he would run for President as an Independent providing his "supporters" got him on the ballot in all 50 states. Later, the "supporters" he mentioned in that initial briefing would prove to be paid campaign workers, but for the moment his colorful candidacy was good press.

Perot appealed to the media for two reasons. First, by denouncing "business as usual in Washington" he gained immediate nationwide approval. Second, by funding his own campaign without special interest contributions, he came across as a man who could not be "bought." Documents suggesting that he may have been "bought" would not be revealed for four years.

Although the network polls suggested those interviewed during the California and Ohio Democratic primaries would vote for Perot instead of Clinton in the general election, the reality was that both Clinton's and Bush's private polls now showed Clinton neck-to-neck with Bush.

During the summer of 1992, the unpredictable and somewhat eccentric Perot suddenly dropped out of the race. Both Bush and Clinton scrambled to attract the Perot "supporters" who were, at that time, still largely paid Perot employees. The reason for Perot's surreptitious last minute return to the campaign would not become known until 1996.

While Perot knocked Clinton during the 1992 Presidential debates by referring to him the governor of the "chicken State," and suggesting that managing the smallest economy in the nation did not qualify Clinton for the job of managing the largest economy in the world, Perot saved his wrath for Bush whose son, he claimed, had falsely maligned his daughter on the eve of her wedding, slamming the President's participation with former President Ronald Reagan in growing the largest federal debt in the history of mankind. Perot, like most liberals, blamed the massive federal debt on Reaganomics, insisting Reagan's "feed the rich" tax cuts in the 1980s, coupled with massive spending increases for the military, caused it.

The reality is, the problem faced by the United States with its rapidly multiplying debt owed to the private banking interests that own the Federal Reserve, didn't happen overnight; nor did it happen in the twelve Reagan/Bush years. Bush merely had the misfortune of having "the watch" when the Democrats opportunistically chose to point it out.

The massive United States federal debt grew into the monster that exists today not because of the Reagan-era tax cuts that fostered the economic growth America enjoys today, but rather it is a direct result of unbridled entitlement spending in the 60s, 70s and 80s to promote the utopian Great Society — during a period when America believed that every social ill could be cured with a federal handout funded through the public treasury that would guarantee every American Herbert Hoover's 1932 promise of "a chicken in every pot."

Because expanding the public trough to include more and more Americans was good for vote-getting, the politicians seeking national office have traditionally promised — and delivered — an even bigger feeding trough every election year by adding more entitlement programs and extending current ones to include even more people until finally, by 1992, one in every five families in America was receiving some form of financial assistance from the federal government that had to be paid by someone else. Added to that was the increasingly intrusive, continually increasing size of government that also had a payroll that needed to be met. Someone had to pay for that as well. The cost of the welfare entitlement programs, the payroll of the government notwithstanding, consumed over half of the government's annual budget. With the federal payroll thrown in, 64% of the budget was

214

spent before any other government expenditures were made or one penny was paid to the Federal Reserve against previously borrowed debt and its rapidly accumulating interest.

Blaming George Bush or Ronald Reagan for the burgeoning federal debt is like blaming General Motors when your Ford has a flat tire. Aside from the fact that the problem started long before either was elected, spending is not controlled by the White House, it's controlled by Congress—in particular, the House of Representatives. And, until the Republican-dominated Congress forced Clinton to keep his 1992 campaign pledge to "end welfare as we know it," welfare and healthcare were sacrosanct. Congress would not let anyone touch entitlements—even though the unchecked growth of entitlements was threatening to bankrupt those who are obligated to pay off the debt incurred by Congress—the taxpayers of the United States.

Be that as it may, both Perot and Clinton blamed Bush, not Congress, for the federal debt. Clinton and the mainstream media also reminded the electorate that Bush had lied to them in 1988 when he promised: "Read my lips—no new taxes!"

The public, which usually buys the lies fostered by politicians but seldom the truth, agreed. The media, Perot, and Bush all ignored the fact that Clinton had also lied. Clinton denied dodging the draft in 1969. He did. Clinton also denied having a twelve year sexual relationship with Gennifer Flowers until a video tape proved he was lying—the day after the Clintons appeared on *60 Minutes* and categorically denied the Flowers allegations to CBS reporter Steve Kroft. The voters, carefully culled by the media, ignored Clinton's lies and punished Bush for his.

On Tuesday, November 3, 1992 William Jefferson Clinton became the 42nd President of the United States on a promise of tax relief for the middle class, a pledge to reduce the size of government, and assurances that he would end welfare as we know it.

Ross Perot, the spoiler, took 19% of the votes—and the election—from George Bush. Clinton who, with less than a mandate to govern, became the President of the United States with 42% of the popular vote[1], only the second candidate in the 20th cen-

---

[1] Only five candidates have won the White House with less than 42% of the popular vote. First was John Quincy Adams who, with 30.5% of the popular vote against Andrew Jackson's 43.1% was elected in the first of two races decided by the House of Representatives. Abraham Lincoln

tury (Wilson being the other) to win the White House with less than 43% of the popular vote. Without Perot in the election equation in 1992, i is likely that Bush would have been easily re-elected with at least a 55% to 45% majority. Those who voted for Perot actually cast their ballots for a Clinton victory.

If Ross Perot was seeking revenge against the Bush family for maligning his daughter "on the eve of her wedding," he got it. He stole the election from Bush for an estimated $45 million. If revenge was truly his motive, it was expensive revenge. Evidence uncovered in the summer of 1996 suggests Perot had a completely different motive for running, or at least, for rejoining the campaign in August, 1992.

By the end of Clinton's first six months Americans found themselves saddled with the largest, most regressive tax increase in the history of the world. Clinton's tax was made retroactive to the last year of Bush's Administration, making him the first President in the history of the United States to tax a previous President's administration. Clinton, who had promised to reduce the size of government began immediately by reducing the Executive staff by some 25% as an example to the other departments of government, challenging Congress to do the same. However, the White House employees cut from the federal employment roster proved, two years later, to consist largely of those viewed by the Clinton Administration as Republican partisans, or at least, those viewed as not likely to be "loyal" to the Clintons.

During the same period, Clinton appointed a national health care task force headed by Hillary Rodham Clinton to propose a government-funded health care system that would nationalize one-seventh of the American economy and create the biggest government bureaucracy in the world.

---

was elected in a four-man race in 1860 with 39.8% of the popular vote and Woodrow Wilson was elected with a 41.9% margin in 1912. Clinton and Wilson are the only two presidents elected to both terms with less than a 50% margin. Even more interesting is the fact that their percentage of victories in their first and second elections mirrored each other. Clinton was elected in 1992 with 42% of the popular vote, Wilson garnered 41.9%. Clinton was elected in 1996 with 49% of the popular vote; Wilson was re-elected in 1916 with 49.4%.

For a brief moment in time Ross Perot, the little Texan whose super ego is exceeded only by the thickness of his billfold, seemed suspended in media limbo. He was yesterday's news. Hillary Rodham Clinton's proposed *Health Security Act* consumed the front pages of the mainstream press. Problems erupted almost immediately.

Hillary insisted her proposal be enacted by Congress precisely as it was written — without change or amendment — which is like telling a little boy he can hold a double scoop chocolate ice cream cone but he can't lick it. Congress has never seen a bill it couldn't change beyond recognition since Roosevelt's New Deal legislation was passed without change or comment in 1933-35. And Hillary, her many spiritual conversations with Eleanor notwithstanding, was not FDR.

By the first of November it was apparent to the Clintons that Hillary's health care plan could not pass without major modification. Even then, it was doubtful that it would pass at all — not even with a liberal, entitlement-minded, Democratically-controlled Congress.

Other than the fact that the program the Clintons were proposing would have been the most expensive social experiment ever attempted in the history of mankind, no one outside the Washington D.C. beltway suspected it was anything other than a very costly entitlement that the taxpayers of America simply couldn't afford. Very few Americans outside of the government knew there was a lot more to Hillary's health care plan than just healthcare; and only a handful of those realized that among those who would financially benefit from the enactment of the Clinton health care plan was H. Ross Perot.

The first clue that there was more than just health care in Hillary's heath care plan is found in what is believed by the author to be a genuine, although heatedly disavowed, White House protocol, dated November 11, 1993[2].

---

[2]A series of five protocols, each bearing the White House seal, were mailed to several traditionally conservative newspapers across the United States on December 6, 1993. The protocols were mailed in a plain white business envelope. It bore a San Francisco postmark. The return address, in the form of a printed sticker, indicated they were sent by a Dr. Calim Robert at 555 California Street in that city.

An investigation by one of the recipients of the envelopes, author

217

Attending that meeting, according to the document, and identified only by initials (aside from the President) were HRC, TFM, RN, IM, GS and RH. "HRC" was, of course, Hillary Rodham Clinton. "TFM" could be none other than Thomas F. "Mack" McLarty who, at that time, was White House Chief-of-Staff. "RN", through the process of elimination, is speculated to be Roy Neel. Neel was a long-time advisor to Al Gore, and served the Clinton White House as deputy Chief-of-Staff under McLarty. "IM" is Ira Magaziner. Magaziner was a Rhodes Scholar like many of the inner circle Clintonoids. Like Clinton, Magaziner had also been an ardent Vietnam era anti-war/anti-government protestor. Hand-picked by Hillary Clinton for the job, Magaziner wrote the text of the *Health Security Act* that would have mandated that roughly 14% of the Gross National Product be surrendered to the federal bureaucracy—which would have become considerably larger if the Clinton health care system had been implemented. "GS" is thought to be Gene Sperling, who became Clinton's National Economic Council chief during his second term. Since the Clinton White House denied that the November 11, 1993 White House protocol is a legitimate document, no source exists outside the White House to confirm the identities of those who participated in this meeting, since the meeting did not, according to the White House, even take place. The author is

---

Gregory Douglas, revealed that 555 California St. was an office building with over a hundred occupants—none of whom appeared to be anyone named Dr. Calim Roberts. At least, Douglas could not find that name in the occupant directory. Determined to either verify or discredit the authenticity of the document in his possession, Douglas did what any good reporter does—he called the White House.

Speaking with a Public Information Officer at the White House, Douglas described the document in his possession, complete with the initials of the participants in the meeting described within its pages, and an overview of the material discussion in the protocol. Douglas was told he had a "classified document" in his possession and if he attempted to use any portion of it, he would be arrested.

Douglas, the author of *Gestapo Chief: The 1948 Interrogation of Heinrich Muller*, which was written largely from both declassified and top secret documents from OSS, CIA, FBI and German Gestapo files, is accustomed to handling top secret and other classified materials, and knew the material in his possession was not classified since it bore none of the markings traditionally found on such documents. He advised

left in something of a quandary. Identifying "GS" for the purpose of this discussion is a coin toss. It could be Sperling; or it could even be George Stephanopoulos, although that is not likely — or, it could be someone else entirely. Between the two known "players," however, Sperling was a much more intimate member of the Clinton White House inner circle, and remained a Clinton policy wonk Therefore, logic suggests if "GS" is one of them, it is more likely Sperling than Stephanopoulos. The identify of "RH" remains a mystery.

In looking over those with close "Arkansas ties" to Clinton whose initials are "RH", only Richard Herget appears. Herget, like McLarty, was a close friend of Clinton during his Arkansas days, and was appointed by Clinton, along with McLarty, to serve on the Arkansas Public Utility Commission. Herget was close enough to the Clinton's inner circle to be invited to ride the presi-

---

the White House Public Information Officer of that fact and was told again that the information in his possession was classified, and that it had to be returned to the White House. Douglas did not return it.

He spent three years attempting to corroborate the authenticity of the five protocols in his possession, or confirm they were frauds. He could do neither, and never attempted to make public the information contained within them. Yet, during that same three year period, most of the programs discussed within the documents became part of the Clinton agenda, and thereby, part of the public record.

Early in 1996, Douglas passed two of the protocols on to this author believing that through this writer's association with the *Washington Times*, *that* the authenticity of the documents could be confirmed. A copy of the November 11 protocol was faxed to a White House contact by Paul Rodriguez, the managing editor of *Insight on the News* magazine. On the fax transmission, Rodriguez wrote, "Tell me this is a hoax..." Nobody did. It was two weeks before anyone in the White House would respond, and at that time they apparently implied that their failure to do so should have obviously suggested to Rodriguez that the protocol was a fraud and did not dignify a response.

Around the same time a Douglas source, a U.S. Army Lt. Colonel assigned to the White House confirmed, in the summer of 1996, that he had heard that some Clinton protocols had been breached by computer hackers who had successfully broken into the White House database, ultimately causing the White House staff to devise a whole new series of security devises and complex passwords to access the system.

Douglas, and all other media people in possession of the documents, refused to cite from them. The decision to quote them in this book is 219

dential merry-go-round, although his name has never surfaced in the volumes of newspaper articles dealing with the Clinton White House, possible Clinton wrongdoing, or coverups of suspected wrongdoing within the Clinton Administration. Although plausible, "RH" may or may not be Herget.

The document, genuine or false, is entitled: *Protocol of White House Conference of November 11, 1993.*

"The **President** opens the discussion by giving an overview of the NAFTA situation. In his view, this matter will probably be passed by the House. Republican support, with a few exceptions, is assured. (**HRC**: After all, it's their bill.) Reluctant Democrats are being lobbied intensively and it appears that a combination of arm-twisting and rewards will prove to be successful. (**TFM**: But we have to be careful not to predict a quick victory. It should go down to the wire...if we are certain of the votes...to make the President look better.) The **President** agrees with this view.

"The second matter on the agenda is the projected final form of the Health Security Act. Here the **President** expresses his opinion that there is probably too much opposition in Congress to pass this as it stands. (**HRC**: If they swallow NAFTA, they can certainly pass this as it stands.) (**IM**: There is absolutely no reason why the same methods used to secure passage of NAFTA cannot apply here.)

---

based on the following logic: (1) Most of the programs discussed in the November 11 protocol were generally not known to the public-at-large during the first year of the Clinton presidency, particularly on December 6, 1993 which is the postmark on the envelope; (2) the protocols reveal a "Clinton-mindset" that has since become public knowledge and therefore we may reasonably conclude that these conversations, which logically fit the personna of the cast of players in the White House, could have occurred; and finally (3) the author feels the reader should have the right to draw his or her own conclusions, based on the other evidence cited in this book, as to whether or not the protocols are genuine or are simply very imaginative frauds written by someone who simply guessed—quite accurately—the agenda that would be forthcoming from the Clinton White House. Again, the author wishes to caution the reader that the November 11 protocol cited in this text not only has not been confirmed by the White House as genuine, it has been refuted as a fraud. The author believes it is genuine. You decide, and place whatever weight you deem worthy on this data.

(**TFM**: The problem here is that NAFTA doesn't entail a huge tax increase and Congress is very nervous about doing this on top of the budget tax increases and the fact that they have elections in '94.) (**HRC**: the public will forget by that time.)

"The **President** states that a major hurdle, namely opposition from the health insurance companies, will be addressed by working out a program whereby these companies will be given no-bid contracts as federal health providers on a regional basis. There will, of course, be no question of public debate on this aspect of the plan. The issuance of contracts will be kept matter-of-fact after the passage of the act and *will not receive media attention at the time of implementation...*" (Bold-face emphasis in original document; italicized emphasis, author's.)

If the November 11 protocol is genuine as the author believes, how could Clinton be so confident that the *Health Security Act* would receive no media attention at the time of implementation? His matter-of-fact statement clearly suggests an agreement, or understanding, already existed between the Clinton White House and the mainstream media not to report any of the negative aspects of the Clinton health care plan, or the fact that some American insurance companies, without competitive bidding, would be allowed to profit exorbitantly from its implementation. At least one of those companies, dealing with medical databases and named in the *Diebold Report,* belonged to H. Ross Perot.

As the protocol continues, it is important to remember that the meeting ostensibly covered by the protocol took place on November 11, 1993, and the contents of the protocol were in the possession of the U.S. Postal Service on December 6, headed to the *Merced Sun-Star* in Merced, California.

"The **President** explores in some detail the increase in so-called "sin taxes," i.e.: increased taxes on tobacco and alcohol. On the one hand, he says, we would very much like to ban totally the use of tobacco and alcohol in the United States. This can be done by presenting the case that both are addictive and harmful and that therefore the Administration has the absolute duty to seek a total ban on both products. On the other hand, the revenues raised by high taxes are very tempting as a relatively painless source of funding for the Health Security Act. (**TFM**: If we ban all cigarettes and alcohol, we would have the same problem

221

we had with prohibition. Most smokers and drinkers won't give up their small pleasures and the result will be that the Mafia will get even richer.) (**HRC**: Perhaps if the tobacco and alcohol people realize that we can indeed cripple their businesses, they might see their way clear to donate substantial sums to help us secure passage of the Health Act. It's something to consider.)

If this protocol is a genuine transcript of an actual meeting that took place in the White House on November 11, 1993, then such a statement by the First Lady of the United States could be construed as the proposed legal blackmailing of two major industries within this nation. Within mere months of this date, in the spring of 1994, the Clintons launched a massive, all-out attack on the tobacco industry — an attack which, by the way, ultimately resulted in the tobacco industry voluntarily submitting to the partial regulation of their industry by the FDA in June, 1997.

A report in the September, 1996 issue of *MediaNomics* stated that over "...a recent twelve month period, television news had devoted significantly more air time to reporting on tobacco than to reporting on cocaine, heroin, LSD, and marijuana combined...[B]etween August 1, 1995 and August 1, 1996 [t]here were 413 stories...about tobacco [and] 340 stories about illegal drugs. This disparity was present despite well-documented...increases in the use of illegal drugs of the past few years, most notably among teenagers...A Nexus search of headlines in American newspapers found that the terms 'tobacco or smoking or cigarette' were employed 26,546 times between January 1, 1993 and September 9, 1996...[while]...the terms 'cocaine or heroin or LSD or illegal drugs' were used only 8,501 times...Eighty-five of the television news tobacco stories were about the Clinton Administration's attack on the tobacco industry."

Is it merely a coincidence, or did that particular November 11 meeting signal the beginning of a concerted White House effort to kill the tobacco industry? If the protocol is genuine, then it is safe to assume the liquor industry is due for some negative press very soon.

"The President discusses the relationship between the White House and the Turner people [CNN]. They, especially Mr. [Ted] Turner and his wife [Jane Fonda], are completely responsive to the White House program to present nothing but positive reporting on the public attitudes towards the Health Security Act. (**HRC**: We really owe this to Jane. She is one of the few people who not only sees the necessity for our programs, but is in a position to do us some good. We ought not to forget this later when we hand out rewards.)

"The **President** brings up the subject of the National Identity Card in conjunction with the implementation of the Health Security Act. *He stresses the necessity of having all Americans be required to possess and carry such a card.* He stresses that it would simplify the task of law enforcement, in cutting down on serial killers and would allow various federal agencies to keep track of a population that is too highly mobile. (**GS**: I think that this issue will present a major problem with Congress. *Most people object to having to carry what amounts to an internal passport.* They will equate this with Nazi Germany or the former Soviet Union.) (**HRC**: We all know this has to be done...just like total gun control. People simply do not realize what has to be done to make their lives easier and safer.) (**TFM**: I think that if we can't get a National Health Card through, we could always turn to the INS issue and fabricate the excuse of preventing illegal aliens from taking U.S. jobs or getting free medical care. I think there would be more acceptance to the card idea if we added this to it.) (**HRC**: Well, I agree with that. After all, if all the provisions of the Health Security Act are passed, as they must be...unaltered in any way...every citizen must by law be registered with the programs even if they have no intention of using its services. That must be made a law...a very important part of this program. Note that it will also help the government track down and prosecute fathers who are delinquent in child support payments. By linking this with the Social Security data banks, we should be able to force the deadbeat males to pay right at the workplace. The key is the Social Security number.) (**TFM**: That's the key to all banks.) (**HRC**: We should make the use of a false Social Security number a federal felony and give every violator five years in jail. A few well-publicized examples would cool off the rest of the country quickly.)" (Boldface emphasis in original; italicized emphasis by author.)

When the *Health Security Act* went down in defeat, some mem-   **223** bers of the House of Representatives, on both sides of the aisle, did attempt to insert a National Identity Card into the *Immigration Reform Act of 1996.* According to the press secretary for Congressman Lamar Smith (R-TX), Allen Kay, in a telephone interview with the author on January 17, 1997, efforts were made on three occasions during the floor debate on H.R. 220 to initiate what Smith's office termed a "National Identity Card dialogue." The Republican majority and Smith, who drafted the legislation that would become Public Law 104-208, Kay said, saw no need for such extreme measures and successfully thwarted efforts to introduce the concept in the immigration debate. "Congressman Smith," Kay reiterated, "as well as most members of Congress, saw no need for a National I.D. Card. Because they did not believe a National Identity Card would solve the problems addressed in H.R. 220, they were not prepared to discuss it."

Like most Americans, even questions about an internal passport made Smith's aide nervous. Sperling was right in his assessment of the American people; McLarty was wrong. The people would view the National Identity Card as a Gestapo-type internal passport; and Congress wasn't buying the "keep-the-jobs-for-Americans" rhetoric suggested by McLarty—at least, not in the House of Representatives. Or, so it seemed.

But those in both Houses of Congress, on both sides of the aisle, who fought so hard and so clandestinely to create a National Identity Card, together with the Clinton White House, did not surrender easily. While the House publicly rejected the idea, the Senate embraced it just as it did the abrogation of the Bill of Rights under the original Senate version of the *Comprehensive Anti-Terrorism Act of 1995.*

A provision that would allow the creation of a National Identity Card was quietly added to the Senate version of the bill before it went to the joint conference where the differences between the House and Senate versions are supposed to be ironed out, and those items without a consensus from both chambers of Congress are to be stripped from the final version of the bill that will be signed into law. According to Congressman Bob Barr (R-GA) no notice of the provision's inclusion was ever sent to the House. There was no Senate floor debate on the subject calling attention to it. As the bureaucrats learned when the provision was debated in the House, talking about it was tantamount to killing it.

224   Other than to those who were party to its creation, both Demo-

crats and high-ranking Republicans alike, nobody seemed to know or would admit they knew that an ID card, however artfully concealed as an innocuous rulemaking provision for the NHTSA, existed. However, before it could be implemented, it had to be approved by the House. This was accomplished at the end of the 1996 session when the omnibus Budget Bill appeared in the House.

According to Barr, who appeared as a guest on the *America's Voice* talk show "Endangered Liberties" hosted by *Coalition for Constitutional Liberties* Director Lisa S. Dean on July 13, 1998, "[T]his was a bill that was several thousand pages long [and] was not distributed to [the House] members." (This was a technique, to be discussed in detail later in this book, that Franklin D. Roosevelt successfully used to ram his blatantly unconstitutional New Deal legislation through Congress.) Congress apparently failed to learn from its New Deal experience and still blindly votes on legislation it has never read. "The only chance any of us might have had to have seen this bill," Barr continued, "was while it was sitting on the floor during the debate. [But] there was no debate on it. No chance for review. It was slipped in as a mickey and was enacted into law because it was part of a very important omnibus spending bill."

Then, taking a politically prudent stand, Barr declared that he, and Congressmen Ron Paul (R-TX) and Mac Collins (R-GA) were introducing legislation to abolish the provision that grants the NHTSA authority to create a national identity card, or any system that would allow the federal government, or any of its agencies, the right to implement such a card by prohibiting the funding of such projects. Of course, as history has clearly confirmed, its rather difficult to milk the cow after its left the barn.

Funding for this infringement of States rights by the NHTSA was not viewed by the federal bureaucracy as a problem since the costs for upgrading driver's licenses falls on the States themselves. Although Congress passed the *Unfunded Mandates Reform Act of 1996* (Public Law 104-4) to prevents the federal government from forcing the States to foot the bill for administering costly, bureaucratic federal programs and regulations, such programs fall under the Act only when the costs are projected to exceed $100 million. The NHTSA conservatively, and deliberately, projected the total cost of implementing the "standardization" of driver's licenses throughout the United States at less than $72 million. NHTSA documents indicate their projections were based on estimates from 5 sparsely populated States that were

225

supposed to be indicative of a cross-section of the nation: Delaware, Iowa, Montana, Utah and Wisconsin.

Clearly, the true intent of low-balling the estimates was to get under the radar scope of the *Unfunded Mandates Act*. Florida estimated its cost to implement NHTSA-98-3945 at over $31 million. The costs incurred by California, Illinois, Michigan, New York and Texas alone would almost double the $100 million cap set by the *Unfunded Mandates Act*. The program is currently being implemented as a devise that is supposed to stop illegal immigrants from taking the jobs of legal American citizens.

The publicized intent of the *Immigration Reform Act of 1996* was to establish a system for employers to identify illegal immigrants. As Lisa Dean pointed out on *America's Voice,* it fails the smell-test on two points. First, most of the employers who have been hiring illegal aliens have been doing so knowingly, and will not be deterred by the new law. It's like passing gun control laws on the pretext that it will prevent criminals from buying guns. Poppy-cock!

Those who enact the laws know better.

"While the Act," Dean declared in a July 15, 1998 open letter to Congress, "places the burden of identification upon innocent and law-abiding citizens, it poses few substantive obstacles for an illegal worker to obtain a driver license that conforms to the proposed standards." In addition, primary and secondary forms of ID (a social security card and a driver's license) are easily forged, inexpensive, and readily available. You can buy either or both on almost any street corner in any border city in America. "This plan," Dean concluded, "pushes us to the brink of tyranny, where citizens will not be allowed to travel, open bank accounts, obtain health care, get a job or purchase firearms without first presenting the proper government papers. The authorizing section of the law and the subsequent NHTSA proposal is reminiscent of the totalitarian dictates of Politburo members of the former Soviet Union, not the Congress of the United States of America."

Barr admitted as much himself. "[T]his, as you know, is not some theoretical exercise. This is a very real, very serious problem with practical ramifications for every citizen in our country, ranging from everything [from] gun control to bank accounts to government programs to travel to seeing a doctor [or] enrolling a child in school. Once this program goes into effect, if we allow it to, then the government will be able to not only track everything that an American citizen does, but they will be able to stop citizens from doing certain things...If we don't do something very quick," Barr admitted, "we will be faced with a government that is all-powerful, and an executive branch that can override either of the two branches of government at will."

But Barr, like Ron Paul, Mac Collins, Lamar Smith and every Congressional member and leader — in particular former House Speaker Newt Gingrich, House Majority Whip Dick Armey and Senate Leader Trent Lott — must share the blame with the Clintonoids that initiated the National Identity Card dialogue on the behest of the Clinton co-presidency. Each of them clearly understands that the provision that creates the platform for a national ID card will not be reversed since it was the most powerful members of Congress who allowed its enactment. To either repeal the provision that gave rise to the authority to create such a card or to enact legislation that would prevent any federal agency using federal funds to implement such a program, requires not only the support of the very Congressmen and Senators who surreptitiously inserted it into both the Senate version of the *Immigration Reform Act* and the House version of the 1996 Budget Bill but it would require the President of the United States, in this case, Bill Clinton (whose program the NHTSA implemented with regulation 98-3495), to sign such legislation into law.

Frankly, it won't happen since the Constitutional conservatives in Congress aren't strong enough to muster the support they would need to override the Presidential veto that would most assuredly result should such legislation land on Clinton's desk — notwithstanding the fact that 90% of the American people polled are abhorrently opposed to anything that even smells like a National ID Card.

And, it won't happen for a second reason.

Impressed with Barr's concern over the ramifications of a National ID Card, Paul Weyrich and Lisa Dean scheduled a meeting with Barr at his office on Tuesday, July 28, 1998 to see how the *Free Congress Foundation* could help gain the support Barr would need to kill the funding the NHSTA required to implement its universal national "driver's license."

Barr arrived after them. The meeting was unexpectedly brief. It lasted less than five minutes before Weyrich and Dean got up and left abruptly, both in amazement and disgust.

Barr apologized to them for the delay and then told them   227 that at the moment there wasn't anything he could do about killing the funding to implement the national ID card as a favor to Lamar Smith—whose aide had specifically and directly assured me that neither Smith nor any Republican in Congress was in favor of, or would even discuss, anything that even remotely appeared to be a national ID card.

Barr told Weyrich and Dean that Smith didn't view the national driver's license as a threat, and wanted to give it a chance. And "...as a favor to Lamar Smith," Barr said, "I'm not going to do anything at this time. Perhaps later," he concluded, "...if it becomes necessary."

Who's fooling who?

The reality is, as Barr well knew, once a national identity card in any form was implemented, it would be too late to do anything. Clearly Barr knew he didn't possess enough political clout to stop it—not even with the help of any as yet untainted members of the Republican Class of '94. The political force behind the National ID Card was too great for Barr. And, even the coalition of Constitutional conservatives like Ron Paul and Helen Chenoweth-Hage—combined with political activists like Free Congress Foundation's Paul Weyrich, the traditionally liberal American Civil Liberties Union, the CATO Institute, and Christian Coalition—was no match for them since the force that successfully launched the National ID Card included most of the senior leadership on both sides of the aisle in both the House and the Senate at the behest of the invisible power that was described so well by both Woodrow Wilson and Franklin D. Roosevelt.

However, within a week Barr and Paul were introducing legislation that would defund the program, effectively suspending it in a bureaucratic limbo, but unable to kill it outright. While the legislation didn't stand a snowball's chance of getting out of Committee and onto the floor for a debate, Barr, Paul, Lamar Smith and then House Speaker Newt Gingrich, who was largely responsible for the fact that Americans would soon be forced to carry a form of what was planned by Clinton Administration to be a national ID card, knew what was more likely to happen was a debate in the public arena. And that was something the leadership did not want. On August 4, 1998, more to appease Barr than to accomplish anything, a hearing was held in the office of the Transportation Subcommittee. Barr, Paul, Smith and several Congressional staffers attended. Barr requested that the comment period on the legislation be reopened. That is, of course, like discussing the changes you would like to make in the script of a movie you have just watched. The moratorium Barr requested would allow "interested parties" to "...have sufficient time to consider the agency's proposals and to provide written comments." Of course, at that point the barn door was wide open and the livestock had scattered all over the countryside. In a press conference held at the time, Barr declared that "I do not believe Americans are interested in giving the federal government unprecedented power to track and identify them. Hopefully, these hearings will be the beginning of the end of efforts to create a national identification system."

Barr quickly learned his statement was premature.

Using the only leverage they could find, Barr and Paul hit the conservative talk show circuit. Smith, the schill for the leadership on an issue that Gingrich, House Majority Leader Dick Armey (without whose participation it could not have been inserted into either the *Immigration Reform Act of 1996* or the 1996 Omnibus Budget Bill), and Minority Leader Richard Gephardt (D-MO) all denied knowing about, doggedly pushed House Appropriations Transportation Subcommittee Chairman Frank Wolf (R-VA) to derail Barr's attempt to suspend implementation of the national "driver's license."

Barr and Paul were now pushing for a one-year moratorium on the implementation of the National ID Card. Barr's resolution was to be added to the Transportation Appropriations Bill and would defund the national "driver's license." This infuriated Smith who, according to Congressional insiders, frantically lobbied Transportation Subcommittee Chairman Wolf to exclude Barr's resolution. On Tuesday, October 6, Smith was reported to have gained an agreement from Gingrich to eliminate this provision from the bill. After an overnight battle, Barr won a temporary victory. Several House members came to his aid, openly questioning Gingrich why it was that Smith was so zealously pushing for something that the American people so vehemently opposed. Gingrich, fearful of voter backlash in an election that would be held in less than a month, finally caved in.

The globalists within our own government who are attempting to fulfill an international mandate to provide a uniform global identity system have been both clever and cautious. The

229

words "national identity card" will never cross their lips since such a devise is quickly identified by most Americans with both the Nazi regime of Adolph Hitler and the Communist overlords of the Soviet Union. In fact, the language used in the legislation clearly and specifically denies that it is one. But then, the Social Security Act of 1933 also mandates that Social Security numbers may not be required for identification purposes — and that is the first thing that will be encoded on the new national driver's licenses. As Stephen Moore of the CATO Institute told Lisa Dean: "[I]f it looks like a duck and quacks like a duck and runs like a duck, it's a duck...I think this has every characteristic of a national ID card, except they don't call it a national ID card."

Borrowing from the pattern developed by the globalists in Europe that requires all of the European Union states to use a standardized EU driver's license (whose only difference is that nation's flag in the upper right hand corner), the National Highway Traffic Safety Administration (NHTSA-98-3945) implemented the obscure provision in the *Immigration Act of 1996* that will force the States to implement Clinton's de-facto National Identity Card by mandating that all State-issued driver's licenses must conform to new "federal regulations" and "federal standards" by October 1, 2000. The new regulation mandates that each new driver's license contain a biometric chip that will record the "traffic history" of each card's owner. Like most government intrusions, this one sounds innocuously innocent on the surface. However, what is not stated in NHTSA-98-3945 is what other data may also be encoded on the chip, and whether the card itself can, and will, be used by the federal government as a tracking devise. Clearly, that *was* the focus of the discussion in the White House on November 11, 1993.

"The **President** brought up the subject of federally funded abortions. In his view, this might not be possible to force onto Congress because of the opposition by religious groups. (**HRC**: I disagree with the use of the word 'force'. The better usage is 'persuade.' As far as the religious right is concerned...and I am not speaking here of the mainline Protestant groups...but rather the religious nuts...fortunately they are not united or we would have far more trouble than we have had. My view, and the President agrees with me en-

230

tirely o [sic] this, is that the religious right is our worst enemy, and we should deal with them directly. The Attorney General assures me that if we can link them...any of them...as organizations, not as individuals...to violence against clinics, medical personnel, and so on, that we could well bring RICO into play. [Rush] Limbaugh is safe for the time being, but if [Pat] Robertson or some of the others get up in their pulpits or, better, go on the air, and encourage what they call resistance to the freedom of choice movement...and by definition can be linked through this to violence and death, Reno can apply RICO to them and seize their property, including their radio and TV outlets. Things would be a lot more pleasant without their fascistic screaming anyway. We can all agree on that.)

"A lengthy discussion follows this comment by **HRC**. It is generally agreed that the religious right poses a danger to the programs of this Administration, especially to the projected Education Reform Bill. If a program of realistic sex education is to succeed in the lower grades, opposition must be neutralized. **TFM** brings up the subject of the Catholic Church. Its views on abortion are well known. (**HRC**: For me, this is a dying religion in this country. They have no power and, if we cannot arrive at a mutual agreement on this, we can proceed against them by increasing the number of priest-pederasty charges...The Turners have already begun the groundwork for this, and we don't need to go too much further with this before the Catholic leadership can recognize mortal danger for them. We can bring them around in the end. And I'm sure the issue of female priests can be solved to our satisfaction in the same way and at the same time. A package deal. The born-agains are most irritating problem [sic]. The Attorney General advises me that some of the Idaho people are deeply involved in criminal and anti-government activity and have a connection with certain right wing churches. We need to stress this. Ted Turner is willing to run a series on CNN about the fascist right wing terrorists and make references to their links with various churches. If we do this a little bit at a time, the public will get the impression that all churches of the right advocate killing abortion clinic people, stockpiling deadly weapons like the Koresh nutties and eventually plan to attack or fight government agencies...like in Waco. We can make the connection in the public mind." (Bold-face emphasis in original.)

Three comments in the aforementioned commentary should stand out. First and most notably has been the dramatic increase in the number of allegations, charges and prosecutions of Catholic priests for pedophilia over the past few years.

Second was the offhand reference to the *Education Reform Bill*. This legislation, proffered as H.R. 1617 in the 104th Congress by Rep. Howard McKeon (R-CA), was originally introduced by Sen. Ted Kennedy (D-MA) as S.143—directly from the blueprint fashioned by Hillary Clinton, Marc Tucker and Ira Magaziner. While Education Committee Chairman William F. Gooding (R-PA) and subcommittee chairman McKeon both insisted the purpose of H.R.1617 was to create "...a cost saving, jobs program consolidation bill and a repeal of [existing] school-to-work [legislation]..." it was merely an extension of the former legislation that would create a powerful monopoly of federal and state appointed boards that could not be regulated, or controlled, by the electorate.

These boards would control all jobs programs in the nation. Once control was firmly in the grip of the bureaucracy, the government would then be in a position, as in any socialist society, to control not only school-to-work programs, but all workforce problems associated with not only the initial job placement but, ultimately, through Out-Based Education (OBE), decision-making authority over the American work force in determining whether workers desiring to make career changes in later life would be allowed to do so—or, in some instances, mandating that they do.

Like most of the proposed Clinton Administration legislation which includes surreptitious database provisions, *The Careers Act* would establish the mechanism which could ultimately lead to the combining of the data banks of the Departments of Education and Labor ostensibly, according to its sponsors, to focus the career orientation of the students on those jobs that the government feels will be available when those students enter the work force. While a laudable objective on the surface, *The Careers Act* smacks of Marxist big-brotherism because the legislation possessed the characteristics which would allow it to subvert the rights of the individual by treating people as mere commodities of the State.

Over the past three decades of politically correct indoctrination, the public school system has increasingly de-emphasized

232

the importance of the both the Declaration of Independence and the Constitution of the United States, and with it, the importance of national sovereignty. In its place has sprung a curriculum that glorifies "natural rights" instead of "national responsibility." The offspring of America are slowly evolving into the proper environmentally-correct blue collar workers needed for the new utopian socialist global society of the New World Order in which people will be measured only in terms of their value to the system as productive human capital.

The Hillary Clinton Education Reform Bill, more commonly known as the second "school-to-work" bill, was virtually unheard of at that time by any of the "extremist rightwing nuts" who might later be accused of concocting the November 11 protocol as a means of embarrassing the Clinton White House. In November, 1993 it is doubtful that anyone outside of either the liberal inner circle of the federal government or the National Education Association had any knowledge that such legislation even existed, or that anything resembling it was even on the drawing table in the Clinton White House.

Finally, there has been a concerted and highly-publicized effort on the part of the mainstream liberal media to ideologically link both Christian and non-religious, issues-oriented nationalist organizations with the more extreme ultra rightwing militia movements, often described by the media as domestic terrorists, in order to discredit the genuine concerns of those organizations over the direction America is heading.

In a 72-page report entitled *"False Patriots: The Threat of Anti-Government Extremists"*, the Southern Poverty Law Center, which is viewed by many in the mainstream media as one of the most authoritative sources on rightwing fanaticism in the nation, declared that "...the Patriot movement is a potpourri of the American right, from members of the Christian Coalition to the Ku Klux Klan..." Evidence, always demanded of the conservative to support its conspiracy allegations, is conveniently ignored by the SPLC. The liberal knows all too well that when an allegation is leveled enough times, it becomes a perceived reality without the need of factual corroboration.

By suggesting that a covert conspiracy exists between all "right-wingers," the liberal media is able to tag all conservatives as fascists, racists, neo-Nazis, homophobics, conspiracy nuts and isolationists — the label successfully placed on 1996 Presidential hopeful Pat Buchanan by the mainstream media.

Media-ordained extremist expert John J. Nutter held a highly acclaimed seminar on rightwing extremism for law enforcement officers in Oklahoma City shortly after the bombing of the Murrah Building. During his syllabus, Nutter detailed the "warning signs" by which law enforcement officers could ascertain the likelihood that "suspects" were active in extremist groups, or were likely to be planning domestic terrorist events. Nutter listed, as warning signs, words like: the Bilderbergers, the Council on Foreign Relations, the Illuminati, the Trilateral Commission and the United Nations — words that drape the fears of most nationalist conservatives in the United States.

Nutter might have also mentioned *black helicopters* but, at that time, the U.S. Army had not yet conducted any of its covert "anti-terrorist maneuvers" over any American city, or built any of the internment camps which are now being photographed outside of many of our military installations across the country, so the phrase had not yet become a "rightwing buzz-word" to describe a growing apprehension among Americans that the United States government was anticipating an "extremist revolution" at some unspecified date in the foreseeable future, or might even be planning to fabricate one if it did not develop on its own.

In a May 13, 1996 op-ed piece in the *Christian Science Monitor*, globalist Ira Strauss, the U.S. Coordinator for NATO's Committee on Eastern Europe, wrote: "What is the milieu in which criminal groups of 'freeman' and Oklahoma City bombers grow? It is the underworld of conspiracy theory, a subculture in which people share fantasies of fighting heroically against a huge conspiracy that is taking over the world...Conspiracy theory is doing America real harm. Long incubating underground, it has grown into the greatest enslaver of human minds since communism. It irrationalizes thinking on every issue. It kills. It turns millions of Americans against their own country. It undermines foreign policy by vilifying our government's every effort."

Not all conservatives believe there is a growing globalist conspiracy to create a one-world government. In fact, less than half do, since most conservatives believe they are amply protected by the Constitution. One such conservative is radio talk show host Rush Limbaugh whose sarcastic anti-liberal rhetoric influences the opinions of well over 5 million conservative Americans. Limbaugh who is indisputedly the king of conservative propaganda in the United States, caustically poopahs the idea that a ruling elite actually exists, or that there is a concerted, organized globalist conspiracy to create a one-world government.

Equally adamant is conservative intellect Robert J. Bidinotto who, in an op-ed piece for *The Freeman* entitled *Conspiracy or Consensus,* argued against the idea of an organized force "...dragging America down..." or that "...the world [is] in the grip of a powerful, malevolently directed conspiracy." He agreed that a conspiracy did exist, but argued the "...undertow is not an international conspiracy; it's an international consensus. What the conspiratorialists fail to appreciate," he declared, "is the power of ideas."

Standing in accord with Bidinotto and Strauss is third term Congressman Peter T. King (R-NY) who, in an *Insight on the News* symposium on whether militia groups threaten the civil order of the nation, said: "...Disaffected groups and individuals on the far ends of the political spectrum often...[imagine] conspiracies involving the federal government...Conspiracy theories have always held a special fascination for those with severely undeveloped intellectual and emotional facilities. This preoccupation has been demonstrated by the far left with Oliver Stone's paranoid cinematic opus *JFK;* [and] by the far right in countless convoluted accounts of the 'Bavarian Illuminati' and the threats possessed by the Trilateral Commission...The common link among these delusional fantasies is the complicity of the federal government." King, who insists he is a Goldwater Republican, admitted that "...while the government often may be inept and ineffectual...[it is] rarely if ever evil or conspiratorial." (*Insight on the News;* September 25, 1995; pgs. 20-22.)

Lyn Nofziger, a former Reagan aide disagrees and proudly called himself a "rightwing wacko." In a rebuttal of King's *Insight on the News* argument, Nofziger, who was privy to the inner workings of presidential power for eight years under Reagan, clearly understands how easily those in power can abuse the authority granted to them by, and for, the people of the United States.

"First," Nofziger began, "understand, we wackos do not trust government. We expect the worst from them. We believe there are many in it who distort the Constitution and seek to impose their will on a free people. We think that such people endanger our liberty. We think, for example, that Bill Clinton is a bigger threat to our freedom than David Koresh ever thought of being ...Those beliefs clearly set us apart from most of today's officeholders...[who]...adhere to a philosophy that says government knows best and must be obeyed and that they have been selected not to serve the people but to rule them...[S]ome Americans fear the advent of one-world government. Some Americans think big government and big business and big media are in a never-ending conspiracy to take away their rights and 'keep them in their place'...The main difference between most of them and the rest of us wackos is that they also believe a massive international conspiracy is to blame for what is wrong and what is going wrong. Of course that is not the case—I hope. Mostly, I don't think it is because I don't think any internationalist groups or any military-industrial combines are smart enough or tough enough to take over this country. Furthermore, I don't think Richard Nixon intended to and I don't think Bill Clinton could get away with it, even with Hillary's help.

"But just in case I'm wrong, I like the idea of having those men and women out there in the woods, trained and ready to take on any conspirators who might stick up their heads. I'd rather depend on them to defend my freedom than almost any member of Congress or the federal government that I can think of." (*Insight on the News*; September 25, 1995; pgs. 20-23.)

Nofziger's argument is well-grounded in historic fact. The federal government, a subservient creation of the various States in 1787, attempted to exert its will over those sovereign States almost from the moment of its inception. Today, it has succeeded beyond its wildest imagination. The most serious and far reaching usurpations of power by the legislative and executive branches of the federal government have occurred since 1913. Today, in a direct violation of the 10th Amendment, the federal government legislates with the authority granted only to the States. Federal law, contrary to the intent of the Founding Fathers to specifically restrict not only the lawmaking penchant of the federal government but its sphere of authority as well, now supersedes State law.

Anyone who has ever taken the time to read the Constitution more clearly understands the dilemma facing America. Those who have been appointed to safeguard the rights of all Americans have slowly usurped those rights until they no longer exist. And, anyone who has studied the course being steered by the commanders-in-chief of the Ship of State since 1913 also have reason to be alarmed. The *U.S.S. United States* is floundering in the shoals of a socialist globalism that will ultimately sink the Constitution of the United States — and its captain and congressional crew appears determined to scuttle the Ship of State and run the nation aground on the nonexistent Island of Utopia.

F ar too many Americans believe, as Nofziger admitted, that the United States is immune from a successful conspiratorial plot by either internal or external forces, believing no national government, military or industrialist group is shrewd enough to overthrow the government of the United States. For that reason most Americans balk at the idea that conspiratorial forces are at work, or that they have been for several decades, slowly eroding the basic tenets of the Constitution until finally, one morning America will awaken and discover all of its constitutional rights were surreptitiously obliverated while they slept.

There is a small but growing contingent of insomniac Americans maintaining a vigilant watch over the Constitution. Most are reminiscent of Ethan Allen, John Hancock and Samuel Adams, although some, admittedly, are simply opportunistic revolutionaries like Adolph Hitler, Vladimir Lenin and Mao Tse-Tung, or ideological revolutionaries like Karl Marx or Adam Weishaupt.

This group, witnessing the erosion of the Constitution while their neighbors confidently sleep, have attempted to warn America with all of the vigor of the boy who cried "wolf" — and with equal success. America has been lulled into a false sense of security by politicians who have convinced them that minor infringements on their liberty are necessary to safeguard their remaining rights.

Shortly after the bombings of the World Trade Center and the Murrah Building in Oklahoma City, President Bill Clinton urged Congress to take "swift, certain and severe" action against domestic terrorism. In patriotic fervor, the bipartisan *Comprehensive Anti-Terrorism Act of 1995* was making its way through Congress. It virtually flew through the Senate with a 91-8 vote and headed to the House Judiciary Committee where HR 666[3] suddenly

---

[3]It is an ironic coincidence that the legislation promoted by Congress to eliminate the Bill of Rights would have such a theologically significant number. However, it needs to be pointed out that the Senate version of the *Comprehensive Anti-Terrorism Act* was S.735; and that other versions later entered in the House as H.R. 896, 1635, and 1710. On March 7, 1996 H.R. 2703 would be the bill that was finally enacted.

came to a screeching halt as an unlikely coalition of powerful lobbyists that included the American Civil Liberties Union, the Competitive Enterprise Initiative, Gun Owners of America, the National Black Police Association, the National Rifle Association and others aligned against it. Their mutual concern was the overreaching power granted to the federal government by this pending legislation that would have virtually abolished the Bill of Rights.

The media immediately trumpeted the *Anti-Terrorism Act* as a necessary evil that would provide an added measure of security for Americans against both domestic and foreign terrorist groups.

H.R. 666 abrogated the following rights under the 1st Amendment: loss of the freedom of religion, freedom of speech, the right to petition, and under extraneous circumstances, freedom of the press; 2nd Amendment: loss of the right to own firearms; under the 3rd Amendment: the use of military force to assist local police; under the 4th Amendment: the loss of the right to privacy from unreasonable search and seizure and the repeal of *habeas corpus;* under the 5th Amendment, the suspension of due process; under the 6th Amendment: the loss of the right to face an accuser, and an enhanced right of the authorities to hold anyone accused of a crime for an indefinite period of time without trial. And finally, the 10th Amendment would be *legislatively* abolished, giving the federal government total dictatorial power over every aspect of human life in the United States in times of a declared national emergency by the President of the United States.

This legislation would have allowed the federal government to wiretap any citizen's telephone without a court order. It would further have allowed federal authorities to search any citizen's home and person without a warrant, and secure any information about that citizen for any reason. *The bill would have allowed Congress to make it a federal crime to possess a firearm of any type.* Those accused of a crime would no longer be allowed to face those who accused them, and could be confined based on an accusation from an unidentified accuser and held without bail until such time as a federal prosecutor had amassed enough evidence to indict them and place them on trial for whatever crimes they stood accused[4].

---

[4]Had the *Comprehensive Anti-Terrorism Act of 1995* been enacted when Richard Jewell became the prime suspect of the Atlanta Olympics boming, Jewell would have been summarily arrested and incarcerated

And finally, what constituted terrorism would be defined by the Executive Branch, based on the whims of the White House, rather than by either State or federal statute. In other words, "crime" could be defined as such after-the-fact—and the perpetrator arrested and held without bail for trial for doing what was ostensibly not legally defined, by statute, as a "crime" when the deed was committed.

The fact that the Congress of the United States could even consider such legislation, or that it could be overwhelmingly passed by the Senate should be cause for grave concern by every American—not just those labeled as rightwing wackos—since it so blatantly and contemptuously violated the Constitution. But, even more frightening is that such arbitrary power was to be entrusted to a President who had proven he could not be trusted.

It is clear from the disavowed protocol that the Clintons viewed the "rightwing nutties" as *the most serious threat facing the Clinton Administration* according to HRC. Clearly it was the intent of the Administration to initiate a variety of ploys to banish not only automatic and semi-automatic weapons, but all weapons of any type. The media would prove to be of incalculable value in this effort.

After Hillary Clinton's alleged comment that people like the Koresh *nutties* "...were stockpiling deadly weapons and eventually planned to attack..." the government, the discussion centered on gun control.

> "This led to an extensive discussion about total gun control. The **President** says that he personally favors the Japanese approach to such matters. *No guns of any kind, even old replica guns, are acceptable to him. No swords or deadly knives can be permitted. Hunting clubs may be allowed where hunters, with scrupulous proof of identity, can rent guns from a federally supervised center, with promise of serious felony charges if the guns are not returned.* He mentions the value of the National Identity Card in enforcing this policy. He points out that the gunshot deaths in Japan are minimal and obviously the total gun control program there is solely responsible for this..." (Boldface emphasis in original document; italicized emphasis from author.)

---

without bail while the FBI conducted its investigation. With all of his Constitutional rights suspended, it is likely Jewell would have been successfully railroaded. As it was, the media virtually declared him guilty when they named him the only suspect in the bombing.

There is a reality which few politicians wish to face when contemplating the differences in capital offenses committed in Japan as compared to those committed in the United States. It is not due to gun ownership or the lack thereof, but rather it is due almost entirely on the value one human places on the life of another. When life has no inherent value, the act of taking it is an insignificant event. America has desensitized itself over the past twenty-five years not only by glorifying random acts of violence as a celluloid form of family entertainment, but by the sanctioning of abortion and the resultant slaughter of well over 39,000,000 innocent babies by their own mothers.

The discussion continued:

"**TFM** asks about duck hunting for example. The **President** replies that a shotgun can do terrible damage to another person. **TFM** asks about the use of bows and arrows. The President will allow that concession to hunters but with reservations. He also mentions various firearms magazines and newspapers with especial reference to the *Soldier of Fortune* publication that he insists must be removed from circulation as quickly as possible and the circulation lists seized for investigation."

Again, this protocol—if genuine—shows a frightening disregard for the Constitution of the United States. It also reveals, as it continues, a President with a few conspiracy theories of his own:

"The **President** explains that the passage of the Brady Bill will greatly facilitate the passage of future, even more effective restrictive legislation. He mentions California laws that prohibit possession of even dummy guns that might be used to simulate deadly weapons. **RN** brings up the matter of seizing weapons in the inner city areas where gun owners use their weapons on a daily basis and are likely to shoot. (**HRC**: We have to approach minorities with caution. We cannot appear to be picking on them or singling them out for punishment. *I suggest we first use records to confiscate all legally registered weapons from white citizens to show the inner city residents that the white population will be disarmed before any minorities are.* Keep in mind that of the fifty-odd deaths in the Los Angeles riots, most were caused by Korean shop owners defending their property. These Koreans should merit special attention in the initial roundup.) The **President** makes reference to the fact that the actual death toll in Los Angeles was triple the official one and wonders how many of those the Koreans were responsible for. *He agrees that the biggest danger in America today is that the white middle class will take up arms against the inner city minorities and start some kind of civil war.* For this reason, the disarming of the public must begin at once. The Brady Bill will be a start and then a ban on so-called assault rifles should follow as quickly as possible."

And, as history records, that is precisely what happened. At that point, according to the disavowed November 11 protocol, Hillary Clinton picked up the gauntlet of middle class elitism when she said:

"(**HRC**: And while we are on this subject, I would like to discuss the white flight issue. I have mentioned this before, but I want to get these views clearly out into the open. *When middle class whites flee from an area that has a significant African-American population, they take the tax-base with them. This only perpetuates a vicious cycle wherein tax money is no longer available for our entitlement programs. These whites are practicing an intolerable elitism when they move into moated communities with fences and guards. This is an offense to the African American and Latino communities. It's the same sort of thing as whites taking their children out of public schools because of what they perceive are dangerous conditions.* If they only realized that this elitism actually propagates these dangerous conditions, they would stop. And, since they won't, I think that all housing projects, regardless of the price of the units involved or the location and regardless of whether these units are public or private in nature, be mandated by Federal law to provide 25% minority low cost housing. *Perhaps the elitists would be forced to come to grips with the plain fact that this is going to be a multi-cultural and multi-racial country very quickly and we are not going to tolerate or perpetuate de facto segregation.* I suggest a Federal Housing Act that could control this in the future. *And it has been suggested to me that given the housing shortage among the economically disadvantaged, the ownership of two houses in these times is in the worst possible taste. Perhaps a Federal Housing Act could make provision to heavily tax these examples of conspicuous consumption. Let us say that if an owner did not live in his second house for...six calendar and consecutive months, he would be subject to this tax. We* 241 *could then show this to those who do not own two homes as an example of our concern for the disadvantaged and our contempt for the flagrant lifestyles of the rich and uncaring. No one cares if a few rich people have to pay more taxes for their economic sins.)*

"The **President** comments that this might pinch a lot more people than the very rich. (**HRC**: You have my view on this.)

TFM mentions that federal programs now emphasize financial assistance to needy African-Americans over whites and this could well be attacked in the courts as reverse discrimination. **TFM** feels that this aspect should be de-emphasized before the courts get their hands on it and cause damage to the structure of the total socio-economic integration to which the current administration is pledged. **HRC** agrees as does **GS**.

"...**HRC** discussed the public education system at length. *Her views in general are that school vouchers are another form of white elitism and must be stamped out.* California and other states have had such measures on their ballots and this should be discouraged. She suggests that the means used against this measure in California be studied. Another topic dealt with home schooling. **HRC** points out that *home teaching is rightwing religious in nature and that children involved in it do not have the opportunity to mix with other racial and religious groups during the children's most impressionable years. She suggests that this practice be stopped by the means of requiring home school parents to enroll in expensive education training and certification programs that would be lengthy in process and expensive.* Church schools have a perfect right to exist but should not be granted any kind of tax-exempt status. This alone would make such establishments unattractive to churches.

"To offset any apparent bias against religious organizations, it is necessary to establish dialogue with the mainstream religions in this country and grant them every mark of respect and cooperation. Tax exemptions can continue and even be enhanced for these people. (**HRC**: *Our children are our greatest resource. We owe them the right to grow up as interacting and socially conscious citizens, ready to take their places in the interracial global community that all of us in this room see as the wave of the future. If we have to be severe or even cruel in furthering this doctrine, we must realize that the end is* *certainly worth whatever means we have to employ.")* (Boldface emphasis in original document; italicized emphasis from author.)

If the disavowed November 11, 1993 White House protocol is a genuine document—as the author believes it is—then the concluding statements by HRC clearly vindicate every "right-wing nuttie" who believes that a conspiracy to create a modular global society does exist.

But even more important, Hillary Clinton's own words: "We owe [our children] the right to grow up...ready to take their places in the interracial global community..." are a foreboding omen of the future of our nation. The globalists have claimstaked America, and our elected officials have recorded their deed.

Hillary Clinton's words were more than privately spoken liberal rhetoric—they were facts uttered by a woman at the pinnacle of power who clearly understands both the agenda and the timeline of the New World Order, and eagerly awaits it arrival.

"Ideal perfection is not the true basis of English legislation. We look at the attainable; we look at the practical, and we have too much English sense to be drawn away by those sanguine delineations of what might possibly be attained in Utopia, from a apth which promises to enable us to effect great good for the people of England."
William Ewart Gladstone,
British Prime Minister
Speech in the House of Commons,
February 28, 1884

"For other nations, Utopia is a blessed past never to be recovered; for Americans it is just beyond the horizon."
Henry Kissinger
The London Times
March 12, 1991, attributed

❖ TEN ❖

The Emerging World Order

Europe, as it prepared to enter the 20th century, was a virtual boiling pot of intrigue as the money barons behind the nation-states on the continent jockeyed for more financial power as the heads-of-state jockeyed for more economic and social power. Assassination was the rule of the day. Treaties between the nation-states were made and just as quickly broken. War was brewing on the continent, but in the opening days of the century it was merely a disdainful rumbling, like the distant thunder of an impending storm that the world chose to ignore. Most convinced themselves that the distant thunder was merely the sounds of a rapidly expanding world economy bulging at the seams as it sought new outlets for its wares. The 20th century offered both the industrialist and the banker a heretofore unimaginable opportunity for increased wealth and prosperity. Only one thing stood in their way—the nations themselves.

Each had their own dreams of the future. The industrialists envisioned a Europe in which they would be allowed to dominate the markets in Paris, London, Berlin, Stockholm, St. Petersburg or Rome without the trade barriers that restricted their marketing activities. The bankers grandiosely envisioned a Europe without borders, ruled by a consortium of men like themselves who possessed not only the wealth but the knowledge to create a profitable global society, an economic utopia in which all men would be productive members of society, but that they would control the counting house that partitioned the wealth and divided the spoils of the working man's labor.

The birth of modern Europe and the end of the feudal monarchies came from the travails of the Franco-German War in 1871 with the unification of the Germanic people. When the War of 1812 was being fought in the United States, Germany was comprised of 38 different sovereign powers joined together in a loose

245

knit confederation called a *staatendbund*. While the *staatendbund* protected the feudal states from more powerful foes like France and Russia, the multiplicity of governing bodies within the confederation created an economic nightmare. The multiple tariff system that existed in the separate German states proved to be not only irksome, but a hindrance to commerce.

Roughly a third of the *staatendbund* was aligned with Prussia and was collectively known as the North German Confederation. Austria controlled the southern alliance, which was known both as the German Austria and the South German Confederation. England owned the principality of Hanover. Two provinces, Schleswig and Holstein, were possessions of Denmark.

The unification of Germany had an unostentatious beginning in 1819 when Prussia formed a *zollverein,* or customs union, among its German territories to encourage commerce. By 1844 the *zollverein* included all of the Germanic states except German Austria, Hanover and five other city-states. It was a major victory for Prussia and slowly shifted the balance of economic power in Central Europe away from Austria.

The empire of the Hapsburgs was an anomalous congery of diverse Germanic people and others previously conquered, who were united only by obedience to the Austrian throne, and then, only to the extent that the Hapsburgs' will could be enforced by the Austrian courts.

Ferdinand I, who assumed the throne in 1837, was a weak-minded monarch who willingly surrendered control of his government to Prince Clemens Wenzel von Metternich the Austrian chancellor who, 22 years earlier, began assembling the Germanic Confederation from the feudal states of central Europe.

While censorship in the Germanic states was strict, Ferdinand mistakenly allowed the universities in Austria too much philosophical latitude. In short order the liberal views of Adam Weis-haupt and other western European liberals took root among the educated classes of Austria and the population began demanding an elected parliamentary form of government that had the power to legislate tax reform. The modest reforms that were initiated by the Hapsburgs stimulated a decade of industrial growth that produced a flourishing, self-confident middle class ready to take its place in the political circles of Austria.

The prosperity of Austria was shattered on February 22, 1848 when an Illuminati-instigated rebellion in France occurred. At that time workers and students began to demonstrate in Paris. The insurrection, which lasted three days, witnessed the bloodiest civil street fighting in Europe to date. On February 24, Louis Philippe abdicated in favor of his grandson Prince Louis Napoleon Bonaparte, giving rise to France's Second Republic.

The flames of revolution spread quickly. On March 3, Louis Kossuth, the vassal president of Hungary demanded independence from Austria. Stimulated both by Kossuth's boldness against the Hapsburgs and the fact that Austria was crippled by its worst economic depressions in decades, Viennese workers and students launched a massive demonstration in Vienna on March 12.

Under the threat of death if caught by the rioters, Metternich resigned and fled the country. On March 15, Ferdinand issued an imperial degree creating a constitutional assembly in Austria. A second manifesto made Hungary an equal trading partner. In 1867 the *Compromise of Ausgleich* joined them together as the dual monarchy known as Austria-Hungary.

But, instead of creating the promised constitutional assembly whose job it would be to write the new Constitution, Ferdinand's ministers wrote the document themselves. While it granted his subjects some semblance of parliamentary government, it reserved all of the real power for the existing nobility.

When a citizens' committee comprised largely of students, workers and national guardsman appeared before the palace on May 15 to protest the broken promise, Ferdinand dissolved the committee. The demonstrations started again with renewed fervor. Fearing for his own life and the safety of his family, Ferdinand fled to Innsbruck two days later. In his absence, the government reconvened the citizens' committee and began structuring a slightly more democratic Constitution.

Sensing that Austria's discontent was stemming from its universities, the government outlawed the Academic Union on May 26, causing another massive demonstration.

The flames of independence were now kindled all over central Europe. On June 12 the Princess Windischgratz of Czechoslovakia was accidently shot and killed by student demonstrators as they fired pistols into the air. Crown Prince Windischgratz, a strong advocate of repressive measures against his subjects even under the best of circumstances, seized the opportunity to bring in troops and quickly crushed the rebellion. Czechoslovakia would not gain its independence from Austria until 1918.

247

The period from 1850 to 1853 in Prussia was one of reaction. Persecution of liberals became the order of the day. Because of internal strife in Austria, Prussia resisted joining the *zollverein*, afraid that the liberal influence of the Illuminati would invade Prussia if the doors to commerce with Austria were opened.

The Prussian conservatives, headed by Count Otto von Bismarck, wanted to abolish the democratic parliament, and openly published their views in a newspaper called *Kreuzzeitung* that condemned not only the liberals but the moderates as well. Bismarck was hated by the liberals and feared by Crown Prince William, a moderate. Prince William was a realist who recognized that the age of the monarchy in Europe was rapidly coming to an end.

When Frederick William IV was adjudged insane in 1858, William, Frederick's brother, became regent of Prussia. Upon the death of Frederick in 1861, the prince became William I of Prussia. William's reign was in trouble almost immediately. While still regent, William appointed General Albert von Roon as his Minister of War and ordered him to reorganize the military in the same manner and style as Louis Napoleon's French army. At the same time, in 1859, he lifted the ban which prohibited liberals from holding public office, feeling his action would eliminate rising discontent from that faction. The liberals had previously refused to vote since their views would neither be recognized nor championed by those elected. However, once the ban against liberals holding office was lifted, they campaigned feverishly for the offices that had previously been denied them, and became the majority party in Prussia that same year.

Roon appointed General Helmuth von Moltke as chief of the general staff with instructions to modernize the army. However, the new liberal majority did not see a need for an army and refused the money needed for reform. The conservatives, who were largely aristocrats, challenged the right of the liberals, who were largely scholars and lawyers, to deny the king who, as both monarch and head of the army, legally possessed the right to initiate military reform without their permission. The liberals argued that what was at stake was responsible government versus autocracy. Unfortunately, the Prussian Constitution was deliberately vague on precisely where the authority lay. A stalemate resulted with neither side yielding. Although the king possessed the authority to dissolve parliament, he knew such an act would court disaster. When he confided to Roon that he was contemplating abdication, Roon summoned Bismarck, now the ambassador to France, back from Paris.

Bismarck returned to Prussia in September, 1862, about the same time that Union troops under General William Starke Rosecrans took Chattanooga, Tennessee and drove General Braxton Bragg's Confederate army into Georgia.

Bismarck was immediately named President of Prussia with an imperial command to solve the problem in Parliament. An avowed enemy of the liberals, Bismarck did not hesitate to use threats. Rather than risk the return of liberal repression, they caved in. Bismarck would fight them until 1867.

In the spring of 1863, a *congress of princes* to reform the Germanic Confederation was called by Austrian Emperor Francis Joseph. The Congress was to take place in August of that year. Bismarck convinced William I to decline the invitation. Fearing an alliance between Austria and Prussia was in the making, Denmark formally annexed the Germanic Duchy of Schleswig-Holstein. This action on the part of Denmark was a violation of the *London Protocol of 1852,* created to protect the sovereignty of both Schleswig and Holstein. The German Diet demanded that Denmark relinquish their claims to the duchy, but Frederick VII refused to even consider their demands.

As a result of Denmark's refusal, the Diet voted a federal execution of Denmark and ordered Hanover and Saxony to invade Holstein, which they did on December 24, 1863.

On January 16, 1864 Austria and Prussia formed an alliance and immediately sent an ultimatum to Christian IX of Denmark (who ascended the throne the previous November with the death of Frederick VII). On February 1, German troops invaded Schleswig. In six days the Danes abandoned their positions and were in full retreat. German troops followed — straight into Denmark.

On April 25 the English called for a cease fire. The *London Conference,* designed by the British to help the Danes save face before the international community of Europe, backfired when the Danes overplayed their hand. Bismarck resumed the war on June 26 and dealt the Danes a crushing defeat that cost Denmark not only Schleswig and Holstein, but the Duchy of Lauenburg as well. A peace accord was signed in Vienna on October 30, 1864.

At the *Convention of Gastein* on August 14, 1865 the joint sovereignty of the Austro-Prussian conquests was formalized. Austria would administer Holstein and Prussia would govern both

Schleswig and Lauenburg. While neither country realized it at the time, an impossible situation had been created. Holstein was an enclave almost entirely within the borders of Prussia.

As far as Bismarck was concerned, it was a small problem that could easily be remedied. Under his skillful hands, Austro-Prussian relations deteriorated rapidly. On April 8, 1866, with the aide of Louis Napoleon, Bismarck negotiated a military alliance with Italy. Under the terms of the alliance, Italy would join Prussia against Austria if war broke out. Venetia was to be Italy's reward.

The following day Bismarck attempted to provoke Austria by introducing a reform measure in the Germanic Diet that he knew Ferdinand I would oppose, hoping Austria would reject it and precipitate a conflict. And, that is precisely what happened. Ferdinand rejected the proposal and Austria began to mobilize its army. Delighted by the turn of events, so did Bismarck. By the end of May, however, the situation remained a political stalemate. Both armies were ready to move, but neither side felt it had been properly provoked. On June 6, Austria made a tactical error. The Austrian governor of Holstein summoned the leaders of the Holstein Diet to discuss the future of the duchy. Bismarck denounced the meeting as a violation of the *Gastein Convention* and, needing no further provocation, sent Prussian troops into Holstein.

Ferdinand I, worried about Bismarck's relationship with Napoleon, secretly negotiated a non-aggression pact with France. In return for French neutrality if war broke out, Austria agreed to cede Venetia to Napoleon the moment hostilities erupted. One interesting detail in the Franco-Austrian treaty concerned Austria's possible victory over Prussia. In the event Austria won, she was free to make whatever changes in Germany she wished — unless those changes disturbed the European balance of power. Also, Austria would be obligated to create a neutral buffer zone along the Rhine to protect the security of France.

On June 14, 1866 the Frankfurt Diet voted federal execution against Prussia. Most of the Germanic states of central Europe joined Austria against Prussia. On June 20, Italy declared war on Austria.

The Seven Weeks War began on June 22, 1866 when the Austrian First Army under the command of Prince William Charles and the Army of the Elbe, commanded by General Herwerth von Bittenfeld, entered Bohemia. The Bohemian campaign was over quickly. Moltke, the Austrian chief of staff, was a student of the recently concluded American Civil War. Moltke attributed the Union's victory over the Confederacy to two things: the telegraph and the railroad. Moltke use both quite successfully.

Bismarck, however, had a secret weapon of his own. While the Austrian troops, like most of the standing armies in the world, were armed with muzzle-loaders, Prussia's army was equipped with breech-loaders. Had it not been the breach-loader, it is likely that Bismarck would have been defeated at Battle of Königgratz on July 3, ending the war in a matter of days instead of weeks.

As it was, Bismarck, whose army was getting the worst of it from a cannon assault throughout the morning, turned the tide in the afternoon and achieved a stunning victory when the Austrian troops advanced, changing the nature of warfare forever. Bismarck's troops fired from prone positions, lying in the craters created by the Austrian cannons. Moltke's troops fought in the traditional manner — advancing in the rigid formation of the British, firing from a standing position and reloading after every volley. Bismarck's troops disseminated them as they advanced in what was the preamble of trench warfare.

On July 5 Napoleon, who was partially responsible for the war by acting as an intermediary for both Austria and Prussia before the war began, now offered to arrange an armistice between the warring factions. Bismarck, the taste of victory still fresh on his lips, was ready to continue the fight and balked at the idea until Napoleon agreed that the terms for peace would be determined before any formal armistice was signed.

Two days after Austria entered Bohemia, the Italian forces, moving towards Austria, were routed by Archduke Albert at Custozza. On July 20, the Italians surrendered after losing most of their naval fleet in a sea battle with Baron Wilhelm von Tegethoff off the coast of Lissa.

The war was effectively over on July 26 with the signing of a preliminary peace accord at Nikolsburg. All of the Germanic states north of the Main River including Electoral Hesse, Frankfurt, Hanover, and Nassau were incorporated into a Prussian German Confederation. The four remaining southern Germanic states were allowed to either become independent nations or form a separate confederation.

Although the formal *Definitive Treaty of Prague* brought the Austro-Prussian War to an official end on August 23, 1866, Bismarck — like Adolph Hitler after him — was determined to bring all of the Germanic states into the German federation. Even before the treaty was signed, Bismarck and Napoleon were carving up Europe. Napoleon wanted Belgium and Luxembourg; Bismarck wanted the four southern German states — and Austria.

Bismarck slowly brought the four southern states into his *zollverein*. While there was still much resistance in the south to a political union with Prussia, economically it made sense. A *zollparlament* (customs parliament) that was politically linked to the German *Reichstag* was established. However, there were still too many cultural and religious differences between the South German states and the Northern Federation to attract the southern alliance. In addition, the South was extremely suspicious of Bismarck, believing him to be a man who could not be trusted.

And, of course, they were right.

Bismarck ultimately came to believe that only a war with France, and the specter of French troops occupying the Rhineland, would bring the South German states around. All he needed to do was to provoke one.

Spain provided the opportunity.

At the end of the Spanish Revolution, the provisional government of Regent Francisco Serrano y Dominguez expelled Queen Isabella. Seeking a new monarch with blood ties to the more powerful thrones of Europe, Dominguez and Prime Minister Juan Prim, the Marqués de los Castillejos, attempted to secure one from the royal families of either Portugal or Italy. From the onset, both had contemplated offering the throne to Prince Leopold of Hohenzollern-Sigmaringen because he was related to both King William of Prussia and Louis Napoleon of France.

William I was indifferent to the idea. Napoleon, who strongly favored an Italian alliance, was adamantly opposed. The diplomatic intrigue that ultimately resulted in the Franco-Prussian War is partially obscured. Only Bismarck's handiwork, revealed in a letter to Prim dated March 15, 1870, is available for scrutiny.

Bismarck, sensing that Napoleon was planning to use the Spanish crown to formalize an Austro-Italian alliance that would also obligate Spain to commit troops in a war against Prussia, urged William I to order Leopold to accept the Spanish offer. Grudgingly, William did so, but only on the provision that Leopold be elected by a substantial margin of the Spanish Córtes. On June

252

19, 1870 Bismarck, acting as the Chancellor, notified Prim.

However, either through a misunderstanding or by deliberate design, the Córtes adjourned before the vote could be taken. Word of what was taking place was mysteriously leaked to the French government, creating a wave of panic. The French, who largely viewed themselves as invincible, suddenly envisioned a dangerous vice-grip alliance between Spain and Prussia with France in the middle. It did not bode well with Louis Napoleon.

The French foreign minister, Antoine Agenor the Duc de Gramont, decried the plot from the floor of the French parliament, threatening war against Prussia if William I did not withdraw Leopold's candidacy. Strangely, the Prussian insisted it had no knowledge of the affair, suggesting that perhaps Bismarck, without the knowledge of either Leopold or William I accepted the throne on Leopold's behalf and arranged for the information to be leaked to the French.

In any event, the French declared war on Prussia on July 19, 1870. The South German states immediately joined the German Federation in anticipation of an attack by the French.

Not content with a mere confederation, Bismarck was determined to build an empire. The support Napoleon expected from his Austrian and Italian allies never materialized. Bismarck was certain, however, that if Prussia fared badly Austria would quickly join the fray if only to share the spoils.

As well-trained and well-equipped German armies launched a three-pronged attack across the Rhine into France, the French army advanced into the Saar and scored a minor victory at Saarbrucken.

Then the German blitzkreg began. By August 6, Bismarck's forces captured Wurth and Weissenburg and forced the French to evacuate Alsace and Strasbourg. By August 18, the Germans had reached Mars-la-Tour and Gravelotte. Both Metz and Bazaine were under siege and all efforts by the French to relieve them were repealed.

On September 2, 1870 the French army, under the command of Louis Napoleon, capitulated after an extremely bloody battle in which a horrendous loss of life on both sides resulted. With nothing between them and Paris, Bismarck's forces swept across France.

When the news of Napoleon's capitulation reached Paris, a mob stormed the Palais Bourbon and demanded that the legislature repudiate Napoleon's claim to the throne and proclaim a new republic. In accordance with the accepted revolutionary standards of the day, a provisional government was quickly established and charged with the responsibility of winning a war that was already lost.

On September 19, German troops laid siege to Paris. The new provisional government suddenly discovered it had no nation to govern. Leon Gambetta, who was charged with the responsibility of forming the new government, escaped Paris in a hot air balloon under the cover of night and devoted his efforts over the next four months towards building a guerilla army of villagers and farmers in a desperate defense of a nation already lost. The surrender, on October 27, of General Achille Francois Bazaine and his army of 173,000 men ended the last organized resistance to the German army. But Paris, even with less than 80 days of rations, refused to capitulate. It was not until those provisions dwindled to nothing that, on January 28, 1871, Paris surrendered.

Gambetta, to his own surprise, proved to be more than adequate as a military leader. The small group of guerillas he organized fought with a ferocity that amazed the Germans. However, Gambetta was outmatched and outgunned. Exhausted, starving and completely without supplies, the resistance movement he started was crushed in mid-January.

Most Frenchman had enough and wanted peace. They were ready to surrender. Only the Jacobins[1] and socialists among the French society wanted to continue the fight.

---

[1] The Jacobins, like the Masons, was a splinter group of the Illuminati, the socialist utopian organization founded by Jesuit scholar Adam Weishaupt. However, unlike the Masons who initially attrracted the emerging, but nevertheless politically disenfranchised low middle class who were predominantly tradesmen, the Jacobins represented the disenfranchised gentry who possessed some wealth but no political power. The Jacobins, as a political force, was founded by Maximilien Isadore Robespierre in 1789 as dissatisfaction in France grew to a revolutionary pitch.

The name, Jacobins, was derived from the "Jacobites." The term was first applied to the Scottish landowners who launched the Stuart rebellion in Scotland in September, 1715. The rebels, who called themselves "The Fifteen," were led by John Erskine, the Earl of Mar. The Jacobites, financed by the French, planned to install James III of France as the King of Scotland when victory was achieved. James III arrived in Scotland in December, shortly after the Jacobites had fought their first two skir-

On March 1, 1871 after suffering a four month siege, the French suffered their final humiliation of the war—German troops marched into Paris to claim their victory at the National Assembly. On March 18, long after the main German army had left the city, the French National Guard, headed by a small conclave of Jacobins whom the Germans had unwittingly failed to disarm, seized a cannon belonging to the regular French army and prepared to start another conflict.

Unwilling to risk a continuation of a war already lost, the new provisional president, Louis Adolpe Thiers sent a French military delegation headed by Generals Claude Martin Lecomte and Jacques Leonard Thomas to negotiate the surrender of the radicals. The mob seized both generals and executed them as traitors. The troop detachment fled, leaving the city in the hands of the Jacobins.

On the demands of the Jacobins, new elections were held on March 26. The *Commune of 1871,* as it was called, contained an equal amount of traditional Republicans and Jacobins as well as followers of socialist Pierre Proudhon and Louis Auguste Blanqui, the French revolutionist. It was a government destined to go nowhere.

O n January 18, 1871 William I of Prussia was proclaimed Emperor of the German Empire. The new Reich included 25 states, 4 kingdoms, 5 grand duchies, 13 duchies and principalities and 3 "free cities." Bismarck had formed his empire. All that remained to be added was Austria. It would come. Of that, Bismarck was certain. It would be his *kulturkampf*—his culture struggle.

---

mishes. However, in the third encounter with the British on Feb. 15, 1716, the Jacobites, overwhelmed by the superior forces before them, broke and ran without engaging in battle. James III fled back to France but the Scot-ish ringleaders were caught and executed. Thirty years later a second Jacobite rebellion took place. This group, again financed by France, called themselves "the Forty-five." Better prepared, better armed, and with an army of 2,000 men, the Jacobites captured Edinburgh on Sept.11, 1745. They defeated the British at Prestonpans on Sept. 21, then marched confidently into England, expecting a quick victory since there was little resistance between them and London. They won battles at Penrith on Dec. 18 and at Falkirk Moor on Jan. 17, 1746. However, once they left the Highlands of Scotland, grumbling and discontent festered like an open boil among the troops. When the Jacobites met the British at Culloden on

Time was on his side.

Or so he thought.

It wasn't.

Emperor William I died on March 9, 1888 and his brother, Frederick III succeeded him — only to die from throat cancer on June 15. His son, taking the name William II ascended to the throne of the German Empire on June 15 and, almost immediately clashed with his uncle's chancellor, Bismarck.

William II, even with an imperial upbringing, favored democracy. This would become increasingly obvious a few months later when a bill to prolong anti-socialist measures was introduced in the *Reichstag* in January, 1890. The Emperor killed the measure and all bans against socialists in Germany were lifted. That single incident caused a rift between the chancellor and the Emperor that only widened over the next three months, resulting in the resignation of Bismarck on imperial command.

The Emperor chose a political neophyte, General Georg Leo von Caprivi as his chancellor. Caprivi's job, however, was reduced to that of imperial messenger since William II decided an emperor's job was to rule.

William II believed socialism existed because social programs didn't. He hoped that by greatly increasing social legislation he would be able to wean the workers away from socialism. Over a period of three years, William II initiated many radical reforms in Germany. Industrial courts were established to adjudicate wage disputes. Shorter working hours were established for women and children. Factories were closed on Sunday. Workers were allowed

---

April 16, 1746, they were decisively beaten and the Stuart rebellion ended. It was the Jacobite's passion and determination to rid their land of a despotic monarch that convinced the "illuminated" French gentry who followed Robespierre to choose the name "Jacobin" when the Illuminati, which sparked the flames of rebellion throughout the continent, was outlawed by the Crown heads of Europe in 1789.

The French Revolution began with a peasant uprising instigated by Jacobins and Masons on July 14, 1789 over the issue of unfair taxation. The Bastille was stormed and the governor, the Marquis Bernard René De Launay was murdered by the mob.

The emerging middle class was being targeted for the majority of the taxes because the rapid expansion of French trade in the Americas had generated unexpected wealth both for the tradesmen who created the products which were now in demand in the new nation across the Atlanto form committees to negotiate working conditions with employers. Factory inspections by the government became more frequent and more effective. Working conditions improved immensely throughout the Empire.

Yet, the Emperor's experiment to wean the workers from socialism failed dismally. If anything, socialism now spread even more rapidly. In the election of 1890, the socialists placed 35 deputies in the *Reichstag*.

Whagen the 20th century broke on the horizon, Germany was rapidly becoming a world power. In return for financial support from the Rothschilds during the Franco-Prussian War in 1870, Bismarck agreed to allow the Rothschild's to create a central bank in the new German Empire. The charter was granted by William I in 1875. The *Reichsbank* opened its doors in January of the following year and played a major role in the development of Germany from that date on.

The privately-owned *Reichsbank* and the *Deutschebank* paid for German expansion in the Mideast and in East Africa, as well as financing the Baghdad Railroad and the Kiel Canal that gave Germany a link to both the North Sea and the Baltic.

Domestically, Germany — in typical FDR fashion — enacted legislation that provided its citizens with tax-financed accident

---

tic, and for the gentry whose warehouses bought the goods and whose ships carried the goods to America. What angered them most was not the excessive taxes they were forced to pay, but the fact that they had no voice in the government to determine a more equitable distribution of the tax load. They demanded that voice. When their demands were not met, they instigated a rebellion and overthrew the monarchy. King Louis XVI was taken captive by Robespierre and held by the Jacobins until his execution by the guillotine on January 21, 1793. A year later, on October 16, Robespierre ordered the execution of Marie Antoinette. A coalition government between the Jacobins, the Cordeliers and the Feuillants was formed. In 1792 the monarchy was abolished. Robespierre, who had amassed the most power, assumed control of the new government. By 1793 Robespierre was a near dictator. Fearful that another faction would rise up and overthrow his government, Robespierre and the Jacobins embarked on a reign of terror, eliminating not only his known enemies but those who might someday challenge his authority. Robespierre began the systematic arrest of all Cordeliers and Feuillants—who were splinter

insurance, old-age benefits and sickness insurance. Internationally, the communities of Europe looked upon Germany with a growing apprehension. In 1898 Germany embarked on an aggressive naval buildup that created diplomatic friction with both England and Russia. Ignoring the concerns of its neighbors, Germany further expanded the program on June 12, 1900 with legislation calling for a 17-year buildup that would make Germany second only to England in the size and strength of its navy.

The tethers that ultimately led to world war were tied, one strand at a time, in Austria beginning in 1867 with the *Compromise of Ausgleich* that formed the co-monarchy of Austria-Hungary and concluded with the annexing of Bosnia and Hercegovina in 1908. The Austria-Hungary Empire was a boiling pot incessantly plagued with internal strife due to its vast multinational and multicultural distinctions. Planning sedition against the Hapsburgs was almost a way of life in most of the captive provinces of the Empire such as Bosnia, Croatia, Hercegovina and Serbia.

Neither Bosnia nor Hercegovina had been independent nations since 1254 when they were conquered by the Huns. Bos-

---

groups of the Jacobins. Both groups broke from the Jacobins prior to the Revolution because of their distrust of Robespierre. With his former partners gone, Robespierre turned his attention on the Girondists with whom he shared power in the government. On October 31, Robespierre ordered the execution of 21 Girondist deputies. With them dead, Robespierre became the virtual dictator of France.

On November 10, Robespierre outlawed the worship of God in France and created the Church of Reason through which he expounded the illuministic views of Adam Weishaupt. However, since Illuminism was pure utopianism, requiring the abolition of all forms of government, Robespierre quietly abolished the Church six months later and declared himself to be the high priest of the Supreme Being. With the passage of Law 22 on June 10, 1793, executions by the guillotine became so commonplace they were no longer a public spectacle to which the crowds flocked. Up to 354 beheadings took place in Paris each month—over ten each day.

It was Robespierre's reign of terror, with nobody knowing when the National Guard would break into their home and lead them off to the guillotine, that finally led to a plot to overthrow Robespierre by the more moderate element of the Paris Commune. On July 27, 1794 Robespierre and 18 Jacobins were surprised at the Hotel de Ville in Paris. Arrested, they were immediately executed. The next day 80 Jacobins were capnia fell to the Ottoman Empire in 1463 and Hercegovina was conquered by the Turks twenty years later. Both remained Turkish provinces for over 400 years.

The Croats and the Serbs, on the other hand, although known as distinct "peoples" since the first century, were largely homeless marauders in central Europe for most of their existence. They, like the Russians, the Bulgarians, the Czech and the Poles were Slavokians by heritage.

---

tured and executed. The *coup d'état* took several days, but the Jacobins were driven from power. Those who escaped the purge did so only because they managed to escape from France before they were captured. Taking what wealth they could carry, or taking letters of credit from the money lenders with whom they entrusted their wealth, most of the Jacobins who escaped the revenge of the Paris Commune made their way to America where they, like the Masons who preceded them, were unobtrusively absorbed into the American society. As a political force, the Jacobins resurfaced in America around 1840, forming first the Liberty Party and later, the Free Soil Party which was headed by Salmon P. Chase. Martin Van Buren, the 8th President of the United States became the Free Soil Party's candidate for President in 1848. By 1860 the Jacobins were instrumental in forming the Republican Party. Chase, who saw himself as the next President of the United States, was forced by the Republican hierarchy to step aside in favor of Abraham Lincoln whom they felt would be more likely to beat the very popular Senator Stephen Douglas [D-IL], who was favored to win the presidential election. Lincoln, who had an immense dislike of Chase, was forced to cede the role of Secretary of the Treasury to him before the Republicans would back his candidacy. Chase, who wanted to be President, settled for the right to control the currency of the United States as he attempted to force Lincoln to back his efforts to create a new privately-owned central bank in America. Thwarted by Lincoln at every turn, Chase engineered a partnership between the State banks and international bankers and created the national bank system which still exists today, and issued the first paper currency in the United States that was not backed by gold.

In 1864 Chase resigned from Lincoln's cabinet, arguing that Lincoln's anti-slavery position was too weak. Lincoln, who wanted also to rid himself of his Jacobin Secretary of War, Edwin Stanton, was relieved to see Chase leave. Yet, a few months later, pressured to do so by the Jacobin Congress, Lincoln appointed Chase to head the Supreme Court. It was Chase who proposed the impeachment of Andrew Johnson; and it was Chase who drafted the articles of impeachment. And, then it was Chase who presided over the Senate trial.

259

By the end of the 10th century, the inhabitants of both Serbia (modern Yugoslavia) and eastern Bosnia were largely Greek Orthodox Christians. Those in western Bosnia and Hercegovina were Roman Catholic. When the Ottomans captured most of central Europe, Islam became the mandated religion, and remained such for 400 hundred years.

By the end of the 13th century the Serbian states, like most of the European powers, had highly evolved secular aristocracies. Because there was no universal law on sucession and inheritance, there was a general trend in all of the smaller Germanic and Slavic states towards dynastic conflict. The weaker states were simply swallowed by the more powerful ones and lost their national identities, but not their national characters — nor their political and theological prejudges and hatred for those who had shackled them in bondage. Such was the case with not only Croatia and Serbia but Bosnia and Hercegovina as well.

Serbia was swallowed by Bulgaria. Croatia was defeated and annexed by Hungary which was itself defeated by Austria. And, as previously mentioned, Bosnia and Hercegovina were annexed by Austria in 1908, setting the stage for the assassination of Archduke Francis Ferdinand of Austria six years later in what would become history's acknowledged catalyst for World War I.

O n January 30, 1889, the Crown Prince of Austria, Archduke Rudolph, committed suicide, paving the way after the death in 1896 of the emperor's younger brother, Charles Louis, for Archduke Francis Ferdinand to succeed his uncle, Francis Joseph I to the throne of Austria-Hungary should the elder statesman succumb before his nephew. Two years after the death of Rudolph, Francis Joseph's wife, the Empress Elizabeth, was assassinated on September 10, 1898 by Italian anarchist Luigi Luccheni who openly advocated the overthrow of the Hapsburgs by the Jacobin socialists.

Small factional wars were breaking out all over Europe as captive nations demanded their freedom, and revolution-inspired people demanded their independence from the shackles of the monarchies that ruled central Europe. The flames of discontent were fervently fanned by the Jacobin socialists who had carefully planted the seeds of revolution across the face of Europe.

260 In 1910, Francis Ferdinand fell in love with a Hungarian com-

moner, Sophie Chotek, and married her against the wishes of his uncle. Because she came from common stock and not from the aristocracy, their union was declared to be a *morganatic marriage* . As such, neither Chotek, who was granted the title of Duchess of Hohenberg, nor her children, could share in the dignities of the Crown, nor could they inherit the possessions of the Archduke upon his death. It was a crushing blow to the Emperor since his nephew was the last of the Hapsburgs. The Dynasty, which had flourished in Europe such 1745 would die with his seed.

When Austria annexed Bosnia and Hercegovina on October 6, 1908, Serbia was outraged. The Serbs had long looked upon both provinces as the future legacy of the Serbian government. The Serbs attempted to negotiate an alliance with Turkey and Greece against Austria. Germany, although visibly disturbed because the Hapsburgs didn't notify them of their intentions in advance, nevertheless, supported Austria. The British, French and Russians demanded an international convocation to consider the ramifications of the Austrian move.

On Christmas Day, 1908 Alexander Petrovich Izvolski, the Russian foreign minister advocated the establishment of a League of Balkan States, that would also include Turkey, to prevent further encroachments of this type. Nothing came of the proposal since Serbia adamantly believed that the provinces rightly belonged to the Serbs, Bulgaria claimed that most of Macedonia rightly belonged to the Bulgarians, and Turkey wanted to create a military alliance to re-establish the Ottoman Empire, which was now collapsing around its ears.

On January 12, 1909 Turkey formally recognized the annexation, followed by a similar recognition on March 31 by Serbia.

As one political crisis after another exploded across the face of Europe, it was inevitable that war would eventually erupt somewhere. As Italy annexed Tripoli, bringing the war cauldron to full boil with Turkey, Germany was making demands on France for entering Morocco in violation of a February 8, 1909 treaty between them that forbade either from doing so. The French-German dispute was amicably settled when Sir David Lloyd George, the British prime minister, stepped in as the arbitrator. The Italian-Turkish situation, however, was not.

War broke out on September 28, 1911. And, like any fire that is not quenched, it began to spread, ever so slowly, until the entire continent was finally consumed with flames.

On April 18, the Italians expanded the war by bombarding the Dardanelles, and in May they conquered the Isle of Rhodes. Germany now began flexing its muscles. England withdrew its battleships from the Mediterranean and moved them to the North Sea because of the growing strength of the German navy. The French, expecting to be attacked by Italy did the opposite. It pulled its fleet from Brest and moved it to the Mediterranean.

On October 18, 1912, Bulgaria, Greece and Serbia declared war on Turkey. Now, all of the Balkan states were at war. That same day, Turkey signed a peace treaty with Italy and turned to face the more lethal enemy. Weakened from its war with Italy, Turkey was no match for the triploid. As the Serbs entered Albania and headed for the Adriatic, the Bulgarians entered Turkey and headed for Constantinople.

The Balkan War was now spilling out into central Europe.

On November 3, Russia warned the Bulgarians against attempting to occupy Constantinople. The Austrians, on November 24 warned Serbia that any attempt on its part to gain access to the Adriatic across Austrian soil would result in war. Soon, every major European power would be involved with threats and counter-threats. Germany, Italy, England supported the Austrians. Russia and France backed the Serbs. It was not until Austria and Germany began to mobilize that Russia, who was not prepared to go to war at that time, abandoned its position backing the Serbs. A dangerous situation temporarily defused, the warring factions sat down to talk in London on December 17.

The peace talks were almost derailed when George I of Greece was assassinated on March 18, 1913 while on an inspection tour in Salonikia[2]. On May 30 the *Treaty of London* ended the first Balkan War. Peace reigned in the Balkans for one month.

On June 29, the Bulgarian army under General Michael Savov attacked a Serb garrison for what it termed "provocation." However, Savov neglected to inform anyone in his government what he was doing, or to seek permission. The Bulgarian government

---

[2]The monarch was the son of the Danish king, Christian IX. He was a cousin the Hapsburgs of Austria. Interestingly, he was placed on the throne of Greece by the English when Otto I, the Bavarian prince, was deposed and assassinated during the Greek Revolution of 1862. The assassin was not caught so the faction responsible, and the motive for the assassination, have never been satisfactorily ascertained.

disavowed the attack, but it was too late. The Serbs, assisted by the Greeks, the Rumanians and the Turks took advantage of the incident to launch a long-planned attack of their own. Bulgaria was quickly defeated.

Serbia launched its second invasion of Albania on September 23, 1913. On October 18 the Austrian foreign minister delivered an ultimatum to the Serb government to get out of Albania in eight days or face the consequences. The Serbs yielded. The same threat was leveled against Greece which held the southern portion of Albania. Interference from England delayed the Greek evacuation until April 27, 1914.

T he trumpets of war had already sounded over Europe when Archduke Francis Ferdinand and his wife Sophie were gunned down by Bosnian revolutionary Gavrilo Princip on June 28, 1914 in the streets of Sarajevo[3]. To claim that this act perpetuated World War I is like saying it's the cigarette after sex that makes a woman pregnant. While it is likely that the brutal murders of Ferdinand and his wife inflamed those already plotting to wage war, and perhaps even gave them a plausible excuse for starting a war already planned, it was not the catalyst most historians claim it was.

Emperor Francis Joseph sent Count Alexander Hoyos to Berlin with a memorandum written four days before the assassination of his nephew repudiating a German suggestion that urged

---

[3]Gavrilo Princip and his young Bosnian revolutionary friends were socialist members of the Serbian *Union of Death* (the Black Hand), an organization founded 1911 to terrorize those whose sympathies were not in sync with Serbian aspirations. While it is believed by many that the Black Hand was both financed and controlled by the Serbian government, no proof has ever substantiated such allegations. It is clear, however, that even if the Serbian government was not an actual conspirator, they were aware of the plot and did nothing to warn either the Austrian government or the Archduke and his wife.

The Austrians were so convinced of the complicity of Serbia that they sent Baron Friedrich von Wiesner to Sarajevo to search of evidence. Wiesner returned to Vienna with no evidence with which to accuse the Serbian government, but the role of the Black Hand in the assassination was clearly established. Fortunately for Austria's plans, the court of world opinion had already condemned the Serbian government.

Austria to reconcile with Serbia, Rumania and Greece "due to threats against the Germanic confederation from France and Russia." On July 5, the emperor penned a note on the bottom of the memo suggesting that steps be taken immediately to resolve the "Serbian issue" while world opinion was still favorable. The July 5, 1914 note clearly, although not conclusively, suggests that plans to attack Serbia were being discussed between Austria and Germany at least four days before the assassination of the Archduke.

Prior to that note, on May 29, 1914, Colonel Edward Mandell House, who was sent by President Woodrow Wilson to get a "first hand" sense of the emergency that currently existed in Europe, wrote the following to the President from Berlin: "...When England consents, France and Russia will close in on Germany and Austria."

The real reason, or more accurately, reasons for World War I must be found on some other page, or pages, of your history book. Gavrilo Princip didn't start the war.

Most conspiracy historians believe that World War I was deliberately staged by world bankers in order to indelibly impress in the minds of the citizens of the world a need for a global governing body. Although no "physical" evidence exists to corroborate such a theory, it is actually more plausible than the assassination conspiracy theory advanced by the traditionally thinking scholars who, in recording the history of the those times, largely ignored the tempestuous moods of most of the nation-states of Europe that had absolutely nothing to do with the assassination of Archduke Ferdinand.

As it has been manifestly established throughout this text, the dichotomy of events leading to most of the significant happenings in history were staged not by the obvious national, regional, or international autocratic or oligarchic players, but rather by the financiers, who, from shrouded secrecy on high, were able to control, or at least manipulate, most of the governments of the world to serve their purpose in creating a supra-national ruling body.

Logic supports no other theory.

Y ou now have a picture of the world and the problems, real or contrived, that faced the leaders of the nation-states of Europe—and the dilemma of the international bankers who financed the economic explosion that resulted from the industrialization of the modern world. The bankers themselves had a monumental problem. There were simply too many countries — and too many borders that restricted trade. The bankers needed a more simple Europe with fewer nation-states. They needed a confederation in Europe much like that found in the United States.

In the United States, however, the problem was even more complex. America was a Republic. The people ruled. There was just so much the bankers could do to influence the affairs-of-state since power in the United States was equally divided between the national government, the States, and the people.

Efforts to change the constitutional balance of power in the United States began with the J.P. Morgan engineered Panic of 1907, and continued with the fraudulently enacted 16th and 17th Amendments to the Constitution. The bankers' plans, however, would not be fully implemented until March 9, 1933 when Franklin Delano Roosevelt used the Wilson-era 1917 *Trading With The Enemy Act* to decree by proclamation an on-going national emergency that still exists to this day. To appreciate how such a thing could occur it is first necessary to understand precisely what happened to the Constitution — and the United States of America — during the first two decades of the 20th century.

Prior to April 8, 1913, America was a Republic. The national government was manageable and was still somewhat unobtrusive. The "voice of the people" was spoken with a mouth that had real teeth; and the States — which held the real power — kept the slowly encroaching federal bureaucracy in check to make certain it did not usurp the mandate provided it by the Founding Fathers through the Constitution.

By stripping the States of their power to participate in the national governing process, the federal bureaucracy was able, within two decades, to steal all but one of the powers reserved for the States by the Constitution. This was done with the enactment of a series of oppressive national emergency laws in 1933 and 1934 that unconstitutionally granted the federal government authoritarian control over every aspect of life in the United States. The "temporary" depression-era emergency mandates forever stripped the States of their authority over the federal bureaucracy and shackled the people to the rapidly burgeoning federal debt that was used by the bureaucrats to finance the overthrow of the Republic through the bribery of the electorate with what would become so self-perpetuating that by 1972 it would simply be called an "entitlement."

265

The problem that exists in America with the perpetuation of an elected bureaucracy through the use of entitlements as bribes for votes is neither new nor uncommon. In the early 19th century, British economist, political scientist and teacher Alexander Fraser Tyler, in comparing the prevalent economic systems of the world, made the following observation: "A democracy cannot exist as a permanent form of government. It can exist only until the voters discover they can vote themselves largesse out of the public treasury. From that moment on, the majority always votes for the candidate promising the most benefits...with the result that democracy always collapses over loose fiscal policy, always to be followed by a dictatorship."

The vision of the one-world government that will slowly and carefully manipulate the eventual dissolution of all formal nation-state borders was more than a dream when the Jekyll Island Seven met in November, 1910—it was a plan on the drawing board in its final stages of development.

The crisis needed to bring about revolutionary change in the world hierarchy was already being engineered in Europe. All that was still needed was the right "visionary" at the helm of the American ship of state in 1913. That man was Woodrow Wilson.

Wilson suited the Morgan interests for two reasons. First, Wilson, even with his impressive scholastic and civil service credentials, was nevertheless a political neophyte who could easily be manipulated by the professional politicians already under the control of the bankers. Second, and most important to Morgan, was the strange and immediate influence Colonel House had over Wilson, and the close personal relationship the pair enjoyed throughout both of Wilson's terms.

Had Wilson's health not failed him during his second term, Colonel House had convinced him—as he did Roosevelt—to seek a third term. Ironically, Wilson ended his second term pretty much as Roosevelt spent most of his—in a wheel chair.

When the United States Congress flatly rejected the Treaty of Versailles because it contained the creation of a supra-nation within its pages, Wilson embarked on a nationwide whistle-stop tour of the United States to sell the American people on the merits of the League of Nations—largely because he expected to be named its first president. Unfortunately, fate was against him.

On September 25, 1919 while hawking the League to the citizens of Pueblo, Colorado Wilson suffered a stroke and was rushed back to Washington. Recovering much of his speech capacity, weak and scratchy though it was, as well as a limited use of his arms and legs, Wilson isolated himself even from his cabinet, attending only one cabinet meeting from October, 1919 until he was succeeded in office by Warren Gamaliel Harding. The severity of his condition was kept from the public. Wilson was so stigmatized by his disability that he virtually refused to meet with anyone other than Colonel House and a few very close congressional leaders. On March 4, 1921, at precisely noon, the man who saw himself as the first president of the world was unobtrusively wheeled from a side entrance of the White House and whisked out of Washington to finish his life in a self-imposed exile.

The political campaign to involve the United States in what could correctly be called "Mr. Wilson's War" by America began with a February 22, 1916 memo from House to the British foreign secretary Sir Edward Grey, in which he stated that Wilson would, whenever England and France felt the timing was right, attempt to negotiate a peace settlement between the Allied Powers and Germany. If Germany refused to sit down at the conference table and negotiate in good faith, America would then enter the war on England's side. (*An Encyclopedia of World History*; Compiled by William L. Langer, Professor of History, Harvard University; Houghton Mifflin © 1956; pg. 935.)

Throughout the fall of 1916, Wilson campaigned feverishly against Republican Charles Evans Hughes, reaffirming his promise to keep America's sons out of the bloody trenches of Europe although less than eight months earlier he had secretly committed the military forces of the United States to the fray. In his campaign he painted Hughes as an uncaring Republican war hawk who would immediately send American troops into harm's way.

Hughes, an associate justice of the United States Supreme Court, resigned from the high court in 1916 to run against Wilson because he was worried not only about what he viewed as the deliberate destruction of the Constitution, but also the socialist legislation coming from the Wilson Congress.

On July 17, 1916 as Wilson prepared for the fall campaign, Congress passed the *Federal Farm Loan Bank Act*. It would virtually assure his re-election. Wilson campaigned on a pledge to keep America out of Europe's war. Hughes campaigned against Wilson's socialist ideas. America wasn't interested in industrial monopolies or domestic reforms in 1916. It was only interested in staying out of the war. Hughes lost the November 7 election by 594,188 popular and 23 electoral votes. Most of his opposition came from the farming states in the west and midwest who showed their appreciation to Wilson for the *Farm Loan Bank Act* by placing him back in the White House for four more years.

Wilson was preparing for war even before he prepared his second inaugural speech. In one year American soldiers would be dying in the trenches of Belgium and France. But much was at stake. At the end of the conflict a new world order would be formed, and with it, a new global hierarchy of governance. Wilson wanted to assure his place at the head of that table.

On December 12, 1916 the German government notified Wilson that the Central Powers were prepared to negotiate peace. Most historians feel that German Crown Prince Wilhelm made the peace gesture to the Americans only because he knew Wilson was preparing, at that very moment, to ask Congress for a declaration of war against Germany.

While Wilson may have privately wanted to do just that[4], the general consensus in America was still one of isolationism. Privately, the British were pushing him to commit American troops without Congressional approval, since the war was going badly for the Allies. Without American assistance, Grey confided to Colonel House, it was probable that Germany would win the war, and all of their plans would be for naught.

Wilson, and Congress, needed adequate provocation. None yet existed. The sinking of the *U.S.S. Lusitania* with the loss of 1,201

---

[4]The private papers of House and several English statesmen including Churchill, Grey and Lloyd-George suggest that Wilson, even before the election of 1916, was looking for a "safe" way to enter the fray that would not cost him the election in 1916. It was believed that the sinking of the Lusitana would create a sufficent outcry to enter the war, reminiscent of the "Remember the Maine," warcry of the Spanish-American war era. However, it did not happen. Numbed as Americans were by the sinking, they were still reluctant to get mixed up in what they viewed as a European war that did not concern them.

lives on May 7, 1915 was now just one of those bitter memories of war. The Germans, however, would provide the opportunity when its high command met at Pless on January 8, 1917.

Although Wilson insisted to his English allies that any overt act of war against the United States would be construed as sufficient provocation to join the fray, that proved not to be true. In February and March, several American merchant ships were sunk by U-boats. The United States neither retaliated on the high seas nor in the halls of Congress. Worried about the midterm elections that were still some twenty months away, Congress refused to act. It was not until the British secret service intercepted and deciphered Zimmermann's dispatch to his ambassadors in Japan and Mexico that Congress, suddenly worried that Germany would bring its war to America's doorstep, reacted. On April 6, 1917 Congress declared war against Germany. It would not be until American troops were actually committed that, on December 7, 1917, a state of war was declared against Germany's ally, Austria-Hungary.

The spring of 1917 was a strange time in America. As the youth of America exuberantly prepared for war, fear gripped the hearts of those who remembered the horror of prior conflicts. While even the faintest memory of war is a living hell for those who endured its pains, the peace that follows eludes those whose loved ones do not return. Wilson's war would affect every man, woman and child in America. It was to be, after all, the "war to end all wars"—climaxed with the formation of the League of Nations, followed by the creation of the new world order that would forever assure the peace and tranquility of mankind.

By July, England was still losing the war and America was still preparing to enter the conflict. While the first American divisions embarked for France on June 13, it would be September[3] before

---

[3]A limited amount of American troops participated, under the general command of the French army, in four prolonged attacks against German strongholds in France between July 18 and September 1, 1917, prior to the American Expeditionary Forces first wholly American assault against the Germans at Saint Mihel on September 12. AEF commander, General John J. Pershing rightfully felt the troops needed to be seasoned under fire before embarking on their own campaigns.

those divisions would see action in the Battles of Saint Mihel and Meuse-Argonne. On August 3, 1917 Frenchman Reginald Baliol Brett, the Lord Viscount Esher, who along with Sir Alfred Lord Milner would serve as the inner circle of Cecil Rhodes' *Society of the Elect*, penned the following in his personal diary: "...No American is likely to be killed before November. This is unfortunate, as Wilson may be required to be steadied before then; and only the death of young Americans can ensure him stability...No one can truly say that the sufferings of the world has been in vain; for they have regenerated all nations, and [France] in particular." (*The Journals and Letters of Reginald, Viscount Esher; Secret Records Revealed;* Dennis Laurence Cuddy, Ph.D.; Plymouth Rock Foundation © 1995; pg. 8.)

On August 11, Brett's diary entry says: "Mr. Henry Morgenthau asked me to call on him...[H]e was one of the principle supporters of President Wilson in the campaign for the Presidency, and he possesses the friendship and confidence of the President...They are ready to sacrifice the lives of American citizens...Mr. Morgenthau realizes the importance upon the morale of the French army and the French people of cementing the Alliance by shedding American blood at the earliest possible moment. If many lives have to be sacrificed, the influence upon the American people can only be beneficent." *(ibid;* pg. 9.) As Brett penned these words, American soldiers were already shedding their blood on French soil — dying for a cause that neither of them, French nor American, understood. Nor did the wives, mothers or sweethearts that were left behind.

Perhaps the words of former President Harry S. Truman, uttered before the U.N. General Assembly on October 24, 1950, might serve as an explanation: "The United Nations..." (created in 1945 by rechartering the grossly ineffective League of Nations) "...represents the idea of a universal morality, superior to the interests of individual nations...The men who died *for* the United Nations in Korea...*died in order that the United Nations might live.*" (Emphasis, author's.) Using Truman's own words, which were unfortunately the truth, we may logically conclude that the 7,940,000 men who died in World War I, and the 16,278,000 men who returned home with broken and torn bodies, suffered the agony of war so that a new world order, a world nation controlled by the supra-government of the League of Nations, could be formed.

That was, after all, the reason the world went to war in 1914.

Even as the first divisions of American troops prepared to embark on the Liberty ships that would carry them to the battlefields of France, Congress enacted the legislation needed to assure that there would be sufficient troops available to see the job done.

On May 18, 1917, using Lincoln's 1861 conscription of troops as a legal precedent, Congress passed the *Selective Service Act*, requiring all American males between the ages of 21 and 31 to register for the draft. By June 5, local draft boards had registered 9,586,508 men. Many did not wait to be called. Business at the local army recruitment centers across the country was brisk as America's youngbloods, bored with life on the farm, were dying to see Paris.

However, those who thought the war would be a Sunday afternoon turkey shoot were quickly educated to the horrible reality of modern warfare. Men died — not by the tens or hundreds, but by the thousands. Tired, wounded and disseminated troops had to be replaced with fresh troops. By September 12, 1918 the Selective Service age requirements had been adjusted to include all men from 18 to 48 years. An additional 13,228,762 conscripts had been added to the draft roster by the end of the conflict; ready, if not willing, to fight "Mr. Wilson's War" for the creation of an exciting new world order.

On October 17, 1917 Congress passed what appeared to be an innocuous piece of legislation designed to protect America from the opportunistic profiteers of war. This legislation was known as the *Trading With The Enemy Act*. Like most pieces of legislation passed by Congress, the name sounded good. In fact, it sounded tough. Severe confiscatory penalties would be assessed against malefactors. Or, so it seemed. It appeared as though the legislation would prevent any and every American profiteer from trading with the enemy while American doughboys were shedding their blood on French and Belgium soil. Of course, that was how it was supposed to appear. Only the reality of the legislation was much different than its perception.

The *Trading With The Enemy Act* prohibited American companies or their foreign subsidiaries from trading with enemy nations except under license of the United States government, or more specifically, the President of the United States to whom that authority was granted under the provisions of the Act.

At that time there were already several multinational companies not only in the United States, but throughout Europe. From an American perspective, the most notable would be Standard

271

Oil. By the outbreak of World War I, the international bankers already held interlocking directorates in most the major corporations of the world, and were rapidly expanding their transnational business. That was, after all, the reason for the war: the dissolution of the feudal nation-states and the creation of a global confederation of trading partners headed by the governing body of the League of Nations.

The *Trading With The Enemy Act* was more of an anti-competition bill than it was anti-trading bill. The president, or those delegated by him to oversee such activities, determined not only what goods or materials could still be traded with Austria and Germany—but also who precisely could conduct that trade. The multinational companies upon whose boards the Warburgs, the Rockefellers, the Lazards, the Rothschilds, the Israel Moseses, the Kuhns, the Loebs, the Sachs and the Goldmans found it easy to gain licensed privilege. No one else did.

H.R. 4960, *The Trading With The Enemy Act of 1917,* codified as Public Law No. 91, begins with a clarification that describes H.R. 4960 as: "An Act to define, regulate, and punish trading with the enemy, and for other purposes." The phrase, *and for other purposes* is the innocuous loophole that allowed trade to continue for favored businessmen and industrialists who could not afford to have commerce stifled during such periods of exorbitant profit-taking.

Public Law 91 defined the *enemy* as "...(a) Any individual, partnership, or other body of individuals of any nationality, resident within the territory [including that occupied by the military and naval forces] of any nation with which the United States is at war, or resident outside the United States and doing business within such territory of any nation with which the United States is at war or incorporated within any country other than the United States and doing business within such territory. (b) The government of any nation with which the United States is at war, or any political or municipal subdivision thereof, or any officer, official, agent, or agency thereof. (c) Such other individuals, or body or class of individuals, as may be natives, citizens or subjects of any nation with which the United States is at war, other than citizens of the United States, wherever resident or wherever doing business, as the President, if he shall find the safety of the United States or the successful prosecution of the war shall so require, may, by proclamation, include within the term 'enemy'." (Public Law 91; Chapter 106, Section 2; October 6, 1917.)

By definition, it would appear that anyone caught trading with the enemy would logically be construed as an enemy of the United States and therefore subject to the confiscatory penalties of Public Law 91. However, Section 5 of that legislation granted Wilson the right to "...suspend the provisions of this Act so far as they apply to an ally of enemy...and the President may grant licenses, special or general, temporary or otherwise, and for such period of time and containing such provisions and conditions as he shall prescribe, to any person or class of persons to do business...and to perform any act made unlawful without such license..."

To find such a provision within any law theoretically enacted to deny comfort to an enemy of the United States while Americans are fighting on foreign soil is shocking, and may be hard to grasp by those who have not come to grips with the fact that there is, and has been for well over one hundred years, a super power behind the seats of government, dictating both national and international policy to all of the world's leaders. But the reality is that such a clause, for the reason stated, was not only part of Public Law 91 but has been the standing policy of the United States government throughout most of this century.

During the Vietnam War, Congress proposed a piece of legislation called the *Export Control Act of 1969* designed primarily, it would appear, to control detenté with the Soviet Union. The legislation wore a name that suggested the government was taking an active role in controlling the exportation of American products and materials to "unfriendly" nations. It didn't. What it did was to further amend the *Trading With The Enemy Act* by authorizing the licensing of goods to Soviet bloc nations. An amendment was introduced by Congressman Earl Landgrebe that would have prevented the sale and shipment of either general consumable goods or the machinations of war to any Soviet bloc nation supplying, or in any way assisting, North Vietnam's efforts against the United States.

Although common sense argued that the *Landgrebe Amendment* should have been overwhelmingly approved, it was defeated. Why? Because the Nixon Administration, like the Johnson Administration before it, was practicing the same type of foreign trade

273

policy as every other wartime president since Wilson. It was a trade policy counterpoised to the best interests of the those charged with the obligation of fighting the war, since it assured a steady, never-ending flow of supplies from the Soviet bloc "trading partners" directly to Ho Chi Minh in North Vietnam for use against American forces in the South.

War is good business. Or, at least, it has always been a profitable business for those who manufacture armaments and the other essentials of war — especially if the industrialists who profit from the carnage can sell both sides of the conflict. That was what the *Trading With the Enemy Act of 1917* was supposed to stop. It appeared, on the surface, to ban any American company from selling goods or materials to an enemy nation, or to an ally of an enemy nation. But, in reality, it didn't. It only banned small companies, without any national or international political leverage, from doing so. The large transnational corporations could apply for "wavers" that would allow them to continue supplying materials or products (ostensibly not war materials) to those with whom America was engaged in conflict. First Wilson, then Roosevelt, Truman, Johnson and Nixon granted wavers that allowed the multi-national corporations to continue to do uninterrupted transnational business during times of war.

Why would they do so, knowing that any aid to the enemy could, and likely would, cost additional allied lives? Because even during the war years in the early half of the 20th century, the existing transnational corporations no longer saw themselves as "American" companies although they were born here. The heads of America's Fortune 500 corporations view themselves as wholly trans-sovereign entities that owe no allegiance to any nation. The chief executive of one American corporation recently boasted to Reform Party candidate Pat Buchanan that the government could no more control the growing giants of industry than a child could redirect an elephant by shouting. In point of fact, the behemoths of government and the behemoths of industry now perform like elephants walking truck to tail. *Insight on the News, Synposium*; Patrick J. Buchanan; February 21, 2000 pg. 41.

Buchanan, in his *Insight on the News* article, further noted that Carl Gerstacker of Dow Chemical Company confided to the media that he envisioned a day when Dow Chemical would severe the tethers that tied it to the apron strings of America. "I have long dreamed," he said, "of buying an island owned by no nation and of establishing the world headquarters of the Dow Company on the truly neutral ground of such an island, beholden to no nation or society." [*ibid,* pg. 41.]

Phil Condit, the head of Boeing, told an *Insight on the News* interviewer in 1997 that he would be delighted if, in 20 years, "...no one thought of Boeing as an American company. My goal," he said, "is to rid [Boeing] of its image as an American company."

A spokesman for Union Carbide, another American corporation gone transnational, agreed with Condit and Gerstacker's views. "It is not proper for an international corporation to put the welfare of any country in which it does business above that of any other." [*ibid,* pg,. 41.] The transnationals have only one loyalty — and that is to the bottom line. Profit. For that reason, it suffers them not to pull up stakes from within those American communities whose sweat equity built them into the international power houses they now are.

Dwight D. Eisenhower, in his last Presidential address to the nation in 1961, warned the American people to guard against the acquisition of "...unwarranted influence [by] the military-industrial complex." He declared that such a combination of interests represented a "...potential for the disastrous rise of misplaced power..." that could threaten not only our liberties but our democratic process as well. (*Funk & Wagnall's New Encyclopedia;* Vol. 8; pg. 408.)

The contradictory trade policy within the *Trading With The Enemy Act* is puzzling when viewed through the eyes of the typical citizen on the street who, according to the politician, doesn't understand the complexity of global politics. Logic suggests that our national interest is always best served by protecting the sons and daughters of America who have been placed by their government in harm's way, and by doing everything within our power to quickly win the conflicts into which they have been thrust.

Global imperialism was supposed to die with the birth of the League of Nations. Wars could no longer be waged for the purely military or political objectives of any single nation-state. Instead, wars were now to be ideologically waged only to advance the economic and sociological agenda of those now shaping the emerging new world order. The threat of force would be applied only to keep belligerent states in lock-step with the global mandate of the League. Ultimately, when force was deemed necessary, it would be applied by the League of Nations, who was to be des- 275 ignated as the police force of the new world order.

Of course, the globalists' plan failed because Congress, seeing the creation of a supra-global state within the League's charter, refused by a vote of 49 to 35 on March 19, 1920, to ratify the Treaty of Versailles in which the League of Nations was hidden. The "war-to-end-all-wars" would now need an encore.

Vigilance, however, had a price.

America had not learned it yet, but its privately-owned Federal Reserve system, which was entrusted with the responsibility of creating the nation's money supply through interest-bearing debt, also possessed the ability to manipulate the economic cycles by expanding and contracting the amount of money in circulation. By rigidly controlling the money supply, the Fed also controlled the amount of credit that would be available at any given time from almost any bank in the nation.

The Fed was about to show America its contempt for their refusal to ratify the League of Nations. Within two months of Congress' rejection of the Treaty of Versailles, the Fed met on May 16, 1920. On May 17, they severely raised the amount of the reserve each bank was required to hold and contracted the money supply. The overall effect of that decision, according to Senator Robert L. Owen, Chairman of the Senate Banking Committee in a 1921 report, was the immediate reduction of the national income by some $15 billion, the depreciation of the value of the ranches and farmlands of America by some $25 billion, and the immediate elimination of over a million jobs on mainstreet America. [*The Congressional Record,* May 17, 1921.]

To finance the war economy, the Fed had greatly expanded the money supply from 1917 to 1919. Tax receipts of the federal government in 1916 were $761 million. The government spent $731 million, and had a tax surplus of $30 million at the end of the year. No long term debt was incurred from the Fed in 1916.

However, the 1917 tax receipts of $1.1 billion fell $853 million short of covering the government's expenses, and those funds were borrowed from the Fed. In 1918, even with $3.645 billion in tax collections, the government still had to borrow $9.03 billion. It was even worse in 1919. The national debt increased another $13.363 billion — although tax revenues reached $5.4 billion. It should be noted that the tax load on the American citizen increased sevenfold between 1916 and 1919. Defenders of the Fed and advocates of the utopian global society were quick to point

276

out precisely how much freedom costs, suggesting that those unwilling to shoulder the tax burden were somehow unpatriotic — or worse. However, it should be pointed out that America's peacetime economy in 1920 cost $6.649 billion to manage, a nine-fold increase over the pre-war 1916 economy — only five years earlier.

Except that in 1920 the Fed compressed the money supply and contracted the economy. Two things happened. First, through taxation, the United States government drained what would have been $5,888 billion dollars in pre-1917 discretionary dollars from the economy. At the same time, the Fed contracted the quantity of money available to the banks to extend credit, creating immediate hardships not only on the working class of America, but also on most of the industries in which those Americans worked, creating massive layoffs, business closures and finally, mortgage foreclosures by the local community banks who owned the notes. When the home owners, who owned the delinquent mortgages, could not find work and were unable to meet their payments, the local banks, forced to do so by Fed rules, foreclosed.

Second, during the war years, the demand on America's farmers increased tenfold since much of Europe's productive farmland served as the battlefields of war. The demand for foodstuffs from America's allies simply could not be satisfied. American farmers were encouraged to mortgage their farms to buy more land. Then they were encouraged to borrow even more money to buy additional seed, materials and equipment to plant their increased acreage in order to produce more crops.

Suddenly the bottom just seemed to fall out of the "good luck bucket." The foreign market for the farmer's increased yield that had materialized from the ravages of war three years earlier just as quickly vanished. The debt that created that yield remained. When the farmers couldn't meet their payments, they returned to their local banks for help, only to find the banker faced with the same problem. All of their money was out on loan. To compress the money supply, the Fed simply raised the bank's fractional reserve requirements. Not only did the local banks not have any money to lend, most of them were short as well. They frantically began calling in loans to stave off foreclosure by the Fed. In the end, over 5,000 community and State banks were forced to sell off substantial amounts of their banking assets at greatly reduced prices to survive a takeover by the Fed. Many of them simply didn't make it, and closed their doors forever.

Welcome to the Panic of 1920.

In less than one decade the Fed had learned it could manipulate the economies of nations at will without war. It would be a tool the central banks would use repeatedly throughout the balance of the twentieth century — each time with more stealth and, ultimately, with more success than each previous cycle. Ever so slowly, the most desirable wealth in the world was being transferred from the hands of private individuals and companies into the portfolios of the international bankers and their various holding companies.

Welcome to the land of opportunity.

The largest transfer of wealth in the history of the world was only nine years away.

❖ ELEVEN ❖

Peace, Prosperity and the Wall Street Affair

The "war-to-end-all-wars" ended with a multitude of unresolved political, economical, and financial issues that would, in less than one generation, bring the nations of the world back to the battlefields of Europe and Asia. Other than the fact that the Europe of 1920 contained fewer nation-states than the Europe of 1914, the political landscape remained unambiguously unchanged as the League of Nations floundered haplessly in a sea of powerless political uncertainty.

The weak alliance would never become the super nation envisioned by its architect, Colonel Edward Mandell House, or its public creator, Woodrow Wilson. In fact, it would prove to be a dismal failure within two decades. Forty-six nations, with high expectations that the League would able to provide solutions to the growing sociopolitical problems of the rapidly shrinking world, would join the newly formed League of Nations. The United States of America would not be one of them. Without the United States, the dream of the multinational bankers and industrialists to create a single global community came to a temporary halt as the world settled back for eight years to catch its breath.

Herbert Hoover had a fairly easy election in 1928 thanks in part to himself. As Secretary of Commerce for both Warren G. Harding and Calvin Coolidge, Hoover, an engineer turned economist, was largely responsible for the economic policies of both Administrations. America had finally recovered from the Recession of 1920, and the nation was experiencing an unprecedented surge of prosperity as the stock market continued a dizzying, five-year upward spiral.

The Federal Reserve returned to its pre-1920 practice of easy credit and began pouring money into the economy. America still

279

hadn't learned it could not trust the bankers at the Fed. Now, however, the floodgates to easy money were opened even wider. From 1921 to 1929 the Fed expanded the money supply by 44%, up from $31.7 billion in 1921 to $45.7 billion in 1929. In addition, vast sums of private money—totalling some $286 billion—from the Morgan and Rockefeller interests were poured into Wall Street. Wall Street financiers grabbed as much of the Morgan/Rockefeller money as they could get their hands on, quickly investing it in an vast array of entrepreneurial ventures throughout America. The country was on a "get-rich-quick" feeding frenzy, and there was no end in sight.

Truly, America was the land of opportunity.

Wall Street utilized a new tool to entice novice investors to speculate in the stock market. The stock exchange was open to virtually everyone from the factory worker to the bored American housewife who invested with the household milk money. The tool Wall Street used was called "buying on margin." Everyone was doing it. And, to listen to them, everyone was getting rich.

Investors were encouraged to purchase stock with a modest 10% down payment, financing the balance with credit supplied by the broker from either a traditional bank or from some large corporation like Standard Oil or J.P. Morgan & Company.

Buying on margin was easy. The small-time investor was led to believe that the "day of reckoning" would not come until the stocks were sold, at which time the loans would then be repaid from the profits. On paper, America had more millionaires and near-millionaires from 1921 to 1929 than any other period in its history. However, the real wealth was actually owned by the Wall Street bankers who financed the debt—and assumed none of the risks.

The margin notes were typically "24-hour broker call loans," which meant the broker could call in the loan at anytime with a 24-hour notice. If the investor did not have the liquidity to meet the call, he or she would be required to sell off the stock—usually at a substantial loss—to meet the obligation. America either ignored the conditions of their loans or failed to take note of the "fine print." In either event, most of the amateur investors greatly over-extended themselves, believing perhaps that the bull market would never end, or at least that their profits would greatly exceed the cost when that day finally arrived.

280   Virtually overnight, ladies' bridge clubs became *investment*

clubs. Taxi drivers provided their fares with the latest stock market tips, and *penny stock* clubs sprang up everywhere. By 1928 there were more people playing the stock market than there were "playing the ponies." It was a much safer bet—and it was legal.

America was having a love affair with Wall Street. Unfortunately, love is blind. When the Wall Street tycoons, financial bankers and America's wealthiest families like the Rockefellers, the Mellons, the Carnegies, the Vanderbilts; the maverick rich like Henry Ford, Joseph P. Kennedy and Bernard Baruch, and high profile Americans like Douglas Dillon (the father of John F. Kennedy's Secretary of the Treasury) and Henry Morgenthau (Roosevelt's Treasury Secretary) began, ever so slowly, diverting their funds from the stock market in the fall and winter of 1928, few noticed. So many "common types" were buying into the market at such a rapid rate that the exit of the wealthiest families in America barely caused a ripple in the wake of the *U.S.S. Wall Street.* By the summer of 1929, only the "expendable" dollars of the middle class investors remained in the market.

During the roaring '20s, America largely ignored Europe. It was, after all, another world—a distant place where the scars of war were still evident. It was a world of old animosities and lingering hates. It was a world of small nation-states still frightened of their more powerful or more aggressive neighbors. It was a world worried about when the bully next door would strike. It was a world wondering what types of alliances could be forged to best protect its national borders from aggression.

Although the League of Nations was created to alleviate those apprehensions, fear persisted. Everyone knew the League was a paper tiger. It was merely a diplomatic alliance with a Court in The Hague that had no real legal standing outside of its membership roster and an international bank funded by all of the central banks of the world to bribe aggression into submission.

When the World War I ended, the cost of the conflict, which was to be assessed entirely to Germany, was calculated to be $337 trillion dollars in both direct and indirect costs. When Germany balked at paying such a sum, the League appointed a reparation committee to study the matter. On April 27, 1921, after debating the issue for over a year, the committee—which included not only an American "political" delegation headed by a young bureaucrat named John Foster Dulles, but a "financial" delegation led by Fed Chairman Paul Warburg and his brother Max, who headed the German *Reichsbank* – set the reparation at 132 trillion gold *Reichsmarks,* or about 30% of the total cost of the war. Believing it was the best deal they were going to get, Germany reluctantly agreed to the terms.

After Germany signed the agreement, British Foreign Secretary Lord George Curzon declared that the *Treaty of Versailles,* due to the extreme amount of reparations assessed to Germany, would not provide lasting peace in Europe. The peace, he insisted would prove to be merely "...a truce for twenty years." He correctly predicted that another world conflict would begin in 1939. Even socialist John Maynard Keyes, who hated the Germans, declared that the *Treaty of Versailles* was "...outrageous and impossible, and can bring nothing but misfortune behind it."

In addition to the monetary assessment which postwar Germany lacked the ability to pay, the *Treaty of Versailles* stripped Germany of all colonial possessions throughout the world, allocated a sizeable portion of eastern Germany (known as the Polish Corridor) to Poland, ceded the rich coal fields of the Saar basin to France for twenty years, and created a League of Nations mandate out of the disputed Mermel Territory.

Germany, from the moment the Treaty was signed, was in both political and economic turmoil. Strife ruled the Weimar Republic throughout the Roaring 20s. As America enjoyed the good life, Germany suffered privation and deepening recession.

By 1922, Germany was in financial trouble. The *Reichsmark* was about to collapse, and with it, the entire German economy. The Reparation Committee met on May 31, and over strenuous opposition from France, granted Germany a moratorium for the balance of the year, easing the situation slightly.

On August 1, Lord Sir William Balfour, the new British Foreign Secretary sent a note to each of the Allied powers suggesting that all further claims against Germany should be abandoned provided a "...general settlement could be made which would end the economic injury inflicted on the world by the present state of things." (*An Encyclopedia of World History;* compiled by William L. Langer, Professor of History at Harvard; Houghton Miffin © 1952; pg. 958.)

The offer was contingent upon the United States – which had not demanded reparation from Germany – forgiving the debts owed to it by the European powers who had borrowed heavily from America between 1914 and 1919. In the event the United States would not cancel those debts then, according to Balfour, England would be obligated to collect at least enough from Germany to repay its obligations to the American government.

Congress, however, failed to see the connection. As far as they were concerned, reparations and inter-Allied debt were not related; nor would the voters likely allow them to be. It was enough that American doughboys had shed their blood to save Europe. The taxpayers would revolt if they suddenly learned they were going to have to pay Germany's war debt as well. Of that, Congress was certain — and it didn't require a public opinion poll to confirm it.

As the good times began to unfold in the United States, the economic situation in Europe continued to worsen. Britain realized if the German mark collapsed it would very likely create a domino affect throughout Europe since all of the central banks were interlinked. French president Raymond Poincaré, who still had vivid memories of German troops marching into Paris, didn't seem to care. France wanted its pound of German flesh regardless of the price. France also had a sizeable debt of its own, owed to the central banks of both Great Britain and the United States.

In exchange for the debt moratorium, France wanted 60% of the capital of the German dye factories on the left bank of the Rhine as well as exploitation rights to the German coal mines in the Ruhr. Such a concession would have bankrupted the Weimar Republic. The stalemate continued.

By the end of 1922, Germany had defaulted twice.

On January 2, 1923 a conference was held in Paris to negotiate a bond issue to satisfy the German debt. France rejected it out of hand. On January 9, Germany defaulted again. Two days later French and Belgium troops moved into the Ruhr in retaliation for what they termed a deliberate default on the part of Germany. In reality, France was ambitiously determined to create a French Protectorate out of the rich coalfields of the Ruhr District.

The Germans protested to the League, and Great Britain protested to both France and Belgium. Nothing happened. On August 11 England issued a white paper declaring the "...Franco-Belgium action...was not a sanction authorized by this treaty..." and demanding their withdrawal from the Ruhr. Of course, by that time it was too late.

When the Franco-Belgium troops invaded the Ruhr, German workers, urged to do so by the Weimar government, went on strike and closed down the mines. Obligated to pay idled workers as well as compensate the mine owners, the Weimar government embarked on a reckless scheme to inflate the German mark and pay off its reparation debt with worthless money. It was a mistake of monumental proportions — and with catastrophic consequences not only for Germany but the rest of the world as well. The Weimar Plot set into motion an irreversible series of events that would eventually threaten all of the world's central banks, and cause the bankers themselves to retaliate with a plan of their own that would not only ensure them of a tighter grip on the monetary policies of the nation-states of the world, but of the governments themselves.

On September 26, 1923 passive resistance to the Franco-Belgium occupation of the Ruhr ceased. The German mark was on a downhill slide, and nothing the Weimar government tried could slow its rapid depreciation. In fact, the Mark was now worth less than the paper upon which it was printed. On October 21, France declared the Ruhr District to be an independent republic.

By the end of October, the French franc fell 25%. Fearful that Germany's super-inflation would destroy the British pound as well, Great Britain's prime minister, Stanley Baldwin, petitioned U.S. President John Calvin Coolidge to ask the Fed to intercede to prevent a complete global economic and monetary collapse.

In America, the Roaring '20s were just getting into full swing. It was the era of the speakeasy, the flapper, and bathtub gin. Life in the United States was indeed a cabaret. Jobs were plentiful; life in the urban areas of America was fast becoming a gigantic, carefree, continuous party. What more was there? Europe? The rest of the world? Who cared?

At the moment, virtually nobody. Within six years, just about everyone.

Reparations Committee Chairman Charles Gates Dawes, who served President Harding as the first director of the Bureau of the Budget in 1921-22, and who would become Coolidge's vice president later that year, completed his report on the state of the Germany economy, or what was left of it, on April 9, 1924. It was alarming. In 1918 a pound of potatoes cost 1/8 mark. In November, 1923 that same pound of potatoes cost 50 billion marks. One egg, which cost 1/4 mark in 1918, cost 80 billion marks in 1923. And, a pound of butter that would have cost 3 marks in 1918 would require a wheelbarrow filled with 6 trillion marks to purchase in November, 1923. Christmas, for most German families, was out of the question that year. But in America, most families were experiencing the best Christmas in at least three years — and, things were already looking even better for the next season. God bless America.

The Dawes Plan, which entailed a complete restructuring of the German mark, called for an immediate loan of 800 million gold *Reichsmarks* by the United States to stabilize Germany's monetary system. In addition, the Reparations Committee, realizing it was the heavy annual assessment that created the current crisis, reduced the reparation payments by some 600%, to one million gold marks per year for five years, after which the payment would increase to 2.5 million marks. It was an acceptable solution.

Just before the Dawes Committee met in November, 1923 a group of nationalist insurgents headed by Adolph Hitler, and hiding behind the respectability of former General Erich Friedrich Wilheim von Ludendorff, attempted to overthrow the Austrian government on November 8 in what history records as the Beer Hall Putsch. It was a wakeup call for the world. The Weimar Republic was in trouble — deep trouble.

In an attempt to stabilize the government of Frederick Ebert, the Dawes Plan also demanded the immediate and unilateral withdrawal of Franco-Belgium troops from the Ruhr. The withdrawal bega in the early summer of 1924, and on November 18 the region was restored to Germany.

Hitler, the leader of the National Socialist German Workers party was sentenced to five years in prison for his part in the Beer Hall Putsch, but he was released after serving only one. Hitler immediately returned to Munich and re-established himself as the head of the Nazi movement that would, two months before Franklin Delano Roosevelt became the 32nd President of the United States, assume the reins of power of the Third Reich.

When Herbert Hoover was sworn into office as the 31st President of the United States on March 4, 1929, the dye was already cast. The stock market would crash that fall. Although

285

documented proof of the Wall Street bankers' conspiracy clearly does not exist, sufficient circumstantial evidence does. As mentioned previously, in the winter of 1928-29, every major financial family in the United States sold off their stock portfolios and moved their money into gold. No "insider" dollars of any major consequence remained in the stock market.

On Tuesday, October 29, 1929 American financier Bernard Baruch brought an illustrious visitor with him to the New York Stock Exchange. His guest was England's former Chancellor of the Exchequer, Winston Churchill. Churchill had resigned his position in the Baldwin government only four months earlier over a political dispute that led to an irreconcilable parting of the ways between himself and Baldwin. Churchill, the consummate imperialist, vehemently disagreed with Baldwin's policy towards India that would ultimately lead that colony towards self-government. Churchill contemptuously viewed Baldwin as a man determined to destroy the British Empire, and he could no longer support his Administration.

But Churchill was not invited to the Stock Exchange that day because of his political posturing. He was invited because, as Chancellor of the Exchequer during the German mark crisis, he convinced Parliament to temporarily return the British pound to the gold standard to avoid its devaluation[1]. To the money barons of the world Churchill, a man with no political scruples, would play an important role in shaping the future of Europe

---

[1]Churchill would later declare that his decision to reinstate the gold standard was among the worst decisions of his career. From a sound monetary perspective, it was not. Churchill's action not only stabilized the British pound, but also helped stabilize the currencies of its European trading partners. Churchill, like Franklin Delano Roosevelt and many years later, William Jefferson Clinton, was a man consumed with blind ambition. Churchill, like Roosevelt and Clinton, was a political piranha who thought nothing of sacrificing his own personal beliefs if it would further his objective to become the political head of his nation—a goal he achieved in May, 1940.

Churchill began his political career in 1900 as a Conservative in the House of Commons. When the Conservatives lost power in 1906 by campaigning for the expansion of colonialism in Africa, an issue favored by Churchill, he switched to the Liberal Party and was rewarded with the position of undersecretary of state for the colonies. In 1908 he was promoted to the Cabinet where he served as the president of the Board

within the next decade.

Most conspiracy chroniclers are convinced that Churchill, who did not hold office again until 1939, was singled out to witness the Stock Market Crash so that he would be able to testify to the power possessed by the international bankers who were, at that moment, preparing to the reshape Europe into a socialist model that would not be to the liking of either Churchill or Great Britain. While there is no physical evidence to support such a conclusion, there is likewise none to dispute it.

In an April, 1970 *American Opinion* article, writer Gary Allen insisted that Baruch bragged to Churchill that he "...began to liquidate [his] stock holdings..." the previous winter and put his "...money into bonds and into a cash reserve..." as well as gold. In the same article, *Federal Reserve, the Anti-Economics of Boom and Bust* (page 63), Allen declared (citing still another writer without documentation) that when Joseph P. Kennedy took his money out of the stock market during the winter of 1928-29 he did not reinvest his dollars in anything. Was Kennedy afraid that when the stock market collapsed every capital asset in the United States would become worthless? Of course, if that was in fact true, then gold and silver—even with government controlled prices—would skyrocket in value.

Kennedy was much too smart to hold all of his wealth in paper money—particularly after watching the super-inflation of Germany only five years earlier decimate the *Reichsmark* in a matter of weeks. Kennedy, like Baruch and anyone else who might have liquidated their Wall Street holdings during the winter of 1928-29 would have placed their money in whatever portable wealth

---

of Trade. He was named Home Secretary in 1910 and First Lord of the Admiralty in 1911. Churchill was 37.

However, his fortune with the Liberals was about to change. As First Lord of the Admiralty, Churchill was blamed for the British losses during the disastrous Dardanelles debacle, and was forced to resign. After serving briefly as an army major in France, Churchill returned to Parliament as a member of Conservative Party where, because of his military experience, he was appointed Lloyd George's Minister of Munitions from 1917-18. In 1918 he was appointed Secretary of State for War. In 1921 he was appointed Secretary of States for the Colonies by Prime Minister Andrew Bonar Law, who resigned due to ill health in 1923. From 1924 until June, 1929 Churchill served as Stanley Baldwin's Chancellor of the Exchequer.

287

was available that would increase in value in a direct relation to the rapidly declining value of the stocks when they pulled the plug on Tuesday, October 29.

Revisionist historians are quick to place the blame for the Crash on amateur investors who they claim simply panicked when they saw their life-savings being erased in the slow-motion ticker-tape charade that began on Black Thursday and climaxed the following Tuesday. If they had simply held their stock instead of selling, revisionists maintain even today, the Crash would not have happened. Of course, they insist, there would have been a major correction, as there is at the end of any bull market, but the market itself would not have collapsed and the ensuing Great Depression would likely not have occurred.

If it was not tragic, it would almost be amusing. As is always the case when revisionists attempt to "tidy up" history, historians affixed the blame for the Crash on its victims — the working class investor.

If the Crash had not been a carefully staged dichotomy, such an analogy might merit contemplation. However, two theoretically unrelated factors came into play simultaneously, guaranteeing that what happened necessarily had to happen. First, the bottom "fell" out of the market as a major sell-off began. The sell-off started with the sale of the "remnant shares" left in the accounts of the same conspirators who had previously sold off the bulk of their portfolios, leaving only enough stock to prime the suction pump that would eventually suck the life from the stock market. Since there were not enough remnant shares left in the market to trigger a crash, a well-planned panic was needed.

Telephone calls were strategically placed to key brokers across the country advising them to dump stock As stock prices edged slowly downward in the morning, brokers all across the country began calling in their "24-hour demand notes." Panic now set in on mainstreet America in earnest. By the time the market closed on Friday, a slight recovery from the afternoon beating offered investors a thin ray of hope that perhaps the worst was over. However, when the market opened Monday morning, the sell-off began again with renewed vigor.

Second, to meet their margin calls on Thursday and Friday, thousands of small investors all over the country beat a path to their local banks to withdraw years of savings in order to protect their stock portfolios, causing major drains on the cash reserves of hundreds of community banks. Meeting this new threat head on, the Fed suddenly and unexpectedly increased the reserve requirements of its member banks and shrank the money supply at the precise moment when an expanded money supply would have ended the crisis on Wall Street.

The well-to-do middle class speculators who had enough liquidity to meet the margin calls on Thursday or Friday suddenly discovered, on Monday or Tuesday, that more margin calls would be received from their brokers until finally, not only were their savings gone, but their local banks no longer possessed the funds to extend additional loans. In the end, not only was the stock lost, so were their savings—and so was the collateral that was originally pledged to the broker when the stocks were purchased.

John Kenneth Galbraith, who in *The Great Crash, 1929,* declared that nobody "...was responsible for the great Wall Street crash..." also said: "Nothing could have been more ingeniously designed to maximize the suffering, and also to insure that as few as possible escaped the common misfortune...*The man with the smart money, who was safely out of the market when the first crash came, naturally went back in to pick up bargains.*" (pg. 111; emphasis, author.)

Of course the smart money was safely out of the market. That was the whole point of engineering the Crash. It should also be noted that those who manipulated the market for their own gain knew precisely why the Crash happened, and they likewise knew the dollars they poured into the Market to buoy the rapidly sinking *U.S.S. Wall Street* would not be lost.

While history notes that most of the working class and middle class speculators were forced to endure mammoth financial losses, it fails to give an accounting of the names of those who profited, other than to acknowledge that several speculators—which included many of America's wealthiest families, and some of the biggest banks not only in the United States but Europe—attempted to restore confidence in the market by buying when everyone else was selling.

Coincidently, none of these "buyers" suffered any appreciable losses when the Crash was first registered on Black Thursday.

While Galbraith conveniently found no one to blame for the Crash, Congressman Louis McFadden, head of the powerful House Banking Committee did. On May 23, 1933, McFadden submitted Articles of Impeachment against the Fed, charging them not only with creating the Depression, but with unlawfully and arbitrarily increasing and decreasing the money supply of the United States to benefit private interests. The Depression, McFadden charged "...was a carefully contrived occurrence [by] international bankers [who] sought to bring about a condition of despair here so they might emerge as the rulers of us all."

The one man in Washington who was absolutely blameless for the economic woes of 1929 was, to no one's surprise, the person who was singularly blamed for it—both by the media and the American people who discovered by the spring of 1930 that not only were their savings gone, so for the most part, were their jobs. He was also blamed by his opponent in the 1932 election. In reality, the decade-long Depression was actually created from the Recession of 1930 by Franklin D. Roosevelt, who used the economic upheaval in a brazen attempt to usurp the Constitution of the United States and create what would amount to a socialist police state that granted him almost absolute dictatorial power not only over the lives of his "subjects," but over the free enterprise system of America as well. Yet, history would be much kinder to Roosevelt than his predecessor, Hoover.

Herbert Clark Hoover, who had resided in the White House for only eight months when the stock market crash shattered the American dream, was doubly stigmatized by the uncontrollable events of his time. The man who campaigned on the slogan "a chicken in every pot" was quickly faced with the reality that far too many Americans were going to bed hungry every night providing, of course, that they still had a bed. Many had been evicted from their homes and were living with more fortunate relatives who still had jobs and a place to live. Some were forced into the streets and were attempting to exist in makeshift cardboard hovels in alleys, under railroad bridges, and in the growing hobo villages that were suddenly springing up across the country. Hoover inherited the most prosperous economy of the 20th century on a campaign promise to make it even better.

Because Hoover was convinced that the solution to the nation's economic problems would not be found in massive governmental intervention, social programs, or intrusive federal regulations, he was characterized by the media as being insensitive to the plight of Americans.

290   While economists have known for some two hundred years

that business cycles — the axiom describing recurring patterns of fluctuation within any given economy — exist, it was not until the mid-1930s that they became a major concern. Prior to the Great Depression, the view of French economist Jean Baptiste Say was generally held as the accepted law. Say's Law, as it is known, argues that the total supply of commodities always equals the total demand, and that temporary imbalances between supply and demand created economic slumps.

Since there was an adequate supply of commodities in the spring of 1930 that was matched by an equally corresponding demand, according to Say's Law, there should not have been a Recession. However, as the slump deepened during the summer months, economists were challenged to find the answer. None of them pointed a finger at the Fed which was, at that time, tightening the economy even more by continuing to shrink the supply of money, thereby further reducing demand by eliminating the means by which goods are bought.

Two conflicting theories were ultimately advanced by America's leading economists, clearly revealing that none of them had any idea why the economy was in a tailspin or, at least if they did, they were not prepared to jeopardize their careers by pointing fingers. Business cycles, they theorized, were not created by the laws of supply and demand; rather, they were initiated by external forces outside of the economic system. On the surface, this conclusion was absolutely correct. It was a theory the Fed had successfully tested and proved in 1920. The Fed had learned it could manipulate the economy at will.

Other equally respected economists counterpoised that business cycles were caused by a variety of as yet "undefined" economic factors. Clearly, no definitive, stable economic law existed by which economic slumps such as the one that was devastating America could be accurately defined, predicted — or corrected.

The prevailing point of view during the early Depression years was the psychological theory first advanced by the British economist Arthur Cecil Pigou. Pigou maintained that his studies supported the view that business trends can be manipulated by the optimism or pessimism of the political and business leaders who are responsible for the economy.

Sensing the logic of Pigou's argument, Hoover, in all of his public appearances, presented himself as optimistic about business prospects, believing this facade would somehow stimulate the rapidly decaying economy. Instead, Hoover came across to the public as a man completely out of touch with reality. And, on election day they would remember his insensitivity to their plight.

Surprising as it may seem, the ploy Hoover attempted was also used—equally as unsuccessfully—by Harry S. Truman in 1949 and Dwight D. Eisenhower in 1957-58. Both tried to reverse economic slumps by declaring themselves to be "optimistic" in their confidence of the American economy to rebound. America had learned nothing in thirty years about the forces that actually controlled its fate.

Roosevelt, James Cox's 1920 running mate and a two-term governor of New York, adhered to the socialist philosophy of British economist John Atkinson Hobson. Hobson believed that economic slumps were caused entirely by the inequality of incomes between the rich and the working class. The principle, known as the "underconsumption theory," suggested the market becomes glutted with commodities because the poor cannot afford to buy all that they need, and the rich cannot consume all they can afford to buy. Consequently the rich, according to Hobson, accumulate excess wealth that is removed from the economy instead of being reinvested in the production/consumption cycle. As a result of this "hoarding" of wealth, the economy grinds to a halt.

Hobson's solution—like Roosevelt's—was to seize this unused hoarded wealth and return it to the economy in the form of subsidy payments to the unemployed underclass of the American society. Roosevelt's "New Deal" was not new at all. The Bolsheviks had been practicing it in Russia since 1917. While most who have studied the policies and practices of FDR would call it Marxism, Roosevelt's New Deal was actually *illuminism* in its purest form.

Politics in America was changing almost as rapidly as the face of America itself changed from an largely rural and somewhat old-fashioned society steeped in traditional values to a mishmash of diverse and increasingly tolerant sprawling urban centers which were loosely interfaced with more the placid suburban communities that relied heavily on the commerce of the urban centers for survival.

In 1932 Franklin Delano Roosevelt changed forever the techniques presidential candidates would use to campaign for the White House. Previous candidates did most of their stumping from the front porch, hitting the campaign trail only when they were trailing in the polls, and then usually only during the final month or so of the campaign. Seldom, if ever, did a presidential candidate attend the nominating conventions. Nor did a sitting President ever debate an opponent.

Roosevelt in 1924, like Bill Clinton in 1984, had already mapped out his own timeline to the White House. Like Clinton, he would use the governor's mansion as his springboard. Also like Clinton, Roosevelt was both a master manipulator and a master of deceit. They shared one other trait: both possessed extremely charismatic personalities. More than one Roosevelt detractor was forced to admit that his or her own firmly held opinions were almost swayed by the hypnotic sincerity of Roosevelt.

Even though radio dramatically changed the nature of campaigning in 1924 Roosevelt, like Al Smith in 1928, was determined to take his case for change directly to the people. Roosevelt promised America a "new deal" that would guarantee a return of the happier days America remembered before his opponent took office. Commenting that "...stumping is for losers," Roosevelt's campaign manager James Farley tried in vain to keep Roosevelt out of the public eye. Farley was more afraid of Roosevelt's polio than was the candidate himself. Roosevelt knew the only way he could dispel the rumors that he was disabled was to prove he was not. He could accomplish that only by stumping.

Farley preferred radio. Radio was good. It allowed the candidate to appear as though he was speaking extemporaneously while using a prepared text. Radio, with its scripted message, also kept the candidate from making serious political gaffs.

Hoover, the non-political bureaucrat, used radio successfully against the slick, big city politician Al Smith in 1928. Hoover, the Great Humanitarian, had the same type of soothing, "you-can-believe-me voice" that became so familiar to the millions of Americans who listened to Roosevelt's fireside chats for twelve years. Smith, the consummate politician on the other hand, built his political career playing the role of the city slicker, and deliberately spoke like a Bronx used car salesman. Although Smith was a product of Tammany Hall, he was very articulate and could, when the need arose, speak in perfect, unaccented English. Smith admitted once to Bernard Baruch that he could easily deliver his speeches in court-of-appeals English, but that it wouldn't be typical Al Smith.

On radio, Hoover sounded presidential. Smith sounded like the used car salesman who sold you a lemon. Hoover won.

Roosevelt was no stranger to radio either. He used it to gain the New York governor's mansion in 1924, and continued to use it throughout his tenure as governor, averaging at least one political speech a month. He could easily have written a textbook on the art of using vocal inflections to convey emotions and was, by 1932, as polished as any radio actor in America.

Even though the economy was bad, Roosevelt was clearly the underdog in 1932. The product of one failed presidency campaign, Roosevelt's record as governor of New York during the past four years was no better than Hoover's. Neither chief executive had been able to mitigate the misfortunes of those who placed them in office. But unlike Hoover, Roosevelt at least had a campaign strategy.

While Hoover attempted to remain presidentially aloof after declaring that "...Except for a few major addresses expounding the policies of the administration, I will not take part in the forthcoming campaign..." Roosevelt went on the offensive, blaming his opponent for the stagnant economy and stressing his "new deal" for the "forgotten man." While Roosevelt's campaign rhetoric was long on promises and deliberately vague on specifics, few seemed to notice, or for that matter, care. Roosevelt's well-rehearsed radio ad-libs were a refreshing change from the subdued and sometimes apologetic voice of Hoover.

A month before the 1932 election Hoover was in deep trouble. Hoover's "Rose Garden" campaign was as ineffective as Jimmy Carter's 1980 campaign against the Great Communicator, Ronald Reagan. Hoover resented being blamed for the Depression, but on the advise of his campaign managers, refused to be dragged into an on-going, mud-slinging debate on the inability of his Administration to solve the economic woes of the nation. Republican Congressional candidates, who watched Hoover's presidential coattails gradually shrink to nothing throughout the summer, demanded that Hoover get off the "front porch" and onto the "stump," hoping somehow that a reincarnation of the 1928 Hoover would magically appear.

294   Hoover's last minute stumping, like former Republican Sen-

ate majority leader Bob Dole's three-day blitz against President Bill Clinton in the waning hours of the 1996 campaign proved to be too little, too late. Hoover, a political paradox, was too honest for politics. His reputation as a problem solver was ubiquitously well-deserved. Hoover built his career on achieving results, and never publicized his own accomplishments. As such, his declaration in a rare three hour speech from his hometown of West Branch, Iowa on October 5, 1932 that the economic crisis had passed must be viewed not as typical political campaign rhetoric, but as the honest statement of an honest man.

On November 7, 1932 America went to the polls. The outcome was predictable. Roosevelt had such a wide lead in the polls that he was already shaping his Administration a month before the election. America wanted a pound of flesh, and the electorate had already decided that Hoover had a pound to spare. Although Hoover had consistently refused to kowtow to big business throughout his term, he was painted by Roosevelt, the big business candidate, as pandering to the interests of the industrialists and Wall Street bankers. Roosevelt, who was an integral part of the banking community portrayed himself as candidate of the "forgotten man," whose raw deal from Hoover would become the New Deal as Roosevelt put America back to work.

Roosevelt took 22,821,857 votes to Hoover's 15,761,841. But even with only 57.3% of the popular vote, it was a landslide for Democrats. Roosevelt won 42 states. Hoover carried only six. Iowa, Hoover's home State, was not one of them.

America's "New Deal" would prove to be nothing more than the final dissolution of the Republic and the entrenchment of a socialist oligarchy in Washington. Even before Roosevelt was sworn in as the 32nd President of the United States, the sound of congressional hammers could be heard along Pennsylvania Avenue as the bureaucrats began expanding the sides of the public trough to provide a feeding place for the thousands of Americans who would be invited to come and dine at the expense of the taxpayers who had greedily hoarded too much of their hard-earned wealth.

"The art of government consists of taking as much money as possible from one class of citizens and to give it the other."

Voltaire
Dictionnaire Philosophique
1764

"Whenever you have an efficient government you have a dictatorship."

Harry S. Truman
Lecture at Columbia University
April 28, 1959

"A goverment that robs Peter to pay Paul can always depend on the support of Paul."

George Bernard Shaw
"Everybody's Political What's What?"
1944

❖ TWELVE ❖

Roosevelt And The "New Deal"

Even before he was sworn in as the 32nd President of the United States, Roosevelt began to create the socialist legislation that would forever change America. The remnants of the American Republic would die during his Administration, and our republican form of limited government which shaped the early years of America would be replaced with the oligarchic socialism found in most of Europe's "democratic" nations.

Roosevelt's biographers justify his actions as necessary under the "emergency situation" that existed at the time. However, according to Herbert Hoover, the crisis upon which Roosevelt publicly acted during his first term of office was resolved before his successor assumed office.

That this was Hoover's belief is confirmed by an entry in the former president's personal diary: "I hardly need restate the fact, now well-established by disinterested economists the world over, that America was shaking itself clear of the depression, under its Republican Administration, in June-July, 1932. The whole world started forward. Prosperity had actually swung around the corner and was on its way up the street of our national life when it encountered the change in national policies. After Mr. Roosevelt's election in 1932 we alone of all the great nations were set back. Most other nations continued forward." (*Public Papers of the Presidents of the United States;* Washburn Law Library.)

However, the "emergency" Roosevelt referred to when he called for a Governor's Conference in Washington, D.C. on Monday, March 6, 1933 had nothing to do with putting Americans back to work, nor did it have anything to do with assuring that every American had something to eat or a place to rest to his or her weary head. The "emergency" that triggered the president-elect's letter to each of the 48 State governors in the winter of 1932-33, some four to six weeks before his inauguration, dealt primarily with two issues. First, Roosevelt needed to broaden the scope of his presi-

297

dential authority to initiate what he knew would be unconstitutional mandates when he assumed office. That authority could come only from the States. Second, he had to deal with the rapidly expanding crisis within the banking community even though it was a crisis the banks themselves had created.

The banking system of the United States, which was complicit in the collapse of the stock market in 1929 due to the Fed's loose money policy in 1928-29, discovered during in the winter of 1932-33 that too much of their liquidity was tied up in foreclosed properties that weren't moving, and not enough was available in cash to meet the demands of its ordinary citizen depositors. While the unemployment rate dropped slightly in October, 1932, roughly 15% of America's workforce still remained idle. Although no paychecks were being earned by those workers, mortgages and rents still had to be paid, groceries still had to be purchased, and families still had to exist until the breadwinner returned to work.

But America was confident. Roosevelt had promised them a new deal; a fair shake. America was anxiously awaiting spring. FDR would be in the White House, and they would be back at their old jobs, turning out widgets or whatevers, and the past four years would be nothing more than a bad memory. They had survived Hoover's Recession.

Few of those who maintained deposits in the nation's community banks in 1932-33 realized that the savings they had deposited during the "good times" might not be there, waiting for them during their own times of economic stress. Granted, several banks across the nation had failed during the Crash, and hundreds of depositors had lost their life savings when those banks closed their doors. But the crisis had passed. The banks which remained open, America was assured by the Federal Reserve, were solvent. Their deposits were safe.

Those who had lost confidence in the banking system between 1929 and 1932 withdrew all of their funds — occasionally in currency, but usually the frightened depositor, believing the entire economic infrastructure of the United States was going to collapse, demanded payment in gold coins. Literally hundreds upon multiple hundreds of Americans lined up at banks all over the nation, withdrawing their meager savings and closing accounts which many had maintained for decades, fearful that the banks would close their doors and a lifetime of scrimping to save a nest egg for the future would be lost.

As Americans withdrew their savings — usually in panic but occasionally in an orderly fashion just to meet their own debt obligations — panic, from inside the Federal Reserve, set in. There wasn't enough gold or silver on deposit anywhere in the United States to cover one more good run on the Fed if the depositors all demanded gold for their script. The Fed had, quite literally, issued too much debt-backed paper money. By March 1, 1933 the Federal Reserve was "legally" bankrupt. Over $264 billion in gold had been withdrawn from America's banks. On Friday, March 3 another $150 billion would be withdrawn.

As America anxiously waited throughout the winter of 1932-33 for Roosevelt's promised "new deal," the Fed plotted feverishly to provide a slightly different version than that promised by the president-elect. The Federal Reserve was preparing a grandiose scheme to steal the wealth of America with the help of its brand new president, Franklin Delano Roosevelt.

Sometime between the middle of January and the first of February, 1933 the president-elect sent a letter to the governors of each State advising them of the "national crisis" facing America, and calling a Governors' Conference in Washington on March 6 to deal with it. Roosevelt, a close friend of New York Fed Governor Eugene Meyer, knew Hoover was not going to allow himself to be bullied by Meyer into declaring a bank holiday, believing as he did that the federal government had no legal right to do so.

Roosevelt took matters into his own hands.

On February 14, 1933, the same day that Texas governor Merriam "Ma" Ferguson penned her reply to Roosevelt's letter reclusing herself from Roosevelt's conference, Michigan Governor Comstock declared a bank holiday. Within a matter of days, several States followed, creating a widespread panic that merely exacerbated the crisis, forcing even more States to follow suit. By the time Roosevelt took office, a banking crisis of almost unbelievable magnitude existed.

Hoover saw it coming.

From the middle of February on, Hoover was in daily contact not only with Meyer, but the other Fed governors as well. On February 17, according to Hoover's personal diary, after several States had declared bank holidays:

"...it had become apparent that a panic was inevitable unless Mr. Roosevelt would cooperate to allay fear. I, as President of all the people, addressed to Mr. Roosevelt as President-elect of all the people a personal appeal in my own handwriting which was delivered personally to him by a trusted messenger. It contained these words: 'A most critical situation has arisen. The majority difficulty is the public mind. A statement by you upon two or three policies of your administration would restore public confidence...by the removal of fear. With the election there came a natural and inevitable hesitation...A number of things have happened on top of this...The breakdown in balancing the budget...The proposals for inflation...a state of alarm...rapidly reaching a crisis [from the] flight of capital [and] foreign withdrawals of gold[1] ...hoarding. It is obvious that you are the only one who can give prompt assurance that there will be no tampering or inflation of the currency, that the budget will be unquestionably balanced."

(Public Papers of Presidents of the United States: Herbert Hoover; Washburn Law Library.)

Hoover's personal note to Roosevelt was triggered by reports from knowledgeable Washington insiders that Roosevelt had no intention of keeping his campaign promises by forcing the president-elect to publicly affirm them once again. Furthermore, by making Roosevelt reaffirm his pledge to America, Hoover hoped to quell rumors suggesting that the president-elect was planning to embark on what Hoover believed was a reckless course of action that could very likely destroy the bedrock of democracy in the United States.

The delivery of Hoover's communique to Roosevelt was delayed for a day because the President-elect was vacationing on Vincent Astor's yacht off the coast of Miami, Florida. Astor, like Roosevelt, did not appear overly concerned about the banking

---

[1]Although the American public was rightfully accused of hoarding gold to the tune of some $150 billion by the Fed, by Roosevelt and by the media in 1933, and was made the scapegoat for Roosevelt's blatantly unconstitutional act of removing the United States from the gold standard—something which legally required a Constitutional amendment, the reality is it was not the demand for payment in gold by the general population that created the Bank Panic—it was the constant, never-ending rumors that the federal government was going to remove the United States from the gold standard and create what many Americans viewed as the same type of inflationary currency that collapsed the German mark only ten years earlier.

crisis which had gripped the country.

On the morning of February 18 the note was delivered to Roosevelt by a Secret Service agent at the President-elect's home at 49 E. 65th Street in New York. Roosevelt would not respond to Hoover's concerns until March 1, at which time he informed the President there was nothing he could do.

In point-of-fact, Roosevelt was the only one who could.

In the unique political situation that existed at that time, Hoover was a lame duck president in more ways than one. Not only was he within two weeks of surrendering the White House to his successor when he wrote the note to Roosevelt, he was also a defeated Republican president with a very hostile New Deal Democratic Congress that was, at that time, already taking its orders from a man who would not become the President for another two weeks. And, to make matters even worse, the American people themselves had already repudiated Hoover as their leader. As far as they were concerned, Franklin Delano Roosevelt was already the President of the United States. They were right. Nothing political happened in Washington D.C. between December 1, 1932 and March 6, 1933 that Roosevelt didn't want to happen. Hoover, an absolutely powerless president, was the Chief Executive of the United States in name only.

Privately Roosevelt found Hoover's concern, and his dilemma, amusing. According to syndicated newspaper columnist John T. Flynn, who closely followed the Rooseveltian dynasty from 1933 to 1945, Roosevelt simply pocketed Hoover's note and showed it to no one until February 19.

On that day, or more precisely that evening, Roosevelt was the guest of honor at the annual Inner Circle press club dinner at the Astor Hotel in New York. During the entertainment that followed the dinner, Roosevelt passed Hoover's note under the table to his adviser, Raymond Moley.

Moley, a professor of political science at Columbia University, was only one of several political, financial and legal "brain trust" consultants employed by Roosevelt during the formative period just prior to the commencement of his first administration. Roosevelt's "brain trust" included Moley, James W. Angell, Adolf Berle, John D. McGoldrick, Lindsay Rogers and Rexford Tugwell. Some would fade away in the opening days of Roosevelt's first administration. Others, like General Hugh Johnson, George Peek and Charles Tausing, would be added.

301

Moley read Hoover's note amidst the gala laughter resulting from a burlesque comedy skit performed on-stage by a myriad of newspaper reporters. As Moley read the opening line:

"A most critical situation has arisen in the country of which I feel it my duty to advise you confidentially..."

he glanced across the table at Roosevelt whose head was thrown back in laughter at the merriment. Moley remembers the event as chilling, mentally comparing it to Nero fiddling while Rome burned. He wondered how Roosevelt could sit there laughing as amateur actors and actresses lampooned various New York politicos while the nation was facing what was described by Hoover as the threatened collapse of its monetary system.

"Hoover pointed out with complete realism the threat to the whole national banking structure, the flight of gold from the country, the rush of cash from the banks into hiding. Fear, he said, had taken possession of the public mind. Hoover believed...that a new element had entered the situation—the appearance of terror. The air was full of rumors of inflation and of going off the gold standard. This was leading to the withdrawal of gold from the banks..." (*The Roosevelt Myth*; John T. Flynn; Garden City Books © 1948; pgs. 17-18.)

Roosevelt was unimpressed, as Moley described it in Flynn's account, "...with the bony hand of death stretched out over every bank in the country." Roosevelt was unimpressed because everything that was happening was happening in precisely the manner in which it was supposed to happen. Roosevelt had no desire to stem the panic. Panic—and more of it—was needed.

The crisis continued to escalate as planned. On March 2, everything came to a head. The Federal Reserve continued to pressure Hoover to declare a nationwide bank holiday. Clearly, Roosevelt wanted Hoover to take that step before leaving office, so that any stigma that might later be attached to it would fall on Hoover's Administration and not his. Uncooperative, Hoover continued to refuse.

On March 2, 1933 Hoover's Treasury Secretary, Ogden L. Mills sent the following note to Hoover:

Dear Mr. President:

Referring to your personal notes of February 22nd and March 1st, 1933, I have submitted to Mr. [William] Woodin in detail the various phases of the present financial and banking situations and the critical nature of the problems that confront the country and the Government. I emphasized the desire of the Administration to cooperate in every way with the incoming Administration and to facilitate the transfer of the government from the present to the incoming Administration.

On the occasion of my first conference with him on February 22nd, I pointed out how enormously helpful it would be were Governor Roosevelt willing at once to declare that it would be his policy to take all necessary steps to bring the budget of the Federal Government into balance and to maintain the credit of the Government and to resist all schemes looking to uncontrolled inflation. Again last night, I stated as emphatically as I could that great as are the present difficulties, their solution would be greatly facilitated by a clean-cut declaration along these lines in the Inaugural Address, while a failure to do so would inevitably increase existing uncertainty and fear and magnify the obstacles to be overcome.

Mr. Woodin evidently was not in any position to commit the President-elect, but he and I have spoken fully and frankly. He certainly knows my views, and I think they faithfully represent yours. I know he will welcome any assistance that I may be able to give him in taking over his own immediate and at present extremely difficult duties.

Faithfully yours,
Ogden L. Mills
Secretary of the Treasury

(*Public Papers of Presidents of the United States: Herbert Hoover;* Washburn Law Library.)

That afternoon Hoover received another call from Meyer. It was imperative, Meyer advised him, that a bank holiday be declared immediately. Hoover declined again, deferring such actions to the incoming president, should Roosevelt find such extreme measures necessary. The transfer of power, Hoover reminded Meyer, would occur in less than 48 hours.

Meyer pressed the issue, insisting the crisis was too volatile to wait even 48 hours. Hoover replied that he had no legal authority to declare the holiday the Fed was seeking. Meyer argued that, under Section 5(b) of the *Trading With The Enemy Act,* he did.

In a hastily scribbled note to the Fed Board of Governors in Washington, Hoover wrote:

Gentlemen:

I understand that the Board is meeting this evening to consider recommending to me the use of the emergency powers under Section 5 of the Enemy Trading Act as amended for the purpose of limiting the use of coin and currency to necessary purposes. I shall be glad to have the advice of the Board. If it is the view of the Board that these powers should be exercised I would be glad to have your recommendation accompanied by a form of proclamation, as it would seem to me it should be issued by me before banking hours tomorrow morning.

I also take this occasion to acknowledge the receipt of your letter of February 28. I am familiar with the inherent dangers in any form of federal guarantee of banking deposits, but I am wondering if the situation has reached the time when the Board should give further consideration to this possibility. I am enclosing herewith a rough outline of a method upon which I should like to have the Board advise me.

Yours faithfully,
Herbert Hoover.

(Public Papers of Presidents of the United States: Herbert Hoover; Washburn Law Library.)

The summary attached to Hoover's memo to the Fed contained a notation that Secretary Mills had rejected Hoover's proposal out-of-hand. Hoover's suggested bank deposit guarantee, which would become the framework for the Federal Deposit Insurance Corporation, took the following form:

1. All member banks shall be eligible. All non-member banks shall be eligible upon appraisal by the Federal Reserve Banks or by the Comptroller or such agencies as he may designate that the net assets of such bank exceed 50% of the deposits. Joining of the plan to be voluntary with the banks.

2. For purposes of the plan, deposits in the joining banks are to be divided into two categories, that is "active deposits" and "inactive deposits."

3. The government to guarantee 100% of the "active deposits."

4. The "active deposits" to be

304

    a. New deposits made in the banks.

    b. 50% of the existing deposits of all depositors except secured or guaranteed deposits.

    5. The "active deposits" to be a first charge of all assets of the bank including stockholders' liabilities. "Inactive deposits" to be subordinated entirely to the "active deposits" and not be available to depositors as long as the guarantee is outstanding.

    6. The percentage of credit to the individual "active deposit" may be increased beyond 50% if on examination of the assets of the bank such assets prove to be more than 50%, but no such increase to exceed more than 75% of the value of existing assets. (This plan could be extended to banks whose assets are below 50% by guaranteeing an active account at some proportion of whatever the assets are, say 75% — if the assets show 40% of the deposits, the "active accounts" could be opened for 30% and be made subject to federal guarantee.)

(Public Papers of Presidents of the United States: Herbert Hoover; Washburn Law Library.)

    Mills, a banker himself before joining Hoover, was opposed to Hoover's plan not only because it made the stockholders of the bank financially liable for any bank failures, but because it mandated that the *ordinary citizen* depositors would get their money back before the stockholders in the event of a failure.

    The plan was proposed by Hoover in lieu of the more drastic measures suggested by the Fed governors. The complexity of Hoover's depositors' guarantee, plus the fact that it had been previously reviewed by his Secretary of the Treasury and declined, clearly suggests that much thought and discussion had attended it, and in all likelihood that its merits had been addressed with at least some of the Fed governors (i.e., the reference to a letter from the Fed on January 28) prior to that writing.

    In *The Roosevelt Myth,* author Flynn maintains that at the beginning of February Hoover proposed such a plan to the Fed, suggesting a one day national bank holiday during which time each "...bank in the country would submit a statement of its assets and liabilities...The Federal Reserve would accept the banks' own statements. The next day all solvent banks would be opened and the government would declare them to be solvent and would guarantee their solvency during the crisis." (*The Roosevelt Myth;* John T.   **305**

Flynn; Garden City Books © 1948; pgs. 17-18.)

It was the opinion of Hoover's Attorney General, William D. Mitchell, that the President did not have the legal authority to declare a bank holiday without the consent of Congress. Congress, however, without specific instructions from Roosevelt, would not work with Hoover to solve the crisis. Hoover's February 17 note to Roosevelt was a request for the incoming President to help him enact his plan to end the banking crisis before it was too late.

However, the fact that Hoover's plan penalized the bankers doomed it from the start. In addition, the Fed Board was not ready to solve the crisis, nor were they interested in guaranteeing the deposits of the average depositor. They wanted nothing less than a national closure that would allow them, through a declared emergency, to "reform" the monetary system of the United States.

On March 2, Roosevelt and his entourage of advisers arrived in Washington and took up residency at the Mayflower Hotel. While Roosevelt was refreshed and in the best of humor, Moley and the others, who had been working with Hoover's people almost non-stop for two days, were exhausted. And, while Hoover was doing everything humanly possible to save the banking system of the United States, Roosevelt was doing everything possible to promulgate the crisis.

Hoover spent the better part of the following day, March 3, on the telephone with various Fed governors as well as Senator Carter Glass (D-VA) and newly-elected New York Governor Herbert H. Lehman. Lehman, himself a very successful investment banker before becoming New York's lieutenant governor, was Roosevelt's hand-picked successor for the governor's mansion. He was also a man who had Roosevelt's ear.

Glass was a former Chairman of the House Committee on Banking and Currency and was one of the key architects of the *Federal Reserve Act.* He also played a decisive role in its passage. He resigned from the House of Representatives in 1918 to become Wilson's Secretary of the Treasury. In 1920, only a few months before Wilson's term expired, Glass was appointed to a vacancy in the Senate. He was subsequently re-elected four times. He would become a co-sponsor of the *Glass-Steagall Act*[2], commonly known

---

[2]The *Glass-Steagall Act*, which was proposed to Carter Glass by John Nance Garner, was greatly opposed by Roosevelt. Roosevelt was

as the *Bank Conservation Act of 1933* that created the F.D.I.C. Glass was offered the position of Treasury Secretary in the Roosevelt Administration before it was conferred on Woodin. He declined it on January 21, 1933 after learning from Henry Wallace, who would become Roosevelt's vice-president in 1940, that the President-elect was planning to take America off the gold standard. Glass was a fiscal conservative who feared such a move would establish a dangerous inflationary precedent that could easily destroy the economy of the United States.

Just before retiring on the night of March 3, Hoover spoke at length with Charles Dawes, his ambassador to Great Britain. Dawes, who had served as Calvin Coolidge's vice president, was retiring from government service the next day. Dawes planned to return to his former occupation as the president of Central Trust Company of Illinois. Hoover recorded the substance of that conversation in his diary:

> "...[Dawes] said that Lehman was within a few minutes [of] having a meeting with both of these groups together [the Federal Reserve and representative banking officials]; that he had no doubt that they would settle it. I asked him if he agreed with my view that there should be no national proclamation closing all the banks. He said he did not want it and would not support it as he wanted to consider the whole question. He told me that he had been talking with Senator Glass for an hour. Glass was opposed to a national closing; that he considered the whole business could be cleaned up through a series of clearinghouses if the bankers of the country would stand up and change their attitude; and that he, Roosevelt, was taking that view..."

Although Roosevelt may have taken that position publicly, his actions on March 6 would be substantially different than his stated views of March 3.

> "...I asked [Dawes] if I might repeat to my colleagues his

---

adamantly antagonistic of any Hooveresque program that guaranteed the bank deposits of the common citizen depositor—and was even more discountenanced with *Glass-Steagall* because the bankers opposed it. *Glass-Steagall* divorced commercial and investment banking and created the F.D.I.C. When Roosevelt threatened to veto it, Glass assured him the New Deal would end with his veto. As a result, it became law without Roosevelt's signature.

statement while he held on to the line. He did so. I told him that I thought that ended all questions of national proc-lamations and he agreed.

[Senate Majority Leader Joseph] Robinson then rang up Chicago and asked them how they were coming on. They expressed the view that the President should not under any circumstances issue a proclamation; that they had the Gov-ernor of Illinois in a meeting at that moment with the Fed-eral Reserve and representative banking officials, together with the clearinghouse people; that the Governor was per-fectly prepared to put in the holiday if the banks asked for it and that a national closing might do much harm.

At 12 o'clock, Dawes rang me up and asked what the situation was. I told him the situation.

I then went to bed.

Saturday, March 4, 1933

At 1:30, I was awakened by the policeman who deliv-ered the attached letter from Eugene Meyer. At 8 o'clock in the morning I checked up and found that two Governors had issued their proclamation. I called up Mills at 9:30 to ask him what had taken place at the Federal Reserve Board that gave rise to the letter they had written to me. He told me he had objected to the letter; that Meyer was merely trying to escape responsibilities; that Meyer had been the origin of the whole movement with Woodin [Roosevelt's designated Treasury Secretary] and was anxious to loom large in the new administration..."

(*Public Papers of Presidents of the United States: Herbert Hoover;* Washburn Law Library.)

Obviously Meyer and Woodin would settle for nothing less than a crisis. The reason should be obvious, since it was mentioned to Hoover by Meyer on March 2. The banking crisis would be the excuse Roosevelt needed to provoke Section 5(b) of the *Trading With The Enemy Act*. America was, according to Meyer, in a state of national emergency. Unfortunately, no one seemed to notice that the *Trading With The Enemy Act* dealt only with hostilities of war, and all of the actions it authorized were directed against foreign powers. In fact, the citizens of the United States were specifically excluded. That was, however, merely an inconvenient oversight that could be corrected later on with subsequent legislation.

308   Meyer's letter, dated March 3, follows:

Dear Mr. President:

The Federal Reserve Board has been in session again this evening reviewing the latest reports of developments. The situation as reported from Chicago has reached the point of extreme tension, with prospects that by the end of banking hours tomorrow the gold reserves of the Federal Reserve Bank of Chicago will be dangerously depleted. Representative bankers are assembled there tonight and have requested that a national holiday be proclaimed as the only method they know of dealing with the immediate exigency with which they are confronted.

There is enclosed a copy of a resolution adopted by the Board of Directors of the Federal Reserve Bank of New York, now in session. This resolution speaks for itself as to the New York situation.

Similar conditions are developing rapidly in other Federal Reserve Districts.

The Federal Reserve Board has considered two methods of dealing with this emergency, one by executive order and the other by joint resolution of Congress. The Senate having adjourned for the day, the issuance of an executive order seems to be the only alternative to meet the immediate situation. A form of executive order is enclosed for your consideration.

The Federal Reserve Board feels it cannot too strongly urge that the situation has reached the point where immediate action is necessary to prevent a banking collapse.

Respectfully,
Eugene Meyer
Governor

P.S. Since this letter was dictated, there has been communicated to us, by telephone, a resolution adopted by the Executive Committee of the Federal Reserve Bank of Chicago, now in session. A copy of this resolution is enclosed.
[The President, The White House]

Hoover's consternation at that point was understandable. When he retired for the night on March 3, the crisis was under control. Now, Meyer renewed his demand for a national bank holiday. Why? Because restoring the public's confidence in the banks wasn't the solution the bankers were seeking. In fact, it wasn't

309

even the problem. It was merely the catalyst the bankers used to create the crisis. What the Fed wanted was the United States off the gold standard. Nothing less. On March 9, 1933 they would begin to get their wish. On June 5, 1934 their wish would be complete.

The proposed executive order Meyer enclosed for Hoover to execute on the morning of March 4, 1933 scant hours before his successor was to take office was substantially the same executive order Roosevelt would issue two days later. It began:

"WHEREAS the nation's banking institutions are being subjected to heavy withdrawals of currency for hoarding..."

The justification for the executive order was found in the allegation of "hoarding." Although whatever gold or currency on deposit within the banks rightfully belonged to those depositors who placed it there, there was something sinful to be construed from the word "hoarding." It implied greed.

In reality, as stated earlier, the "hoarding" the American depositors were guilty of totalled $150 billion compared to the $114 billion which had already been removed from the country by a handful of wealthy foreign investors (who had been encouraged by American investment bankers to bring their debt-backed francs, pounds, lira and marks to the United States where they could be exchanged for gold). Yet, the "solution" which would be sought by the bankers would be focused entirely on the American wage-earner whose "hoarded wealth" was still within their grasp. By that time, the foreign investors had already withdrawn most of their funds—in gold—and had them securely sequestered in European vaults.

"WHEREAS there is increasing speculative activity in foreign exchanges; and

WHEREAS these conditions have created a national emergency in which it is in the best interest of all bank depositors that a period of respite be provided with a view of preventing further hoarding of coins, bullion or currency or speculation in foreign exchange, and permitting the application of appropriate measures for dealing with the emergency in order to protect the interests of the people; and

WHEREAS provided in Section 5(b) of the Act of October 6, 1917, as amended, that "The President may investigate, regulate, or prohibit, under such rules and regulations as he may prescribe, by means of licenses or otherwise, any transactions in foreign exchange and the export, hoarding, melting, or earmarking of gold or silver coin or bullion or currency***; and

WHEREAS it is provided in Section 16 of the said Act that "Whoever shall willfully violate any of the provisions of this Act or of any license, rule, or regulation issued thereunder, and whoever shall willfully violate, neglect, or refuse to comply with any order of the President issued in compliance with the provisions of this Act shall, upon conviction, be fined not more than $10,000, or, if a natural person, imprisoned for ten years, or both***..."

The Fed was engaging in smoke and mirrors legal chicanery. First, prior to March 9, 1933 the *Trading With The Enemy Act* had not been amended to include American citizens. The Fed assumed — on good authority — that Congress would cave in to Roosevelt's demands when he assumed the White House. But, when the executive order was penned by the Fed for use by Hoover, no such legislated authority, legal or otherwise, existed that granted the President the right to seize the lawful assets of the citizens of the United States.

Second, the United States Supreme Court in its 1921 *Stoehr v. Wallace* decision, made that fact clear when it said: "The *Trading With The Enemy Act*, originally and as amended, is strictly a war measure, and finds its sanction in the provision empowering Congress to 'declare war, grants letters of marque and reprisal, and make rules concerning captures on land and water.' Constitution, Article I, Section 8, clause 11. P241."

Third, by virtue of that decision, Congress could not legally expand the perimeters of the *War Powers Act* to include peacetime emergencies since the *Trading With The Enemy Act* gained its authority solely from the constitutional provision granting Congress the right to declare war.

Finally, the Fed's proposed executive order deliberately edited and misquoted the Act of October 6, 1917, Public Law 91, to fit their current needs. To understand the legal manipulation more clearly it is necessary to look at the defining clause of Public Law 91 to determine precisely whom the law targeted, and by virtue of that, precisely whom it excluded.

"Be it enacted by the Senate and House of Representatives of the United States of America in Congress assembled, That this Act shall be known as the "Trading with the enemy Act."

311

SEC. 2. That the word "enemy," as used herein, shall be deemed to mean, for the purpose of such trading and of this Act—

(a) Any individual, partnership, or other body of individuals, of any nationality, resident within the territory [including that occupied by the military and naval forces] of any nation with which the United States is at war, or resident outside the United States and doing business within such territory, and any corporation incorporated within such territory of any nation with which the United States is at war or incorporated within any country other than the United States and doing business within the territory.

(b) The government of any nation with which the United States is at war, or any political or municipal subdivision thereof, or any officer, official, agent or agency thereof.

(c) Such other individuals, or body or class of individuals, as may be natives, citizens, or subjects of any nation with which the United States is at war, *other than citizens of the United States...*"

(Emphasis, author.)

As you can clearly see, the Act of October 6, 1917 dealt specifically with trading with an enemy power during times of war. Not only that, but it also specifically excluded American citizens from its tenets. Precisely what authority did Public Law 91 give the President, and under what circumstances could he use it?

"If the President shall have reasonable cause to believe that any act is about to be performed in violation of Section Three hereof he shall have authority to order the postponement of the performance of such act for a period not exceeding ninety days, pending investigation of the facts by himself.

(b) [T]he President may investigate, regulate, or prohibit, under such rules and regulations as he may prescribe, by means of licenses or otherwise, any transaction in foreign exchange, export or earmarkings of gold or silver coin or bullion or currency, transfers of credit in any form [other than credits relating solely to transactions to be executed wholly within the United States]; and transfers of evidence of indebtedness or of the ownership of property between the United States and any foreign country, whether enemy, ally of an enemy or otherwise, or between residents of one or more foreign countries by any person within the United States; and he may require any such person engaged in any such transaction to furnish, under oath, complete information relative thereto, including the production of any books of account, contracts, letters or other papers, in connection therewith in the custody or control of such person, either before or after such transaction is completed."

As you can see from reading the text of Public Law 91, the Fed merely excerpted that portion of Section 5(b) that served its purpose, and edited the balance since it unequivocally delegated that authority to the President only in times of war—and only when those transactions were being made to an enemy, or an ally of an enemy, of the United States.

It is important to grasp the significance of what you are reading. For years the politically correct "mainstream" liberals have ridiculed the rightwing, conspiracy harbingers as extremist fanatics who are mesmerized by words and phrases like Illuminati, Bilderberger, Trilateral Commission and Council on Foreign Relations. They have scoffed at the suggestion that a secret "money power" exists behind the seats of government, or that a group of elitist bankers have contrived to control all of the currencies of the world. Yet, here it is.

The Federal Reserve Board of the United States conspired, on March 3, 1933, to force the President of the United States to exercise a power he did not possess to declare a national bank holiday he had no legal authority to mandate. When Hoover refused, they turned to his successor, Franklin Delano Roosevelt, who became a willing conspirator on March 6. On March 10, 1933 the Federal Reserve seized possession of every ounce of gold in America, and Roosevelt seized almost dictatorial power over the people of the United States.

In response to Meyer's letter, dated March 3 and accompanied with the draft of the executive order the Executive Board of the Fed expected Hoover to issue, the President shot this reply, dated March 4, 1933, back to Meyer:

"My dear Governor Meyer:

I received at half past one this morning your letter dated March 3rd. I must assume that this letter was written on the basis of information received by you prior to 11:30 o'clock last night for the reason that before your letter was sent you had certain information as follows:

a. At 11 o'clock last night the President-elect had informed me he did not wish such a proclamation issued.

b. The Attorney General had renewed the same opinion which had already been given to the Board that the authorities on which you were relying were inadequate unless supported by the incoming Administration.

c. That groups of representative bankers in both Chicago and New York embracing members of the Board of Directors of the Federal Reserve Banks in those cities, were then in conference with the governors of the states of Illinois and New York, and that the governors of those two states were prepared to act if these representative groups so recommended. It appears that the governors did take action under their authorities, declaring a temporary holiday in these two critical states, and thus accomplishing the major purposes which the Board apparently had in mind.

In view of the above I am at a loss to understand why such a communication should have been sent to me in the last few hours of this Administration, which I believe the Board must now admit was neither justified nor necessary.

Yours faithfully,

Herbert Hoover.

[Hon. Eugene Meyer, Federal Reserve Board, Washington, D.C.]"

(Herbert Hoover Presidential Library, West Branch, Iowa.)

Hoover's letter to Meyer was his last recorded act as President of the United States. Hoover left office not realizing that Roosevelt was playing both ends against the middle. Hoover the bureaucrat simply wasn't a politician. He was too honest. With all of his years in Washington, Hoover never learned the rules by which the game of politics is played. When Roosevelt told him he didn't want the executive order closing the banks issued, what Roosevelt really meant was h didn't want to issue it—he wanted Hoover to take the flack if the American public started firing salvos at the White House. It was, after all, their gold the Fed was stealing.

R oosevelt was forced to do his own dirty work. On Monday, March 6, 1933 Roosevelt issued the first two of a series of Executive Orders and Presidential Proclamations that would launch his "New Deal." On the surface, the general public heartily approved of what he was doing since it appeared as though he was doing something. America's complaint against Hoover was that for four years it appeared as though the Great Humanitarian was doing nothing.

Roosevelt's first act, which actually occurred on March 5, was to issue *Proclamation 2038* calling Congress into a special session on March 9. His second act, issued as *Proclamation 2039*, was to declare a national bank holiday and stop the withdrawal of gold from America's banks by the owners of that gold. Roosevelt's proclamation differed only slightly from the verbage prepared by the Federal Reserve for Hoover, clearly indicating Roosevelt's proclamation was prepared from their text, if not by them.

"WHEREAS there have been heavy and unwarranted withdrawals of gold and currency from our banking institutions for the purpose of hoarding; and

WHEREAS continuous and increasingly extensive speculative activity abroad in foreign exchange has resulted in severe drains on the Nation's stock in gold; and

WHEREAS these conditions have created a national emergency; and

WHEREAS it is in the best interests of all bank depositors that a period of respite be provided with a view of preventing further hoarding of coin, bullion or currency or speculation in foreign exchange and permitting the application of appropriate measures to protect the interests of our people; and

WHEREAS it is provided in Section 5(b) of the Act of October 6, 1917 (40 Stat. L 411) as amended, 'That the President may investigate, regulate, or prohibit under such rules and regulations as he may prescribe, by means of licenses or otherwise, any transaction in gold or silver coin or bullion or currency***;' and

WHEREAS it is provided in Section 16 of the said Act 'that whoever shall willfully violate any of the provisions of this Act or of any license, rule or regulation issued thereunder, and whoever shall willfully violate, neglect, or refuse to comply with any order of the President issued in compliance with the provisions of this Act, shall, upon conviction, be fined not more than $10,000, or, if a natural person, imprisoned for not more than ten years, or both; ***;'

Now, THEREFORE, I, Franklin D. Roosevelt, President of the United States, in view of such national emergency and by virtue of the authority vested in me by said Act and in order to prevent the export, hoarding, or earmarking of gold or silver coin or bullion or currency, do hereby proclaim, order, direct and declare that from Monday, the sixth day of March, to Thursday, the ninth day of March, Nineteen Hundred and Thirty-three, both dates inclusive, there shall be maintained and observed by all banking institutions and all branches thereof located in the United States of America, including all territories and insular possessions, a bank holiday, and that during said period all banking transactions shall be suspended...As used in this order the term "banking institutions" shall include all Federal Reserve banks, national banking associations, banks, trust companies, savings banks, building and loan associations, credit unions, or other corporations, partnerships, associations or persons, engaged in the business of receiving deposits, making loans, discounting business paper, or transacting any other form of banking business.

IN WITNESS THEREOF, I have hereunto set my hand and caused the seal of the United States to be affixed.

Done in the City of Washington this 6th day of March — 1 A.M. in the year of our Lord One Thousand Nine Hundred and Thirty-three, and of the Independence of the United States the One Hundred and Fifty-seventh.

FRANKLIN D. ROOSEVELT

By the President:

Cordell Hull

Secretary of State.

[No. 2039]."

The "***" in the proclamation indicates that not all of the cited law is quoted in the text. The paraphrasing is ostensibly done to highlight that portion of the applicable law relative to the Proclamation. Of course, as it has already been pointed out, the balance of the text was omitted from *Proclamation 2039* not as an expediency, but rather, because the cited law pertains only to powers that may be exercised by the President in times of war, and even then, never against citizens of the United States.

On Wednesday, March 8 Roosevelt extended the bank holiday for an undefined period with *Proclamation 2040*. Also on March 8, the Federal Reserve issued instructions to every banking institution in the nation to prepare for the Secretary of the Treasury a list of every individual in the United States who had withdrawn their savings in gold prior to March 6, as well as a list of those who did not redeposit that gold by March 13. At noon the following day, Congress convened to "legalize" Roosevelt's actions. Before them that day was the *Emergency Banking Relief Act of 1933*.

Again, the Fed was moving before any legislation authorizing them to do so had been passed by Congress, or signed into law by the President. The "law" amending the *Federal Reserve Act* and expanding the authority of the Secretary of the Treasury to impound the gold legally possessed by citizens of the United States would not even be "debated" in Congress until the following day.

When the Congressmen and Senators filed into their respective chambers at noon on March 9, they were greeted by the weighty *Emergency Banking Relief Act*, waiting on immediate passage. The leadership suspended the traditional rules on the reading of the legislation due to what they termed a "national emergency" and called for an immediate vote. None of the members of the House had been given an opportunity to examine the law, or study its ramifications — nor would they be granted a chance to do so before voting.

After a very heated and sometimes partisan debate that afternoon, the most controversial banking bill in the history of the United States (with perhaps the single exception of the *Federal Reserve Act of 1913*) was passed — in less than one day!

The debate on the House floor that was recorded in the *Congressional Record* clearly revealed both the anger and the frustration of several House members — including Louis McFadden, the Chairman of the House Banking and Currency Committee, who declared on the record that his first knowledge of the legislation came when the bill was announced by the Clerk. (*Congressional Record;* March 9, 1933; pg. 80.)

The legislation — a currency bill — didn't go through McFadden's committee, or for that matter any Congressional committee. It was written by Roosevelt's brain trust with the assistance of the Federal Reserve before Roosevelt assumed office. The legislation to cure the Banking Crisis of 1933 was actually written before the banking crisis officially became one.

317

McFadden was frustrated over the fact that Congress had not even been allowed to read the *Emergency Banking Relief Act* before being asked to vote on it. He was even more apprehensive of what he viewed as an attempt by the Fed and Roosevelt to impose a dictatorship over the finances of the United States.

"Mr. Speaker," he began, "I regret that the membership of the House has had no opportunity to consider or even read this bill. The first opportunity I had to know what this legislation is was when it was read from the Clerk's desk.

"It is an important banking bill. It is a dictatorship over finance...It is complete control over the banking system of the United States...I have been calling attention for some years past in the manner in which the Federal Reserve has been conducted, and have predicted that it would lead to this kind of a situation. We have, step by step, been proceeding down the lines of centralization. Attempts in past meetings of this Congress have succeeded in enacting increasingly centralized banking plans. This gives supreme authority to those people who have wanted to control the finances of this government, through a centralized system...No one wants the new administration, under the leadership of President Roosevelt, to succeed any more than I do. I shall go as far as any other man to see that success comes to it, but I say now to that leadership that the first thing that must be done is to audit the United States Treasury!

"We want to know," McFadden continued, "—the people of the United States want to know the condition of the Public Treasury and the obligations that are outstanding. We want to know the amount of gold in the United States Treasury, and we want to know the amount of gold in the Federal Reserve System...This is a time to draw a line, and I may say to you Democrats here that if you do not draw a line through the Treasury operations...and the Federal Reserve operations, you will be enmeshed in all the things that they have been doing—and they have been doing some things as I have pointed out heretofore—or we would not be in the condition we are in today.

"I want to know...[if]...this bill represents the ideas of the new administration—the new deal. I shall help carry it through if it is that. If, on the other hand, this bill has been proposed and written by the same influences that are responsible for this financial situation, I shall fight it and do everything that I can to defeat it.

"The first section of the bill — as I grasped it," McFadden continued, "is practically the war powers that were given back in 1917, with some slight amendments. The other gives supreme authority to the Secretary of the Treasury of the United States to impound all the gold in the United States in the hands of individuals, corporations, or companies for the purpose, I suppose, of bringing together that gold and making it available for the issuance of Federal Reserve notes."

Clearly, the purpose for impounding the wealth of America was not detailed. However, it was not to support the currency of the United States, because as Representative McGugin declared on page 83 of the Congressional proceedings of March 9, "The money so issued will not have one penny of gold coverage behind it, because it is not really needed. We do not need gold to back our internal currency...Our people do not actually use gold as a medium of exchange; paper money is just as good and is much easier to handle."

In McGugin opinion, basing the nation's money supply on "...a mortgage of all the homes and other property of all the people in the Nation..." was far superior to backing it with gold. The dollar, McGugin argued, would still be worth 100 cents on the dollar. That is, it would be until January 4, 1934. When the New Deal Congress passed the *Gold Reserve Act of 1934*, Roosevelt immediately devalued the dollar to 41¢[3].

McFadden continued to demand to know exactly who wrote the banking bill, since the legislation was not properly introduced in either the House or the Senate, nor were copies provided for any of the members — or, in particular, to the Committee chairmen

---

[3]Most Americans today do not realize exactly what has caused the retail prices the consumer pays for goods in America to double, triple or quadruple over the last two or three decades. Contrary to popular myth, it is not due to the rising cost of the materials used to create those products, nor is it the costs associated with the labor needed to manufacture them. While it is true that as the hourly wages paid to the factory workers increased, those costs have been passed on the consumer in the form of higher prices. But all of the combined cost increases for materials and labor do not translate into the increased prices the consumers are forced to pay if they want to buy those goods. In reality, the lion's share of these price increases are caused by the elasticity of our currency. The American dollar has an invisible "benchmark" value that remains pegged to

of the House and Senate—to read.

His objection was echoed by Representative Lundeen, who addressed Speaker of the House Henry T. Rainey.

"Today," Lundeen began, "the Chief Executive sent...a banking bill for immediate enactment. The author of this bill seems to be unknown. No one has told us who drafted the bill. There appears to be a printed copy at the Speaker's desk, but no printed copies are available for the House members. *The bill has been driven through the House with cyclonic speed after 40 minutes debate – 20 minutes for the minority and 20 minutes for the majority!*" (Emphasis, author.)

"I have demanded a roll call," Lundeen continued, " but have been unable to get the attention of the Chair. Others have done the same...Fifteen men were standing, demanding a roll call, but that number was not sufficient. We therefore have the spectacle of the great House of Representatives of the United States of America passing, after a 40-minute debate, a bill its members never read and never saw; a bill whose author is unknown!

"The great majority of the members have been unable to get a minute's time to discuss the bill; we have been refused a roll call; and we have been refused recognition by the Chair...I want to put myself on record against a procedure of this kind and against the use of such methods in passing legislation affecting millions of lives and billions of dollars. It seems to me that under this bill thousands of small banks will be crushed and wiped out of existence, and that money and credit control will be still further concentrated in the hands of those who now hold the power...I am suspicious of this railroading of bills through our House of Rep-

---

gold even though we are no longer on the gold standard. When FDR devalued the dollar to 41¢ in 1934, consumer prices remained static until the FDR price controls were suspended. Then, prices escalated rapidly since the "material value" of the goods already manufactured did not decrease in value when the dollar lost 59% of its buying power, requiring more "new" dollars to buy what "old" dollars, worth more, had created.

As the Fed "stretches" the dollar by putting more dollars into circulation, the value of each of those dollars already in circulation decreases in a direct proportion to the new dollars added to the economy. The net result is that the value of the paychecks of the American workers shrinks accordingly. The higher price tags we are forced to pay to buy the goods we require is largely the result of that anomaly.

320

resentatives, and I refuse to vote for a measure unseen and un-known!" (*Congressional Record* of March 9, 1933; pg. 83.)

Quite frankly, Lundeen's vote—and McFadden's for that matter—were not needed. The New Deal Democrats comprised a majority in both the House and the Senate. The *Emergency Banking Relief Act,* with only 40-minutes of debate by a Congress that had not even read the bill, was passed and sent to the White House. Roosevelt signed it into law that evening. The "cyclonic" passage of the *Emergency Banking Relief Act* would be the litmus test for other pieces of Roosevelt's New Deal which would be forthcoming from the assembly line Congress.

The sterile debate over the gold standard has continued al-most unabated since the *Congressional Gold Repeal Joint Resolution* of June 5, 1933. Unquestionably, even though the Joint Resolu-tion was upheld by the U.S. Supreme Court in the *Gold Clause Cases* (294 US 240) on February 18, 1935 in a five-to-four deci-sion, it was nevertheless an unconstitutional act[4].

Revisionist historians argue that the widespread adoption of bimetallic monetary systems is a recent event dating back only the mid-19th century, and that it was brought about by the In-dustrial Revolution. They further insist the United States did not formally adopt the gold standard until 1873 with most of the European nations following around 1900.

Such declarations are, of course, ludicrous.

---

[4]While the Supreme Court upheld Roosevelt's actions by the narrowest of margins, it did so, it declared, only because of the manner in which the government presented its argument: that the government's action was necessitated by the "national banking emergency." Homer S. Cum-mings, Roosevelt's Attorney General argued that the compelling interest of the United States government to protect the assets of America super-ceded all other issues under debate. The Court agreed. In its ruling, however, the Court left open the door to further debate by declaring that the abrogation of the gold clause was not legally valid, but since the petitioners (those holding government bonds) were not injured, they were not entitled to recover damages.

Justice Harlan Fiske Stone, a Coolidge appointee, argued that since the petitioners had not proven they had been "damaged" by the abroga-tion of the gold standard, the Court had no reason to allow them to test the validity of the *Gold Repeal Joint Resolution,* since the ambiguous ruling of the Court itself might later interpose serious obstacles to the stabilization of the dollar.

The Constitution of the United States mandated a bimetallic monetary system. From the creation of the Republic in 1787, the monetary system of the United States has been based on gold and silver. Other than during the Civil War, it has only been during those periods when central banks have been allowed to control to our monetary system that the currency of the United States has been debt-based rather than asset-based. And even then, gold was still used to stabilize the currency by affixing the value of the dollar on the international money markets. Gold reserves theoretically equalled 25% of the money in circulation.

The Civil War ended without the bankers' realizing their goal of rechartering a central bank in the United States. Instead, on January 14, 1875, on the heels of the failure of Jay Cooke & Company in September, 1873 and the ensuing *Bank Panic of 1873,* Congress passed the *Resumption Act of 1875* which officially ended the use of Lincoln's war script and restored the nation to species.

As in any economic debate, the advocates of a debt-based rather than asset-based monetary system advance only one logical argument in defense of the current Fed position, although the basic premise upon which they base that argument is flawed since, for some strange reason, most economists fail to link inflation to the increased circulation of script.

Unlike most ordinary American citizens who decry the repeal of the gold standard as the rape of the wealth of the nation, most non-Fed related economists in the United States wrongly believe the gold standard itself caused the Great Depression, arguing, in defiance of empirical evidence to the contrary, that the money supply in 1929 could not be expanded by the Fed because it had reached its 25%/75% threshold, thereby bringing about the collapse of the stock market and the ensuing Depression.

In a March, 1997 article entitled *Gold: Been There, Done That* in *The World & I* magazine, former chief economist for the New York Stock Exchange William C. Freund, in his ardent defense of the *status quo,* confirmed that point himself when he said: "Few people know that in the 1930s, our central bank did exactly the wrong thing. Instead of encouraging the money supply to expand, [the Fed] allowed [it] to contract by some 30%. No wonder the economy when down the drain." (pg. 79.)

Prior to that admission, Freund argued that Fed Chairman Alan Greenspan was correct when he said basing money on the gold standard paralyzed the Federal Reserve's ability to stabilize prices and production. "Imagine," he hypothesized, "that our country is in the grip of a serious economic downturn...If the money supply cannot be expanded, the country may be destined to suffer through a long period of depression and stagnation...Governments everywhere became determined to do something about unemployment and to gain control over their domestic economies. The gold standard would have condemned them to a policy of standing there and doing nothing." (*ibid;* pg. 77)

"What we have learned since then," he concluded, "is that giving control over the money supply to able board members of the Federal Reserve is better than leaving control to the unpredictable consequences of the gold standard. In fact," he said — as if the statement somehow validated his argument, "we have not had a major worldwide economic depression for over 60 years." (*ibid;* pg. 79.)

Of course not. The international banking community now controls virtually every currency in the world. All they have left to take from us are the rest of the world's tangible capital assets.

O n Friday, March 3 the New York and Chicago Fed branches were forced to pay out another $110 billion in gold to foreign investors and $20 billion to others. In addition, state banks across the nation coughed up another $20 billion in gold to small depositors, bringing the total gold drain to $414 billion, and triggering the March 3 midnight crisis by Meyer.

What is most disturbing about the gold drain of 1933 is that the foreign entities that pulled at least $224 billion in gold bullion from the Treasury of the United States from December 1, 1929 to March 3, 1933 did not invest gold in the economy of the United States — they invested their own national script, backed by the debts of their own economies.

In exchange for that script they were given gold. None of that gold was seized under Roosevelt's emergency proclamation. What was seized was all of the gold lawfully held by American citizens who had actually deposited gold certificates — redeemable in gold — into the banks of America, and who were legally and morally entitled to redeem those certificates in either gold coins or bullion. In exchange for their gold they were given debt-backed script — that would be devalued by 59% less than one year later, reducing the net worth of every citizen in the United States by a like amount.

323

On Tuesday, January 30, 1934 Roosevelt signed the *Gold Reserve Act of 1934* into law, followed on Wednesday by the issuance of Presidential Proclamation 2072 reducing the weight of the gold dollar from 25 4/5 grains to 15 5/21 grains — a reduction of 59%. The immediate windfall to the government was approximately $4 billion. Of that, $2 billion created Roosevelt's Economic Stabilization Fund — taken directly from the pockets of America by a new form of taxation — the devaluation of the dollar.

Interestingly, the authority for Roosevelt to create fiat money was not found in the *Gold Reserve Act of 1934*, nor was it found in either the *Emergency Banking Act of March 9, 1933* or the *Banking Act of June 16, 1933*. It was found, unobtrusively concealed within Title 3 of the Thomas Amendment in the *Agricultural Adjustment Act of May 12, 1933*. Also interesting is the fact that when the authority to create fiat money from gold coins in Proclamation 2072 was cited by Roosevelt, it was referred to only as *Title 3 of the Act approved May 12, 1933* and never as the *Agricultural Adjustment Act*, in order, one might logically conclude, to avoid the question why such an important and completely unrelated delegation of monetary power to the President of the United States would be included in a farm bill rather than, say, in the *Gold Reserve Act*. Or, was it perhaps because it was an unlawful delegation of authority to the President by Congress, since the unassignable right to coin money and fix the standards of weight and measures is reserved exclusively to the Congress by the Constitution?

What was included in the *Gold Reserve Act of 1934*, however, was the issuance of new currency by the Federal Reserve. Since the United States was no longer on the gold standard, the gold clause on the dollar had to be changed. The 1900 U.S. Treasury certificate contained this simple pledge: "*Redeemable in gold on demand at the U.S. Treasury.*" The 1928 Series Federal Reserve certificate contained this promise: "*Redeemable in gold on demand at the U.S. Treasury or in good or lawful money at any Federal Reserve Bank.*" What did lawful money in 1928 consist of, if not gold or silver?

The new 1934 Federal Reserve note, however, said: "*This note is legal tender for all debts, public and private and is redeemable in lawful money at the Treasury or at any Federal Reserve Bank.*" First, it was no longer a "certificate" — it was now a "note." A *note* signifies debt. The *lawful money* of 1934 was debt-based rather than asset-based.

Does that mean if you took a handful of Federal Reserve notes to the Treasury and demanded they be exchanged for *lawful money* you would be given with a handful of debt, or would you simply exchange the notes in your possession for a like amount of identical, although possibly newer, Federal Reserve notes?

Quite possibly the government itself found the phrase ambiguous, because it was changed again in 1963. This time it simply said: *"This note is legal tender for all debts, public and private."* It was no longer redeemable for anything.

"Democracy never lasts long. It soon wastes, exhausts, and murders itself. There never was a democracy that did not commit suicide."

John Adams
In a letter to John Taylor
April 15, 1814

"The arts of power and its minions are the same in all countries and in all ages. It marks a victim; denounces it; and excites the public odium and the public hatred, to conceal its own abuses and encroachments."

Henry Clay
Speech to the United States Senate
March 14, 1834

"It has eternally been observed that any man who has power is led to abuse it."

Montesquieu,
French Philosopher
The Spirit of the Laws
1748

❖ THIRTEEN ❖

War Powers: Codified

During the first 100 days of Roosevelt's administration Congress passed a litany of legislative programs ostensibly designed to stimulate the economy and send America back to work. Most of this legislation was expediently enacted with about as much Congressional forethought as the *Emergency Banking Relief Act*. And, a great deal of it, like the *Agricultural Adjustment Act*, the *National Industrial Recovery Act* and the *Congressional Gold Repeal Joint Resolution*, violated the Constitution of the United States.

The first of three laws designed to wrest control of the United States away from the States and the people was engineered on May 9, 1933. This law, enacted without a single Congressman reading it — and after only 40 minutes of debate — was the *Emergency Banking Relief Act*.

There were at least two reasons Roosevelt didn't want Congress looking too closely at the language of the *Emergency Banking Relief Act*. First, it restructured the banking system of the United States and placed even more monetary control in the hands of the central bankers. Second, it gave Roosevelt *war powers* control over the United States of America in peacetime. But most important, it changed the language of the *Trading with the Enemy Act*, effectively classifying the citizens of the United States as enemies of their own federal government.

And, it did one other thing. It granted Roosevelt the right to redefine the ownership of private property in the United States. Such redefinition was necessary since the "war powers" authority Roosevelt was being accorded to deal with the "national emergency" granted him the right to seize the property of those who failed to comply with the laws which were being enacted.

The right to seize the property of American citizens without due process would be one of the paramount weapons the govern-

327

ment would continue to use long after the "emergency" expired.

It would be a much-used weapon by the Internal Revenue Service, which has not hesitated to seize any asset or property of any American citizen without due process since 1934. In the last few years, that "right" has also been assumed by State and federal police agencies who now seize the assets of drug dealers and those charged with violations the RICO act — at the time of arrest, not conviction. Gone forever is the presumption of innocence until guilt is proven beyond a reasonable doubt.

Municipalities do the same when they seize the vehicles driven by "johns" arrested for seeking the illegal and illicit pleasures of prostitutes in hundreds of sting operations launched each year by a countless brigade of city and county police agencies throughout the country. All such laws, regardless of their deterrent qualities, and regardless if they are upheld by the courts, violate the Constitution of the United States because they deny the accused the right to due process before seizure takes place.

It is a troubling sign of our times that any court of law in America, regardless of the compelling interest of society to eradicate the proliferation of illegal drugs that is taking such a devastating toll on human life and dignity while breeding all other forms of crime from petty larceny to murder, would wantonly violate the Constitution of the United States under the guise of providing a safer and more secure America.

The redefinition of private property rights is found in *Senate Document 43* that examined, and attempted to justify, the ramifications of the powers delegated to the President under the *War Powers Act* — albeit after-the-fact. On page 9 of that document, we find: "*The ultimate ownership of all property is in the State; individual so-called 'ownership' is only by virtue of the Government, i.e., law, amounting to mere user...*"

That particular facet of *Document 43*, further clarified by *Senate Report 93-549*, has become codified by precedent. As the Senate began to examine exactly what powers they had granted the President by amending the *Trading With the Enemy Act* on March 9, 1933, they concluded that: "*Under these powers the president may: seize property; organize and control the means of production; seize commodities; assign military forces abroad; institute martial law; seize and control all transportation and communication; regulate the operation of private industry; restrict travel, and in a plethora of particular ways,* 328 *control the lives of all American citizens.*" (Senate Report 93-549.)

It is important to note that every dictatorship in the modern world has abrogated the rights of private ownership, seized property at will, organized and controlled all production within its society, seized and controlled the transportation infrastructure of the nation, nationalized communications to censor the free expression of opinion — *and restricted the movement of its citizens.* This is usually done with an internal passport which the citizens of every authoritarian country are required to carry with them at all times[1].

Whenever these steps are accomplished by any government, democracy dies a bittersweet death and totalitarianism is born in the ashes of lost freedom.

The Roosevelt "brain trust," in paving the way for Roosevelt to implement his New Deal programs, privately acknowledged that most of the economic and social programs they were constructing even before Roosevelt assumed the White House would be legally problematic when viewed in the context of the constitutionality of a United States president's authority in peace-

---

[1] Two of the strangest features of the aborted *Clinton Health Security Act of 1993* would have been the introduction of both a National Identity Card and a global monitoring system that would allow government officials to restrict interstate travel.

In the disavowed November 11, 1993 White House protocol, the discussion centered on the Identity Card since it was obvious at that time that Hillary Clinton's health care reform bill was in deep trouble in both the House and the Senate. The subject was first broached by the President who "...stresses the necessity of having all Americans being required to possess and carry such a card...[to]...simplify the task of law enforcement...and...allow various federal agencies to keep track of a population that is too highly mobile."

As the various reports of the Clinton Healthcare Task Force were uncovered by the *Freedom of Information Act* and retrieved from their "documental tombs" in the National Archives where they had been adroitly buried among other meaningless reams of White House papers, a curious and alarming pattern of deception began to take shape.

Among the promises of the swan song of universal healthcare in the Clinton documents is one "ugly duckling" that does not belong in any bill dealing with healthcare—the Intelligent Vehicle/Highway System (IV/HS). In its synopsis of IV/HS, the Diebold Group (which prepared the study for the Clinton White House) declared that the work they had

time. In times of war, the Constitution itself allows for the broadening of presidential powers by the Chief Executive to deal with extraneous, albeit temporary, emergencies that seriously threaten the security and welfare of the nation.

However, in 1933 America was not at war.

It was a dilemma the "brain trust" would quickly solve by modifying the *Trading With the Enemy Act of 1917* to include any national emergency. In doing so, it was also necessary to redefine the "enemy" since the extraneous authority granted the President under the terms of *Public Law 91* was directed only at the enemies, and allies of the enemies, of the United States. A peacetime application of the *Trading With the Enemy Act* without some form of universal modification that would allow Roosevelt to apply the tenets of that law against the citizens of the United States would be meaningless.

That fact is supported by a conversation that transpired between Roosevelt and Glass shortly after 11:30 p.m. on March 3,

---

undertaken "...is an international cooperative effort whose goal is to assess the value of information technology in societal infrastructures and, where appropriate, bring about the policy conditions which facilitate its development and application...Public infrastructures that could be improved by information technology include road transportation...

"In the next stages of the project, we expect to carry out the work outlined in the above paragraphs. Our results will be reviewed with the key participants and public policy groups. In parallel, we shall be disseminating our results both in the United States and abroad. This process has already begun with presentations to the Council on Foreign Relations...and the Centre for European Studies, Brussels."

In Diebold Working Paper #6, prepared by Professor Kan Chen on the IV/HS vehicle tracking system, it is noted that the system is already being used experimentally in England, where it is called *TrafficMaster*. The system was set up on the M25 motorway, but the British Department of Transport is contemplating expansion into the "A-roads" in the London-area.

Looking at its use in America, the report cautions that "...IV/HS may be perceived by some as conflicting with other important societal goals such as privacy, environmental control, local democracy and competing with other solutions to highway problems. First and foremost in people's minds is privacy. Automatic vehicle location could be misused by unauthorized persons or organizations. It could be used by the government for purposes other than originally intended."

From a public relations perspective, IV/HS offers some beneficial

1933. Twelve and a half hours before his term in office expired, and shortly before he retired for the night, Hoover called to apprise Roosevelt of the situation concerning the banking crisis which he believed, at that moment, had been resolved.

Earlier that day Roosevelt had visited Hoover at the White House where they discussed the crisis at length. Hoover informed the president-elect that Attorney General William D. Mitchell had advised him that the *Trading With the Enemy Act* did not give him the authority to close any State or community bank, but he would nevertheless do it — if Roosevelt would agree to publicly approve and support the effort.

Instead of agreeing, Roosevelt told Hoover that Thomas Walsh, whom he had originally selected as Attorney General-designate had advised him it could be done. Unfortunately, Walsh was not around to advise either of them how this could be done legally since Walsh had recently died. The question was also posed by Roosevelt to Homer Cummings, who would become his Attorney General the following day. Cummings was noncommit-

---

aspects which will very likely be touted by the White House that ultimately seeks to implement the program as a means to continuously monitor the highway system in America for signs of "...deterioration and structural weakness in bridges and tunnels..through a network of probes embedded into the physical infrastructure." These probes, however, are necessary to monitor the whereabouts of vehicles between the major "checkpoints" which will be established at major highway intersections.

The report details that "Traffic will be managed on the main roads of major metropolitan areas through controlling road junctions and access to major routes..."

IV/HS can, and likely will, be used to control the flow of traffic on congested arteries around the major cities as an alternative to HOV restrictions since it will allow the government the ability to assess tolls on all vehicles (automatically withdrawn from your e.money account) as you pass a checkpoint. "Through automatic vehicle identification and automatic toll collection, the way is opened to variable pricing of access to roadways [congestion pricing]."

Most motorists who travel the beltways around most of the major cities of America will be affected, but few will complain since those who do not wish to pay an access toll to travel the congested roadways will be obligated to seek alternate routes, thereby lightening the traffic. However, there is a downside the government, in promoting IV/HS as an alternative to HOV lanes, will likely not mention. Just as the government will have the ability to permit access on these arteries, they will also have

tal on the subject, wanting to review the law before offering a legal opinion. "Roosevelt thought Hoover could act legally, but *he was not sure* and this was as far as he would go. Roosevelt left Hoover at 5 p.m., saying: 'I shall be waiting at my hotel, Mr. President, to learn what you decide.'" (*The Roosevelt Myth;* John T. Flynn; Garden City Books © 1948; pg. 26.)

At 11:30 that evening when Hoover called before retiring, the President reiterated again that he would sign the Proclamation sent by Meyer if Roosevelt would join him in the matter but wanted the President-elect's assurance that Roosevelt agreed with him that there should be no universal national bank closings. "Roosevelt answered: 'Senator Glass is here. He does not think it is necessary to close the banks—my own opinion is that the governors of the states can take care of closings wherever necessary. I prefer that you issue no proclamation of this nature." (*ibid;* pg. 26.)

Of course, as the events of the next three days mutely affirm, Roosevelt lied. He wanted Hoover to declare the bank holiday, but he wanted Hoover to do it by himself. Roosevelt did not want his fingerprints to be found anywhere on the proclamation, which was clearly illegal. Congress, however, would correct that when they passed the *Emergency Banking Relief Act* six days later without demanding full disclosure of the bill.

At that time, according to Flynn's account in *The Roosevelt Myth,* Roosevelt was then forced to explain to Glass that the Fed-

---

the ability to deny it.

Part of the plan is centered on an experiment to control interstate access of those commercial vehicles that currently come under the jurisdiction of the Interstate Commerce Commission.

"Commercial vehicle operators will receive regulatory documents [permits, registrations, etc.] for multiple states in a single transaction, and automatic weight checking as needed, without requiring the vehicle to stop." Again, it sounds like progress. However, when viewed next to Bill Clinton's concerns about the mobility of American citizens in the disavowed White House protocol of November 11, 1993, warning flags go up.

IV/HS could be used just as easily to restrict interstate travel. Add to that the statement in the disavowed protocol that the National Identity Card could, and likely would, be used as an "internal passport," it is obvious that it, combined with IV/HS, the use of an internal passport is the logical first steps in restricting the movement of a population.

eral Reserve Board had urged Hoover to close the banks.

"Glass asked Roosevelt what he was going to do. To Glass' amazement, he answered: 'I am planning to close them, of course.' Glass asked him by what authority. He replied: 'The Enemy Trading Act' — the very act Hoover had referred to and on which Roosevelt had said he had no advice from Cummings as to its validity. Glass protested such an act would be unconstitutional and told him so in heated terms. 'Nevertheless,' replied Roosevelt, 'I'm going to issue a proclamation to close the banks.'" (*ibid*; pg. 26.)

Roosevelt knew something at that moment that Glass, a staunch party-line Democrat, did not know. The legislation which would mysteriously appear in both chambers of Congress on Thursday, March 9 would "legalize" the action Roosevelt was taking on March 6 — as well as steps that he would take later to nationalize the economy of the United States.

For Roosevelt to successfully usurp the Constitution of the United States, a national emergency of such monumental proportions had to exist that only such drastic measures would forestall the collapse of the nation. At least, that was the legal opinion Roosevelt had previously received from Walsh.

Within hours of Roosevelt's inauguration on March 4, the "brain trust" had moved from the Mayflower to their new offices in the White House. Moley, the policy coordinator, immediately started his first day in the new Administration reviewing the content of the *Emergency Bank Relief Act* with Cummings and Roosevelt to make certain that when the bill was signed into law the Administration would be standing on legal ground.

Later that afternoon, Roosevelt called the Fed bankers and apprised them of a meeting that would be held on Sunday, March 5 at the Treasury to discuss the impending proclamations. Roosevelt knew it would be easy to close the banks; the unanswered question in his mind was, once closed, how does the Administration reopen them? He wanted a concrete plan before Monday, March 6.

The Fed bankers attending the Treasury meeting were Adolph A. Berle, Jr., G. W. Davidson, George Harrison, Eugene Meyer, Adolph Miller and Melvin Traynor. From the Morgan bank were Leffingwell and Gilbert. From the Senate was Glass and from the House, Congressman Henry B. Steagall. From Hoover's administration was Ogden Mills and the former Treasury Undersecretary Arthur Ballentine. (Like Hoover, Roosevelt wanted to make certain if the flack starting flying, he could direct a good portion of it at the other Administration.) From his own Administration, Roosevelt sent Moley, Cummings and Woodin.

After arguing all day, the sun set on Sunday, March 5 without a solution. Roosevelt could close the banks, but there was no certainty they would ever re-open. Unfortunately, Roosevelt had already issued *Proclamation 2039*, effective the following day.

The group returned to work the following day. The banks were now closed. The drain on the gold reserve had finally stopped. Foreign investors had drained roughly $264 billion in gold from the Treasury of the United States. American depositors had taken almost a $150 billion in gold, which they were privately holding. The Fed wanted the gold returned, and would not agree to any proposal that did not include the seizure of all gold coins and bullion held by private citizens of the United States.

Resistance to the notion of seizing the gold from its rightful owners came only from Steagall and Glass who argued it was the lawful money of the United States. However, by removing the dollar from the gold standard, gold would no longer be species—it would simply become "property," which under the amended *War Powers Act* was subject to seizure at the discretion of the President. Although there are no public records to support the notion, it is likely that the redefinition of "private property" occurred during this meeting. Clearly that was the intent since gold was not, prior to that meeting, defined as "property"—gold was species, the lawful "currency" of the land.

Once that hurdle was cleared, solving the balance of the problem became relatively easy. On March 7 the group had put together the rudiments of a plan. Congress would issue a fresh supply of new Federal Reserve notes—totalling some $20 billion—and recall the old currency. The new currency would be backed by both the assets and bond issues of the banks themselves. The Fed would issue instructions to each member bank to supply a list of all depositors who had been paid in gold, and each would be required to surrender all gold and gold certificates to the conservators of the banks under penalty of law.

Obvious, however, was the fact that since Congress had to
334   authorize the printing of a new series of Federal Reserve notes,

and they were not scheduled to convene in special session until March 9, it would be impossible for the solvent banks to re-open on Friday, March 10. On March 9, Roosevelt issued *Proclamation 2040* extending the bank holiday. The banks—or at least a portion of them—would finally begin reopening on Monday, March 13.

When Roosevelt issued *Proclamation 2039* there were approximately 20,000 banks in the United States. By March 16, some 9,883 banks had reopened and were again offering full service to their customers. Another 2,678 would ultimately be restored. But over 6,000 banks remained closed, victims of an overplayed hand by politicians and bankers alike. Had Roosevelt acted prudently instead of helping to promulgate a situation that only "war powers" could solve, it is very likely that many of these banks would have reopened, and the deposits lost by many of their customers could have been saved. However, Roosevelt had an agenda—a grand experiment—to try out on America, and he was blinded by his own vision.

Public Law 1 of the Roosevelt Administration, stemming from H.R. 1491, will long be remembered both as the bill nobody read and the legislation that gave the President of the United States almost complete dictatorial power over America.

As Americans, each of us are prone to criticize those citizens who blindly vote for candidates based solely on their political affiliation without possessing any knowledge of the issues at stake in the election in which they are casting their ballots. Yet, in the Congress of the United States, on March 9, 1933, those we elected to represent us before the federal government of the United States did precisely that. Is it any wonder the electorate of America has a herd mentality?

What happened that day in 1933 is more terrifying than the stock market crash and the ensuing Depression combined. Clearly those we have elected, and continue to elect, no longer represent the constituents who placed them in office—and have not for several years. Most career politicians have been "institutionalized" and clearly represent only the interests of big government—and the special interest groups that contribute massive amounts to keep them in office so they can manipulate the reins of government from behind the scenes in the name of the general public they have sworn to serve.

The special session of Congress that met on March 9, 1933 did so because the President of the United States called them to address a national emergency of such extraordinary proportions that it required extraordinary legislation to cope with the crisis. If that fact, in and of itself, was not a red flag (pardon the pun), the failure to read the legislation being considered for rushed passage (another red flag), or the preamble of the legislation itself should have been.

"Be it enacted by the Senate and the House of Representatives of the United States of America in Congress assembled, That the Congress hereby declares that a serious emergency exists and that it is imperatively necessary speedily to put into effect remedies of uniform national application.

TITLE I.

Section 1. The actions, regulations, rules, licenses, orders and proclamations heretofore or hereafter taken, promulgated, made, or issued by the President of the United States or the Secretary of the Treasury since March 4, 1933, pursuant to the authority conferred by subsection (b) of section 5 of the Act of October 6, 1917, as amended, are hereby approved and confirmed."

A very large red flag was being waved. The Emergency Bill begins with an admission that the new President and his Treasury Secretary had already broken the law; and were now seeking not only retroactive exoneration for those deeds, but absolution from future infractions of the Constitution as well.

Clearly, Roosevelt and his Attorney General Cummings did not want Congress scrutinizing the bill too closely because some of the very subtle textual changes they made in their revisions of the *Act of October 6, 1917* might not stand up under the light of day. Many Congressmen believed the only revisions were those found in Section 5(b) (italicized).

"During time of war *or during any other period of national emergency declared by the President,* the President may, through any agency he may designate, or otherwise, investigate, regulate, or prohibit, under such rules and regulations as he may prescribe, by means of license or otherwise, any transactions in foreign exchange, transfers of credits

336

between or payments by banking institutions as defined by the
President, and export, hoarding, melting, or earmarking of gold
or silver coin or bullion or currency, *by any person within the*
United States or any place subject to the jurisdiction thereof..."

In fact, the *Act of October 6, 1917* expressly forbade the President
from interfering in banking transactions executed wholly within
the United States. Furthermore, *Public Law 91,* Chapter 106, declares itself to be "An Act to define, regulate, and punish trading
with the enemy, and for other purposes" — none of which dealt with
citizens of the United States, clearly defined by Section 2(c):

"(c) Such other individuals, or body or class of individuals, as may be natives, citizens, or subjects of any nation
with which the United States is at war, *other than citizens of*
the United States..."

Again, we see the same exclusion. As defined under the *Act of*
October 6, 1917, American citizens were exempted from the clas-
sification of an "enemy." However, in the Rooseveltian version,
the only people under scrutiny for punitive action are American
citizens — or those who haplessly fall within the jurisdiction of the
United States government. Roosevelt sought, and was granted
by Congress, power to engage in an economic war against the
people of the United States.

It may well be that the only use Roosevelt intended to make
of the expanded war powers authority was to protect his Administration from any potential problems that could have arisen from
assuming prerogatives he did not legally possess when he closed
the banks over which he had no Constitutional authority. More
likely than not, either he or his brain trust — or both — realized
that his far-reaching socialist agenda to nationalize the industrial base of America would usurp not only the separation of
powers between the executive, judicial and legislative branches
of the federal government, but would create insurmountable sovereignty issues between the federal government and the States
as well. Realizing such, possessing supra-wartime powers would
weigh heavily in disputes with either the States or with Congress.

Whatever the logic, Roosevelt assured the American people
that the proclamation under which he had operated the country
on a wartime basis since March 6, 1933 would be lifted at the
end of World War II. However, he died on April 12, 1945.

On August 6, 1945 under direct orders from President Harry S. Truman, the United States Army/Air Corps dropped the first of two atomic bombs on Japan. The target, Hiroshima, was actually an alternative. The primary target was clouded over and had to be bypassed. The death toll was staggering. Over 129 thousand men, women and children perished in the world's first nuclear holocaust. Thousands more were wounded. Thousands more eventually died from radiation poisoning. The blast leveled a four square mile area.

On August 9 the devastation was repeated on Nagasaki. The Japanese surrendered on August 14 although the formal surrender was not completed until September 2 on board the *U.S.S. Missouri* in Tokyo Bay, ending the conflict known as World War II.

However, even though the war had ended, the *War Powers Act* remained in effect in the United States. Truman found a valuable tool in war powers authority, and he would not willingly relinquish it — nor would any President after him.

It would not be until the spring of 1973 that the 93rd Congress, determined to dilute the power of the Presidency, decided it might be time to declare an end to the "national emergency" that had existed unabated since 1933. The decision to do so was made largely because the supra-powers granted the President by the 65th Congress, and enlarged by the 73rd, were then held by the most unpopular President in the history of the United States since Herbert Hoover. His name was Richard Nixon.

The decision to hold hearings in the Senate on the advisability of repealing the *War Powers Act* was not based on Nixon's 29% popularity polling, but rather it was due to Nixon's expansion of America's role in Vietnam and his own obvious involvement in the Watergate scandal.

When he was first elected in 1968, Nixon promised to get the United States out of the Vietnamese civil war, but soon found himself so deeply enmeshed in the southeast Asian political conflict that escape seemed virtually impossible.

Unlike his predecessor, Lyndon Johnson, Nixon believed the war in Vietnam could be won. Johnson knew it wasn't supposed to be. In March, 1969 Nixon, encouraged to do so by both National Security Council Director Henry Kissinger and his deputy, Major General Alexander M. Haig, Jr., secretly authorized the bombing of the North Vietnamese and Viet Cong supply lines and troop havens inside the borders of neutral Cambodia.

The Cambodian air strikes continued until May 9 when the *New York Times* broke a by-lined front page story. The man who had promised to end the conflict if he was elected expanded the war less than three months after his inauguration.

Congress responded to Nixon's secret aggression by repealing the *Gulf of Tonkin Resolution,* passed after the Tet Offensive, authorizing Johnson to conduct war in southeast Asia. Nixon denounced the action as not binding on the President, citing his authority under the *Trading With the Enemy Act.* Congress was not pleased, and threatened to cut funding for the President's Vietnamese excursion unless Nixon got the troops out of Vietnam. Nixon backed down—for the time being. A troop withdrawal was announced, and some troops were actually pulled out, completely demoralizing those who were left behind.

On August 15, 1971 Nixon incurred the wrath of Congress again when he exercised Section 5(b) of the *Trading With the Enemy Act* by declaring a "national emergency" existed due to America's declining global economic position. Nixon issued *Presidential Proclamation 4074,* imposing a surcharge on imports, and devaluing the dollar. The following year when the *Export Control Act* expired, he invoked Section 5(b) again, basing his authority not only on *Proclamation 4074* but also on *Proclamation 2914* issued by Truman on December 16, 1950 during the Korean War.

But the final straw probably came on December 12, 1972 when Nixon ordered American B-52 bombers to drop over 36,000 tons of conventional bombs on Haipong and Hanoi, North Vietnam. Fifteen B-52s were shot down during the 12-day raid, and 44 pilots and crew members were captured. North Vietnam claimed that over 1,600 civilians were killed during the sorties, and that one civilian hospital was completely destroyed.

Congress decided it was time to clip the President's wings. Congress, at that time, was more than just a little afraid of Nixon, whom it viewed as a paranoid loose cannon with too much power. Nixon had discovered the *Trading With the Enemy Act,* and did not hesitate to exercise it whenever the Democrat-controlled Congress got in his way. On top of everything else that was happening, on February 9, 1973 the Senate voted overwhelming to appoint a special committee headed by Senator Sam Ervin,

Jr. (D-NC) to investigate the well-publicized Watergate scandal that appeared to be centered in the Oval Office.

Congress then appointed Senator Frank Church (D-ID) Chairman of Senate Special Committee on Aging to head a Special Committee on the Termination of the National Emergency. Hearings began in July, 1973.

A week before Richard Nixon became the first sitting President to resign from office, Church and Senate Republican co-chairman Charles Mathias, Jr. sent letters to every House and Senate Committee Chairman whose extraordinarily-assumed powers under some portion or another of the *Trading With the Enemy Act* could be affected — or eliminated — by its repeal. The purpose of the letter was to determine what portions of the *War Powers Act* needed to be codified to protect the bureaucracy it created before the Act was repealed.

One such reply to their letter, from Senator John Sparkman, Chairman of the Banking, Housing and Urban Affairs Committee is listed here in its entirety:

> "Committee on Banking,
> Housing & Urban Affairs
> Washington, D.C. -Aug. 1, 1974
>
> Hon. Frank Church
> Hon. Charles Mathias, Jr.
> Cochairmen, Special Committee on the
>   Termination of the National Emergency,
> U.S. Senate, Washington, D.C.
>
> Dear Senators Church and Mathias:
>   This is in reply to your request for the recommendation of the Senate Committee on Banking, Housing and Urban Affairs as to whether national emergency statutes under the jurisdiction of this Committee should be repealed, recast as permanent legislation, or amended to meet present circumstances.
>   A review of the compilation provided by your Special Committee has been accomplished. This Committee's recommendations pursuant thereto are attached in memorandum form.
>   A nine month grace period between enactment and effect of legislation terminating any state of national emer-

gency should provide sufficient time in which to recast or amend those statutes considered to be of permanent utility.

I trust this review will prove satisfactory.

With best wishes, I am

Sincerely,

John Sparkman

Attachment

LAWS APPLICABLE TO
PERIODS OF NATIONAL EMERGENCY

Title 12 Banks and Banking

Title 12 USC Code 95 and 95a

It is the Committee's recommendation that these sections of Title 12 be retained in their present form.

The executive replies also.

12 USC 95. Emergency limitations and restrictions on business of members of Federal Reserve system:

In order to provide for the safer and more effective operation of the national banking system and the Federal Reserve system, to preserve for the people the full benefits of the currency provided for by the Congress through the national banking system and the Federal Reserve system, and to relieve interstate commerce of the burdens and obstructions resulting from the receipt of an unsound or unsafe basis of deposits subject to withdrawal by check, during such emergency period as the President of the United States by proclamation may prescribe, no member bank of the Federal Reserve system shall transact any banking business except to such extent and subject to such regulations, limitations, and restrictions as may be prescribed by the Secretary of the Treasury, with the approval of the President. Any individual, partnership, corporation or association, or any director, officer, or employee thereof, violating any of the provisions of this section shall be deemed guilty of a misdemeanor and upon conviction thereof, shall be fined not more than $10,000 or, if a natural person, may, in addition to such fine, be imprisoned for a term not exceeding ten years. Each day that any such violation continues shall be deemed a separate offense. (March 9, 1933, ch. 1, Title 1, 4, 48 Stat. 2.)

341

Recommendation: the Treasury Department recommends retention of this statute in its present form.

This section should be retained. The Congress may wish to enlarge the scope of the statute to cover all banks and other financial institutions located in the United States, including foreign banks having offices or branches here."
(*Constitution: Fact or Fiction;* Dr. Eugene Schroder; Buffalo Creek Press © 1995; pgs. 109-110.)

Interestingly, when the Special Committee notified the Federal Reserve of their request, the Fed responded that they were not aware of any emergency laws still in force that had not been made part of the United States Code. (*ibid;* pg. 110.)

On September 14, 1976 Congress passed H.R. 3884, the *National Emergencies Act* (50 USC 1601), *Public Law 94-412,* to terminate the broad powers previously granted to the President.

Exempted from the law were any and all actions taken before the bill became law; or, any fines, assessments or penalties due the government from those actions.

However, what Congress erased with one hand, it rewrote with the other. The only thing permanently taken from the President was autonomy. Section 201.(a) granted virtually the same powers to the Congress, who may now "authorize" the President to declare states of national emergencies that he could formerly declare without their consent. This slight of hand was important to Congress because it now allows Congress, through a concurrent resolution, to terminate any state of emergency declared by the President.

Retained, almost in its entirety, was the infamous Section 5(b) which classified the citizens of the United States as enemies of their government. The *Trading With the Enemy Act* has now been duly codified, and is now a permanent part of the U.S. Federal Code.

❖ FOURTEEN ❖

Politicizing the Judiciary

The third New Deal law, enacted on May 12, 1933 was the *Agricultural Adjustment Act*. It was the first Roosevelt law to be declared unconstitutional by the U.S. Supreme Court. It would not be the last. Hidden within this piece of legislation was a clause that shifted the authority to coin money from Congress to the President, as well as one which gave the Fed control over the expansion of consumer credit in the United States. However, it was neither of these clauses that brought the *Agricultural Adjustment Act* before the high court. What brought the farm bill into question by the Court was the fact that it sought to nationalize farming by controlling all of the production and pricing of agricultural products in the United States.

Theoretically enacted to establish parity for farm products through the elimination of surplus crops by means of compensated crop curtailment, the *Agricultural Adjustment Act* dictated to the farmer what he could and could not produce on his land — and the price he was to arbitrarily receive for his labor.

The farm bill's compensation was derived from a tax assessed against the processors of farm products, passed directly on to the consumer who bought the products for consumption. In other words, the American consumer was taxed to pay the farmer for not growing enough of a particular crop so that a planned shortage would result. Those planned "shortages" would artificially inflate the crop's price. In the end, the consumer would have to pay more for the privilege of buying the crops that were grown.

In the October, 1935 term of the Supreme Court, the case of *United States v. Butler et al., Receivers of Hoosac Mills Corp.* appeared on the high court's docket. Although Hoosac Mills was bankrupt and in receivership, the Internal Revenue Service sued Franklin Process Company, the receiver, for unpaid processing and floor taxes owed by Hoosac. When Franklin refused to pay, 343 the Internal Revenue filed suit in the U.S. District Court. The District Court ordered Franklin to pay the claims against Hoosac. Franklin appealed to the First Circuit Court of Appeals which upheld the District Court. Franklin then appealed to the Supreme Court. The case was argued on December 10, 1935. The decision, ruling the Act unconstitutional, was entered on January 6, 1936.

At issue was whether or not the government had the authority to levy a "processing and floor-tax" on the processors of food stuffs. The Solicitor General's office insisted that right existed under the "general welfare" clause of the Constitution which gave the federal government the right to lay and collect taxes in order to provide for the common defense and general welfare of the nation (Article I, Section 8 § 1).

The Solicitor General argued that the general welfare clause endowed Congress, not the courts, with the power to determine what best served the country's interests in times of national emergency. The high court, growing weary of a "national emergency" that no longer existed, saw a much larger and more threatening issue. The *Agricultural Adjustment Act* invaded the separation of powers and usurped the powers reserved for the States.

In its decision the majority opinion stated: "The Constitution is the supreme law of the land, ordained and established by the people, and all legislation must conform to the principles it lays down. It is a misconception to say that, in declaring an Act of Congress unconstitutional, the Court assumes power to overrule or control the actions of the people's representatives. The Court is not required in this case to ascertain the scope of the phrase "general welfare of the United States," or to determine whether an appropriation in aid of agriculture falls within it...*The Act invades the reserved powers of the States. Regulation and control of agricultural production are beyond the power delegated to the Federal Government. The tax [is]...the means to an unconstitutional end...The regulation of the farmer's activities under this statute, though in form subject to his own will, is in fact coercion through economic pressure; his right of choice is illusionary...Congress cannot invade State jurisdiction by purchasing the action of individuals any more than by compelling it...Existence of a situation of national concern resulting from similar and widespread local conditions cannot enable Congress to ignore the constitutional limitations upon its own power and usurp those reserved for the States.*" (Emphasis, author's.)

344   A portion of the high court's ruling was an admonition di-

rected against Congress for enacting what it should have known was an unconstitutional law that infringed on States' rights. (Of course, for Congress to realize the *Agricultural Adjustment Act* was unconstitutional, they would have had to have read it before voting on it.) Furthermore, it must be noted that since the Senate no longer represented the States, there was no inherent interest in that chamber to protect the separation of powers — and an even more self-serving reason for abusing it. Power.

Just as the invisible power behind the seat of government controlled them with the promise of money, they were able to do the same to their constituents by enlarging the public trough to accommodate those who voted for them. Most of the New Deal Democrats found there was immense job security in socialism; and most of the "new left" is still campaigning on the failed socialist agendas of both Roosevelt and Lyndon B. Johnson — and, they continue to get elected. The power of the "dole" will never lose its appeal because those who take Big Brother's gratuities don't understand, first, from whose pockets the "gift" is actually coming; second, they don't care; third, they have never looked beyond the handout at the cost assessed to their own dignity as a human being; and finally, they do not realize the personal liberties and rights they have surrendered to the State in order to share in the Rooseveltian socialist utopia. All they know is that Big Brother is willing to support them. Why should they refuse?

O n May 17, 1933, Roosevelt made a rare appearance before Congress to personally lobby for what he would promote as the flagship piece of legislation in his recovery package: the *National Industrial Recovery Act.* Roosevelt knew the program, which contained special collective bargaining rights would be a "hard sell" since it allowed the President to usurp Congressional authority in determining "codes of fair competition," as well as violating the separation of powers between the federal government and the States. The *National Industrial Recovery Act* would be ruled unconstitutional by the Supreme Court on May 27, 1935.

"Before the special session of Congress adjourns," the President began, "I recommend two further steps in our national campaign to put people to work.

"My first request is that the Congress provide the machinery necessary for a great cooperative movement throughout all in- **345** dustry in order to obtain wide re-employment, to shorten the work week, to pay a decent wage for the shorter week, and to prevent unfair competition and disastrous over-production. Employers cannot do this singly or even in organized groups because such action increases costs and permits cut-throat underselling by selfish competitors unwilling to join in such a public-spirited endeavor.

"One of the greatest restrictions upon such cooperative efforts up to this time has been our anti-trust laws. They were properly designed as a means to cure the great evils of monopolistic price-fixing. They should certainly be retained as a permanent assurance that the old evils of unfair competition shall never return. But, the public interest will be served if, with the authority and under the guidance of Government, private industries are permitted to make agreements and [establish] codes insuring fair competition." Roosevelt's comments are both interesting and revealing. The President viewed capitalism as an evil that needed to be regulated by the government. The program he would outline to Congress that day would nationalize the industries of the United States under the benevolent tutorship of the Roosevelt Administration, allowing them to "compete" in the free enterprise system only as long as they followed the rules that would be mandated by the government.

"However," he continued, "it is necessary, if we limit the operation of anti-trust laws...[that we] provide...rigorous licensing power in order to meet rare cases of non-cooperation and abuse. Such a safeguard is indispensable." (*The Roosevelt Papers, Vol. 2*; pg. 202.)

The purpose of the law was to force employers to hire more people by mandating shorter work hours. Then, rather than allow the business owner to pay the worker based on his current wage, less money each week, the law would establish a minimum wage. The worker, under Roosevelt's utopian plan, was to receive essentially the same paycheck each week for anywhere from ten to twenty fewer labor hours. To compensate for the labor shortfall, the business owner would be obligated to hire more workers from the surplus of unemployed laborers on the streets of the nation. Those who failed to do so stood in violation of the law and would be subject to fines, boycott or prosecution. Those who complied were exempted from the *Sherman Anti-Trust Act.*

346   In reality, it didn't quite add up to the sum total of the Roose-

veltian equation. The work week was reduced by 1/3, but the pay raised guaranteed by the minimum wage laws only increased the worker's paycheck by some 10% to 15%, leaving most with a net deficit at the end of the week. As a result, the discretionary income the Roosevelt plan counted on to purchase the goods industry would create never materialized until 1942 when severe manpower shortages due to the war created voluminous overtime and an excessive amount of discretionary income for the American workers in the booming wartime economy.

The additional labor costs would be passed on to the consumer in the form of higher prices. Or at least, in a free enterprise system, that is supposed to logically happen. However, in the utopian Roosevelt world, prices would be controlled by the government to make certain that they did not escalate at the same rate as earnings, thereby theoretically assuring that those returning to work would have buying power in their pay envelopes each week. Of course, we now know Roosevelt's grand scheme didn't work. His utopian programs crippled both the worker and the employer — and stretched the Depression out for an entire decade.

Under the *National Industrial Recovery Act,* businesses were expected to operate without profits until such time as the President decreed the emergency had expired. Of course, in the 65 years which have since transpired, that has not yet happened. The United States government still functions under the national emergency declared by Presidential Proclamation on March 6, 1933. Even Roosevelt's closest supporters in Congress were having a problem with the President's industrial recovery plan since the bulk of their campaign dollars came from the very industries they were now being asked to regulate.

The *National Industrial Recovery Act* would establish a national minimum wage that most of the legislators felt was outrageous since it would create an immediate and largely unbearable hardship on all but the largest corporations in America.

In addition, the bill would guarantee workers the right to collective bargaining — a sure way to lose the financial support of most labor-intensive business owners during an election year. One third of the Senate would be up for re-election in eight months, as would all of the House of Representatives. Roosevelt's plan was, in the opinion of many in both Houses of Congress, a "kiss-of-death" piece of legislation that most believed would undo the

347

good accomplished by the *Civil Conservation Act* that put Americans back to work without angering the business owners who usually contributed to their re-election war chests.

By the middle of June the bill was stalled — not because it was unconstitutional, or even because it smacked of socialism, but rather because it could potentially curb campaign donations from wealthy businessmen who might be tempted to throw their support behind opposing legislative candidates.

On June 16, Roosevelt scurried angrily back down Pennsylvania Avenue for his second address on the matter. Although he recited a carefully scripted message, his words did not conceal their Marxist rhetoric. "...It seems to me," he said, "that no business which depends for [its] existence on paying less than a living wage to its workers has any right to continue in this country.

"It is, further, a challenge to this administration. We are relaxing some of the safeguards of the anti-trust laws. The public must be protected against the abuses that led to their enactment, and to this end, we are putting into place of old principles of unchecked competition some new government controls...[N]o man who stands on the constructive side of his industry has anything to fear from them. To such men the opportunities for individual initiative will open even more amply than ever. Let me make it clear, however, that the anti-trust laws still stand firmly against monopolies that restrain trade, and price-fixing which allows inordinate profits or unfairly high prices.

"If we ask our trade groups to do that which exposes their businesses, as never before, to undermining by members who are unwilling to do their part, we must protect those who play the game for the general good against those who may seek selfish gains from the unselfishness of others. We must protect them from the racketeers who invade [the] organizations of both employers and workers...Finally, this law is a challenge to our whole people. There is no power in America that can force against the public will [the] action...we require. But, there is no group in America that can withstand the force of an aroused public opinion. This great cooperation can succeed only if those who bravely go forward to restore jobs have aggressive public support, and those who lag are made to feel the full weight of public disapproval.

"...A Labor Advisory Board appointed by the Secretary of Labor will be responsible that every affected labor group, whether organized or unorganized, is fully and adequately represented..."

(Eventually, the Labor Advisory Board would evolve into the National Labor Relations Board.) "An Industrial Advisory Board appointed by the Secretary of Commerce will be responsible that every affected industrial group is fully and adequately repre-sented...A Consumer Advisory Board will be responsible that the interests of the consuming public will be represented and ev-ery reasonable opportunity will be given to any group or class who may be affected directly or indirectly to present their views.

"At the conclusion of these hearings and after the most care-ful scrutiny by a competent economic staff, the Administrations will present the subject to me for my action under the law.

"I am fully aware that wage increases will eventually raise costs, but I ask that managements give first consideration to the improvement of operating figures by greatly increasing sales to be expected from the rising purchasing power of the public. That is good economics and good business...We cannot hope for the full effect of this plan unless, in these first critical months — and, even at the expense of full initial profits, we defer price increases as long as possible..." (*The Roosevelt Papers,* Vol. 2; pgs. 253-55.)

Of course Roosevelt knew if Congress passed his *National Industrial Recovery Act,* he wouldn't have to worry about price increases, since they would not be allowed. It never occurred to Roosevelt that in a free enterprise society, competition — which he had just stifled — controls prices.

It didn't really matter because on May 27, 1935 the Supreme Court ruled the law unconstitutional. On July 5, 1935 Congress passed the *Wagner-Connery Labor Relations Act* and created the *National Labor Relations Board* to guarantee American workers the right to collective bargaining. However, no legislation was ever enacted to guarantee business the right to address its griev-ances against labor.

On June 27, 1934 Congress passed the *Railway Pension Act* that forced all railroads to contribute a percentage of their profits into a pooled fund for the retirements of their employees. The Alton Railroad refused. The Railroad Retirement Board sued. The government argued that the law was a valid exercise of its power to regulate interstate commerce. The high court ques-tioned the relationship between providing benefits to aged em-ployees and that of the interstate transportation of cartage. On

May 6, 1935 the Supreme Court in a five-to-four decision ruled that the Act deprived the railroad of its property [money] without due process, and violated the 5th Amendment.

On August 30, 1935 Congress passed the *Guffey-Snyder Bituminous Coal Stabilization Act* in an attempt to nationalize that industry through regulation. The Act established both the minimum and maximum prices in order to kill competition. At the same time, it guaranteed coal miners collective bargaining rights. The bill also provided that wage and hour rates would be mandatory on the whole industry. The Act further attempted to regulate the conditions under which coal could be mined — a provision that would have bankrupted the small mine owner who would have been forced to meet the same standards as the large conglomerates with millions of dollars of capital.

The Supreme Court ruled, in a six-to-three vote on May 18, 1936, that the *Guffey-Snyder Bituminous Coal Stabilization Act* was unconstitutional not on one, but three, counts. It violated the separation of powers by granting the President legislative rights; it violated the due process clause of the 5th Amendment; and it assumed powers for the Commerce Department not in existence under the Constitution.

R oosevelt was not a happy camper. One-by-one, nine old men were destroying the New Deal almost as fast as Congress could legislate it. Most of the laws that ignored the separation of power between the States and the federal government, or between the Executive, Legislative and Judicial branches of the federal government were being struck down almost as fast as they were contested. The *Guffey-Snyder Act* was invalidated when the Carter Coal Company sued itself.

Slowly, Roosevelt got the message. Not even extraordinary circumstances could grant the President the unbridled right to expand his authority beyond that provided by the Constitution. The Supreme Court was not impressed with Roosevelt's claim to increased authority under Wilson's Act of October 6, 1917, as amended on March 9, 1933. That left Roosevelt no choice but to change the configuration of the Supreme Court before the rest of his New Deal went down in flames.

On January 20, 1937, Roosevelt started his second term as the first President to be inaugurated on that date. Fifteen days after his inauguration, on February 4, Roosevelt summoned Senate Majority Leader Joe Robinson, House Speaker John Bankhead, Senator Henry Ashurst, and Congressman Hatton Sumners, chairmen of their respective Judiciary Committees, to a special cabinet meeting at noon in the White House.

None of those present, except Attorney General Cummings, knew why they had been summoned. Roosevelt, as was his custom, was late. His aide wheeled Roosevelt into the room to his customary place at the center of the table. Another aide placed, in front of each cabinet official and summoned guest, a sheaf of documents. In a predetermined move, Roosevelt glanced at a pocket watch and informed those present he had another appointment and therefore did not have time for a lengthy discussion.

Then he dropped his bombshell.

The documents before them, he declared, were both a message and the draft of a new bill he was sending to Congress in the morning. The bill, when enacted, would reorganize the Supreme Court by allowing him to appoint a new Associate Justice for each jurist on the high court who had reached what he viewed as the mandatory retirement age of 70, but refused to step down from the bench.

The new legislation, he added, would empower him to add six new Justices to the Supreme Court. This action was necessary, he explained, due to an *emergency* that existed within the high court. It was just too backlogged with cases, and many of the Justices were simply too old to handle the caseload before them.

With that, he glanced at his watch again, apologizing for the conflict in his schedule, and was wheeled from the cabinet room.

Those present were flabbergasted. The President was going to use his now trite and well-worn national emergency as a pretext to stack the Supreme Court.

Not that it should have come as a surprise to anyone in the room. Tommy "the Cork" Corcoran, who would be used by Truman to stop leaks in his Administration, told Senator Burton K. Wheeler (D-MT) a year earlier that Roosevelt was trying to figure out how to add two additional Justices to the high court. Wheeler, at that time, advised Corcoran to tell Roosevelt to "forget it."

The idea of stacking the court, which was attributed to Cummings by Roosevelt historians, was initially postulated by one of Roosevelt's inner circle brain-trusters who noticed that most of Roosevelt's high court losses were by margins of one or two votes. The idea was run by Cummings who immediately saw the merit

351

of it. Cummings reasoned if the Administration could add just one or two more Justices to the high court, it would tip the scale in their favor on the close calls, and perhaps even influence the other ones. Roosevelt, of course, immediately fell in love with the idea and swore Cummings to secrecy lest the Republicans find out what he was up to.

The next morning Roosevelt's message was read in both chambers of Congress. He asked for the enactment of legislation empowering him to appoint "...additional judges in all federal courts without exception where there are incumbent judges of retirement age who do not choose to resign..." (*An Encyclopedia of World History;* Edited by William L. Langer; Houghton-Miffin © 1952; pg. 1056.) The reason given was precisely the same as that stated previously — the court was hopelessly backlogged and the nine *old* men on the bench obviously did not possess the strength, the determination, or the stamina to catch it up. Too many important issues, Roosevelt declared, that were key to the recovery of the nation were at stake. Therefore, drastic measures were needed to solve the crisis in the high court.

It was obvious to everyone that Roosevelt intended to politicize the judiciary. The President didn't give two hoots about age — he cared only about political philosophy of the judges!

Roosevelt's request aroused an immediate protest from the Republican minority; but then, Roosevelt anticipated such. The dye was cast. The Republicans could rant and rave all they wanted; it was too late.

What he didn't expect was problems in his own camp. Overnight, when the reality of what Roosevelt was really up to sank in, opposition from Democrats in the Senate began to swell.

Carter Glass, who was recuperating from an illness at his home in Lynchburg, Virginia when news of Roosevelt's court-loading plan reached him on Sunday, cursed both Roosevelt and his plan, declaring that Roosevelt was "...completely destitute of all moral understanding."

The task of killing Roosevelt's plan was assigned to Burton Wheeler, one of the most powerful liberal Democrats in the Senate. Wheeler was a realist who knew it was not good politics to cross Roosevelt, particularly since he had just won one of the biggest landslides in the history of American politics, and was viewed by many working Americans as a political icon. But, Wheeler was also one other thing. He was a believer in the Constitution.

Unlike many of the new breed of quasi-socialist Democrats swept into Congress in 1936, Wheeler had faith in the free enterprise system and believed, with just a little help from the government, it would continue to serve America well for another 200 years.

It was quite a different story in the House of Representatives. When House Judiciary Chairman Hatton Summers left for the White House that day, reporter John Flynn followed him, sensing something important might be underfoot. When he spied several Congressional bigwigs sneak into the White House his hunch was confirmed. He hung around outside the gate until the meeting concluded. When he spied Summers he asked what was going on. Summers, not being sworn to secrecy, told him with a grin: "This is where I cash my chips!"

In point of fact, most of the Democratic representatives felt the same because, by evening the following day, Bankhead and Summers had enough votes in their pocket to pass the legislation. The "Huey Long Syndrome" had captured the House of Representative. Between 1933 and the 1936 elections, New Dealers had learned they could get elected simply by promising enough people enough chairs at the feast-laden public trough. To get their share of the federal budget to take back to their districts, most of the members of the House became very compliant tools of the White House. Ethics didn't matter. Nor, for that matter, did constitutionality. All that mattered was how much "pork" the Congressman could send to the folks back home. How little things have changed in sixty years.

When word of Roosevelt's plan reached the Senate leadership, Burton Wheeler called Chief Justice Charles Evans Hughes to learn just how backlogged the Court really was. To his surprise, Wheeler learned the high court was not backlogged at all, and had, in fact, cleared up all outstanding motions on its docket[1].

Wheeler opened the special session, after Roosevelt's remarks were read by Robinson, with a bombshell of his own. He produced a letter from Hughes in which the Chief Justice reiterated what he had told Wheeler the previous day. There were no cases lagging in the Court. What Wheeler did not tell the Senate was something else Hughes told him about the President. [*The Roosevelt Myth;* John T. Flynn © 1948; Garden City Books; pg. 108.]

During the previous summer, in one of his rare visits to the White House at the behest of the President, Roosevelt suggested an accommodation with the Chief Justice that Roosevelt believed   **353** would make both of their jobs easier. Roosevelt suggested the two meet occasionally to "exchange ideas." Hughes would share with the President some of the more problematic constitutional issues found in Roosevelt's legislation before any decisions were made, ostensibly to find an accommodation that would prevent the laws from being overturned. In turn, Roosevelt would share pending legislation with Hughes for his views on strengthening them so they wouldn't end up on the high court's docket. Hughes was shocked that a President would suggest such an impropriety, but kept the visit a secret until Roosevelt angered him by suggesting he was not a competent administrator of the Court's agenda [*ibid*, pg. 106].

The Hughes letter embarrassed Roosevelt.

The President didn't take the time to check his facts. The ploy was the brainchild of White House advisor Samuel I. Rosenman. Rosenman, who had been with Roosevelt since his New York days, hadn't checked, either. When Bankhead called the President to let him know what had happened, Roosevelt crucified Rosenman. Rosenman would survive to become one of the intimate inner circle advisors and speech writers of the Roosevelt Administration. Rosenman's wife, Dorothy, would later prove to be one of many wives of White House insiders during the Truman Administration to leak embarrassing White House gossip to the media.

E ven though he had the votes to enact Roosevelt's judiciary reform bill, and knew it would pass once it hit the floor, Hatton Summers suddenly got cold feet and buried the measure in the House Judiciary Committee. While publicly voicing their support of the bill when polled by the House leadership, all but the most strident New Dealers privately admitted the bill was as unprincipled as its sponsor, and were pleased that Summers had shelved it.

Roosevelt, Bankhead, Moley and Cummings met to decide if they should demand a vote to force the bill out of Committee and onto the floor. Bankhead advised against it, knowing the private sentiments of a good many of the Congressmen. He suggested they try to run it through the Senate first. Once it passed in the Senate, Bankhead argued, the House would obediently follow suit.

Receiving word from Robinson that they were expected to

carry the President's banner on this one, the Senate prepared for battle. Wisely, the Republican leadership, after conferring with Glass, Wheeler, and Harry Byrd (D-VA), decided to sit it out and let the Democrats — particularly the *liberal* Democrats — slug it out with the White House.

It was a good plan.

Roosevelt expected the Republicans to parade a battalion of Constitutional conservatives onto the Senate floor to denounce the President and his socialist agenda, and he planned his counterattack accordingly. Wheeler did the opposite.

Wheeler's "experts" were all well-known and well-respected liberals whose credentials Roosevelt could not challenge. Almost without exception, the myriad of lawyers, teachers, business leaders and constitutional scholars all had one thing in common — each had previously either challenged the authority of the Supreme Court, or had at least publicly criticized it.

Each argued that while they had some dispute with the decisions coming from the Supreme Court it would be destructive to the Constitution — and the country — to allow the bulwark of an unbiased judicial system to be torn asunder just to serve the personal goals of an ambitious and overly aggressive chief executive.

Wheeler made certain the hearings received good press coverage. As the Senators listened to the arguments against expanding the nine member Court to fifteen, so did the American people. With each passing day, Roosevelt's chances for success got slimmer and slimmer.

Moley and Cummings urged Roosevelt to seek a compromise with Wheeler that would limit the increased jurists to two, and raise the mandatory retirement age to 75.

Roosevelt, still basking in the memory of his recent defeat of Alf Landon, erred again. He refused. Had he agreed to a compromise, it is likely the House would have immediately passed his measure, followed almost certainly, by a similar vote in the Senate. But Roosevelt, who had grown accustomed to having it all, wanted it all.

With each passing day, things looked more and more bleak for the White House. Then, quite unexpectedly, the sun began to shine on the Roosevelt administration. The Hughes Court ruled on five New Deal motions, upholding the Constitutionality of all of them. Adding to Roosevelt's delight, Associate Justice Van-

Devanter unexpectedly announced his retirement. Roosevelt now had an opportunity to select a Justice who was more sympathetic with his political philosophy[1].

The powerbrokers on Capitol Hill wanted the appointment to go to Senate leader Joe Robinson as a reward for his many years of faithful service to the party. Robinson, whose lifelong dream was to sit on the Supreme Court, expected it. Over the past four months, he alone had kept Roosevelt's judicial reform bill alive in the Senate, and by virtue of that fact, alive in the House as well. He had been a loyal party man throughout his political career, and it was his time.

Roosevelt, however, had other plans. He wanted — or rather, needed — a New Dealer on the Court who not only understood what he was trying to accomplish, but would be obligingly sympathetic. He needed someone he could count on — or rather, control — on the bench. Robinson definitely was not that man. While he was reasonably reliable to "do the right thing" for the party, far too often he voted against the "mainstream" with the opposition on programs he viewed as too controversial.

Roosevelt had already picked his first Justice. It would be Alabama Senator Hugo Black. Black either sponsored or co-sponsored most of the New Deal legislation including the *Fair Labor Standards Act,* which he wrote. Not only were Black and Roosevelt *politically* aligned, they were *philosophically* aligned as well. Black was of the view that the Supreme Court should be used as an instrument of social reform. He, Felix Frankfurter and Harry Blackmun would first advance the theory that the Constitution was an evolving document that must periodically be reinterpreted to fit the changing needs of an evolving society.

Now, on top of the unresolved Senate battle over his judicial reform package, the leadership of the Congress had squared off against him as well, forcing him to back down and offer the bench

---

[1]More likely than not, the Court was playing a little "politics" of its own with those decisions. Since almost every piece of New Deal legislation abrogated either the separation of powers between the federal government and the States, or between the Executive, Legislative and Judicial branches of the federal government, very few New Deal laws could pass genuine "Constitutional muster" unless the Justices, with one eye on the preservation of the nine-member high court, closed the other one while they were studying the briefs presented by the litigants.

appointment to Robinson instead of Black. A few days later, while fighting the Wheeler forces on the floor of the Senate, Robinson suffered a heart attack. He died later that evening, alone in his Washington apartment.

However, instead of simplifying Roosevelt's life, Robinson's death only exacerbated Roosevelt's congressional problems. The Democratic leadership gathered on a special train bound for Little Rock, Arkansas to take their fallen comrade home for burial.

What started as commiseration over Joe Robinson fables and foibles ended up as a full-fledged political debate over Roosevelt splitting the Democratic Party wide-open with his court-stacking scheme. Tempers flared and the division between the New Dealers and the moderate Democrats widened.

After the New Dealers buried their fallen comrade, they returned to Washington and told Roosevelt they doubted that any type of compromise was possible that would salvage any part of his court-stacking plan. Roosevelt called Vice President John Nance Garner and told him to cut any type of deal he could with Wheeler — the addition of only one or two Justices instead of six; or if nothing else, even a bill that would force the Justices to retire at a particular age, say 65, but not later than 70. Garner approached Wheeler to see under what terms they could resolve the matter so they could all get back to the business of governing the nation.

Smiling, Wheeler replied: "Unconditional surrender!"

The court-stacking bill was dead.

The relationship between the President and Attorney General Cummings, whom Roosevelt blamed for the failed court stacking plan, deteriorated rapidly from that point. Finally, in January, 1939 Cummings resigned and was replaced with former Michigan governor Frank Murphy. Murphy, a likeable Irishman, was a womanizing playboy. After serving only one year as the Attorney General, Murphy became Roosevelt's second appointee to the Supreme Court. Felix Frankfurter, Roosevelt's long-time friend and the legal mind behind most of the New Deal legislation, joined the Supreme Court in 1939.

E ven though Roosevelt had not been able to stack the Court, thanks to Hatton Summers he was able to infuse it with New Deal thinkers, saving countless Court challenges that would   357 likely have torn down even more of the New Deal and made it much more difficult for Lyndon Johnson to create the Great Utopian Welfare State.

While Summers deeply believed in our constitutional system, he also believed that with lifetime appointments, some of the Justices were simply too old to make incontestable judicial decisions. Taking it upon himself, he approached Associate Justices Sutherland and VanDevanter and broached the subject. Both expressed a desire to retire but wouldn't because their incomes would be cut in half. Neither could afford to live on the pensions they would receive. Both assured him if they could retire on full pay, they would have been gone long ago.

After discussing it with Roosevelt, Summers introduced a bill in Congress that would allow the Justices to retire with full pay. Because there was still a lot of residual bad feelings over the court-stacking incident, a good many New Dealers complained that Summers was "...trying to make a soft berth for a bunch of old tories." (*The Roosevelt Myth*; John T. Flynn; Garden City Books © 1948; pg. 113.) Resistance to the legislation mounted.

Summers withdrew the legislation.

When the same New Dealers complained, the following year, that the Supreme Court was destroying the future of the nation, Summers dragged his bill back out, promising his colleagues that at least two of the "old tories" would retire if the bill was passed.

They passed it.

VanDevanter and Sutherland retired.

Black and Stanley Reed, the Solicitor General, took their places.

From that moment on politics, not constitutional qualifications, became the yardstick by which Congress measured the cloth of every candidate for the high court.

The Supreme Court had been politicized[2].

---

[2]Probably the two best examples of the politicizing of the United States Supreme Court was the 1939 addition to the Supreme Court of Vienna, Austria-born American jurist Felix Frankfurter and the unsuccessful 1985 nomination of federal judge Robert Bork by President Ronald Reagan.

Bork was clearly recognized, by friend and foe alike, as the leading Constitutional authority in the United States. His reputation was spotless; his judicial credentials were impeccable. Not one of the more than 400 judicial decisions that Judge Bork had written or joined into were ever reversed by the Supreme Court. The "flaw" in his character as far as liberals were concerned was his private stand on abortion

From 1937 on, Supreme Court appointees would be selected not as much for their judicial credentials and an indisputable knowledge of Constitutional law as their political and sociological philosophies. Furthermore, most of those appointed in the future would hold one common belief: that the Constitution was an *evolving* document that could to be reinterpreted and updated periodically to meet the changing needs of an evolving society.

The reason for politicizing the Supreme Court is obvious. A president serves a four-year term. His appointees to the high court serve for life. Felix Frankfurter, who was the architect of most of the New Deal legislation, was appointed to the high court by Roosevelt in 1939 and served until his retirement at 80-years of age in 1962 due to ill health. Traditionally, unless they die or are forced into premature retirement due to illness, most Justices choose to step down only when their political party holds the White House, thereby maintaining, as best they can, the political slant of the Court in order to protect their rulings.

Such was the case with both Justice Byron "Whizzer" White and Harry A. Blackmun. White, a John F. Kennedy appointee who was not in the best of health, announced his intention to step down

---

and his view that the Constitution was not an *evolving* document that was subject to reinterpretation by the high court.

In what proved to be the most controversial Supreme Court nomination in U.S. history, the liberal majority in the Senate Judiciary Committee headed by Senator Joseph R. Biden, Jr. (D-DE) amassed a plethora of feminist activists to argue against Bork's nomination on the grounds that he would somehow single-handedly overturn *Roe v. Wade* if he was placed on the high court, or that he would set the woman's movement in America back a hundred years. On the streets of America, the AFL-CIO fervently campaigned against Bork as a fascist who would destroy the bedrock of democracy in America. Reagan refused to withdraw his nomination, forcing it to a floor vote where the most qualified Constitutional jurist in the United States was denied on seat on the high court because his conservative political beliefs threatened the utopian agenda of the liberal Congress.

On the other hand, Frankfurter's nomination was rubber-stamped by the New Deal Democratic Senate when it should have been repudiated by them.

Frankfurter, who was likewise viewed by his peers as a Constitutional scholar, was something of an enigma since he, like Roosevelt, largely viewed the Constitution as an archaic and out-moded document. He believed the Constitution must be construed as an *evolving* document

359

in 1992. He waited for Bill Clinton to assume office before finally doing so in the spring of 1993. He was replaced by Justice Ruth Bader Ginsberg.

Blackmun, a law professor who was appointed to the Eighth Circuit Court of Appeals by Dwight D. Eisenhower in 1959, was named to the high court in 1970 by President Richard Nixon. A centrist on most issues and a conservative in matters of criminal

---

that could be reinterpreted by the Court to better serve the changing needs of an evolving society, or more accurately, the evolving needs of its government. Although the practice of legislating by judicial decision was specifically forbidden to the high court by the Constitution Frankfurter, and other justices like him, have not hesitated to do just that by reinterpreting the Constitution to fit the needs of the federal bureaucracy as it reshaped the American system of government.

While most Americans are not aware of it, Frankfurter was the prime architect of most of Roosevelt's New Deal programs, and was instrumental in writing the *Securities Act of 1933; the Securities Exchange Act of 1934; the National Industrial Recovery Act of 1933; the Public Utility Company Holding Act of 1935* and the *Railroad Pension Act of 1934*. In addition, Frankfurter personally recommended to Roosevelt most of the executives who were ultimately picked to head the new federal agencies that controlled the New Deal Administration.

Frankfurter and Black because of their direct roles in the creation of the New Deal, should have ethically reclused themselves from every case that came before the high court dealing with any of that legislation. Neither did. In fact, they were both instrumental not only in shaping the court's opinions on the legality of the New Deal, but also in defining the legality of the federal government's supra-authority over the States.

Roosevelt appointed Black, Frankfurter and Murphy to the bench of the high court for one reason and one reason only: to protect the New Deal. Even before those appointments were confirmed by the Senate, the 1937-38 Court began making "political" rather than judicial decisions. This was due almost entirely to Roosevelt's efforts to force most of them into unwanted retirement. Because of Roosevelt's ease in successfully passing a myriad of illegal laws, the high court had no reason to believe that his efforts against them would not succeed as well. The 1937-38 Court, intimidated by Roosevelt, mitigated their stand on the unconstitutionality of the New Deal laws, believing Roosevelt would give up his attempt to force them into retirement if they backed off of the New Deal.

The Supreme Court, since 1938, has been a political device designed not to protect the Constitution of the United States, but rather, to promulgate the political ideology of whichever party simultaneously controlled both the White House and the Senate.

law before arriving at the high court, Blackmun proved to be the most liberal Justice ever to sit on the bench. Although his health began to fail during George Bush's watch, Blackmun refused to step down, afraid that a conservative Bush appointee might alter the philosophical makeup of the Court and jeopardize *Roe v. Wade.* Blackmun finally retired in August, 1994. The abortion president, Bill Clinton appointed Stephen Breyer to succeed him.

Breyer and Ginsberg were selected by Clinton because both were believed to be philosophically far left of "center," and were viewed by most liberal activists — and Hillary Clinton, who according to former FBI agent Gary Aldrich in his book *Unlimited Access,* had "first refusal" rights on all of her husband's political appointments during *their* first administration — as stalwarts not only of abortion rights but defenders of most of the other important feminist issues. While Breyer proved to be worthy of the liberal label, Ginsberg, like Blackmun, proved to be a surprise.

Obscured behind Ginsberg's public record of championing women's rights and liberal causes, was an equally impressive record of defending States' rights that was largely overlooked or ignored by the Clinton White House. On the high court, Ginsberg, who wrote the majority opinion in the Virginia Military Institute case that forced the sexual integration of the traditionally all-male military college, is usually found siding with conservative Justices Clarence Thomas, Anthony Scalia and Chief Justice William H. Rehnquist on States' rights issues. Ginsberg, the feminist liberal, is rapidly becoming known in liberal circles as a rightwing extremist — the epithet used by the elitist left to describe all States' rights advocates on sovereignty issues.

Twice in the 1995-96 session of the Supreme Court Ginsberg became the tie-breaking fifth vote in 5-to-4 votes for the "conservative right." Even in the closely watched appeal of the excessive awards granted by a jury in the *BMW v. Gore* case (in which the plaintiff was awarded obscene damages because his new BMW had been repainted by the dealership to cover a small scratch suffered during shipment), Ginsberg sided with Thomas, Rehnquist and Scalia in a 5-to-4 decision which they lost to Justices Breyer, Anthony M. Kennedy, Sandra Day O'Connor, David H. Souter and John Paul Stevens.

Ginsberg, in the dissenting opinion, insisted that the federal court had no jurisdiction. She said: "The court, I am convinced, unnecessarily and unwisely ventures into territory traditionally

361

within the states' domain."

Yet, even with her "conservative" concerns about States' rights, Ginsberg nevertheless still remains a somewhat faithful "card-carrying liberal." Her vote has traditionally been cast with the left, particularly when social justice issues are at stake. However, in the opening days of the 21st century, States' right issues will increasingly dominate much of the high court's agenda. At that time, Ginsberg's true colors will show, since those cases will test the Constitutional right of the federal government to impose its will, through a myriad of global trade laws like NAFTA and GATT, as well as the government's right — as the *legal* owner of the Internet — to assume ownership of all information databases[3] contained within it, and then to sanction the surrender of that ownership to the United Nations.

---

[3]An interesting chart, entitled "Deployment of Health Care Infrastructure" was found within the pages of the Hillary Clinton *Health Security Act's* interdepartmental working group's papers that gives some insight to the complexity of a program designed more to control the people of the United States than to provide them with health care. *(National Archives, Box #1748.)*

This document deals with the ownership of the various information databases that are currently deemed to be owned by either the private sector service providers and/or those citizens whose personal histories are compiled within those databases.

The timeline of the report, written in 1993, suggests (contingent on the anticipated passage of the *Health Security Act*—which failed to clear the Democratically-controlled Congress that year) that the Supreme Court would rule, somewhere between 1997-2001 that the government's assumption and use of the medical records of all Americans did not constitute "practicing medicine without a license." The fact that such a timeline appears in this report further suggests, first, that a test-case would be staged by the federal government. And finally, that the court's decision was predetermined. Another "decision" that will be forthcoming, according to the working papers, somewhere between 2002-2006 will be designed to (a) affirm the government's ownership, or co-ownership of the Internet database, particularly in the area of "patient information," (b) affirm the trans-jurisdictional licensing of the Internet database, and (c) affirm a "universal directory standard" for these databases.

Concluding the timeline, according to the working papers, the United Nations would then be assigned the role of regulating the universal information database utilities sometime between 2007-2011.

❖ FIFTEEN ❖

The Demise of the Republic

If you were to ask any American, including most of our State and national politicians, what form of government exists in the United States today and you will more likely than not receive an incorrect answer. Most without thinking will reply that we live in a Democracy. Others, realizing that America's system of government is based on a Constitution, will respond that we live in a Republic.

Both would be wrong.

The United States of America was created on June 21, 1788 when New Hampshire, the ninth State to do so, ratified the Constitution. The United States was created as a constitutional Republic. The Constitution of the United States is the most unique legal document ever penned: its power resided entirely within itself, delegated equally to the States and the people.

The federal government was created subservient to the States. It was, in other words, created to be the servant of its creator — the people. State law, in the minds of the Founding Fathers as well as in practical application, superseded federal law. For over 100 years, it pretty much remained that way.

In a Republican form of government, power is divided to limit the authority of both the government and the people in order to restrict the claims of supra-authority by either the majority or the minority. All men, under the Constitution, were equal in the sense that their voices — and their votes — were equipollent.

The voice of the People was spoken through the House of Representatives. Congressmen were elected as the direct representatives of their constituents — the people. The people, through their elected representatives, controlled one-third of the power in the federal government. The voice of the States was spoken through the Senate. Senators were elected by the States, and were responsible to make certain that the interests of the States were protected in the nation's capitol. The States, through their Senators, controlled

363

one-third of the power in the federal government[1].

The balance of the power was granted to the President of the United States, who is directly elected by the States. Under the Constitution, the overwhelming bulk of the power was granted to the States and, jointly, to the People. Lesser power was granted to the President because it was intended by the Founding Fathers that the President would serve the lesser role.

However, that changed with the passage of the 17th Amendment on April 8, 1913. At that time, America was transformed from a Republic into a democracy. Instead of having a government equally representative of all factions of the American society, we suddenly found ourselves with a form of government that, in theory only, represented the majority. In reality, because the "majority" no longer possessed the power to check the abuses of those they elected except during the next election cycle, "we the people" saddled ourselves with an oligarchy — a far cry from the form of government created by the Founding Fathers.

Without the Constitutional failsafe that gave the States an

---

[1] With only modest exceptions the Representatives and Senators were not "career" politicians—such an animal did not, in any practical sense of the term, exist. Serving in Congress was a patriotic obligation for all but the bureaucrat, since it took the Congressman away from the more important task of running his business or managing his farm or plantation. Most of the most important names in the political history of the United States were "part-time politicians".

The "career" politician as a standard fixture in the nation's capitol is a fairly recent phenomenon, dating back only to the mid-19th century. Prior to that time, all but the pure bureaucrats were citizen-politicians, honestly representing their communities and their State governments before the Congress. Today, politicians serve big money special interest groups whose creation was spawned by Roosevelt in 1934. The motivation to serve in Congress has changed over the years as well. The colonial politician served to create a better America. Today's politician serves to amass power and fortune. Not since Ulysses S. Grant died a pauper from throat cancer in 1885 have politicians left Washington with less personal wealth than they possessed the day they were elected. No more fitting example affirms this than that of Nelson Aldrich whose efforts single-handedly led to the creation of the Federal Reserve System. Aldrich had a net worth of $50,000.00 (including the value of his home and business) when he arrived in Washington. When the Federal Reserve was created, Aldrich's net worth was conservatively estimated at well over $30,000,000.00.

equal voice in the affairs of the federal government, and protected the sovereign authority of the States over the federal bureaucracy, the authority of the States was quietly and subversively diluted in the flood of New Deal laws and Supreme Court decisions that have forever muddied the separation of powers not only between the States and the federal government, but between the Executive, Legislative and Judicial branches of the federal government as well.

Each facet of the federal government from the White House to the Congress and the Supreme Court have aided and abetted the overthrow of the Republic and the destruction of democracy as the power to govern was wrenched from the people and placed exclusively within the grasp of the oligarchy.

M ost of the national laws that have been enacted by Congress since 1934 are technically unconstitutional. But that fact has not hindered their passage, nor has it stopped any President from signing unconstitutional legislation into law. To give the laws passed by Congress a semblance of legality, each law that infringes on States rights now requires an enabling bill to be passed by the States to "legalize" the national legislation.

Ignored since 1913 has been the Constitutional separation of powers between the federal government and the States. There have been few cries in the night since the voice of the States was silenced with the ratification of the 17th Amendment. The successful bribery of the working class with a myriad of entitlements that now encompass roughly one fifth of the electorate in some form or another has effectively silenced the people.

The Constitution of the United States deliberately limited the authority of the federal government to prevent it from intruding into the affairs of the States and into the lives of the people. Specifically, the authority of the federal government, according to the Constitution, is restricted to building roads, maintaining a post office, raising and maintaining military forces to protect the nation from either external or internal aggression, establishing patent and copyright laws, establishing maritime laws, establishing uniform banking regulations, coining money and, when necessary, declaring war on an aggressor nation.

Afraid that the federal government might be tempted to try to usurp additional authority in the future, the Founding Fathers inserted the following in the form of an amendment: "The powers not delegated to the United States by the Constitution, nor prohibited by it to the States, are reserved to the States respectively, or to the people."

While they were reasonably certain they had covered every contingency, the Founding Fathers were wrong. Some of the clauses, like Article I, Section 8 § 1 and 8 § 3 were broadly interpreted not only by Congress but by the Court: "The Congress shall have the power to lay and collect taxes, duties, impost and excises, to pay the debts and provide for the common defense and *general welfare* of the United States..." Three harmless words did them in. *General welfare* and *commerce.* Sixty years of entitlement spending and precedent-building was based on those three words. Everything Congress does today, or has done for the past sixty years, is done ostensibly to promote *commerce*, or to protect the *general welfare* of its citizens.

And, although most of these laws usurped the authority of the States, creating by application, a legal precedent that federal law supersedes State law, the Supreme Court has almost universally upheld them based, to a large degree, on the 1794 *Gibbons v. Ogden* case in which Chief Justice John Marshall ruled that States cannot interfere with the power granted to Congress by passing conflicting legislation. Marshall declared that the commerce power of Congress included everything affecting "...commerce among the states," thus construing that authority to cover *intrastate* as well as *interstate* commerce.

Marshall based his decision on Article I, Section 8 § 3, which states that Congress shall have the power "...To regulate commerce with foreign nations, and among the several states..."

Infuriated by the high court's blatant assumption not only of the supremacy of federal law over State law, but that the federal government could interfere with the *intrastate* commerce agreements of the various States within the confederation, the States retaliated by passing the 11th Amendment which declares that: "The judicial power of the United States shall not be construed to extend to any suit in law or equity, commenced or prosecuted against one of the United States by citizens of another State, or by citizens or subjects of any foreign state."

Although the 11th Amendment was ratified on February 7, 1795 and effectively negated the Court's decision in *Gibbon v. Ogden*, the decision was on the books for future generations to see and use as a legal precedent.

Over the years, the high court has interpreted the *commerce clause* both to expand or contract the authority of the federal government. At the close of the Marshall era, the Court generally adopted a more restrictive view, choosing to protect the sovereignty of the States over the federal government.

The Supreme Court did not return to the broad view of the commerce clause until 1937 when, due entirely to the Roosevelt threat to force many of them into retirement, the high court capitulated. The Justices did this knowing they were opening the door to an unconstitutional centralized government. They didn't care. It was more important to them, at the moment, to protect both their jobs and the structure of the high court.

Article I, Section 8 became the legal loophole through which the *Civil Rights Act of 1964* was passed. The congressional logic is found in Title II, concerning public accommodations. Broadly, and probably with a smile as it was written, Congress boldly declared that the "...operations of an establishment affect commerce...if...it serves or offers to serve interstate travelers or a substantial portion of the food which it serves or the gasoline or other products which it sells, has moved in commerce..."

Congress knowingly reached beyond its Constitutional mandate to enact the *Civil Rights Act of 1964.* However, since it has been doing so since 1937, it had grown accustomed to exercising its broadened authority under Section 8.

While few Americans would deny any citizen equal rights or equal opportunity, it is alarming that, regardless how beneficial or socially significant such a piece of legislation may be, those who have been elected to represent the people of the United States would deliberately usurp the Constitutional separation of powers to achieve their objective. Apparently to Congress, the White House and the U.S. Supreme Court, the end always justifies the means.

America is in trouble. The Constitution no longer works.

What troubled the Supreme Court most in 1937 when the Justices capitulated to Roosevelt was that they knew full well what the President was attempting to do. Roosevelt was determined to legislate a planned economy with a highly strengthened, totalitarian centralized government. And, they allowed him to   367 do it to save their jobs, believing the President had the votes to force their retirements.

By capitulating, they proved the high court was vulnerable to politicalization — precisely what the Founding Fathers desperately tried to avoid. From that day forward, the role of the Justices changed forever. Appointments to the bench are now political rather than judicial, and decisions are now increasingly based on ideological positions rather than on sound Constitutional principles. Further, when no valid legal precedent or constitutional grounds exists for an opinion, the Justices now legislate judicially and judiciously. Unfortunately, when they do, the country has no appeal other than to pass a Constitutional amendment.

None of this concerned Roosevelt.

In fact, Roosevelt was pleased.

The Republic was dead. Long live democracy!

There have been only a few instances over the past sixty years when the federal court system temporarily resurrected the commerce limitations. One happened during Gerald Ford's administration, appropriately during the nation's bicentennial in 1976, and the two most recent occurred during Bill Clinton's first term. In a 1996 U.S. District Court decision, Judge Jackson L. Kiser stuck down the *Violence Against Women Act of 1994,* using as his legal precedent a 1994 Supreme Court decision in *United States v. Lopez.* In the Lopez case the high court ruled that Congress could not apply the commerce clause to justify a ban on guns near school buildings.

In *Brzonkala v.Crawford and Morrison,* Christine Brzonkala, a student at Virginia Tech sued Antonio Morrison and James Crawford for punitive damages following a failed criminal action. Brzonkala alleged Morrison had raped her while Crawford watched. Morrison and Crawford claimed Brzonkala was a willing participant and that the sex was consensual. After a two-month investigation, a grand jury failed to indict either Morrison or Crawford. Brzonkala's attorney, Eileen Wagner, sued for damages under the *Violence Against Women Act.*

Kiser, a Ronald Reagan appointee, wrote: "Without a doubt, violence against women is a pervasive and troublesome aspect of American life which needs thoughtful attention. But Congress is not invested with the authority to cure all of the ills of mankind. Its authority to act is limited by the Constitution, and the constitutional limits must be respected if our federal system is to survive." In rendering his opinion, Kiser stated emphatically that such attacks have nothing to do with interstate commerce — the sole meaning of the commerce clause of the Constitution.

Congressional sponsors and advocates of the law which passed during the 103rd Congress, argued that it did affect "interstate commerce" since many times it prompted the victims of violence to travel across state lines to seek new employment, or to seek medical care outside of their home state. Kiser, however, didn't buy the argument. In his decision, Kiser also found that an assault on a woman was not "...an action of the state" and therefore the 14th Amendment could not be applied.

At about the same time, a similar case was upheld by a Clinton-appointed U.S. District Court Judge, Janet Bond Arteton, who declared that "...violence against women has a substantial effect on commerce." Congressional scholar and Stanford University law professor William Cohen predicted the Supreme Court would uphold Kiser's decision in a 5-4 ruling. In the event it does, it will effectively overturn Arteton's decision and bring that case before the high court as well.

At the time, a Justice Department spokesman, Gregory King, insisted the law was supported by a "bipartisan majority" — a common phrase used to defend unconstitutional legislation passed over the past sixty years in the Democratically-controlled Congress as a "...historic effort to rectify the real problems that exist."

In 1976, *National League of Cities v. Usery* (426 US 833) was heard by the high court. At issue in that case was the question of whether Congress could regulate government activities that were an integral part of a State's sovereignty. A U.S. District Court, in an action filed under the *Fair Labor Standards Act,* ruled the States' employment laws must conform to federal standards.

A sharply divided Supreme Court, in its first "about-face" in 39 years, ruled that the States had the right, under the sovereignty rule of the Constitution, to decide for themselves how they would manage their own public sectors.

It was a short-lived victory for the States.

The Court reversed itself again nine years later.

In 1985, in *Garcia v. San Antonio Metropolitan Transit Authority* (83L. Ed. 2d 10 16) the high court, again in a 5-4 decision, ruled that Congress could mandate minimum wage laws on State, county and local governments.

369

While a sharply worded dissenting opinion was rendered, the majority opinion set the tone, reaffirming the stance the Court has taken since 1937: "We doubt that courts can identify principled constitutional limitations on the scope of Congress' commerce clause powers over the states merely by relying on a *priori* definition of state sovereignty." If the high court upholds the 1996 Kiser decision, a whole new plethora of questions concerning the application of the commerce clause will open.

If, on the other hand, the Supreme Court strikes it, the supremacy of federal law over State sovereignty will likely have been decided for all time. Tragically, the precedent used to abrogate State sovereignty—although repudiated by the States in 1795—was successfully used by Roosevelt in 1937 when he blackmailed the Supreme Court because the States no longer possessed a voice in Washington. Congress and the Supreme Court had joined forces with the White House to create Roosevelt's utopian planned economy. Today, the federal government's superior authority over the States has been irreversibly codified by hundreds, if not thousands, of legal precedents, the Constitution of the United States notwithstanding.

The door was now opened wide for Roosevelt's New Deal to continue. Privately, Roosevelt had blamed everyone from his vice president, John Nance Garner, to the Wall Street bankers, the American business community, to the union leaders he empowered, and finally to the Supreme Court itself, for the failure of the New Deal.

Everyone, Roosevelt said, had conspired against him.

Then the Court suddenly revisited some of the legislation it had previously found to be unconstitutional. Viewing them under the revised concept of Article I, Section 8, the Court found most of the previously rejected New Deal laws were within the scope of authority of Congress—particularly since the blackmailed 1937 Supreme Court determined this new-found authority under Section 8 existed because the Constitution was an "evolutionary" document, subject to reinterpretation at the whim of the Court.

The planned economy of the United States, controlled exclusively by the oligarchy in Washington, was now under way. Nothing could stop Roosevelt now.

370   To make matters even worse, the New Deal legislation itself

would serve as a precedent-setting platform upon which the welfare state of Lyndon Johnson would be constructed in less than three decades.

Within eight years Roosevelt succeeded in doing what most Americans would likely have imagined to be impossible. He had completely dismantled the framework of the Republic. By the end of 1939, it no longer existed. The legislative, executive and judicial branches had all but solidified into a single, unified cohesive bureaucratic governing body. The check and balance system, so carefully fashioned by the Founding Fathers, was gone. The voice of the States was muted; and the voice of the people, now happily feeding at the public trough was muffled as they filled their mouths with the feast unwillingly provided by the taxpayers of America. The Republic had died. Regretfully, nobody noticed.

D uring his first 100 days in office, Roosevelt nationalized well over 50% of the economy of the United States, seized the monetary assets of the American citizens and replaced their gold-based currency with debt-backed script, and assumed for himself supra-powers under the wartime *Trading With the Enemy Act.* He abrogated the gold clause in all public and private debts, and then, with a well-placed but little-noticed clause in the *Agricultural Adjustment Act,* transferred the authority to coin money from the Congress to the Executive branch.

By the end of his first 150 days, Roosevelt had nationalized all food production in the United States and controlled the pricing of all food stuffs. He regulated both industry and labor, again controlling production, prices, and the wages which would be paid for that labor. Still not content, he then assumed control of transportation and communication.

On June 16, Congress enacted the *Emergency Railroad Transportation Act,* followed three days later by the *Communications Act of 1933.* Three weeks later Congress passed the *Motor Carrier Act* which placed all interstate bus and truck lines under the jurisdiction of the *Interstate Commerce Commission.*

On August 26, Roosevelt gained control of all public utilities with the passage of the *Public Utility Holding Company Act.* It appeared that the Utility Act would benefit consumers by dissolving many of the utility monopolies that controlled the price of

371

electricity. But, all Roosevelt wanted to do was control them. The *Federal Power Commission* was created to oversee, regulate and license public utility enterprises and make sure that each utility holding company was limited to a single fully integrated system — except in instances where Roosevelt, as the tutorial head of the agency, granted an exception or waiver — which he did for every major utility holding company.

Then he went after the coal industry, passing the *Guffey-Snyder Bituminous Coal Stabilization Act.* Under *Guffey-Snyder*, Roosevelt was able to seize control of the mining industry. Within his grasp was the power to control the entire economy of the United States. Under the new codified regulations, Roosevelt determined what would be produced on the farms and in the factories; he determined the prices at the mill and on the street; he forced business to accept labor organizations and negotiate union contracts. He set the wage standards, and determined the work week. He determined what was a fair profit for industry, and heavily taxed what he termed were "unearned profits" — those in excess of what he personally felt they were entitled.

Most Americans do not give a second thought to the implications of the regulatory actions taken by Roosevelt and subsequent occupants of the White House, believing that the President has the Constitutional authority to intrude on free enterprise at the State or local level. He doesn't. Most Americans believe that the increased regulations are designed to provide the consumer with more uniform service and lower prices. The reverse was more often true.

In reality, Roosevelt was not in the least concerned about providing service, better or otherwise. He was structuring an oligarchic economy, with control centered in the White House. To succeed, he needed not only a centralized government, but centralized control over the private sector of the nation as well. It is important to note that, while Roosevelt was the man implementing this socialist agenda in America he, like Wilson before him, was not the master crafter of the agenda he was fostering. The blueprint for totalitarian control over the entire infrastructure of America came from the global model created by the transnational bankers and industrialists who, in 1920, tried in vain to tear down the walls of national sovereignty and create a stateless international nation controlled, for all time, by them through the League of Nations. Their plan failed only because of the unwillingness of the United States, at that time, to surrender its sovereignty to the money barons who have, for almost a century, called the tune to which the nation-states of the world have danced.

On August 15, 1941 the League of Nations model, which called for the dissolution of the nation states, would be fitted with a more stylish and much more acceptable suit of clothes. It would then be gift-wrapped in a glittering red, white and blue star-studded package and presented to the American people as a home-grown American idea. This "refashioned" totalitarian world government-in-the-making, created by the money cartel at the pinnacle of global power, promised to be the champion of democracy for all oppressed people. The public relations rhetoric of the Roosevelt Administration was that the UN would be an instrument that free nations would use to break the shackles of tyranny all over the world in order to free the masses from totalitarian governments. But, like most of the hyperbole spoken by most of the world's politicians — all of whom who are merely regional pawns in a global chess game for the control of all the world's assets, human as well as capital, by a handful of powerful elites at the pinnacle of global power — what was promised in the patriotic rhetoric that accompanied the birth of the UN in June, 1945 is antithetical to the reality of a global agenda that has become all too frighteningly transparent.

The blueprint for socialism in America was not much different than the blueprint for socialism in the Soviet Union or fascism in Germany and Italy since those who created the prototype for socialism that Roosevelt championed also created the blueprints for totalitarianism not only in Germany and Italy, but the rest of Europe as well[2]. Most of the democratic monarchies

---

[2]In 1870 John Ruskin was given the chair as Professor of Fine Arts at Oxford University. In his inaugural address to the students at Oxford, Ruskins declared that it was the obligation of the privileged ruling cast of England to "save the world" by creating a global order based on freedom, the rule of law, decency and self-discipline. Ruskins words had a major impact on the students—and one student in particular. His name was Cecil Rhodes. As Ruskin spoke, Rhodes scribbled his words in longhand on a notepad. Rhodes, according to Carroll Quigley in his massive tome, *Tragedy & Hope: A History of the World In Our Time*, kept that hastily written note with him at all times for 30 years.

Ruskin made such an impression on Rhodes that the Oxford under-in Europe had legislated Enabling Acts in the 1920s or 1930s that would allow those holding the reins of power within those governments to circumvent the rule of law and, based on some real or perceived national emergency, to rule as a dictator for a specified period of time — ostensibly until the crisis that triggered the national emergency had ended. Three of those nations, Germany, Italy and France, had Constitutions that should have prevented their leaders from usurping enough power to abolish the rights of their citizens and to establish permanent dictatorships. Only France and England — which has no written Constitution — constrained those holding, and exercising, that power. Interestingly, both France and England had socialist democracies at that time.

---

graduate made it his life's mission to accomplish the challenge placed before the student body that day at Oxford.

When he graduated from Oxford, Rhodes went to South Africa to seek fame and fortune. Rhodes became a diamond and gold prospector, finding both. With the financial help of Baron Rothschild and Alfred Bret, Rhodes, over many years, was able to secure a monopoly on the diamond mines of South Africa through their joint corporation, DeBeers Consolidated Mines. As his wealth and influence grew, Rhodes formed a secret society that was singularly dedicated to creating a new world order whose task it would be to bring all of the habitable world under the control of the English-speaking people.

The group, formally chartered on February 5, 1891, was so secret that it has always been known publicly only as "The Society." It included several of Rhodes' former Oxford classmates: Arnold Toynbee, Alfred Lord Milner, Arthur Glazebrook, Sir George Parkins, Philip Lyttelton Gell, Sir Henry Birchenough, and a British journalist, William T. Snead, who introduced Rhodes to a group of similiar-minded Ruskin devotees from Cambridge that included: Reginald Baliol Brett (Lord Esher), Sir John B. Seeley, Lord Albert Grey, and Edmund Garrett. New inductees were added as they proved their worth to The Society. Jan Smuts, a Cambridge graduate who would rise to become the Prime Minister of South Africa, and one of those who forged the League of Nations, would become a member, as would Louis Botha, another South African prime minister. The core group consisted of Rhodes, as the leader, Stead, Brett, and Milner who served as the "executive committee." The "Circle of Initiates" consisted of Alfred Lord Balfour, Sir Harry Johnson, Baron Rothschild, and Albert Lord Grey. Others were later added. An "outer circle" was formed that was known as the "Association of Helpers." Those members were inducted from another group formed by Alfred Lord Milner, that was called "Milner's Kindergarten." Milner's inductees were likeminded English glo-

Roosevelt, with the help of his brain trust and the Federal Reserve bankers who were determined to force the American people to surrender the gold which they legally possessed and legally owned, subtly changed a few words in the 1917 *Trading With the Enemy Act* and created the means by which Roosevelt could legally usurp the rights guaranteed to the American citizen by the Constitution. However, the Bill of Rights attached to the end of the Constitution kept getting in their way.

Most of Roosevelt's 1933-35 problems with the Supreme Court came in this area. The authority Roosevelt assumed, or was granted under the March 9, 1933 *Emergency Banking Relief Act* that contained the amended version of the *Trading With Enemy Act* that Congress was not allowed to read before enacting, was unconstitutional.

In its reversal of the "planned economy" New Deal laws, the Supreme Court ruled that Congress could not grant a President supra-authority that Congress itself did not possess. In addition the high court ruled that the Executive branch, through proclamation or Executive Order, could not "legislate," since the President possesses no Constitutional authority to do so. Nor could the White House adjudicate disputes since it likewise possessed no judicial authority. In other words, the Constitution of the

---

balists, but they either did not have the necessary "pedigree," or had not yet proven their trustworthiness for full membership into the "Circle of Initiates."

Rhodes' initiates all had to have one thing in common: an absolute dedication to the achievement of world government, and a lack of morals on how those objectives were achieved.

When Rhodes died in 1902, his vast wealth was left to the Society in the form of the Rhodes Trust. Milner was selected by Rhodes before his death to head the Trust and administer the funds. Gell, Birchenough and several other inner circle members became the head of Rhodes' holding company, the British South Africa Company. Most of those Milner and Rhodes recruited eventually became members of the various British Empire governments. In 1910, Milner's Kindergarten became known as the Round Table. The Round Table has functioned now for almost 100 years, recruiting, indoctrinating and positioning "society" members in the governments around the world. The organization's objective has not changed from 1891—its sole objective is to abrogate the sovereignty of all nations and create a world government—headed by them—that will forever perpetuate the ideals of the British Empire. More times than not, their objectives were achieved only through violence and bloodshed.

United States was designed to prevent a President from becoming a dictator.

During his first term in office, Roosevelt issued 1,489 Executive Orders and 182 President Proclamations, creating a massive bureaucracy that was surreptitiously granted authority to implement, regulate and adjudicate the planned economy. These agencies, which sprouted from the New Deal legislation of the 1930s, have now assumed not only regulatory authority over the citizens of the United States, but in many cases, are allowed to arbitrarily levy fines and seize the property[3] of those who violate their codified regulations—practices that clearly violate the Bill of Rights. Yet, Americans meekly accept these commonplace excursions into their Constitutionally-protected rights as legal intrusions, assuming one might imagine, that the federal government would not initiate such action if they did not have the *constitutional* authority to do so.

When Roosevelt autocratically assumed control of the private industry sector of the American economy and imposed federal guidelines over the conduct and nature of private enterprise in the United States, he created a bureaucracy that would even-

---

[3]Among those agencies is the Internal Revenue Service (IRS), created as the collection agency for Lincoln's illegal income tax in 1862. The power of the IRS was greatly expanded, not by law, but through internal regulations, in 1863 when the agency was used to seize the assets of southern loyalists during the Civil War under the emergency war powers of a president may assume in times of insurrection or open war.

The IRS never surrendered its wartime "emergency" authority once Reconstruction ended, nor did Congress whose responsibility it was to clip the wings of the IRS, do so. Frankly, the IRS was a demon that even Congress feared. The unconstitutional practices of the IRS have become "codified," and thus by precedent their unconstitutional practices are generally construed to be "legal" by the federal court system even though the IRS regularly denies those they assess with the Constitutional right of due process.

Most federal agencies, like the Environmental Protection Agency (EPA), the Federal Trade Commission (FTA), the Federal Communications Commission (FCC), all have quasi-judicial authority; and all have Congressional authority to codify regulations. Each of these agencies have the right to arbitrarily assess fines—a judicial function not granted them under the Constitution. Under the Constitution, the Executive branch has no legal authority to legislate, nor does it have

376

tually become even more powerful than Congress itself, further weakening the rapidly eroding separation of powers. The real power of the American oligarchy, thanks largely to the amended *War Powers Act of 1917* that legitimized the federal bureaucracy, is now clearly vested in the Executive. Although the Church Committee was commissioned by Congress to terminate the national emergency powers of the President in 1973, those powers have themselves been codified.

The Church Committee, in the forward of its report on the

----

authority, on its own standing, to seize the assets of its citizens, or to assess fines or penalties on those who do not march lockstep to the beat of Washington's politically-correct drum. That is a prerogative of the court system exclusively, since the concept of a supra-executive itself violates the constitutional separation of power between the Executive, Legislative and Judicial branches of government.

The United States government has regretfully evolved beyond the Constitution. The ageless document that safeguards the rights of Americans is now considered, by most in Congress, the courts and the Executive branch as an archaic, obsolete document that hinders the creation of the socially-correct laws the politically-correct government mandates.

In order to create new "politically correct" federal laws—and in many cases, "politically correct" State laws as well—the Constitution has been conveniently set aside to allow a rapidly increasing caseload of civil suits to move through the court system at a faster pace. The 7th Amendment to the Constitution guarantees every American the right to a trial by jury in all actions of common law (civil suits) where the value of the controversy exceeds $20.00.

While the 7th Amendment was understandably penned to prohibit the assumption of supra-authority by the federal government and not the States, the U.S. Supreme Court created a binding legal precedent by coupling the 14th Amendment with any actionable constitutional challenge in order to expand the tenets of the Bill of Rights to cover the States. As such, the 7th Amendment, coupled with the 14th, guarantees petit court litigants the right to trial by jury in disputes exceeding $20.00 until such time as the 7th Amendment is amended to raise the sum to an equivalent amount in highly inflated 20th or 21st century dollars or monetary units.

Every State in the Union denies the right of jury trial to petit court litigants on the grounds of expedition. Elected magistrates who are many times not even lawyers, violate the Constitution every time they open the general sessions of their courts. Yet, nobody complains, and few appeal the arbitrary rulings of judges who are far too often not even schooled in the fundamentals of common law—let alone statutory law.

termination of the national emergency, issued on November 19, 1973, declared that:

"Since March 9, 1933, the United States has been in a state of declared emergency. In fact, there are now in effect four presidentially proclaimed states of emergency...These proclamations give force to 470 provisions of Federal law [that] delegate to the President extraordinary powers, ordinarily exercised by Congress, which affect the lives of American citizens in a host of all-encompassing manners. This vast range of powers, taken together, confer enough authority to rule the country without reference to normal constitutional processes.

"Under the powers delegated by the statutes, the President may: seize property; organize and control the means of production; seize commodities; assign military forces abroad; institute martial law; seize and control all transportation and communications; regulate the operation of private enterprise; restrict travel; and plethora of particular ways, control the lives of American citizens." (*Report of the Special Committee on the Termination of the National Emergency;* United States Senate; November 19, 1973; Report 93-549.)

Every president from Roosevelt to Nixon held, and exercised, this authority with restraint. Only three presidents — Roosevelt, Richard Nixon and Bill Clinton personally abused the power within their grasp. Since Roosevelt used the power to promulgate a planned economy, his actions were acceptable to Congress. Nixon and Clinton, however, used their power as a defense mechanism to protect their Administrations from scrutiny from Congress and the people of the United States. All three used their high office to attack their political enemies in the media, in Congress, and in business and industry[4].

---

[4]One of the more recent favorite attack dogs of the Presidency has been the Internal Revenue Service. Richard Nixon legitimized the use of the IRS to audit the tax records of his political enemies during the heyday of the Vietnam War. Clinton perfected its use.

Although Nixon was the first President since Reconstruction to use the IRS as a weapon against his detractors, every President since Herbert Hoover used the FBI to investigate their political enemies—and many times, as did Roosevelt, to investigate their friends and political allies

While *Public Law 94-412* (H.R. 3884) ostensibly terminated the national emergencies declared by Roosevelt, Truman and Nixon on September 14, 1976 with the passage of the *National Emergencies Act* it did nothing to rescind the extraordinary powers previously assumed by the Executive Branch—it wasn't intended to. *Public Law 94-412* was enacted specifically to curb the power of minority-party presidents like Nixon, Ronald Reagan and George Bush by granting Congress oversight authority over the White House—an act that is, in and of itself, unconstitutional because it violates the separation of powers.

But then, why not? If Congress can grant the President unconstitutional non-wartime emergency powers, why should it not grant itself equally unconstitutional oversight authority in order to control the unconstitutional presidential abuse of power?

Since the federal bureaucracy was created under the auspices of national emergencies, real or imagined, Congress had to be careful when they terminated the emergency situations that en-

---

as well. J. Edgar Hoover, who headed the FBI from May 10, 1924 until his death from a heart attack on May 2, 1972, according to Curt Gentry in his 1991 best-selling exposé, *J. Edgar Hoover, The Man & the Secrets,* not only encouraged the practice but even offered to carry out surreptitious investigations and illegal wiretappings for the occupants of the White House as a form of "job security."

Roosevelt standardized the practice of using the FBI in a Gestapo-like fashion, investigating everyone from Congressmen to labor leaders—and even authorized the investigation of his own wife. Johnson had Hoover investigate every suitor that called on either of his daughters. According to Gentry, it was Hoover that first suggested to President Richard M. Nixon that he use the IRS to audit his political enemies.

Learning the names of many of those who appeared on Nixon's "enemy list" in 1969 Hoover searched his own files to determine which of Nixon's "enemies" would most likely have trouble passing an IRS audit and then provided that information to the President, who in turn passed the information on to Attorney General John Mitchell. Those causing Nixon the most trouble suddenly found themselves enmeshed in legal problems of their own—in many cases to such an extent, they could no longer direct their attacks against the President—at least, not to the degree or intensity devoted prior to the onset of the IRS investigation.

Nixon, and most recently, Bill Clinton found the IRS to be a very effective political device in cooling the zeal of their detractors and critics. Since 1993, Clinton's Treasury Department has authorized IRS investigations on many of the country's leading conservative activist and

379

dowed the bureaucracy with life. A universal abrogation of the emergency status would have arbitrarily ended the federal bureaucracy as well. And, killing the bureaucracy was the last thing the kingpins of Utopia wanted.

Title I, Section 101(a) (50 USC 1601) of the *National Emergencies Act* began:

> All powers and authorities possessed by the President, any other officer or employee of the Federal Government, or any executive agency, as defined in section 105 of title 5, United States Code, as a result of the existence of any declaration of national emergency in effect on the date of enactment of the Act are terminated two years from the date of such enactment. Such termination shall not affect —
>
> (1) any action taken or proceeding pending not finally concluded or determined on such date;
>
> (2) any action or proceeding based on any act committed prior to such date; or
>
> (3) any rights or duties that matured or penalties that were incurred prior to such date.

---

advocacy groups such as the *Heritage Foundation*, the *National Rifle Association, Christian Coalition, Citizens Against Government Waste, Freedom Alliance, the Western Journalism Center,* and the *National Center for Public Policy* to name a few—all of whom are outspoken critics of either the Clintons personally or their Administration. In addition, *National Review, American Spectator* and *Media Bypass* magazines—all critical of Clinton—have been targeted.

On January 25, 1997 *Technopolitics,* the television news magazine of the *Public Broadcasting Service* reported that the IRS was "...aggressively auditing conservative public policy groups who oppose Clinton administration policies." Two days before the *TechnoPolitics* report, when then White House spokesman Michael McCurry was asked to comment on similar reports in the *Washington Times, the Wall Street Journal* and the *Chicago Tribune,* he dismissed the allegations as falsehoods declaring flatly that "...no credible news organization had reported such audits..." were taking place. By that he meant the *Washington Post* or the *New York Times.*

TechnoPolitics host James Glassman, a columnist for the *Washington Post,* opened his January 25 program with a question: "Is the White House using the IRS to punish its political opponents?" He continued by saying, "Here at the IRS headquarters in Washington, agency officials won't comment. They say it's illegal for them to discuss the details of any tax investigation. But our own investigation found that a

(b) For the purpose of this section, the words 'any national emergency in effect' means a general declaration by the President. *(Public Law 94-412; [50 USC 1601])*

With one hand, Congress killed the existing national emergencies only insofar as they affected the ability of the President and the executive branch of government to act on current situations using prior authority. However, they left the bureaucracy virtually intact in Section 101 (a) (2). Once Congress had stripped the President of all extraordinary powers, they could then generously return them — under their complete control. Which they did, with the other hand, in Section 201(a) (50 USC 1621):

"With respect to Acts of Congress authorizing the exercise during the period of a national emergency, of any special or extraordinary power, the President is authorized to declare such national emergency. *Such proclamation shall immediately be transmitted to the Congress and published in the Federal Register...*" (Emphasis, author's.)

This is an important clause because it was inserted to prevent a President from doing precisely what Bill Clinton did when

---

remarkable number of Bill Clinton's critics have recently become the target of IRS audits."

The *National Center for Public Policy* incurred the wrath of Hillary Clinton when it came out against the *Health Security Act.* The NCPP provided national talk radio show hosts with information about the Clinton health care reform plan, helping to defeat the measure in Congress in 1994. A few months later, according to NCPP president Amy Moritz Ridenour, the IRS showed up on her doorstep.

Ridenour quoted the IRS auditor "...as saying he did not know the reason the audit was ordered but guessed that someone had filed a 'political complaint.' 'I asked how we got to be audited, and he came back with "Somebody probably didn't like what you were doing," Mrs. Ridenour said...following up with 'You mean it's political?' And then he said, "Right, probably, but my boss tells me to go audit people. I don't always find out why."'" (*The Washington Times National Weekly Edition;* Rowan Scarborough; Vol. 4; Number 6; February 9, 1997; pg. 8.)

Joseph Farrah, head of the *Western Journalism Center* and *WorldNet Daily,* a popular conservative Internet newspaper, said the IRS auditor sent to audit his books was even more blunt. "The auditor told the center's accountant the probe was a 'political case' and that the final decision on its tax-exempt status would be made in Washington, not the regional office." (*ibid;* pg. 8.) Farrah's name and organization fighe issued Presidential Decision Directive 25 (PDD-25) in February, 1996. PDD-25 was a secret agreement between the Clinton Administration and the United Nations that ostensibly contains the conditions under which America will surrender the control of United States troops to the UN. Abrogation of U.S. authority over its own troops, according to the 15-page summary the Clinton Administration reluctantly provided to then House Security Subcommittee Chairman Robert K. Dornan, would occur whenever U.S. troops were placed into cooperative ventures with the UN or NATO—with the UN possessing the right to call up American troops whenever international emergencies arose.

Immediately after issuing PDD-25, Clinton classified the document as being so top secret that not even the Chairman of the House Security Subcommittee—with nation's highest security clearance—could see the actual document. Dornan's security clearance, of course, only granted him access to the nation's most sacrosanct military secrets. Dornan, a hardcore conserva-

---

ures prominently in an internal White House report, "Communications Stream of Conspiracy Commerce" due to Farrah's promotion of the Chris Ruddy reports on the death of Clinton friend and former assistant White House counsel Vincent Foster.

In the audit of the *National Rifle Association,* which began in June, 1995 and continued well into 1999, the NRA was forced to pay over $2 million in legal expenses and accounting fees to defend itself. In February, 1997 the IRS demanded that the NRA turn over all of its confidential membership files—in all likelihood so the IRS could investigate everyone who contributed to them—or at least, to intimidate the NRA's supporters to the point that many would stop supporting them, and help bring about the financial collapse of the organization.

That was precisely the same ploy the IRS used with *Media Bypass* magazine. The IRS demanded a list of all advertisers and subscribers from publisher Jim Thomas in 1996. As a result of "intimidation," virtually every business, except the most militant, that promoted its products in the magazine stopped advertising. By January, 1997 according to the magazine's marketing director, Chris Coleman, *Media Bypass* had lost many of its regular advertisers.

While White House spokesman McCurry described the IRS as a "...friendly, professional government agency that would never harass anyone," a spot survey conducted by the *Washington Times* revealed that not a single group favorable to the Clinton Administration has been targeted for an audit by the IRS during Clinton's tenure as President.

tive, didn't have a "FOB Clearance." Only diehard, inner-circle *friends-of-Bill* — even some even who couldn't pass a standard FBI security check for admission into the White House — were allowed access to many of Clinton's *Nixonesque* political secrets, which was exactly what 201 (a) sought to prevent. To date, Clinton has not released the text of PDD-25. It remains a closely guarded top secret document, denied to all except those Clinton feels have a "need to know."

Sec. 202. (a) Any national emergency declared by the President in accordance with this title shall terminate if —

(1) Congress terminates the emergency by concurrent resolution; or

(2) the President issues a proclamation terminating the emergency.

Section 401 (50 USC 1641) made the President directly accountible to Congress for actions arising from any declared emergency situation, civil or otherwise. While the *National Emergencies Act of 1976* has served, at least to some degree, to check current Presidential abuses of power, it was a piece of legislation made necessary by the abuse of power of the Congressional leadership in the first New Deal Congress in 1933.

Under the *National Emergencies Act*, President William Jefferson Clinton issued Executive Order 13010 on July 16, 1996 establishing the *President's Commission on Critical Infrastructure Protection* the day before Paris-bound TWA Flight 800 mysteriously exploded in mid-air just off the coast of Long Island, New York and fell into the Atlantic Ocean, killing all 230 persons on board.

Although it appears as though it was merely a coincidence that Executive Order 13010 appeared in the Federal Register on the same day TWA Flight 800 went down amid unconfirmed rumors that a CIA black helicopter, a land-based military missile, or that a missile accidently fired from the cruiser *U.S.S. Normandy* which was operating 200 miles off the coast of New York shot it down, a good many anti-Clinton conspiracy buffs immediately "read" into the tragedy a Clinton plot to declare martial law and seize the transportation and communications systems of the nation. He didn't — nor does it appear anywhere in the public record that he even tried.

Executive Order 13010 was the result of several other related   **383** and unrelated events which had taken place in the country even before the bombing of the Murrah Building in Oklahoma City in retaliation, it is believed by many in the media, for the Clinton Administration's ill-conceived use of violent force on April 19, 1993 at the Branch Davidian compound in Waco, Texas that resulted in the deaths of cult leader David Koresh and 88 of his followers.

In fact, the events that triggered Executive Order 13010 began long before William Jefferson Clinton cajoled his way into the White House. America's growing militia movement troubled George Bush's Administration for precisely the same reasons that it worried Clinton.

Because Council on Foreign Relations member George Bush served as Ronald Reagan's vice-president for eight years, most Americans view him in *Reaganesque* terms: constitutionalist, conservatively nationalist, anti-socialist, pro-free enterprise, and a stout protector of the Bill of Rights — particularly the right of an American citizen, under the 2nd Amendment, to keep and bear arms. While all of those terms faultlessly describe Reagan, none of them accurately depict Bush.

No one can argue that George Herbert Walker Bush was not a heroic American. Unlike Clinton who illegally dodged the draft during the Vietnam War[5], Bush became America's youngest bomber pilot during World War II. Unlike Clinton whose only wounds in the Vietnam War may have come from wood splinters received as he carried anti-war posters in front of the American Embassy in London, Bush was shot down over the island of Chichi Jima in the Pacific. For bravery under fire, Bush was

---

[5]On March 20, 1968 Clinton's Hot Springs draft board re-classified the Georgetown University graduate 1-A (ready for induction). Between that date and the arrival of his official notification of induction into the United States Army at his mother's home on or about May 13, 1969, ordering him to report for active military duty on July 28, 1969, Clinton did a frantic 14-month scramble to find a deferment from the draft that ultimately resulted in his convincing Senator J. William Fulbright (D-AK) to intercede on his behalf to secure an exemption from the draft by allowing Clinton to join the University of Arkansas at Fayetteville's ROTC program—where he pledged to serve in the United States Army for 7-years upon graduation of UAF's law school. The exemption itself was illegal since Clinton had already been drafted. (*Clinton Confidential: The Climb to Power;* George Carpozi, Jr.; Emery Dalton Books © 1995; pg.485.)

awarded the Distinguished Service Cross and three air medals. Bush was like Clinton in only one respect, but for an entirely different reason. Both men were globalists.

Both men stoutly believed that America's destiny would be best served by the United States becoming an integral part of the emerging New World Order — a global community of nation-states governed by the laws of the United Nations — as did his father, Senator Prescott Bush.

Bush was the first Republican since the Civil War to be elected in the heavily Democratic Houston-area congressional district. Elected to the House of Representatives in 1966, Bush was then, and has steadfastly remained, a well-credentialed political insider who is very comfortable in the global arena. His congressional career ended when he angered his Texas constituents by voting for Lyndon Johnson's 1968 *Civil Rights Act.* Bush ran unsuccessfully for the U.S. Senate in 1964 and again in 1970. In 1971 Nixon named Bush UN Ambassador to China. It was a job made for him since Bush had been exposed to the utopian principles of globalism years earlier by his father, who was one of the original "one worlders."

From that period forward, Bush became a more vocal advocate of the merging of the nation-states into a cohesive global unit called "the New World Order," which would contain internally sovereign self-governing units, but without external sovereignty — much the way the Founding Fathers envisioned the loose knit confederation of separate sovereign States that aligned in 1787 to become the United States of America. Bush was, in fact, the person who legitimized, in the minds of millions of Americans, the term "the New World Order" at the end of the Gulf War when patriotic fever was at an all time high In doing so, Bush legitimized a phrase that, to those who had never heard of the New World Order, denoted a new world political and military coalition that would be headed by the United States. In a matter of months, the coalition had vanished.

Only the New World Order, now legitimized by the Gulf War, remained. Unfortunately, there was not, nor is, anything American about the New World Order — nor is there anything "new" about it. The New World Order is totalitarianism in its worst form because when world government is established there will be no place left to which those wanting to escape Utopia can flee.

Like Franklin D. Roosevelt before him, Bill Clinton was an amoral, apolitical chameleon who, for votes, switches political philosophies faster than most people change their underwear. Clinton was by far a more dangerous politician than Roosevelt because FDR had no fixed philosophical moorings. Roosevelt only had an agenda. Roosevelt's agenda transcended all political philosophies. While his agenda was partly socialist, partly fascist, partly Illuministic and partly democratic, it was, nevertheless, uniquely and completely Rooseveltian.

A vote for Roosevelt was a vote for a bigger, more intrusive government, the erosion of the Constitutional separation of powers, higher taxes, and a greatly enhanced welfare state. Everyone stepping into the polling booths of American from 1932 to 1944 understood that. But America, in that era of uncertainty, was willing to surrender a certain amount of freedom for the security of a steady job, and the knowledge that they would still be able to feed their families if they were suddenly thrown out of work. Thousands of Americans who had gone without paychecks in the early days of the Depression grudgingly paid Roosevelt's steadily increasing income tax believing that he had singlehandedly provided them with the job they now had. Few of those workers realized that had Roosevelt not been elected in 1932 many of them would never have lost their jobs in the first place, and that the economic recovery would likely have been completed by 1935. Even fewer realize that if Roosevelt hadn't happened, America's monetary system would very likely still be supported by the gold standard instead of the world's debt.

Clinton on the other hand, like most Rhodes Scholars (even single semester Rhodes Scholars), is both a socialist and a globalist. Although his glib political rhetoric changes from day-to-day and season-to-season, his Cecil Rhodes mentality remains clearly and concisely focused on the task at hand: creating an even bigger, even more intrusive and more controlling federal government. Clinton is clearly dedicated to the global agenda of reshaping the political structure of America in order to make it more compatible with a socialist New World Order.

America is, and has been for at least the past five decades, a nation sorrowfully mourning the death of the Republic and the surreptitious destruction of the Bill of Rights by Congress, the federal courts, and the White House. America is concerned, and rightfully it should be. Those who have been entrusted with the

386

care and upkeep of the Constitution have been criminally negligent in their responsibilities.

Most Americans realize it is too late to restore the Republic in the current existing political order. They feel threatened by the utopian global government they see just around the corner, just a few steps away. Few realize it's too late to restore the Republic. The Republic is dead. All that remains is the tattered remnants of a social democracy that has likewise reached the zenith of its years; an obsolete form of government in a rapidly evolving global society controlled by a well-financed and very powerful international oligarchy.

Americans are both concerned and frightened because every "road" they travel today, whether geographic or electronic, leads to the same destination. It is a place few Americans want to visit — the global society of the United Nations where instead of being economic equals with other sovereign States, they will become the human capital of the masters of Utopia.

"They that can give up essential liberty to obtain a little temporary safety deserve neither liberty nor safety."
Benjamin Franklin
Historical Review of Pennsylvania
1759

"Man's capacity for justice makes democracy possible, but man's inclination to injustice makes democracy necessary."
Reinhold Niebuhr
American theologian
Children of Light & Children of Darkness
1944

"A democracy—that is a government of all the people, by all the people, for all the people; of course, a government of the principles of eternal justice, the unchanging law of God; for shortness' sake, I will call it the idea of Freedom."
Theodore Parker
The American Idea
May 29, 1850

❖ SIXTEEN ❖

The Destruction of Democracy

The Constitution of the United States is one of the most unique instrument for governing that exists in the world. It was not contrived by accident. The safeguards that were woven throughout the fabric of the document were deliberately stitched, one thread at a time, to prevent the usurpation of power by any branch of the newly created national government. The Founding Fathers clearly understood that the Constitutional Republic they created would flourish only as long as the powers of that government remained equally divided between the Executive, Legislative and Judicial branches — with ultimate authority clearly vested in the States.

Franklin Delano Roosevelt was the first President to attempt the complete overthrow of our Constitutionally-mandated form of government, using the foundational building stones of socialism that were clearly, cleverly, and with much forethought, laid in place just prior to the onset of the Wilson Administration to guarantee that the Federal Reserve System which Wilson would sign into being on December 23, 1913, would have unfettered control over the economy of America — without any interference from the States, who were themselves rendered powerless on April 8, 1913 with the ratification of the 17th Amendment.

When Roosevelt assumed office on March 4, 1933 there were 11,385,000 unemployed workers in America. By the spring of 1936, due to a myriad of government works programs, the unemployment rate stood at 4,464,000. However, by the summer of 1937 the unemployment rate skyrocketed to over 10,000,000 and was growing at an astronomical rate. By year's end it would surpass the 1932 figure. The January, 1938 Department of Labor statistics — before they were diluted by bureaucratic interpretation — showed 11,800,000 Americans were now without jobs.

389

To compound the problem, industry was still stagnant. There had been no growth in private sector in five years. That, of course, should not have come as any real surprise to the Roosevelt Administration since FDR had very pointedly declared war on business in 1933 — and had waged that war very successfully. In his view, unbridled free enterprise was the "Great Satan." Unfortunately, far too many politicians in Washington hold that view. It is a perspective based not on sound economic logic, since the desire to control free enterprise is a desire to stifle competition. In the transnational economic hierarchy, there is no room at the top for uninvited guests, and the price of admission for the newly rich is astronomical — if they are even allowed to play. Bill Gates, the founder and genius behind Microsoft, is an example of the latter. CNN founder Ted Turner, who personally contributed $1.5 billion to the United Nations, is an example of the former.

Like far too many of our contemporary politicians, Roosevelt believed he could manipulate the societal structure of America and create a utopian democracy in which all men would be truly equal; in which all would share equally in the harvest of a land of plenty. He believed, as his diaries and personal papers suggest, that this could not happen in a republican form of government based on the principles of private property ownership and personal profit.

Roosevelt was convinced he could build a productive, cooperative commonwealth through the gradual nationalization of all of the public utilities in the nation, plus the communications industry, and the coal, oil and steel industries by the federal government. What convinced him this idea would work is not clear. His views were shared by both German Chancellor Adolph Hitler and Italian dictator Benito Mussolini. Both Hitler and Mussolini nationalized the pubic utilities of their respective nations shortly after assuming power.

There is much historic significance to the parallels that existed between the various governments of the world during the turbulent Depression years preceding World War II. The political unrest and financial strife were, in each instance, manufactured by the power barons behind the national seats of gov-

390

ernment to perpetuate the existing crisis in order to weaken the governments in power. In each case, as most conspiracy theorists would quickly agree, the instigators, whether they were conscious of the fact or not, originated from the same source and for the same reason. The objective in 1935-1945 was no different than it was in 1914-1920 — the formation of a global government and the dissolution of the nation-states.

While it is unlikely that Herbert Hoover understood the ultimate goal of the globalists, he very clearly saw the plan that was being implemented throughout the world in 1938, and addressed the issue as he campaigned for Wendall Willkie in the fall of 1940. Roosevelt, he was convinced, did not represent the solution — he represented what was wrong with America.

Hoover, who had remained silent during Roosevelt's second campaign, became an active advocate for change during Roosevelt's third campaign for two reasons. First, Hoover, like most Americans, believed "tradition" had clearly established a two term precedent for Presidents. Second, he was concerned that Willkie and his running mate, Senate minority leader Charles McNary, could not win against the New Dealer unless they could convince the American people that Roosevelt was deliberately destroying the fabric of the Constitution one thread at a time.

Hoover, as the keynote speaker at the Republican Convention in 1940, was ready to take on the New Deal. However, not only was America not listening, Hoover's solemn address was lost on most of the Republican delegates attending the Convention.

Hoover began by talking about the "...weakening of the structure of liberty in our nation." He continued, detailing Europe's 100-year struggle for independence and liberty from centuries old feudal systems, and how those much deserved freedoms were lost in twenty years.

"It was not due to communism or fascism," he declared, "those were merely the effects. Liberty," he continued, "had been weakened long before the dictators arose."

Which is precisely why, when Chancellor Hitler was granted temporary dictatorial powers, Germany fell; and why, when Prime Minister Mussolini was granted extraordinary authority, Italy fell. Freedom is won through bloodshed; liberty is lost by apathy.

Colonial Americans paid a high price for liberty, and cherished their hard-won freedom so much they carefully crafted a

Constitution that would guarantee liberty for all time. However, Depression-era Americans, like Depression-era Germans and Italians, sold those hard-won freedoms for the promise of a stipend at the taxpayer's expense, and the price of a meal at the feast-laden table of the State.

"In every single case," Hoover declared in his keynote address, "before the rise of totalitarian governments there has been a period dominated by economic planners. Each of these nations had an era under starry-eyed men who believed that they could plan and force the economic life of the people...They exalted the State as the solvent of all economic problems...These men shifted the relation of government of free enterprise from that of umpire to controller. Directly or indirectly they politically controlled credit, prices, production of industry, farmer and laborer. They devalued, pump-primed and deflated. They controlled private business by government competition, by regulation and by taxes...Then came chronic unemployment and frantic government spending in an effort to support the unemployed." (*The Roosevelt Myth;* John T. Flynn; Garden City Books © 1948; pgs. 205-206.)

The scenario painted by Hoover could just as easily to applied to Germany or Italy as the United States. The causes, symptoms and effects were the same. Germany, before Hitler, was a weak Constitutional Republic. Italy, before Mussolini, was a democratic monarchy. Each had written constitutions that guaranteed and protected the sovereign rights of its citizens. Each allowed despots to suspend those rights in the name of expediency in order to provide government-sponsored jobs, food, healthcare and retirement benefits — all of the same things every citizen provides for himself without the added repressions of an oppressive, totalitarian government in a free enterprise society.

Roosevelt, from 1933 to 1937, did to the United States what the Jacobins, the socialists, the communists and the fascists did to Europe from 1880 to 1933. America survived not because our Constitution was stronger than Germany's or Italy's, but rather because attached to the American Constitution was an addendum called the Bill of Rights. Although the Bill of Rights has been severely battered by all three branches of the federal government in recent years, it has — thus far — withstood the assault of government to abrogate our constitutional rights in the name of a more secure nation.

Regardless of his personal motives or philosophical belief, Roosevelt, whether deliberately or accidentally, created the model blueprint for socialism in the United States. And, the bureaucracy he established to manage his utopian society was, and still is, determined to carry out its plan. Not only were all of the obstacles that had thwarted the planners of American utopianism in the past removed, the framework of socialism — control of business, industry, agriculture, labor and finance, combined with a progressive income tax — were solidly in place. The blueprint of Roosevelt's planned economy was frighteningly similar to those steps described by Karl Marx as essential to the creation of a communist society.

First is the abolition of private property. While the 5th Amendment prohibits the government from unlawfully seizing private property for public use, the U.S. Supreme Court in *Brown v. Welch* declared that "...the ultimate ownership of all property is vested in the State. Individual so-called ownership is only by virtue of Government...and use must be in accordance with law and subordinate to the necessities of the State[1]." (Senate Document 43.)

Second is the introduction of a progressive income tax that allows the State to redistribute the wealth of the nation. This, of course, was accomplished with the certification of the ratification of the 16th Amendment on February 15, 1913.

Third is an inheritance tax that allows the State to confiscate the accrued "family" wealth that was earned before the socialist State came into being. This was accomplished with the passage of the *Wealth Tax Act of 1935.* The relevant "theory" behind this type of law was that it was a weapon the government could use "...against unfair concentration of wealth and economic power."

---

[1]While the government cannot seize your property without adequately compensating you for your loss, they can regulate how you can use it—or even regulate it so you cannot. This fact is evidenced every day in every community in America where zoning ordinances are enacted to either encourage or forbid one type of development or another. In the fall of 1996, President Bill Clinton declared 18 million acres of the State of Utah to be a protected National Reserve, preventing the mining of millions of tons of sulfur-free coal, and forcing American industry to meet their growing demand for this grade of coal by buying from the Indonesian Riady family's Lippo Group—a major Clinton campaign contributor who, by some strange quirk of chance, just happened to control approximately 25% of the world's known reserves of sulfur-free coal.

In reality it was a law created to make it difficult for themiddle-class to amass inherited wealth. Although the *Wealth Tax Act* imposed a surtax on incomes in excess of $50 thousand per year, it also provided loopholes for the ultra-wealthy to conceal their vast fortunes in tax-free trusts and foundations. In essence it, like every tax passed by Congress, was a tax levied against the middle class. While an income of $50 thousand in 1935 was a virtual "fortune" by the living standards of that day, it is impor-tant to remember that when speaking of "wealth," we are talk-ing about incomes not counted in the simple thousands but in the hundreds of thousands or millions of dollars.

Most revealing about the Money Trust is exactly whose wealth was exempted from seizure by the tax collector. The money bar-ons were not interested in protecting the first or second genera-tion wealth of the "up-and-comings." They were the target of the oppressive tax laws since they would most likely become the "competition" of the truly wealthy if left unchecked.

That was the philosophy of not only John D. Rockefeller, Sr. whose life and financial exploits were documented by author Ron Chernow in the book *Titan, the Life of John D. Rockefeller, Sr.* in 1998, but also the other robber barons of the 19th and early 20th century: Andrew Carnegie, Jay Gould, Cyrus McCormick, Cornelius Vanderbilt, J. Pierpont Morgan, Andrew Mellon, Sid-ney Dillon, and William Rockefeller — who created the organi-zation — were members of what was privately known as the Jekyll Island Club[2]. This largely invisible group collectively possessed, or controlled, over half of the accrued wealth in the United States. The free enterprise system allowed them to amass the wealth they enjoyed. But, when they reached the pinnacle of success in their respective fields, they did everything they could, legally and extralegally, to destroy the system that assured their success.

---

[2]Jekyll Island was a posh, exclusive retreat of the ultra-rich off the coast of South Carolina that was originally purchased by William Rockefeller in 1888 in order, he later maintained,to create a private retireat for America's ultra rich. Rockefeller bragged that 100 of the richest families in America maintained seaonal homes there.

It was at J.P. Morgan's home on Jekyll Island that the legislation for the Federal Reserve Act was drafted, and it was there that the final strat-egy to secure the ratifications of the 16th and 17th Amendments were devised. Clearly, the American members of the global political hierarchy lived there early in this century.

There is probably no better example of this than Henry Ford[3], the founder of Ford Motor Company. Ford, the pioneer of the moving assembly-line produced automobile, fought the money powers from 1908 until he finally surrendered to the Roosevelt Administration in 1941—and was rewarded with contracts to manufacture parts for aircraft, and then in 1942 with the completion of a huge plant at Willow Run, Michigan, the airplanes themselves. Despite the fact that Ford had no experience in aircraft manufacturing, he was awarded lucrative contracts to build war planes for the military. By the end of World War II, Ford had produced more than 8,000 planes.

Although the most successful auto manufacturer in the United States for most of his 44 years in the industry, Ford remained a troublesome "outsider." Sometime between 1933 and 1936 he was reluctantly accepted by the very small and very elite group of international power brokers who determine the causes, courses and conclusions of most global events. Ford, however was not an "invited" member.

Ford, who was not well educated, was something of an enigma

---

[3]Ford's tutorial membership in the elite society came only through his association with the newly-structured German chemical conglomerate I. G. Farben in 1928, and Ford's investment in Farben at that time.

During World War II, Farben built a synthetic rubber plant in Auschwitz, Poland specifically to capitalize on the cheap, captive Jewish, Polish, and Czech labor available from the concentration camps. Farben, bankrupt at the end of World War I, enjoyed an inauspicious rebirth during the reconstruction of Germany. I.G. Farben was singled out as one of those German companies who was to benefit from the Dawes Plan when the Allies stabilized the *Reichsbank* with a loan of 800 million gold *Reichs-marks* from the United States because of an interest in Farben's hydrogenation technology by Standard Oil. Farben was experimenting with a process to extract gasoline from coal. Farben scientists had successfully converted coal to gasoline in 1909, but the technology was far too costly to have any commercial merit.

In August,1927 Standard Oil entered into cooperative agreement with Farben to develop the process. This working agreement was formalized on November 9, 1929. It stipulated that Standard Oil would own 50% of the rights to the hydrogenation process in all of the countries of the world except Germany; and second, that both companies agreed not to compete in the other's areas of expertise. In other words, Farben agreed not to enter the oil industry and Standard Oil agreed not to enter the field of industrial chemicals.

to the elitists. He was, to many of them, simply a very rich mechanic with a workingman's mentality. Although he was something of a philosophical utopian, Ford was also a loose cannon and a vocal anti-Semitic[4]. There was no telling when he would fly off the handle, or what he was likely say when he did.

Shortly after the passage of the *Federal Reserve Act,* Ford denounced it and the Morgan forces which created it when he said: "It is well enough that the people of the nation do not understand our banking and monetary system, for if they did, I believe there would be a revolution before tomorrow morning."

By 1913, like a good many self-sufficient industrialists, Ford found himself the target of bankers like J.P. Morgan who were attempting to carve out a share of what promised to be a growing and potentially lucrative industry. During those hard money times, the fledgling auto industry was alternately squeezed and massaged by the bankers.

Unlike Charles and Frank Duryea and many other early automobile manufacturers whose operations were ultimately assumed by the bankers when they couldn't meet their obligations, Ford fought back. To cut both costs and retail prices, Ford adopted the moving assembly line. Although the idea worked, by 1914 the Ford Motor Company faced a monthly turnover of from 40% to 60% because of the monotony of the work and Ford's incessant demand for increased production. To combat the problem, Ford doubled the daily wage of his workers from around $2.50 to $5.00 per day, ending his turnover problem immediately. The increased stability of his work force ultimately translated into much lower costs. In 1914 the Ford Motor Company earned approximately $30 million in pre-tax profits. In 1916, with an even

---

[4]In 1919 Ford purchased the *Dearborn Independent,* a small, unprofitable weekly newspaper in his hometown just outside Detroit. Almost immediately, the editorial slant of the publication became ardently anti-Semitic, one might imagine because Ford believed all bankers were Zionist conspirators—and those who were not Jewish, like Morgan, were controlled by them. It was no secret, even then, that Morgan was a Rothschild puppet, and owed his vast fortunes to the Rothschild Bank of England.

It was not until there had been considerable public protest against the *Dearborn Independent* and the Ford Motor Company that Ford directed the publication to cease printing inflammatory articles about Jews. (Funk & Wagnall's New Encyclopedia; Vol. 10; pg. 169 © 1973.)

higher tax assessment, Ford earned $60 million.

During the *Banking Panic of 1920* Ford again found himself the target of what he believed was a "Zionist bankers' conspiracy" to take over Ford Motor Company. To combat the bankers from 1920-28, Ford created what has become known in the auto industry as "floor-planning." Ford produced the vehicles and placed them in the showrooms on consignment. When they were sold, the dealers paid Ford.

W hat brought Ford and the I.G. Farben Chemical Company together in 1928 is not clear. But it changed Ford's perception of the world and of global politics for all time. Ford was no longer the naive American utopian who, in 1915, chartered a "Peace Ship" that took him and several likeminded industrialists to Europe where they attempted, without success, to convince the British, French, German and Italian governments to sit down at a peace table and end World War I. To Ford's surprise he discovered that, individually or collectively, the warring nations seemed powerless to act in their own best interests. Determined to fight this frightening invisible force, Ford "bought" the Republican nomination for the U.S. Senate in 1918, but not even his vast wealth could unseat his Democratic incumbent during the mid-term elections.

By 1935 Ford was convinced that a very powerful global hierarchy was being created that could result in a ground-swell of such of monumental proportions that it would ultimately capsize every ship of State in the world. In 1936 Ford and his son Edsel, taking the lead from both Andrew Carnegie and John D. Rockefeller, created the Ford Foundation—their ante to play in this new, high stakes global poker game.

The public mandate of the Ford Foundation was to serve the general welfare of the people of America and the world. It was an auspicious calling. However, while the Ford Foundation was, and still is, a model of philanthropic generosity by creating such things as the National Merit Scholarship Program and donating countless millions of dollars to private colleges and universities as well as providing grants to the arts and helping to fund the Public Broadcasting System, it also has a more covert agenda that includes control over the philosophical slant of the "education" taught in the colleges and universities that it endows.

397

By 1940 Congress was alarmed by the sheer number of anti-American organizations, including both fascist and communist groups, that openly advocated the overthrow of democracy in America and who were operating with impunity in the United States. Congress responded by passing the *Smith Act of 1940.* The *Smith Act* made it illegal for any person "...to knowingly or willfully advocate, abet, advise, or teach the duty, necessity, desirability, or propriety of overthrowing or destroying any government in the United States by force or violence...with intent to cause the overthrow or destruction of any government in the United States; to print, publish, edit, issue, circulate, sell, distribute, or publicly display any written or printed matter advocating, advising or teaching the duty, necessity, desirability, or propriety of overthrowing or destroying any government in the United States by force or violence...or to be or become a member of, or affiliate with, any such society...knowing the purpose thereof." (*The Smith Act;* Section 2.)

The *Smith Act* was tested in the high court with *Dennis v. United States* (341 U.S. 494) in 1951. The leaders of the Communist Party of the United States were indicted under the *Smith Act* in July, 1948. They were found guilty of conspiring to overthrow the government of the United States on October 14, 1949. When the U.S. Court of Appeals upheld the conviction, it was brought before the Supreme Court. The high court upheld the convictions because, in their view, "...the leaders of the Communist Party...intended to initiate a violent revolution whenever the propitious occasion appeared..."

What is interesting in this case is that, as it was pointed out by Associate Justice Hugo Black in his dissenting opinion, the conspirators did not, in fact, initiate any action to overthrow the government—they merely advocated it. Likewise, they were not charged with the overt act, but rather, only with its advocacy.

While Black and William O. Douglas believed the *Smith Act* violated the free speech rights guaranteed by the Constitution, the majority of the justices headed by Chief Justice Fred Vinson (a former banker who served as Truman's Secretary of the Treasury) saw in that advocacy a clear and present danger to the United States. They agreed that while the communists had not yet acted, they clearly intended to do so when the opportunity arose.

However, the high court also clearly drew a distinction between those who advocated the violent overthrow of the government and those who advocated its destruction by peaceful and legal means.

The fractured decision on the part of the high court posed something of a dilemma for Congress, which believed it could stem the rising tide of anti-democracy rhetoric promoted by a myriad of tax-exempt groups and organizations sponsored by some of the major foundations in America.

When *Dennis v. United States* was upheld by the Supreme Court, Congress believed it had found a way to curtail the anti-democracy mongers in the various Foundations. Instead, the Foundations and their advocacy groups found protection under the *Smith Act* as long as they only advocated the peaceful overthrow of the America's constitutional form of government. Because they could no longer use the *Smith Act* against the Foundations, Congress decided to revoke their tax-exempt status.

In 1952, the House of Representatives passed Resolution 561 calling for an investigation of all Foundations and tax-exempt organizations in the United States. One of those called before the Committee was H. Rowan Gaither, the president of the Ford Foundation.

According to Alan Stang, writing for *American Opinion* magazine at the time, Gaither invited Norman Dodd, the chief investigator of the Committee, to visit him at the Foundation in order to question him about the investigation.

Supposedly, during the conversation that took place, Gaither was quoted as saying: "All of us here at the policy-making level have had experience either with the OSS or the European Economic Administration, with directives from the White House. We operate under those directives here. Would you like to know what..[they]...are?" To which, hypothetically, Dodd affirmed he would. Gaither is then quoted as saying: "The substance of them is that we...use our grant-making power...to alter our life in the United States that we can be comfortably merged with the Soviet Union." (*American Opinion; Foundations Pay The Way* © January, 1977; pg. 5.)

While current events, including the passage of both NAFTA and GATT, clearly confirm that was precisely the policy agenda not only of the globalists within the Rockefeller, Carnegie and Ford Foundations, but also the Bush and Clinton White Houses as well, it is hard to imagine that in 1952, during the height of the Cold War, that Gaither or any other Foundation head would make any such statement, in confidence or otherwise, to an investigator of a Select House Subcommittee who was looking for precisely that type of "evidence" for the Committee.

Gaither may have suggested that the Ford Foundation was utilizing its grant-making powers to elevate the economies of all of the underdeveloped or undeveloped nations — including the Soviet Union — in order to prepare them for entrance into a one-world global community, but it seems highly unlikely he would confide to Dodd that the true intention of not only the Ford Foundation, but the Carnegie and Rockefeller Foundations as well was to merge the Soviet and American societies — even though that goal was common knowledge due to the published writings of many of their respective leaders and more outspoken members.

It was also common knowledge at the time that the Royal Institute of International Affairs and the Council on Foreign Relations (originally called the Institute of International Affairs) were both funded by, and still receive a substantial amount of their current support from, the Carnegie and Rockefeller Foundations.

What had not been public knowledge was the political philosophies of these Foundations, and thus, the reason for the 1952 House investigation. Even with volumes of published statements affirming their ultimate goal, the House Select Committee never reached any substantive conclusions on the subversive agendas of the Foundations, the nihilistic rhetoric of those they funded notwithstanding.

In December, 1922 the Council on Foreign Relations journal, *Foreign Affairs,* published an article by Philip Kerr in which the British globalist says: "*Obviously there is going to be no peace or prosperity for mankind as long as [the earth] remains divided into 50 or 60 independent states*...until some kind of international system is created which will put an end to the diplomatic struggles incident to the attempt of every nation to make itself secure...*The real problem today is that of [how to get] the world government."* (Emphasis, author.)

The June, 1923 edition of *Foreign Affairs* contained an article written by none other than Col. Edward Mandell House in which he said: "If war had not come in 1914 in fierce and exaggerated form, the idea of an association of nations would probably have remained dormant, for great reforms seldom materialize except during great upheavals...If law and order are good *within* states [nations], there can be no reason why they should not be good *between* states [nations]." (Emphasis, author.)

A July, 1948 *Foreign Affairs* article written by Sir Harold Butler raised the question: "*How far can the life of nations, which for centuries have thought of themselves as distinct and unique, be merged with the life of other nations? How far are they prepared to sacrifice a part of their sovereignty without which there can be no effective economic or political union? Out of the prevailing confusion a new world is taking shape...which may point the way towards the new order.*" (Emphasis, author.)

On April 5, 1954, Rene Wormser, general counsel for the House of Representatives responded to a letter received from former Assistant Secretary of State Spruille Braden concerning the Foundations under investigation by the Select Committee. Wormer privately conveyed her own personal thoughts. On April 10 Braden would reply: "*I have the very definite feeling that these various foundations you mention very definitely do exercise both overt and covert influence on our foreign relations and that their influences are counter to the fundamental principles upon which this nation was founded and which have made it great.*"

Over the past twenty years, the globalists have been very open with their views, which are eagerly supported by such liberal newspapers as the *New York Times,* the *Washington Post,* the *Los Angeles Times,* the *Baltimore Sun,* and the *Christian Science Monitor* as well as ABC, NBC, and CBS News, and CNN.

Fourth on the Marxist "short list" of things to do to successfully overthrow a democracy is to *centralize the media under the general government.* That was a fairly simple task for Lenin in 1917, for Mussolini in 1924, and for Hitler in 1933. It was not an easy task for Roosevelt. The United States Constitution prevents the general government from interfering with, or abridging, the freedom of the press in America.

Since Roosevelt was not constitutionally allowed to censor the media — something he attempted to do several times between 1933 and his death in 1945 — he did the next best thing. He decided to regulate it through licensing so he could threaten to revoke the licenses whenever he felt the need to control the flow, or content, of the news reaching the American people.

Among the first priority pieces of legislation pushed through Congress by the new president was the *Communications Act of 1933,* 401 enacted on June 19. It created a commission to license and regulate the transmission of news communications by telephone, telegraph, cable and radio. Since radio stations had to apply for a federal license to use the airwaves, Roosevelt had a large degree of leverage over them since each needed the Commission's approval to gain their initial license to broadcast, and at regular intervals, to secure a renewal of their franchise.

However, newspapers have operated with almost complete impunity from government interference of any type in the United States since the formation of the nation. No special licenses or consents from the general government were ever required since a truly free press must be under obligation to no one.

At least one effort was made by the Roosevelt Administration to create a federal agency to regulate the newspaper industry. Since newspaper advertising rates are largely based on circulation, Roosevelt decided an agency was needed to police the circulation statistics of the industry to protect the advertisers from the unsubstantiated circulation claims of unscrupulous publishers. However, before Congress could act, the *American Newspaper Guild* funded the creation of an independent circulation auditing body, the *Audit Bureau of Circulation,* to police the circulation claims of its respective members, thereby depriving Congress of its excuse to act "in the compelling interest of the American people."

Roosevelt was not pleased. But the creation of the Audit Bureau of Circulation did not deter him from further attempts to enact legislation to regulate the fourth estate. Roosevelt was determined to muzzle the media because he was convinced that the American people, if they understood the full ramification of what the New Deal meant in terms of controls not only over business and industry, but over their own liberties as well, would mount such a storm of protest that it would derail the New Deal before it could be implemented.

One of Roosevelt's strongest detractors concerning his attempts to censor the press was Senator Thomas D. Schall, whose chastising correspondences to Roosevelt were also sent to the newspapers in Washington who glorified in printing the exchange between Roosevelt and their arch defender, Schall.

"...For me," Schall wrote in one such discourse, "to chronicle all the attempts of your Administration to throttle the press and free speech—all known to you and approved by you in advance—would be but to recite incidents with which you are entirely familiar. If it were not for the fact that I see in your request for 'information' an attempt on your part to appear as a victim of your own bureaucracy instead of its chief organizer, I would be inclined to ignore your telegram.

"But since you assume a cloak of innocence and since your telegram to me is in the hands of the press, it becomes my duty as a sentinel of the people to do what little I can to mitigate their deception by citing specific evidence of your intention to force a censorship of the press so that your acts and the acts of your communistic bureaucrats might be hidden from public gaze.

"I refer, as you are quite aware, to the statement of your chairman of the Judiciary Committee, Mr. [Hatton W.] Summers of Texas, in connection with the passage of the press censorship bill by the House in the special session of congress called by you. Under your whip, it passed the House. And if the Senate had not taken out the poison, a publisher who had not gained your approval, or the approval of some of your appointees, could be sentenced to ten years' imprisonment. The evidence convicting you of a desire to censor the press twenty-five days after you swore to uphold and defend the Constitution is in print in the archives of the House of Representatives. Mr. Summers in his statement says the bill was introduced at the request of the "Executive," and is necessary to the success of the recovery legislation. Mr. President, in my opinion, secrecy and press censorship are never necessary when motives are pure...You demanded and sanctioned passage of a bill permitting you to secretly fix tariff rates and clothe your acts with a press censorship second to nothing ever before even suggested in the legislative annals of the United States...The Communications Bill originally introduced by you contained a press censorship clause which was stricken out before the bill was passed, but it still gives you the power to inaugurate a Government telegraphic news service, under which as one example you immediately put out-of-business the three radio stations of Mr. [Henry] Ford." (*The Roosevelt Papers, Vol. 3;* pgs. 365-389.)

Roosevelt responded immediately with another telegram, also sent to the media, denying the allegations and demanding that Schall provide proof of his charges. Roosevelt also attempted in that telegram to justify his policies — not to Schall, since the Senator knew all too well what the President was about, but to the public, which still viewed him as the economic savior of the nation. It would not bode well for his re-election efforts if America saw him in the same light as Adolph Hitler.

Schall's second letter to Roosevelt was more scathing than the first:

"My dear Mr. President:

"Your second open telegram to me in no wise explains the various attempts of your Administration to secure legislation censoring the press of the United States.

"You requested evidence from me concerning your own acts. I cited you three instances of your efforts to keep the public from securing, through the press, facts concerning the attempts of your bureaucracy to communize the United States.

"You say you are acting in 'good faith.' Then why not as a starter remove the censorship bars against the press that you have placed in all your departments?

"Your conclusion to me that the 'incident is closed' will in no way, Mr. President, satisfy the people of their fear of where you are unconstitutionally steering their Republic. As a Representative of the people I dare not, under my oath to support and defend the Constitution, let it rest there. The people of the United States want to know from you why their Republic is being gradually cast aside for a dictatorship.

"If you desire specific information as to the basis of my reasonable inference, that the Government is about to co-ordinate its various and sundry publicity functions into a national press service, you have only to assemble the following 'makings' thereof:

"The White House...press code which aims to dominate the publishers in the conduct of their business, and your opposition to include therein the freedom of the press demanded by the publisher's association of which there should have been no dispute, since it is a part of the Constitution and is guaranteed in the Bill of Rights...In short, it seems to me your Administration's intent is evident. It has become lock, stock and barrel, simply a group of publicity machinery not yet assembled for efficient and smooth operation.

But if the people return to you another spineless Congress, the defects no doubt will be remedied and 'what we fear will come upon us.'

"Your Administration has set up its magazine, called *Today*, edited by brain truster Raymond Moley and financed by Admiral Vincent Astor of the flagship *Nourmahl*...All dictatorships and most kings and emperors have their official organs. In Germany, President Hitler has created his ministry of publicity with [Joseph] Goebbels at the head. The Russian Soviet has the Tass Agency. Nothing goes out of Italy without Mussolini's sanction. The news service of the Washington Administration might appropriately be called the WHP — or White House Press — which would function as the official news service of the 'New Deal.'" *(ibid; pgs. 365-389.)*

It is difficult to look at the Roosevelt Administration and not see the similarities between Roosevelt, Hitler and Mussolini. As Schall declared in his second letter to the President, if Roosevelt had been blessed with a slightly weaker Congress during his first administration, or even during his second term after he had successfully blackmailed the Supreme Court, it is likely he would have become America's first dictator — the Constitution of the United States notwithstanding.

As it is, the damage Roosevelt caused to the Constitution has proven to be irreparable. As in any oligarchic system, the architects of Roosevelt's political shell game successfully manipulated America's perception of precisely where their "rights" originated, and upon whose authority those rights were granted.

The Constitution has successfully been undermined with the federal government assuming the paternal role as "grantor" of individual rights and liberties. Once the federal government has been legally construed as the "source" of all individual rights, it then stands to reason that same government will possess the legal authority to withdraw, or amend, whatever individual rights it feels are either unnecessary or unwarranted, or are counter-productive to its overall agenda.

That is exactly what has happened to America.

One need look no farther than the disavowed November 11, 1993 White House protocol for a very clear, and very frightening, example of a President determined to undermine the constitutionally-protected rights of the American people.

405

If you will recall from earlier text in this book, President Bill Clinton decided that cigarette smoking was a scourge that needed to be erased from the American landscape. He also advocated a prohibition on alcohol — a suggestion which, as you recall, provoked Mack McLarty to say: "...*If we ban all cigarettes and tobacco, we would have the same problem we had with prohibition.*"

With the willing assistance of a myriad of liberal activist organizations that are overzealously eager to curtail someone else's rights, Clinton tried unsuccessfully to enact legislation that would allow him to strangle the manufacture, sale and use of tobacco products. The fact that Congress had no constitutional authority to pass such legislation seemed of little importance. Cigarette smoking is, after all, detrimental to the smoker's health — and "second-hand smoke" is, as we all know, even worse. We know this not because we have seen evidence to support that conclusion, but rather because the anti-tobacco lobbyists in the Clinton Administration have told us they have seen the evidence to support it.

The abrogation of the rights and liberty in any society always begins on the outermost fringes of that society, targeting first those things which are, or theoretically should be, either socially abhorrent or morally repugnant. Slowly, over a period of time as we become accustomed to these abrogations of our constitutional rights or liberties, the government then unobtrusively intrudes into our lives even more by enacting "big brother laws" that are designed to protect us from ourselves. Seat belt laws are such types of legislation. Arguably, seat belts are not only a good idea, but common sense dictates that they should be worn while either driving or riding in a car. Seat belts, particularly harness-type seat belts, save lives.

However, the use of seat belts for adult passengers in any vehicle should be a matter of choice. Today, in almost every State in the Union, if you are stopped for any traffic violation and are not wearing a seat belt, an additional fine is levied for that infraction. This unlawful "tax" is assessed not because the wearing of seat belts will protect the driver or passengers of some other vehicle, but because it will protect you. Your "right" not to wear a seat belt does not exist. It has been arbitrarily denied by the State. Several States have now expanded their seat belt laws to give police officers the right to stop your vehicle for no other reason than because you are not wearing a seat belt.

Many Americans refuse to wear a seat belt not to abuse the Big Brother laws which mandate that they do, but because they have heard about serious injuries sustained by those wearing them, and they are convinced the State has no legal authority, the seat belt laws notwithstanding, to mandate that they do.

What is interesting is that the media never reports any statistics about the number of deaths, or types of serious injuries, caused by seat belts or airbags — or attributed to them by litigious attorneys — although the government is quick to advise us how many avoidable deaths occur each year by those who ignore seat belt laws.

Sometimes Americans refuse to buckle up because seat belts are a nuisance, or because they are uncomfortable and restrict their movement. Or, it may be that they refuse to buckle up because seat belts "wrinkle" their clothes. But what is really at issue is not whether the reason they offer for not buckling up is valid enough to avoid the ticket they are likely to receive for refusing to obey a law designed specifically to protect them from themselves; but rather, does the State has a constitutional right to insist that they do? The courts in every State have thus far ruled that seat belt laws are legal.

The purpose of most of these types of laws is not the well-publicized politically correct rhetoric that makes them appear both reasonable and well-intentioned. Rather, it is the subtle snipping away at the tattered edges of the Constitution itself, combined with the further unraveling of the fabric of our republican form of democracy that is so artfully being rewoven with a patchwork of socialism not only by the Executive and Legislative branches of government, but by the courts as well. Seat belt laws, like all Big Brothers are not about helping people — they are about control. *We are being conditioned to do what we are told.*

W e, the people, have enjoyed the protection of the Constitution as our insurance policy against tyranny for 220 years, but like a great many people who buy insurance, most Americans have never read the policy to see exactly what type of coverage they possess. They simply assume they are adequately protected. It is not until tragedy strikes that they pull out their "policy" and begin to read the terms of coverage. Of course, at that time, it's too late. The barn has already burned to the

407

ground and the livestock has scattered over the countryside.

Congress, over the past eighty years, has surreptitiously amended our "constitutional insurance policy" thousands of times with a myriad of innocuous and seemingly harmless laws, ostensibly enacted to benefit the citizens of the United States. Many of these faceless laws and Constitutional amendments actually changed the terms and conditions of our "insurance policy." But, because Congress gratuitously increased our "benefits" each time they deleted some of our "coverage," we failed to either notice or protest.

The "insurance policy" provided to us by the Founding Fathers was a Life Income Endowment. In 1913, it was reduced to a Whole Life Plan, with premiums due for the rest of our lives. In 1933, it changed from a permanent form of protection to Term Insurance. Now, in the opening days of the 21st century it has been modified to a 10-year Renewable Term plan whose premiums now exceed the benefits — and may well extend beyond the life of the "insurance policy" itself, since our coverage is now in global jeopardy.

Americans have not been good stewards of their freedom.

❖ SEVENTEEN ❖

Reshaping Democracy

Franklin D. Roosevelt, like Karl Marx before him, envisioned himself as the champion of the working man against those — the capitalist business enterprises of America — who sought to "exploit" them. To those feeding from the public trough throughout the 20th century, the *helping hand* of the New Deal era slowly evolved into the *gravy train* of the Great Society. However, by 1990, the gravy train had derailed. The Great Society had exacerbated into an ugly, self-debasing cycle of dependency that trapped multiple generations of American families who found not only themselves but their children — and sometimes their children's children — permanently shackled to the public feeding trough. Welfare, to far too many Americans, had become an inescapable way of life. The recipients of welfare served only one purpose in the grand socialist scheme: to perpetuate the system that spawned them.

Since the New Deal accomplished what it was designed to accomplish — the nationalization of the States themselves — it must be acknowledged that Roosevelt succeeded far beyond the wildest expectations of the globalists who advised and supported him. However, the "planned economy" of the New Deal, expressed in terms of the Great Society, failed miserably.

To more fully understand the true nature of the society that Roosevelt envisioned for America, it is important to note precisely what a "planned economy" is, and what types of adjustments were needed in our current form of government to allow the planned economy to blossom into full bloom.

But first it is important to understand what the planned economy was not. It was not Roosevelt's idea. It was Mussolini's.

Under socialism, the oligarchy controls every facet of life within the society. The fascist, on the other hand, acknowledges that private enterprise, to some degree, has to exist to keep the economy from stagnating. It is, however, rigidly controlled.

409

The State assumes ownership of approximately 25% of the economy and by law, controls the balance. Banks, railroads and all other forms of mass transportation, public utilities, mines and other natural resources, as well as the news media must necessarily be nationalized. Ownership of factories, stores, farms and recreation facilities can remain in private hands. The State, of course, assumes a supervisory role over the whole affair with regulations designed to make certain the system works, and to provide for the general welfare of all of its citizens.

In other words, unlike communism which completely suppresses the middle class and creates a single working class controlled by a ruling oligarchy, fascism recognized the need for "free" enterprise, albeit controlled by the State. Private initiative is needed to keep the gears of the economy well oiled and moving forever forward. Mussolini recognized the fact that when society becomes deincentized, the economy will grind to a halt — regardless of the amount of state funds infused into it. That was, he felt, the single biggest problem with communism as an economic system.

Like communism, fascism imposes totalitarian controls over the people it claims to serve, and subjects them to a myriad of confiscatory taxes since all governments feed like a giant predatory cancer on its citizens. Control is achieved first by offering the electorate a grand gratuity — like Social Security, or a national healthcare system — and then creating an intrusive bureaucracy to oversee it through a series of rules, regulations and finally, laws that ultimately supersede the mandate of the entitlement and restrict, rather than assist, those the gratuity was ostensibly created to help. Nothing illustrates this point more completely than the working papers of the failed Clinton *Health Security Act*.

First, in typical fascist form, the *Health Security Act* would have nationalized approximately 22% of the economy of the United States. Second, buried within the text of the *Health Security Act* working papers, discovered in four boxes in the National Archives, were two other measures. One was completely unrelated to healthcare, and appears to have been designed to either monitor or control the whereabouts of American citizens.

Interestingly, the fifth item on Karl Marx's short list of things to do to create a communist society out of a democracy is the control of the movement of the people within that society. Roosevelt accomplished control over transportation by creating the Interstate Commerce Commission to regulate commercial interstate traffic. Hillary Clinton's proposal, included among the *Health Security Act* working papers, would take transportation control a step beyond Roosevelt's wildest fantasy and into the world of George Orwell's *1984*.

Control of movement in the Clinton plan, if you will recall, began with an internal passport. Roosevelt himself debated how to create an internal passport, and even attempted to use the newly created Social Security card as one. However, Congress refused to cooperate with him, and specifically wrote into the law that the Social Security Card could not be used for identification purposes. Of course, in this day and age, your Social Security card and your driver's license — which is also not to be used for identification purposes — are the first thing demanded as proof of your identity.

The biometric *Health Security Identity Card,* to be used by its recipients to secure benefits, would also double as an internal passport. While the term "internal passport" was not used in the text of the proposed law, it was clearly viewed as such by the Clinton Administration.

When Hillary Clinton's shackles-encased *Health Security Act of 1994* died a well-deserved death, the conservative watchdog groups who had discovered a bonanza of wrongdoing in the secretive activities of her task force took their eyes off healthcare and focused their attention elsewhere. For that reason, none of them saw the Clintonesque slight of hand that moved the personal identifier "pea" from under the *Health Security Act of 1994* "walnut" and into the *Healthcare Portability Act of 1997* "walnut" as the inside the beltway shell game continued unnoticed.

The stealth used by several key legislators on both sides of the aisle to keep the American people from learning about the identification system clearly suggests nefarious intent on the part of the government. The argument that a unique numbering system was needed to create an accurate medical record-keeping database does not wash, since the Social Security numbers the medical community currently uses provides those who need them with an identification system that is personally unique.

The problem with the Social Security Card is that it is too easy to steal the social security number, and the identity, of a recently deceased person; or counterfeit a new card and with it, a new identity that is not recorded in the Big Brother's ever-growing   411 electronic database. For that reason the government has been exploring various ways to create a counterfeit-resistant Social Security Card. Coupling the personal identifier found in the *Health Portability Act of 1997* with the universal drivers' license found in the Senate's *Immigration Reform Act of 1996* and the House of Representative's 1996 Budget Bill House solves that problem for all time.

It must be remembered, however, that the national identity card that so innocently appeared in the *Health Security Act of 1994* was not uniquely a "Clinton thing." It was in fact a "globalist thing," and is part of a universal global identification effort that did not originate with the Clintons.

When the use of a universal European identity card — in the form of an EU driver's license — was first announced by the governing elite of the European Union in 1994, most Europeans immediately thought of Nazi Germany, and of the consequences of being "enrolled" in a government identity registry. Resistance to the idea was both fierce and immediate, even though every citizen in each of the 12 nations were assured by their governments that the new card was not an internal passport, nor would it ever be used as one.

Of course, as anyone who has ever been stopped by the police for any reason, even while walking, knows: the officer will always ask to see your driver's license — for identification. Write a check at the local department store or supermarket and the clerk or cashier will ask you for your driver's licence. Does a driver's license verify whether or not you have funds in your account at the bank? Of course not. It's for identification. The idea of the government creating a national identity card and then not using it to both identify its citizens and monitor their whereabouts is as easy to believe as the trite, oft-quoted phrase: "I'm from the government and I'm here to help you."

When the British Parliament began to debate the identity card issue in 1995, Prime Minister John Major announced that it was being issued to help prevent crime, welfare cheating and illegal immigration. What made Major's program initially controversial was the fact that carrying the British card, like the Clinton identity card (that was to be disguised as a health care benefits card), would be compulsory.

As a mandatory form of identification, Major's Conservative Party could not muster the support it needed from within its own ranks to pass the measure through the House of Commons, and was forced in the end, at least for the time being, to make it a voluntary card.

The initial EU card design featured the European Union symbol — 12 stars in a circle — in the upper left corner of the card, and the EU member's own national flag in the upper right. A growing number of Great Britain's citizens are Europhites who eagerly await the unification of Europe, believing that the waning glory of the British Empire will somehow be reborn through that economic confederation. Conservative Party legislator John Redwood, who was labeled by the liberal British press as a "Europhobe," raised a question on the floor of Parliament that concerned a good many Britishers: "Does the presence of the European symbol mean we are in the process of giving up our independence on...important justice, law and order, and immigration matters?" (*The Washington Post*; August 23, 1996; pg. A23.) Because that argument could not be settled to the satisfaction of the British people, England waived membership in the EU until the Euro becomes the official "currency" of Europe in 2002.

I n either a socialist or fascist system, one of the first restraints that must be exercised over the people is the control of movement. Controlling what Bill Clinton termed "*...a population that is too highly mobile*" remains a top priority not only in the United States but around the world. Because before any population can be controlled, government must know where any given member of that population is at any time. For that reason, a considerable amount of taxpayer money was earmarked for the *Intelligent Vehicle/Highway System,* with a start-up cost totaling several hundred billions of dollars when all cost factors are weighed[1].

---

[1] It should be noted that IV/HS, like globalism itself, predates the Clinton Administration. George Bush, Clinton's predecessor in the White House, a globalist of a much wider stripe, initiated the IV/HS ground-breaking in the United States with the *Intermodal Surface Transportation Efficiency Act of 1991* (ISTEA) which provided $151 billion over six years to improve surface transportation in the United States. Over $660 million of those dollars were earmarked for experimentation in IV/HS. Additional funds were set aside for building automated toll booths on private toll roads built by, or purchased from, the State by private investors. The Diebold Institute numbers suggest an additional $22 billion

413

Interestingly, IV/HS, like the national identity card, originated in Europe. Both are now in use there. The prototype from which the Diebold Institute cast its American model was borrowed from a pilot program in England where the experimental system was installed on the heavily travelled M25 beltway around of London. M25 was selected not only because of the amount of traffic on the roadway, but also because the terrain was ideally suited for the constant measurement of speed.

The UK Department of Transport was encouraged by the program, and expanded the system into the arterials (A-roads) of London itself. The UK system, according to the Diebold Report, had a dual purpose. First, *TrafficMaster*, as its name implied, monitored traffic and electronically assessed speeding tickets which were levied against the owner of the vehicle.

Second, *TrafficMaster* served as an electronic toll collector.

---

will be needed for "start-up" costs.

In April, 1992 Bush issued an Executive Order on the privatization of State and local infrastructure assets built in whole or in part with federal money. These assets, by definition, are roads, tunnels, and bridges. An interesting incentive is found in the decree. Prior to the Executive Order, the Office of Management and Budget (OMB) "...had insisted that the federal government be repaid its past grants in the event the infrastructure was sold. The Executive Order does away with this disincentive. State and local governments will be able to keep the majority of the proceeds from privatization. The Executive Order goes a long way toward removing any remaining blocks to actions along the lines envisioned by ISTEA." (*Clinton White House Health Care Interdepartmental Working Group; Working Paper #1; Box 1748.*)

By allowing the States to keep the majority of the funds from privatization—believed to be around 90%—they will become active participants in the rapid development and deployment of IV/HS. Likewise, with the 1997 announcement by the Clinton White House that the States may convert the interstate systems within their borders into toll roads, IV/HS will likely occur more quickly since the States will initially be allowed to plow 90% of those tolls into their own treasuries as well.

To the Clinton White House, the most important consideration at this time is the establishment of an IV/HS infrastructure—the electronic monitoring stations without which the plan would fail. Once the automatic toll booths are set at every major road intersection in the nation, and all of the vehicles on the road are equipped with some sort of sensory devise, the monitoring of America's highly mobile population can begin in earnest.

As mentioned earlier, the Diebold group's working papers, found in Box 1748 of the Clinton Health Care interdepartmental working papers in the National Archives, suggests that the system can be used to regulate interstate commerce by controlling road junctions and access to major roadways.

Before any electronic vehicle monitoring system can be implemented, two very important problems must first be solved. Both are troublesome. First is the task of installing a honing devise in every vehicle on the road. This will initially be accomplished with the introduction of a new electronic license plate, developed under a $20 million research fund established during the Bush Administration.

The development program was global in scope. In the United States, the project was called HELP (Heavy Vehicle Electronic License Plate). In Europe, the program was called LLAMD (London, Lyon, Amsterdam, Munich and Dublin), and is part of the Drive System. In Japan, the system was called VICS (Vehicle Information and Communications System). The experimental *TrafficMaster* system on the M25 beltway around London is privately owned by General Logistics, and has been in operation since 1990. It is this program which is currently being hawked by the media as the electronic system for travelers in the United States in the not to distant future[2].

Second, before the government can regulate access to the interstate system, toll booths necessarily have to be installed at every on-ramp of our vast interstate system. This mind-boggling problem was solved on March 10, 1997 when Bill Clinton unveiled a sweeping plan that would allow each State to charge access tolls to motorists on the federal interstate systems within their boundaries.

---

[2]An experimental program was also launched in the United States in 1989. It did not, however, include the use of the Global Positioning System. Instead, the program—called *Smart Corridor*—integrated traffic sensors, computer and a variety of communications links to coordinate traffic and disseminate traffic information along the San Diego Freeway, and from the five major highways leading from downtown Los Angeles to the freeway. The program was a cooperative venture between Los Angeles, the Federal Highway Administration, the California Department of Transportation and several local agencies. The program, which cost over $100 million before it was completed, has been operational since 1993.

On March 29, 1996 the Clinton White House announced that the government was granting civilian access to 24 Pentagon Global Positioning System (GPS) satellites to provide motorists, airline pilots, hikers and anyone else with a small hand-held receiver the ability to pinpoint their locations anywhere on Earth to within a few yards. (*The Washington Post;* Section A1; March 30, 1996.)

"Enthusiasts of this decades-old technology..." wrote *Post* staff writer John Mintz, "envision a world in which drivers no longer have to pull over and ask directions, hikers never get lost in the woods and airline pilots don't have to talk to air traffic controllers. Any stolen car could be found in a jiffy." (*ibid;* pg. A1.)

Clinton's announcement was greeted with some trepidation by the military community and a considerable number of civilian security experts since the privatization of the top secret GPS spy system, which was first deployed in 1970, will provide both enemy governments and terrorist groups a far more sophisticated tracking system than they currently possess to guide cruise missiles to very precise targets anywhere in the world.

One question that begs an answer is why the Clinton Administration, or any U.S. Administration for that matter, would jeopardize the security of the nation in order to make GPS available to the private sector to monitor the whereabouts of civilian cars and trucks on the roadways of America. After all, GPS is a system that was so secret, according to former senior Pentagon advisor to the Bush Administration Henry Sokolski, that the United States denied its existence for over ten years.

Another question that begs an answer arises from an indirect statement attributed to Vice President Al Gore in the March 30 *Post* Mintz article. "Proponents of the GPS industry envision that within a few years the receivers will be implanted in every *telephone,* car, truck and boat in the world." (Emphasis, author.) Why would a GPS *tracking device* ever need to be implanted in a telephone? Is it to make it easier for you to find your phone when it rings? Somehow, I don't think so. The most logical answer suggests such a devise would be needed only if someone wanted to either randomly, or specifically, monitor the telephone calls of certain Americans at will without their own efforts coming under scrutiny from anyone else—including the courts who, legally, must authorize any wire tap made by the government. Big Brother has arrived and is standing at the gateway to the 21st century.

416

IV/HS offers a myriad of benefits to the motorist, such as the monitoring of other vehicles on the roadway with the use of in-cabin "virtual" displays that alert drivers of vehicles in their "blind spots," or the ability to warn them if oncoming traffic is approaching too rapidly, or is on the wrong side of the road. The use of enhanced imagining will assist drivers to "see" through fog by defining the lane markers on the road. Add to that global tracking, and you have a option most motorists will want in their new 2010 GM, Ford, Chrysler, Toyota, BMW or Volkswagen vehicle — only it will be standard equipment on every car manufactured anywhere in the world. Because, as beneficial as this space-age technology will be to the motorist, it will absolutely essential to a rapidly evolving global government to both monitor and restrict the movements of its society-at-large.

In Japan, the National Police Agency was one of the forces behind the creation of IV/HS. In the United States "...law enforcement authorities...are discouraged from involvement in IV/HS because involvement would generate concerns about invasion of an individual's privacy, for example, using IV/HS to identify traffic violators." (*Clinton White House Health Care Interdepartmental Working Group; Working Paper #1; Box 1748;* National Archives.)

The feeble excuse put forth by the Diebold Group to discourage the "open" involvement of police agencies on the pretext that the objection of the American people would be based on IV/HS being used to identify traffic offenders simply doesn't hold water. IV/HS has been in use as a traffic control tool since 1993 on the San Diego Freeway. Most Californians are already very familiar with the IV/HS system in the "Smart Corridor." Integrated traffic sensors, computers and a variety of communications links disseminate traffic information along the freeway, and from the five major highways leading from downtown Los Angeles to the freeway as well.

Most Americans realize that speed limits are not intrusive, nor do they violate the Constitutional rights of U.S. citizens. No American is going to take up arms against the government of the United States because the police agencies have developed a sophisticated method to identify and apprehend speeders. Controlling speed on the roadways of America saves lives. Everyone clearly understands and expects it — that's part of highway safety. On the other hand, what most Americans will not understand,   417 nor tolerate, is an effort on the part of the United States government to restrict or monitor the free movement of American citizens throughout the country. That is, after all, one of the reasons the Revolutionary War was fought.

Clearly, the universal intent of IV/HS is to provide the governments of the industrialized nations the ability to control all vehicular movement within their borders. Most of the advocates of IV/HS will readily admit this — with a single exception. They stoutly maintain the "control" will be limited to restricting access to roadways that are overburdened with traffic by assessing special tolls during peak traffic hours to reduce congestion.

The public relations hype matches neither the private 1993 White House rhetoric about controlling a population that is too highly mobile, nor the massive amount of funds being committed by both private enterprise and the public sector to implement such a system by the year 2010. Once government possesses the means to control the movements of its population, it will quickly and unilaterally exercise that control. The society that awaits the world in the 21st century will be a rigidly controlled global community governed not by the Constitution of the United States but rather, by the Constitution of the United Nations.

But before any government can successfully restrict the movement of its people, there is one other thing it must do first. It must outlaw the private ownership of firearms.

To more clearly reveal the private mindset of the government with respect to the ownership of firearms — including shotguns, it is necessary once again to refer to the disavowed November 11 protocol.

Clinton, in that meeting, declared that the private ownership of guns of any kind — including replica guns — was not acceptable to him. Neither, for that matter, were swords or knives. In an ideal utopian world, according to the protocol, American sportsmen would be allowed to hunt only in closely supervised federal centers "...where hunters, with scrupulous proof of identity, can rent guns...with the promise of serious felony charges if the guns are not returned." Clinton "...mentions the value of the National Identity Card in enforcing this policy." *(Protocol of White House Conference of November 11, 1993.)*

The Founding Fathers believed the private ownership of fire arms was essential to assure the freedom of its citizens from a dictatorial government. The reason for the inclusion of the 2nd

418

Amendment wasn't because the colonial citizens were redneck "good old boys" or macho militia-types who carried a rack of shotguns and rifles on their plows or wagons as decorations so they could shoot an occasional stray dog or an illegal deer on the side the road. Nor was it so they could, whenever the whim struck them, decorate road signs with close patterns of buck-shot to affirm their marksmanship.

Nor, as you may have been led to believe, was it solely to enable the colonials to defend themselves from hostile "native Americans"—although the risk of attack from hostiles remained a constant threat until civilization pushed the frontier west of the Mississippi River. The Founding Fathers were convinced that the private ownership of guns was essential for the fledg-ling States to defend themselves against the unlikely, but never-theless real, possibility that the central government might some-day attempt to usurp the Constitution and overthrow the sover-eignty of the States. In addition, it was also the Constitutional prerogative of the States to maintain their own militias in order to safeguard against such a threat, unlikely as it may have been.

Every State maintained a citizens' militia that answered only to the State government. The central government had no au-thority over it, and none was ceded by the States.

The Founding Fathers had an inherent mistrust of central government—even the one they had created—for good reason. History had proven time and again that omnipotent central gov-ernments cannot be trusted.

Although each of the American colonies maintained their own militias to protect themselves against random attacks from hostiles, these civilian militias were largely ill-equipped and poorly trained—if trained at all. Prior to 1760 the formation of civilian militias was encouraged by the British government, who believed the colonials should actively participate in their own defense. These militias were not free-wheeling, ad hoc guerilla outfits but were judicatory, albeit temporary, companies within the British army. While the militia could be activated only by the colonial governor, once activated the militia commanders reported directly to the British garrison commander, and took their instructions from him.

The Founding Fathers took great pains to create an orderly society governed by Constitutional law. The militia spoken of in the 2nd Amendment was to be "well-regulated"—in other words,   419 legally established and controlled by law. Clearly, the formation of the militia was the lawful prerogative of the States to protect them against threats to their sovereignty by the central government. Further, the Constitutional mandate that "...the right of the people to keep and bear arms shall not be infringed" was another safeguard against an intrusive central government. It was, after all, "citizen soldiers" — farmers, shop owners and day laborers — who responded when British troops marched on Lexington and Concord, Massachusetts to confiscate the military armaments stored there by Samuel Adams and John Hancock. Had the colonial citizens not possessed arms, the British army would have successfully confiscated the colonial stores of munitions and guns on April 18, 1775, ending the American Revolution before it began.

It is interesting that the issue of gun ownership never surfaced with the English until the British Parliament enacted the *Intolerable Acts* that eliminated many of the "rights" granted to the American colonists and greatly restricted most others. Likewise, the issue of gun ownership — and the alarming growth of the paramilitary movement in the United States — did not publicly surface in contemporary America until towards the end of the Bush Administration in 1992 when FBI agents attempted to arrest suspected Idaho militiaman Randy Weaver.

The federal government's war on the 2nd Amendment, blamed on Bill Clinton by most diehard well-right-of-center conservatives, actually began during George Bush's watch. Granted, in a frightening premonition of an entire series of unconstitutional acts to come, the Clinton Justice Department quickly expanded the "front," first by laying siege to the Branch Davidian compound in Waco, Texas in February, 1993 that resulted the fiery deaths of David Koresh and 88 members of his commune on April 19, 1993; and later, with the federal government's bloodless siege of the 960-acre farm that Montana Freemen called Justus Township, located some 30 miles from Jordan, Montana from March 25 to June 13, 1996.

The Waco fiasco, the tragedy at Ruby Ridge and the Montana Freemen standoff each raise an important constitutional question, since the underlying core issue in each incident was centered on gun control. Advocates of the abrogation of an American citizen's constitutional right to own firearms insist that the circumstances which led to the inclusion of the 2nd Amendment no longer exist:

420

namely attacks from hostile "native Americans." A settled, law-abiding society, they argue, has no need to personally possess firearms since it is clearly unlikely that there will be an Indian uprising in any typical American neighborhood any time soon. Security, they maintain, is amply and equally provided by the government.

As previously stated, the inclusion of the "right to bear arms" clause of the 2nd Amendment had little to do with Indian uprisings. The Founding Fathers learned from experience that the first thing any central government wanting to establish rule by tyranny will do to suppress freedom is disarm the population. A society without the means to fight an oppressive government cannot, for very long, resist a dictatorship.

There exists today a genuine fear within the federal government of the United States that America is close to armed rebellion. That fear is not without merit.

Worried Americans have watched the steady erosion of their Constitutional rights for over six decades. During that same period, the federal bureaucracy has increasingly assumed authority over the lives and lifestyles of the American people, and over the States themselves that it does not constitutionally possess—yet, its intrusion into mainstream America has been consistently upheld, since 1935, by the federal judiciary it created.

The American family has been plagued with steadily increasing taxes which now consume up to 40% of most gross household incomes, forcing wives and mothers into the workplace in order for families to survive. Efforts on the part of citizens groups in several States to enact term limits legislation have been thwarted in the courts whenever such bills have been either successfully passed in the State legislatures or voted for by a majority of those casting ballots in the general elections of their States. The "will of the people" has been, is currently, and will likely continue to be, ignored by the powers that govern this nation since that "will" is, quite simply, at odds with the planned economy of the New World Order and the utopian society of the 21st century.

That agenda was not formed in secret. Americans, believing the Constitution will protect them from harm, have chosen to ignore or mitigate the global rhetoric, believing our participation in the global community will be a voluntary partnership with other global

421

trading partners from which we can extradite ourselves if the terms of the covenant are found not to our liking. Sadly, this will prove to be a tragic miscalculation. The dye is already cast and the wheels are in motion. All that remains is the final dissolution of an archaic document called the Constitution of the United States.

Since the Roosevelt years, or more precisely, from the ushering in of the Great Society, the understanding of what social democracy in America really means has ever so slowly drifted to the left. This has happened because the original intent of the Constitution has become shrouded behind the philosophical veil of social justice and the liberal's ever-changing view of what democracy means, and whose rights are to be safeguarded. No longer is the Constitution a clear and unambiguous document that protects all Americans equally and without bias under the rule of law. Today, even the legal reasoning of the judiciary seems clouded as the Supreme Court searches for new societal meanings in old legal precepts.

To arrive at what may best be described as politically correct legal rulings, the high court has initiated the practice of "coupling" clauses and amendments to reinterpret the original intent of the Constitution for which there is no constitutional basis. When there are no legal points to be gained from "coupling," the original meaning is simply reinterpreted on the grounds that the Constitution, like society itself, must evolve to survive.

Democracy floats in a sea of socialist rhetoric as the courts debate to what extent, and for what purpose, democracy still exists. Clearly, the visionary democracy of the Republic has vanished, usurped long ago by those who desired to weaken the power of the various States over the central government. Gone also is the freedom of the 1940s and 50s, which now lie buried under the tombstone of the greater "socialist freedoms" of the 1960s and 70s.

Democracy still exists in America, but it is an epistemic democracy — pragmatic in nature, political in scope, and grounded in new theories of implied equality. It is a democracy in which politically correct rhetoric forms public opinion, and public opinion redefines truth. Reality is no longer pertinent. Only the perception of a fabricated reality matters since the entire constitutional issue and the relevance of the Constitution itself has become the defining intellectual debate in America.

The erosion of the Constitution as the defining principle of legal positivism in America must be laid at the doorstep of socialist judicial activists. The bulk of the destruction, which began with the self-reversals of the Hughes Court in 1935 was perpetuated by the Warren Court which mastered the original art of "coupling" as a means of reinterpreting the Constitution.

The logic for yoking unrelated amendments and constitutional clauses together was defended by liberal jurist John Hart Ely in his 1980 book, *Democracy and Distrust: A Theory of Judicial Review* as a means of enforcing "fundamental values"[3] and, at the same time, eradicating what he viewed as "clause-bound interpretivism." The principle of tethering amendments allows the Justices to apply current moral philosophy to the rendering of judicial decisions. While high-minded in principle, the practice is wrong because it allows, and in fact even encourages, the Court to judicially legislate from the bench — a practice expressly denied them by the Constitution they swore to uphold.

The problem with Ely's theory is threefold. First, the Constitution, combined with its 26 amendments, was written over two centuries. The original document, penned to establish the framework of a government of the people (not of career politicians), was never intended to be the tool used to solve all of the social injustices which are inherent to any society. Those were problems to be solved

---

[3]In Ely's view, according to U.S. Court of Appeals Chief Justice Richard A. Posner, coupling amendments allows federal judges to make constitutional law a vehicle to enforce the ever-changing societal values based on the evolving redefinition of moral philosophy—which Ely calls "clause-bound interpretivism." In Ely's view, when the fundamental values of society shift, the court must be allowed to adjust its judgment based on what society accepts as a "norm," even if the legislature has not succumbed to "populist pressures." The result, in Ely's view, is that "substanative injustices" are avoided, justifying the tethering of laws and amendments. Ely argues "...that the Court, far from acting in elistist fashion with or without the permission as it were of the framers, was making America more democratic by promoting the foundational democractic principles of partipation and representation." Representation, according to Posner, was promoted by identifying minority groups whose interests were unlikely to be weighed sympathetically by representatives drawn primarily from the majority and by forbidding government to place unequal burdens on such groups without a compelling and noninvidious reason for doing so." [*Overcoming Law;* Richard A. Posner © 1995; Harvard University Press; pg. 200.]

exclusively by the States. The central government had no legal constitutional authority to address them. Second, 200 years and hundreds of thousands of pages of legal decisions, judicial interpretations, and case law precedents, have now provided the high court with a virtual cornucopia of coupling devises that is guaranteed to even further muddy the original intent of those who penned the Constitution. And, finally, beginning with Roosevelt's politicizing of the Supreme Court with likeminded New Dealers, every President since has attempted to do the same thing, creating philosophical and political biases where none should ever exist since the Supreme Court is the "court of last resort" in the nation.

America, by failing to exercise its lawful prerogative to impeach high court justices and other federal magistrates who have politicized the bench, has allowed the federal court system to become an instrument for manipulating and controlling the social environment of the United States. Liberalism, under the guise of increasing tolerance and expanding diversity in America, with the stated aim of expiating human rights has, in fact, neutralized the Bill of Rights.

❖ EIGHTEEN ❖

Agents of Change

R apidly becoming the clearinghouse of political debate for all the nations of the Earth, the United Nations was initially the vision of a small group of international bankers and industrialists centered in a half dozen nations on two continents from the seeds planted in the fertile mind of Woodrow Wilson by American socialist, financier and diplomat, Colonel Edward Mandell House in 1915. Even before House, the utopians dreamed of creating a transcontinental government in which all of the wealth of the world would be within their grasp.

Colonel House, who was truly one of the few genuine political enigmas of the 20th century, mysteriously appeared from the closet of history to influence the thinking of two American presidents: Thomas Woodrow Wilson, who brought the League of Nations to life but could not convince America to join it; and Franklin Delano Roosevelt, who converted the weak and ineffective League into the United Nations that is now preparing, through subterfuge, to politically overwhelm all of the nation-states of the world.

The dilemma facing the utopians who had employed Colonel House to plant the seed of globalism into the fertile minds of both Wilson and Lloyd George was how to alter public opinion in America sufficiently enough to bring about a peaceful transition from nationalism to globalism — something that necessarily had to occur before any meaningful form of world government could be implemented.

Just as the faceless international banking cartel learned by trial and error that they would have to remove the States from the equation of national governance in order to create a tamper-proof central bank in America, the equally faceless power barons — the super-wealthy transnational industrialists and the equally rich former nobles of Europe, whose power had been stripped from them by the democratization of Europe — were also

425

quick to realize that world government could not be successfully established until the American people were thoroughly indoctrinated in the utopian principles so adroitly expounded by the
League of Nations Charter that they would willingly surrender
their sovereignty to a world governing body in exchange for the
promise of peace and prosperity for all time.

Admittedly, it would prove to be a herculean task. In our Republic the people, not the government, are sovereign. Under the
League of Nations — and the United Nations — the governing
body, not the people nor the individual nations, is sovereign.

In 1919 America stood united against Wilson's brand of internationalism. Had either Teddy Roosevelt or Taft been elected
in 1912, it is very likely that America's view of globalism would
be quite different today. Likewise, had Hoover been re-elected
in 1932, and Franklin D. Roosevelt remembered only as the handi-
capped former governor who ran on the Democratic ticket that
year, America would be a much stronger Constitutional democracy today because the Rooseveltian programs that drained the
States of power would not have been legislated.

T he vision of world government did not die with the 49 to 35
Senate vote against the ratification of the League of Nations
charter that was buried in the Treaty of Versailles in 1921, although the plans of the globalists were thoroughly eviscerated
without the participation of the United States.

America's rejection of the League of Nations put the globalists in a quandary. The League could not initiate its globalist
plans of a one-world government without the United States, nor
was it strong enough militarily to force its will on America. From
a financial perspective, the League needed the contributions of
the wealthiest nation in the world to fund its grandiose social
agenda.

The League of Nations was, from its birth, a weak and ineffective multinational fraternity that lacked the military or economical clout to curb civil disputes, or to protect its weaker members from attack from their more powerful neighbors. By the
time Germany came under the steel grip of the Nazis, the League
had lost every trace of prestige and global influence.

The world changed radically during the first three decades of
426   the 20th century. A new dynamic effused from the rubble of the

rapidly collapsing British Empire in the form of a virtual pancopia of independent third-world nation-states. Colonialism, the umbilical cord to the grandiose global-nations of the past century, was abruptly severed with the surgical scissors of Marxism.

One by one, the colonial dynasties of the 18th and 19th century world powers disintegrated. The League of Nations, due to its plenary structure, offered the former colonial powers the opportunity to regain some semblance of that former glory. However, because the most powerful military and economic force in the world rejected it, the League of Nations remained a paper tiger for its entire 26-year existence.

With their immediate plans for world government temporarily shelved, the globalists embarked on a new course of action, focusing on new angles of attack against the globalphobes. Although the arsenal of the globalists has greatly expanded over the ensuing decades, one weapon is preferred. It is a long-term strategy since the globalists were forced to acknowledge that world government would not happen overnight. It was aimed at educating both the electorate and those who represented them in the seats of government. The focus was on "educating" the children of America — the future generations of voters — on the benefits of world government.

The instrument used by the globalists to subtly brainwash America was created by an act of Congress. Prior to 1906, school teachers in America were represented by the National Teachers' Association, a "union" created in 1857. The NTA flourished until it was superseded by yet another union with a "non-union" name in 1870: the National Education Association. While the NEA, prior to 1906, was largely focused on advancing teachers' causes, it was equally committed to the improvement of both traditional education and traditional values in America. Marxism would not begin to creep into the NEA and the classrooms of America for at least two more decades.

While documentary evidence in the form of letters, diaries or sworn statements does not publicly exist to support the author's contention, clearly the "invisible" force that steers the engines of State had already realized that to change the philosophical direction of any nation over a long period of time, it is necessary first to control the minds of its children. Logic suggests this 427 awareness actually existed in 1906 because during that year the NEA, which had existed as a legal corporation since 1870, was incorporated by Congress, becoming the first official NGO (non-government organization) in the United States.

Most Americans—liberal and conservative alike—view the NEA merely as an extremely powerful teachers' union and lobbying force without any patriarchal link to the federal government other than in the form of federal grants. In reality, the NEA was chartered, and funded, by the federal government of the United States to create and manage a uniform government-approved national curriculum. The NEA would be the instrument the powers behind the government would use not only to educate, but to indoctrinate the offspring of America. And, America's parents, eternally vigilant and forever suspect of the motives of its overly-intrusive federal government, were none the wiser.

NGOs like the NEA and the Council on Foreign Relations, as well as those that would later be created by the UN, would play key roles in reshaping the opinions of Americans over the next six decades with respect not only to globalism, but with societal issues and national policy as well.

Colonel Edward House, like Morgan, Rockefeller, Rothschild and the other transnational bankers, industrialists and the former nobility of Europe who struggled so hard to create the League of Nations recognized that their failure was a direct result of American isolationism. It was a puzzling paradox. The Progressives in the eastern and midwestern United States, as well as the Populists in the west, supported both the creation of the Federal Reserve and the direct election of the U.S. Senate. They supported America's entry into World War I, and what they believed would be the Americanization of post-war Europe.

Yet, they were opposed to further American involvement in Europe—particularly when it came to the issue of a world parliament. For them it was not an issue of national sovereignty—it was simply a repudiation of Europe. America blamed Europe for the loss of American lives during the war. Most Americans believed that the only way the nation could be certain that it would never again be dragged into another European conflict was to divorce itself from that continent.

Although isolationism and an enhanced nationalist pride became the vogue throughout the entire decade of the 20s, there was still much division on the subject throughout the nation. Although a minority view, there were those who believed, as did Wilson, that the United States had a golden opportunity to bring an American version of democracy to the world.

In the final days of his association with the Wilson Administration, House shuttled back-and-forth across the Atlantic, speaking with government figures, bankers and business leaders. The League of Nations, as far as the United States was concerned, was dead. The purpose of House's transcontinental meetings was provide the European globalists with some insight into the minds of those Americans whose opinions they needed to sway to make world government a reality; and to help formulate the massive, decades-long public relations campaign that would be needed to re-shape public opinion in America about the merits of world government. From those clandestine meetings, the Royal Institute of International Affairs and its American counterpart, the Council on Foreign Relations, were born.

Until the mid-1960s the Council on Foreign Relations was a largely invisible political think tank of liberal policy wonks whose name did not trigger any raised eyebrows from conservatives, most of whom had never heard of it. Or, if they did, they thought the CFR was merely an agency of the State Department. America would not shed its political naivete about globalism until Jimmy Carter descended on Washington—even though America had lost its trust of its political leaders during the Nixon years.

In 1966 McMillan & Company published a voluminous 1,348 page work entitled *Tragedy & Hope: A History of the World In Our Time* by liberal Georgetown University history and political science teacher, Dr. Carroll Quigley—the man who Bill Clinton had said, more than anyone else, influenced his political perspective. When he accepted the Democratic Presidential nomination at Madison Square Garden on July 16, 1992, Clinton credited his success in the political arena to two people: former President John F. Kennedy and Quigley.

Quigley, an avowed globalist and a Professor of History at Georgetown University clearly described (in an August 9, 1927 *Chrisitian Science Monitor* article that covered an address Quigley made to the World Federation of Education Associations in Toronto, Ontario) the CFR as an organization created by and for   429

"...J.P. Morgan & Company in association with the ...American Round Table Group..." The CFR, Quigley declared, "...grew up in the 20th century [as] a power structure between London and New York which penetrated deeply into university life, the press, and the practice of foreign policy...The American branch of this English establishment exerted much of its influence through five American newspapers." The newspapers Quigley cited by name were the *New York Times,* the *New York Herald Tribune,* the *Christian Science Monitor,* the *Washington Post* and the now defunct *Boston Evening Transcript.* (*Tragedy & Hope:* A *History of the World In Our Time;* Carroll Quigley © 1966; The MacMillan Company; pg. 953.)

First, as a CFR insider, Quigley was privy to the inner workings of that organization. Second, in writing about it, he exposed it for the world to see in his book *Tragedy & Hope: A History of the World In Our Time,* Quigley, like Woodrow Wilson—who was exposed to the invisible power in 1911 and described it in his own book—was mesmerized by the raw power he witnessed. Convinced that these powerful men held the key to the future peace and prosperity of the world, he felt obligated to share both their vision and their agenda with his fellow man.

However, unlike Wilson who merely referenced the existence of this powerful group, Quigley named names—and placed each within the invisible power structure, defining the roles each played not only in their day-to-day activities, but named each member's role in the reshaping of the world order.

Through *Tragedy & Hope,* Quigley becomes a tour guideof the CFR as it came under fire from Tennessee Congressman B. Carroll Reese in 1953. America was a nation transformed in 1952. Everything and anything communist was repugnant. Isolationism was once again the rule of the day. It was the age of communist-hunter Joe McCarthy. During that period, Eisenhower's Attorney General, Herbert Brownell, Jr. revealed that President Harry S. Truman, knowing that CFR member Harry Dexter White was a Russian spy, promoted him from Assistant Secretary of the Treasury to Executive Director of the U.S. mission to the IMF in 1946. Congressman Harold Velde, Chairman of the House Un-American Activities Committee subpoenaed the ex-president to testify, but Truman ignored the summons. [*Tragedy & Hope: A History of the World In Our Time;* Carroll Quigley © 1966; The McMillan Company; pg. 991.] McCarthy attacked Truman for ignoring the subpoena; but most of all, McCarthy attacked the CFR and its British counterpart, the *Royal Institute of International Affairs*, as a communist "front" whose aim it was to obliverate national boundaries and establish a communist, one-world government.

The Republican platform at the GOP Convention of 1952 promised to repudiate any secret "understandings" with the Soviets which would aid the communist "enslavement" of mankind. It also agreed not to enter into any political arrangements that could lead to world government—the core mission of the CFR since its creation in 1921—since such arrangements were suddenly viewed as antithetical to America's best interests.

White, whose NKGB code name was "Lawyer," was viewed by Moscow as one of the most promising agents in America because of his position in the American government, and his ideological beliefs—and because he was one of the few known commuunist sympathesizers that Truman did not jettison from his administration after the death of Roosevelt. (*The Haunted Wood;* Allen Weinstein and Alexander Vassiliev © 1999; The Modern Library, pg. 157.) With the death of Roosevelt, the Soviets recalled their Washington station chief, Anatoly Gorsky—and with him their entire "spy" corp in Washington—and replaced them with one man, Grigory Doblin. Doblin was sent as a diplomat, and used the Soviet Embassy as his cover. Doblin's job was to cultivate old acquaintances to find out how many, if any, of them still viewed themselves as "Roosevelt Democrats," and were still willing to "meet" with Soviet officials. On Doblin's short list of "old friends" to contact were a few former Executive Branch officials, a handful of Congressmen, former Roosevelt aides Henry Wallace and Harold Ickes—and the Council on Foreign Relations. (*ibid;* pg. 289.)

In July, 1953 the 83rd Congress formed the *Reece Committee* and launched an investigation not only of the CFR but every tax-exempt trust and foundation in the United States. The investigation was instigated after Reece, and likely McCarthy, tracked the movements of known communists like White and Whittaker Chambers—first through Alger Hiss, and from Hiss, through the Carnegie Endowment to the Morgan Bank—and through the Morgan Bank into a complicated network of interlocking global tax-exempt foundations (*ibid,* pg. 954-55). But, what startled Reece most was that from the foundations, the link reached some of the nation's most powerful mainstream newspaper, including the *New York Times*   431 and the *Washington Post* – two of the loudest voices of socialist liberalism in America.

The media, it appeared, was serving as a shield that either ignored "negative press" linking the foundations and major trusts to known communist agents; or, it successfully spun the stories to make the foundations and their benefactors appear to have been duped by the communists who manipulated the foundations and "...misused the power of the international financial coterie." (*Tragedy & Hope: A History of the World In Our Time;* Carroll Quigley © 1966; The McMillian Company; pg. 954.) According to Quigley, "It soon became clear that people of immense wealth would be unhappy if the investigation went too far...in terms of votes or campaign contributions." (*ibid;* pg. 955.) In 1954, the Reece Committee quietly, and without any fanfare, issued its report on left-wing tax-exempt associations and their subversive, communist-aided, activities to create world government.

Shortly after the release of the *Reece Report* – which did everything it could to mitigate the roles of the "financial coterie" that filled their campaign war chests – Congress took its wrath out on the "messenger." In December, 1954, Congress censured McCarthy. Leading the charge against McCarthy was the rising star of the Democrats, Texas Senator Lyndon B. Johnson.

As liberal Democrats in both the House and Senate were threatened with the loss of financial support from angry canpaign contributors if all the communist conspiracy nonsense sparked by McCarthy in 1948 didn't stop – and stop quickly – they, in turn, "...badgered Johnson relentlessly to launch a Democratic counteroffensive. Aware of the danger of taking on McCarthy too early, Johnson resisted. 'If I commit the Democratic Party to the destruction of McCarthy,' he told his friend William S. White, 'first of all, in the present atmosphere of the Senate, we will all lose and he will win. Then he'll be more powerful than ever. At this juncture, I'm not about to commit the Democratic Party to a high school debate on the subject, "Resolved, that communism is good for the United States," with my party taking the affirmative.'" (*The Walls of Jericho: The Struggle For Civil Rights;* Robert Mann © 1996; Harcourt & Brace; pg. 137.)

No sooner was the *Reece Report* duly buried without a wake than the media began to hammer McCarthy in an attempt to dilute his popularity with the electorate. No longer was McCarthy the patriotic crusader ferreting communist infiltrators from every corner of government, from the colleges and universities where they were indoctrinating the youth of America, and from Hollywood where they were subtlely brainwashing movie-going audiences with subtle socialist messages. McCarthy was now an ogre who "...unjustly ruined many lives and brilliant careers...[with the]...smear of 'guilt by association'." By the time the media finished their smear campaign, McCarthy was ajudged guilty of "...pander[ing] to the resentment of the less well-off against the privileged...[because] McCarthy declared that the traitors were not found among the poor or minority groups, but among those who have had all the benefits." (*A History of the World Within the 20th Century;* J.A.S. Grenville © 2000; The Belknap Press of the Harvard University Press; pg. 510.)

When the McCarthy hearings began, crowds of McCarthy supporters from all over the United States appeared. Many carried picket signs denouncing both Congress and communism. In the end, McCarthy was censured. And, even though the Wisconsin Senator attempted to pick up his soiled mantle and continue his fight, he was blocked at every turn by the same Congressmen and Senators who had championed his cry only a year earlier before the red trail led through the Morgan Bank to the "financial coterie" at the pinnacle of power.

D isgusted with the congressional coverup — or "downplay" of the role of the tax-exempt transnational trusts and foundations in the *Reece Report,* the Committee's general counsel, René A. Wormser, issued her own report four years later in book form: *Foundations: Their Power and Influence.* But, without the support of the mainstream publishing community, or solid reviews from mainstream newspapers, Wormser's book was largely viewed by the public as just one more spiteful, rightwing conspiracy book that was more fancy than fact.

While the CFR stoutly maintains that its sole purpose for existing is to provide America with a steady,ever-ending stream of scholarly literature that deal with the political and social issues which face a rapidly shrinking world, conspiracy writers have long insisted that on November 25, 1959 the CFR published a white paper called *Study No. 7* that actively encourages dissidents to create whatever social and economic upheaval is needed to draw all of the nations of the world, including those in the

433

former Soviet bloc, into a single economic and political confederation.

Publicly, the CFR claimed it sought only to inform, but not necessarily to influence, American public opinion. In point of fact, the opposite is true. The agenda of the CFR has always been to "sell" the intellectuals who were teaching the youth of the nation in the colleges, universities and primary schools of America (as well as the opinion-shapers in the local communities), on the benefits of world government. It was a grassroots effort with malignant intent.

Today — as it was in McCarthy's heyday — the CFR membership roster is a venerable *who's who* of elite globalist leaders not only in government, but also in business, industry, finance, communications, the media — and the judiciary. Because typical CFR members represent such a broad and diverse cross-section of domestic views, they cannot easily be labeled or identified. Ideologically, many politicians who are viewed as domestic liberals are, in reality, nationalists; and many who take the conservative high ground on domestic issues are globalists. In other words, being a globalist or a nationalist has nothing to do with political party affiliation.

George Bush, mentioned earlier, who inherited the Reagan mantle of conservatism, and who personally championed many 1st and 2nd Amendment issues during his presidency, is an avowed globalist. Conversely, many social liberals like Senator Robert C. Byrd (D-WV), who have consistently voted to expand the welfare state, are flag-waving constitutionalists.

The media-hyped watershed issues which usually consume the bulk of the political debate in America — abortion, homosexual rights, welfare, crime and violence, and expanded health care rights are admittedly issues that will continue to remain on the centerstage as the 21st century unfolds. But, each of these advocacy issues are merely well-staged, well-fabricated smokescreens — albeit serious and very real problems — created by those who actually determine what "issues" will be important each political season. These agendized issues are then hawked by the media in order to promote the "politics" of particular candidates while carefully concealing any abhorrent philosophical ideologies those candidates might possess — such as a predisposition to surrender the national sovereignty of the United States to the United Nations.

434

Anyone who doubts the validity of that statement need look no further than the 1996 Presidential campaign season. The underlying issue throughout the 1996 race was the character of Bill Clinton. Clearly the American people, even those who honestly believed the Clintons were being unjustly maligned by conservatives, wanted the character issue on the table. They wanted to see the tangible evidence from which the allegations of wrongdoing arose that would either confirm or refute from the charges that had dogged Clinton almost from the moment he announced his candidacy for the White House in 1991.

Yet, both Republican Presidential contender Bob Dole in his first televised "debate" with Clinton, and veep running mate Jack Kemp in his only TV appearance with Vice President Al Gore, made it quite clear that *character* — their only chance to win the White House in 1996 — would not be an issue in the election. It was not until the last few days of the campaign, when he was trailing by some 10 to 15 points, that Dole brought "character" into the race, closing the gap between them to between 2% and 5% on the eve of the election.

Why was "character" not an issue in the 1996 race? Because it wasn't supposed to be. If "character" had been the defining issue in that campaign, hindsight clearly indicates that Clinton would have been repudiated by the voters and Bob Dole, the man nobody wanted, would have been elected the 43rd President of the United States.

W ho decides what core issues will be debated each year? If we do not pick the candidates who will seek our votes, who does? Most Americans, particularly those who have been engaged in advocacy issues, or have campaigned for the candidates offered by their political party, will immediately dispel as myth the notion that such a contemplation has any reasonable standing.

Yet, it does.

The social issues that have come to the forefront of the political debate in America over the past fifty years or so did not surface from a festering American groundswell. The "groundswell" was media-created to coincide with a concept or program which had already been agendized.

Abortion, the most controversial advocacy issue in America, is the best example to cite since most feminists believe abortion-   435 rights was a home-grown issue even before *Roe v. Wade/Doe v. Bolton* found its way into the United States Supreme Court.

The grassroots abortion-on-demand movement gained real life in October, 1963 when British jurist Granville Williams argued the concept before the Abortion Law Reform Association in London. The ALRA quickly rejected his proposal. Williams' crusade for universal abortion-on-demand was a movement without legs because abortion was clearly recognized, even by its staunchest advocates, as murder. The idea that women should be allowed unrestricted access to abortions based on their personal desire was just beyond their comprehension.

The view of the American judiciary, as well as the public's perception of human life prior to 1973, coincided with the published view of the United Nations in its 1959 document, the *Declaration of Human Rights* in which the following statement was contained: "...The child, by reason of its physical and mental immaturity, needs special safeguards and care, including appropriate legal protection before as well as after its birth."

However, on April 22, 1970 as the world celebrated its first *Earth Day*, the UN's official position on abortion was undergoing a radical change. The about-face on abortion would initially go all but unnoticed by the public, but George Gallop of the Gallop Poll seemed well-advised that a major shift in public opinion was in the making—and that his organization was playing a key role in shaping it.

Between 1962 and 1969 Gallop, funded by the Rockefeller Foundation, polled the country four times to determine its position on abortion. Asked if they approved of abortion as a means of terminating an unwanted pregnancy, the respondents of the 1962 poll repudiated abortion by 91%. In the 1965, 1968 and 1969 polls, a majority of Americans consistently opposed abortion as a means of "family planning." Asked if they approved of abortion as a solution to economic problems, 74% voiced their opposition in 1965. However, by 1969 after a seven year media blitz on the "population explosion" that was depleting the world's natural resources, the disapproval rating dropped to 68%. (*The Zero People: The Right to Life*; C. Everett Koop © 1983; Servant Books, pg. 62.)

In June, 1972 Gallop changed the question. The poll now simply asked if abortion should be a private matter between a woman and her physician. Nothing more. Some 67% of those sampled indicated it should. Without asking those polled whether they believed abortion was right or wrong, Gallop announced to the nation that "...two-out-of-three Americans now favored legalized abortion." They didn't. They simply believed abortion should be a private matter between a woman and her doctor, not the lead story on the evening news. Their personal views on abortion had not changed. That fact is supported by a Michigan plebiscite held the same year *(ibid;* pg. 63).

In November, 1972, Michigan residents voted on a proposal that would legalize abortions in that State up until the 20th week. The measure was rejected by 62% — almost two out of every three voters *(ibid;* pg. 63).

Clearly the grassroots abortion-on-demand movement in the United States had not sufficiently altered public opinion throughout the "free-thinking" decade of the sixties to cause the United States Supreme Court to justify judicially legislating a *right to privacy* that did not formerly exist, into the Constitution.

Why, then, did it happen?

Was it because the Supreme Court accidently stumbled over a heretofore undiscovered constitutional right? Of course not. Such a right did not exist prior to *Roe v. Wade*—nor did it constitutionally exist up until the very moment the justices voted. That fact is clearly revealed in the majority opinion of the Court itself, when Associate Justice Harry Blackmun wrote: *"We feel that the right is located in the 14th Amendment's concept of personal liberty...* [but it could also be rooted]...*in the 9th Amendment's reservation of rights to the people..."* (*Roe v. Wade;* pgs. 37-38; italics, author.) Quite frankly, Blackmun had no idea where the "right" was located, because such a "right" simply didn't exist.

Over the past two dozen years constitutional scholars have attempted, in vain, to coherently define the constitutional clause-by-clause logic of the Burger Court in order to find a legitimate *home clause* for *Roe v. Wade,* since it clearly didn't fit under the equal protection clause the 14th Amendment.

The language and unambiguous meaning of the equal protection clause of the 14th has not been lost on the constitutional scholars who have attempted to find *Roe v. Wade* a home. Constitutional scholar Laurence Tribe, in *American Constitutional Law,* tried to force the adoption of *Roe v. Wade* into the 1st Amendment, but could not justify it even in his own mind. Liberal jurist and constitutional scholar Ronald Dworkin tried combining the free

437

exercise clause with the equal protection clause, but couldn't justify it, either.

In *Overcoming Law,* a complex and somewhat controversial 1995 scholarly dissertation on legal pragmatism, Chief Judge Richard A. Posner, U.S. Court of Appeals, 7th Circuit, wrote: "...*Roe v. Wade* has been the Wandering Jew of constitutional law. It started life in the due process clause, but that made it a substantive due process case and invited a rain of arrows...Feminists...have tried to squeeze...[it]...into the due process clause. Others have tried to move it inside the 9th Amendment; still others [including Tribe] inside the 13th Amendment, which forbids involuntarily servitude...It is not, as Dworkin suggests, a matter of more the merrier; it is a desperate search for an adequate textual home, and it has failed." (*Overcoming Law;* Richard A. Posner; Harvard University Press © 1995; pgs. 180-181.)

If it has proven to be an impossible task for the best legal minds in the United States to justify *Roe v. Wade,* how could the United States Supreme Court legalize abortion-on-demand? And, why, in the face of such a complete lack of Constitutional mooring, would they do so? Obviously, *Roe v. Wade* was not a constitutional decision—it was a political decision whose time had come.

By the late 1960s the globalists were consumed with a new fear: overpopulation and its related environmental threats. This new threat to mankind was promoted as a time bomb that was slowly detonating in all of the urban centers of the world. America was suddenly flooded with a barrage of articles and books by "population experts" decrying the fact that within 20 to 40 years the world would no longer be able to sustain its own population. At the same time, a rash of articles and news stories also began appearing that claimed, as fact, that the forests of the world were being depleted faster than they could be replaced; and that by the end of the century most of the world's known oil, gas, and coal reserves would also be gone.

While rampant population growth was problematic in places like India, Pakistan and China, as well as many of the emerging third world African nations, there was no "population explosion" in the United States—nor was there in any industrialized nation in the world. Of course, that fact would not be substantiated until December, 1974 when the results of a study done by the Rockefeller Foundation financed Population Council were finally released under the title: *Population and Family Planning*

438

Programs: A Factbook. Statistical data extracted from the report by the Office of Population Research at Princeton University stated: "Of the 31 countries that are usually listed as highly developed, 21 now have birthrates below replacement."

While the population growth rates were higher in most of the underdeveloped or economically distressed nations of the world where birth control devices were virtually nonexistent, the statistics cited by the UN that triggered the panic were grossly exaggerated. The UN concluded that the population of the world would exceed 16 billion by the end of the 21st century.

The funds needed to study the "population time bomb," the devastating affect people had on the ecology, and man's careless destruction of his own environment were supplied by the Rockefeller Foundation. At the same time, the Rockefellers contributed handsomely to other organizations that were dedicated to curbing population growth. Among them was Planned Parenthood. An August 10, 1975, *Washington Post* article on the subject noted that the Ford Foundation and General Motors had devoted considerable financial resources to the "problem" of population control.

In 1968, a small but very elite group of international industrialists, bankers, economists, and various government bureaucrats who expressed concern over the peripheral environmental issues caused by over-population, formed an organization that would become known as the Club of Rome. Spearheading the formation of the organization was the Rockefeller Foundation. From the onset, the world's attitude on abortion—or at least that of its governments—changed dramatically. Abortion would quickly become an essential tool in the globalist's efforts to control population growth.

The Club of Rome's influence on the UN was immediate. In 1972, its first book, *The Limits to Growth,* called for the creation of a world forum on population and environmental issues where statesmen, policy-makers, and scientists could discuss the creation of a global environmental system without being hamstrung by formal, time-consuming intergovernmental negotiations. The ink on its pages had barely dried before the UN issued *Resolution 2997* calling for a Conference on the Human Environment in Stockholm, Sweden. From 1972 until the present day, every UN Conference has advocated the need to control population through abortion.

While most Americans accept their "constitutional right" to an abortion as the result of an American grassroots initiative, clearly it was not. Frightening is the as yet unanswered question: why did the U.S. Supreme Court, on January 22, 1973, legislate into the Constitution of the United States a UN decree mandating abortion rights when there was no legitimate constitutional provision for them to do so? Can the invisible power that intimidates every world leader reach, so easily, into the highest court in America? If so, who protects us when the invisible power decides the enfeebled, the chronically ill, or the unemployed, are too much of a burden on society to continue to exist because they do not contribute to the economy that is forced to support them?

Clearly, the average American citizen doesn't pick the issues which gravitate to the political forefront. If they did, the political debate would be centered on taxation, a reduction in government and government spending, the strangulation of the Bill of Rights, and a return to the concept of "citizen" legislators through the enactment of term limits for all of the entrenched politicos—regardless of their political party affiliation.

That is not to suggest that real, non-agendized American grassroots issues do not surface from time to time. They do. However, they seldom get any meaningful "play" in the mainstream media. The only "legs" many of those issues receive are found on the conservative talk radio circuit or on the Internet. Most of the major issues that America debates are carefully selected and thoughtfully agendized by a handful of special interest groups—after they are meticulously laundered and starched by the media to prepare those "issues" for consumption by the American public.

Far too often the framework of the government-initiated programs that need to be implemented to solve the issue-related problems raised by special-interest groups, were created before the *problem* became a problem.

The task of defining and agendizing the relevant social, economical, environmental and ecological issues—as well as establishing the framework of the solutions—falls today on the quasi-official non-government organizations [NGO]. In the first half of the century, before the myriad of UN-created NGOs existed, it was a task that fell largely on the Council on Foreign Relations, which was created solely for that purpose.

The Council on Foreign Relations has, on many occasions, been called the "shadow government" of the United States for good reason. Very little happens politically, or has happened politically over the past eighty years in this country, that was not first blessed by the CFR.

Former Massachusetts governor Michael Dukakis lost his bid for the White House long before election day in 1988. The CFR, which traditionally backs "liberal" candidates like Bill Clinton, put their money that year on "conservative" George Bush. Bush had the "right" political credentials: he was the vice president of one of the most admired Presidents in the history of the United States, he was the former head of the CIA, a former UN ambassador and most of all, he was an avowed globalist with memberships in both the CFR and the Trilateral Commission. Bush, in successfully forging the first cohesive UN coalition between historic enemies legitimized the phrase *the New World Order*.

Bush was, in fact, the first major concession California governor Ronald Reagan made to the CFR in order to become the 40th President of the United States in 1980. Bush was the person they had picked for the job that year.

Ronald Reagan was convinced that the Council on Foreign Relations was the driving force behind the movement to create a global government headed by a group of very powerful international bankers and industrialists. That was to be the defining issue in the presidential debate of 1980 and one of the planks in the 1980 Republican platform—exposing the CFR.

And, largely because Madeleine Albright, a longtime CFR member headed the Carter[1] team that negotiated the surrender

---

[1] During the televised political debates in 1976, Jimmy Carter sparred with President Gerald Ford over that very issue since a proposed giveaway of the Canal was already being discussed in some of the more liberal corners of Washington. Democratic presidential nominee Carter explained his position to the viewing audience: "I would never give up complete or practical control of the Panama Canal Zone. But I would continue to negotiate with the Panamaians...I would not relinquish the practical control of the Panama Canal Zone anytime in the foreseeable future." (*Review of the News;* January 25, 1978, pg. 40.) A year later, Carter signed the Panama Canal Treaty. But, true to his word, Carter did not surrender the canal to the Chinese PLA-controlled Hutchinson-Whampoa Company until August, 1999—long after his term of office expired.

of the Panama Canal to Omar Torrijos, Reagan was convinced that the CFR hierarchy was behind the Carter Administration's decision to surrender the Panama Canal to the Marxist dictator so Panama could pay off its $14 billion dollar debt to the international bankers. And, according to one reporter in a position to know, Reagan was also convinced that Jimmy Carter forced pro-U.S. Iranian Shah Muhammed Riza Pahlavi to abdicate in favor of anti-U.S. Shiite Muslim Ayatollah Ruhollah Khomeini due to pressure applied by the CFR.

Only the CFR did not become a political issue in 1980, nor did that issue become a plank in the party platform.

On March 17, 1980 during the Florida primary Reagan was specifically asked if he would allow any members of the Trilateral Commission to sit in his cabinet. Candidate Reagan replied that while he didn't think the Trilateralists were a conspiratorial group, he believed "...its interests are devoted to international bankers [and] multi-national corporations. No," he concluded, "I would go in a different direction." (*Ronald Reagan; American Opinion Magazine;* September, 1980; pg. 99.)

Reagan's different direction was a 180° turn.

When Reagan accepted George Bush as his running mate in the summer of 1980, he also made two other concessions to the power barons. He abandoned his crusade against the CFR, and privately agreed to appoint CFR and Trilaterialists to every key post in his administration. Twenty-eight of the 59 members of Reagan's transition team (those who would both screen and recommend the presidential appointees for the Reagan Administration) were members of the CFR. Ten others were Trilateralists. His transition team recommended, and Reagan appointed, 64 CFR members, 6 Trilateralists, and 6 globalists with combined CFR/TC credentials. Casper Weinberger, Donald Regan and Alexander Haig were active CFR members. (*The Unseen Hand;* A. Ralph Epperson; Publius Press © 1985; pgs. 198, 248. *Silent Coup: The Removal of a President;* Len Colodny and Robert Gettlin; St. Martin's Press © 1991; pg. 89.)

While it appears likely to most contemporary chroniclers of American politics that the groundswell that catapulted Reagan into the White House would have been sufficient without any deal-cutting or backroom concessions with political power brokers to assure the outcome of the election, the average American citizen 442 is privileged only to viewing history from the perspective in which the events studied actually occurred, and not from a perspective of what might have more logically occurred under an entirely different set of circumstances. Those who control the flow of power in Washington and around the globe role carefully weigh every possible political scenario with every potential player and every combination of potential players as they chart the course of the events that will shape our time. They seldom err. No candidate who served his entire term in office since Andrew Jackson has been elected President of the United States without the tacit approval of the power brokers behinds the seats of government.

While it appears so from the perspective of hindsight that whoever ran against Carter would become the 40th President of the United States, Reagan was not assured of an electoral victory in 1980. The notion that Reagan cut a deal to win the White House is clearly supported by the fact that he entered the race as a vocal foe of the globalists within the CFR and the Trilateral Commission who were, at least in his own mind, the cause of Carter's problems. Yet, he personally quashed the movement within the Republican Party to insert an anti-Trilateral Commission plank in the party's platform that year — and then, over the opposition of most of the conservatives in the party, selected the CFR's candidate, Bush, as his running mate.

On September 17, 1980 then Congressman Larry McDonald, on the floor of the House of Representatives, laid the blame for the overthrow of the pro-U.S. Nicaraguan government of West Point-trained Anastasio Somoza by Cuban-backed Marxist Daniel Ortega on the doorstep of the CFR. McDonald declared that the "...policies of this administration...[Carter's]...were deliberately and calculatingly designed to destroy the elected government of the people of Nicaragua and to bring the Cuban-dominated Sandinistas to power."

A few days before McDonald's impassioned speech, Somoza himself spoke out in a book entitled *Nicaragua Betrayed*. In his book, Somoza declared that "...There [was] a planned and deliberate conspiracy in the United States of America to destroy [the] republican form of government [in Nicaragua]...[and that]...the betrayal of steadfast anti-Communists allies places Mr. Carter in the company of evil worldwide conspiratorial forces...[T]his treacherous course charted by Mr. Carter was not through ignorance, but by design." (*Nicaragua Betrayed*; Anastasio Somoza;   443

Western Islands; © 1980; pgs. 227, 291.) Within a matter of weeks of his book's release, Somoza was assassinated.

Even more than the betrayals of Nicaragua and Iran, America demanded an accounting of the Canal Zone giveaway, which a majority of Americans, Democrats and Republicans alike, believe to be the lawful property of the United States—and essential to our national security. Carter, who was now viewed by a majority of Americans as an inept, bumbling small town politician who was completely out of his elements in the international arena, received the full brunt of the broadside from the American public. The CFR and the Trilateralists remained virtually unscathed—except that there was now a growing suspicion of both organizations in places where none had previously existed.

In the end, the forces that Somoza described in *Nicaragua Betrayed* turned on Carter. Shiite militants under the control and direction of Khomeini—who gained power in Iran because of Carter's actions—stormed the American Embassy in Tehran in November, 1979 and took the embassy and its personnel hostage, holding them until Reagan was sworn in as the 40th President of the United States at 12:15 p.m., January 20, 1980.

Carter's popularity dropped to 25%—worse even than Hoover's in 1932. Carter's fall from public grace was completed when Senator Edward Kennedy (D-MA), who was probably the only man in America with a worse national approval rating than Carter, announced he would seek the Democratic nomination for President of the United States.

With rapidly spiraling double digit inflation that was devastating the American economy, Democratic Federal Reserve Chairman Paul Volcker seemed singularly determined to remove Carter from the White House. It appeared obvious, even to a blind man, that with all of Carter's economic and foreign policy problems, the CFR would be backing a dead horse if they placed their chits behind the Carter/Mondale ticket in 1980.

They didn't.

They cut a deal with Reagan.

What makes such a contemplation even more convincing is the fact that Carter, who did not join the CFR until 1983, was clearly the Council on Foreign Relations' choice against Bilderberger initiate Gerald Ford in 1976. The fact that nobody knew who Carter was didn't seem to matter. After all, few people (except those who keep up on the governorships around the country) knew who Woodrow Wilson was, when J.P. Morgan tapped him for the presidency in 1912.

Several "unknowns" have risen from the abyss of obscurity in America, and almost overnight overcame a better known and beat a more popular opponent—most notably was Abraham Lincoln's defeat of Stephen A. Douglas in 1860. But each of those successful candidates for the White House all had one thing in common: the invisible, but very influential, support of the invisible power behind the seat of government.

Carter sought, and was granted, the support he needed from the CFR in the fall of 1973. In fact, on December 13, 1973 the peanut farmer who wanted to be the President of the United States appeared on the popular television program *What's My Line?* and stumped the panel.

Prior to his prime-time television debut, Carter met privately with CFR chairman David Rockefeller in London, England. At the time of their meeting, Rockefeller was clearly recognized as one of the most powerful men in the world. His influence in geopolitics was legendary. In 1973 alone, Rockefeller—who has never held public office—met with 27 heads of state, many times before those heads of State met with President Richard Nixon.

In July, 1964 during a visit to the Soviet Union, Rockefeller met for two-and-a-half hours with Nikita Khrushchev. Publicly, the meeting between the head socialist and the head capitalist was due to the severe Ukrainian drought of 1963, and the need for the Soviets to import grain from the west. Privately it is more likely the talk centered on the fact that Khrushchev had simply outlived his usefulness, based as much on Khrushchev's removal of the Russian missiles from Cuba as the rapidly declining standard of living in the Soviet Union. On October 24, four months after Rockefeller's visit, Khrushchev's colleagues in the Presidium of the Central Committee fired him.

In January, 1974 Rockefeller—who is anything but a Roman Catholic—was granted an audience with Pope Paul VI. Within four weeks, Cardinal Josef Mindszenty, an outspoken critic of the Communist regime of Janos Kadar in Hungary, arrived in Rome. When the primate returned to Budapest he was no longer allowed to speak out against Communism—a right he had earned after years of confinement in a Hungarian prison where he was physically tortured by then Interior Minister Kadar for his religious stand.

Former Senator Barry Goldwater (R-AZ), the Republican standard-bearer in 1964 felt the full wrath of the CFR when he campaigned against Lyndon Johnson's Great Society. Johnson hired Doyle Dane Bernbach, the New York advertising agency to destroy Goldwater, depicting the outspoken conservative as a right-wing radical, trigger-happy extremist who planned to slash Social Security to fuel the military which he would then use to start World War III.

But it would be a Democratic National Committee consultant, Anthony Schwartz, who would forever destroy Goldwater's presidential aspirations—as well as those of any conservative Republican until 1980—when he created an television ad depicting a little girl picking flowers in a summer field that suddenly erupts with the mushroom cloud of a nuclear explosion. Exit Goldwater.

For the rest of his life, Goldwater was remembered as the trigger-happy extremist who almost caused the total destruction of the world. Before he died, Goldwater was able to retaliate at least in part against the CFR and its offshoot, the Trilateral Commission, which David Rockefeller formed on July 23, 1972. In his book, *With No Apologies,* Goldwater declared that, in his view, the Trilateralists intended "...to [create a] worldwide economic power superior to the political governments of the nation-states ...[that they represent]... a skillful, coordinated effort to seize control and consolidate the four centers of power: political, monetary, intellectual and ecclesiastical." (*With No Apologies;* Barry M. Goldwater; Berkley Books © 1979; pgs. 297, 299.)

While Goldwater's detractors viewed his book as merely "sour grapes," Goldwater's opinion was well supported by other writers outside of the United States with no a political axes to grind. The London, England based *Review of the News* carried an article on page 45 of its October 12, 1977 edition that declared: "...International Communism of the Moscow order has many features in common with David Rockefeller's Trilateral Commission—such as undermining the national sovereignty of the United States."

When the Carter Administration began drawing up its plans in 1977 for America's participation in the proposed new electronic global currency based on "special drawing rights" (SDRs) in 1977, Jeremiah Novak, writing for *American Opinion* in its combined July/August summer issue, observed: "The Trilateral Commission's most immediate concern is the creation of a new world monetary system to replace...the dollar as the international exchange..." (*ibid;* pg. 240.) It was, fortunately for America, an idea before its time. It was not, however, a new idea. Its roots were found first in the League of Nations, and then in the United Nations. Today, it is tomorrow's reality of the New World Order—starting with the introduction of the American "international" dollar that will, ever so slowly, replace the currencies of Canada, Mexico and the remaining Central and South American nations, and concluding with the formalization of the Euro as the official currency of Europe in July, 2002. By 2006, the *all-America* dollar, a Federal Reserve note that will monetize the debt of all of the nations in North, Central and South America, will become the official currency of the Americas. During that same period, unified African and Asian currencies will be introduced. All that will remain is to merge all of the regional currencies into a single global monetary unit. That will occur sometime between 2008 and 2010. At that time, the global economy of the global community will be complete.

"Current experience suggests that socialism is not a stage beyond capitalism but a substitute for it—a means by which the nations which did not share in the Industrial Revolution can imitate its technical achievements; a means to achieve rapid accummulation under a different set of rules of the game."

James Robinson
British economist
Marx, Marshall and Keynes
1955

"A general association of nations must be formed...for the purpose of affording mutual guarantees of political independence and territorial integrity to great and small states alike."

Woodrow Wilson
Speech to Congress
January 8, 1918

"Those who exercise power and determine policy are generally men whose minds have been formed by events twenty or thirty years before."

Hugh Trevor-Roper
British historian
From Counter-Revolution
to Glorious Revolution
1992

❖ NINTEEN ❖

The United Nations

Utopian fantasies of a human paradise on earth, a universal society in which mankind lives in harmony not only with one another, but with nature as well, is clearly reminiscent of Adam and Eve strolling sanguinely through the Garden of Eden. Mankind, however, surrendered its Edenic privileges long ago. Just as Nimrod failed in his attempt to build a tower to heaven at Babylon, the utopians among us, encouraged and financed by the world's financial elites whose goal it is to control the wealth of the world, will fail in their lofty effort to create Heaven on Earth. Mankind, because of its inherent greed and egocentric needs, cannot create that which is antithetic to its own nature.

Within the next decade mankind will succeed in creating its grand substitute, a new world order—a global community of government-approved trading partners controlled by a world government that is bonded by a universal Constitution which supersedes the sovereignty of all of the nation-states of the world. With it comes a universal economy and a diverse, multi-cultural system of "social religion" that offends no one while offering a utopian vision of economic and cultural salvation to everyone.

Visitors to the sixteen-acre United Nations headquarters complex at 1st Avenue and 42nd Street in New York are generally impressed with the striking simplicity of the soaring 39-story Secretariat Building, architecturally well-executed in steel and glass. The UN Building was intended, by its design, to reflect the utopian aspirations behind which its creators mask their true goal of world domination.

Unfortunately, the lofty and Edenic precepts of the United Nations do not match the reality of its rhetoric since its private mission is antithetic to its public stance. The UN is, and has been since its ideological inception as the League of Nations in 1919, a socialist world government waiting to assume power.

Franklin Delano Roosevelt began to publicly promote the United Nations in 1942 based on an empirical need to create a more "permanent system of general security." Roosevelt spoke of creating a "union of nations" fashioned after the American system of governance. It would be a flexible association. Unlike its predecessor, the League of Nations, the United Nations would not demand that its members surrender their sovereignty; nor would the UN be allowed to possess a "police force." The alliance would rely on the military forces of its more powerful "partners" — the United States, Great Britain, France and the Soviet Union (all allies at the time) to resolve geopolitical disputes.

Roosevelt's version of world government, like Wilson's, was shrouded in Americanism and the American flag. Both men spoke of a union of nations fashioned in a somewhat constitutional manner, similar to that of the United States. And, where Wilson was driven by an egotistical desire to be the first President of the world, Roosevelt was fueled by a desire to usurp Churchill's role in history.

While Roosevelt, like Wilson, was obsessed with creating the New World Order, Churchill and Soviet Premier Josef Stalin were obsessed not only with the division of Europe, but their relative positions within the political and economic megasphere that would emerge from the chaos of World War II. The CFR, on the other hand, was concerned about the further expansion of colonialism in the post-war world, and the affect it would have on the plans of the globalists to shatter the remnants of the rapidly decaying empires of Great Britain, France, Spain and Portugal. The globalists were convinced there was no room for "empires" in the New World Order.

Neither Roosevelt nor Churchill, when they met off the coast of Newfoundland on August 10, 1941 to establish the framework of what would ultimately become the United Nations, had any idea of the direction United Nations would take, since both came to Placentia Bay with differing views on the organization they were about to create. Churchill clearly recognized Roosevelt's United Nations as nothing more than the League of Nations in a new suit. As such, he fully expected the UN to travel the League's well-ex-

450

plored path to world government, with the same entrenched global bureaucracy still at the helm. The concept of the United Nations was, after all as both of them knew, only so much media hype
conceived more or less to convince the American public that a completely new global peace-keeping organization, one without world
governing aspirations, was being formed.

Roosevelt, who knew the American people would flatly repudiate anything that even smelled like the League of Nations, viewed
the failed League as an entirely European venture, and the United
Nations as an American one. And, while both Roosevelt and Churchill would likely have agreed that the governing principles of the
League failed because the United States, the most powerful military and economic power in the world, refused to join it in 1920;
only Roosevelt sailed to Newfoundland with the conviction that
the UN would likewise fail without the participation of the Soviet Union.

O n Sunday morning, August 10, 1941 the *U.S.S. Augusta* and
the *H.M.S. Prince of Wales* met in the Placentia Bay just off
the coast of Newfoundland. In the seas around the two ships
was a virtual armada of war ships and destroyers. In the skies
overhead, American war planes patrolled. On board the *Augusta*
was Roosevelt. On board the *Prince of Wales* was Churchill. With
them was an entourage of high-ranking military figures and mid-
level bureaucrats.

They met, according to banner headlines in most of America's
newspapers on Friday, August 15 to sign, a day earlier, what the
media called the *Atlantic Charter* – a resolution expressing the
mutual goals of both nations in the post-war world – even though
America would not be at war with Japan for another 107 days.
The document they signed would become the *United Nations Declaration* on January 1, 1942 after being signed by 26 of the governments currently at war with the Axis powers. It would be this
same document, signed by most of the free nations in the world
over the course of the next three years, that would become the basis of the UN, established in San Francisco in June, 1945.

The UN, like the failed League of Nations before it, is historically remembered as having risen from the ashes of world
war. Yet, the frameworks of both organizations were established
long before the first cannons of war in either conflict were fired.   451

Roosevelt's participation in the House dream of world government began in January, 1935 almost two months before Colonel House joined his team of advisors, during the period when Hull, Cummings, and Daniel Roper were unofficially consulting him on the Supreme Court matter.

On January 16, 1935 Roosevelt sent a message to the 74th Congress advocating that the United States agree to adhere to rulings made by the League of Nations' World Court. This was his first step in reversing the repudiation of the League of Nations. Interestingly, the ploy used by Roosevelt to subject America to the terms and restrictions of the League of Nations covenant—a treaty the nation had soundly rejected 15 years earlier—was precisely the same tactic applied by the Clinton Administration in 1998 to implement, by Executive Order, the restrictions of the rejected UN *Global Climate Change Treaty* voted on in Kyoto, Japan resulting from the UN *Declaration on Global Warming.*

In 1935 Senator Hiram Johnson (R-CA) led the charge to denounce Roosevelt's efforts to reinvolve the Senate in the League of Nations and to entangle America in the affairs of Europe. Even Huey Long, Louisiana's capricious Roosevelt-clone, and Idaho's William Borah joined in the fray. The controversial measure quickly made national headlines. Within days, 50 thousand letters and telegrams poured into Washington demanding that America stay out of the League of Nations—and the political affairs of Europe.

The resolution, which had been introduced before the Senate by Majority Leader Joe Robinson had enough support for safe passage. However, when the Senate voted on January 29, the resolution was defeated by a vote of 52 to 42—seven less than two-thirds required for ratification. It was shortly after that vote that Ernest Gruening[2] was asked by Interior Secretary Harold Ickes to call Colonel House. It is very likely that the initial plans for the United Nations, the same animal in a different set of skins, be-

---

2Gruening was a Wilson-era bureaucrat with ties to the Morgan banking interests through his old friend Col. Edward Mandell House. He was also a close personal friend Maine Congressman Owen Brewster and several other Wilson-era Congressmen and, thus, knew his way around the Hill. A well-credentialed liberal, Gruening was given a minor post in the Roosevelt Administration, serving as the Director of the Division of Territories and Island Possessions in the Department of the Interior, where he reported to Ickes.

gan to be constructed by Roosevelt and House at that t ime.

Euphorically, the globalists were already discussing it. Shortly, they would be writing about it. The first notable text on the subject, *Union Now: A Proposal For A Federal Union of the Leading Democracies* was published in 1939. Written by Rhodes Scholar Clarence Streit, who was the League of Nations' correspondent for the *New York Times,* the book was promoted by the Council on Foreign Relations in its magazine, *Foreign Affairs.* Hundreds of copies were donated to various educational institutions throughout America by the Carnegie Foundation. A year after the publication of *Union Now,* Streit incorporated an advocacy group called the Federal Union. On his board would be Frank Aydelotte and William Yandell Elliott who, in 1941, would publish *The City of Man* in which they would argue: "...Universal peace can be founded only on the unity of man under one law and one government...All states, deflated and disciplined, must align themselves under the law of the world-state...when the heresy of nationalism is conquered and the absurd architecture of the present world is finally dismantled."

Elliott, interestingly, was Professor of Government at Harvard University. Not at all surprising is the fact that both Elliott and Aydelotte were also Rhodes Scholars. So was P.E. Corbett who wrote an article entitled *Post War World* as part of the 1942 Institute of Pacific Relations *Inquiry Series* in which he reiterated that "...a world association [of] states may evolve towards one universal federal government...[the process of which]...will have to be *assisted by the deletion of the nationalistic material employed in educational textbooks and its replacement by material explaining the benefits of a wider association...*World government is the ultimate aim, but there is more chance of attaining it by gradual development ...[through]...common economic agencies for advise and control...An economic and financial organization, embracing trade, development and migration...and a central bank. The functions of these organizations...would be to regulate the production and distribution of raw material and food, [and to] control the flow of inter-regional investment and migration." (Emphasis, author.)

What Corbett was describing in 1942 was global totalitarianism. He, and others like him, were cautiously preparing America for the global government that will eventually evolve from the United Nations — which itself would not be born until the guns in Europe and Asia were silenced in 1945.

453

Corbett's totalitarian dream started to become a reality when Congress, in 1993, ratified NAFTA; and the following year, GATT. Both were UN projects that stemmed from the World Economic Development Congress of 1989. If there is any doubt, one need only review a July 18, 1993 issue of the *Los Angeles Times* to see the following comment by former Secretary of State Henry Kissinger concerning NAFTA: "What Congress will have before it is not a conventional trade agreement but the hopeful architecture of a new international system. A regional Western Hemisphere Organization dedicated to democracy and free trade would be a first step towards the New World Order that is so frequently cited but so rarely implemented."

Although NAFTA[3] was actively promoted both by Congress and the White House as a program which would stimulate economic growth and create more jobs in the United States, in reality as most American citizens quickly discovered, the reverse was true. That fact was not lost on those—on both sides of the aisle—who voted for passage. Although Republicans have traditionally voted for "free trade," NAFTA was not a free trade issue—it was an issue of economic osmosis—a concerted, well-devised globalist plan to transfer jobs and personal wealth from the

---

[3]While the Senate Republicans were almost unanimous in their vote on NAFTA, only 40% of the Democrats voted for passage, fearful that they would "anger" the labor lobbies that most needed to get re-elected.

Since the passage of NAFTA—over the protests and threats of both American labor unions and isolationist conservatives like 2000 Reform Party presidential candidate Patrick Buchanan, America is facing an economic upheaval as the devolution of the American free market system continues unabated. What is happening in America at this time cannot be called, by any stretch of the imagination, "business as usual." Both the *Washington Times* and its companion investigative news magazine, *Insight on the News,* constantly monitor the American job market. In the month of May, 2000 alone, American cities lost 17 thousand jobs. As shocking as it seem, America is currently losing between 10 thousand to 20 thousand jobs every month. Over 1.8 million U.S. jobs disappear from the American employment landscape annually. Factories are closed and boarded. Employers leave, taking a portion of the community's tax-base with them as they head south to Mexico, leaving the remaining industries within the community—or those taxpayers within the community who still have jobs—to cover the tax revenue shortfalls caused by the exodus.

United States to its impoverished neighbors to the south in order to raise the standards of living in those countries — at the expense of the wage-earners in the United States.

The same can be said about the UN *Global Warming Treaty*, and for that matter, the attack in 1998 on the tobacco industry by the Clinton Administration. The *Global Warming Treaty*, touted by as an environmental or ecological issue, is actually a jobs issue.

On September 29, 1992 Winston Lord, the former CFR President who served as Ronald Reagan's Ambassador to China before becoming Clinton's Assistant Secretary of State, spoke at a town hall meeting in Los Angeles on the subject of *Changing Our Ways: America and the New World.* Lord admitted that "..[t]o a certain extent, we are going to have to yield some of our sovereignty...[and] some Americans are going to be hurt as low-wage jobs are taken away."

The truth of Lord's statement came as no shock to those Americans, who like 2000 Reform Party presidential candidate Pat Buchanan, has studied the ramifications of NAFTA. It didn't take a Rhodes Scholar to see that American industry, attracted south by the contemplation of paying lower wages, having fewer government regulations to hinder them, and not being required to pay the costly fringe benefits demanded by the labor unions in the United States, would simply move their factories — and their jobs — to Mexico. Only, the jobs that were going south were not "low-wage" jobs when they passed through Brownsville, Texas on their way south. The jobs lost were in the $30,000 to $60,000 per year income range — not your typical "Mickey D" pay scale. Of course, by the time the jobs got to Mexico, they had a "Mickey D" paycheck attached to them. Everyone won except the American wage-earner.

The same type of job exodus, only on a much grander scale, is expected to take place once the *Kyoto Protocol*, agreed upon in Kyoto, Japan by Vice President Al Gore, is implemented. The U.S. Senate, which must ratify all treaties, in a 95-0 vote on the *Hagel-Byrd Resolution*, advised the Clinton Administration not to sign the treaty since it would penalize every industrial nation in the world while exempting 136 emerging nations — and Japan. The *Kyoto Protocol* is a very transparent effort to impose such costly and demanding environmental regulations on every industrial plant in the world that burns fossil fuel, that many of them will be forced to relocate to the exempted nations in order tocompetitively survive.

On March 9, 1998 the *Washington Times* received a copy of an

455

Environmental Protection Agency document which led it, and several House and Senate leaders, including Senators Trent Lott (R-MS) and Jesse Helms (R-NC), to believe that the Clinton Administration was going to implement the treaty without Senate approval. The document claimed that the EPA already possesses the authority, under the existing *Clean Air Act,* to implement the greenhouse gas restrictions mandated by the *Kyoto Protocol* — without Senate approval. Since it already had the authority to do so, the EPA declared, it was simply requesting that the specific language to force electric power plants to reduce their greenhouse emissions by 37% be inserted in the Energy Deregulation Bill that was expected to be voted on in the fall of 1998.

It is difficult for most Americans to accept the fact that their elected officials would implement regulations that would deliberately cause the industries in which they are employed to shut down forever and move their operations to another country. For that reason, it is essential to understand why the transfer of jobs is taking place at this time in history, and why the forced closures of industrial plants in America are sending jobs, by the thousands, to the second and third world countries in Central and South America.

Living in the most affluent nation of the world, we view wealth in terms of financial assets — money, property, and investment portfolios. These are capital assets. Tangible wealth. Prior to the redefinition of wealth in terms of *human capital* by the World Bank in 1996, wealth was measured in terms of capital assets. That is, after all, what we have strived for throughout our adult lives.

Economists have been watching the economic growth of the industrialized nations with growing trepidation for the past two decades. The slow down of the world's economies began in 1973 and continues unabated today. While not obvious to most of us who may be enjoying a better standard of living than we did a decade ago, it is persistently obvious to those in the industrial and banking communities who view growth patterns not from one year to the next, but from one or two decades to the next. Despite the economic expansion of the 1990s, the core economic problems remain.

The problem resides in a $12 trillion shortfall between the production and consumption of capital goods. Historically, the United States has experienced an average annual growth of 3.4% per year since the Civil War. Since 1973 — the year *Roe v. Wade* was legislated by the Supreme Court, our economic growth rate has plummeted. From 1973 to 1993, our economic growth averaged only 2.3%, resulting in a net production loss (those goods not produced because there was no consumer demand) of $4,600 for every man, woman and child in America. This loss occurred even though the workforce was expanding. If our economy continues to grow at the current rate without improving, the production shortfall by 2003 will reach $25 trillion. While America has the capacity to produce the goods, we do not have a sufficient amount of "human capital" to cover this shortfall.

Since January 22, 1973 America has "produced" 39,000,000 fewer consumers who, had they not been aborted, would have been available to buy all of the products our industries didn't produce. Likewise those same consumers do not exist to pay the taxes needed to keep the Social Security fund liquid. Every industrialized nation in the world is now well below population replenishment levels. Because of that, it is easy to see from where the consumers of tomorrow must come — from the underdeveloped, overpopulated second and third world nations. All they require are jobs.

The industrialized nations are now supplying them to the detriment of their own citizens.

In July, 1994 the UN released a Ford Foundation-financed study, entitled *Renewing the United Nations System* in which its authors, both former UN officials, Erskine Childers and Sir Brian Urquhart, repeatedly described the need to "...chip away" at the edges of traditional sovereignty until there was a "...notable abridgement of national sovereignty." They also stressed in their report that the "...gradual limitation of sovereignty [must necessarily to be taken in]...small steps [to achieve a]...trans-sovereign society" in order, one might logically assume, not to awaken the patriotic fervor in the American people who have unwittingly slept through most of the abrogation of their rights under the Constitution.

There can be no sustainable argument levied by the globalists today to deny that their objective is anything less than the complete elimination of the national sovereignty of the American people and the abolition of the Constitution of the United States. The evidence, circumstantial as it is,it is far too overwhelming.

They are not too concerned, however, because they believe they have generated enough momentum to carry the freight train of globalism to its planned destination on time—even if the American people suddenly wake up and attempt to derail it. The railroading of America will remain on schedule simply because the globalists fill over 60% of the elected offices at both State and federal level—on both sides of the aisle. There is not enough time for America to disenfranchise the globalists at the national level and replace them with others who must then, in turn, disenfranchise the United Nations. The merging of the economies of the world is scheduled to take place between 2002-2008. The timeline for the implementation of a trans-sovereign world government, according to a virtual plethora of mainstream newspaper and magazine articles touting the formalization of a cohesive, unified global society, is somewhere between 2004-2012.

Throughout *Renewing the United Nations System* Childers and Urquhart detail the interim strategies which must necessarily be implemented before the world has been effectively transformed into a cohesive global community headed by a single trans-sovereign government. Among these are various global taxes that would allow the UN to fund its own operations and, in a direct contradiction to its charter, raise its own army. Among the contemplated tax levies is an assessment on all oil production, a surcharge on all international arms sales as well as international commerce of all types, and finally, a tax on international travel. Such an international travel tax was implemented by the Clinton Administration shortly after the 1996 Presidential election. Whether the revenues gained from that tax were retained by the Treasury of the United States for its own domestic purposes, or was quietly surrendered to the UN remains unclear.

Clearly, a worldwide tax on travel was an issue prior to the 1996 general elections in the United States. On January 16, 1996 the UN announced it was contemplating the assessment of a global surcharge on international travel to support its sagging coffers.

Instead of demanding to know where the UN gained its authority to tax American citizens and American industries, former Senate Majority Leader Bob Dole (R-KS), the 1996 Republican presidential candidate, responded the following day by declaring that if the UN persisted with its plans for a global travel tax, the United States Congress would have no alternative but to withhold funding from the UN—suggesting by his statement that the UN somehow already possessed the prerogative to tax American citizens. From where did its authority to tax nations come? Certainly not from its charter. The United Nations Charter, as it was ratified, was very specific in this area, since it was a concern of the U.S. Congress when the UN was created. Funding for the UN was to come entirely from the voluntary contributions of the governments of its member States. (Of course, the federal government now insists that the United States income tax is "voluntary" as well.)

In 1996 the UN also proposed the establishment of what it termed a worldwide "one day" income tax, assessed against one day's labor of every employed person in the world. The tax, of course, would be minimal—like the 1% or 2% tax that was proposed when the ratification of the federal income tax was debated in the State legislatures between 1909 and 1913. However, once the legal precedent for a global income tax is irrevocably established it, like the income taxes of every industrialized nation in the world, would rapidly escalate. Of all forms of taxation, an income tax is essential simply because socialism, by its very nature, requires one. *It is the only way an oligarchy can suppress its middle class without bloodshed.*

Proceeds from such taxes, according to the agenda of Habitat II in Istanbul, Turkey in June, 1996, would help eradicate poverty in the third world and provide a quick and effective means of debt relief for the most severely indebted nations—at the expense not only of the American workers but those in the other industrialized nations of the world as well.

The eradication of poverty in the third world will not occur until the transfer of wealth from the industrialized nations to the "emerging" second and third world nations of Central and South America, Africa and Asia has been completed; or until a global income tax has been successfully implemented. In all likelihood, both will occur before 2006.

The working papers of Habitat II reveal the addition of a paragraph that was neither negotiated, nor adopted, by either the working group or the plenary during the third session when the agenda for Habitat II was finalized. Yet, it was this paragraph that became the basis for a vote, by those in attendance, for a worldwide tax.

Interestingly, those who voted in favor of the global tax, while serving as quasi-official representatives of their respective governments, were not official representatives of the UN with State-authorized power to vote on such matters. Most of those voting

459

were members of NGOs and other global special interest groups like the CFR, the Club of Rome, the World Federalist Movement, the Wildlife Federation, and other lesser known entities together with "official" members of most of the world's major Foundations. Many were American citizens who are prohibited by the Constitution from entering into international covenants on behalf of the people of the United States. Such a vote was tantamount to someone asking your ten year old son if they can borrow your car, and then taking it if he says yes — even though he possessed no real authority to loan it.

In each of the following global UN Conferences: Habitat II (Istanbul, Turkey — June, 1996); the 4th Women Conference (Beijing, China — September, 1995) an the UN World Summit for Social Development (Copenhagen Denmark — March, 1995) resolutions for UN authority to assess a global tax were introduced, beginning with the Social Summit in March, 1995. In September, 1995 the matter was reintroduced in Beijing and those in attendance unofficially voted the UN that right. By January, 1996 the UN was trying to determine precisely what type of tax to assess.

The international taxes discussed at the Social Summit included a 0.7% tax on the gross national product of all of the UN member States and a 0.5% surcharge on all international investment transactions. (Since the GNP tax was assessed on the "governments" of the member States [i.e., the middle class taxpayers], those voting had little problem "unofficially" concurring on its implementation. However, because the 0.5% surcharge was to be levied on transnational corporations and not individual people, those voting reluctantly deferred any decision on it to Habitat II.)

The United Nations originally drove its claimstake of sovereign authority where none, from any nation, formerly existed: in the largely invisible world of internationalism — an empery that did not physically exist, but has yet somehow still managed to control not only the national policies but the economic direction of most of the industrialized nations of the world for well over 100 years. This is the invisible world of the transnationals.

It has been a slow, tedious journey, fraught with countless pitfalls, detours, and delays. The objective is in sight. Only one last hurdle needs to be vaulted: the Constitution of the United States. With that final obstruction comes a final question: do the

460

globalists go through it or around it? Two plans of attack are currently being implemented. One is designed to abolish the Constitution as we know it, the other is designed to circumvent it.

To abolish, or radically alter, the Constitution it is necessary to call a Constitutional Convention. In the history of the United States, only one such convention was ever held. If a Constitutional Convention cannot be called, the Constitution can be suspended under a declaration of martial law. That, also, happened only once in our history when the nation was divided over the issue of States rights, and 11 southern States seceded from the Union. Abraham Lincoln declared martial law and suspended the Constitution. For a brief, tragic period in our history the citizens of the United States were not protected by the Bill of Rights. While most Americans dismiss out of hand the possibility that any state of emergency could arise in the United States that would necessitate a declaration of martial law and a suspension of the Constitution and the Bill of Rights, they should understand that all of the mechanisms to do just that have been quietly, and without fanfare, implemented by the Clinton Administration over the past six years. All that is required to trigger those mechanisms is the right, real or perceived, national crisis.

Likewise, most Americans also dismiss out of hand the idea that its leaders could arbitrarily call for a Constitutional Convention for the expressed purpose of abolishing the Constitution of the United States – and be successful in their effort. But then, most Americans don't realize that it already happened once in their history. And, if a Constitutional Convention is successfully called, it will very likely happen again.

Since the nationalists among us have thus far resisted the globalists' bait – a State-initiated Constitutional Convention to reverse the Supreme Court's stance on school prayer or abortion, the globalists did precisely what their 18th century counterparts did to abolish their first Constitution: they called for a Conference of the States to set the wheels in motion.

Since the American people did not snap up either the school prayer issue or the abortion amendment bait, the Council of State Governments, which Republican Utah Governor Michael O. Leavitt was elected to head in 1994, prepared the most tantalizing bait yet: reducing the scope of authority of the federal gov-

461

ernment. On the surface, the resolution which was sent to the governors of all 50 States on December 22, 1994 sounded "conservatively correct." Even the name, "Restoring Balance in the Federal System," had the right conservative tone. So did the names of the high profile conservative Republican participants urged by Leavitt to lend their support to the petition: Wisconsin Governor Tommy G. Thompson, North Carolina Senator Jesse Helms, and Colorado Senator Hank Brown. All of the correct conservative buzzwords were included. Nothing was left to chance.

Conveniently absent from the resolution, however, was an affirmation that this Conference of the States would not be used as a springboard to call a Constitutional Convention. There was also one other red flag: Leavitt, who was elected governor of Utah in 1993, had been appointed by President Bill Clinton to serve on the U.S. Advisory Commission on Intergovernmental Relations—a UN cell group. Leavitt was a globalist.

On the surface, there appeared to be nothing improper about the resolution offered by the Council of State Governments. In fact, if anything, it identified the problem it sought to address very well. But then, so did the bait offered by Alexander Hamilton in 1786 to establish the first privately-owned monopoly of our money.

Although the Resolution sounded harmless enough at a glance, there were several problems with it which were, very likely, the reasons most of the States chose to ignore the Committee's call for a Conference of the States.

Most of America's governors realized that, contrary to all of the political rhetoric denying it, the Conference was being organized explicitly for the purpose of calling a Constitutional Convention.

A Constitutional Convention is called by the States only when a resolve to abolish, alter or amend the Constitution exists. Since States rights were greatly diluted as a result of the first Constitutional Convention, there has been a genuine, overwhelming fear on the part of most Americans to ever allow a second one to take place. Most of the State's political leaders clearly understand that the power behind the seat of government at the national level is not interested in strengthening States rights, nor does it wish to restore balance to the separation of powers.

As Lloyd Cutler so aptly put it in his 1980 *Foreign Affairs*

462   article, the globalists want to completely change, or simply abol-

ish, the Constitution. It is just too troublesome, and it offers the common citizen too many superior rights. [*American Government: Readings and Cases, 10th Edition;* Peter Woll © 1900; Scott, Foreman, Little & Brown; pg. 58-59.] Only by radically restructuring the Constitution can they either eliminate those otherwise inherent rights, or condition them on the revocable whim of government—much as they are in those countries that have adopted the UN's *International Covenant on Human Rights* to define the "rights" of their citizens.

In a May 17, 1995 letter to the governors, Leavitt insisted that the purpose of the Conference was not to destroy the federal government, or to make the States the dominant player in the area of national governance. He didn't lie. His statement, in both respects, was true. It was, however, deceitfully incorrect. Whether it was Leavitt's plan, or the plan of the globalists, is irrelevant. In reality, the end result would be the same.

It was a classic example of "bait and switch."

The ultimate objective of the globalist is to strengthen, not weaken or destroy, the federal government's control of its citizens. In the United States the globalists' dilemma is focused on the remnants of power held by the States. The Conference was, in point of fact, not designed to destroy the federal government but to endow it with even greater authority by either weakening or replacing our existing Constitution with a more up-to-date 21st century global version much like that proposed by Cutler in 1980. The destruction of our current Constitution, or at the very least the modification of the Bill of Rights to make our inherent rights conditional, is necessary for the globalists to achieve their objective.

Therefore, most assuredly, it was not the purpose of the Conference to make the States the dominant player in the sphere of national governance—unless an end-run around the Constitution was needed to meet the globalists' timeline for world government. Again, Leavitt spoke the truth.

Under a utopian UN-styled Constitution, which the globalists hope to substitute for our archaic 1787 version, a new Bill of Rights will be offered that will appear more like the UN's *International Covenant on Human Rights* in which the inherent, inalienable, God-given *rights* of man have been transformed into retractable *privileges* that may be granted or recanted by the government at will. The differences are best viewed by comparing the language of our Bill of Rights with that of the *Covenant on Human Rights*.

"Congress shall make no law respecting an establishment of religion, or prohibiting the free exercise thereof..." (1st Amendment, the Constitution of the United States.) Note first, the Founding Fathers placed all of the restrictions on the government. Of course, somewhere along the road to the toll bridge to Utopia, the meaning of the 1st Amendment has become fuzzy, because now all of the restrictions are placed on the citizen who no longer possesses an inherent right to practice the free exercise of religion. In fact, the Supreme Court now interprets the exercising of religious freedom more in the manner of the privileges described in Article 13 of the *Covenant on Human Rights: "Freedom to manifest one's religion or beliefs may be subject only to such limitations that are prescribed by law..."* For this reason alone any sitting federal judge or Supreme Court Justice who votes in this manner should be impeached and removed from the bench. The Justices are sworn to uphold the Constitution of the United States, not the UN.

The 1st Amendment further guarantees the American citizen the right to free speech when it declares: *"Congress shall make no law...abridging the freedom of speech...or the right of the people peaceably to assemble, and to petition the Government for a redress of grievances."* Article 14 of the *Human Rights Covenant* deftly abridges those rights while appearing to grant them: *"The right to seek, receive and impart information and ideas carries with it special duties and responsibilities, and may therefore be subject to certain penalties, liabilities, and restrictions, but these shall be only as such as are provided by law."*

One need look no farther than the 1st Amendment to see a clear distinction between the quality of freedom guaranteed under the Bill of Rights and that promised by the *International Covenant on Human Rights*. One applies to the individual, the other to a collective society. In our Republican society, each individual has the right to life, liberty and the "pursuit" of happiness. Happiness is not guaranteed — only the right to pursue it is. Man, in a republican democracy, is not guaranteed work, nor is he guaranteed that he will be successful in his economic endeavors. Nor is he guaranteed income parity with his neighbor. Nor does he possess an inherent "right" to expect such "equality."

On the other hand, in the controlled society of the New World Order, equality — in the form of income parity — will be achieved at the expense of the American middle class both through oppressive taxation and the transfer of jobs from the United States to the emerging economies of third world nations where the opportunity for profit-taking for the industrialists and those who finance their efforts is much more to their liking.

While the masters of deceit in the New World Order hide their chicanery behind the politically-correct garb of humanitarianism, it is important to understand that the form of socialism fostered by the United Nations has little, if anything, to do with equality. Equality is the smoke and mirrors rhetoric that conceals the "bait and switch." It is, quite simply, a matter of power — the power of an omnipotent world government to control every facet of life in the global community.

O mnipotence permeates throughout every fiber of the New World Order from the core of the United Nations to its growing international and transnational partnerships around the world. Although world government does not yet exist, the UN is preparing to assume its role as the caregiver of the nation-states of the United Nations when national sovereignty collapses — perhaps as soon as sometime during the next decade.

As Habitat II convened in Istanbul in June, 1996, Wally N'Dow, Secretary General of the UN Center for Human Settlement in a press conference declared: "What we are doing here is building ...the global brain." An explanation of what he meant was found on page 6 of Discussion Document #23, presented by the World Assembly of Cities and Local Authorities during Habitat II. "The UN must help governments at all levels forge and nurture new and renewed intersectoral alliances of public, private, non-governmental and community-based organizations to make a positive difference in the quality of life in human settlements...The need to build alliances with local authorities and NGOs and to draw upon and empower the mobilization capacity of community-based organizations and neighborhood groups in order to address these problems in a holistic way is now increasingly recognized."

Since 1976 the UN has been carefully weaving a global network of "partnerships" that include transnational corporations,

NGOs, individual State governments within the United States, as well as governments at county and local levels[4].

N'Dow, quoted in a May 31, 1996 Habitat II press release, affirmed that the UN member States "...in a historic General Assembly decision, had not only acknowledged the changing role of local authorities in governance, but had, for the first time, accorded them the opportunity to participate in deliberations of Habitat II..." Suddenly the "unofficial" partnerships between the UN and various American State and local officials — ostensibly created for the purpose of sharing concerns and visions for collective humanity — is clothed with the texture of officiousness.

Lest he be misunderstood, N'Dow reiterated his understanding of the official nature of all of the participants, from each of the nations, in attendance during his opening address to the Conference on June 3 when he said: "...It is indeed gratifying that governments, the private sector, *local authorities*, NGOs, women's coalitions, youth, the entire civil society of many nations, banded together in mutually supportive partnerships to forge and successfully advance a very demanding preparatory process..." (Emphasis, author.) (*United Nations Global Business Plan*; Linda Li-

---

[4]While these "working arrangements" between State, County and Local governments and the UN are cautiously and judiciously referred to as "partnerships" in which only "ideas" are exchanged, any "agreement" between an international body (such as the UN) and any agent of the United States—authorized or unauthorized—in which UN agendized physiological, ecological or sociological programs are being implemented in the United States must be construed as a "treaty." As such, these "arrangements" are unconstitutional, and therefore, illegal.

According to Article II, Section 2 of the Constitution, the negotiation of Treaties is a prerogative of the President of the United States, but only with the advise and consent of two-thirds of the Senate—a fact sometimes lost on the White House. Of course, all parties—including the White House—insist these arrangements cannot even remotely be construed as treaties, since no official action is being taken by any member of the federal government. Ishmael Serageldin, a vice-president of the World Bank summed it up for the globalist position in an interview at Habitat II when he said: "...What we are looking for here is not individual agreements to be signed. What we are looking for here is a consensus on the principles that really come together around our shared concerns, our shared vision, and our collective humanity." (*United Nations Global Business Plan;* Linda Liotta; © 1996Americans For America; pg. 20.)

otta © 1996; Americans For America; pg. 20.)

It appears quite obvious that then-UN Ambassador Madeleine Albright, who had characterized the UN as nothing more than "...a business with 185 members on the board[5]," was part of that historic General Assembly decision, and that an end-run around the Constitution had the tacit approval of the Clinton Administration — and the Republican Congressional leadership, which failed to challenge the notion that the UN possessed some "superior" right to negotiate directly with a State, county or municipal government.

Since the Istanbul Conference in June, 1996 Maryland governor Parris Glendening became the first chief executive of a State to introduce a UN Habitat II program into a State legislature, circumventing the constitutional process through which the political agenda of an international body is recognized. On April 8, 1997 the Maryland legislature passed Senate Bills 388 and 389, giving rise to America's first UN-style public/private partnership.

To those who have been watching Maryland politics, it came as no surprise that Glendening would be the first governor to enact a UN-style public/private partnership law in his State since he was also the first United States governor to sign an accord with the United Nations — clearly a questionable, if not unconstitutional end-run around the Constitution of the United States.

On August 15, 1995 the World Health Organization issued a press release announcing that an agreement had been signed between the State of Maryland and WHO that was aimed at "...improving the health of the world's poor."

> "In an unprecedented accord between an international organization and one of the fifty states of the United States of America, the World Health Organization [WHO] and the State of Maryland have signed a three-year agreement to share expertise and experience to improve the health of the world's poorest nations."

Clearly, Glendening, as the governor of one of the 50 sovereign States, stepped outside his constitutional prerogatives in signing what amounted to a "treaty" with WHO. Yet, no angry

---

[5]Quote from the *Washington Times*, "The United Nations We Deserve; July 25, 1996. Albright became Secretary of State for the Clinton Administration when Bill Clinton named his second term department heads in January, 1997.

protest bellowed from the White House. The State Department was not outraged, nor did the media question by what constitutional authority did a State governor sign a binding agreement with an international organization. Was it ignored by the media because Glendening's agreement was *called* an "accord" and not a "treaty"—as *in the Camp David Accord?* Was it ignored by the media because the "accord" ostensibly affected only the State of Maryland? Or, was it ignored by the media because the plan had the tacit approval of the Clinton Administration?

Granted, the States have been involved at that level and below with the UN, and with UN programs, for over four decades. Many Americans proudly recall "trick-or-treating" for UNICEF as they raised money each fall for the United Nations International Children's Relief Fund. Americans, particularly American educators, and through them the children they teach, have been involved in UNESCO programs since that organization's premature birth in April, 1944—over a year before the UN itself was chartered.

Americans have, in other words, been carefully desensitized to the threat of globalism and world government by UNESCO. While the UN is, and always has been, a European enterprise, it is viewed by most people in the United States as American as Chevrolet and apple pie. The media has done its job well. Even though the United States does not have a single senior level official in that body, most Americans still view the UN as an American institution that is responsible for forging the path to peace and global democracy—based almost entirely on the fact that the UN Building is located in New York City.

Unlike most unofficial cooperative ventures between the States and NGOs like UNICEF, the Maryland/WHO Accord links WHO's *Division of Intensified Cooperation with Countries* (ICO) into Maryland's public health database. Promoted as a partnership to share technical expertise in order to improve the health all of the citizens of the world, the Maryland/WHO Accord was actually the initial phase of a global plan to create and manage an international database that would eventually include every citizen in the soon-coming global society of the New World Order[6].

---

[6]Under the *Freedom of Information Act*, Potomac, Maryland-based *Americans For America* secured copies of most of the working papers of the Clinton White House's Health Care Task Force from the National Archives

For that reason, Maryland was selected as the first State to collaborate with the UN on "information management system development." In 1996 Maryland became the first State to activate a government-run computerized medical records database. In accordance with State law, all patient encounters with health care providers are compiled into the database. Patients in Maryland health care facilities do not have the right to deny the State access to that information. A few months after Maryland enacted the first medical database law in the nation, Congress passed legislation creating a clearinghouse for medical records, creating a national computerized medical database into which the States will feed the data accumulated at the local level.

In light of the deliberations that were taking place in the Maryland State Legislature in March, 1997 on Senate Bills S388 and S389, USA Radio correspondent Joan Veon requested an interview with Baltimore mayor Kurt Schmoke, who served as an official U.S. delegate to the UN Habitat II Conference, and was one of the prime movers behind S388 and S389 that were, at that time, pending before the legislators in the State capitol. Veon had previ-

---

in September, 1996. Buried among those papers was a study performed by the *Diebold Institute for Public Policy Studies* that establishes tentative timelines for various events that relate directly to the Clinton agenda with respect not only to universal health care but the creation of an international database on patient history as well and the creation of a high tech global tracking system that will allow the government to closely monitor what Bill Clinton calls, in the disavowed November 11, 1993 White House Protocol, a "...population that is too highly mobile."

Among those papers, mentioned in an earlier footnote, exists the framework for creating an international health records database, ostensibly for the humanitarian reason of providing health care providers, regardless of the location of inquiry, with the patient's full medical history on the grounds that such a database will improve the quality of medical care and reduce costs. Both, on the surface, are logically true.

The Diebold Report continues by saying that our current system provides few opportunities for third-party organizations which provide health care analyses to obtain this information due to concerns about privacy issues and the real threat of information misuse, creating a liability exposure to information providers.

The question at that point became one not only of potential liability,   469

ously interviewed Schmoke for USA Radio in Istanbul. He granted her the second interview in Annapolis on April 1, 1997, exactly one week before *Rural Legacy* and *Smart Growth,* which were the UN-styled public/private partnerships, became law in the State of Maryland.

Veon, a savvy financial services executive when she is not investigating the ramifications of the social, political and economic issues that threaten the security of the Republic, dove into the heart of the matter with her first question to Schmoke: *"Rural Legacy,"* she said, "appears to be a fulfillment of the public/private partnerships spoken about in Istanbul. Is that a correct assessment of what is going on with *Rural Legacy* and *Smart Growth?"*

"Well, I'm not sure about that," Schmoke replied diplomatically, "I think it is probably consistent with the ideas. I'm not sure whether anybody from the State actually looked at what came out of Habitat—the specific documents. But clearly, *Smart Growth* policy is consistent with what was being talked about in Istanbul, and that's why I have been supportive of what the governor is trying to do."

---

but ownership. Who legally owns that information? In exploring the logic of that argument, the Report states: "In considering the deployment of information technology, it is important to recognize that unlike highway transportation...the highway infrastructure is almost completely owned and operated by the public sector, health care is operated very differently in the United States from Japan and the European Community. In the United States, the delivery of health care is operated on a professional, commercial basis..." The report pointed out that in Japan and the European Union, the central governments control the system and can mandate "new approaches."

The Diebold Report, which clearly calls the private sector health care system in the United States a failure, not because 7% of the American people did not have health care in 1992 but because as Drs. Paul Ellwood and Harry Wetzler stated in Diebold Institute Working Paper #8, "...it has been documented that coronary bypass procedures are performed more than twice as often in Boston [Massachusetts] as in New Haven [Connecticut]..." although there is no discernible difference in mortality rates between the two cities. Are they suggesting that doctors in Boston perform too many bypass operations, or that the physicians in New Haven do not perform enough?

470   In any event, the Report addresses the obstacles faced in the United

"How important is it to the people of Maryland?" Veon asked, "And what will it mean?"

"Hopefully," Schmoke answered, "it will mean better planning in the future not only as we look at our population growth, but as we examine our economic development and what kind of impact it will have on our quality of life. If we are able to use our existing resources better and plan for the future, we might be able to preserve some of our natural resources and also improve the quality of family life so that people will be in more village-like settings and also have better planned communities."

The politically-correct rhetoric, dripping with Hillary Clinton "it takes a village" logic was, according to Veon, an almost flawless textbook description of sustainable development, the foundational cornerstone of the UN's Agenda 21 — the environmental program from which Habitat II was blueprinted.

Veon continued: "What are the holdups right now?"

"Well, the holdup is politics — it's politics and tradition. There is a sense that this is a new idea that is in conflict with old traditional zoning and local planning prerogatives. I don't think that it is in conflict, but it takes a while to persuade people that we can come up with a new idea and a new planning strategy that will

---

States with creating a medical information database, comparing those to the obstacles and/or advances in the European system on determining how to decide "...whose authorization is needed to release the various types of information."

Buried in the report was a graph entitled *Deployment of Health Care Infrastructure* in which a timeline for creating an international health care database was charted. (It must be remembered that since the Clinton Health Security Plan failed in Congress, the entire timeline for creating this database has been thrown off.) Between 1992-96, *community-based information utilities* would be established on a test basis. Local physicians were to be paid for each patient's medical history downloaded into the system. Sometime between 1997-2001 the *"...Supreme Court rules that providing information services is not practicing medicine without a license."* During that same period, [r]eimbursement of information charges approved for Medicare and Medicaid," and the "possibility that single payer insurance will be instituted in the U.S." (Emphasis, author.) *That statement is noteworthy since the report is not only predicting what issues will be heard by the high court, but also the judicial ruling that will be issued from the bench.*

Between 2002-06, transjurisdictional licenses will be approved in the United States and Europe. Again, the psychic Diebold Group is prophes-

471

benefit them at the local level. My hope," Schmoke declared, "is that at least part of what the governor is talking about will get through this year and serve as the basis for building on a more comprehensive policy in the future."

"Some people are concerned about personal property rights with growth to be legislated," Veon interjected, adding: "Do you see that as a problem?"

"No," Schmoke answered, "I don't think so. I don't think there is any intention to undermine personal property rights, but I think that like all rights that we have in this country, there has to be some compromise because individual rights run up against collective rights and, in this instance, we are trying to plan for an entire state and some of the individual prerogatives—the local prerogatives—really will have to be compromised to a certain extent in order to deal with the greater good." Schmoke's comment read like a page out of Karl Marx's *Communist Manifesto*.

"Then," Veon asked, "do you see collectivism as the new wave of the future for the 21st century?"

"I would prefer to call it *partnership*," Schmoke replied. "I think that's better—it's *partners in progress*. That's what the governor is trying to achieve, and I support him."

"Public/private partnerships?" Veon shot back.

Schmoke nodded. "Correct," he said. (*Dialogue from transcripts of a taped interview;* supplied by Americans For America. April 1, 1997; Annapolis, MD.)

To grasp the significance of this interview, and the program that was launched in Maryland on April 8, 1997, the reader needs to possess a rudimentary understanding of socialism, and one of its fundamental principles, affirmed by the language of Habitat II. The first plank in the *Communist Manifesto* is the abolition of private property rights. Interestingly, the ninth plank centers

---

izing—probably with extreme accuracy—on actions that will be taken by an Administration two or three national elections removed from the one which retained their forecast. During the same period, another Supreme Court decision, will be handed down ruling that "...patient information [is] co-owned with [the] government insurer."

Diebold's final prophecy deals with the UN, somewhere between 2007-11. "International licensure approved; information utilities interconnected across national boundaries; [and] UN assigned role in regulation of information utilities."

on the forced redistribution of the population into "population centers" where they may be more easily controlled. Both planks were hammered into Agenda 21. Both became part of Maryland's public/private partnership.

To more fully understand and appreciate the significance of the parallels that exist between Communist collectivism and Maryland's *partners in progress,* it is necessary only to look at some of the statements of the policy framers of Habitat II:

Then UN Secretary General Boutros Boutros Ghali opened Habitat II with a special message to the *World Assemblies of Cities and Local Authorities:* "The Habitat II Conference addresses the future of humankind in a very comprehensive way. It is bringing together the different strands of development: the issues of population movement and urbanization, employment generation, environmental infrastructure and living conditions, participation and governance, legislation and finance, and sustainable use of resources. These issues must be considered in light of current trends in globalization, liberalization and privatization. In short, the Conference is addressing nothing less than the economic and social survival of millions of people, in particular, the poor and disadvantaged, in both the developed and undeveloped nations." *(ibid;* pg. 13.)

In response, the *World Assemblies of Cities and Local Authorities,* a UN-created NGO, issued their own statement, contained within Discussion Document #23, page 6: "The UN must help governments at all levels forge and nurture new and renewed intersectoral alliances of public, private, non-governmental and community-based organizations to make a positive difference in the quality of life in human settlements. The recommendations of Habitat I were largely assigned to national governments for implementation. The need to build alliances with local authorities and NGOs and to draw upon and empower the mobilization capacity of community-based organizations and neighborhood groups in order to address these problems in an holistic way is now increasingly recognized." *(ibid;* pg. 19.)

What problem?

The problem the national governments failed to solve in 1976: private land ownership. In 1976 during Habitat I the UN declared that "...[p]rivate land ownership is a principal instrument of accumulating wealth and therefore contributes to social injustice...Public control of land is therefore indispensable...Public

473

ownership of land is justified in favor of the common good, rather than to protect the interests of the already privileged." (*UN Conference on Human Settlements;* Habitat I; Vancouver, British Columbia, Canada.)

"To ensure the adequate supply of serviceable land, Governments at the appropriate levels should...consider fiscal and other measures, as appropriate, to prevent the hoarding of vacant land for speculative purposes and thus increase the supply of land shelter." (*UN Conference on Human Settlements;* Habitant II; Discussion Document #56e.)

During a Habitat II press conference N'Dow affirmed that the agenda was centered on "...a whole revision of laws and institutions which will allow...many, many poor people to access lands that have been left unoccupied, or owned by absentia owners[7]. Traditionally, this debate...[advocated]...that the big holdings...like in America and Africa...be the object of great study and great scrutiny, so that the poor and the landless will have access to it."

"To avoid unbalanced, unhealthy and unsustainable growth of human settlements, it is necessary to promote land-use patterns that are a precondition for minimizing transport demands, saving energy and protecting open spaces." (*UN Conference on Human Settlements;* Habitant II; Discussion Document #83.)

Under Marxism, collectivism is a critical and necessary tool in the successful transformation of a society into a communist

---

[5]In the disavowed November 11, 1993 White House protocol, under the heading of "Combating Middle Class Elitism," Hillary Clinton, according to the document, reportedly said: "...And, as it has been suggested to me that given the housing shortage among the economically disadvantaged, the ownership of two houses in these times is in the worst possible taste. Perhaps a *Federal Housing Act* could make provision to heavily tax these examples of conspicuous consumption. Let us say that if an owner did not live in his second house for...six calendar and consecutive months, he would be subject to this tax. We could then show this to those who do not own two homes as an example of our concern for the disadvantaged and our contempt for the flagrant lifestyles of the rich and uncaring. No one cares if a few rich people have to pay more taxes for their economic sins." Although the President did not share his views about land hoarding, he did quickly squash the idea of a "land hoarding tax."

If the right to own private property was not guaranteed by the Constitution, as well as the protection under the 5th Amendment from having that property seized by the government for public use, it would not have

state. Most Americans, largely because they were told as much by their government, believe that communism collapsed because it could not compete with capitalism, and that communism itself was a failed political philosophy. Nothing could be farther from the truth, particularly since the global government fostered by the UN is merely an extension of that communist system.

T he report, entitled *Renewing the United Nations System,* outlined the procedures needed to create an effective, omnipotent world parliament. Unlike the current system which simply provides each the national governments of the world with an international forum to debate geopolitical and social issues in which each member State has one vote, the proposed world parliament would be the first giant step towards dissolving national sovereignty—a step that is essential to the establishment of a world government.

It is critical for Americans to understand the difference, since

---

surprised the author to see a suggestion from the First Lady that all properties not in use by the owners be seized for use by the economically disadvantaged—much the way she suggested that a federal *Animal Control Act* be designed to "...readjust the emphasis now given by Americans to domestic animals over people." In that discussion, under the title *The Animal Control Act,* the First Lady purportedly said that "...there are nearly 100 million documented pets in the United States today and that hundreds of millions of dollars are spent on the care and feeding of these creatures to the detriment of more deserving groups. Many cats and dogs live better and eat higher quality food than residents of many inner cities and this is a status quo that must change. The new bill would limit each household in the United States to two pets, be it two dogs, two cats, two birds, and so on...To finance this program it is projected that every owner of animals must pay an annual tax of $100 per animal. Given the huge number of pet owners in America, the revenue would be satisfactory. Most pet owners will object but it can be put forward that this is to benefit all Americans, not a few. The amount of money spent annually on dog food alone could feed the entire inner city poor of Los Angeles for two years." (Disavowed White House Protocol; November 11, 1993.)

It should be noted that this one statement reportedly made by the First Lady is the reason that most of the newspapers and magazines that received the protocol discarded it out-of-hand as a hoax. None of the editors who received the document believed the First Lady would make such an outlandish statement. You must judge it for yourself.

clearly, before such a plan can be implemented it will be preceded by a massive amount of public relations extolling the virtues of the concept — complete with all of the politically-correct assurances that the differences between the current system and the proposed world parliament will be purely cosmetic.

Again, Americans need to understand that the only thing standing between them and world government today is the Constitution of the United States. When it is abolished, the elitists who have been planning world government since before 1917, will move quickly to weaken, and then eliminate, the sovereignty of the nation-states. At that time, the nucleus of world power will be centered in, but not controlled by, the United Nations.

Before the globalists' plan can proceed much farther, the Constitution has to go.

❖ TWENTY ❖

Forming The New World Order

The issue of gun ownership must necessarily come to a head and be resolved to the satisfaction of the federal government within the next few years since it is imperative to those planning America's grand entrance into the communist global society of the New World Order that the United States be a submissive partner when American sovereignty is surrendered to the United Nations sometime between 2008 to 2012.

It would not bode well if America's "rightwing extremists" were still "armed to the teeth" with the virtual arsenals of high powered rifles, shotguns and illegal Soviet AK-47s that the federal government's public opinion spinmeisters insist exists in far too many American homes, since there is little doubt that a second Revolutionary War would erupt overnight if the globalists prematurely abolished the existing Constitution of the United States, or attempted to surrender our national sovereignty to the United Nations.

That is precisely the reason the Founding Fathers wanted to make certain that Americans retained the right to bear arms. Aside from the fact that in an emerging frontier nation, each citizen soldier would likely be called upon to fight threats to the security of the community, the State or the nation, there was, as repeatedly stated throughout this text, a lingering fear in the minds of the Founding Fathers that the central government they created to serve them might some day attempt to force the people to serve it.

Testimony to that extent is found in the writings of both James Madison and Noah Webster. Madison, one of the authors of the *Federalist Papers,* wrote: "Americans never need fear their government because of the advantage of being armed, which the Americans possess over the people of almost every other nation." (*Federalist Paper #48.*)

Madison believed that hereditary monarchies posed a threat to the liberty of any nation and, he was certain that an even distribution of power between the States and the Federal government would keep the enterprising ambitions of the Executive Branch in check. Furthermore, since access to the pockets of the people was left entirely to the discretion of the States and the people through the Congress, Madison was convinced that each facet of the gov-ernment would be adequately restrained. (*Federalist Paper #48.*)

Webster, the States' right scholar, declared in his *Examination into the Leading Principles of the Federal Constitution*: "Before a standing army can rule, the people must be disarmed, as they are in almost every kingdom in Europe. The Supreme power in America cannot enforce unjust laws by the sword, because the whole body of the people are armed, and can be, on any pretense, raised in the United States."

Two facts should now be crystal clear.

First, the Founding Fathers did not insert the 2nd Amendment into the Constitution, as today's liberal revisionists insist, simply because of the clear and present danger from hostile "native Americans," or because of a persistent threat from other nations. Rather, the Constitutional right to "keep and bear arms" was clearly and specifically inserted to serve a twofold purpose. Each State maintained a *citizen* militia to meet whatever threat to the security of the community might arise from natural enemies; and even more important in the minds of the Founding Fathers, a well-armed population all but eliminated any threat from an *unnatural* enemy — the central government of the newly created United States — which they feared might attempt to overwhelm the States, abrogate the Constitution and establish totalitarian rule in America.

Second, it should be apparent to every American by this time that the professional politicians who now make up the federal government have proven time and again they cannot be trusted to protect their constituents from abuses of power at the hands of the federal bureaucracy. Evidence clearly exists to substantiate decades old charges that well-placed, high-ranking officials in all of the branches of the United States government are, and for many years have been, in collusion with powerful international personalities, corporations and financial institutions which are intent on destroying the Constitution of the United States and the sovereignty of all of the nations of the world in order to create a universally-sovereign global government. The United Nations 478 will become the global governing body of that organization which will be controlled by an international oligarchy comprised of industrialists, global bankers and the royal families of Europe who have waited patiently for over two hundred years to have their subjects returned to them . Interestingly those same international bankers and industrialists who have manipulated the strings of government from on high for over a century have proposed amending the United Nations charter to provide a sixth seat on the UN Security Council — a seat controlled by the trans-national corporations and banking establishments — who would then have the right to overrule any proposal by any nation, or groups of nations, within the Council. Just like in the plot of any good mystery story, in the final chapter, the culprit — who has remained largely invisible throughout the storyline — suddenly decides to become highly visible at the end. When absolute power is at stake, absolutely nothing can be left to chance.

B efore the globalists within the federal government of the United States can proceed with the remaining steps that must imperatively be accomplished before America can successfully join the global society of the New World Order, it must disarm America. It must surrender the vast arsenals of its military — but, first, it must disarm its citizens.

At the end of the Gulf War in 1991, the United States stood alone and unrivaled not only as the most powerful military force in the world, but the most technically-advanced nation as well. As American Stealth Fighter-Bombers successfully evaded Iraqi radar on the evening of January 15, 1991 and unleashed a frightening display of 21st century laser-guided weaponry on Saddam Hussein, the world stood in awe, marveling at jet fighters that could not be detected by enemy radar and bombs that did everything short of knocking on the door before entering.

Just as they did at the ends of both World War I and II, America stood alone and unchallenged for a brief, suspended moment in time before beginning to dismantle the awesome military machine that guaranteed both its security and its sovereignty.

While most Americans blame the evisceration of the American military war machine we are witnessing today on Bill Clinton and George Bush, the dismantling of America's security umbrella actually began much earlier — 30 years earlier, in fact — during the Kennedy Administration.

479

Shortly after the Bay of Pigs fiasco, Kennedy issued an explosive document that detailed plans for the universal disarming of all of the nations of the world—beginning with the United States. The plan, State Department Publication #7277, was entitled *Freedom From War: The United States Program for General and Complete Disarmament in a Peaceful World.*

Publication #7277 called for the gradual transfer of all of America's military assets—men and machines—to the United Nations. The authors of the Kennedy plan were Secretary of State Dean Rusk, Secretary of Defense Robert S. McNamara and presidential advisors Robert Lovett and John McCoy. McCoy would be appointed to head the newly created U.S. Arms Control and Disarmament Agency the following year. Each were members of the Council on Foreign Relations. All were globalists. Lovett was reportedly offered his choice of cabinet positions in the Kennedy Administration and declined all of them. He chose instead the more invisible role of advisor. In that capacity, he carefully hand-picked the inner circle of the Kennedy Administration—most of whom were retained by Johnson after Kennedy's assassination.

On May 3, 1962 a revised and expanded version of Kennedy's plan, Publication 4, General Series 3, was issued by McCoy. This report, called the *Blueprint for the Peace Race: Outline of Basic Provisions of a Treaty on General and Complete Disarmament in a Peaceful World,* detailed the strategy under which the United States, by example, would lead the "race" to disarm themselves to a point, according to Publication #7277, where no nation would have a sufficient arsenal of either traditional or nuclear weapons to challenge the progressively strengthened UN Peace Force.

The global disarming of private citizens is, and has been since 1995, a primary objective of the United Nations. During the 9th Annual UN Conference on Crime Prevention that was held in Cairo, Egypt, Japan introduced what became known as "Resolution 9"—a well-financed but highly prejudicial and completely nonobjective 137-page study aimed at justifying a global UN ban on the private ownership of guns of any type. From that study came *Resolution 19*, a rudimentary draft of what would become the *Universal Declaration of Principles on Firearm Regulation,* a global ban on the private possession of firearms that was substantively agreed upon in Vienna, Austria between April 28 and May 9, 1997. At that time, the UN Crime Commission voted on *Resolution 19* and referred it to newly elected UN General Secretary Kofi Annan to develop the *Global Gun Ban Treaty* that was expected to be offered for ratification sometime in 1998.

Ignored in the study, according to the *National Rifle Association*, was the legal defensive use of firearms. Ignored also was the use of firearms for hunting and competitive sport shooting. Blatantly ignored was the Constitutional right of American citizens to own and "bear" firearms. And, for good reason.

According to Congresswoman Helen Chenoweth-Hage (R-ID) the "...federal courts have ruled that international treaties...supersede the Constitution [of the United States]." That being the case, if the U.S. Senate ratified a UN gun ban treaty, it is likely, pursuant to Chenoweth-Hage's logic, that the U.S. Supreme Court could — and based on its past rulings in support of the superiority of the UN, would — rule such a treaty superseded the 2nd Amendment, effectively banning the private ownership of guns in America. For that reason, Chenoweth-Hage introduced a Constitutional Amendment in the 105th Congress that would have stopped "...any treaty which establishes any foreign power or international organization as legally superior to matters of domestic jurisdiction." (*Washington Times National Weekly Edition;* Vol. 4; Issue 30; July 27, 1997.) Given both the globalist attitude and the mushrooming anti-gun sentiment in Congress, Chenoweth-Hage's *American Sovereignty Amendment* never saw the light of day. The feisty Bill of Rights advocate could not muster the support she needed to force it through Congress. Neither nationalism nor American sovereignty are now politically correct.

Without a doubt, a complete and total global ban on the private possession of firearms is just around the proverbial corner. According to an August, 1997 *American Rifleman* article, during the 1997 *UN Commission on Crime Prevention,* "...approximately 20 countries spoke in favor of Resolution 19...and several, including the United Kingdom...openly advocated reducing the number of civilian firearms." India, *American Rifleman* reported, took the position that "...self-defense was never a justification for civilian possession." (Tanya K. Metaksa; Global Gun Control is on the March; *American Rifleman* © 1997; pgs. 42-43.)

In June, 1997 British Labor Party Prime Minister Tony Blair pushed a complete ban on the private ownership of handguns 481 of any type — even .22 caliber — through the House of Commons on a vote of 384 to 181. British handgun owners were given 120 days to surrender their weapons to the British government, after which, instead of receiving the "fair market value" for their handguns, they would be charged with felony possession and sent to prison.

Former British Foreign Secretary Douglas Hurd declared during an interview at the United Nations in New York that the UN must assume an "imperial role," and be prepared to usurp national sovereignty and assume control when national governments collapse. And this, of course, is precisely what the European Union did in 1999 when it ordered NATO to invade Serbia, a sovereign but non-member European nation, because the EU had received, but could not — or conveniently chose not — to substantiate the reports the UN had received detailing human rights atrocities committed upon Islamic Kosovar Albanians by Serbian eastern orthodox Christians. The "protecting human rights" rhetoric aside, the aerial invasion of Serbia by England, the United States and a coalition of European Union states was designed to accomplish three primary objectives.

First, the invasion of Serbia was designed to show the European nations, and the rest of the world, that a new governing body existed which had supra-sovereignty over the nation states under its control, and that it would not hesitate to invade any nation which chose to ignore the new supra-authority's self-proclaimed prerogative to interfere in the internal affairs of any nation within its sphere of influence. Second, the invasion of Serbia made it clear that this new supra-government claimed the authority to redefine national boundaries and, if it so desired, to create additional nation states from the States or provinces of existing sovereignties as it did when it recognized Kosovo's right to secede from Serbia. And, third, the new supra-government wanted to create a precedent it could use in the future to invade any sovereignty nation which either threatened or questioned its authority.

The overlords of Europe, who created the master plan for global government — and who now controls most of its vast, lethal arsenal of war through NATO — are now flexing their muscles. While the human capital the transnational industrialists require to create the consumers they need to buy the products and services they will

482

create over the next few decades in order to grow the global economy—and their profits—will come from the people-rich, job-poor impoverished third world nations which currently hold most of the important jobs in the United Nations. Although the overlords of Europe appear more than eager to surrender not only jobs, but entire industries, to their neighbors to the South and East in order to expand their profits in the new millennium, it is not likely they will eagerly surrender real power to the emerging nations who control the "public" affairs of the United Nations.

The aerial invasion of Serbia was planned and executed by the European Union with the United States, which unleashed most of the devastation that destroyed the Serb infrastructure, joining the EU as a willing co-conspirator. While the "operation" was billed as a UN-controlled action by the media, it clearly was not one since the UN's angry voice was among those who protested the senseless killing of over a hundred Kosovar Albanians who were attempting to escape—not from the Serbs who, according to the media, were slaughtering them by the thousands —but from the NATO planes that were bombing their cities and indiscriminately killing those they were ostensibly sent to protect. The UN was obviously neither "in charge," nor "informed" of the actions being taken by NATO in either Serbia or Kosovo. It was a European Union action from start to finish.

More clearly than anything else, the dichotomy of events that transpired during the brief Serb military excursion gave the world a clear indication of precisely who controls the United Nations, and who is the real power behind the New World Order. The former rulers of the kingdoms of Europe and their industrialist and banking partners who control the European Union flexed their political muscle and savored the sweet taste of victory. They had breached sovereignty and no cries of outrage were heard.

According to Grant Jeffrey in *Final Warning*, "...Secretary Hurd drew attention to what he called 'a new phase in the world's history.' There is a need," he continued, "for the UN to intervene in crisis situations earlier to prevent things from getting to the stage where countries are run by corrupt warlords, as in Somalia." (*Final Warning*; Grant R. Jeffrey; Frontier Research Publications © 1995; pgs. 99-100.)

Hurd's opinion on the authority of the UN, or the European Union, to usurp national sovereignty is simply one of many. In

483

June, 1991 former CIA Director Stansfield Turner defended the UN's role in the Gulf War while admitting that the United Nations had intruded on Iraq's national sovereignty; adding that the UN had created a precedent that would, in the future, be used "...in all of the countries of the world." (*Secret Records Revealed;* Dennis Lawrence Cuddy; Ph.D.; The Plymouth Rock Foundation © 1995; pg. 40.)

On July 20, 1992 *Time* magazine published an article entitled *The Birth of the Global Nation* by Strobe Talbott, the former Oxford classmate and personal friend of Bill Clinton, in which Talbott wrote: "All countries are basically social arrangements...No matter how permanent or sacred they may seem at any one time, in fact they are all artificial and temporary...Perhaps national sovereignty wasn't such a great idea after all...But it has taken the events in our wondrous and terrible century to clinch the case for world government." (*ibid;* pg. 41.) Talbott, who is probably best remembered as the "credible" *Time* editor who came to Clinton's defense when then Governor Clinton was confronted with accusations that he had dodged the draft during the Vietnam War, was rewarded for his loyalty by being named to the second highest post in the State Department.

In August, 1992 former Citicorp Chairman Walter Wriston's book, *The Twilight of Sovereignty,* was published. Wriston wrote: "...A truly global economy will require...compromises of national sovereignty...There is no escaping the system." (*ibid;* pg. 42.)

During the winter of 1992-93, *Foreign Affairs* printed an article by former UN Secretary General Boutros Boutros Ghali entitled *Empowering the United Nations* in which the Egyptian statesman said: "It is undeniable that the centuries-old doctrine of absolute and exclusive sovereignty no longer stands...Underlying the rights of the individual and the rights of people is a dimension of universal sovereignty that resides in all humanity...It is a sense that increasingly finds expression in the gradual expansion of international law...In this setting the significance of the United Nations should be evident and accepted." (*ibid;* pg. 44.)

The issue, and the empirical need for the unilateral disarming not only of nations but of the people within those nations, is based solely on anticipated resistance to the worldwide dissolution of the nation state. If a nation, or a people, lack the means to resist, resistance to tyranny will be short-lived. Conversely, a well-armed population cannot easily be enslaved. As long as Americans retain and exercise the right to own firearms, the New World Order cannot be created. The minute that right is taken from, or voluntarily surrendered by, the American people, liberty will die a bittersweet death. The Constitution as we know it will die shortly thereafter, as will the Bill of Rights and the remaining rights and liberties that Americans so freely enjoy but so casually take for granted.

The elitists among us, while rhetorically affirming our Constitutional right, but not our actual need, to own firearms insist that it is necessary to disarm Americans to protect us from themselves. Steps must be taken, the custodians of law and order steadfastly maintain, to get guns off the streets. They stubbornly insist that the availability of legal firearms has substantially contributed to crime in America. Tighter gun control laws, they insist, will reduce the rate of violent crime and murder in America.

Organizations like the *National Rifle Association* and *Gunowners of America* have frequently and accuratelyquoted John R. Lott's[1] research that less than 7% of the weapons used by criminals were either purchased legally or stolen from those who originally legally purchased them. (*More Guns, Less Crime: Understanding Crime and Gun Control Laws;* John R. Lott, Jr. © 1998; University of Chicago Press.)

A cornucopia of unconstitutional confiscatory gun control laws are regularly enacted in almost every session of Congress

---

[1]John R. Lott, Jr., the author of *More Guns, Less Crime,* is one of the nation's leading authorities gun violence. Currently he teaches Law, Economics and classes on Criminal Deterrence at the University of Chicago, where he is the John M. Olin Visiting Law and Economics Fellow. Lott was the Chief Economist at the United States Federal Sentencing Commission for two years, in 1988 and 1989.

Participating in the research that went into *More Guns, Less Crime* was the University of Chicago, Harvard University, Yale University, Stanford University, Northwestern University, Emory University, Fordham University, Valparaiso University, the American Law and Economics Association, and the Cato Insitutute. And, even though *More Guns, Less Crime* is a tome of actual federal statistics on gun violence, from the moment the book was published in 1998, its conclusions has been attacked by both the political and academic advocates of gun control.

with hardly a murmur of protest by an outraged public which has largely failed to grasp the reality that all of the other "inherent rights" guaranteed them under the Bill of Rights will remain unconditional only as long as the 2nd Amendment stands. When the 2nd Amendment is successfully breached, the Bill of Rights will die, as will the Constitution as we know it.

While most diehard antigun lobbyists insist that increasingly restrictive measures are necessary to keep guns out of the hands of the criminal, it is interesting to note that the most restrictive gun laws are enacted with retroactive grandfather clauses that are specifically designed to make it illegal for law-abiding citizens to possess the weapons they legally purchased before the law was created. It is important to remember, as difficult as it may be to believe, restrictive gun laws are not, nor were they ever, intended to keep guns out of the hands of the malefactor—they are designed solely to take the guns out of the hands of the law-abiding citizen since it is the law-abiding citizens, and not the criminals, who will most likely rebel against the central government that attempts to steal their liberty and surrender their sovereignty to a foreign power.

Because it violates the Constitution to forbid its citizens the right to own firearms, the government of the United States has chosen to nibble away at the edges of the 2nd Amendment rather than try to take a giant bite out of the middle of it, believing somehow that America wouldn't notice "baby bites" or that America wouldn't object too strenuously to the "regulation" of what they call the nation's most lethal industry, since Big Brother emphatically declared it was not trying to eliminate the citizen's right to own a firearm, but was merely attempting to control which citizens could legally do so—and what types of firearms those citizens might buy.

Germany's citizens did not object to the registration or the regulation of guns. Nor did Russia's. Neither remained free. Registration, as any government well knows, is the first step towards elimination.

When Hitler came into power in 1933, he began by freeing Germany of the shackles of the Treaty of Versailles. It was his first step in restoring Germany to its pre-war economic eminence. That was, after all, what the German people wanted. They were unemployed and wanted jobs. They were hungry and wanted to be fed. In exchange for jobs and food, the German citizen willingly surrendered what each individually believed was "just a little" personal freedom. Unemployment in Germany dropped from slightly over 6 million in 1934 to roughly 1 million in 1936.

Censorship cloaked the media. The government issued a national identity card to each citizen, ostensibly to make certain that Jews didn't steal jobs—and food—from hard-working Aryans. And, because the need might arise to defend the motherland from foreign aggressors, every firearm in the Third Reich was registered.

First to vanish was free elections.

Second to vanish was freedom itself.

Fed, and armed with a job, the German worker barely noticed. It didn't matter. One politician, he reasoned, was pretty much the same as another. And, what value was freedom to a starving man?

Adequately confirmed by history, it is reasonably safe to say that gun registration ultimately leads to gun confiscation. It is also reasonably safe to assume that if gun ownership in America is not abrogated before the proponents of the New World Order attempt to abolish the Constitution and tear down the walls of national sovereignty in the United States, there will be a second American Revolution. Therefore, logic alone mandates that such an attempt must necessarily be made very soon.

Americans who, for whatever reason, don't understand what they believe is a "fetish" other Americans have for guns, but who cherish the other liberties provided them by the Constitution of the United States clearly need to fight to preserve the 2nd Amendment because when the right of Americans to own a firearm is swallowed up by the federal government, our remaining liberties will be consumed in the next couple of bites.

The next globalist bite will likely consume private property rights, affecting not only the diehard gun rights folks, but those Americans who simply want to be left alone to enjoy the American dream. A home in the city, a cabin in the woods, and possibly a shared condo at the beach—and enough money to enjoy each of them. The right to own property, and its freedom from seizure without due process is, of course, guaranteed under the Constitution. That being the case, why worry?

487

The abolition of private property rights is one of the primary tenets of the New World Order, which abhorrently views property ownership as a stigma on a modern society reminiscent of colonial times. "Public ownership of land is justified," the UN declared during Habitat I in Vancouver, British Columbia in 1976, "in favor of the common good, rather than to protect the interests of the already privileged."

UNESCO, in its vision of the cities of the world at the dawn of a new century, views life in a "global urban frame." Accordingly, the urban revolution, in its own words, is a "...qualitative leap [that is] closely linked with globalization." Urban centers, the UN maintains, promote globalization and are, in turn, transformed by it, rewriting the rules of the geopolitical game as they grow in strength. By doing so, the cities will challenge the role of the State and assume for themselves a more important role in the lives of those residing within the frameworks of their communities. Thus, both the federal government and the State governments will be weakened by the downpouring of authority to the lowest common denominator. Theoretically this returns "power" to the people. In reality, it strengthens only the oligarchy at the top of the pyramid. Yet, to the political bottom feeders at the community level who are merely pawns in the game of geopolitics, the sense of new found authority is sufficiently overwhelming to achieve what is otherwise incomprehensible: the self-abrogation of what limited rights of sovereignty are possessed at that level: the ownership of property within the community.

The power barons learned long ago that the smallest of men will surrender the most to gain the least. The infusion of power at the community level was just the spark needed to ignite a firestorm of debate on sustainable development and the regionalization of economic governance.

The *Smart Growth* and *Rural Legacy* programs in Maryland are two such examples. The dual programs — one cannot work without the other — are designed specifically to ultimately control not only the movement, but the economic direction and productivity of the human capital within the "population centers." Which is, of course, what any socialist State attempts to accomplish since people are the sole capital assets of any oligarchy.

That is the essence of sustainable development. It is both the most massive land grab in the history of the world, and the most
488   massive collectivization of humanity for the purpose of economic

exploitation.

In the Agenda Documents of Habitat II, the following statement, #56d, is found: "To ensure an adequate supply of serviceable land, governments at the appropriate levels should...apply transparent, comprehensive, easily accessible and progressive taxation and incentive mechanisms to stimulate effective, environmentally sound and equitable use of land..."

Programs like Maryland's *Smart Growth* and *Rural Legacy* are designed to create what the environmentalists call "legacy areas" — areas that are completely devoid of human settlement. Legacy areas are "passed on," in their virgin state, to future generations — who may also not use them.

To discourage human settlement in rural areas, *Smart Growth* eliminates the funding needed to maintain the infrastructure, rechanneling all tax-based funds to designated urban/suburban areas. Zoning regulations will be used to curtail capital improvements in rural areas, greatly reducing property values and, in many cases, rendering homes in those areas uninhabitable as the infrastructure disintegrates over time. Property values in rural areas will plummet as critical utility services such as electricity, water, gas, telephone and even trash pickup become too expensive to maintain; or, that those services, due to special *rural legacy* taxes assessed both on the utility and the consumer, become too expensive for homeowners to afford.

Conversely, with increased tax dollars funneled into the urban areas, and tax-concessions made to those buying homes in the decaying inner cities, together with an increased demand for homes in the designated urban/suburban areas, urban property values will skyrocket, creating immense profits for the speculators who had the "foresight" to buy the urban real estate nobody else wanted.

While the speculators in these ventures will be afforded an almost unbelievable opportunity to realize obscene profits, the urbanization of humanity is not about profits, nor is it about protecting the environment, nor the conservation of the world's natural resources. Plain and simple, it is about control. The control of human capital, the most valuable asset in the world.

The core debate in the New World Order is centered on the redefinition and control of economic wealth, based on social cohesion within the global community, computed not simply in terms of economic capital — which has largely been monopolized by the industrial nations — but rather in terms of natural capital, human

489

capital and social capital.

By redefining the very nature of wealth, the geopolitical transformation — and integration — of the global community is made easier. The World Bank, declaring that no true measure of wealth actually existed, began the complex task of reassessing per capita wealth based on natural, human and social capital rather than on the accumulation of financial and produced assets.

An analysis, completed by Ishmael Serageldin, the World Bank's Vice President for Environmentally Sustainable Development "...found that produced assets [man-made capital] represent only 16 to 20 percent of the wealth of most of the [192] countries studied. Astonishingly, with the exception of some raw materials exporting countries, the value of human resources is equal to or exceeds both natural and produced assets combined, accounting on average for 64% of national wealth...This research ...sends a challenging message to the worlds' policy makers who, with a few exceptions, measure their wealth and focus their economic policies almost exclusively on measures of financial and pro-duced assets." (*Business As Partners In Development;* Jane Nelson, the *Prince of Wales Business Leader Forum, Executive Summary* © 1996; pg. 1.)

It is the New World Order's definition of wealth in terms of human capital that has caused the invisible overlords of business and high finance to shift their vision of the future away from the industrialized, economically solvent nations in the west and north to seek out the new and even potentially more profitable virgin horizons in the Far East and southern hemisphere. Human capital means far more than just cheap, non-union labor. The emerging nations of Africa, Asia and South and Central America are also emerging markets in which the products of the overlords of the New World Order will be sold. However, before these "emerging" consumers have a commercial value to the global community, their standards of living must be elevated substantially. Unfortunately, in the process, the standard of living in the United States will decrease proportionally, since the jobs needed to fuel the economic growth of the emerging nations must come, initially, from the industrialized nations.

That was, after all, specifically, the purpose of NAFTA.

Serageldin summed it up when, in an USA Radio interview at Habitat II, he said: "We cannot accept...that our concern for others stop when we cross an invisible line that we call a political frontier — that we are all citizens of Planet Earth, and that we cannot foresee a situation where the richest 20% are getting 84% of the world's income, and the bottom 20% are getting 1.4%...The ruth-less...market has to be tempered by a caring and nurturing State." (*UN Global Business Plan;* Linda Liotta; Americans For America © 1996; pgs. 33-34.)

"We cannot rely," Richard Jolly declared in the 1996 UNDP Annual Human Development Report, "on growth trickling down [to developing countries] automatically...it takes government policy and action to insure that income helps citizens to expand their choices and to...achieve human development." (*ibid;* pg. 34.)

"In a world of change," Clinton Administration Undersecretary of State Timothy Wirth concluded, "everyone doesn't *remain* advan-taged." (*ibid;* pg. 31; emphasis, author.)

Like the Civil Rights Acts of 1964 and 1968, treaties like NAFTA, GATT, and the UN Treaty on Global Warming, which the United States Senate, in a 95-0 vote on July 24, 1997, asked President Bill Clinton to reject, are now being punitively applied to correct what are perceived by the globalists as intolerable economic imbalances worldwide. Enacted and ratified by the United States Senate, a Treaty on Global Warming that greatly restricts or eliminates what environmentalists call industrial greenhouse pollutants in the United States while exempting the emerging nations from the same restrictions, solves no ecological problems, although it does resolve a major economic one—how to get small to medium-sized American factories that cannot competitively afford to meet these tough, new emissions standards and remain in business to relocate their plants in the emerging, human capital-rich nations of Central and South America, and Africa and Asia.

When this occurs—as it necessarily must for the globalists' plan to succeed—America will no longer remain an "economically ad-vantaged" island in the sea of humanity. Universally, average income levels in the United States will plummet as they skyrocket in the emerging third world nations. Since human reproductivity in the industrialized nations, due to the proliferation of abortion, is now well below replenishment levels, a new class of consumer must be created to purchase the new products and services created by the global merchants and industrialists. And, those new consumers—the human capital of the 21st century—must possess the financial wherewithal to purchase those new products and services with money earned from jobs that have been surrep-titiously plucked from America.

491

The draft of the standards of Habitat II was hammered out in New York between February 5 and 16, 1996. The Habitat agenda, containing its game plan and goals, was finalized on April 13 and prepared for consumption in Istanbul in June.

The Habitat II preparatory draft, which had a very limited distribution, is interesting in that it acknowledges that according to current projections "...by the turn of the century, more than 3 billion people — one half of the world's population — will live and work in urban areas...Rapid rates of...internal migration as well as population growth in cities and towns, and unsustainable patterns of production and consumption raise these problems in especially acute forms." Yet, instead of focusing on deurbanization to eliminate what it admits is overcrowding, the report focuses instead on methods of alleviating the sordid living conditions within the urban centers that are, the report explains, exacerbated by inadequate inner city planning, lack of investment and the unfair allocation of the financial resources stemming from tax revenues.

Why? Because populations are more easily controlled in an urban setting. The mobility of Americans was, after all, one of the concerns addressed by President Bill Clinton in the disavowed November 11, 1993 White House Protocol — and it was a concern that was extensively addressed in the Diebold Report, contained within the working papers of the Clinton White House Healthcare Task Force.

Like *Smart Growth* and *Rural Legacy,* the creation of the *Intelligent Vehicle Highway System* detailed in the Diebold Report, which will ultimately be used to monitor the mobility of the population of the global community, will be funded by private/public partnerships at the state and community levels.

Together with the IV/HS vehicle monitoring system that will ultimately be able to track specific vehicles on any roadway in the world, each global citizen will be obligated to carry an internal passport, which will be issued in the form of a biometric national driver's license, as it already is in all of the European Union nations. Imbedded in each card will be a microchip that can, and ultimately will, be used to track individual citizens.

GPS civilian tracking and IV/HS vehicle monitoring will likely take place in the U.S. government's recently completed National Identification Center in the mountains in western Virginia. Plans of the secret installation were first revealed by former House Appropriations Subcommittee Chairman Neal Smith (D-IO), who was defeated by political neophyte, Dr. Greg Ganske (R-IO), in 1994 after Smith mentioned the Center in an October, 1993 fund-raising newsletter to his constituents.

Smith, an anti-gun advocate, mentioned the Center to curry favor from those constituents who were opposed to unregulated gun rights, declaring that the "...Subcommittee on Appropriations which I chair has been actively pursuing an effective solution to this problem...But the program we are implementing will take more time. The solution to screening people...is to have a National Center computerized so that local law enforcement offices can instantly access information from all states." (*Final Warning;* Grant R. Jeffrey; Frontier Research Publications © 1995; pg. 212.)

Whether or not Smith realized it at the time, such a "Center" already existed. It's called the FBI. On file at the FBI is every piece of data on every American citizen who had ever come into contact with any law enforcement official—whether local, county, State or federal. Of course, that may be precisely why the FBI intelligence gathering network was not used. The database to be assembled by the National Identification Center is not to be collected on those who, for criminal reasons, have come into contact with the various law enforcement agencies of the United States; rather, it was to be used to compile a complex information database on those who have not, nor likely ever would, come into contact with the FBI. The database would include not only all of the personal data—medical as well as financial—on file any-where in the United States about every American, it would also include a digital image of that American and, in many cases, a digital fingerprint scan as well, secured from each State's drivers' licenses digital photo database and secured for the government by Image Data, Limited—a well financed CIA-created, government funded "private enterprise" venture that began buying up the digi-tal photos of every licensed driver in America shortly after the CIA funded its start-up in 1997.

"We have invested," Congressman Smith concluded, "$392 million so far in such a Center...and we hope to have it completed and equipped in about two years...We hope all States will be on the system by 1998 and will supply the information on a continuing basis... Mean-while, we will continue to establish the...Center for this and other law enforcement purposes." (*ibid;* pg. 212.)

While Jeffrey expressed concern about the use of the NIC to amass intelligence on gun owners; my concern, and his as well,

493

was more focused on the "other law enforcement purposes" for which the Center could, and likely would, be used—including not only the ability of Big Brother to eavesdrop electronically on any and all telephone calls in America—a technology the government already possesses, but even more important, that the Center will likely be used to monitor population movement in the United States through GPS and IV/HS tracking on an ongoing basis. In addition, the Center will be used as the repository for an electronic database on every citizen, procured from their credit files, police records, scholastic records, employment and wage histories, and their medical records—psychological as well as physical.

The United States government spent billions of dollars to harness cyberspace—only to give Americans free and completely unbridled access to it. Not only that, but in June, 1997 and again in its annual Conference of Governors in February, 2000 the Clinton Administration declared cyberspace was so sacrosanct that neither Congress nor the States could not impose "tolls" at the "on ramps" of the information superhighway to assess those who use the Internet to promulgate business (although several federal and State legislators are curently attempting to levy such tolls) . Clearly, the United States government wants every home and business in the nation linked to the Internet. Why?

The answer may be found, at least in part, in the second of the five disavowed White House protocols. Just before the conclusion of a purported November 12, 1993 meeting between Clinton, senior adviser David Gergen, Gene Sperling, and a fourth participant identified in the protocol only as "JFS[2]," the President commented that the project to get American businesses involved on the Internet was going "...far better than expected." The basic goal of the Administration was, according to the disavowed protocol:

---

[2]Since part of that particular disavowed protocol dealt with a Clinton plan to permit the government to engage in some banking practices by offering no-interest loans to "cooperating business entities," it is possible that the unidentified "JFS" was Joshua Steiner, the Treasury official who, when called to testify before a Congressional committee headed by former Senator Alfonse D'Amato (R-NY), found his sworn testimony somewhat at odds with notes of those particular relevant conversations recorded in his diary. Steiner recanted the diary entries, suggesting to the Committee to that he had "lied" to his own diary.

"...to have an unobstructed overview of American business trends without apparent observation [which] will materially assist him and his planners in [the] further integration of the business community into his overall industrial policy. *As a side issue, several investigative agencies have suggested that cooperative chip makers build trap doors into their products to permit selective observation of information that will be of great value not only to future planning but to permit heightened and more effortless observation of the public sectors.*" (*Disavowed Protocol of White House Conference of November 12, 1993;* Emphasis, author.)

Clearly, in November, 1993 such "backdoors" already existed in the computer software programs created and sold in America although Clinton's people did not appear to be aware of that fact. According to two computer program designers interviewed by the author, it has been a common, if not highly secretive, practice for years. But, regardless if such access did or did not exist at that time, the protocol — if it is a genuine transcript of a White House meeting — clearly establishes that on November 12, 1993 the Clinton Administration was discussing the possibilities of having secret trap doors designed into all programs and systems that the government could use to surreptitiously access the stored hard drive databases of "civilian" website servers sometime in the future.

Clinton's scheme to access the computer databases of Internet website users began to take shape in the summer of 1997 when the controversial "bipartisan" *Oxley-Manton Encryption Amendment* was introduced in the House of Representatives by seventh term Congressman Thomas J. Manton (D-NY) and eighth term Congressman Michael G. Oxley (R-OH).

Like most of the pieces of intrusive and highly unconstitutional legislation being touted as necessary to safeguard America from the more unsavory elements of our society, the *Oxley-Manton Amendment,* according to its sponsors, grew out of a concern by Congress to protect its constituents from the criminal element of society who, one imagines Oxley and Manton believed, were detailing their nefarious schemes to bomb buildings, sell illegal drugs or record the transactions of their illicit criminal operations in the hard drives of their computers which were linked to the Internet. *Oxley-Manton* was the high tech equivalent to the anti-gun legislation that is ostensibly designed to prevent criminals

495

from purchasing legal weapons from lawful gun dealers. The *Oxley-Manton Amendment* was not designed to provide Big Brother with access to criminal databases, it was designed to allow a very intrusive federal government unconstitutional, and very secretive, access to the databases of unwary American citizens who frequent the information superhighway.

Just as most of the gun control laws enacted over the past 20 years violate the 2nd Amendment, *Oxley-Manton* violated the 4th Amendment because it allows any government official to casually browse through the files on your personal or business website or on the hard drive of your personal computer without your knowledge or consent—and with a court-approved warrant—seeking incriminating evidence that can then be used against you in a court of law.

Since it appears that only one major computer software manufacturer had, at that time, voluntarily agreed to accommodate the Clinton White House's private request for access, *Oxley-Manton* was needed to force encryption developers, by law (albeit unconstitutional) to provide law enforcement officials with access keys that will now provide the government with unbridled access to the data stored in your home or office computer. Welcome to George Orwell's world.

The final phase of the plan of the New World Order is now in effect. No longer is it a question of whether or not world government can be achieved. It can be, and it will be. Now, the only question that remains unanswered is "when." Over the past two decades, the globalists have become bold. Nor longer is the global agenda of the New World Order a secret spoken wistfully in liberal circles. The publicists of Utopia herald the arrival of the New World Order as the triumphant victory of mankind.

The spinmeisters have done their jobs well.

Big Brother is coming and America awaits his arrival with the gleeful anticipation of children impatiently waiting for Santa Claus. Only, in this case, Santa Claus is not a cheery old man in a red suit carrying a bag full of shiny new toys. And, the "toys" Big Brother is bringing will be used to control not only the political systems of all the nations of the world, but the economic and societal infrastructures of those nations as well. Under the socialist world system of this utopian Santa Claus, religion—or rather those forms of religion practiced by the Christians and the Jews — will be banned or greatly restricted since any religion that recognizes the "God of exclusivity" rather than the "gods of inclusivity" are antithetical to the all-encompassing universal inclusiveness of the New World Order which will recognize the universal, collective rights of society while greatly restricting, or eliminating, the personal rights of the individual.

While the foundation of the New World Order was cast in secret, its construction has not only been largely accomplished in the open for the whole world to see, but the elitists have boldly told us what they were doing as they calmly paved the road to Utopia. Apparently, we weren't listening — or, we didn't care enough for liberty to protect our right to enjoy it.

Should the boundaries of the world's sovereign nation-states remain standing beyond 2012, logic suggests the very clear likelihood that World War III will commence, on schedule, both in the Mideast and in heartland of American shortly thereafter to bring about world government. In the aftermath of a nuclear holocaust that will decimate much of the North American continent, and with no superpowers except China left to challenge their supremacy, the New World Order will be established.

At that time, the final conflict of man on Earth will be only seven years away.

"We of the sinking middle class...may sink without further struggles into the working class where we belong, and probably when we get there it will not be so dreadful as we feared, for, after all, we have nothing to lose but our aitches."

George Orwell
The Road to Wigan Pier
1937

"Mankind always sets itself only such problems as it can solve; since, looking at the matter more closely, it will always be found that the task itself arises only when the material conditions for its solution already exist or are at least in the process of formation."

Karl Marx
Critique of Political Economy
1859

"No soceity can survive, no civilization can survive, with 12-year olds having babies, with 15-year olds killing each other, with 17-year olds dying of AIDS, with 18-year olds getting diplomas they can't read."

Newt Gingrich
The Washington Times
February 5, 1995

❖ TWENTY-ONE ❖

Afterwords

We are living in perilous times. Like most nations in the modern world, America is not without its societal problems: rampant crime, senseless violence, racism, drug abuse, poverty, bigotry and a multitude of other sins found in any advanced multicultural, multiracial society. Most of the nation's ills are of recent vintage, surfacing to crisis proportions only within the past four or five decades. Some, like racism and bigotry, have been with us as long as the nation itself and, in some cases, even before. For the most part, some of the more recent societal enigmas that now plague our nation stem directly from the proemial efforts of the societal planners of the emerging New World Order to prepare America for its membership in the state-less multicultural, multiracial society of tomorrow. America, a nation of immigrants who earned the equality they enjoy among their peers through the sweat equity of their own labor as they strived collectively to build the greatest nation on Earth, has only grudgingly been willing to cede what they struggled to achieve to those who have gained imputed, but not earned, equality from the federal courts and through the civil rights and equal rights legislation enacted by Congress and enforced by the societal planners of Utopia.

Few Americans would argue against the theory that, under our Constitutional form of government, all men—and women—are equal, regardless of the circumstances of their birth or their earned stature in the community. However, being equal under the rule of law in a purely Constitutional perspective is much different than being granted imputed equality. Imputed equality is a device used by the societal planners to correct what they view as "past injustices" to either racial or societal minorities. Imputed equality is designed to elevate minority groups or to legally protect those who practice activities which, in a moral and ethical society, are

499

viewed as both reprehensible and repugnant; and to grant those groups an "unearned" status in the community. It is the imputing of equality without the investment of sweat equity that flies in the face of many Americans. Further, it is the demands of the societal engineers, backed by the threat of government intervention by force, that has created much of the current racial and cultural unrest in America.

Americans, who have established a unique historic precedent of fighting — and even shedding their own blood — to protect the civil rights of beleaguered people in distant lands, are generally willing to accept anyone, from any nation, as an equal. However, few Americans who earned what they possess through sweat equity, are well-disposed to stand aside and surrender, without a fight, the equality they earned through their labor to those who ask that equality rather than equalness, be imparted to them by decree. It is the edicts of socialism and not the rule of law which mandate preferential — not equal — treatment based on race, ethnic culture, or sexual orientation which created the renewed wave of racism in America.

Racism is a blight on any society. It is divisive. Racism is a weapon that is currently being used, quite successfully, to divide America against itself. Most Americans, particularly those born in the war years in the first half of the 20th century, remember a nation of English speaking people, unified by a love of country, regardless of their nation of origin. During that period, there were no hyphenated Americans. No African-Americans, no Chinese-Americans, no Japanese-Americans, no Hispanic-Americans, no Indonesian-Americans, no French-Americans, and no Vietnamese Americans. There were only Americans. The adopted land of these new citizens quickly became their home and, as adopted children of the greatest nation on Earth, the heritage of America became their heritage. As quickly as they could, the adopted Americans of the early 20th century usually wanted to be assimilated into their new society. Speaking English was a prerequisite to citi-zenship because to become a functional member of the American society, each new citizen had to be able to communicate. People who can communicate with one another are unified not only by a common language but by the immigrant heritage of America. Assimilation is, and has always been, virtually assured. At home the Italian remained an Italian, the Jew remained Jewish, and the Irishman remained Irish. Collectively, they were assimilated Americans—and each was as proud of his or her adopted homeland as they were of their own native heritage. During World War II, naturalized German, Italian and Japanese American soldiers fought side-by-side with native-born American soldiers to defeat their ancestral nations.

On the other hand, the various nationalities forcibly absorbed into the Soviet Union, largely through conquest, remained ethnically, culturally and nationalistically separate from the ethnic Russians. As captive peoples, they had no interest or desire to be assimilated into the Soviet society. For that reason, the natural assimilation of its conquered peoples was a problem for the Lenin government in 1917, and it continued to be a problem for every Soviet leader throughout the history of that oppressive regime—and it remains such today even though the former captive satellite nations are theoretically independent, free nations.

National separatism grew stronger over the years, making it even more difficult for the Soviet bureaucracy to manage its troubled economy. Compounding the economic dilemma of the Soviets was the need of the Russian oligarchs to buttress their occupation-level garrisons in most of the captive nations under their control with invasion-strength armies, further agitating their financial woes by forcing the Soviet government to spend millions of rubles it did not possess on military payrolls it could not meet. Every ethnic group in the Soviet Union retained not only its native language, but its cultural diversity as well.

Efforts on the part of the government to assimilate those diverse peoples into the Soviet society met with such resistance over the years that forced assimilation would have resulted in a continuous series of Civil Wars. Josef Stalin was finally forced to recognize the national diversities of his captured peoples by making both his commissars, and the Soviet bureaucrats assigned to those captured lands, learn the native languages rather than forcing the cultural separatists to learn Russian.

It was a problem that did not get better with time. While the separatists were integrated into the Soviet society, national unity was never achieved. Each sect remained diverse peoples within a foreign land. Ethnically, each remained ideologically linked with the cultural moorings of their former national identity. Granted, the communist philosophy of the Soviet Union transcended the national politics of the separatists, which is really all Stalin wanted.

501

Force is, after all, a universal language.

The national loyalties of each ethnic group remained bonded to their separatist pasts. Internal strife, whether from years of forced collectivism or ethnic separatism remained a bitter fact of life throughout the history of the Soviet Union.

From the Soviet experience, the utopians learned a valuable lesson that would pay them huge dividends over the next fifty years. Diligently and ever so unobtrusively, they worked inside the societal structure of America using ethnic separatism and cultural diversiety to weaken and then ultimately destroy the fabric of patriotic unity one thread at a time. Ethnic and cultural separatism would prove to be the Achilles heel of this nation of immigrants which rose to become the strongest nation on Earth by providing economic opportunities to the outcasts of the other nations of the world.

Separatism would be the weapon the globalists would use to destroy the national unity of America through the deliberate fractionalization of the people of the United States into sub-cultures within the societal structure of the nation. This has been achieved over time not by promoting America as a nation of immigrants forged into single society of freemen who are unified to protect the inherent rights of all men under the banner of the Stars and Stripes, but rather as a multi-lingual, multicultural society in which diversity, not unity, is encouraged. That this was a deliberate policy of the United States government during the Clinton years is confirmed, you will recall, by the words of Hillary Rodham Clinton in the disavowed White House Protocol of November 11, 1993 when the wife of the President of the United States said:

> *"When middle class whites flee from an area that has a signifi-*
> *cant African-American population...[they perpetuate]...a vicious*
> *cycle wherein tax money is no longer available for our entitlement*
> *programs. These whites are practicing an intolerable elitism when*
> *they move into moated communities with fences and guards. This*
> *is an offense to the African-American and Latino communities.*
> *It's the same sort of thing as whites taking their children out of*
> *public schools because of what they perceive are dangerous*
> *conditions. If they only realized that this elitism actually propagates*
> *these dangerous conditions, they would stop. And, since they won't,*
> *I think that all housing projects, regardless of the price of the units*
> *involved or the location and regardless of whether these units are*

*public or private in nature, be mandated by Federal law to provide
25% low cost minority housing. Perhaps then the elitists would
be forced to come to grips with the plain fact that this is going to be
a multicultural, multiracial country very quickly and we are not
going to tolerate or perpetuate de facto segregation."*

This thought is further evidenced by an examination of the
working papers of the past four UN Global Summits which reveal
the high priority given to its multiculturalism and multiracialism
agenda in the United States by those controlling the emerging
policies of the New World Order. The issue of multiculturalism
angrily championed by Hillary Clinton on November 11, 1993
was not uniquely a Hillary Clinton platform — it was, and remains,
a part of the ongoing agenda of the United Nations to merge all
of the nationalities of the world into a blended societal homology
that is neither black nor white, yellow or tan, rich or poor, theist
or atheist.

When you look at the world as a single unit rather than as
individual nation-states you will gain a perspective seldom noticed by Americans — particularly middle class white Americans.
Globally, Caucasians are a minority race. Caucasians control
over 85% of the world's tangible wealth; but its work force —
which controls over 80% of the world's jobs and a like amount
of its buying power, is comprised of less than 20% of the world's
population. While it may appear that it is this "inequity" that the
societal planners, who are currently dealing with a hodgepodge
of multicultural issues, are attempting to change, it is not. NAFTA
and GATT have already solved that problem. The largest job
transfer in the history of mankind is currently under way as
American, European, and Japanese industries are slowly being
uprooted from their native lands and are being transplanted into
the human capital-rich nations in the southern hemisphere and
in Asia, where a new whole generation of consumers are eagerly
awaiting their promised soon-coming affluence.

During the past decade, America has become increasingly
alarmed over what is now classically referred to as the
"dumbing-down" of the schools in America. The federally-
funded public school systems of America today have de-
emphasized the need for its students to learn such things as U.S.   503

history and mathematics, and few students who graduate from America's high schools can accurately tell you why, and in many cases when, the Revolutionary War, the Civil War or either of the world wars were fought. Nor do they understand the significance of the Constitution of the United States or the Declaration of Independence. Yet, many of them can explain the primary tenets of the UN's Declaration on Human Rights. In October, 1999 Virginia state education officials posted copies of the 1998 uniform Standards of Learning [SOL] Test on the Internet, creating an immediate firestorm of criticism from teachers, parents and testing consultants—some of whom thought the test promoted racial tension, and others who thought it should not have been made public, believing, as they did, that the parents of those students did not possess a "need to know."

Versions of the SOL test that was posted on the Internet have been administered annually to all third, fifth, and eighth graders as well as some high school students in the public school system of Virginia since 1997. Other States have used similar tests for much longer. Many parents, particularly those in the conservative South, were alarmed by what they saw when they went to *http://www.pen.k12.va.us* on the Internet.

So was *Washington Post* reporter Jay Mathews, since his newspaper had already published an article in September, 1996 that called teaching standards in America's public schools a disgrace. Mathews was granted an interview with Cameron Harris, Virginia's assistant school superintendent at her office in Richmond to discuss the questions on the SOL test.

Asking for her assessment of the scholastic accuracy of the SOL test, Mathews focused on the question which disturbed him most: *"Which statement best explains the main idea of the Declaration of Independence?"* The correct answer, according to the SOL, was: *"All people are born free and have equal rights."* While it is true that John Adams attempted to insert an anti-slavery plank in the Declaration that would have outlawed slavery in the United States when it approved by the Continental Congress, making the United States slave-free from its inception, he could not gain the support of enough legislators to have such a clause added to the finished text. Thus, the Declaration was not about people being born free—as Mathews pointed out to Harris. Nor, the reporter advised her, did the Declaration of Independence deal with equal rights. Clear and simple, the Declaration of Inde-

504

pendence was just that: an announcement to the nations of Europe that the United Colonies of America had declared their independence from England, and that a government established on the principles of the rule of law was being created.

Harris, according to Mathews, made an exasperated sound and said: "We are talking about third-graders! This is not a seminar on constitutional law and the Declaration of Independence!" (*Adults Answer SOL Tests;* Jay Mathews, *The Washington Post,* page B1, Oct. 25, 1999).

Another of the questions that bothered Mathews appeared in the high school version of the SOL test. It asked how Northerners reacted to the influx of African-Americans from the South at the end of World War I. The correct answer was: "*Many saw them as cheap labor and a threat to their jobs.*" Many of the parents, black and white, who complained to the Virginia Board of Education viewed that particular question as being racially insensitive. Many of them complained that, instead of teaching tolerance of other ethnic groups, questions like that one would serve only to inflame subsurface ethnic prejudices.

Although the *Washington Post,* in a front page article did call teaching standards a "national shame," the reality of the problem goes much deeper than the teachers themselves, since NGOs like the NEA have a virtual stranglehold on the curriculum taught in America's schools. The evolution of that control was not accidental. The agenda of the NEA was meticulously sculptured within the bureaucracy of the federal government beginning with the NEA's "congressional incorporation" in 1906.

The collapse of educational standards, and the polarization of America through a curriculum of cultural diversity that mandated bilingual education is akin to the biblical tale of the Tower of Babylon, and the confounding of languages to prevent a unified people from building a tower to Heaven. Clearly, culturally diverse and ethnically divided people cannot easily align to fight common causes since they will have few causes in common — particularly when the cultural distinctions between them are used as a wedge to create racism where it may not have previously existed.

Admittedly, racism and bigotry exists — they are human traits. They exists in the United States, and have since before the colonies ever became a nation. They existed in the Europe from which our forefathers came, and they existed in the Africa from which the slaves who cultivated the crops of the South and built the factories of the North came.

The debate, however should not be over the fact that racism exists, but rather why it does. To solve that problem, or for that matter any problem that we encounter in life, it is necessary to understand why the problem exists. Racism is a problem that simply should not exist in contemporary America since we are, after all, a nation of diverse nationalities, cultures and ethnocentricities. For over 200 years we worked together, not as diverse peoples, but as Americans, to build the greatest nation in the history of the world.

However, every society has its share of home-grown racists and bigots who need no prompting to promote hate. In the United States racism was, to a large degree, regionalized. In the east and northeast, racism was initially focused on the cultural distinctions between the Jews and the Gentiles. In the North, where most of the racial violence occurred in the first half of the century, it was a Black and White issue that spilled into the South at the end of World War II when the Black population rightfully claimed the liberty they were guaranteed under the Constitution of the United States. In the West, racism was largely directed against native Americans. In the deep South and far West, racism was a two-headed dragon, rearing its incendiary head not only against Black Americans but Hispanic Americans as well.

There was, of course, enough bigotry and fear of diversity in every quarter of America to hate anyone culturally or ethnically different. But in no part of the nation was bigotry historically universal because bigotry, whether racial, societal, or philosophical, is an "acquired taste" — it must be learned — and it is always learned best by those who, academically, know the least.

Few would argue that racism — violent racism — in America, not only between Blacks and Whites but between all ethnic segments of the population, is growing at an alarming rate and is, today, almost at the crisis level. The wedge of cultural and ethnic diversity has been driven into the spine of America and has crippled our nation. But then, it was supposed to.

E very dictatorial society in the modern era has been quick to realize that the key to the future stability of the political system it spawned was in the psychological exploitation of its children. The manipulation of the mind to rid children of their home grown moral values begins with desensitization—sometimes centered on death, but more likely, as has been the case in America, with brainwashing to eradicate what the NEA calls "the ignorance of the religious right," either with elaborate exercises on evolution to prove man was not created by God, or by inducing the children to accept deviant lifestyles as a normal alternative to heterosexuality—and, in many cases, both.

It was this dichotomy that created the societal mess America now faces. Whether such was deliberate or accidental is unclear. In either event, it has served the global masters well to help obscure their agenda by forcing the nation to focus on the symptoms of the illness rather than the cause.

Today, according to Dr. Jim Nelson Black, "...[t]he United States has roughly 28 million functional illiterates and approximately 83 million people who are in some way learning impaired....And the problems do not end at the school door. The suicide rate among young people has gone up 300% since the 1960s; drug and alcohol abuse and promiscuity have become commonplace... As a result, more than 2.5 million young people graduate from the public schools of this nation as functional illiterates each year." (*When Nations Die;* Jim Nelson Black; Tyndale Publishing © 1994; pgs. 75-76.)

The agenda of the NEA is twofold. First, it calls into question the moral values children learn at home by providing them with a politically-correct, value-neutral curriculum that questions the rights of parents to impart their traditional values and religious beliefs on their own children. It is this hostile ideology that has fostered the war zone mentality inside of our public schools.

William Kilpatrick, in his book *Why Johnny Can't Tell Right From Wrong,* reveals that every month as many as 525 thousand robberies, shakedowns and physical attacks occur in the public schools of America. Further, he declares, over 16,000 crimes per day are committed in, or near, America's schools—and that one out of every five students carries a weapon of some type to school each day. (*ibid;* 76.) It is no wonder that rape is commonplace in our public schools. Or that school authorities would have such a cavalier attitude about it, as they did in Washington, DC when four girls and five 9- and 10-year old boys disrobed in an empty classroom and engaged in oral sex; or when a 14-year old Queens, New York girl was raped in another empty classroom by boys supplied with condoms only minutes before by a school guidance

507

counselor—and the incident could go unreported to the police by the school system for a month[1].

Second, the educational system in America is no longer designed to educate our youth with the 3 "R's." The role of the "teacher" is to indoctrinate America's children with what the NEA terms essential knowledge: multiculturalism, sexual diversity and a desensitization towards nationalism. Instead of readin', 'riting and 'rithmatic, the deconstructionists of the NEA are now focusing on the four "isms:" environmentalism, multiculturalism, globalism and bilingualism.

The bonus in all of this for those bent on implementing world government is, of course, the societal wedges of bilingualism and multiculturalism which are touted by the spinmeisters of Utopia as one of those "inherent rights" any nationality possesses to maintain its own distinct cultural or ethnic identity—and language.

---

[1] When Winston Elementary School principal Ronald Parker learned that four girls and five boys, ages 9 year to 12, disrobed in an empty detention room and, for 30 minutes with the lights turned out and the door locked, engaged in oral sex, he did nothing. The incident took place on Monday, April 7, 1997, but most of the parents did not hear about the incident until Friday of that week when those involved began talking about it.

The parents of the girls charged that their daughters were raped at the southeast Washington, DC school. Three of the students were sent, by a teacher, to a small "detention" room next to the classroom, because they were "disrupting the class." The other six students, according to a school official, "snuck" out of the classroom and joined them. Once inside the room, they locked the door and turned off the lights. After some "light" sexual foreplay, some of them disrobed, and began to engage in oral sex with one another. When the teacher discovered some of her students were missing, she went to the detention room to check.

Parker decided not to report the incident to either the parents or the authorities because, in his words, "...the sex was consensual." Once the story leaked, Parker—still refusing to call the police or report it to the DC School System—called a meeting between the students involved and their parents. But even then, Parker played down the incident, making it appear as though all that happened was a little innocent childish "sexual exploration." It was not until the DC police were called in that it was learned that the 9 to 12 year-olds were engaging in oral sex. (*The Washington Times; Gingrich Calls For Principal's Dismissal;* Stephen Dinan; April 14, 1997; pg. A1.)

But, the sex acts which took place on April 16, 1997 at the August Martin High School in Springfield Gardens in Queens, New York, were

It was estimated by the federal government in 1996 that over 100 languages and dialects are now spoken in America — and every government form that is available to the general public is now published in all of them.

America's socialists learned well from the failure of the Soviet system to absorb the ethnically diverse peoples it had conquered into the Soviet society. Because the conquered vassals kept their own separatist identities, they remained ideologically and culturally distinct from the Russians, and the communists were never able to unify the populations they had conquered under the scepter of the hammer and sickle. Where Lenin and Stalin attempted to force the conquered peoples they controlled to learn the Russian language in order to assimilate them into the Soviet society, the socialists in the American educational system are doing the opposite. There has been, and there continues to be, an effort on the part of the NEA — usually against the expressed wishes of the parents — to force the children of ethnic minorities to maintain a separatist identity. This "bill of goods" is peddled,

---

anything but consensual.

Four teenage boys lured a 14-year old female student from the cafeteria to an unused classroom. Three of the boys: DeShawn James, 17; Valijean Lee, 18; and Vincent Dowdy, 17, allegedly gang-raped her as she was being held by the fourth teenager, Charles Baskerville, 18. Police investigators, who were called in over a month later, said that just minutes before the attack two of the boys went to the guidance counselor's office and asked for, and were given, condoms. The school, it seems, was urging the students to practice "safe sex."

When the school officials were interviewed by the *New York Times* on May 20, they were very guarded and defensive, saying that the reason the incident was not reported sooner was that the "...girl initially gave an incomplete account of what happened..." then added that the girl "...did not want to press criminal charges" against the boys. The police were called by Principal Richard Ross on Monday, May 19, 1997—33 days after the incident happened.

On May 20, a 17-year old junior at the school told investigating officers that she was sexually assaulted by four boys in the basement of the high school on May 14—38 days after school officials knew that a 14-year old freshman girl had been raped by four boys whom she had identified to them as students at that school. (*The New York Times; Four Teen-Agers Charged in Rape of Girl in a Classroom in Queens;* Norimitsu Onishi; May 21, 1997, Metro Section.)

with all of the slick rhetoric of a snake oil salesman, as an "inherent right"—the right of every ethnic minority in America to retain their cultural diversity. Of course, those who emigrated from their native lands in the 19th and early 20th centuries had little difficulty doing precisely that—and still learned the language and the customs of the American people.

In most cases, the minority students in multilingual areas of the nation today are taught only in their native languages, further exacerbating the racial tension that already exist within their communities. Most are denied bilingual educations even when it is requested by their parents—who all too clearly understand, usually because of their own economic circumstances, that if their children cannot read or speak English they will be denied the economic advantages provided to those who can. That fact is not lost on the educators. It is, in point of fact, part of the over-all strategy to keep the "boiling pot" of America boiling.

W hat makes it difficult for most Americans to realize that something terrible has happened to America is that most don't realize that the political system under which we now live is not the same political system that was created by our Founding Fathers. Nor is it the same system our grandparents lived under before the "ratification" of the 17th Amendment. Nor it is the same system that our parents lived under in the 1940s and 1950s before our Supreme Court Justices learned they could "rewrite" the rule of law from the bench of the high court; or before our lawmakers cast aside the constitutional rule of law in favor of "engineering" legislation to fit the new concepts of social justice. Our democracy has, unfortunately, devolved through most of the 20th century.

Frankly, none of those who signed the Constitution of the United States—not even those who would have preferred a much stronger central government—would have placed their signatures on any document granting the federal oligarchy the type, or degree, of power that has been unconstitutionally conferred upon it by both the Congress and the Supreme Court of the United States.

But then, too few Americans care. Too many for too long have taken freedom for granted. It is, after all, an inherent right. America has been watching the elitists slowly and meticulously revise the history of the United States and of the world over the past decades without barely a whimper of outrage, not realizing that to change the future of a nation it is first necessary to alter the motives of its past. The revisionists have edited the history of the 20th century to fit the reality of the 21st.

The die is cast. Those bent on the destruction of America are too deeply entrenched in the governments of the world to be stopped. And while the timetable of the New World Order may yet be delayed, it is, as the globalists have told us repeatedly over the past decade, now inevitable. World government is the reality of the 21st century. When America and its citizen warriors are effectively disarmed, the walls of national sovereignty will fall like children's building blocks all around the globe, and the New World Order will rise from the rubble.

And the souls of the martyrs of America's past will cry out in anguish.

❖ About the Author ❖

Jon Christian Ryter

The author of this work, Jon Spokes, has been writing under the pseudonym of Jon Christian Ryter since the mid-1980s. He is a former newspaper reporter who wrote for the Parkersburg, WV *Sentinel*. The author also wrote a syndicated newspaper column from the mid-1970s until 1986 entitled *Answers From the Bible,* which had a weekly following of over a half million people.

It was during this period, when the author expanded the topic of his column to include contemporary social and political issues, that he began receiving threats of violence that included three death threats from those who did not like the conservative political tone in the author's writings. It was at that time that the author, being first and foremost a Christian writer, assumed the pen name of Jon Christian Ryter.

In 1996 the author's first book, *The Baffled Christian's Handbook* was published. Writing under both his own name and that of Jon Christian Ryter, the author had, by that time, written over 500 articles on a plethora of subjects.

Today, the author works for *The Washington Times* as an advertising executive where he now interacts with some of the most notable conservative advocacy groups in the United States on a much more personal level than most traditional reporters are able. In addition, his Internet website, *Jon Christian Ryter's Conservative World* at *http://hometown.aol.com/baffauthor/jonchristianryter.html* has helped him establish a network of mid- to senior-level Washington insiders who now provide the writer with a steady stream of material to use both in his books and in the investigative reports found on his website.

❖ Subject Index ❖

513

Subject Index

Subject Index

Subject Index

Subject Index

531

Subject Index

Subject Index

BOOKS OF INTEREST
ON
SIMILAR SUBJECTS

Available through all bookstores
or directly from the publisher,

HALLBERG PUBLISHING CORPORATION
P.O. Box 23985 • Tampa, Florida 33623
Phone 1-800-633-7627 • Fax 1-800-253-7323

memoirs
of a
superfluous
man

Albert
Jay
Nock

"*Those whom Nock has reached do not form a movement or
a clique; such diverse scholars as the eminent sociologist,
Robert Nisbet, out in the South Pacific during World War II
where he "practically memorized" Nock's Memoirs; or the
influential Russell Kirk, at an army camp reading Nock and
corresponding with him . . . This is the kind of book that gets
under a person's skin, performing catalytically to persuade
the reader into becoming what he has it in him to be.*"
— Edmund A. Opitz

ISBN 0-87319-038-6
352 pages, Trade Paper, $16.95

Albert Jay Nock

OUR ENEMY, THE STATE

An essential history of Colonial America and critique distinguishing "Government" from "The State"

Foreword by:
EDMUND A. OPITZ

Expanded Edition Featuring Nock's Essays:
"Life, Liberty and . . ." as an Introduction
and
"The Classicist's Opportunity," Epilogue

An essential history of Colonial America and must reading for students of government and advocates of man's right to Life, Liberty and Property.

ISBN 0-87319-023-8
180 pages, Trade Paper, $14.95

Seventeen thought-provoking essays, many of which have never before been published in book form.

Albert J. Nock (1870-1945) was a radical, in the venerable sense of the word: one whose ideas cut to the root and make you think again about things previously taken for granted.

— Edmund A. Opitz

ISBN 0-87319-041-6
224 pages, Trade Paper, $14.95

"A must read to better comprehend the important linkage between religious principals and individual liberty."

— RON PAUL

THE
LIBERTARIAN
THEOLOGY
OF
FREEDOM

by

The Reverend
Edmund
A. Opitz

"This book by Rev. Opitz will go a long way to help those in mainline churches appreciate the critical importance of liberty in the construction of a just society. It will disabuse all readers of the notion that to be a libertarian, one must be a libertine."

— FR. ROBERT A. SIRICO
ACTON INSTITUTE FOR THE STUDY OF RELIGION AND LIBERTY

"I have never before been aware of the debate between Ed and the Rev. Bennett. It is fascinating! It alone needs to be published for it gets to the very core of the issue from both a theological and political standpoint."

— MILLER UPTON
PRESIDENT EMERITUS, MILTON COLLEGE

ISBN 0-87319-046-7
160 pages, hardcover, $18.95